THE POET AND THE KING

The Poet and the King

JEAN DE LA FONTAINE AND HIS CENTURY

Marc Fumaroli

TRANSLATED BY
Jane Marie Todd

UNIVERSITY OF NOTRE DAME PRESS
Notre Dame, Indiana

Manufactured in the United States of America

Translated by Jane Marie Todd from *Le Poète et le roi: Jean de La Fontaine en son siècle*, published by Éditions de Fallois, Paris, France.

The publisher is grateful to
THE FRENCH MINISTRY OF CULTURE—CENTRE NATIONAL DE LIVRE
for support of the costs of translation.

© Éditions de Fallois, 1997

Library of Congress Cataloging-in-Publication Data
Fumaroli, Marc.
[Poète et le roi. English]
The poet and the king : Jean de La Fontaine and his century / Marc
Fumaroli ; translated by Jane Marie Todd.
    p.   cm.
Includes bibliographical references and index.
ISBN 0-268-03877-5 (cloth : alk. paper)
1. La Fontaine, Jean de, 1621–1695.   2. Authors, French—17th
century—Biography.   3. France—Intellectual life—17th century.
4. Louis XIV, King of France, 1638–1715.   I. Title.
PQ1812 .F8513   2002
841'.4—dc21
2002007576

∞ *This book is printed on acid-free paper.*

Contents

Acknowledgments

The shortcomings of this work, of which I am only too aware, are my own. If the book has some merit, I cannot adequately acknowledge the debt I incurred while writing it, toward my listeners at the Collège de France, who faithfully followed and commented on the first version, in the form of lectures; toward the devoted collaborators of my chair at the Collège, who generously helped me to bring this outline to maturity and to give shape to it; toward the Société des Amis de Jean de La Fontaine, who re-created in Paris and Château-Thierry a fervent environment favorable to a better knowledge of the poet; toward my colleagues and fellows, French and foreign, writers, philosophers, historians, and professors of literature; toward my friends and students, who were all kind enough to listen, read, and reread attentively, at one stage or another, the various drafts of my manuscript; and, finally and most of all, toward my publisher Bernard de Fallois, whose intelligence and affection have never failed to support me in my research, and to whom I dedicate this book with all my heart.

Preamble

Neither she nor any of us could have tolerated Mme de Sévigné being called "witty marquise," any more than that La Fontaine be called *le Bonhomme*.

—Marcel Proust, *Sodome et Gomorrhe*

*O*f all the "great" French writers, La Fontaine is the only one to whom the epithet "great" seems unsuitable. He has continually been the most popular of all, the most highly praised for three centuries, but also the most unclassifiable, the most evasive, the least respectable of all our literary lares. It is as if something has always prevented the French people from identifying completely with a poet who declared "grace even more beautiful than beauty," and who did not give the Gallic cock the leading role in his *Fables*. That world-famous book has been acclaimed for three hundred years, but a secret impulse keeps the French from allowing its author, whose stature seems too modest, into the club of Shakespeare, Cervantes, Dante, and Goethe. No M. de Norpois ever considered naming France's cultural representatives abroad "La Fontaine Institutes." Even on the Mount Parnassus of our classics, the Muse who does the table seating reserves a place for him only at the far end, if she does not send him away with the servants to eat with the children. The Maison de Molière works toward the comic playwright's glory; Boileau can rely on his authority as the lawmaker of classicism, Racine on his success with the king at Saint-Cyr, Bossuet on the impact of his funeral orations at Notre-Dame. All participate in the grandeur of the state. All are monuments. La Fontaine is only *le Bonhomme*.

Of all the French tributes paid him, that of the poet Léon-Paul Fargue is the friendliest: the "Pedestrian of Paris," as Fargue is called, unself-consciously empathizes with the man La Fontaine, and attributes to the poet not only the superior knowledge of form Valéry had first recognized

I

in him—"a studied elegance, a suppleness of thought, a willingness to feel the exquisite torments of the soul, and the perpetual triumph of sacrifice"—but also a rare lyric genius. Fargue does not place the author below and to one side of his works, he does not apologize for one by means of the other, but shows them to be in solidarity and of a piece.[1] He is not bothered that La Fontaine's format differs in appearance from that of the demigods of which other national literatures boast; he even sees it as the superiority of a self-effacement that is rare, even unique, at that altitude. In rejecting self-importance, in agreeing to demean himself for fools, the poet La Fontaine has descended to the invisible center of things, which he displays in their natural light without batting an eye, smiling through his tears. He is an Oriental from Paris rather than Champagne, a French Zen master.

French literature, however, produced an impressive series of eulogies of La Fontaine before and after Léon-Paul Fargue's. The tradition began in 1771 with a purple passage from Chamfort, written for a competition at the Académie de Marseilles. It is the starting point for a true literary "genre," which has its ranking, its limits, and its conventions, which are themselves modest.[2] The genre is academic in origin, but from a provincial academy: "O La Fontaine," Chamfort exclaimed, "your glory is the greater for it! It is the triumph of art to be so misunderstood." The author of this piece of oratory was young at the time, thirty-three years old; he had always felt marginalized and unhappy, even when he had the appearance of success. That bitterness led him to understand La Fontaine's marginality and to envy the poet's unassailable cheerfulness and sweetness. The long procession of eulogies that followed Chamfort's *Discours* has every chance of becoming an expiation and excuse for the pale figure La Fontaine cut within the great and true edifices erected to "all the glories of France." Celebrated by La Harpe, Sainte-Beuve, and Giraudoux, but celebrated for his *Fables*, which conceals its author, La Fontaine is relegated to the wings when, on the stage of the great national amphitheater, the honors list of the truly great is read aloud.

Orators seem to have remembered that, during the reign of Louis XIV, the king ignored the fabulist; that Boileau, the "regent of Parnassus," did not even mention La Fontaine's little apologues in his *Art poétique*; and that the Catholic Church condemned his *Contes* (*Tales*), which were also banned by the *lieutenant-général de police* in 1675. All the same, La Fontaine was no martyred *poète maudit*; he was not Cervantes, gravely wounded at the battle of Lepanto and brought to Algiers as a slave; he was not Dante, who died in exile; or the blind Milton; or Baudelaire, paralyzed in Brussels; or Rimbaud, a victim of gangrene in Marseilles. Neither faction of the French intelligentsia can turn him to its advantage. Leftists seek suffering to be vindicated. Rightists look for honors to be dispensed: to represent France, they seek counterparts to the privy councillor Wolfgang von Goethe, poet laureate of the Weimar court.

And La Fontaine was not received at Versailles! He described its gardens in *Les amours de Psyché,* when Versailles was still a mere country château, fussed over by Louis XIV but not yet set up as the theater of his state. La Fontaine described them as any visitor whatever, almost furtively. He was denied the presence of the king, whom he never saw except from afar, the day of the festival of Vaux. In France, however, that snub, which continued indefinitely, ought to be considered as cruel as Cervantes' wounds or as the rope Nerval tied around his own neck. When he was received at the Louvre, which had been deserted by the court, in the out-of-date apartments Louis XIV abandoned to the Académie Française, the abbé Cureau de La Chambre fired off a terrible reply to La Fontaine's acceptance speech of 2 May 1684, a reply that ought to have struck fear in the poet: "Therefore, count for nothing all that you have done in the past."[3] The path for his new life as an academy poet was thus set out, in what was already the "Empire" style, in these terms: "To work for the glory of the prince, to devote all one's nights of labor solely to his honor, to set no other goal than the immortality of his name, to direct all one's efforts to it."

The poet's reaction to his judge was that of Ariel. He confined himself to smiling and to taking flight. Reclaiming the floor after the interruption, he ignored the reprimand and the lecture, and read the enchanting *[Second] Discours en vers adressé à Madame de La Sablière:*

> Le temps marche toujours; ni force, ni prière,
> Sacrifices ni voeux, n'allongent sa carrière:
> Il faudrait ménager ce qu'on va nous ravir.
> Mais qui vois-je que vous sagement s'en servir?
> Si quelques-uns l'ont fait, je ne suis pas du nombre.
> ·
> Si j'étais sage, Iris (mais c'est un privilège
> Que la Nature accorde à bien peu d'entre nous),
> Si j'avais un esprit aussi réglé que vous,
> Je suivrais vos leçons, au moins en quelque chose.
> Les suivre en tout, c'est trop; il faut qu'on se propose
> Un plan moins difficile à bien exécuter.

Time marches on, and no force or prayer,
No sacrifice or vow can lengthen its stay:
We must make good use of what we will lose.
But who besides you employs it with such wisdom?
If some have done so, I am not of their number.
. . . .

Were I but wise, Iris (but that is a privilege
That Nature gives to few among us),
Were my mind as disciplined as yours,
I would follow your lessons, at least in some things.
To follow them in all would be too much to ask;
One must make a plan less hard to execute it well.

The trills rise and are inflected with a grace so perfect, addressed to his
only lady friend and his chosen one, that the academy itself could only
have felt it was in the way. The abbé de La Chambre must have been furious to have provoked a public confession as imperceptible as it was unassailable. He refused to allow his own welcoming speech to be published
in the same volume as the impure poet's acceptance speech.

But for Proust's immortal duc de Guermantes and no less immortal
Mme Verdurin, that high-wire escape was only the latest development in
a delicious high-society scandal. A poet and member of the Académie
Française, yes; but though he placed himself in the line of such an affront,
he will bear the scars forever. The pummeled Voltaire knew how to exact
a terrible revenge on the race of his insulters. The humiliated Rousseau
claimed to be a martyr and stirred up Europe with his laments. La Fontaine, who poked fun at himself when his pride ought to have been
wounded, could not decently represent the national character as he himself defined it:

Se croire un personnage est fort commun en France,
    On y fait l'homme d'importance,
    Et l'on n'est souvent qu'un bourgeois:
    C'est proprement le mal françois.
            ("The Rat and the Elephant," 8.15)

Believing oneself a somebody is common in France,
    One puts on airs of a man of importance,
    And often one is nothing more than bourgeois,
    That's the French malady to be sure.

Vanity, common to the left and the right in France, has kept us from feeling any sympathy for a man who did not deign to defend himself; and a tin ear has made it difficult to discover fully a poetry that wants to be defenseless, except in the cause of poetry.

In *Enfantines*, Valery Larbaud tells how, as an adolescent, he was called upon to choose between Lamartine (who, along with Rousseau, was one of the rare avowed naysayers of *Fables*) and La Fontaine, whom he knew only through his fables. He was very tempted to prefer the languorous author of *Le Lac*:

> And then, those animals who made speeches, who appeared to be concerned with the same things as grownups—were they men disguised as beasts, or beasts to whom the passions and ideas of men were being attributed? In any case, they were not animals: they were given that name, but they were not shown to be so. It was as if the fabulist had never looked at them. And, at the end of every fable, there was a moral, some very banal and very prosaic reflection, which gave us the impression that everything that preceded had served only to come to that point, as a sort of theorem: Q. E. D. If only there had been at least a perceptible rhythm for us, a well-marked cadence, repeated sounds, the beautiful dance of rhyme. But not at all, the poet seemed hardly to have begun when he fell gracelessly into a line that was too short. How, after the great organ chords of Lamartine, could one bear that shrill little flute solo?[4]

His annoyance was exacerbated by the smug and generally agreed-upon admiration of friends of the family. But disgust gave way to a provisional moral:

> Not only did we need crude rhythms, but we also demanded sentimental inspiration and even sensual images from poetry. To be sure, there was in *Fables* the quintessence of poetry, the fruit of experience by an artist who had not written until he was past forty: a taste of honey, a drop of incense, which gave the entire book a flavor and a scent. Later, when we were men, when we had lived, we too would no doubt discover this precious honey, and would know how to savor it. In the meantime, it was better not to tire ourselves looking for it.

The future author of *Amants, heureux amants* was right to wait. His poetry and prose adequately attest that he had matured in *Fables* and with

Fables. Toulet's *Les contrerimes* cured him of Lamartine and guided him toward a chamber music he could only guess at in his student years:

> C'était sur un chemin crayeux
>   Trois châles de Provence
> Qui s'en allaient d'un pas qui danse
>   Le soleil dans les yeux.

> Following chalky trails
>   Three shawls from Provence
> Tripped along in a dance
>   The sun in their eyes.

In this lively and dreamy ballad by Toulet, Perrette from La Fontaine's "The Dairymaid and Her Milk-Pot" (7.10) is multiplied by three, into Mireilles "walking with long strides" on the same sunny path as that of "The Coach and the Fly" (7.9).[5]

The music of *Fables* is profound, and it takes a fine ear to hear it. La Fontaine is the most discreet of lyric poets. He requires the most attentive and the least hasty surrender. He knows this and does not conceal it:

> L'homme lettré se tut, il avait trop à dire.
>   ("Knowledge Avails," 8.19)

> The man of culture fell silent, he had too much to say.

Montaigne, a great reader of poets, defined for himself the discipline of this art of saying much less than one intends to communicate, a symbolic art in the most literal sense.

Nothing is easier than to pass by that art without hearing it, inasmuch as La Fontaine took care to make allowances for the public's lack of an internal ear and of internal memory, by supplying social charms more within reach of the simple passerby. In a letter to their mutual friend Trébutien, Barbey d'Aurevilly reports the sense Maurice de Guérin formed of this secret La Fontaine:[6]

> What comments he might have made about La Fontaine! Sometimes he transposed him, as one says in music, by the sheer force of profundity. He found the comic under the sadness, and the sadness under the comic, and that was a discovery, but it was not an invention. Hence,

for example, I heard him read and perform the fable "The Hare and the Frogs," which is so charming in its gaiety *on the surface of the expression*, and he turned it into a never-before-heard poem of desolate melancholy. Neither *René* nor *Oberman* nor any of our darkest *humorists* have achieved the feeling of desperate isolation he was able to give to that piece. I recall when, with one finger raised between his ever-so-black eyes—since his eyes are *black* in both senses, *black* in color and *black* in their expression—he said, as he knew how to say:

> Dans un profond ennui ce lièvre se plongeait.
> ("The Hare and the Frogs," 2.14)

Into a deep ennui this hare was thrust.

It was wonderful! And the greatest actors had to admit defeat.[7]

The Fables, reduced to a brief anthology for school use (when they are not learned by heart) or to a small number of animal sketches ending in a proverb, have been stripped of these resonances and shadows where, at the edge of silence, their all-seeing gaze lurks. But at least they have linked the French nation as a whole, a people so divided in other respects, to a "wisdom of nations" that may seem to be the exact opposite of poetry.

The origins of that wisdom go back to the Greece of Aesop, to the Middle East, and to the Far East of Bidpai. Lamartine's mistake, his sentimental romanticism, was to have believed that such a harsh education in reality was incompatible with the quiver of lyricism, even though, among poets who are truly the friends of mortals, the two imply each other. La Fontaine's Orient is not that of Hugo's *Les Orientales* or even Goethe's *Westeasterly Divan*. It is an *orientation*, both internal and external. One may not sense its vigorous nervures or their delicate articulation. One may merely travel a piece of the road with the man called the "butterfly of Parnassus." But, as soon as one has journeyed down the first section of road and caught a glimpse of the design, the trail is marked out and one feels free to follow it on one's own. This is as true of *Fables* as it was of *Essays*, of which Montaigne wrote: "How many stories have I spread around which say nothing of themselves, but from which anyone who troubles to pluck them with a little ingenuity will produce numberless essays. . . . They often bear, outside of my subject, the seeds of a richer and bolder material."[8]

This art of the conjurer, skilled in the fertile science of the unsaid, has often been reduced to the exaggeration of received ideas. The author of *Fables* has been named the French master of rural "common sense," composed entirely of caution and malice. In France it is well known, and a matter of pride, that the Fables are not the rosary of maxims on marriage to which Arnolphe wanted to confine the readings of the young Agnes. "Our Homer" is not just "our Aesop" or "our Bidpai." We are easily persuaded that, in *Fables,* the French core that makes the slightly bitter but very substantial old nuggets of Aesop's apologues so flavorful is combined with the nectar that the bee La Fontaine, held aloft by "his time," gathered and collected in the gardens of the great seventeenth century. Stendhal referred to love as a "crystallization" that occurs around the slightest dead branch when it is immersed in water supersaturated with salt. La Fontaine, somewhat by chance, somewhat by the mere good fortune of having been born at the right moment, dipped his paltry bines in the salty waters of the "French genius" at the time of its greatest degree of concentration.

Two very different, but in many ways complementary, great books have erected a dissymmetric monument to the glory of this "classical moment" of France and literary France, a monument that bears witness to national memory for eternity. Voltaire's *Le siècle de Louis XIV* and Sainte-Beuve's *Port-Royal* seem to speak to each other. One freezes the features of the historic grandeur of France at its zenith in a majestic "history painting"; a universal propriety, in keeping with the will of the absolute state and its enlightened despot, makes a sort of unanimity reign in this "grand century" of "grand taste," a unanimity that assigns official talents and private talents the same pitch. *Port-Royal,* no less ambitious in its design but more lackluster in its style, does not so much oppose the historic grandeur established by Voltaire, as supplement it with a symmetrical but entirely spiritual grandeur. That spiritual grandeur, misunderstood and persecuted by Louis the Great, was the mirror image of his own grandeur, and all the loftier, all the more worthy of the nation in the century of its grandeur. Port-Royal, "an early experiment in a sort of superior Third Estate governing itself within the Church," was, in Sainte-Beuve's view, the true Christian and French Reformation (as opposed to sixteenth-century Calvinism, said to be "an effort on the part of the aristocracy or, at the very least, of the petty nobility"). It was an entirely internal religion, fertile for the history of spirit, productive for literature, and unjustly persecuted by a king outwitted by the Jesuits.[9]

Standing between these two great frescoes, one organized around the royal state, the other around an elite of grand bourgeois draped in sublime meditations, La Fontaine, and even his works, became imperceptible.

In the *Catalogue des écrivains français*, which served as supporting evidence for his justification of Louis XIV's reign, Voltaire is as offhand in his manner toward the author of *Fables* as he would be toward Corneille in *Commentaire*, his book on Corneille's theater:

"Young people, and especially the adults who choose what they read," he writes pedantically, "must be very careful not to confuse his natural beauty with the colloquial, vulgar, careless, and trivial faults into which he very often falls." Louis XIV and Boileau were therefore not wrong to keep this gifted but uncouth *bonhomme* away from Olympus.[10] Voltaire never wavered. A few years earlier, he had written to Vauvenargues: "The character of that *bonhomme* was so simple that, in conversation, he was hardly above the animals he made speak; but, as a poet, he had a divine instinct, and all the more *instinctive* in that he had only that talent. The bee is admirable, but only in its hive; outside it, the bee is nothing but a fly."[11] Later, having donned Boileau's wig in his *Connaissance des beautés et des défauts de la poésie et de l'éloquence dans la langue française*, Voltaire did not hesitate to grossly confuse literary criticism with the snobbery of a parvenu: "I hardly know of a book [*Fables*] more filled with traits made for the common people, and with those befitting the most feeble minds."[12] *Fables* judges those that judge it. In his correspondence, in fact, Voltaire was the first to use the Fables, not, like Mme de Sévigné, as poems one savors musically, but as sketches or burlesque proverbs capable of enlivening his commentaries on current events or his own domestic disappointments. Jean is for Voltaire what Françoise is for Tante Léonie.

It is to Sainte-Beuve's *Causeries du lundi* that we owe one of the most beautiful purple passages, of which the genre "eulogy of La Fontaine" has produced so many examples.[13] In short order, Voltaire and his strict hierarchy of styles and social rankings are put in their place. Sainte-Beuve also refutes Lamartine. He very wittily shows that the humanitarian author of *Jocelyn* was, in the end, a prisoner to the same courtly prejudices Voltaire held. He vindicates La Fontaine the man, whom the most discriminating circles of the Paris of his time were vying for. He awards him the laurel of "Gallic genius" and French "good sense, enlivened with mockery, animated by charm and imagination." "The Homer of the French people" is his ally against the invasion of French literature by a "sentimental" and "picturesque" school, which Mme de Staël and Chateaubriand initiated, and to whom Lamartine was the successor. The popularity of the author of *Fables*, which did not fall off in the nineteenth century, made him a recruit of some weight in this battle of taste. The greatest consideration was due this ally of circumstance.

But when Sainte-Beuve comes to truly "elevated" things—in a word, to serious things—to the sublimity of religion, which he ruminated on throughout his life, he replicates all the deficiencies of *Causeries du lundi* for which Proust would later reproach him: he grants three condescending pages in *Port-Royal* to the humble collaborator of the great Messieurs.[14] Now, it seems, La Fontaine's foremost claim to fame was to have published, under the direction of the Messieurs, his *Recueil de poésies chrétiennes et diverses*, designed to chastise high society for its tastes. But the Port-Royal with which La Fontaine found himself associated was not that of Pascal, or that of Racine, or that of the Arnaulds, or that of Mother Agnes, or that of M. Hamon. It was not even the Port-Royal of the duchesse de Longueville, the duc de Luynes, or the marquise de Sablé, to whom Sainte-Beuve, however worldly these converts may have been, devoted all his perspicacity as a portraitist. It was an ancillary Port-Royal, which was obliged to resort to an external service provider when the comte Loménie de Brienne, former state secretary (to whom Sainte-Beuve devotes a full-length portrait), shirked his duty to compose a poetry collection for the layman's use. La Fontaine's unworthiness in such lofty and grave company is indicated by a brief and vicious parenthetical remark: "the author of 'Joconde'"!

Voltaire had left La Fontaine on the doorstep of the school of well-bred France, which learns from good models to speak and write tastefully. Sainte-Beuve, in his most ambitious work, and the one into which he put himself entirely, relegated him to the kitchen in the château of the French soul. At Port-Royal, the "French Homer" of *Causeries du lundi* was now only a relatively anonymous kitchen boy.

La Fontaine did not confine himself to speaking of the "French malady" with sweet irony. In his own way, without insisting, he indicated his clear preference for the English "character," whose gravity impelled it to *think profoundly* ("The English Fox," 12.23), and especially for the Spanish "character":

> Les Espagnols sont vains, mais d'une autre manière:
> Leur orgueil me semble en un mot
> Beaucoup plus fou, mais pas si sot.
> ("The Rat and the Elephant," 8.15)

> The Spanish are vain, but in a different way:
> Their boastfulness, in sum,
> Seems madder by far, but not so dumb.

The commonplace of the "character of nations" gives a veneer of banality to these comparisons. At a profound level, it is a choice of the heart. La Fontaine is faithful to the Hispanophilism of Voiture and Corneille. That would also be Saint-Simon's and Stendhal's preference. This choice by an internal exile is also the forthright confession of a temporal or, if one prefers, historical inability to adapt. As of 1661, the defeated Spain ceased to dazzle. The "Spanish character" was no longer in fashion under Louis the Great, as it had been among the high-spirited adversaries of Richelieu. French "vanity," carelessly set in motion by Louis XIV, had become the driving force behind a courtly science of mechanics. La Fontaine was not "distrait," he was elsewhere. His "far-off look" was only the more piercing. This melancholiac by circumstance as much as by temperament, unclassifiable, at home everywhere but keeping an internal distance, was very much behind, or in advance—as you like—of the mass of French troops in the age of Louis XIV. Since 1661 they had marched in step, in regular formation, under the eyes of a lynx king. La Fontaine's lyric sensibility and his kingdom, his untimely "states of mind," date from the regency of Anne of Austria and the Fronde, which themselves harked back to King Henry, Francis I, and Saint Louis. He needed all the grace he could muster—and this was not altogether the effective grace of Port-Royal—not to make himself intolerable to the new reign. This troublesome delay with respect to history did not affect the little marquis of Molière's *Le misanthrope*, but it tormented Alceste. It could also be observed in Mme de Sévigné and Mme de La Fayette, in the duc de La Rochefoucauld and the prince de Condé, in the marquis de La Fare, the great love of the "turtledove" Sablière, in Mazarin's pretty nieces, for whom any adventure was fine provided it got them away from court, and even in Colbert's daughters, who zealously rallied behind the worst adversary of their father's work: Fénelon. All these men and women were friends of La Fontaine. Were they merely a handful of worldly people no longer "in the know"? They did not carry much weight, compared to the bureaucratic king, his state, his armies, and the order they imposed on France and Europe. They also did not carry as much weight as the great Christian consciences of Port-Royal, bearing witness to the City of God against the great king of the earthly City.

But these famous figures, by their talents and their names, stood for a much larger number of "back shops" with less brilliant facades, which were nonetheless thinking and feeling. In their private homes gardens could be found, but also libraries, where things other than *Le Mercure Galant*, *La Gazette de France*, and panegyrics of the king were read:

Montaigne, Charron, Boccaccio, and Ariosto, in short, a literature that did not fit the mold of the official public opinion of the moment. The *Gazette de Hollande,* and soon, Pierre Bayle and Jean Leclerc would also be read there. The public hid in that semidarkness: even though it no longer took action, as it had in the time of secret assemblies and plots, it still lived its own uncontrolled life. What was seen publicly was only what was officially visible and acceptable.

So long as Molière (who also came from somewhere else, but behind a mask) was alive, a balance was offered even on the official stage between acquiescence to the new regime and a concern to safeguard the rights of private life and private feelings. Louis XIV knew how to use the great comic actor and playwright to emphasize that there were more opportunities for individuals within the state than among the religious zealots and their inquisition, which was insinuating itself even into the secret life of the conscience and of families. La Fontaine undoubtedly felt the same way as Molière. He was not a rebel or a member of the opposition.

But he was also a lyric poet, whose antennae were more sensitive to vibrations and whose internal demands were more radical than those of a comic author. In many respects, despite everything that separates the tragedy *Othon* from the fable "The Animals Sick of the Plague," La Fontaine was more profoundly in harmony with Corneille's way of thinking. Corneille's judgment of the regime became darker and darker, until his admirable cry of despair, *Suréna,* which remained unanswered.[15] The ironic alexandrine that concludes La Fontaine's "The Daughters of Minea" (12.28)—"Les jours donnés aux dieux ne sont jamais perdus" (The days we give to the gods are never lost [line 562])—is a less lofty equivalent of the affirmation made by Eurydice, the heroine of *Suréna,* and addressed to King Pacorus: "Que l'empire des coeurs n'est pas de votre Empire" (The heart's empire is not of your Empire" [4.4, line 1310]).

La Fontaine inclined toward the elegy and the idyll, but he impelled the elegy and the idyll to move against their own inclination. He liked Ariosto, the poet who went so far with fantasy and the supernatural only because they were able ironically to reconcile the cruelty of the things of life with the gentleness lying latent within hearts, to reconcile wearisome action with restorative contemplation. (Cardinal de Retz and the marquise de Sévigné also worshiped Ariosto.) By what miracle was this French reader of Ariosto able to transpose the succulence and richness of *Orlando furioso* into individual tales and fables? It is as if, in order not to betray itself, the genius of the Renaissance in the age of royal academies and state art, which liked large formats, had to adopt the small, suggestive format and produce a multitude of interstices where a great deal remained to be discerned. Posterity, which never neglected La Fontaine, did not always give proof of its perspicacity. It usually took his "absent-mindedness" and naive "gaiety" for one of the most delectable, but also the most inoffensive, ornaments of the great, regular spectacle of classical France, whose center and principle stood at a loftier height, in the king's immediate sphere of influence and in accord with His Majesty. It did not see to what extent this poet had his own center and that, in this respect, there was an essential dissymmetry between him and his "age."

In 1936 Jean Giraudoux delivered a series of lectures entitled "The Five Temptations of La Fontaine."[16] As soon as they were published in 1938, they became the most widely quoted of all the encomiums of which the poet had been the object. The author of *Bella* wanted to outdo Léon-Paul Fargue, whose essay on La Fontaine was rightly considered a remarkable example of perspicacity and critical poetry.[17] If Giraudoux praised *Fables*, he did so, once more and by contrast to Fargue, at the expense of its author, whom he painted as a *bonhomme*, inferior to his works, which, like Voltaire and in contrast to Valéry, he wanted to see as the product of the "inconsistency" and "absent-mindedness" of a "dear fellow from Champagne," a fabulist of genius. The greatest merit of *Fables*, according to the lecturer, was to have anticipated unawares the program of the Popular Front, and to have given a glimpse of "the poor anemic face of France crying out in hunger" under a regime in which "the first great operation of state propaganda" had succeeded, "thanks to Molière, Boileau, and company," in putting a muzzle on the miserable, starving nation.

In that paradoxical eulogy, sprinkled throughout with delicious and intuitive insights, La Fontaine appears as a servant in the great house and, inadvertently, as a popular orator, in the company of La Bruyère ("One sees some wild animals"), Fénelon (the notorious letter to Louis XIV), and Vauban (*La dîme royale*). These last three, to be sure, were perfectly aware of the significance of what they were writing.

Giraudoux thus pleasantly planted the seeds for the first Marxist interpretation of *Fables*. According to that reading, La Fontaine was, in the "superstructures" of absolute monarchy, the ventriloquist of social suffering and class conflict, which, reduced to silence by the violence of "power," manifested, within the bowels of the kingdom, the "silent labor" of History, a new, immanent Providence worshiped by scholars. Marxist History is undoubtedly not Maurrassian History; it leads to the proletarian state and not back to the monarchical state. But both are merciless toward latecomers and dawdlers. Giraudoux, who was neither doctrinaire nor a purist or snob, at least did not have that brutal side. Nevertheless, he was the interpreter, as conformist as it was brilliant, of a national tradition intent on rushing to assist in the victory of *Fables*, but only on the condition that the peculiar poet who was its author, and who, by the way, had other works to his credit to prove it, be hidden or suppressed.

．．．

Chamfort, in a trying time that resembled our own in its noisy, garrulous pretentiousness, had already found the clearing where La Fontaine awaits us: "A loyal friend, who penetrates the heart without doing it any harm."[18] La Fontaine's unique contribution to French literature was to combine the "charm" of a profound musicality with a lesson in balance—entirely modern and difficult to achieve—between the education of the soul and the art of living at peace with oneself, but not just for oneself. That poetry of private life teaches us how to be both here and not here, present for the best things, which are within our control, and elsewhere for the worst things, which are not.

In its essence, lyricism is public and choral, like the art of praise. Of the two poets La Fontaine publicly embraced, the first, Malherbe, was primarily the author of royal odes, hymns of praise addressed to the king and to his ministers in the name of "the good French people," receiving in exchange for his immortal words participation in the grandeur of the state. The second, the Roman poet Horace, celebrated, but much more intimately, the happiness rather than the grandeur of the century of Augustus: he publicly thanked Caesar, but also Maecenas, for the charms of private life, the pleasures of friendship, travel, and the refuge of reading, which the Augustan peace had given back to the Romans. Elegiac lyricism, for which La Fontaine had a vocation, the lyricism of the ancient Latins as well as that of the French of the previous generation—Théophile, Tristan, and Saint-Amant—broke cleanly with what, for Horace, still joined the poetry of private life to the commonwealth. Error, absence, sorrow, desire—the stuff of private emotion—are by definition jealous: even in the century of Augustus, they sought refuge in the home of Tibullus and Propertius, in a sort of ardent and wholly internal melancholy, which public life aggravated or assaulted. But that melancholy, the pains of which were adequate in themselves, was also defenseless against the external world, which it would have liked to negate and which interrupted its contemplation with rude reminders of reality. The exiled Ovid had been through that ordeal. The elegy of love existed within a circle of friends and accomplices, and, when they were dispersed or far away, it became an elegy of despair. In his *Tristia* and *Epistulae ex Ponto,* Ovid no longer laments his mistress, but rather his fierce solitude among the barbarians.

Lyricism, which began in Greece with Pindar, the public poet of Olympic victories, continued in Rome with an internalization on the frontiers of desertion, a virtual desertion which the prince's punishment, in the case of Ovid, transformed into actual exile. The young La Fontaine, born to be a lyric poet, did not rush to follow in Malherbe's footsteps, though he admired him, or in those of Ovid, the devastated elegiac poet. He undoubtedly wavered between these two choices, which ought to have drawn the poet either toward the impersonal and public poem or toward poems expressing his innermost feelings. He was careful to refrain from the first temptation, but he also did not succumb unreservedly to the second.

The poetic tradition in itself is not sufficient to explain La Fontaine the poet or to assess his extreme originality. This virtuoso metrist also wrote a great deal in prose. *Le voyage en Limousin* is a collection of letters, *Les amours de Psyché* a novel, intermingled with verse to be sure. Even when his lyric inclinations pushed him in that direction, his freedom, inseparable from his feeling for diversity, kept him from being locked into the tradition of a single genre, however sharp in contrasts and rich in possibilities it might be. He enjoyed "love stories"; he liked the dialogues of Plato; he was not unfamiliar with the philosophical prose of Descartes and Gassendi. He was not a poet of one style, especially if that style proudly affirmed itself "poetic." He was profound and lucid enough as a lyric poet to go back to the source of all lyricism, of all song, to the intimate beginnings of his unique voice. He did not rush that search for his own voice, but once he had reached the source, he discovered he was capable of a plurality of voices, a polyphony, which made him the lyre not of the state, like Malherbe, nor of his particular aggrieved "self," like the elegiac poets, but of the entire human kingdom, judged by the gazes of animals, plants, and gods, and by their oracular pronouncements:

> J'ai fait parler le loup et répondre l'agneau.
> J'ai passé plus avant: les arbres et les plantes
> Sont devenus chez moi créatures parlantes.
>   ("For Those Impossible to Please," 2.1)

> I gave the wolf speech and made the lamb reply.
> I went further yet: every plant and tree
> Has become a speaking creature for me.

Is this not a translation into emblematic language of Montaigne's project? "I set forth a humble and inglorious life; that does not matter. You can tie up all moral philosophy with a common and private life just as well as with a life of richer stuff. Each man bears the entire form of man's estate."[19]

That coincidence of opposites between a lyric poet whose poetry can be compared, in French literature, only to that of Baudelaire and the master of the "experiment" of *Essays*, is so improbable, and supposes a genius for synthesis so superior, so unique, that not one of the poet's panegyrists has ever dared attribute it to him. How could one attribute it to *le Bonhomme?* Some, like Odette de Mourges in her admirable study,[20] have emphasized the lyric splendor of the author of "The Two Doves" and "The Mogul's Dream." Some have been more likely to expound on the moral and philosophical profundity, and the political science, of *Fables*. But that incredible symbiosis between poetic musicality, self-knowledge, and acceptance of reality, that hybrid of *Orlando furioso* and *Essays*, could not be perceived, and a fortiori admitted, so long as the legend of the "fabulist" cast a shadow on the disproportionate but well-deserved glory of his *Fables*. If we admit that coincidence of opposites, that union of true lyricism— so rare and intermittent in France—and the great "moderation" achieved by Montaigne (also against the general French current, which favors display and fashion), we are obliged to place "poor La Fontaine" at the vanishing point of all French literary perspectives. If the stature of *le Bonhomme* from Château-Thierry—both an Orpheus and a Socrates—was to be recognized and understood, we would have to do a comprehensive reassessment of both the scale and arrangement of the great immutable edifices that, in the French public memory, have been erected around the royal square of the seventeenth century.

That alliance between musicality and wisdom might seem too paradoxical for a single author, especially for the lovable fool protected by Mme de La Sablière. It was improbable, but not impossible. Perhaps we have a reductive and all-too-prosaic notion of Montaigne and the wisdom of his essays, though they too have been celebrated ad nauseam. Montaigne became a master of wisdom through a patient exertion of control over himself and his tendency toward melancholy. And although it is true that the aim of the introspective *Essays* is balance, moderation, and the health of the soul, what Montaigne's meditation drags up is painful, choppy, and more tempted than we might believe to deliver itself from anguish through lyric song. It was Montaigne who wrote:

Here is a wonder: we have many more poets than judges and inter-preters of poetry. It is easier to create it than to understand it. On a cer-tain low level it can be judged by precepts and by art. But the good, supreme, divine poetry is above the rules and reason. Whoever discerns its beauty with a firm, sedate gaze does not see it, any more than he sees the splendor of a lightning flash. It does not persuade our judgement, it ravishes and overwhelms it. The frenzy that goads the man who can penetrate it also strikes a third person on hearing him discuss it and recite it, as a magnet not only attracts a needle but infuses into it its own faculty of attracting others. And it is seen more clearly in the the-ater that the sacred inspiration of the muses, after first stirring the poet to anger, sorrow, and hatred and transporting him out of himself wher-ever they will, then through the poet strikes the actor, and through the actor consecutively a whole crowd.[21]

That is the poetics of Plato's *Ion* (so dear to La Fontaine) and of *On the Sublime* (and the author of *Fables* did not have a naive understanding of its lesson on enthusiasm). But it is also an inner experience revealed with a burst of excitement and joy that is itself inspired.[22] It was in *Essays* that the improbable alliance first manifested itself in France between the lyric capabilities of the otherworldly and the sober understanding of the here and now. The famous commentary in book 3 on the verses of Lucretius and Virgil led Montaigne to find an outlet for skepticism and decline via the gushing voice of poetic energy and vision:

Horace is not content with a superficial expression; it would betray him. He sees more clearly and deeply into the thing. His mind unlocks and ransacks the whole storehouse of words and figures in order to express itself; and he needs them to be beyond the commonplace, as his conception is beyond the commonplace. Plutarch says that he saw the Latin language through things. It is the same here: the sense illumi-nates and brings out the words, which are no longer wind, but flesh and bone. The words mean more than they say.[23]

Under the reign of Louis XIV, Montaigne was to become an "old author" whose freedom of expression and hybrid language was a depar-ture from propriety. He was still a master of style and of life for the gen-eration of Molière and La Fontaine. Ariosto—the joy of imagination, the rage of the liberating fantasy—would also be relegated to the squalid or disreputable neighborhoods of the town of classical poetry. The French lyric poets of the two previous generations, who had for the most part been in the service of the princes who revolted against Richelieu, were themselves out-of-date. Under the new regime, the duc de Liancourt, once he had become a penitent at Port-Royal, turned away from a poem that, though religious, was too colorful in its lyricism, the poet Saint-Amant's *Le Moyse sauvé*, even though it had delighted him in 1653.[24] People read Montaigne at Port-Royal, though only to refute his doctrines and condemn "the foolish plan he had to portray himself." Under Louis XIII, *Essays* had been the bedside reading of the young nobility: it was taken to the camps and into exile; it was read and reread as the "gentleman's breviary," the antidote to servitude and hypocrisy. It was not to Richelieu's taste. Montaigne had written, in fact:

> In truth, our laws are free enough, and the weight of sovereignty scarcely touches a French nobleman twice in his life. The real and essential subjection is only for those among us who go seeking it and who like to gain honors and riches by such service; for anyone who wants to ensconce himself by his hearth, and who can manage his house without quarrels and lawsuits, is as free as the Doge of Venice.[25]

This reminder of the "natural state" of political France inspired a friend of Corneille's, Alexandre de Campion—lieutenant to Gaston d'Orléans, then to Louis II de Bourbon, comte de Soissons—to execrate the cardinal-minister and the new yoke he had imposed on the French people's freedom of movement, and even on the frankness of their speech.

In a circle of friends meeting secretly in Paris in 1641 (the year La Fontaine entered the Oratory, a religious institute protected by the leader of the conspirators, Gaston d'Orléans), Campion said: "It is certain that, when I reflect on the total liberty that French people have always taken to murmur and complain, under the most moderate regimes, not simply in their homes and in the country, but even in town and at court, and when I see that now one hardly dares speak of one's own affliction at home and within one's family, I hardly recognize France in this reformed state."[26]

The Fronde had attempted in vain, and in a disordered manner, to return the kingdom to the state of freedom that de Retz too wildly praised in his *Mémoires*, written in secret by the disgraced and exiled cardinal during Louis XIV's reign. De Retz was the friend, almost the idol, of La Fontaine's best seventeenth-century reader, the marquise de Sévigné. Both were "mad" about Corneille, *Amadis*, and *L'Astrée*. The state, "reformed"

by Louis XIV and Colbert after 1661, imposed a fear even more intimidating than that inspired by Richelieu's police, and much stricter restraints on speech, since all the centers of resistance and independence (except, for a few decades, Port-Royal) had been harshly quashed. "Diversity," La Fontaine's motto, was a literary but also a political choice, profoundly out of step with the centralizing and authoritarian will of the new regime. He rejected a unity that went against nature. That diversity was faithful to the spirit of freedom behind the resistance to the iron reign inaugurated under Louis XIII, which saw that reign of terror as direct violence done to the living mosaic of the kingdom: it could be tamed by less brutal means. Montaigne had found a successor, another French Socrates: Pierre Gassendi. At the home of Mme de La Sablière, La Fontaine became very close to Gassendi's best disciple and popularizer, François Bernier.[27] Between 1643 and 1655, he probably knew the master himself, who spent the end of his life in Paris, in a mathematics chair at the Collège Royal. Through Foucquet, he met another of Gassendi's disciples, Samuel Sorbière. Gassendi was the foremost philosophical adversary of René Descartes. An ecclesiastic, he was a friend of Nicolas Fabri de Peiresc, but also of the "erudite libertines" François Lhuilier (the father of Chapelle, a friend of La Fontaine's), and François de La Mothe Le Vayer (the father of the libertine abbot Le Vayer, a friend of the young Racine, of Molière, and of La Fontaine). Gassendi had set out, as a metaphysician and a physicist, to rehabilitate Epicureanism, whose modernity Montaigne had pointed out, especially in his last essays. In establishing an equitable division between the rights of *private* life and conscience and the public duties of life and conduct, Montaigne had already asked Epicurus for a philosophy of "modern freedoms" in a very Christian kingdom that *was not* the classical Greek commonwealth. In France the freedom of the king's subjects was not exhausted in service to the state, but reserved its most precious dominion for the *conscience*. There was a kinship between this conscience, which transcends the political order and the elementary duties it can legitimately require, and lyric interiority as the Latin elegiac poets and the Swan of Ferrara had postulated it, freed from the tasks of active life and even from duties toward the prince. And nowhere did that kinship appear more clearly than in Montaigne's *Essays*:

> We must reserve a back shop all our own, entirely free, in which to establish our real liberty and our principal retreat and solitude. Here our ordinary conversation must be between us and ourselves, and so private that no outside association or communication can find a place;

here me must talk and laugh as if without wife, without children, without possessions, without retinue and servants, so that, when the time comes to lose them, it will be nothing new to us to do without them. We have a soul that can be turned upon itself; it can keep itself company; it has the means to attack and the means to defend, the means to receive and the means to give: let us not fear that in this solitude we shall stagnate in tedious idleness.[28]

That extraordinary "Declaration of the Duties of the Individual" and of the right to an interiority "turned upon itself" was nonetheless destined to be published: it is part of the "matter of my book," that mirror of "myself" that Montaigne gives, if not as an example, then at least as fodder for "back shops" other than his own. In these back shops, *Essays* would be read and meditated upon in solitude, in the silent retreat—"without wife, without children, without servants"—particular to the reader.

This is a paradoxical co-implication of the *public* and the *private:* the private is made public to prevent the "tedious idleness" that threatens the truly private and free conscience, in other words, the reader, in the seclusion of his unobserved meditation. A book of this sort initiates conversation with these scattered solitary souls, it keeps them occupied, nourishes them, leads them to meditate together in an invisible society. Just as he was the first to define "modern freedoms," Montaigne drew the defining features of a republic that was very different from the ancient republic, a republic "by lamplight," composed of private and free individuals, whose forum, a conversation of consciences, was the reading of books. And not just any books, no doubt, but "books of good faith": books of experience and books of dreams. *Essays* gives some idea of these two sorts of books. Montaigne fostered a complete internal experience that claimed to be *individual;* it was not destined to be emulated or to be respected as an authority, but rather to initiate a dialogue of one conscience with another, to "confer" with a friend and equal, the reader. "An open way of speaking opens up another man's speech and draws it out, as do wine and love."[29]

This assumes both Epicurus's "conceal thy life" and the public utterance of a confidence; it combines in a single mode of conduct the political reserve of the sage and the inspired frankness of the poet: the maxim and the fable. A balance between ruse and innocence, in-depth analysis and cordial naïveté: such behavior originates in grace rather than artful intent. But it is only books with that quality of interiority that deserve to occupy the reading public, a community of solitary souls who labor to be "by themselves," but without haggling with the public, the duties of family, society, and state, over what is their due and only their due. There is therefore a close kinship between "the freedom of moderns," literature (its appropriate nourishment and law), and lyricism, the open door to the revelation of dreams. But, via other connections, that freedom also stems from Epicurean philosophy, which teaches that salvation lies within and owes nothing to civic and historical life. That notion of freedom is still indebted to the Christian religion, in the Augustinian interpretation given by Montaigne in his "Apology for Raymond Sebond," where the right to religious conscience is clearly asserted against the earthly City, against Caesar, and against the corrupt and corrupting "world" onto which Caesar, in the best of cases, imposes a provisional semblance of order.

These "modern freedoms" that Montaigne asserted and illustrated during the religious wars, in a century when the king of France, assailed on all sides, was not in a position to enslave consciences, had an entirely different fate in the seventeenth century. From one crisis to the next, there was an increasingly vigorous assertion of a military, political, and cultural state whose summonses, reinstituting the full-time civic duties of the ancient commonwealth, can be encapsulated in the exorbitant demands spelled out by the abbé de La Chambre the day La Fontaine was admitted to the Académie Française: "Understand that henceforth you are working under a prince who will be informed of the progress you make on the path of virtue, and who will have consideration for you only insofar as you aspire to advance in the proper manner."[30]

Beginning in 1684 at Versailles, that was how poetic freedom and, more generally, private freedom were viewed. In spite of the moderation of La Fontaine's prose and poetry, it was clear that they emanated from an *entirely free back shop*, built on the same model as Montaigne's, and as those of the Renaissance poets and small opposition courts under Louis XIII, who celebrated their friends the princes in the intimacy of châteaux that were not state palaces. That lost poetic freedom, which could not be found at the Louvre or at Versailles, could at least seek its revenge by gathering around itself an invisible republic of readers who escaped the discipline and official conventions of King Louis the Great's court.

Far from being a minor "ornament" to the seventeenth century, La Fontaine's poetry truly burst forth from what may have been its most perilous zone of tension. It required a miraculous degree of understanding and tact for the poet to produce poems as he chose, without leaving himself open to the direct reprisals of the state. In the midst of Louis XIV's reign, that fidelity to a vocation of freedom, which had been taken for granted in France under Louis XIII and during the regency of Anne of Austria, indicated no "meekness," no "servility." On the contrary, the poet's courage did not fail, despite his superior diplomatic skills, when he judged it appropriate to take a stand, with the utmost clarity, in the quarrel concerning the souls of animals, where nothing less than the legitimacy of his poetry and of his wisdom were at stake, or in the quarrel between the ancients and the moderns. He saw very clearly that the ancients (the better readers) were on the side of "modern freedoms," whereas the moderns (readers who were more easily satisfied) were the sycophants of power and fashion.

Above all, he took sides, with a modest heroism whose audacity and rarity have not been adequately measured, in the political drama behind the Foucquet affair. After Foucquet, the dream of a reconciliation between the king and the Fronde, order and freedom, evaporated. For La Fontaine this was also the end of a wholly amicable patronage, more stable but not more constraining than the "service of princes" characteristic of poets in the Renaissance courts or of their French successors in the early part of the century: Montmorency and Orléans, Soissons and Liancourt. With Colbert, the regime of "creatures," imposed by Cardinal de Richelieu on the writers who had rallied behind his cause, was about to be revived in the form of a "list of gratifications for French writers." The gravity of Foucquet's fall went far beyond the injustice done to the *surintendant*. La Fontaine's political lucidity was equal to his lyric genius. Ariosto, a poet he "held dear," had, like him, combined these two sorts of intelligence. It was a moment of tragic crisis for La Fontaine, and that crisis led him to mature within a few months. In that terrible light, he "understood his age," but he especially understood who *he* was, and that he would not abjure himself. The best of his writings date from the Foucquet affair, and the two magnificent poems he wrote and published to obtain a pardon for the *surintendant*, facing a death sentence, marked his second birth to poetry and wisdom. That tragic ordeal obliged him to look deep within himself and, at the same time, to appeal to the most intimate and profound part of the French public.

In *Le voyage en Limousin* La Fontaine was bold enough to write, from the safety of a letter addressed to his wife and destined to circulate only in manuscript form, that, standing before Foucquet's first prison in Amboise, he became very emotional for a long time. Quoting that passage, Giraudoux allowed himself this comment: "It is the friendship of a dog who stands in front of the door of a house where the master is no longer."[31]

This misinterpretation is also a retrospective pettiness. Sainte-Beuve, more at home in the seventeenth century, had better glimpsed the true nature of La Fontaine's fidelity, and his attachment to the French "frankness" of which Montaigne boasted, and on behalf of which Richelieu was so fiercely combatted. In the section of *Causeries du lundi* devoted to the author of *Fables*, he cites Boileau's striking account of the foundation of La Fontaine's thinking. "M. Racine," wrote Brossette at Boileau's dictation,

> was conversing one day with La Fontaine on the absolute power of kings. La Fontaine, who loved independence and freedom, could not adjust to the idea M. Racine wanted to present of that absolute and unlimited power. M. Racine found support in Scripture, which speaks of how the Jewish people wanted to choose a king, in the person of Saul, and of the authority this king had over his people. But, replied La Fontaine, if the kings are masters of our possessions, of our lives, and of everything, they must have the right to look upon us as ants when compared to them, and I shall give in if you can show me how that is authorized by Scripture. "So," said M. Racine, "then you don't know the passage from Scripture, *Tanquam formicae deambulabitis coram rege vestro?*" This passage was his own invention, since it is not in Scripture. But he offered it to make fun of La Fontaine, who quite simply believed him.[32]

Few texts introduce us so brutally to the "captive thinking" that reigned in France under Louis XIV. "M. Racine" appears as the interpreter of the doctrine of the state (he may have been a much more wily interpreter, and one more in complicity with La Fontaine, than Boileau realized). In my view, the author of *Fables* (who, in this story, does not have the right to be addressed as "Monsieur," which is reserved for gentlemen of the king's chamber) has the leading role. As a reader of the Bible, he knows the God of Israel's bias against kings, whose illusory power neglects or openly combats his own. When the Hebrews, like the frogs in the fable, asked the prophet Samuel for a king, he replied with a vehement exhortation. He painted a terrible portrait of the tyranny that awaited them. But the people were hungry for voluntary servitude, and Samuel, having taken counsel with God, ceased to resist: he anointed Saul and had him elected king. He was a warrior-king, and he died with his sons on the battlefield. Monarchy by divine right was in this sacred text the punishment of the people, who were incapable of a freedom regulated solely by the prophets: it was a further instance of their fall.

Racine accepted this punishment as a consequence of Adam's sin. La Fontaine, who did not accept equality in servitude and the exile of the divine, was on the side of the prophet Samuel. He would have preferred that the bitter cup be spared poets, even if the people wanted it. If he surrendered to Racine's facetious response in Latin, it was only because everything was understood implicitly between them.

La Fontaine—altogether lagging *behind* the age—remained faithful to the liberal conception of the kingdom, which the princes and the Parlement had set up in opposition to Richelieu, and which inspired the various Frondes. Beyond it, he remained faithful to the hopes that Foucquet's magnificence, intelligence, and charm had elicited in him. Racine was a stranger to these loyalties. He accepted (without being duped, and as Pascal had also done) the royal dictatorship, a still very small-scale, but already oppressive, version of the modern state. Racine was a tragic poet. In his "back shop," however, the author of *Phèdre* remained faithful to Port-Royal, which had been savagely persecuted and was eventually dispersed by the king.

La Fontaine was the only lyric poet in the century of Louis XIV. His internal resistance to political servitude, unlike that of Port-Royal and Pascal, was not simply an affirmation of God's primacy over the kings he gave to nations to punish them. It was also fed by the ideal of "French freedom" that Montaigne, despite his monarchical loyalty, held for his most precious possession, which the chroniclers of the opposition to Richelieu and of the Fronde invoked, and which Racine no longer understood except in its purely religious dimension. It was that moral, philosophical, and political ideal that sustained Saint-Evremond all his life: exiled in England in 1661, he was one of La Fontaine's closest friends. That same ideal was also shared in the following generation by the marquis de La Fare, another friend of the fabulist and the author of vengeful memoirs compiled at the end of Louis XIV's reign. That liberal ideal was at the heart of the politics of Fénelon, a man who admired La Fontaine: the education the author of *Télémaque* gave the duc de Bourgogne amounted to making the latter a king capable of moderating his will to power, and of accepting the free play of a "polysnyody." La Fontaine, even in the most oppressive years under the autocrat of Versailles, was not alone in sharing these sentiments in his private thoughts. He was not an anachronistic eccentric. The princes, the Parlement, and the Messieurs of Port-Royal submitted to the yoke, kept quiet, and even pretended to echo the official panegyrists: they were thinking nonetheless. It is obvious that a lyric poet had to make himself understood among the princes through the slightest hints, since it was among them, in a friendly domesticity that had none of the *political* servitude characteristic of the writer pensioned by the state, that his art traditionally had meaning. Mme Ulrich, La Fontaine's friend in his final years, who was cloistered with the Madelonnettes after the poet's death, wrote, in an edition of La Fontaine's works augmented with previously unseen material, which she published in 1696: "All those who loved his works (and who does not love them?) also loved him personally. He was received by the finest people in France. Everyone wanted him, and, if I tried to list all the illustrious people and all the superior minds who were eager for his conversation, I would have to give a list of the entire court."[33] What Mme Ulrich meant by "court" was the princes, high magistrates, grandes dames—high society—who saw La Fontaine in Paris. What an elegant revenge on Louis the Great and his decision to take his leave! With La Fontaine, in his company, free France read his master-pieces or occasional poetry, savoring in private, even under the oppression of Louis XIV, the very thing for which they had developed such a passion in public, during the mad disorder of the Fronde and the miraculous fireworks of the *surintendant* Foucquet. It is striking that, until his last moments, the poet who saw the political and religious trouble ahead found, in spite of Versailles and Marly, such lofty, generous, and grateful appreciation around him. No poet from Louis XIV's reign, not even the most official ones, left so many portraits, including portraits commis-sioned from the most famous painters of the time: François de Troy, Hyacinthe Rigaud, Nicolas de Largillière.[34] These portraits, which depict him as a high magistrate of letters, adorned with all the attributes of pub-lic ceremony, counterbalance the appearance of marginality of Mme de La Sablière's friend. It is well known that, in the seventeenth century, the portrait was a prestige industry, but also an industry of love tokens, like locks of hair and jewels. It is a good wager that the portraits of La Fontaine, though stemming from the former, also owe a great deal to the latter. This man was an object of friendship even more than an object of admiration.

To be sure, the fantastic escapade of the Fronde and the seductive ambitions of the charmer Foucquet, though they reveal a passion for free-dom with which everyone can identify, were powerless to build, or even to outline, a political rationale worthy of that passion. Freedom, even private freedom, can endure only under a free form of government, and one that deserves to be so. In France between the seventeenth and the twentieth centuries, there has been a striking generational contrast between the tal-ent for freedom and the political incapacity to guarantee it. Every time the French people's love of freedom leaves the private sphere to invade the public square, the uproar caused is enough to make these same French people rush toward voluntary servitude to escape the disorder. Is that any reason to prefer the sinister boredom of Versailles to the absurd swarms of young madmen in the Fronde, to prefer Dangeau's *Journal* to Cardinal de Retz's *Mémoires?*

But are we condemned to choose between these two extremes? In essence, it is this very French question that has been raised, and with greater clarity today than ever before, by the person and works of La Fontaine. As soon as it is raised—and the question has come up repeatedly throughout French history and is even constitutive of the national character—the *Legenda minor* of the fabulist is no longer relegated to the footnotes of the *Legenda major* of Louis the Great. There is undoubtedly in La Fontaine something of the reed of freedom that withstands all storms and ignores the scorn heaped upon it by the oak, which is soon brought down by the North Wind. All the same, he was not just an underground fighter in the Fronde, courageously persevering under his vanquisher. He was generous enough to be faithful to the fire of his youth, but he was also ironic and superior enough to see its vanity and weakness. He was the only Frenchman who understood, with such a degree of political intelligence and detachment, that freedom is not a flame: because he did not resign himself to being snuffed out by the state, he rose above both freedom without vigilance and long-lasting order within servitude. He made his life and work an unbelievable and supreme alliance between caprice and rigor, wild abandon and composition, impulsiveness and a discipline that this life and this work found solely within themselves. Better than the majestic order of Louis XIV, who trampled so many living shoots, La Fontaine's life and works indicate what France could be, or could have been, if it were to unite the private genius of freedom with a living political form capable of disciplining it, but only to better realize it. None of the subsequent administrations in France have been able to find the secret of that balance, for which La Fontaine and his works are at once the most obvious, the most famous, and the most ignored receptacle. We find the harmonic of that secret, however, in the masterpieces of French literature, which, from Chateaubriand to Proust, and from Marivaux to Larbaud, have contrasted a politics of "lost time," composed of abrupt leaps forward and brutal failures, to the ironic and victorious kingdom of "time regained," which is reserved for their readers.

· · ·

In the national tradition of La Fontaine eulogies, Taine's *La Fontaine et ses Fables* stands apart.[35] It is the most famous of all, and the least read.

Taine wrote it in 1851, to console himself for being flunked for political reasons at his *agrégation* in philosophy. This early work has something of the purple prose of a writer floundering about, and something of the thesis of a great mind putting his skills to the test. But what a writer, and what a mind! It is remarkable that this young titan chose to flex his new muscles by interpreting a winged poet, as far as could be from his own prose and the architectonic genius he already bore within himself. The encounter between these two great personalities, who were hardly made for each other, is all the more striking. They illuminate each other better than any natural resemblances and affinities might have done.

As a literary critic, especially if he is judged by his *La Fontaine*, Taine passes for the father of everything that is now despised: poetry "explicated" in terms of what is most alien and external to it. He believes that the three coordinates of historical positivism—"race" (in the sense that Chateaubriand speaks of "the race of the Bourbons"), milieu, and moment—will allow us to understand La Fontaine and to read his Fables *scientifically*, in their objective truth, as a "product" of a particular human type (the Gallic), within a particular context of human geography (provincial, ancien régime), and within a particular historical period (the reign of Louis XIV). It would be hard to be more diametrically opposed to the finesse of Ariel. The modern reader, alerted to Taine's avowed agenda, reaches an impasse. In fact, in the first pages of *La Fontaine*, the initial description of the "Gallic character" over the long term, the realistic depictions of the landscape and fauna of Champagne at which Taine excelled, have the effect (like some introductory sections of Balzac's *La comédie humaine*) of a museum of realist paintings in the style of Courbet, worthwhile in themselves, but clashing with the Watteau and Oudry paintings that decorate the pavilions in the gardens of *Fables*.

And yet, once we have overcome our first sense of impatience, that laborious preparation, as in Balzac's novels, creates a climate and a world. Taine the artist, hidden under the ferocious modesty of his Victorian scholar's redingote, has sought and found his own palette and his own brushstroke, a transposition, truly his own but still faithful, of La Fontaine's poetic kingdom, his landscape, and his characters. With the tools of Teniers and Ruysdael, Taine has been able to create his own metaphor for the comic and tragic Arcadia of *Fables*, where the clear waters, the barely outlined vegetation, and a symbolic meteorology serve as the setting for little dramas, oftentimes horrible, sometimes simply disturbing, as quickly concluded as they began, and leaving no other trace than the ironic stela and inscription that a poet has dedicated to them. The doctrinaire Taine, assisted by the vision of a writer he has within himself, manages to give us a glimpse of the Champagne poet's *Et in Arcadia ego,* even as he paves it over. He is able to highlight the contrast between this unique universe, both lyric and realistic, and the official version of King Louis the Great's reign. The "Gallic" La Fontaine, rooted in the kingdom for the long term, remained unaffected by the conventions that governed the pomp of Versailles; he perceived and revealed the human comedy and tragedy behind the machine-made spectacle of the royal state, and in its metal gears and cogs.

Taine is a very subdued romantic, but more forcefully romantic for all that. The scholar and philosopher in him conspire with the artist to withhold easy emotion, but also force him to pursue his intuition and feelings to the end. In Taine's reading of *Fables,* the seeds for his extraordinary analysis in volume 1 of *Origines de la France contemporaine* are already sown.[36] And, if we listen with the same ear that Taine lent to *Fables,* that close reading can be heard for what it truly is: the lively, but already threatening, overture to the tragic symphony of *Origines,* the masterpiece of Taine the artist and historian, his *Ancien régime.*

Even more than Auguste Comte's notions, Balzac's *Comédie humaine* helped the young writer to recognize the ambition and honesty, the irony and melancholy of the fabulist's universe. Bypassing the trees in favor of the forest, Taine goes directly to the principal characters—monstrous and grotesque—into which amour propre metamorphoses the human form in *Fables,* and which invade an Arcadia ideally suited to the shepherds of *L'Astrée.* He gathers together the scattered traits of the king, the courtier, the country squire, the monk, the bourgeois, the financier, the judge, the pedant, the peasant, and the whole animal cast of characters from "The Companions of Ulysses" (12.1). He undoubtedly slants *Fables* too far in the direction of La Bruyère and coarsens the poet's satirical touch. But the magnifying optics and acoustics he chooses have the enormous merit of doing justice to the powerful vision of La Fontaine the painter and to the originality of his music, which has been downplayed and aestheticized by the whole French critical tradition. Taine the philosopher and historian sees the author of *Fables* as a prince of poetic thought to whom he surrenders his weapons, and a superior artist who inspires a trembling respect in him. He shows the teeming life of his satire, which sees, shows, and gives us to hear with an impartial serenity the very thing that broke the poet's heart, but which he leaves it to his reader/beholder/listener to understand and experience, according to how finely tuned his inner senses are.

This restraint in judging reality, and the freedom the poet gives his interlocutor to draw his own conclusions, are in themselves a response to the "French malady." Taine's English-style empiricism recognizes in La Fontaine a sincere experience of France, a lucidity, a sorrow, and a tact akin to his own. The critic shows the poet mobilizing his harmonic powers so that his listeners can hear the dissonance that Descartes's and Malebranche's mechanistic metaphysics, and the abstract administrative order of absolutism, have superimposed on the old "Gallic" nature and on the nature of the kingdom itself. Taine the historian, instead of locking La Fontaine inside his time, succeeds in establishing the meaning that is still alive, now more than ever alive, for himself and for France in the wake of the Revolution, a poetry powerfully poetic enough to have seen and heard, in the seventeenth century, the main lines of the political drama of France and of modernity as a whole.

The first volume of *Origines de la France contemporaine* brings to the fore all the virtualities that were still latent in *La Fontaine*, written a quarter of a century earlier. This overview of the kingdom caught within the network of a presumptuous state, at once all-powerful and powerless, indefatigable and paralyzed, providential and bloodsucking, this depiction of the pleasant and temperate mores that allowed the French people of the ancien régime to enjoy the established disorder by seeing to their own affairs and averting their eyes, borrows its formal power, its black comedy, and its detached impartiality from *Fables*. With a modesty that is also very artful, the implacable rigor of the Tainian analysis veils the powerful undercurrent of emotion that makes the vigorous prose of *Origines* rumble, like that which sets to vibrating the delicate lyre of "The Schoolboy, the Pedant, and the Man with a Garden" (9.5) or "The Gardener and the Squire" (4.4): love and pity for a masterpiece of nature, history, and art, bursting with talents and resources, ruined by a geometrical mind-set in the service of a proud and predatory egotism. Taine's *Ancien Régime* is an overture or prologue that carries *La Révolution* within itself, just as a cloud carries a storm. The two subsequent volumes of *Origines* demonstrate, with the same methodical and controlled precision as the first, but now with a roiling undercurrent of dread and pity, the "storms of steel" that were laying waste the oldest kingdom in Europe, and which within a few months created the desolate and devastated landscape of modernity. In what sense is this historicism? Taine, in situating La Fontaine and his *Fables* within his century, reveals to what extent the poet and his works, concealed behind their cheerful familiarity, get to the heart of a great human and French tragedy and, without displaying it in the slightest, hold the keys to it for all eternity.

Nothing is more fantastic or more contrary to the monotonous laws that govern the unsurprising order of things than to see a poetry mature and blossom over time, a poetry that, from the beginning, had been whispered and shared by the poet as a way of recovering from the ills of time. With his poetry, the poet finally revealed himself, and today this *bon-homme* looks like a major contemporary.

Many perspicacious friends of the poet, French and non-French, who did not let themselves be discouraged by his legend or intimidated by the classic shadow cast by his king, have prepared the way for the conversation with La Fontaine you are about to read. I cannot give their names here: many will be cited in the notes, and if this book helps readers to understand a little better La Fontaine's silences, to appreciate the intelligence, kindness, and sense of the divine they hold in store for us, I will clearly owe it to these young and not-so-young predecessors, the contemporaries, like myself, of another fin de siècle, it too worn down by grandeur and dread.

CHAPTER I

Olympus and Parnassus

Pendant le doux emploi de ma Muse innocente,
Louis dompte l'Europe, et d'une main puissante
Il conduit à leur fin les plus nobles projets.

As I with my innocent Muse am at play,
Louis tames Europe and with powerful hands
Sees to their end the most noble plans.
> —Jean de La Fontaine, 11, *Epilogue*

M. de La Fontaine was a simple and true man, who on a thousand matters thought differently than the rest of mankind.
> —The abbé Pouget, priest of Saint-Roch,
> La Fontaine's confessor in the last months of his life

*L*a Fontaine wrote poems about sleep, desire, solitude, and leisure. To top it all off, as if to better highlight all these luxuries of contemplation, he forever engraved in his readers' minds a portrait of the world of passion and self-interest as captivating on the surface as it was terrifying at a deeper level.

These were serious crimes. To conceal them, the legend of a sweet fool was no more than what was required.

Among the numerous quasi-Franciscan *fioretti* embroidering that legend, and which the poet mischievously allowed to spring up on his path, there is one that tells of him suddenly deserting his hosts in the middle of a conversation, later explaining that it was time to follow and admire the orderly funeral of an ant.[1] During his lifetime such stories camouflaged what was essentially incompatible, or even dangerously contradictory, between the great public favor enjoyed by *Fables*, written by a lightweight of belles lettres, and the very official fervor of which the king, heavyweight champion of action in love, politics, and war, was simultaneously the object.

The disproportion between this distrait man and the Sun King, between the pleasing fictions of which the former was capable and the monumental history of which the latter was the protagonist, in itself barred any comparison or worrisome resemblance.

But the legend was no more than was necessary. It led his contemporaries to a guilty sympathy with the author of *Fables* and *Contes*, even as it generally freed them from disentangling whatever scandal the contrast between the poet's melodious idleness and the king's tireless activity might conceal. Even over time, people's first notions of this overgrown child kept them from plumbing the depths of a body of writing that carefully refrained from displaying the fact that it had depth.

Hence, in the fond collective memory of the French nation, that legend has contributed not a little toward protecting the author of *Fables* from the suspicion formulated in the eighteenth century by another "madman"—this one much more dangerous—namely, Jean-Jacques Rousseau. In his *Emile*, the citizen of Geneva accuses *Fables*, which, like its author, passes for charming, of actually conspiring in the demoralization of children, future adults who would be held responsible for the advent of the Republic.[2]

Nonetheless, even during the Revolution and the Empire, *Fables* continued to be taught to schoolchildren. Beginning in the nineteenth century, care was taken to have the pupils themselves refute Rousseau, by making the accusing passage in *Emile* (prettied up by Lamartine for his own purposes) into a composition topic.[3] By humble means, and thanks to numerous misunderstandings, *Fables* thus continued imperturbably and surreptitiously to influence a wide audience, without in the slightest disturbing the authorities in charge, who were respectful of a canonized author in the national pantheon, like Hans Christian Andersen in Denmark or Lewis Carroll in England.

How, in fact, could the French commonwealth be considered in peril from an innocent who, according to Marguerite Hessein de La Sablière, his best friend and host for twenty years, produced fables the way an apple tree produces apples?

Chateaubriand paid a high price at the hands of his posterity for his boast, openly declared in his *Mémoires*, that his pen had provided a counterweight to Napoleon's sword. The biographical legend of the author of *Mémoires d'outre-tombe*, hardly inclined to smile at his own expense, or so it was believed, presented no obstacle to the indignant accusation of

French high treason and of the writer's ridiculous megalomania: it still afflicts him today. One might wonder why Victor Hugo, who, from Guernesey, launched the firebrand of *Les châtiments* against Napoleon III, never passed for a braggart, even though he took the trouble to put England and the sea between himself and the Second Empire. But in the orthodoxy of French thought, that empire, despite recent efforts to rehabilitate the regime and its leader, has been encapsulated in the disaster of Sedan. And the author of *Les châtiments* was given great national recognition for having retrospectively—in his *Légende des siècles*—draped the defeat of Waterloo in sublimity.

A Young King, Ancient Sphinxes

With La Fontaine, one can dispense with such epic quarrels between literature and the state. The poet lost no opportunity to deprecate himself and make people smile at his innocuousness. His modesty was taken so literally that the rare efforts by modern criticism to depict him as a renegade from his times and—prior to Fénelon and Saint-Simon—a merciless painter of the comedy of power under Louis XIV have remained without influence, or have been ridiculed. Such excessive zeal in countering his legend does honor to him, however, and is closer to the truth than the sympathy of his biographers. The poet has even been made into a Balzacian peasant arriving in Paris, who keeps the ploys of a somewhat crafty social climber carefully under wraps.

The character of a "daydreamer," attributed to the poet during his lifetime, has survived him. It even foiled Rousseau's posthumous indictment. It did not protect La Fontaine so well against the public reprobation that, as of 1675, clung to his *Contes*. It was and remains utterly unlikely that an innocent, even one marvelously gifted at verse, always a bit drowsy, could have been involved in lampooning, however subtly, the Sun King and the ever-glorious operation of his state.

In contrast, it was or is only too obvious that the same poet, politically incompetent and inoffensive (with Laziness, Sleep, and Desire along for the ride), really was guilty of corrupting morals. The harsh crackdown on him from the police, the Church, and the Académie Française may cause indignation today, like the morality trials to which Flaubert and Baudelaire were summoned under the Second Empire. But no one has ever doubted that the author of the exquisite "Lettre à l'abbesse de Mouzon" (anticipating the best of Toulet) and *Nouvelles en vers tirées de Boccace et de l'Arioste* (anticipating the best of Apollinaire) had breached the limits of decency; and he did so, undeniably, in full possession of the facts.

Under the reign of Louis the Great, this was undoubtedly a grave sin. But, in the end, it was not a state crime. Under Louis XIV, there was no comparison between the crime of political high treason and the crime of offense to morality or even to religion. In the king's eyes, the wrongs of the Compagnie du Saint-Sacrement, of Port-Royal, of the Protestants, and of Fénelon were theological only in the final analysis. It was not so much the suspicion of heresy that condemned these suspect religious fanatics as their political revolt disguised as theology. For some of them, heresy may have been the root of their error, but the true error consisted in meeting as a private "sect," separated from the body of the state. France had to proceed as a single individual under the guidance of a sacred leader.

It was not so much their relatively heterodox mores, discovered when their correspondence was seized, that elicited Louis XIV's anger against the young princes, nephews of his cousin Condé, who had deserted the court and in 1685 had waged war against the Turks in the emperor's armies. Rather, it was their cruel words against the king and Mme de Maintenon. Their epigrams gave a criminal significance to their departure from Versailles and seemed to reveal in these young people the most culpable form of libertinage, namely, political libertinage.[4]

Accused only of corrupting morality, the lovable fool La Fontaine tactfully, and without too much difficulty all in all, extricated himself from the morality trial to which his *Contes* had given rise. In many respects this minor scandal was even a lucky excuse that allowed his supporters and his enemies, at the time of his candidacy to the Académie Française, to face off on a relatively secondary front. There, the poet could confess his errors, even as he benefited from the leniency that was granted in advance—in Paris and even at the academy—to bad subjects who were not freethinkers.

The very literary libertinage of *Contes* and the virtuous indignation it elicited even had the enormous advantage of further concealing the true crime. That crime was still on the king's mind when he held up the triumphant election of La Fontaine and made his approval depend on his historiographer Boileau's admission to the academy before La Fontaine. The political crime was the suspicious role the poet had once played in the "Foucquet affair" and the imperceptible whiff of independence that the language of *Fables*—undignified, moreover—had, since that time, continued to give off.

This supposedly distrait man, like the title character in his "Simonides and the Gods" (1.14), had a great deal of luck. But he assisted Fortune by displaying a flair for diplomacy that belies his legend. The poet's reverse Machiavellianism stemmed not from the sociology of ambition but from what Leo Strauss has analyzed in *Persecution and the Art of Writing*. Strauss, a great commentator of Hobbes, shows that in times of tyranny (that is, most of the time) the contemplative man of genius must set up a camouflage even more intricate than the suspicions and traps of which he is the object.[5] Rilke said nothing less in his poem *Mensonge, arme d'adolescent*, written in French.[6] And, already in the rather dark scene from *Le malade imaginaire* (act 2, scene 11) in which Argan has his daughter, little Louison, appear before him and tries to force her to denounce her sister by threatening her with a whipping, Molière had shown what serpent's ruse the innocent dove is capable of when she must extricate herself from the talons of a bird of prey without giving herself away, even when that bird bears the honorable name of "father."

La Fontaine was not "persecuted," even though, by the criteria prevailing under Louis XIV, his being kept away from the court was equivalent to the "bad luck" or "curse" of a romantic poet. He was not persecuted only because he did not count enough, and did not seek to count more; he knew better than anyone the perils of thinking "differently than the rest of mankind." He was willing to demean himself, especially since that sacrifice of personal authority protected his body of work and prevented suspicious people from catching him where he knew he was the most vulnerable. Rousseau's clairvoyance (which was in fact off the mark) came far too late: it could not posthumously do damage to a masterpiece of poetic caution that the Argus of classical France had not been able to find wanting.

Although in his heart the poet may have accepted for himself the stag's tragic fate in the fable "The Eye of the Master" (4.21), he did not seek it for his "favorite book":

Chacun donne un coup à la bête.
Ses larmes ne sauraient la sauver du trépas.

Everyone strikes the beast.
His tears cannot save him from death.

All the same, La Fontaine made a narrow escape. The Lion of the Louvre and of Versailles did not wish to know that the lion and its court of wolves and foxes, which wreak havoc in *Fables,* had some relation to himself or his entourage. The king thought it beneath him to exclaim: "Away, you puny insect, dung of the earth." He preferred to act as if he had not heard the gnat of the fable (2.9) "sounding the charge" at the periphery of his august mane. How could the "king of glory" (as a historian of our own time has called Louis XIV, using a title that, even under that idolatrous reign, was reserved for God alone)[7] have condescended to recognize himself and his entourage in little children's stories as old as time?

Pupils had stumbled through them in every little Latin school since antiquity, and their translation by an insignificant poet, known in town but ignored at court, had been tediously routine in the nation since the Middle Ages and Marie de France.[8]

The king, as his son Monseigneur and his grandson the duc de Bourgogne would later do, had himself translated and imitated Aesop's tales. Would his tutors have subjected him to such exercises if they had believed that the most insignificant of his subjects could fashion a mask out of them that would allow him to look directly at the king with impunity?

Animals, the main characters of these fictions for nurses and tykes—horses and dogs, cats and monkeys, mice and rats—abounded in the palaces of the Crown, though they did not speak. The more exotic animals—lions and tigers, camels and elephants, birds from Africa and river fish—populated the royal grounds, their aviaries and ponds. A great hunter like his forebears, Louis XIV was no less familiar with stags, hinds, wild boars, and even, occasionally, wolves and foxes, which he tracked in his forests. The king, a genealogist and heraldist (though Saint-Simon pointed out the "grossest absurdities" he propounded in that discipline, which was key for any French gentleman who knew his world),[9] was at ease among heraldic animals, which appeared everywhere in his kingdom, painted, engraved, sculpted, or embroidered, on the sides of coaches, on the doorsteps of dwellings, on the pediments of tapestries and portraits, on crockery and furniture, on cannons and swords. In many respects the king of France was at that time the king of animals as well.

That domestic, cynegetic, and heraldic dominion over the animal world meant that Louis XIV would not condescend to be annoyed at a kite, if some gamekeeper, after capturing the pretty bird of prey, had humbly wished to offer it to him; no, not even if that kite had taken it into its head to plant its talons "into His Majesty's nose":

Le roi n'éclata point; les cris sont indécents
A la Majesté Souveraine.
("The Kite, the King, and the Hunter," 12.12)

The king did not explode; screams are indecent
To his Sovereign Majesty.

The king's stoicism toward an animal committing treason against his majesty is amusing. Would the king have used such restraint if he had discerned that the poet, who for once invented this impertinent fable from whole cloth, and who was himself a former gamekeeper, did not hesitate to let his own captive birds sink their talons into the royal nose?

Furthermore, La Fontaine dedicated the fable of the kite to the prince de Conti, one of the young Frondeurs of 1685. At the time, La Fontaine was no longer, and had not been for a long time, a "gamekeeper" for the duchy of Château-Thierry. He was not in the king's service at all. A lowly subject, he did not even have the inferior position held, in the outbuildings of Versailles, by an animal painter of genius, François Desportes, who had the official job of following the royal hunts and immortalizing the spoils in still lifes; or the position later held, in the retinue of the hunts of Louis XIV's great-grandson, by the great Jean-Baptiste Oudry, who in 1764 provided sumptuous illustrations for La Fontaine's *Fables*, on the orders of Louis XV.[10]

But La Fontaine might easily have become the animal poet of Louis XIV, had the king so ordered. The poet had tried his hand at this genre to please Nicolas Foucquet. In 1658, in the conclusion of the idyll *Adonis*, dedicated to the *surintendant*, he had composed the long tale in verse of a boar hunt. The purple prose of the piece, if we are to believe Paul Valéry, is deadly dull. Is it less so when we know that it imitates the tragic hunt of Actaeon in Ovid's *The Metamorphoses*? Even La Fontaine did not succeed in making venery a subject of French poetry.[11]

That was how Louis XIV himself felt: he liked venery and painters of tables of game, but hated it when other hunters told of their exploits in front of him. After a performance of *Les fâcheux* during the festival of Vaux on the night of 17 August 1661, he asked Molière to add to his parade of bores a garrulous huntsman character. This was done for the performance at Fontainebleau a week later:

Parbleu! chemin faisant, je te le veux conter.
Nous étions une troupe assez bien assortie,
Qui, pour courir un cerf, avions hier fait partie.

(2.7)

Oh Lord! On the way, let me tell you about it.
We were a fairly well-assorted gang,
Who set out yesterday to hunt a stag.

La Fontaine would have been properly ensnared if, on the faith of a first attempt in honor of the lord of Vaux, the king had appointed him to the office of poet of royal hunting gear, stables, menageries, and kennels. After all, Louis XIV "annexed" to his service all the other artists and writers chosen and assembled with keen intuition by his superintendent of finances. The king even made Foucquet's former right-hand man, Paul Pellisson, his historiographer. Subsequently, he practically reduced to silence Boileau's satirical genius and Racine's tragic genius by making them Pellisson's successors in his court and in the armies. To be sure, La Fontaine made a narrow escape in every respect.

The author of *Adonis*, even in the very inferior rank he held as one of the faithful of the disgraced Foucquet, had the good fortune to displease, particularly and definitively, not just Colbert but the king as well. He had compromising friendships, protectors with too-important titles, and independent ways. During the trial of the *surintendant*, he had committed more than a crime—he had committed a sin. But it was a much greater error on the king's part to have noticed that sin. Instead of sentencing Foucquet's minor poet to a lifetime of tedious descriptions of the king's hunts and encomiums of his hounds, which he might very well have done, Louis XIV believed he could destroy him by ignoring him.

As of 1668, the king had to resign himself to seeing the large menagerie of *Fables* running about everywhere; the book was not the slightest bit indebted to him, he was neither its king nor its master, he could not even condemn it without losing face. And, for three centuries, it has obstinately provided a counterpoint to the grandeur of his reign.

Fortunately for the king, who did not like to admit his errors, he was not short on amour propre. La Fontaine, a painter in verse of barnyard animals, cocks and goats, donkeys and ewes, was, in the king's eyes, never anything but a burlesque miniaturist, who worked for a private clientele for lack of something better. By his conduct, La Fontaine did everything to shore up that fiction, which was his best safeguard. In the end he was even admitted to the Académie Française in 1684, in spite of *Fables*, in spite of *Contes*; he took over Colbert's own chair and with Louis XIV's

approval, delayed for a time, but in the end granted in spite of everything for the sake of peace and quiet, after more than twenty years of
open indifference.[12]

The "greatest king in the world" willingly let himself be persuaded that
only the major genres of art were worthy to speak of his own art of government: harangues by the Académie Française for the feast of Saint
Louis, Latin inscriptions by the Petite Académie, Boileau's Pindaric epistles and Horatian odes, Racine's neo-Greek tragedies, Benserade's mythological ballets, Quinault and Lully's operas, Le Brun's large history paintings. The epic, abundantly practiced and zealously theorized under his
reign, still counted for little in the hall of mirrors set up for the king. That
is one of the literary mysteries of the monarchy. As for lyric poetry, it
withered away.[13]

Over the course of Louis XIV's reign, that royal, hierarchical, and almost regimental conformity hardened into a system, namely, academicism. Since then that yoke, periodically restored after periods of "Fronde"
such as the rococo, which became fashionable after 1715, has never ceased
to weigh heavy, majestic or carictural, on the arts and letters of France.
Nothing has done more damage to an understanding of that literary age
than the continuing confusion, thanks to the deceptive name "classicism," between the official academicism of the regime and the freedom
that several poets of genius, heirs to an age of freedom without "grandeur,"
managed for a time to exercise in opposition to the gradual glaciation of
seventeenth-century literature. La Fontaine's robustness allowed him to
resist the summer, autumn, and even the first part of the long and terrible
winter of a reign that lasted more than half a century.

In Molière's comedy, a "lowly genre" in which Louis XIV took pleasure
during the troubled beginnings of his personal power, all sorts of inferior
creatures—peasants, valets, bourgeois, courtiers of the worst sort—show
their true colors, ridiculous and valiantly alien to the sacredness of the
state, like the animals in *Fables*. The king could not be associated with
these performances for commoners and that comic troupe, except in the
dance interludes, those, for example, in *Le mariage forcé* of 1668 (the year
of *Fables*), when he appeared disguised as an "Egyptian." He did so at the
Louvre, in front of a handpicked audience, and in the guise of a leisure
activity beneficial for the state and misleading as to its great military plans.

In *Tartuffe, L'impromptu de Versailles,* and *Le misanthrope,* Louis XIV
was evoked as a king who fully exercised his sacred authority only from a
great distance and by hints, like a transcendent, omniscient, and invisible
power seated on Olympus. The one time Molière had Olympus descend
onto the stage, in the mythological comedy *Amphitryon*, it was to ensure

a framework worthy of Jupiter, king of the gods, and his love affairs: in the mirror of the production, he showed Louis XIV another of his diversions, which was also very much in favor among his subjects.

Olympus had already appeared in the ballet libretto composed by Molière for the festival of "The Pleasures of the Enchanted Isle,"[14] which in May 1664 (in the heat of the Foucquet trial), before a very limited audience, inaugurated the first Versailles of Louis XIV: it was the king's response to the festival of Vaux. The Apollo that Molière presented on the first day was not the Apollo who created the Muses, not the god of Parnassus, patron of the arts, with whom Foucquet had been identified in the decoration of his château and by virtue of his generosity toward poets. Rather, he was a god of Olympus, a Jupiter at rest, who was nonetheless considering going to war so that "the laws of Charles V, the rights of Charlemagne," added to his own via his Spanish marriage, would be respected in Europe. In the gardens of Versailles, transformed into a romantic set, Molière put on stage an official declaration, in alexandrines, of foreign policy. It was a "useful" attraction, which Foucquet had not been able to combine with the "agreeable" entertainment at the festival of Vaux.

In official art at the beginning of Louis XIV's personal reign, Molière's comedies, skillfully inscribed within the decorum of royal grandeur, held the same rank and function that, in the papal Rome of the Renaissance, had been assigned to Giovanni da Udine's "grotesques" on the walls of the Vatican Stanze and on the ceilings of the Farnesina. The latter served to set off, by virtue of their "frames" teeming with comical chimera, the sublimity of Raphael's frescoes, worthy mirrors of a universal and sacred sovereignty.[15]

A fortiori, then, Louis XIV and his reign could not be the subject of La Fontaine's animal depictions, marginal inventions of a new Scarron working on his own behalf, representations alien to the architectonic coherence of royal art, roving locusts living off the charity of a private audience. In the eyes of anyone who had some idea of the true weight of current affairs at court, they counted infinitely less than the entertaining spectacle of the beasts and winged creatures behind their bars in the royal gardens, or the magnificent daily ritual kill by the royal pack of hounds.

In 1674, on the grounds of Versailles, among the other "factories" that set about to entertain the king and the court in the intervals between serious matters (as a pleasant counterpoint to the splendid underground cave of Thetis, where the king himself, in a setting worthy of him, was depicted by Girardon as Phoebus at rest), sculpted animals from Aesop's fables, animated by water fountains, were scattered throughout a laby-rinth of greenery.[16] This menagerie made of lead, painted in trompe l'oeil, which escorted a statue of its counterfeit shepherd, Aesop, indicated quite well the legitimate but inferior rank reserved for animal poetry and art within the hierarchical and harmonic totality of royal art. The Aesop of Champagne, who had published his *Fables* in Paris in 1668, did not even have access to that rank: banned from the jubilation, he must have judged himself extremely lucky that the king of animals and men, from his high perch, pretended to ignore his existence.

The king, strolling in front of the fountains of his labyrinth, could relax with a sense of satisfaction from his days of labor, on which the fate of France, Europe, and the world depended. The animals never spoke to him of anything, except of the talent of his own artists, the gallant spirit of his own poet, Isaac de Benserade, author of the quatrains engraved in bronze at the foot of each fountain. In the king's eyes, La Fontaine's *Fables* could not and should not be anything but the poor man's version—left to the amateurs in the city—of his luxurious labyrinth of Versailles, reserved for his own enjoyment and that of his noted guests.[17]

Charles Perrault, who had thought up that ingenious "factory" and who had given shape to it with the gardener, the water engineer, and the sculp-tors of Vaux, knew La Fontaine very well. He had met him in Foucquet's entourage, where he had once made his way. He admired *Fables* as a con-noisseur, imitated it himself, and was inspired by it not only for the "fac-tory" of the labyrinth of Versailles, but later for his own *Contes*. In stealing from it, he indirectly did the great disgraced poet a favor. The Aesop of the gardens of Versailles was an expensive screen that prevented Louis XIV from pausing to look at the inexpensive Aesop in Parisian bookstores.[18]

Boileau has been reproached a great deal for not mentioning *Fables* in his *Art poétique*, which was published in 1674. This silence cannot be due to some disdain for the fabulist's genius, or even for the genre of the fable: Boileau knew better than anyone that this genre had literary letters of nobility going back without interruption to antiquity and the Renais-sance. In his later writings, he himself boasted that he had convinced the bookseller Barbin to publish the first collection of *Fables*, whose author had been his friend since at least 1664.[19] The silence maintained by *Art poétique*, strange and shocking to modern eyes, was only what was required of anyone who wished to obtain the king's favor, as was the case for Boileau in 1674. It was only fitting to respect the silence of Louis XIV himself, who made it a point to ignore the significance and even the existence of *Fables*.

To consider matters in their best light, it was also an act of compassion toward a colleague with no future, whom this official silence at least left in peace. After all, the author of *Fables* had all he needed to be satisfied; the esteem of the public, manifested in the extraordinary success his brief collections enjoyed from the moment they were put on display in bookstores, compensated somewhat for the king's indifference and the petty behavior of his fellow writers. Such a success, which even the marquise de Montespan could not resist, was augmented by *Le Mercure Galant*, the only magazine of that era, and it no doubt enriched bookstores much more than the poet. But that made it even more difficult for the king to publicly express any annoyance whatever.[20]

Although his literary education had been sadly neglected, Louis XIV had too many talented people around him not to sense the difference in scope between an ordinary translation of Aesop and its lively re-creation, sparkling with wit, by La Fontaine. But no magistrate of the kingdom, however servile he can be imagined to be, could have engaged, without ridiculing the king's justice, in the exegesis necessary to establish that the gap between the obvious moral meaning and the ironic significance of *Fables* was a crime of high treason. Only Holy Scripture and theological writings were open to exegesis at the time—and then only at the Sorbonne, not at the Parlement. To sanctify the puny *Fables* through such an inquiry was out of the question.

Fables was therefore published and became a great best-seller in the seventeenth century, slipping into one of the modest literary nooks of the kingdom that Louis XIV's blind spot keep him from seeing: the service entrance set aside for beasts of burden, the nook of the poor man's Aesop.

There was nothing in what La Fontaine wrote in his *Fables* that had not already been written, published, and learned by heart thousands of times since time immemorial. Was he even an "author"? As a translator, the latest arrival in an age-old tradition, he spoke a symbolic language as familiar to everyone in France, Europe, and the Orient as natural languages themselves. The uniquely alluring inflection he gave to that symbolic and universal language has remained keen and enigmatic over time. Is it something more than the strong impulsion he gave to the long parade of fables, which might otherwise have slowed or been interrupted? Another impulsion, sharper and more aggressive, had occurred sixteen hundred years earlier, in the first century A.D. under the reign of Augustus, in the fables of a Romanized Thracian slave named Phaedrus. That chain of fables was very resistant to time, and, at the desired moment, found champions as resistant as itself. Even today, the veiled and enchanted meaning of *Fables* drives exegetes to despair: there is something impossible to grasp in the way it oscillates between tired platitudes that have been repeated too often and the astounding freedom of an intelligence grappling with the transmigration of souls.[21]

A fortiori, it must have escaped the grasp of seventeenth-century readers, like the disappointing and alluring tenches and gudgeons that slip away in the fable "The Heron" (7.4):

L'onde était transparente ainsi qu'aux plus beaux jours.

The wave was transparent as on the finest days.

Is the incredibly vivacious poetic life of *Fables* to be attributed to its ancient pedigree, which makes it a separate realm of heraldic animals forever evolving in the purest form of the French language? Or might it be to the exciting and always-new pleasure of secret locks and keys opening up the other, hidden side of a century of which we know only the facade? It is both at once. That, in fact, is what gives La Fontaine's fables, officially ignored by the court, the same troubling, almost oracular vitality as Racine's tragedies and Molière's comedies, which were performed with great ceremony in front of the king. Fortunately, Louis XIV did not suspect, even in the most splendid mirror where he innocently took his pleasure, that there were sphinxes looking upon him who had seen many other kings, dating to a time more remote than the origins of the French monarchy, even though it was the oldest in Europe. Neither the comedies of Molière, the French Menander, nor the tragedies of Racine, whose literary genealogy went back to Homer, Euripides, and Virgil, raised any suspicions in him—nor, a fortiori, did La Fontaine's Parisian knickknacks. It would be very naive to attribute to the king the major credit for these masterpieces, written by spies too well educated for him to see through them.

It is worth taking the trouble to consider this misunderstanding between the king and the poets, who were in fact the most valuable thing about his reign—a misunderstanding as strange, and even more volatile, than that which prevents Racine's heroes from ever looking each other in the eye.

The official, conventional, and contextual meaning that poets, writers, and sacred orators, docilely acquiescing to Colbert's, Chapelain's, and Perrault's wishes, attributed to the deeds and victories of a great king in the great genres worthy of a great century, was, from the outset, a cold and dead monument, ridiculed abroad, that is, beyond the range of French armies.

In reality, Louis the Great and his grand era remain vibrant only in the mysterious mirrors that were not dupe to his grandeur. Even in the prime years of his reign, *Phèdre*, *Le malade imaginaire*, and *Le lion devenu vieux*, with infinite tact in regard to the king, gave the ancient signal—thumbs down—that dismisses the gladiators from the limelight. In 1720, on the sign in front of the shop *Au Grand Monarque* (To the great monarch), Watteau had the little servant of Gersaint make the gesture of a grave-digger; in so doing, he packed away in straw Rigaud's official portrait of Louis XIV. Like Molière in *Le malade imaginaire*, Watteau knew in 1720 that he was going to die. The continuity of art preserves art, but leaves in its wake the artist who has ensured that continuity. The great artist, the great poet, knows that. What tact he must use, at the risk of displeasing, to conceal and yet reveal to his king that the same is true for his art of governance.[22]

The fact that Racine and Molière managed, even for a brief period of time, to triumphantly present on the stage a discourse that was flattering on the surface and troubling below the surface, thanks to a sublime double game within and at the center of official art, is, in Europe, one of the great moments in the power of literary wit. But the fact that La Fontaine and his *Fables* were able to thrive to the degree they did during Louis XIV's lifetime, without even hiding behind the grand appearances of state art, is even more surprising. La Fontaine was the first to have fully assessed the degree of disgrace, but also of grace, involved in the very different reception given to his *Fables* by the king of France and by the French public.

In his first collection of 1668, the poet Simonides, "saved by the Gods," was himself. In the second collection, in 1677–79, one can sense something more: the triumphant delight of Pascal's wagerer, who plays for the highest stakes and wins. The brief, lilting verses with an odd number of syllables that introduce "The Faithless Depository" display a modest and serene triumph:

Et même qui mentirait
Comme Esope, et comme Homère,
Un vrai menteur ne serait.
Le doux charme de maint songe
Par leur bel art inventé,
Sous les habits du mensonge
Nous offre la vérité.

L'un et l'autre a fait un livre
Que je tiens digne de vivre
Sans fin, et plus, s'il se peut:
Comme eux ne ment pas qui veut.

(9.1)

And even one who might lie
Like Aesop and Homer do
Would not a true liar be.
The sweet charm of many a dream
By their fine art made real,
Under the costume of a lie
Offers us verity.
Each wrote a book
That I believe
Worthy to live eternally,
And longer, if it can:
Like them, not everyone
Who wishes to do so lies.

Such a power of revelation, even when enveloped in the fiction of the fable, still exposed itself to the supreme risk faced by true poets' lies, which are always threatened with being discovered and unmasked. That risk, which La Fontaine took, fully cognizant of what he was doing, gives his life and words a suspense as intense as that which made Scheherazade's outwardly calm voice tremble within, during the thousand and one nights she held off King Schahryar's anger by telling him tales. At the beginning of the first collection of *Fables choisies mises en vers,* that sort of suspense quietly underlies "The Life of Aesop the Phrygian." For a long time, Aesop artfully dodges the blows his wit ought to have attracted. Finally, however, he encounters the force that does not give him quarter: "Everything Aesop was able to say did not prevent him from being treated like a notorious criminal. He was taken back to Delphi in chains, jailed, then condemned to be cast down. It was no use defending himself with his ordinary weapons, the telling of apologues; the Delphians made fun of them."

There was no dearth of precedents for the persecution of writers and poets, and more than one was burned at the stake, even under Louis XIV. A careless act or a too-obvious meaning in their works had doomed many writers and their printers. The flames that consumed Etienne Duran, the imprisonment of Théophile de Veau, the torture of Claude Le Petit, the most famous of these unfortunate seventeenth-century poets, served as salutary warnings. The Foucquet affair, which in 1661 had brought down a cherished patron of poets and writers, a "minister" whom they had believed powerful and whom they considered one of their own, was experienced by a portion of the community of writers as the threatening prelude to hard times.

Among the many anonymous pieces in verse with which Colbert was bombarded during the trial of the *surintendant* in 1661–64, there was this one, from the *Recueil Conrart:*

> On ne connaît plus le Parnasse,
> Apollon, ni ses doctes soeurs:
> En ce triste temps de douleurs
> Le Mont-Gibet a pris sa place;
> C'est là que Sainte-Hélène, Héraut,
> Pussort et six autres bourreaux,
> En font l'épouvantable base,
> Et que Colbert, leur demi-Dieu,
> Est au sommet, et tient le lieu
> Du renommé cheval Pégase.[23]

> Parnassus is no longer seen,
> Nor Apollo and his learned sisters:
> In this sad time of sorrow
> Mount-Gallows has taken their place;
> There the tormentors Sainte-Hélène,
> Héraut, Pussort, and six others
> Constitute its fearsome base,
> While Colbert, their demigod,
> Stands at its summit, in the place
> Of Pegasus, horse of renown.

Parnassus (in other words, the community of readers and writers) believed it had found its "Apollo" in the person of the *surintendant* Foucquet, and had ardently wished that the musician-god, whom the Valois had so loftily claimed as their own, would, with Foucquet, again find his place beside the young king and reestablish a lasting peace between Parnassus and Olympus. La Fontaine gives voice to that illusion, dissipated in 1661, in his fable "Simonides and the Gods" (1.14):

Les grands se font honneur dès lors qu'ils nous font grâce.
　Jadis l'Olympe et le Parnasse
　Etaient frères et bons amis.

Great men honor themselves when they are kind to us.
　At one time Olympus and Parnassus
　Were brothers and dear friends.

THE BIBLE OF POETS

　The symbolic language of Olympus and Parnassus is unfamiliar today. We take it for an allegorical convention, which it was undoubtedly becoming under Louis XIV, but it was not yet so for poets of the previous generation—Tristan, Saint-Amant, Colletet—or for La Fontaine. We have no inkling of the seriousness of meaning with which it was charged for them. In 1663 La Fontaine submitted his *Ode au roi* to the imprisoned Nicolas Foucquet for his approval, in the midst of the political tragedy. Here is how he explains his intent in the poem: "I have thus composed this ode for the consideration of Parnassus. You know well enough the interest Parnassus takes in matters relating to you."

　For La Fontaine, to speak of "Parnassus" was to signify something more and other than the community of readers and writers moved by the fate of its patron. It was to recall in brief the founding myth of belles lettres itself, to invoke an allegiance that no doubt wanted to be in harmony with the allegiance every "good Frenchman" owed his king, but which was more ancient and more sacred than the kingdom itself. That allegiance must have been very holy to La Fontaine, in that he drew from it an audacity likely to incur the king's rage, and pled as a poet for clemency toward a cultivated minister and a friend of belles lettres.

　To understand this symbol, and the mythical story that founds it, is also to understand all that is at stake, politically and spiritually, in *Fables*, which was in gestation at the time, and which has always been considered a beautiful garland, placed—albeit in vain—at the foot of the equestrian statue of the Sun King.

　To understand it, we must learn again this forgotten symbolic language, the "language of the gods," which La Fontaine himself said he spoke, which the poetic Renaissance had bequeathed to him, and which was still

understood, though less and less well, by the educated public. In this symbolic language, Parnassus plays a determining role: since the early Renaissance, it had been both its key word and its interpretive key.

In the Middle Ages, Ovid's *The Metamorphoses* was called the "Bible
of poets," and the great poem played that role more than ever in the
Renaissance and the so-called Neoclassical Age. Like the Bible, it begins
with a cosmogonic tale and with a narration of the first cycle of the four
ages humanity passes through. The gods put an end to the iron age and its
horrors via a universal flood. An innocent couple, Deucalion and Pyrrha,
are the only ones spared. They come to the only dry land remaining, in
Phocis:

> Before all turned to sea, lay peaceful Phocis
> Where the twin-horned Parnassus pierced the clouds.[24]

It is from that haven of innocence that humanity, brought back to life
by the couple Jupiter has spared, begins a new cycle, with which the gods
are at first closely involved. From the beginning, Apollo comes to the aid
of human beings: with his spear, he strikes down the serpent Python, which
had risen from the foul mud of the flood at the foot of Parnassus, and which
posed a threat to the rebirth of humanity. From one canto to the next, *The
Metamorphoses* sketches out a whole myth of Parnassus, which the Renaissance systematized, complementing it with original accounts by Greek
poets (Hesiod and, especially, the Alexandrians: Callimachus, Apollonios
Rhodius, and Nonnus). Since Dante and Petrarch, a myth of the holy
mountain had been reconstructed, and a republic of letters, the secular
order of Mnemosyne, was built on its framework.

In 1627 the second edition of a treatise on mythology was published in
Frankfurt: *Parnassus biceps, cum imaginibus Musarum Deorumque praesidum*
(The two-peaked Parnassus, with images of the Muses and Gods who preside over it). The author was a humanist scholar from Besançon, Jean-
Jacques Boissard. He was appreciated by La Fontaine, who paraphrased
in French verse a Latin inscription the scholar had published.[25] That
inscription tells of an episode from "The Daughters of Minea," one of the
tales from Ovid's *The Metamorphoses*. In fact, in his treatise on Parnassus,
Boissard uses Ovid to develop and illustrate all the facets of the central
myth of the poetic and literary Renaissance.

Boissard begins by citing Cicero, both his doctrine of contemplative
leisure (drawn from *De officiis*) and his conception of wisdom as an admission of ignorance and an appetite for knowledge (from the *Quaestiones*

Tusculanae). He praises belles lettres, the eternally lit lamp in the temporality and darkness of the world, rescuing from oblivion "eternal lessons" and providing the sage with the experience of the past, superiority over his present fortunes, and a view of the future. The Muses, daughters of Jupiter and Mnemosyne, are the sources and inspiration for this stream of light, which does battle with the flood of darkness engulfing mortals in the iron age.

Boissard recalls that, on the very site where Apollo had killed the serpent Python, Cadmus, the brother of Europa, founded Thebes on the advice of Apollo, after following the god's example and spearing a monstrous serpent to death. He consecrated the higher of the two summits of Mount Parnassus, with its spring, Castaglia, and the neighboring site of Delphi, to the Muses and the god who created them. Cadmus brought belles lettres from Phoenicia to Greece. Within the mythic triangle of Thebes, Delphi, and Parnassus, the ever-changing destiny of men is played out. According to other poets, Cadmus, with his musical gifts, had once aided Jupiter in defeating Trypho, who was threatening Olympus with the lightning bolts the rebellious giant had stolen from the king of the gods. As a reward, Cadmus was given Harmony, daughter of Venus and Mars, to be his wife. The wedding of Cadmus and Harmony, which all the gods attended, was the perfect hour of "friendship" between Olympus and Parnassus, the prime moment of a fleeting golden age.

Apollo, Minerva, and the Muses, Jean-Jacques Boissard tells us, have presided ever since over Mount Parnassus, the "liberal disciplines and the science of belles lettres," which convey divine wisdom to human beings. He adds: "It is right that poets gifted with genius make the supreme god, Jupiter, the ultimate source of all the sciences, the father of the Muses, who dispensed 'literary knowledge' to mortals." The other summit of Parnassus was subsequently dedicated to Bacchus.

What Boissard does not say, but what every reader of *The Metamorphoses* knew very well at the time, is that, since the wedding of Cadmus and Harmony, belles lettres, the vehicle of divine wisdom among mortals, have been condemned to live in peril and against the current of the times: "These days of happiness," wrote Chateaubriand, himself a reader of Ovid, "vanished so quickly that they were taken for a dream among unhappy posterity."[26] The poets are the interpreters and propagators of the forgotten wisdom enveloped in this dream.

The descendants of Cadmus (Semele, Actaeon, Pentheus, Ino) and Cadmus himself, metamorphosed, along with his wife, Harmony, into a serpent, were by turns the objects of the gods' anger; and a whole bestiary, the bestiary of the fables, a whole flora, perpetuated the memory of that growing misunderstanding between the gods and the family of Cadmus. Later still, in Thebes, the tragic histories of Oedipus and of his sons, Eteocles and Polynices, marked the return of the iron age and the retreat of the gods.

The landscape of *The Metamorphoses* must be glimpsed in the background of La Fontaine's *Fables*. Only the songs of poets (in his *Parnassus biceps*, Boissard particularly praises Anacreon and the melodious, fluent sweetness of his verses) bring the memory of the wedding of Cadmus and Harmony down from Parnassus, and keep alive mortals' affinity for the divine from within the storms of time and the pathos of human error. Belles lettres and poetry, far from being "escapes" from the sad reality of the new iron age, continue the eternal battle of Apollo against the serpent Python; they are the auxiliaries, the teachers, the consolers of a humanity bereft of the friendship of the gods by virtue of its vanity and blindness.

Each "figure" of the "Bible of poets" thus became an interpretive cipher not only of the human condition adrift in historical time, but of present reality: in every age, the witness to the lost harmonic light is intentionally rejected out of ignorance, which blind humanity adds on to its fate, which is itself vacillating and fleeting. In "The Companions of Ulysses," the first fable in La Fontaine's last book, the animals of *Fables* are men metamorphosed into beasts, like the descendants of Cadmus— Actaeon, Ino, Philomela—and like Cadmus himself and the beautiful Harmony, daughter of Venus and Mars. But the Fables themselves, daughters of the Muses, are there to give back to men, through the art of memory and by holding up a mirror to them, the desire for the divine within their reach: the shared consciousness of their humanity. They are a response to Cicero's maxim, endlessly repeated during the Renaissance and quoted by Boissard: "Through belles lettres, human beings surpass themselves to a degree as great as the superiority of humanity to animality."

The logic of symbolic language, in terms of which the light of belles lettres conceives itself, wants there to be two sorts of Olympuses. The Olympus from which the gods descend to attend the wedding of Cadmus and Harmony is not the earthly Olympus, which strangely resembles the throne of Oedipus in a Thebes ravaged by the plague. That historical and political Olympus can even harbor the serpent that Apollo struck down, but which is always reborn again. That human, all-too-human Olympus is not the friend of Parnassus.

La Fontaine, trained in Renaissance literature, its adages, its emblems, and its oracles, was able to transpose onto the royal religion of France the universal attributes of the myth of Parnassus. The Olympus from which Richelieu, in de Retz's expression, had "thundered" down upon France, and where the serpent (which decorates the coat of arms of the Colbert family) had seized hold of the king after the wedding of Cadmus/Louis XIV and Harmony/Marie-Thérèse of Austria in 1660, was the very symbol of the return of the iron age. The abbé Pouget was right to say that the "distrait" poet, "on a thousand matters thought differently than the rest of mankind." He viewed his times through "a forest of symbols." And it was by the power of symbols that, in his time, he sought to favor the little light, joy, and harmony of which the century was capable.

THE PARNASSUS OF 1660

In a curious one-act play, *Clymène*, which La Fontaine wrote (but did not publish) at the same time as *Adonis*, during the finest hours of his "poetic contract" with Foucquet, the author gives a sketch of his very personal notion of Parnassus, which was very compatible with the liberality of his patron of the time, and very out of place a few years later under Colbert's authority.[27]

The poet lets Apollo and the Muses speak from the holy mountain. The god of poetry complains that he "hardly sees good love poems anymore." "Love" should be understood here as the Platonic desire for light, which seeks a partner in order to reconstitute the lost harmony, but only for a brief, perfect instant, on the dark and gloomy earth. There is still love in this "century," but only a "cavalier" love, without the lyric "ardor" that makes true poets and true lovers.

The god, disappointed and even "disgusted" by the proliferation of "versifiers" still worried about meeting the expectations of the *surintendant* and the king, wants to light anew the beautiful lyric fire on earth. This will be a difficult task:

Ce langage divin, ces charmantes figures,
Qui touchaient autrefois les âmes les plus dures,
Et par qui les rochers et les bois attirés
Tressaillaient à des traits de l'Olympe admirés,

Cela, dis-je, n'est plus maintenant en usage.
On vous méprise, et nous, et ce divin langage.
"Qu'est-ce?" dit-on. "Des vers." Suffit: le peuple y court.
Pourquoi venir chercher ces traits en notre cour?
Sans cela l'on parvient à l'estime des hommes.
(Clymène, ll. 520–28)

That divine language, those charming figures,
That once touched the most hardened souls,
And by which the rocks and woods, drawn in,
Trembled at the traits so admired of Olympus,
All that, I say, is no longer in fashion.
You are despised, as are we, and that divine language too.
"What is it?" they ask. "Verses," you reply.
That's all it takes: the people run off.
Why come looking for such things in our court?
We earn the respect of men without them.

To bring about—in spite of it all—the lyric Renaissance he desires and which is requested of him, Apollo chooses a couple as the subjects of his experiment: Acante and Clymène. They are the Deucalion and Pyrrha of this new cataclysm. Acante is a born poet, who wants to ply Clymène with love. She has "spent her life in the provinces" and has thus not fallen victim to the affectations of the city, which are coarsening feelings and distorting words:

Ce qu'on n'a point au coeur, l'a-t-on dans ses écrits?
(Clymène, line 5)

Can what is not in one's heart be in one's writing?

She is not naive, however: the Muses know and appreciate her. And so she is not easy to persuade. She has been forewarned through her readings and her personal sense of the ephemeral fate of all human love.

The Muses engage in a competition (very similar to that which the surintendant Foucquet, under the name "Oronte," presides over in La Fontaine's Le songe de Vaux), trying to find the right tone and words that will allow Acante to persuade Clymène, or Clymène to resist him. Apollo, a difficult and subtle musician ("Il me faut du nouveau, n'en fût-il point au monde"; I must have something new, though it be not in the world [line 30]), comments, evaluates, and directs these variations and the diversity of modes the Muses propose one by one, from the pathetic to the agreeable, the serious to the light, the Malherbe style to the Marot style. The La Fontainian art of pastiche, which will also be found in the fable "For Those Impossible to Please" (2.1), is here practiced with astonishing virtuosity. We have the feeling that we have entered the poet's workshop, that we are hearing him tune his instrument, venture in several directions, criticize himself, begin again, abandon most of his efforts, and pause only after he has found the right-sounding tone.

That tone is found when Acante takes the place of the Muses, and, inspired by the god of love, who also captures Clymène, dares make the gesture that leads the young woman to assent. This wedding of Cadmus and Harmony, of more modest proportions than that of Ovid's heroes, attests to the return of inspired poetry and the golden age.

The second Renaissance celebrated by Apollo ("our troupe is content") is less springlike than that of Petrarch. It seeks to save lyricism through a skillful naïveté, a naturalness. The autumnal harmony at the origin of this naturalness stems much more from Epicureanism than from Platonism. The five senses, within reach of human weakness, feed the aspiration for the divine. Visible, sensible, voluptuous beauties, more than abstract Beauty, fan the "flames." In Clymène, the Muse Polyhymnia regrets that overly carnal conception of poetry.

But at least it is the "something new" required by Apollo to keep alive lyricism, which has been threatened with extinction. Clymène, written by La Fontaine during the period when he was Foucquet's poet laureate, and when he expected to one day become the king's poet, is the program for a new-found royal lyricism, which would place the desire for private happiness, associated with an art of grace, in the service of the kingdom and its "good government."

APOLLO IN HELL

During the trial of the *surintendant* Foucquet in 1661–64, La Fontaine was not the only poet or writer to understand that an iron age of Parnassus was coming into being. The Olympus of the Louvre was now able to use writers, and not, as the *surintendant* had briefly given reason to hope, by leaving them free to participate according to their vocation in the harmony of the kingdom. Belles lettres, and their cutting edge, poetry, had to learn again how to play cautiously with imperious masters, even more cautiously than in the previous age, when they were given some latitude as they oscillated between resistance to Richelieu and ridicule of Mazarin.

La Fontaine, though not a Stoic, was still very sensitive to the peril that, during a return to order, weighs upon true poets and prophets. He had the melancholic and anxious temperament of the artist, even though, within the safety of a circle of friends, a spirit of joy was quick to awaken in him. Maurice de Guérin was right to recognize the poet's self-portrait in a "melancholic animal" in the fable "The Hare and the Frogs" (2.14):[28]

> Il était douteux, inquiet;
> Un souffle, une ombre, un rien, tout lui donnait la fièvre.

> He was full of doubts, troubled;
> A breeze, a shadow, nothing at all, everything made him feverish.

For a very long time, then, he kept "the cautious silence of a Conrart," even during Anne of Austria's regency and the Fronde, which, between 1642 and 1652, had, in a lush disorder, loosened tongues, talents, and printing presses. The light occasional pieces, the "comedy" Clymène, and the rather mysterious idyll Adonis, which La Fontaine composed between 1658 and 1661 as part of a wholly fictive and charming "poetic pension" for the surintendant Foucquet, remained confidential. This reserved poet, whose genius slowly matured, had a decided aversion to breaking his silence. He was the exact opposite of Rimbaud, whose strange impatience of an overly precocious genius led him quickly back to silence.

Although La Fontaine allowed a manuscript of his poems composed for Foucquet to circulate in 1658–61 (but without publishing it through an editor), this decision must unquestionably be attributed to the climate of trust and playful friendship he enjoyed and in which he himself engaged during a few months in the entourage of a rare bird: a cultured prince of the Renaissance, well disposed to reinstall Harmony on the throne of Cadmus, and in a lasting manner.

Even when La Fontaine had become a famous writer, read and recited by a vast audience, half-compromised, half-protected by his astonishing celebrity, a portion (and not the smallest portion) of his works obstinately remained in manuscript form, unpublished during his lifetime. Le voyage en Limousin, the epistles to M. de Nyert and to Pierre-Daniel Huet, and many other short masterpieces were read in the seventeenth century only by very rare confidants and trusted colleagues. The greater part of his regular correspondence with his most faithful and closest friend, François Maucroix, has disappeared, probably destroyed by the recipient at the express request of the poet.[29] The works published during his lifetime were always done so judiciously: they did not so much respond to formal constraints, which he always interpreted in his own way, but to constraints beyond his control, and with which he could play only with a very steady hand.

In 1661 La Fontaine saw the thunderbolt that struck his protector Foucquet and his friend Pellisson, Foucquet's right-hand man. He himself was burned slightly, seriously enough, however, to make him realize what new bolts of lightning could rain down from the heights of the royal Olympus.

It was then that, against all expectations, this timid poet, a "provincial" like his Clymène and naturally inclined toward contemplation and inner luxuries, set aside his reserve: he spoke up to plead a lost cause and to come to the aid of a patron struck down by "the greatest king in the world." With a disconcerting audacity—which confirms his legend as a likable fool for some, while belying it for a small number of others—in the heat of a trial for crimes against the state, the man who had failed to become the king's poet found the courage to have two poems printed in defense of his battered patron. Although they were published anonymously and circulated under the table, no one was fooled: the author's talent and style made him instantly recognizable. Ten years later, in 1671, he published them under his own name: he had nothing left to lose, the damage had long been done and everyone knew it, including, in the first place, the king and Colbert. His official fate was sealed, and these petitions, which were without effect, had over time become trophies of the king's amour propre and absolute power.

The public testimonial in favor of Foucquet was not an isolated case. Many other poets had printed clandestinely, or circulated in manuscript, pieces of verse much more violent (and much more damaging to Foucquet's cause) than the two poems by La Fontaine. *L'Elégie aux Nymphes de Vaux* and *Ode au roi* may have been written by a fool unaware of his temporal interests, but the fool knew exactly what he was doing, what he wanted to obtain for his friend facing possible death, and the risk he himself was taking. That fool did not lose hope of being heard and *recognized* by the king. That imprudent act, carried out with a high level of tact and delicacy calculated to soften the king's heart and careful not to harm him, attests that the poet's usual silence had nothing to do with cowardice or presumptuousness. In the midst of peril and anxiety, he, like the swan in the fable "The Swan and the Cook" (3.12), knew how to find in his throat the bold and melodious song best suited to quell, if possible, the king's anger without offending him.

He straightforwardly demonstrated his intrepid and delicate solicitude toward a "misfortunate soul," who was himself being held by the throat for reasons of state. In identifying with his patron cursed by the king, the poet experienced what the royal curse could entail: the worst possible anguish, along with death and hell, for a seventeenth-century Frenchman.

His words were honed by the ordeal of the king's anger. The king's subsequent silence regarding him, imitated by Boileau in 1674, never really eased the tension between the poet and his king concerning the doomed Foucquet.

In their own domain, the domain of charity, the two poems for Foucquet were themselves bolts of lightning that dared flash, albeit faintly, in response to the king's bolt. They cast a light on the poet's truth, as brief and as brilliant as that of the sudden coup d'état of September 1661, which revealed the prince's truth. They give us a glimpse of the heart of hearts from which startling lyric and meditative patches of light would yet burst forth, exploding into streaming skyrockets of tears over the comic scenes of Fables—so luminous, so colorful, so lively, but often on a path toward darkness.[30]

Those two lightning bolts illuminated the secret life of a poet, well defended against indiscretion, for only a moment. But that instant was enough to decide his fate, both temporal and spiritual. It kept him from a career at court, after earning him a period of exile in Limoges.[31] But, above all, his audacity showed him something about himself; it awakened in him words of which he did not at first believe himself capable. These words, which tried in vain to soften the king toward Foucquet and to get him away from Colbert, did move the public, just as Pascal's clandestine Provinciales had done several years earlier, in 1658. The little letters of "Louis de Montalte" did not obtain any practical result either: the Great Arnauld was not absolved by the Sorbonne or by Mazarin. But truthful testimony had been given, and it resonated deeply in people's hearts. In Pensées, Pascal speaks of the "trognes armées" of the king's bodyguards that make the reign of force temporally effective. La Fontaine discovered in turn, and from within, that the word of truth, even when powerless in the temporal order, is able to get by "the guard watching the gates of the Louvre," and to exert a power of its own in the secret recesses of people's hearts. The public had silently voted for Foucquet's acquittal.[32] La Fontaine played a role in that. Up to that time, he had sensed that sort of power within himself and had feared it: in the illusory safety he felt around

Foucquet, he even hoped that that test of strength would be spared him. But once he had exerted that power, the swan's quill against the eagle's claw, something essential was loosed in him, and his poetic genius underwent a second birth.

POETIC FIDELITY AND POLITICAL COMMITMENT

The man who went through that ordeal without repudiating his opinions, who even got a second wind from it, is not the lovable fool of legend, but a deep thinker with a resolute soul. Never mind what unseeing, indifferent, and spiteful people may have reported about his outer life as a man distracted by poetry. One can presume anything of such a man, even that he persisted in "crime," surrounding himself with every sort of camouflage necessary to keep from being caught off guard. That does not prevent the poet's most recent commentators from seeing *Fables* as a collection of "short forms"; the Fables may be ingenious, such readers claim, but their originality lies entirely in the Alexandrian education their author received and in the indisputably subtle aesthetic flavors he was able to instill in his prose models.

The blinding power of a legend that once kept the king himself in the dark does not explain everything. The excesses of rare but penetrating interpreters, René Jasinski in particular, who thought they saw a kind of disguised *Mazarinade* in every fable from the first collection, that is, an attack on Mazarin that sought to rehabilitate Foucquet and satirize Colbert, went a long way toward creating a reaction, which has culminated in the aestheticization that prevails today in "readings" of La Fontaine.[33]

The politically "militant" La Fontaine put forward by Jasinski, a La Fontaine who distilled his convictions in the "coded" language of allegory, was unconvincing. After that failure, it was inevitable that an exclusively "literary" La Fontaine should appear, a poet fully absorbed in the delicate sampling of many different pleasures, a connoisseur of tasty seasonings in the manner of François Vatel, as he in fact presents himself in the preface to *Les amours de Psyché* ("I sought this temperament with great care"), and as Paul Valéry later presented him in his essay on *Adonis*, the poem La Fontaine composed in Foucquet's honor.[34]

Neither of these readings is wrong. But one reduces the poet to a political pamphleteer, and the other trivializes his poetry by refusing to see the terrible dialectic that, as in all great poetry, links and opposes it to politics.

The first interpretation has the merit of establishing that there are "unrecognized markers" that link the Fables to the drama of freedom played out behind the facade of the Invalides in the age of Louis XIV. It was bolstered by the post–World War II period and its "age of suspicion," and by the theories of *littérature engagée* that prevailed at the time among Marxist critics and those writing for *Les Temps Modernes*.

There is a temptation to move from one extreme to the other and to confine this poet within an aesthetics adequate to itself. The "power of fables" La Fontaine speaks of is not political commitment, but it is not aesthetic dilettantism either. In the short term, all that a poet—yesterday, yesteryear, or today—can hope from his poem (*chant*) is that it will extort a kind of blackmail (*chantage*) from people of power and authority: he is sure of the public that listens to him and that accedes through him to a truth "close to the heart." This blackmail is very little no doubt, but it counts—for the poet himself in the first place. How could he renounce the strange resonance of his words? Poets are defenseless, but they have a spiritual force that is of a completely different order than aesthetic or decorative force. Too many writers of our own century have doubted that force or feared it, preferring to seek patrons for their works among the powerful: states, parties, mass movements. La Fontaine can do no more than please and charm—he says so openly—but he does so only to better instruct, to lead the way toward an internal truth that all can know and that frees everyone from the weight of the latest slogans.

The Fables have been considered a disguised Foucquetist *engagement* in the manner of György Lukács or Jean-Paul Sartre, a calculated act of historical "praxis" in an "age of crisis"; or, conversely, a sophistic and virtuoso game in accord with the views illustrated by Umberto Eco, the manufacture—already utterly modern—of objects of "interactive" communication. In each case, they have been wrested from their original magnetic field. That field is neither completely political nor completely aesthetic, but quite simply poetic in the fullest sense: "I have thus composed this ode for the consideration of Parnassus" (letter to M. Foucquet, 20 January 1663).

Poetry does not need to commit itself politically to be political. On the contrary, it is precisely when it commits itself politically that it ceases to be both politics and poetry, ceases to be the politics of poetry. If every great poetry is political, it is so by definition, since it seeks a foundation for the commonwealth in the truth of the heart, guaranteed and restored through the integrity of language.

"Telling the truth," André Suarès writes, "as a function of what is greatest and least animalistic in man is the only excuse the poet has to leave the enchanted and pure world in which he lives, and where it would be easy for him to live always. He must betray himself only to serve, if he can, the cause of spirit in the world."[35]

That is why the politics of poetry must not be confused, as Sartre confused it, with the politics of politics, which Niccolò Machiavelli and Thomas Hobbes wanted to make a moral norm, and which modern states, discarding the classical and medieval imperative for "good government," the "good prince," the "good father" in the service of the "common good," have made the more or less violent, more or less hypocritical motive for their actions. The politics of poetry seeks the unanimity that lies at the foundation of politics in a truth of the heart ("Beautiful language," Suarès writes, "is the most vibrant form of the commonwealth"), whereas the politics of politics seeks it in a strength and cunning unburdened by "qualms." The latter form of politics takes an interest in words only for their utilitarian and aesthetic uses, to reinforce the alliance between the lion's strength and the fox's cunning, and to veil, for the time being, its own true nature and true designs.

The seventeenth century remains intensely alive in late-twentieth-century thought because, in France and in England, it was the theater (and the theoretical laboratory) where the first victory of the politics of politics occurred. But that victory did not come about without resistance. It was particularly relentless and deep-seated in the France of the Fronde, the France of Mazarinades, Port-Royal, the moralists, of the Foucquet affair and the Fénelon affair.

Overtly or covertly, seventeenth-century French poets were all on the side of resistance to Machiavelli, to Hobbes, to modern politics. Their politics differed from that of the poets who came after the Revolution: they could draw on an uninterrupted literary and philosophical tradition, which gave weight to their lyrical remonstrances. They had the kingdom's commonplaces and the public on their side. Even when disgraced and splattered with mud, they were not yet *poètes maudits*.

All the same, one must not confuse Corneille (despite his well-established sympathy for the resistance to Machiavellianism) or La Fontaine (despite the support he found in several of the circles opposing Louis XIV) with a politics of opposition to absolutism, which was in France only another courtly politics, an alternative Machiavellianism, less internally logical and more poorly armed than the other.

A great poet is a great poet, and he does not compromise the higher politics proper to poetry. What distinguishes a lampoon by Mathieu de Morgues from Corneille's tragedies, a Mazarinade or a Colbertiade from La Fontaine's fables, is not just genius or form; it is the intransigent attachment of these poets to the word of truth they inherited from their predecessors. They also have faith in the power that only poetry possesses to open hearts, not to the victory of one faction over another, but to the underlying and unifying truth, to the moment when all the masks come off. These politicians of poetry, who can be traced back to Sophocles and Virgil, Horace and Ronsard, have a "loftier and more beautiful ambition" than state and party politicians.

That is why their actions in the order of contemplation—though apparently without effect—so successfully survive the "praxis" of the actors of political history. They act on the "heart of hearts," their vehicle is "the profundity of language"; they can count on a public more loyal and resistant, from generation to generation, than the short-lived, though imposing, powerful, and maleficent coalitions that attract the Tartuffes and Machiavellis to their side.

Sartre went after surrealism with hammer and tongs. He ridiculed Breton's "impure" mixture of contemplation and action, a mixture that Richelieu, targeting Corneille, had already called "the lack of a systematic mind." In a note to his essay *Qu'est-ce qu'écrire?* in which he dismisses in a throwaway line the "stupidity" of Parnassian art for art's sake, Sartre dispatches Baudelaire in a paragraph: "Baudelaire's poetry is certainly a 'choice,' a 'commitment,' but only to lose himself, and with the secret hope of gaining everything in the end in 'the total failure of the human enterprise.'" Poetry, even by one of the poets who most heroically made it a destiny, is in Sartre's eyes a waste of freedom and a betrayal of the great hope in historical action that good literature owes itself to maintain. In Pascal's footsteps, Baudelaire egotistically took the risk of driving Billancourt to despair![36]

Sartre, a Jesuit in Pascal's sense, asks literature to "become committed," but with a complicity that is wily and "shady" (and his fondness for this adjective is not accidental)—a complicity between the spiritual and the temporal, between contemplation and action, between the profound politics of the poetic word and the Machiavellian politics of force and success. That conflation of the two orders, irresistible for less-skilled writers, is also found in its naive state among the "political" interpreters of *Fables*. According to them, La Fontaine's shift to a universal wisdom, which gives *Fables* its lasting power over the "heart of hearts," is only a tactic for making his ad hominem political attacks all the more urgent, attacks that sought to avenge the good Foucquet from the wicked Colbert. To believe them, La Fontaine was not a likable fool but an idiot.

But if poetry is the antithesis of Machiavellian politics, as Sartre so haughtily reproaches it for being, can it activate the contemplative pole of language by disregarding the other pole, which makes language subservient to the strategies of force and to the powerful appetites and interests magnetically attracted to force? How can it be itself, without indulging in a radical and perilous criticism of what negates it? How can it posit itself as the "shepherdess of language" without contrasting its own task to the well-recognizable descriptions of lions, wolves, foxes, and asses that threaten or betray their own packs? Paradoxically, the more poetic it is, the more active it is in both glorifying its contemplative ministry and ruining the reputation of the corrupters of "holy language." It is at that altitude, worthy of La Fontaine but just as worthy of his partner, King Louis XIV, that his *Fables* must be read and his life "in poetry" understood.

What is more contemplative than *The Divine Comedy*? It is an uninterrupted ascension to the heart of hearts and the divine source of language, finally regained and worshiped in silence. Along the way, however, what is more ferocious than Dante's words against all the forms and degrees of the possessive usury—public and private—of language? The two movements are indissociable, and together give Dante's poem a prodigious power to awaken what has been forgotten.

Dante was the first to give the name "Parnassus" to the pole of contemplative language reserved for poetry, and that of "Apollo" to the protective inner fortitude that allows the poet, in spite of his inner terror, to utter the words that reveal his heart. These are terrible words, because they threaten the deceptive foundations of the illusory commonwealth; and they are irresistible and sweet words, because they show us and make us desire the sharp edge upon which the inner commonwealth is balanced. As he is leaving Purgatory, on the sacred threshold of Paradise, Dante invokes the god of Parnassus:

O good Apollo, for the final quest
   Make me such vessel of thy worth as thou
   For the loved laurel-gift requirest!
One summit of Parnassus until now
   Sufficed me, but henceforth the twain beneath
   Into the last arena must I go.

Into my bosom enter thou, and breathe
  As when thou didst pluck Marsyas amain
  And from the scabbard of his limbs unsheathe!
Virtue divine! if thou wilt lend me a strain
  To manifest the blessèd realm above,
  Whose shadowy signature is in my brain,
Shalt see me pluck the laurel of thy love
  And crown me with those leaves, which this my
  Matter and thou shalt make me worthy of.
                    (Dante, *Paradiso*, canto 1)[37]

For European poetry since Dante, Parnassus has symbolized its proper home, the vertical and contemplative abode where it maintains its rights to the word of truth and beauty, within the commonwealth compromised by lies and crime.

That mountain of "holy language" quite naturally seeks to be acknowledged and heeded (Dante wanted to persuade the emperor; Petrarch, the pope) by the earthly—political or sacerdotal—Olympus. The properly spiritual duty of Parnassus—its "powerless" power—as counselor, educator, instructor, and therapist, consists of seeing that the word of which it is guardian, and which it holds on behalf of the Muses, is respected and adopted through the authority of the powers that govern the earth, so long as the waning times of human affairs allow it.

APOLLO AND THE KING OF FRANCE

Unlike Italy, France was an empire and a church in itself, an ancient family over which the father/king held both sacerdotal and political authority through God, an authority given him to promote charity and concord among the warring factions that members of the same family nearly always constitute. The figure of the king of France, bishop of foreign lands, sacred in Reims, repository of the miraculous power to heal scrofula, or "king's evil," the descendant of Clovis and Saint Louis, is one of the most original fictions invented by the Christian Middle Ages. It is also the fiction that was put most cruelly to the test in the sixteenth and seventeenth centuries by the development of modern states and the Machiavellian reason of state that dictated their conduct toward rivals abroad and subjects within.[38]

Henry III, the Machiavellian assassin of the duc de Guise, was himself assassinated, stripped, in the eyes of most of his subjects, of the love due a king of France. Even Henry IV, king of reconciliation and clemency, was accused by the Calvinist d'Aubigné, and by an ardent Catholic minority, of hypocrisy and double-dealing: he too was assassinated. Louis XIII, called "the Just," obsessed with the example of Saint Louis, had to delegate his sovereignty to Richelieu because he was unable personally to apply a policy he found repellent and which his contemporaries recognized as the imprint of the Machiavellian "Prince," the modern version of the serpent Python.

The politics of politics, in Machiavelli's sense, was not only the object of Christian criticism in France, modeled on the criticism that Roman theologians propounding the apostolic power of the pope made of the profane abuses of temporal princes. It was felt as cruelly by the Calvinists as by members of the Catholic leagues, and as sharply by the "good French people" faithful to the king as by Fronde rebels. Depending on the perspective particular to the various opposing parties, it was a family misfortune, an emotional drama, or a revolt from the heart against the betrayal of the essence of French royalty, which was summoned to make order, concord, and justice reign in the love—freely given and freely received— between the father and his children. It was also an insult to "French character," as the kingdom of benevolence and freedom had naturally shaped and postulated it over the centuries: "frankness," "good faith," "loyalty," "gaiety." This "generous" character of Francion was the very antithesis of the disconcerting mixture of lies, hypocritical ruses, and cynical cruelty that has spared from scruples the force of modern politics. The parasitical presence, on the monarchy and its Christlike vocation, of "monsters" bold enough to act on the authority of the providential "goodness" of the king of France, was the scandal that tormented seventeenth-century France, even under Louis XIV.[39]

In his *Mémoires*, Cardinal de Retz, the most powerful leader of the opposition to absolutism, did not for a moment place in doubt the traditional form of the kingdom of France or the divine character of its kings. He simply regretted that French royal authority, because it was considered divine in the family of the kingdom, could not be "regulated" like that of the kings of England. It followed that, in France, the "wise middle ground" to which the kingdom had a right (and which it had maintained "once upon a time") rested entirely in the hearts of its kings. If that heart was "wise" and "good," it made the kingdom a garden; if it deviated too far from the king's imitation of God, and from the equally royal "good faith" on which the French people had made the entire political edifice of their monarchy rest, it produced a terrible muddle.[40] The growth, within the heart of the kingdom, of the "serpent" of ministers under Louis XIII broke with the political "wise middle ground," more or less maintained until then, which even the Calvinist schism and the civil wars of the sixteenth century had not definitively prohibited from reappearing with the "wise" and "good" king Henry. Richelieu and Colbert introduced deeper cracks into French royal religion than Calvin had done. The revocation of the Edict of Nante would lay waste the monarchy as the Reformation had never done.

The rise of "seventeenth-century ethics" was linked to the divorce that occurred under Louis XIII between royal authority and its exorbitant exercise, which made it necessary to examine the king's heart and recognize in it the same principles—enemies of "wisdom" and "goodness"—that kept most men from being "honorable." The disappointment of discovering that amour propre could rule the king, and could place him in the hands of ministers themselves governed by their own self-interest, had an impact on his subjects, left to their own devices in a "family" corrupted by suspicion, profoundly uprooted, and haunted by the fear that the harmony of the kingdom was now no more than a memory.

For all the poets of the French Renaissance, the royal religion, elevated as it was by the tragedy of the civil wars, was the very principle of their lyricism. Faith in the "wisdom" and "goodness" natural to their king was so great that the poets offered divine Renaissance poetry as a pure and simple reflection, luminous and contagious, of that ancient and modern French secret. Ronsard speaks to everyone in the name of the poets when he declares to Henry II, in the final antistrophe of his *Ode 1*:

> Presque le los de tes aïeux
> Est pressé du temps envieux
> Pour n'avoir eu l'expérience
> Des Muses, ni de leur science;
> Mais le rond du grand univers
> Est plein de la gloire éternelle,
> Qui fait flamber ton Père en elle
> Pour avoir tant aimé les vers.
> (Ronsard, *Le premier livre des odes*)

> Since the praise of your forebears
> Is hurried by envious time

Not to have had the experience
Of the Muses, or of their knowledge;
But the circle of the great universe
Is full of eternal glory,
Which makes your Father blaze in it
To have so loved poetry.

This is, in fact, the French version of the wedding of Cadmus and Harmony, the friendship of Parnassus and Olympus. In Guillaume Postel and his disciples, Henry III's poets, it even took on millenarian overtones: the dark ages of the kingdom bore within themselves the promise of a King David, a King Daphnis, a Christ the King, called upon to restore the harmony of the golden age throughout a Europe corrupted by the melan-choly of the iron age.[41]

Augustus, Maecenas, and Daphnis

Traces of that royal millenarianism can still be found in Honoré d'Urfé's *L'Astrée*, dedicated to Henry IV, with which the entire seventeenth cen-tury was inebriated, beginning with La Fontaine. The disappointment would be equal to these poetic and religious expectations.[42]

D'Urfé was weaned on the late poetry of the Valois, directly inspired by the philosophy of the esoteric prophet of monarchy, Postel. That mys-tical French doctrine was easily combined with a great Roman example, the principate of Augustus, witnessed by Maecenas and celebrated by Horace and Virgil. It was taught in all the humanist schools, and was revived by the advent of Henry IV, when he established civil peace dur-ing his reign. Horace's *Odes*, the fourth of Virgil's *Eclogues*, and even his *Aeneid* were not without millenarian overtones of their own, announcing to Augustus's subjects Asteria's return to earth, the birth of the redemp-tive shepherd Daphnis, and the beginning of a new golden age. In France, Augustus's name, glorified by poetry, associated with his favorite god, Apollo, the god of poets, and with his minister Maecenas, the friend of poets, sym-bolized the reign of clemency, reconciliation, and peace that had always been the destiny of the kingdom, thanks to its unique vocation. One day, sooner or later, an Augustus and a royal Daphnis would heal the divisions within France, redeem old errors, and shine upon the world.[43]

In the seventeenth century, the king of France, possessed of that Christ-like and Augustan vocation, remained the object of great hopes. There was too violent a contrast between what had always been expected of the beneficent, thaumaturgic king and modern "politics," which since 1635 had been associated with the war "against nature" and a voracious tax system that Richelieu directed under Louis XIII's authority. His heir, Mazarin, did not even have the excuse of being born French. The regent Anne of Austria, who had delegated her powers to him, was also a for-eigner grafted—by marriage and maternity—onto the French royal vine. Hatred of the state minister, almost by definition a bad adviser who pre-vented the immortal king of France from deploying his own ever-latent virtualities of good government, was universal in France under Louis XIII and Anne of Austria. It was reborn with comparable virulence after 1661, as a general execration of which Colbert was the object from the outset. Foucquet had done too good a job of embodying the old trust the French people placed in the harmonic virtues of their monarchy. Louis XIV had quite a task before him to rid himself of the serpent's scales attributed to Colbert, and dress himself in the plumage of the pretty bluebird Foucquet.

The great princely families, who had appealed to these feelings of revolt to take up arms against the wicked ministers, but who were always ready to negotiate advantageous "accommodations" with the court at the opportune moment, never offered a convincing political alternative. They would have their hour of glory during the Fronde: it was brief. The failure of the nobility, combined with that of the magistrates in 1653, made English-style "liberty" impossible in France. In 1642 the great poet Tristan L'Hermite, devoted to Gaston d'Orléans (Louis XIII's brother, long the heir presumptive to the Crown and worshiped by the French), had freed himself of that French-style Hamlet—smiling, warm, witty, and literate, seeing what was expected of him but prevented from truly desir-ing it. As de Retz saw, "Prince Charming" remained a fiction that never quite became a reality.

Louis XIV and His Poets

In the end, the Parnassus of France, understood in Dante's and Petrarch's sense, had always had profound affinities with the favor attached, if not to the person of the present king, then at least to the redemptive vocation always open to the monarchy: this was all the more true in the seventeenth century, with its reason of state. Although Parnassus, the site par excellence for the language of contemplation, had its own politics, harmony, and happiness, in France it was the natural ally of the royal office, a sacerdoce higher than any faction, and an object of love because, like the poet's "prayer," the king's "reason" could "dawn in people's hearts," founding order and justice on a truth that took root in everyone.

In *Tartuffe* (1699), Molière attributes this theologico-political analysis of royal infallibility to the "Exempt":

> D'un fin discernement sa grande âme pourvue
> Sur les choses toujours jette une droite vue;
> Chez elle jamais rien ne surprend trop d'accès,
> Et sa ferme raison ne tombe en nul excès.
> Il donne aux gens de bien une gloire immortelle;
> Mais sans aveuglement il fait briller ce zèle,
> Et l'amour pour les vrais ne ferme point son coeur
> A tout ce que les faux doivent donner d'horreur.
> (Tartuffe 5.7, ll. 1909–16)

> With clear discernment his great soul is full
> And casts his eyes always on things as they are;
> He is never too surprised by anything he sees,
> And his unfailing reason is never subject to extremes.
> He gives immortal glory to men of good birth;
> But without blinding him that zeal shines forth,
> And love for true men does not close his heart
> To all the horror that false men impart.

La Fontaine said the same of Louis XIV in 1662, in the *Elégie aux Nymphes de Vaux:*

> Il aime ses sujets, il est juste, il est sage.

> He loves his subjects, he is just, he is wise.

At least, that was the vocation of the monarchy in France, a vocation more properly religious than even political, the cornerstone of the kingdom, the touchstone of kings. And the kings themselves could not repudiate it or take offense at hearing their glory reaffirmed by their poets, even if it was a poetic fiction. They might well betray the vocation out of political necessity: under such circumstances, it was up to poets to gather it up intact in their golden vessels. It was that vocation, uttered publicly as an oath when the king was anointed, that conferred on the royal office its transcendent character and religious legitimacy.

That act of faith, the principle of an ever-renewed hope and of an ever-expected charity, rarely coincided with the actual state of the "Olympus" of the Louvre, and the divergence between them was usually cruel. In 1653, after the overwhelming failure of the "Fronde of princes," ridiculed even by Cardinal de Retz, all the old hopes of France fell upon the young king Louis XIV, whose birth in 1638 had been unanimously celebrated as a miracle. The French Daphnis had appeared. It was anticipated, not without impatience, that he would finally break free from the tutelage of Mazarin, universally despised but indisputably the victor of the civil war and one of the architects, in the king's name, of the general peace in Europe. That anticipation of the "return of Asteria" and the rebirth in France of an Augustan golden age was all the more ardent given that, for an attentive and increasingly broad public, Nicolas Foucquet, the superintendent of the king's finances, seemed destined, after the death of the old cardinal, to ensure that Louis XIV's reign would truly be that "reign of grace and peace" so long awaited and desired. It had been delayed until that time only by a series of misfortunes, mishaps, and crimes that had afflicted the kingdom since the catastrophic assassination of Henry the Great in 1610.

The arrest of the *surintendant* in September 1661 suddenly dissipated that grand illusion. With a clap of thunder, Olympus had made its choice known, and it was not Parnassus. The alliance between the two "peaks," which had raised hope that the winners and losers of the Fronde would unite around the king, and that there would be a government enlightened both by Minerva and by the Muses, gave way to the triumph of a reason of state reestablishing its ties with that which had made Richelieu and Mazarin so despised. Now, in the guise of Colbert, a Minerva without the Muses was imposing the king's rule more coldly than ever. "Demolition of the hero"? "Disenchantment of the world"? Or doubt introduced into the royal religion just when the young king was entirely free to keep his old promises?

This "coup d'état" deprived Parnassus of its "Apollo/Maecenas" and, with him, of the Augustus that France was hoping for.

It would be tempting to reduce Parnassus's response to this coup d'état to the two extremes of revolt and servitude. The servitude of the "rallied troops" is well known: Boileau himself fulminated against it in his first *Satires*. The revolt remained underground, but there were rumblings of it, powerless to combat openly the new master of the king's mind, and all the more ardent to rip him apart in verse. A regular "samizdat," circulating in manuscript form (both the talent represented in it and its vastness can be measured by the handwritten *Recueils* compiled by Maurepas and Conrart; unfortunately, these collections have as yet been little studied for themselves), attacked Colbert and took up Foucquet's defense.

But, at that time, the highest function of French poetry could not be to "commit oneself" to a "resistance" stance—desperate and criminal moreover—in the presence of a king as monumentally legitimate as Louis XIV. It could at most, and this was a very narrow and perilous path, gather up the "reason" and "truth of the heart" obscured by the wicked ministers and take it to the king.

CLANDESTINE POETRY

Only the greatest writers succeeded in walking the fine line between the extremes. However, to understand the secret tension persisting between Parnassus and Olympus, but veiled by Molière's and Racine's sterling successes, and which began just after Foucquet's conviction, we must descend to the subterranean depths of clandestine literature, where the tension between the kingdom's "conscience" and court politics bursts forth unencumbered by the veils of fable.

Without a doubt, the masterpiece of clandestine literature contemporary to the Foucquet affair was the sequence of five dialogues entitled *L'innocence persécutée*, of which only a single manuscript remains. That six-thousand-line work, written between 1662 and 1664 during the Foucquet trial, may be the "abominable book" alluded to by Alceste, standing in for Molière, a book whose "very reading . . . is to be condemned" and which merits "the utmost severity."[44]

That "tragedy," destined solely for readers in secret, is composed of five dialogues, or rather, of five long harangues vaguely arranged into dialogues in alexandrines. The burning immediacy and suspense of the Foucquet trial make up for the absence of plot.

There is a remarkable flash of political intelligence in this ambitious satire, which suggests that its author paid an indignant, but accurately informed, attention to the power struggles going on in court. Several indications (indifference to dramatic technique, hence contempt for theater; disdain for the academic refinements of language and efforts at euphony, hence an aversion for profane poetry; horror at any sort of Machiavellian exercise of political power; and, finally and especially, hatred of the Jesuits) make it possible to recognize the author as someone belonging to the religious faction, most likely to Port-Royal. Moreover, during the summer of 1664, a time when the Foucquet trial was threatening to slip out of Colbert's control, violent persecutions resumed against the nuns and Solitaries faithful to Saint-Cyran. The friends of Port-Royal and those of the *surintendant*, in danger for his life, combined their resistance networks.

L'innocence persécutée, then, did not come from "Parnassus," even though that "tragedy" wanted to captivate its clandestine public with a few sober and almost transparent literary charms. The tragic satire was the most extreme expression—more theological than poetic—of the bitter conflict that was tearing apart the royal religion from within, just as the kingdom was crystallizing into an absolute state. It was the Jansenist counterpart, in the Foucquet affair, of Emile Zola's "J'accuse."

The first dialogue depicts Colbert and his damned soul Berryer, whom the king's "favorite" assigned to preside over the special court named to judge Foucquet. The culminating point of the secret meeting between the two accomplices is Colbert's reading of the last will and testament, dictated to him by the dying Mazarin:

> Sache que le chemin le plus sûr pour régner
> Est celui des tyrans ou bien celui des crimes;
> Car, dans tous les puissants que les siècles ont eus,
> L'injustice a pour eux mieux fait que la vertu.
> Donne au roi le mépris des choses les plus saintes,
> Qu'il ait un Père Annat seulement pour l'honneur.
> Ote-lui de l'enfer la chimérique peur;
> Que si son peuple crie, il soit sourd à ses plaintes;
> Imprime-lui qu'un roi sensible à la pitié,
> Perd de tout son pouvoir la plus belle moitié.
> Dis-lui que la révolte, aux princes si funeste,
> S'engendre dans les coeurs, se nourrit par l'argent;
> Que lorsqu'un sage roi rend son peuple indigent,
> Bien loin des ses Etats il chasse cette peste;
> Dis-lui que, pour remède à la rébellion

Il faut dépouiller l'homme; et régner en lion.
Fais qu'il se rende enfin par son humeur farouche
Cruel à ses sujets et dur à ses amis,
Et qu'étant sur le trône où le hasard l'a mis,
La disgrâce d'autrui point ou peu ne le touche.
Qu'il pense que l'orgueil, avec sa fierté
Fait avec plus d'éclat briller la majesté.

Know that the surest path for a reigning king
Is that of tyrants or that of crime;
In every powerful man the centuries have seen,
Injustice has served him better than virtue.
Give the king contempt for the holiest things,
May he keep a Father Annat for the honor alone.
Take away his chimerical fear of hell, so that
If his people cry out, he may be deaf to their pleas.
Persuade him that a king sensitive to pity,
Loses the greater half of his power.
Tell him that revolt, so deadly to princes,
Is produced in the heart and feeds on money;
So that, when a wise king makes his people indigent,
He banishes that plague far from his states.
Tell him that, as a remedy to rebellion
He must make man destitute, and reign as a lion.
And finally, make him become, by his savage moods
Cruel to his subjects and severe toward his friends,
And, sitting on the throne where chance has placed him,
Let the disgrace of others leave him unmoved.
Let him think that arrogance, with its pride
Makes his majesty with more brightness shine.

Possessed by "hell's reason," the Colbert of *L'innocence persécutée*, loyal heir to Mazarin, seizes in his turn the king's soul, whose sacred office he despises ("the throne where chance has placed him"), making him a docile instrument of his thirst for power and money at the expense of the French people and their common good.

The other acts in the tragedy allow Colbert's principal accomplices to speak: Chancellor Séguier, Foucquet's first "judge"; the Jesuit Annat, the king's confessor; the entire coalition of "imposters" who, under Colbert's leadership, have seized hold of the king of France's will.

It is impossible not to compare Molière's *Tartuffe*, whose first version was performed before the judgment ending the Foucquet affair: Molière's religious hypocrite also becomes the absolute master of Orgon's "house" by circumventing the "head of the family." In both works, a conspiracy of masked men has seized hold of legitimate paternal authority, and it uses this authority to crush the innocent, placed in principle under its benevolent protection. The similarity between the two dramatic situations, mirror images of each other, explains why this Jansenist tract could have been attributed to Molière. Each is a dramatic creation: the first a transparent depiction of the reality, the second a metaphorical representation, accomplished by a shift from the public to the private sphere. Both refer to the same French commonplace of the "kingdom as family," the "king as father," and "bad government" as the unnatural fruit of a usurpation of authority, of which the king is (in *L'innocence persécutée*) or might be (along with Orgon, in *Tartuffe*) the dupe. The large-scale modifications to which Molière had to agree in 1667 may not have been simply the result of the scandal caused, among the devout of the "old" court, by the small ecclesiastic collar worn by the first "Imposter." They may also have been required out of a concern to shelter the king from any suspicion that he was ignoring or covering up, albeit unawares, the slightest "imposture" harmful to his subjects, even in their private lives. Molière performed on a stage constructed over gunpowder.

The last act of *L'innocence persécutée* presents Foucquet in his cell in La Bastille. He converses with his jailer, d'Artagnan, in the moments preceding his departure for the Arsenal, where the verdict will be read to him. He is expecting a death sentence. All the sympathy that the *surintendant*'s loyalists—and an increasingly large public—felt for Colbert's victim could be projected onto that tragic situation, comparable to that of Socrates in Plato's *Phaedo*. But the anonymous playwright refrained from idealizing the persecuted innocent or making him into a hero:

Je suis homme, Monsieur, et tel, je sens mon coeur
Avoir de la faiblesse et craindre la douleur.

I, Sir, am a man, and as such, I feel
The weakness of my heart and its fear of suffering.

With d'Artagnan as his witness, Foucquet acknowledges his "sins" and even his "crimes," for which he believes he has been justly punished by

God, whom his ambition led him to neglect. This is not the misappropriation of funds of which Colbert accused him. He himself dismantles the
machinery that made possible his ascension, begun under Richelieu and
continued under Mazarin. He confesses that he served hell, but that he
has paid the price through the hell endured within his conscience:

> Il faut, pour soutenir ce malheureux emploi,
> Donner une parole et n'avoir point de foi;
> Il faut nourrir son coeur des plus dures maximes
> Accoutumer son âme aux plus énormes crimes,
> Et, sans en sourciller, voir le peuple innocent
> Verser par vos forfaits ses larmes et son sang,
> Et de vos cruautés le rendant la victime,
> Auprès de votre maître établir votre estime.
> . . . .
> Ainsi dans cet emploi, si l'on conserve une âme,
> De la moindre pitié qui quelquefois s'enflamme,
> Parmi tant de forfaits s'il reste dans un sein,
> Pour rendre encor sensible, un sentiment humain,
> Hélas! que l'on éprouve altérer de délices,
> Quand on ne peut agir sans faire des supplices,
> Et que de votre emploi le destin le plus beau
> Est de savoir, l'oeil sec, égorger en bourreau.

> To continue to pursue that unhappy employ,
> One must give one's word and be without good faith;
> One must nourish one's heart with the harshest maxims,
> Accustom one's soul to the greatest crimes,
> And, without flinching, see the innocent people
> Spill their tears and blood for your misdeeds,
> And through your cruelty make them the victims,
> And so before your master establish your own worth.
> . . . .
> Hence, in that employ, if one preserves a soul
> With the slightest pity that sometimes flashes up,
> Among so many misdeeds, if there remains in the heart
> A human sentiment to make one feel,
> Alas! how one senses one's joys fade away,
> When one cannot act without causing torments,

And one realizes that, in this employ,
The best fate is to know, dry-eyed and cold,
How to be the tormentor who cuts another's throat.

That "confession" by Foucquet, which attributes to the *surintendant*
sincere repentance for his ambition, also sets out the arguments for his
release that the prisoner had developed in his *Défenses*, addressed to his
judges, but distributed clandestinely to the public. The last act ends with
an eloquent "letter in verse to the king," which d'Artagnan, fearing Colbert, refuses to send to its addressee, and which Foucquet must be satisfied
to read aloud as a last will and testament. It is the exact antithesis of the
Testament de Mazarin, read by Colbert to Berryer in act 1:

Je ne condamne point, Sire, votre Justice;
Je baise votre main qui m'envoie au supplice;
Mais c'est la Vérité, qu'on bannit de ces lieux,
Qui condamne la main qui la cache à vos yeux;
Mais, malgré les efforts de cette main funeste,
Qui retranche mes jours, Sire, ce qu'il m'en reste
Je le dois employer à me conduire aux Cieux
Et vous rendre un grand roi digne de vos aïeux.

I do not condemn your justice, Sire;
I kiss the hand that sends me to the fire;
But it is Truth, that, banished from this place,
Condemns the hand that hides it from your gaze;
But, despite the efforts of that deadly hand,
Which shortens my days, Sire, the time I have at hand
I must use to strive to reach heavenward
And make you a king worthy of your forebears.

The pedagogy of "hell's reason," taught by Mazarin on his deathbed to
Colbert, is now balanced by Foucquet's counterpedagogy, enlightened by
misfortune, repenting of his errors, and finding in disgrace and in the face
of torment the authority of a Christian Socrates of the monarchy.

In this very French tragedy, everything rests on the assumption that the
king has a conscience. That royal consciousness of the Good can be
blinded and numbed by the imposture of ministers who have sold out
to Evil; and, because it is inherent in the essence of his function, it can
always be reawakened and enlightened by the voice of his true and faith-

ful subjects. Foucquet is not a saint, but, like the vizier in "The Mogul's Dream" (11.4), he "sometimes sought solitude" even when he enjoyed favor at court; and that beginning, fully developed in his disgrace, can now make him a depository of and martyr for the royal truth perverted by the "favorite" Colbert, but latent in the king's heart of hearts. One already finds, in the words of the Foucquet of *L'innocence persécutée*, the unassailable faith in the awakening of the royal conscience that Racine would later attribute to Queen Phaedra, finally banishing the "faithful" Oenone:

> Détestables flatteurs, présent le plus funeste
> Que puisse faire au roi la colère céleste.

> Despicable flatterers, the deadliest gift
> That the wrath of heaven can make to the king.

In this "last will and testament of Foucquet," one also finds the same distance taken from earthly kingdoms that are not inspired by the charity of Christ, as in Pascal's *Pensées* (still unpublished in 1665):

> C'est ainsi qu'un grand roi voit croître chaque jour
> Dans le coeur de son peuple, et le zèle et l'amour:
> Cet amour pour sa garde est plus fort qu'une armée,
> Et l'âme d'un sujet de ce zèle animée
> Sert toujours à son roi d'invincibles remparts
> Que sait rendre l'amour plus fort que ceux de Mars.
> Tant de soldats, en vain semés dans les provinces,
> Y pensent maintenir la puissance des Princes;
> La force en cet endroit n'a qu'un masque trompeur:
> Elle marque des rois la faiblesse et la peur.
> Un prince environné de soldats et de gardes
> Imprime la terreur avec leurs hallebardes,
> Mais tout cet appareil et dont se sert un roi
> Dans l'esprit de son peuple à jeter de l'effroi
> Fait voir qu'un souverain, en régnant par la crainte,
> En a comme un tyran le premier l'âme atteinte.
> Un sage Ministère évite ces excès.

> So it is that a great king sees increase day by day,
> In the heart of his people, both their love and their zeal:
> That love, as his protection, is stronger than an army,

And the soul of a subject animated by this zeal
Always serves his king as invincible ramparts
Which love can make stronger than those of Mars.
So many soldiers, scattered in vain in the provinces,
Believe they are maintaining the power of princes;
Force in such a place is only a deceptive mask:
It marks the king's weakness and his fear.
A prince surrounded by soldiers and by guards
Sows terror with their halberds,
But all the equipment that a king uses
In the minds of his people to inspire fear
Shows that a sovereign, in reigning by fright,
Sees, like a tyrant, his soul the first attacked.
A wise ministry avoids such excess.

L'innocence persécutée thus distinguishes quite clearly between the always-possible king and the real king, and between the real king and the evil spirits that prevent him from exercising his royal duty—divine in origin and Christlike in its essence—as he should and as he wishes to do in his heart of hearts. Nevertheless, the Foucquet of *L'innocence persécutée* warns Louis XIV that a too-obvious and too-lasting identification of the monarchy with Colbert's Machiavellian policies will deprive him of the love due the true kings of France and reduce him to the notorious rank of the tyrant, and to the execration the tyrant attracts. The king of France can be "absolute" only insofar as he himself does not stand apart from true "natural and divine right," that of Socrates and that of Christ. The French monarchy is founded on the image of the God of love in the king's heart of hearts: if that foundation is effaced, if the people lose faith in the sage-king, in the Christ-king, then the French monarchy is threatened with the fate that awaits tyrannies everywhere.

It would be difficult to push further, at least with pen and paper, the freedom of a prophetic spiritual power to "set aright" temporal power gone awry. The anonymous author of *L'innocence persécutée*, probably backed by Port-Royal, wrote and made known what was secretly on people's minds in the devout circles that supported Foucquet's cause. It elevated the Foucquet affair, officially limited to accusations of misappropriation, embezzlement, and rebellion against the state, to the level of a violent theological and political debate on the essence of the French monarchy. The anonymous author of *L'innocence persécutée* has many traits in common with the Zola and Péguy of the Dreyfus affair. Dante had spoken from deep within the conflict between the priesthood and the empire. This conflict was now being reconstituted within the kingdom of France, and the king's conscience was at stake. The great writers in the early part of his personal reign, under the protective and flattering veils of the theatrical poetry condemned by Port-Royal, remained very close to the tempest. But they did so as poets, to identify the political drama of the monarchy with the universal human drama, the struggle between good and evil, truth and lies, grace and freedom, not only within the heart of the king of France but within all human hearts.

CORRUPTION OF THE WORD, CORRUPTION OF THE CENTURY

It is very likely that *L'innocence persécutée* was indeed the "abominable book" mentioned by Alceste, the "misanthrope" whom Molière shows us rebelling, during the reign of Louis the Great, against the "corruption of the century":

Je ne trouve partout que lâche flatterie
Qu'injustice, intérêt, trahison, fourberie.

Everywhere I find only base flattery
Injustice, self-interest, betrayal, treachery.

But, in the same scene, Molière also presents Philinte, the friend of Alceste, a philosopher who says: "It is good to hide what one has in one's heart," and advises Alceste to "hold his tongue." But it is no use: that "honorable man" admits, in private conversation, that, in his heart of hearts, although he conceals it under a veneer of courtesy that Alceste finds too "obliging," he shares his friend's very dark view of contemporary political society:

Oui, je vois ces défauts dont votre âme murmure,
Comme vices unis à l'humaine nature,
Et mon esprit enfin n'est pas plus offensé
De voir un homme fourbe, injuste, intéressé,
Que de voir des vautours affamés de carnage,
Des singes malfaisants et des loups pleins de rage.

(act 1, scene 1)

Yes, I see those faults that your heart murmurs of,
As vices inherent in human nature,
And my mind is no more offended in the end
To see a man treacherous, unjust, self-interested,
Than to see vultures hungry for slaughter,
Evil-doing monkeys and wolves full of rage.

Alceste's "frankness" is insulting and crude in private life. Is it necessary to say when face to face with an aging coquette that she is ridiculous or obnoxious? Such language would be boorishness, not frankness. Devotion to the strict truth is no less absurd in public life, where it is "quixotic" and sows disorder. The dilemma that torments the friendship of Alceste and Philinte, in the early scenes of acts 1 and 5 of *Le misanthrope*, is the same as that which preoccupied writers during and after the Foucquet affair. Was the "frankness" that the Fronde had abused, which Pascal had put in the service of a holy cause in the last *Provinciales*, and with which Port-Royal continued to appeal to the French conscience, but only in secret (like the author of *L'innocence persécutée*), desirable in a kingdom that was once more enjoying civil peace under an utterly legitimate king, but where treachery, injustice, and self-interest, the slaughter of vultures, the evil-doing of monkeys, and the rage of wolves, nonetheless wreaked havoc at the highest levels of the state?

That undisguised freedom of expression, ready (at least on principle) to face martyrdom, can also take on the meaning of an "abominable" sacrilege against the keystone of the kingdom, the royal office. That office is less compromised by "slavish" lies that heap flowers on vultures, monkeys, and wolves. That mercenary flattery no doubt compromises the honor of Parnassus, but it at least rescues the principle of peace, which this contemplative peak is fond of by definition. Is there no path of transcendence for the poet, one that does not compromise truth, of which he is the depositary and which he guarantees with the fidelity of language, but which also does not compromise the good faith with which every French person is obliged to credit his king, even if he believes him misled, deceived, deceiving, and swallowed up by his ministers in their tyrannical roles as predatory animals?

Parnassus is not Port-Royal. Even though La Fontaine, who studied at the Oratory and remained close to the Solitaries for a long time, respected their apostolic intransigence, he never confused the words he used in his own "Christian and diverse poetry" with those of "saints" of both sexes who were bold enough—almost to the point of martyrdom—to oppose "truth" to "lies," the word of God to that of men.

The French Parnassus is also not Jesuit. La Fontaine ridiculed the "velvet way" in a ballade and in stanzas on "Escobar." He did so in 1666, with the verve of a libertine Christian, but that verve was combined with irony, if not with Pascal's holy wrath.[45] At the time, he wanted to support the nuns and M. de Sacy, who were being persecuted, just as he had supported the persecuted Foucquet in 1662–64.

Voltaire saw very well who had saved Foucquet's life: "Several men of letters openly declared themselves for him, and served him with so much warmth that they saved his life" (*Le siècle de Louis XIV*, chap. 25: "Particularités et anecdotes").

In saving him, they saved their own souls. In other words, they saved the aptitude of the French language to assume the legacy of Cadmus and Harmony. But they also saved their own capacity to escape the serpent's coils, to rise, each according to his vocation, to the sovereign role—worthy of their sovereign—of the kingdom's poetic conscience. In 1661–64, the Foucquet affair had itself taken on a tragic dimension devastating for men of letters only because of the question of language, which transcended by far the person of the *surintendant* and even the beneficent function of patron he had skillfully fulfilled and symbolized.

Despite his caution and intelligence, Foucquet had been trapped by his own naïveté, frankness, and good faith regarding his king's word. His error—if it was one—went to the very core of the French royal religion. In his *Mémoires*, probably compiled by Paul Pellisson, Foucquet's former right-hand man, the king took great care to turn the suspicion of which he was the object into an accusation against Foucquet: of all the reproaches addressed to him, the most violent was to have dared *lie* to his king.

Who had lied? Who, after the death of Mazarin, had reintroduced the corruption of language into the sanctuary of the monarchy? On the brink of a reign from which so much good was expected, could poetry and belles lettres repair that wound, or could it simply conceal it under praise? The origin of that drama, like the range of literary reactions it elicited, openly raised the question of the loyal and royal word, and hence of the very foundation of the political family that the kingdom of France was supposed to have been since Clovis. Foucquet's impeccably loyal career in the king's service, his unassailable trust (despite all the opinions of his friends, servants, and spies) in the pledges of friendship the king had heaped upon him to better lower his guard, even if people attributed the king's conduct to Colbert's advice, compromised all the "frankness" of language in France and, among other things, all the dignity of poetic and literary language.

But, in another respect, the indignation against the appalling hypoc-risy covering up Colbert's conspiracy, as it was set forth undisguised in *L'innocence persécutée*, compromised the most precious thing the kingdom had accomplished: internal and external peace, the unanimity surround-ing the king, whom his subjects had always been obliged to trust. No one wanted to return to the Fronde. Holy violence could only harden the king, push him a little deeper into error—supposing he was in error—and lead the kingdom a little farther in the direction of tyranny.

Even Port-Royal felt and knew what Molière was expressing through the plot of *Le malade imaginaire*: it was not the reproaches of the "rational" Béralde or his open protests, however well founded, that might one day make Argan, blinded by the self-interested lies of his doctors, see reason. The king, image of God on earth, was also the image of man, quick to be deceived and willingly rearing up in error. Port-Royal, however, was not ready to admit, with Molière and his friends the poets, that the indirect method of the plucky Toinette—ingratiating, ironic, a wizard of disguise and fiction—was more in harmony with the humanity of men and kings than the method of theologians and prophets.

All the same, acceptance of lies, slavish complacency toward hypocrisy, and denial of the word of truth could not be part of the mores of the princes of Parnassus. Parnassus could not be content to blindly worship Olympus.

CULTURAL POLITICS

In 1663–64, the years when the Foucquet trial reached its dénoue-ment, Colbert's agent and the tempter of poets was Jean Chapelain. An erudite and veteran critic, he had had many titles, and, at the death of his friend and correspondent Guez de Balzac in 1654, he became the French prince of the republic of letters. But with his epic *La pucelle*, about which he had been saying wonderful things for a long time, he had fallen into a slavish and pompous versification, at a time when a sense of respect had not yet returned, and when a sense of the ridiculous was the most com-mon thing in the world in Paris. Chapelain's *La pucelle*, when it finally appeared in 1656, produced the effect of monumental boredom and set off a general outburst of laughter.[46] The French epic as a whole never recovered. The freedom of the years 1643–61, the degree of irony it had made possible, the requirement of "naturalness"—between the excesses of Chapelain and the excesses of Scarron—that it had finally set up as the principle of the "Foucquet" taste, continued to exert their salutary effects during the first twenty years of Louis XIV's personal reign. From the outset, it formed a blockade against pompous commissioned literature, the responsibility for which Colbert at first made the mistake of entrusting to Chapelain.

In 1661 this learned and ridiculed man had a score to settle with the people of culture and high society who had injured his *Pucelle*. He despised Foucquet: choosing between two evils, the *surintendant* had preferred and awarded a pension to the unfortunate Scarron, who knew how to laugh and make others laugh, at himself in the first place. Very early on, Chapelain had discerned Colbert's character and decided to serve him. What brilliant revenge for him to become, under Colbert, the arbiter of royal gratifications and the official evaluator of literary talents! Unable to be the prince of the French republic of letters, Chapelain became, after Foucquet's fall and in the service of Colbert, its general director and censor.

The contrast between that enlistment of writers by a bitter writer and the elegance with which Nicolas Foucquet had practiced patronage was all too glaring. Even the sometimes less-graceful patronage of bankers and businessmen, which had prevailed under Mazarin, a stingy minister indifferent to French literature, had appeared very compatible with the freedom of poets. People had poked fun at Corneille, who in 1642 dedicated his tragedy *Cinna* to the banker Pierre Montauron in exchange for a fat gratification. But it was very clear to everyone that *Cinna*, a masterpiece of political intelligence as well as of dramatic poetry, had been conceived by Corneille in full independence and, in fact, verged on a challenge to the "tyrant" Richelieu. The price paid by Montauron for the dedication honored the patron, without casting the slightest shadow over the integrity of the work or its author. French belles lettres were even grateful to Corneille, as they would be in the nineteenth century to Honoré de Balzac, for having greatly increased the price of works of the mind under all circumstances, with booksellers and theater directors, as well as with private patrons.[47]

That was not the case for the pensions and gratifications granted by Colbert on Chapelain's recommendation: in exchange for bags of gold from the king, Chapelain required panegyric works, whose design and form—not to say format—he himself set out in advance, under threat, and not even a veiled threat, of disgrace. His definition of the pensioned poet—"one of the instruments of the king's glory via works of the mind"—

was brutal. Corneille, who had joyfully benefited from Foucquet's patronage in 1660, and who, moreover, still held a grudge for the hateful *Sentiment de l'Académie,* which Chapelain had written on *Le Cid* in 1637, was nonetheless placed at the top of the list for official pensions in 1663. Corneille was "the French Sophocles." It would have been impossible to exclude him, without creating a scandal, from the list of poets pensioned by the king. The poet showed no gratitude. He later confined himself to pointing out, in a petition to the king, that the pension had been paid to him only after long delays.

The painter Charles Le Brun, whose art made him much more dependent than Corneille on what must in effect be called Colbert's "cultural policy," was obliged, as soon as Foucquet was arrested, to go into the service of the new administration; but, in private and in the presence of trusted friends such as Olivier Lefèvre d'Ormesson, he did not conceal the fact that he missed the manners and taste of the disgraced *surintendant.*[48]

The Colbertist pension list has been celebrated as the crowning moment, in the form of royal patronage, of a movement begun in the Renaissance in support of a social status for writers. It can also be seen as the radical inversion of that movement. Nothing was more alien to that administrative and distant measure, which humiliated more than one person, than the familiarity enjoyed in sixteenth-century Italy and France by poets and artists in the entourage of princes. Charles IX and Henry III, in imitation of Leonello d'Este or Lorenzo di Medici, participated on equal footing with an academy of intellectual princes, where humanist friendship attenuated or veiled the difference in rank. The favor that Gaston d'Orléans, the duc de Montmorency, and Foucquet himself enjoyed among writers and poets rested a great deal upon the ties of affection that united these patrons and their protégés, and removed the cold calculation and humiliation of servitude from the "duties" mutually rendered. Recognition and respect, preferably well informed, mattered at least as much to poets and artists as the subsidy and status. Colbert and Chapelain offended the people in their debt more than Montauron had done.

In that matter, the king remained above the fray much more than he had in the Foucquet affair. By virtue of an admirable and very French fiction that had protected Louis the Just, Louis the Great (who had declared he wanted to govern "alone") could allow himself to have tastes and manners quite different from those of his "favorite." The French royal religion postulated that it was always possible to appeal to the king's "heart of hearts" and, by extension, in the "post-Foucquet" era, to the infallible taste which the grace of his state office was to provide him. He alone could go over the heads of his blundering functionaries. He had the merit to sense this.

The minor and undistinguished writers therefore accommodated themselves with good grace to all of Chapelain's and Colbert's requirements, provided that, in the shadows, they could cash pensions and subsidies and have their mediocre works preceded by promotional dedications to the king or a major figure at court.

The truly talented and more delicate consciences very quickly understood that they would demean themselves in the public's mind, and in their own eyes, if they did not gracefully dissociate themselves from the herd of recipients of the administration's subsidies. The "public," which, within their own consciences and the safety of private conversations, had not been intimidated or silenced by the military apparatus deployed by Colbert against Foucquet, was even less blinded by the large sums dispensed by Chapelain. How to obtain the approval of "honorable men" without offending the minister and the agents of his power?

This was not difficult for celebrities such as Corneille, or for great writers protected by birth and fortune, such as La Rochefoucauld, La Fayette, and Sévigné, who, moreover, jeered at the idea that they were "authors." For those obliged to live by the pen, but who also had a poet's conscience, Molière, a vile histrion by the criteria of the time, provided a model of conduct from the beginning. The direct "friendship" he had been able to establish with the king during the festival of Vaux, after the performance of *Les fâcheux*, was a tribute to his political intelligence and to his urbanity. It also implied that the king, even before having Foucquet arrested, had discerned the superiority of his future victim's taste, and had sworn not to neglect that heretofore un-Bourbonian aspect of the king's duties.

That personal bond between Molière and the king somewhat resembled the liberal playfulness that had reigned between La Fontaine and Foucquet between 1658 and 1661. Molière did everything he could to let the king believe it. That pretty fiction spared him any overly restrictive dependence on Colbert's staff.

That extraordinary example was difficult for the "authors" to follow. Unlike Molière, they were not on the margins, but they also did not have the opportunity to play on the solidarity of "stage people," so quickly established between King Louis XIV, an actor and dancer at heart, and Molière, whom the king quickly sensed was the Diaghilev of comedy ballet. The path leading from the Parnassus of writers to the Olympus of the king was therefore much "steeper, more slippery, and more difficult," though "exposed to the sun on every side," than the path of a man of the theater. How to get around Jean Chapelain, and even his successor, Charles Perrault, who stood at the ticket window in front of Colbert's offices, and attract the interest and attention of the king himself? Louis XIV knew how to flame desire.

Finally, in 1677, Racine and his friend Boileau definitively escaped the common fate, by obtaining from the king the positions of historiographers of the regime, which brought them into close proximity with him on almost a daily basis and attached them directly to his person. In 1677 Jean Chapelain had been dead for three years. The proprieties had been carefully respected.

The "long march" of Racine and Boileau began very early and followed very different tracks, reflecting the enormous differences between their two forms of genius. The two poets crossed paths, however, understood each other, and united in an indestructible friendship the very year that the king sent Foucquet to the Pignerol dungeon.

That year, in the company of the libertine Chapelle and the sour Furetière (who joined the Académie Française in 1662), they sat around a cabaret table and conceived a parody of Le Cid entitled Chapelain décoiffé (Chapelain doffed), which would be published anonymously the next year. For Racine and Boileau, it was a discreet and inoffensive, but effective, manner to let it be known they were not Chapelain's "clients." This was already very clear in Boileau's case, much less so in Racine's.[49]

In 1660, with remarkable foresight, the unknown young poet, fresh from the Petites-Ecoles of Port-Royal, had acquiesced to Chapelain's corrections of his ode La Nymphe de la Seine à la reine, written to celebrate Louis XIV's Spanish marriage.[50] At that time, he had also become closely associated with La Fontaine, his elder and a relative, who was then the poet laureate of the surintendant Foucquet and potentially that of the king. Racine therefore had no trouble commanding respect from Chapelain as well, when Chapelain became Colbert's literary assistant. In 1664 he was placed on the famous list of "grantees," with a modest pension equal to his still-nascent reputation. That in no way prevented him, that same year, from participating with Boileau in the burlesque "doffing" of the old periwig who was wreaking havoc around Colbert. He betrayed his Port-Royal masters in the cause of poetry; he could much more easily "betray" Chapelain, the functionary of poetry. He had the literary stuff of the greatest tragic poet of his age. But he also had personally experienced the crisis of confidence plaguing that generation.

Did he also, like Corneille, have a true vocation as a playwright? He had begun with the lyric poetry of pomp, in the tradition of Malherbe. But in 1664, the example of Molière, with whom he was associated, showed him the way: to touch the eyes and ears of Louis XIV, the most direct path was the dramatic scene. The king did not have time to read and annotate much more than dossiers and reports, and, unlike Henry III, a student of Ronsard's contemporary Amyot, he did not have the reading habit. He divided his leisure time between sermons, theater, and love affairs. Conversation filled in the gaps.

Since the festival of Vaux, Molière had been the "new Terence," discovered by Monsieur, the king's brother, recognized by Foucquet, and adopted by Louis XIV. A place of choice remained for Racine: in the king's mind, he would be the Euripides or Seneca of the new regime. That choice became all the more clear since Corneille, the "French Sophocles" dear to the queen mother and the "old court" (and compromised since 1659 by an enthusiastic dedication to Foucquet in his *Oedipe*), apparently had little chance, because of his age and character, of taking in hand the secretly equivocal and devious climate that the Foucquet affair had created. He would do so, however, but as an increasingly ironic and gloomy witness.

Racine refrained from following in Corneille's footsteps, and from overtly making tragedy the "political breviary of kings." After *La Thébaïde*, a "Senecan" effort that enjoyed modest success, he hit the right note with *Alexandre le Grand*. The king let his satisfaction be publicly known. But, if he believed he had found a flattering portraitist in Racine, he was wrong. He too was betrayed. Racine betrayed everyone except Parnassus.

In itself, the dedication to the king in *Alexandre le Grand*, performed by Molière and his troupe before the court in 1665, is a true diplomatic manifesto of the equitable exchange, for which the poet takes the initiative, between revelation, his "divine" duty, and magnificent illusion, the king's duty, it too "divine" in its way. With extraordinary tact, the poet managed to create a direct dialogue, almost of equals, between the author of *Alexandre le Grand* and his delighted royal spectator. "Despite the efforts that had been made to disguise my hero from His Majesty, he had no sooner appeared before Him, than He recognized him as Alexander."[51]

In an instant, that "recognition," occasioned by Racine's poetry, eradicated the sacred distance that separated a subject from the majesty of a "king whose glory extends as far as that of that conqueror, and before whom one can say that all the peoples of the world fall silent, as Scripture said of Alexander."

Against the background of that vast universal silence, the exchange between the poet's spellbinding words and the king's enchanted approbation wondrously stood out. That *fiat lux*, which revealed the poet to the king and the king to the poet, effaced and offset the destruction of Foucquet/ Maecenas by the royal word. Parnassus suddenly saw the bridge that connected it to Olympus, and which it had believed in ruins, rebuilt by Racine, diligently and with added genius, but rebuilt for him alone.

All the same, the most astonishing thing is that Racine in no way renounced poetry's vocation to tell the truth. Skirting danger even in that dedication, the poet indulges in the luxury of emphatically celebrating the glory—in peace, not war—with which the king's great soul knows (or ought to know) how to be satisfied. In the midst of clouds of incense, he insinuates the principle intrinsic to the entire Virgilian poetic tradition to which the playwright is connected: peace and the wisdom of peace are more glorious than the victories of conquerors; they are even more meritorious in Louis XIV since he obtains them (or ought to obtain them) by himself, he "who owes the thriving state of his kingdom only to his councils," and who, if he desired (but must he so desire?), could "make himself feared by all of Europe." This amounted to launching a spearhead into the secret realm of the royal councils, but without hitting them, and orienting Olympus in the direction desired by Parnassus.

It would have been impossible to go over Colbert's head in a bolder manner and to instill, deep in the conscience of a barely literate—but flattered—king, a keen interest in poetry, and perhaps even in the things the most elevated poetry has always taught kings.

In 1671 Colbert was only too happy to accept the brief and pompous dedication of *Bérénice*, from the hand of a poet long favored personally by the only true patron of the arts, the king.[52]

Racine was only just beginning as Louis XIV's "privileged interlocutor." But his "diplomacy of poetry" was already completely set in place in 1665: it presupposed that the integrity of the poetic word and its vocation as a truthful mirror could be maintained intact at the perilous center of sacred authority, and could even find there, between a protective illusion and the intimation of truth, a surplus of tragic intensity.

Boileau, less gifted and more outspoken than Racine, also took a much less roundabout path. That worthy and deserving route, as Albert Thibaudet saw and expressed so well, allowed him to become the grand magistrate of the French republic of letters under Louis XIV, to be respected and honored by the king, but with a more visible autonomy and moral authority of sorts over his peers than Racine had ever obtained or sought.[53]

The first move by the young Boileau, in 1661–64, was revolt. That revolt was all the more meritorious in that Boileau owed nothing to Nicolas Foucquet: it was the anger of a true writer, an anger in the manner of Jean

Paulhan, against any downgrading of belles lettres, whatever its origin and motives.

His first satire, composed during the Foucquet trial, was presented in the voice of François Cassandre—under the "Parnassus name" Damon—an erudite libertine who had been very close to La Fontaine since his youth. The young Boileau, without venturing in the slightest into the realm of the "Affair," identified somewhat with his literary elders and their confusion at that moment of crisis between belles lettres and the court. The Damon of *Satire I,* though preceding Molière's misanthrope by several years, has more than one trait in common with Alceste:

> Puisqu'en ce lieu jadis aux Muses si commode,
> Le mérite et l'esprit ne sont plus à la mode,
> Qu'un Poète, dit-il, s'y voit maudit de Dieu,
> Et qu'ici la Vertu n'a plus ni feu ni lieu;
> Allons du moins chercher quelque antre ou quelque roche,
> D'où jamais ni l'Huissier, ne le Sergent n'approche;
> Et sans lasser le Ciel par des voeux impuissants,
> Metton-nous à l'abri des injures du temps.
>
> (*Satire I,* ll. 21–28)

> Since, in this place, once so obliging to the Muses,
> Merit and wit are no longer in vogue,
> Where a poet, it is said, is cursed by God,
> And virtue no longer has fire or place;
> Let us seek at least some cave or some rock,
> Where neither the bailiff nor the sergeant will approach;
> And, without boring heaven with impotent vows,
> Set ourselves apart from the ravages of our times.

He even allowed Damon to judge Colbert and Chapelain, and had the courage not to suppress the judgment when he published the first edition of his *Satires* in 1666:

> Il est vrai que du Roi la bonté secourable
> Jette enfin sur la Muse un regard favorable,
> Et réparant du Sort l'égarement fatal,
> Va tirer désormais Phébus de l'hôpital.
> On doit tout espérer d'un Monarque si juste.
> Mais sans un Mécénas, à quoi sert un Auguste?
>
> (*Satire I,* ll. 81–86)

It is true that now the king's helpful kindness
Is finally casting on the Muse a favorable glance,
And, repairing the deadly error of Fate,
Will now save Phoebus from the hospital.
One should hope everything from a monarch so just.
But without a Maecenas, what use is an Augustus?

The strike, carefully prepared and protected by praise of the monarch, is ferocious against his minister, much more ferocious than the trifle *Chapelain décoiffé*, which simply ridiculed one of Colbert's elderly employees. But it is not merely a strike: it is an axiom of literary policy, which Boileau will henceforth embrace, and which will govern his entire strategy, both audacious and cautious, and (not without sacrifice) will safeguard the integrity of belles lettres under a new regime that appears at first sight to endanger them.

To his credit, Boileau was a close friend of Molière's at the time (he dedicated his *Satire II* to him), and the two authors shared the same feeling: one must prefer the king to his ministers, one must flatter his pride in "reigning alone" to educate a Maecenas within him. Racine, on his own behalf, had quickly come to the same conclusions.

In dedicating the first collection of *Satires* (published in 1666) to the king, Boileau rigorously obeyed the rules of conduct he had set for himself. He lavished Louis XIV with the praise he knew the king would find most sympathetic ("Et qui seul, sans Ministre, à l'exemple des Dieux / Soutiens tout par toi-même, et vois tout par Tes yeux"; And who alone, with no minister, following the example of the gods / Sustainest everything by thyself, and seest everything through thine eyes). But, taking him at his word, he drew none of the consequences that Colbert and Chapelain wanted to impose on the kingdom's belles lettres. Following a "heroic" convention established by Malherbe and Corneille, he addressed the king as "thou," positioning himself firmly as the prince of Parnassus, addressing, with utmost dignity, the god of Olympus. This is far from the servility of the "instrument of the king's glory," required by Chapelain in exchange for a pension. And the poet, with a frankness that sought to do honor to the king of France, plainly declared to him that he himself did not have enough genius to excel at the great panegyric genres, the only ones worthy of praising such a great king. But he made this confession in such terms that it was also possible to understand that he had no taste for praising unwillingly, under threat, or in exchange for money:

Mais je sais peu louer, et ma Muse tremblante
Fuit d'un si grand fardeau la charge trop pesante.

(ll. 9–10)

But I little know how to praise, and my trembling Muse
Flees the great weight of such a heavy load.

He would not abandon his "naturalness"; like Horace (but under an Augustus/Maecenas), he would continue to write satires and epistles. In this *Discours au roi*, he gave the king an appealing glimpse of his natural talent by ripping apart with relish the literary proletariat recruited by Colbert and Chapelain. He also imperceptibly led the king to understand that he was being deceived about the merchandise, that he had to form his own taste and prefer poets with an independent but sincere talent to mercenaries who did no honor to his reign:

Le mal est, qu'en rimant, ma Muse un peu légère
Nomme tout par son nom, and ne saurait rien taire.
C'est là ce qui fait peur aux Esprits de ce temps,
Qui tout blancs au dehors, sont tout noirs au dedans.
Ils tremblent qu'un Censeur, que sa verve encourage,
Ne vienne en ses écrits démasquer leur visage,
Et fouillant dans leurs moeurs en toute liberté,
N'aille au fond du Puits tirer la Vérité.

(ll. 81–88)

The trouble is, when she rhymes, my frivolous Muse
Names everything by its name, and cannot hold her tongue.
That is what frightens the wits of our time,
Who, all white on the outside, are all black within.
They tremble that a censor, encouraged by her verve,
Will come to her writings and unmask their faces,
And, rifling through their mores in full liberty,
Will reach the bottom of the well and draw out the verity.

That same king, suspected of having bowed to Colbert's duplicity in the Foucquet affair and betrayed his royal vocation, was now ingeniously summoned by Boileau (as he was by Molière in *Tartuffe*) to personally stand as guarantor and protector of poets, the friends of truth and the critics of hypocrisy, the only ones worthy and capable of speaking the true king's own truth.

In the end, Louis XIV tired of Molière, who died early enough not to witness his disgrace and the favor shown to Lully. But he gradually took Boileau's holy ruses literally, until, in 1677, he chose to make this poet of truth ("Grand roi, c'est mon défaut, je ne saurais flatter"; Great king, that is my fault, I cannot flatter) one of the two historiographers of the kingdom. A weighty honor, which Boileau might perhaps have done without, but which he assumed for a few years, shifting a large part of the load onto his colleague. This was the consecration of the pious and happy lie of the *Discours du roi* of 1665, which had had the merit of assuring a certain play between liberty and authority, both for himself and for his friends, the greatest writers of his generation.

La Fontaine, who had also been a friend of Boileau's since 1664, benefited in his own way from that narrow margin. But he was great enough to defend himself alone and save his poet's soul his own way, in a regime more formidable for him than for his younger friends.

For him, in fact, Parnassus and Olympus would never be "good friends."

SURVIVING FOUCQUET

On Monday 27 December 1661, at eight o'clock in the morning, d'Artagnan brought Nicolas Foucquet down from his cell at La Bastille in the former high chapel of the château, where the prisoner, after a brief interrogation, was read the sentence of banishment imposed by the Chamber of Justice, and its immediate commutation by the king to life imprisonment in the fortress of Pignerol. A coach equipped with barred windows immediately took the condemned man, who did not even have the chance to see his family, to his permanent prison. When the coach left La Bastille and reached the Porte Saint-Antoine, a large crowd composed of the lower classes, which had mysteriously been informed, greeted the poor man with cheers and lavished blessings upon him.

Less than three weeks earlier, on 10 December, the bookseller Claude Barbin had put a thin collection on sale on rue Saint-Jacques. It was entitled *Nouvelles en vers tirés de Boccace et de l'Arioste par M. de La Fontaine.* The poet was making his literary return with these deliciously libertine tales, which became an immediate best-seller, and at a time when there was every reason to believe that he shared the same anguish as the marquise de Sévigné and the other friends of the *surintendant*.

Was that major impropriety to be ascribed to the likable fool, who, all too soon, had turned over a new leaf? In reality, the first Tales, like the Fables the poet had already begun to compose, spurted from the same vein as the *Relation d'un voyage de Paris en Limousin*, written between August and September 1663. The poet wrote these news reports as private letters to his wife, who was also a friend, as he traveled with his uncle Jannart into exile in Limousin. In them, he bravely made the best of a bad situation, sparkling with wit, curiosity, and appetites. But that gaiety of a "nursling of the Muses" was an act of defiance against misfortune. The "tragic sense of life" ran deep and silent, and was all the more forceful and somber for that. Crossing the Tréfou Valley (between Montlhéry and Etampes) by coach, La Fontaine abandoned prose for verse:

> République de loups, asile de brigands,
>   Faut-il que tu sois dans le monde?
>   Tu favorises les méchants
>   Par ton ombre épaisse et profonde.
> Ils égorgent celui que Thémis, ou le gain,
> Ou le désir de voir, fait sortir de sa terre.
> (Letter of 30 August 1663 from Amboise)

> Republic of wolves, refuge of bandits,
>   Must you be in the world?
>   You favor the wicked
>   With your thick and deep shadows.
> They cut the throat of anyone whom Themis, or profit,
> Or the desire to see, lures out of his lair.

And when the coach carrying the exiles passed through Amboise, they stopped to make a pilgrimage to the château, one of a series of prisons that had held Foucquet:

> Qu'est-il besoin que je retrace
> Une garde au soin non pareil,
> Chambre murée, étroite place,

Quelque peu d'air pour toute grâce,
   Jours sans soleil,
   Nuits sans sommeil,
Trois portes en six pieds d'espace?

What need have I to draw again
A prison like no other,
Walled-up room, narrow walk,
A little air its only grace,
   Sunless days,
   Sleepless nights,
Three doors in six feet of space?

The poet added simply:

"Had it not been for nightfall, no one could have torn me away from that place." (Letter of 5 September 1663 from Châtellerault)

It was not only caution but also piety and propriety that led him never to publish the remarkable *Voyage en Limousin*. It still revealed too much of "his heart laid bare."

Like Mme de Sévigné, during the Foucquet affair the poet began to train himself in the patience and private gaiety that belles lettres can secure against the terror emanating from Olympus. Mme de Sévigné, whose great anguish about Foucquet did not prevent her from keeping her verve and humor intact in her own epistolary news reports to Pomponne, was undoubtedly one of the first to read La Fontaine's verse *Nouvelles* and to aid in its success.

Far from being a betrayal of the beloved victim, this first masterpiece of a new La Fontaine was a rallying sign addressed to the public that supported Foucquet, and an indirect challenge to Colbert. For the poet, it was also the first stage in a second career, in keeping with the profound lessons the Foucquet affair had inculcated.

Breaking the king's silence was still, and for a long time yet, beyond his reach. He also had no gift for theater. Unlike his friend Molière, he could not make the free, liberating, and conciliatory gaiety for which he had a knack burst forth publicly, in the midst of the court. His only expedient was to share it with this public of readers that had recognized themselves in his *Elegie* and in his *Ode au roi*. Deprived of the condescending favor of Augustus/Maecenas, which his Parnassus colleagues—Boileau, Racine,

and before long Pellisson himself, after his release from jail in 1667—
knew how to attract, and which his old comrade Furetière basely solicited,
he could create a new family and many friendships for himself among the
Paris public he had been able to touch, and that he now knew how to
entertain. The success of his *Contes* had proved this to him.

He did not remain at that point. Like a new Voiture, and pointing
the way for Chaulieu and Piron in the eighteenth century, he might
well have worked out an agreeable life as a high-society poet in a Paris
too happy to drink from that wellspring of charm and irony, even as it
was forced to submit to reductions in income, high taxes, and the court's
insolent impunity. But the author of *Adonis* and *Clymène*, though without personal ambition, was ambitious about his art. And then too, could
Nicolas Foucquet's poet laureate, in essence disgraced for that crime,
retrospectively contradict the elect status his unfortunate Maecenas
had given him, and "on behalf of Augustus," by keeping too low a pro-
file? Since Louis XIV was ignoring him, since his poetry was not fit for
the king's grandeur, he would inwardly aim even higher by outwardly
pretending to aim very low. Great musician that he was, that was not
out of reach.

ROYAL POET IN SPITE OF IT ALL

He would be a royal poet after all, in spite of the king. The king he
would address would be that other king in whom Nicolas Foucquet had
believed, the desirable king, the king capable of a king's poetry and a
king's wisdom. The curious choice to rise to that knowledge of men and
the good government of men by the path of the "puerile" little Aesop's
fables, which no one wanted at the time, will never cease to be baffling. In
essence, having failed to get a hearing from a deaf Louis XIV, La Fontaine
wagered not only on the Dauphin, the future king, but especially on the
reader-as-king. The king who had failed Foucquet was now internalized by
Fables, which made all its readers witnesses to Louis XIV. Montaigne's
Essays had won a similar wager in the previous century. Voltaire and the
philosophes would win it on a grander scale in the next.

In the preliminary pieces of the first collection of *Fables*, triumphantly
published in 1668, four years after the first collection of *Contes*, that
wager, that challenge, and that tour de force were quietly articulated,

but enveloped in veils arranged with such moderation and care that they may annoy the unprepared reader and attract the complicity of the witty one.

The first collection was dedicated to the Grand Dauphin, eldest son of Louis XIV, who in 1668 was six-and-a-half years old. Far from looking to the past, Foucquet's poet was a reign ahead. He was wagering on Louis XIV's heir presumptive. This was a flash of brilliance that would not have occurred to any man of crude ambition.

Even so, he had to get approval to dedicate these little fables to a child of France. La Fontaine indirectly owed this signal favor—signal especially for him, poorly regarded by the king and Colbert—to Foucquet. It was in the *surintendant's* entourage that he had met Périgny, magistrate and high-society poet when he chose to be, and now, like so many others of Foucquet's clients, annexed by the king and named tutor to the Dauphin. Bossuet succeeded him in 1670. It was Périgny, within the context of the primary education dispensed to the Dauphin, who accepted in the name of his pupil the dedication of *Fables*.

One might have expected that the disgraced poet would seize upon that modest perch, offered by an obliging friend, to lavish praise on the little dedicatee's father, the king. To be sure, in his prose dedication, La Fontaine made this obligatory compliment, but only in a few lines in the second half of his text, and as if adopting the child's adoring gaze at his father to write them.

In contrast, what was solemnly presented from the first lines was the refusal to let *Fables* be confined to pedagogy. Olympus had reduced Foucquet's poet laureate to showing up in the nursery, but to no avail; the public had to know that *Fables* was addressed to the adult king the Dauphin would become and, in the meantime, to adult readers, even the kingdom's most refined and subtle readers: "If there is anything ingenious about the republic of letters, it must be in the way Aesop delivered his morals."[54]

The elegant show of modesty that followed could not erase the indomitable pride of that initial sentence, where the "republic of letters," its "ingeniousness," and its "morals" were presented from on high to the eyes of a king's son, in a cloud from Parnassus that was certainly the equal of the clouds of the paternal Olympus: "It would have been truly desirable if hands other than my own had added the ornaments of poetry, since the wisest of the ancients judged they were not useless."

After Aesop, Socrates. La Fontaine ironically called his fables "puerilities," but in vain; such childish stuff, he added, as if casually, "serve as an envelope to important truths." The ambition of being both the modern Aesop and the modern Socrates of the French language was not small, especially since it was formulated in an epistle officially addressed to a child. That ambition even took on the dimensions of a remarkable act of faith in the "power of fables." The poet spoke of them as something obvious he shared with the greatest men: "The reading of his book [the collection known under the name of Aesop] imperceptibly sows the seeds of virtue in a soul, and teaches it to know itself without being aware it is studying, and while it believes it is doing something else entirely."

The fable, the Latin *fabula* (from the old verb *fari*, "to say," which is the root of *fata*, fairy), is in truth not only fiction, but the poetic word itself, in its supreme power to undo the dark tangle within souls and expose them to its own light. The paradoxical and captivating power of that word is that, without lying, it always says something other than what it seems to be saying. It gives a glimmer of the truth that does not wound but awakens.

In that dedication, signed by a "very humble, very obedient, and very faithful servant" of the royal child, La Fontaine hid in plain sight nothing less than his new poetic program. This is a bit as if André Breton, taking the opposite course from Marinetti, who had launched "futurism" on the front page of *Le Figaro*, had, to fool the censor, been able and obliged to slip the "Manifesto of Surrealism" into the pages of *Le Journal des Voyages*.

The rites that had to be performed on the threshold of the palaces of Olympus, even at the service door, were the occasion for the poet to proffer his truth of Parnassus, without raising his voice, without awakening attention, and seemingly in the interstices of the expected and obligatory words. Let those who can and will heed him.

A preface followed the dedication. Nothing surprising about that at first sight. Racine and many other authors of the time proceeded in the same way. But the length of the preface and the insistent exegesis it presented of the poetics outlined in the dedication had something peculiar about them. It was as if, to compensate for the low place to which he had been reduced by Olympus, the poet took it upon himself to show at what altitude of Parnassus he stood, in the proximity of the true Apollo and his Muses.

One of his peers on Parnassus, Olivier Patru, a member of the Académie Française since 1640—"one of the masters of our Oratory"—had pointed out to him that the Aesopian apologue did not belong to poetry, and a fortiori to great poetry. It was by definition a brief moral genre in prose. The Boileau of *Art poétique* and Louis XIV himself stood by that article of literary law. La Fontaine apologized to Patru, as was fitting to do to a master, but he intended to take the liberty of understanding the word "fable" in Ovid's fuller sense, not as a narrow genre, the apologue, but as a synonym for "poem," open to all the possibilities of poetry, even the most lofty ones.

Hence, not only did his poems, like Aesop's apologues, say something other than what they seemed to say, but, in the never-before-seen version created by the poet, which he himself was bold enough to declare without precedent, ancient or modern, the fables "set to verse" and "dressed in the livery of the Muses" (the livery of Parnassus is not the same as that of Olympus) could, beginning from Aesop's seed, conceal and deploy all the powers of poetry, from Terence's comic effects to Homer's and Virgil's sublimity. In themselves, these apologues dressed up by the Muses stood in for all the tasty treats that could have been offered to the greatest kings. And not only treats of the senses, since, under their delicious husks, they also distilled for the mind the "back thought" (*pensée de derrière*) to which only true kings were attentive.

Aesop, then, but also the Muses. Music, then, but a music that conveyed the truth of the "wisest of the ancients," Socrates. And suddenly, with that name, the somber and terrible note of "torment" surged forth in the heretofore entirely harmonious score. If Socrates was the first to introduce Aesop's apologues into poetry, as Plato reports in *Phaedo,* it was at the order of the gods, during his sleep, as a spiritual exercise in keeping with the most agonizing situation the human soul can endure, that of a man condemned to die, waiting in prison for the signal.

The earthly Olympus holds the supreme power of life and death, but the gods of heaven are more benevolent: to the wise man condemned by the earthly Olympus, they offer the refuge of Parnassus, and they invite him to carry his condemned truth even unto death by making it into a poem that will last. Through song, the persecuted innocent does not confine himself to defeating the unjust punishment, death, and his anguish; he rises above his tormentors, purges their crime, and transfigures it into a sacrifice to the gods on high.

In his first collection, La Fontaine introduced variations and resonances on this Orphic and Rilkean motif: "L'oiseau prêt à mourir se plaint en son ramage" (The bird ready to die complains in its song) ("The Swan and the Cook," 3.12); "Dans un bois où chantait le pauvre Philomèle" (In a wood where the poor Philomela was singing) ("Philomela and Procne," 3.15).

The motif reappeared a quarter century later in the last book of *Fables*, this time dedicated to the son of the Grand Dauphin (the king's life was long and slow, but hope had remained keen). "The daughters of Minea" had "whiled away the time" with their innocent and delicious tales, but in vain; despite their devotion to Pallas, they would not escape the vengeance of Bacchus, whom they had neglected during that sweet prattle. In that tale or fable inspired by Ovid, Olympus is not divided, and remains unmoved. The song of the "daughters of Minea," for which the punishment is death, is its own reward:

> Quand quelque dieu, voyant ses bontés négligées,
> Nous fait sentir son ire, un autre n'y peut rien:
> L'Olympe s'entretient en paix par ce moyen.

> When some god, seeing his bounty neglected,
> Makes us feel his ire, another cannot do a thing:
> Olympus maintains peace by this means.
> (12.28, "The Daughters of Minea," ll. 556–58)

Yet it is the mouth closing around innocents and poets, ready to devour them as the wolf devours the sheep, that makes the least wrenching tones possible rise up from their defenseless throats, tones marked by a strange and contagious joy that conceals and wards off the cruelty of its origins: "I do not see gaiety as that which excites laughter, but rather as a certain charm, an agreeable tune, given to all sorts of subjects, even the most serious ones" (preface to *Fables choisies*).

Between the lines of these prefatory texts, as if the poet were planning a close reading of his fables, a supremely ambitious poetics of the sublime can be read, veiled by grace and modesty, by the word of truth that has agreed to sacrifice external brilliance, only to deploy, at a deeper level, the whole delicate lyre of light and shadow. Rarely have the lines of a purely contemplative language been drawn with more exquisite or firmer strokes, through an implicit contrast with the language of power, predation, possession, and flattery.

Thus La Fontaine did not hesitate to link the "fable," as he reinvented it, to Gospel parables. Although poetic language and the language of redemption are not on the same order, they are analogous, parallel, and joined at the cutting edge of the heart. Both speak mysteriously under the veil of fictions that, despite all resistance, knows how to insinuate that lost truth, beauty, and love into the oppressed heart of hearts, which hungers for them.

After his dedication and preface, La Fontaine found it fitting to add a "Life of Aesop" to these preliminaries (in keeping with the custom of Aesop's editors and translators). As he well knew, and this suited him well, it was in reality a myth, not true history. This myth, which he imperceptibly bent to fit his design, was the mirror in which he wished to be seen, his greatest contribution to his own legend, but also the most complete contradiction of it. Aesop, a runaway slave? "Ugly and deformed," deprived "almost entirely of the use of language"? Undoubtedly, but also "gifted with a very keen mind," and, above all (the phrase was added to the ancient Greek text La Fontaine was supposed to be translating): "his soul stands ever free and independent of fortune."

Like *Fables* itself, its author and his forefather had received a coarse and unpleasant husk from Fortune but also, from nature and heaven, a fruit bright and flavorful enough to hold, against the efforts of Fortune, infinitely more than it seemed to promise. At the beginning of his *Fables*, La Fontaine was more than a biographer: he demanded a reader who was a friend of Aesop, of Socrates, and of Orpheus, and who, venturing beneath the husk, offered himself the royal luxury of savoring the fruit of his poetry, fully apprised of the situation, even though the king snubbed and ignored him.

CHAPTER 2

The Years of Obscurity

From Arcadia to the Academy

In the fourteenth, fifteenth, sixteenth, and seventeenth centuries,
imperfect civilization, superstitious beliefs, and alien and
semibarbarian practices diluted the Romanic everywhere: characters
were strong, the imagination powerful, existence mysterious and hidden. . . .
　　Not only did one face chance dangers and brave the sword of justice,
one was also obliged to defeat the reign of regular habits within oneself,
the authority of the family, the tyranny of domestic customs,
the opposition of conscience, the terrors and duties of the Christian.
All these obstacles redoubled the energy of the passions.
　　　　　　　—Chateaubriand, *Mémoires d'outre-tombe*, book 4, chap. 8

CHAMPAGNE OR PARIS?

A poet is a creature of borders, and of border crossings. He can come and go among several worlds, since he is always both there and elsewhere. He does not need to travel far. Travel is the poetry of prose writers. The vehicle and the passports of poetry may be powerless on the brink of the next world, but they have powers on earth verging on magic: the power to get across barriers, span bridges, trifle with distances, and make different moments in time converge.

In Ariosto's *Orlando furioso*, one of the poems that most influenced La Fontaine, the true hero is not Orlando, despite an ironic and somewhat misleading title.[1] Orlando is a formidable warrior, given to splitting Saracens in two, a fearless knight-errant beyond reproach. But the poem's heroine, the *bellissima* Angelica, daughter of the Great Khan of Cathay lost in Europe, flees Orlando's passion like the plague. The athlete Orlando is lacking in grace, charm, and wit, the wit that, even in love, one takes pleasure in sharing. He has made great, invincible parries with his sword and has ridden his famous steed at no risk of being thrown off: it is no use, he is still an oaf. Angelica, weary of being pursued by him, falls in love at first sight with a ravishing young Moor, who does not have a fraction of Orlando's glory and valor, but whom she will make her husband, come hell or high water, and place on the throne of the Great Khan of Cathay.

One of the finest stories in *Orlando furioso* is the rescue of Angelica, the new Andromeda, by Astolfo, the new Perseus. That brief encounter between Angelica and Astolfo is one of the keys to the poem: it briefly links two great destinies in love, in an epic that pretends to be about the terrible battles that, in Paris and outside its walls, set the knights of Charlemagne against the Saracen lieutenants of the king of Spain. Just as Angelica is the true heroine of the epic, it is Astolfo, and not Orlando, who is its true hero. He is loved by men and by women. His tutor, the magician Atlant, has provided him with a splendid hippogriff, and on that living airplane, which he maneuvers with the virtuosity of Roland Garros, he flies over continents swift as the wind, nose-dives to save Angelica, and even lands on the moon to retrieve the soul of the poor Orlando, who has become a "lunatic" after discovering the "betrayal" of Angelica, whom he loves but who never made him any promises. Astolfo's Pegasus is the symbol, within the poem itself, of the poetic imagination, the powers of the word when it is combined with the fable and freedom. Ariosto's imagination, like Astolfo's winged horse, moves easily between the Christian camp and the Moorish, between love affairs in the forest and on the rocky coasts of northern Europe and those set in the sensuous cities of the Orient. The narrator of *Orlando furioso* is just as much at home within the councils of God and his archangels as with the tricks of the magician Atlant and the beautiful sorceress Alcina, both mad about the irresistible Astolfo.

Like Ariosto, the poetic generosity that keeps La Fontaine aloft allows him to pass through walls, transgress prohibitions, and eliminate distances that might appear insurmountable to men apparently of much higher birth and much better armed than he. And this in an age much less favorable to poetry than was Ariosto's time.

Poetry, which has such powers, is not a "means of success," however. Even Ariosto, who was one of the most gifted diplomats of his time, and a poet celebrated in his lifetime throughout Europe, made only a modest fortune from the dukes and cardinals of Este, his "patrons" and friends. But at least the intelligent and touching gentleness he radiated earned him, in Rome and Venice, among princes and popes, everywhere he went, the benevolent favor La Fontaine wished for his friend Paul Barillon, ambassador to London, in the fable "The Power of Fable" (8.4). In a France much more compartmentalized and restricted than Ariosto's Italy, Jean de La Fontaine's hippogriff carried him from one world to another, finally transporting him, not to the Olympus of Versailles, which Racine reached, but to a Parisian society more in tune with his deepest affinities. There, libertine princes, liberated women of letters, independent duchesses, and shrewd bankers welcomed him with open arms for what he was: a prince of Parnassus and a shepherd of Arcadia in possession of Astolfo's hippogriff.

La Fontaine's biographers, from Walckenaer to those of our own time, have had little gift for astonishment. They have watched him move from Champagne to Paris, as if that went without saying, and from practical life to dreams, bourgeois life to the life of high art. They have seen him moving out of step and against the current, but always with ease and in a timely manner, in the spheres of French society most alien to one another: the provinces and Paris, the legal profession and the salon, Port-Royal and the cabaret, the Luxembourg Palace of the dowager duchesse d'Orléans and the Hôtel de Bouillon of the young and very free Marie-Anne Mancini, the society of Mme de La Sablière and that of the Condé family, the bourgeois bohemia of Mme Ulrich and the princely bohemia of the Vendômes, the venal "Jeannetons" and the confessional of the abbé Pouget.

In addition, they have watched him stroll about, as if at home, in eras and among authors the most distant from one another, an ancient among the moderns, a modern among the ancients, a Renaissance Italian in the "utterly Catholic France" of the Revocation, a Frenchman from the adventures of the Round Table among the contemporaries of Malebranche and Bossuet. Nothing has surprised them. In the person of La Fontaine, they have had before them an Alceste infatuated with the good old days of Henry IV and Foucquet, who was nevertheless in vogue in Paris under Louis XIV. That vogue survived his own death and that of the king and, without spending any time in purgatory, he became all the rage under the regency of the duc d'Orléans and then the reign of Louis XV. No matter: it all goes without saying. His biographers sometimes catch a glimpse of something abnormal in these wonders and miracles of genius, but their explanation is ready to hand: it never has anything to do with the power of fables, the magic of literature, or with poetry.

His friend Mme Ulrich wrote in 1696:

It is true that with people he did not know, or who did not suit him, he was sad and even dreamy, and even at the beginning of conversations with people he liked, he was sometimes cold; but as soon as the conversation began to interest him . . . he was no longer the dreamer, he was a man who spoke well and a great deal, and who quoted the ancients, and who gave them a new charm. He was a philosopher, but a gallant philosopher, in a word, he was La Fontaine, and La Fontaine as he is in his books.[2]

La Fontaine was a little provincial raised in Château-Thierry: unlike Corneille, who came from Rouen, he was not even a student at a major Jesuit college; unlike Racine, a native of La Ferté-Milon, he was not a student at the prestigious and persecuted Petites-Ecoles of Port-Royal. One wonders what ambition, what calculations, what sociological motivation could have allowed him to be recognized and embraced by the most exclusive, the most elegant, the most free, and the most fussy society there ever was, not the society of the court, but that of Louis XIV's Paris.

Mme Ulrich (a Mme de Tencin born too soon) also wrote: "Everyone wanted him, and, if I tried to list all the illustrious people . . . who were eager for his conversation, I would have to give a list of the entire court."[3]

None of his biographers have been concerned with the very Parisian literary celebrity which, in the end, surrounded the poet with empathy and indulgence, desired and admired him as an original, a genius, the first of his kind, as Charles Perrault wrote in 1696.[4]

La Fontaine was so completely and so warmly adopted that, in 1664, disgraced by the court, prosecuted for usurpation of a noble title, he was the object of a Parisian plot that made him a gentleman of the House of Orléans. In 1674 he left his wife, child, and business interests in Château-Thierry and, as an adulated bachelor, moved into lodgings in the mansion of Mme de La Sablière, the brightest center of intelligence and charm in Paris at the time, the first eighteenth-century salon, in the middle of the Sun King's reign.[5]

It took him time to cross the border between his province and the capital city. He took to it slowly, beginning in 1642, gradually increasing the number of trips back and forth from Château-Thierry to Paris.

The acclimatization of this man of Champagne into a true Parisian was so complete that even Léon-Paul Fargue, an expert in the matter, posthumously awarded him a certificate of residency and went so far as to make the author of *Fables* the foremost arbiter of the refinement of "Parisian wit." A plebiscite dating back to the seventeenth century, whose margin of victory has not fallen off, anticipated by nearly three centuries that official consecration by the "Pedestrian of Paris."[6]

"Parisian wit"? But what an insult to a poet! Was it not in Champagne, in the forest, along the rivers, around ponds—as a little boy following his father, "master of the waters and forests of the duchy of Château-Thierry,"

or as an adult, himself awarded the post in 1652 of "special triennial master of the waters and forests" in that same duchy—that this "daydreamer,"
familiar with fallow land, found inspiration for his *Fables*? The trouble
with that romantic fiction, given credence by Taine, is that *Fables*, like *Le
songe de Vaux* and *Les amours de Psyché*, is, in André Gide's words, a "masterpiece of culture"; it owes at least as much to library books as to walks in
the great outdoors.

Even today, when the "miracle of culture" from which *Fables* proceeded
has come to light, its vivacity, its evocative power, its insight lead us to
believe that it was painted "from life" and not worked over in Paris in front
of open books. The big city is still supposed to sharpen the wits, but at the
expense of poetic feeling and a sense for nature. It is as if wit and poetry
were incompatible, as if one had to be a bit dull-witted to be a poet, as if
poetry were not the cutting edge of the melancholic wit placed in the service of the imagination, of memory, and of the heart. That conjunction is
rare, but the big city is indispensable for it. Since Montaigne's—not to say
Jean de Meung's—time, "Parisian" has always meant "French" to the utmost degree of wit, just as, in Greek antiquity, "Athenian" encapsulated the
wittiest aspects of Hellenism, common to Sophocles and to Plato, and just
as, in Latin antiquity, *urbanus* (from the *Urbs*, that is, Rome) signified what
was most full of wit in the Latin world, common to Cicero and Horace.

It is undoubtedly as difficult to define "Parisian wit" as it is to define the
Atticism of Athens or the urbanity of Rome. These essences result from
the conjunction, in a single locale, of intellects and talents that cross-
pollinate, that are unforgiving toward one another, but that also know
how to indulge in the luxury of being moved and amused among themselves. They define themselves negatively for the most part, by ridiculing
and intimidating the barbarians within, the pedantic and the precious,
the oafish and the pretentious, who leech off and mimic them. The Paris
of the young La Fontaine was the Paris of the young de Retz, the young
Tallemant des Réaux, the young Mlle de Rabutin-Chantal, the Paris of
the poets Saint-Amant and Tristan L'Hermite, Voiture and Scarron. It
was an academy that led one to the summit of Parnassus. Even if one
admits that Château-Thierry and Champagne were La Fontaine's original Arcadia, what Forez had been for Honoré d'Urfé's shepherds, that
Parisian academy, with its society of poets, its patrons, its public, was for
the Arcadian shepherd, with an inner gift for contemplation, the ordeal
that made him a more highly civilized and refined poet, an Athenian or a
modern French Alexandrian.[7]

Paris seems incompatible with poetry only when one reduces the wit of
which it is capable to "Parisianism." To understand how Paris can itself be

the best corrective, in terms of wit and poetry, to intellectual and high-society "Parisianism," to the Verdurins of yesterday and today, one has only to read Proust's *A la recherche du temps perdu*. Léon Daudet, the learned author of *Paris vécu*, confers on the young Marcel the title that Léon-Paul Fargue retrospectively gives to La Fontaine: an Ariel of "Parisian wit," a poet of true "urbanity."[8] Marcel did not have La Fontaine's provincial and rural roots, but he too had his Arcadia, and the Paris he knew was little more than an academy and a Parnassus. His life and works were an odyssey, departing from an Arcadia and returning to it only at a higher stage of poetic consciousness, after a long journey. Along the way, the literary, musical, and artistic academy of Paris, that of la Berma, Vinteuil, Bergotte, and Elstir, thrilled and refined his poetic antennae; even the Paris of "Parisianism," unbeknownst to itself, continued to hone his intelligence of things and beings, and his knowledge of his own heart, by virtue of the ironic resistance the writer had to mount against it.

Yet, in *A la recherche du temps perdu*, Mme de Sévigné and La Fontaine, who are almost inseparable, are the infallible measure by which the grain is separated from the chaff, the urbanity of intelligence and feeling of which Paris is the crucible, from its dark shadow, Parisianism. Proust, an excellent radiographer, studied with curiosity the progress of that shadow in the brains and lungs of the capital.

The Paris of Parisianism—coarse snobbery, hard-heartedness, ostentatious culture, political feeble-mindedness—is the tormentor and the back-handed educator in the academy of poets, artists, and musicians, an academy that is nevertheless its true glory, and whose Arcadia is the remote provinces. In the seventeenth century, Parisianism, which the comedy of *Les femmes savantes*, the irony of *Le misanthrope*, and the wit of *Fables* kept at a respectful distance, was already the parasitic presence of courtly mores—servility, ostentation, and self-interested asperity—on true urbanity.

THE ARCADIA OF A BORN POET

La Fontaine turned his back on Château-Thierry, the Arcadia of his childhood and adolescence in Champagne. When he reached adulthood, that Arcadia was spoiled by professional and familial duties and conflicts of interest. He became a Parisian only in stages. But, in the end, he did establish a home in the forest of the capital and create a clearing there in harmony with the freedom and contemplation of his provincial child-hood. An essential part of himself—his vocation as a man of letters and his appetite for knowledge—first called him to Paris. But another part of himself, his poetic nature, enraptured by solitude, a stranger to any society other than friendship and love, might just as easily have led him to accommodate himself externally to his preordained fate and to follow in the footsteps of his father, an obscure bourgeois in his small town and native province. Fortune, more than La Fontaine's own will or even his vocation, decided otherwise.

At first, he was both attracted to Paris and repelled by it. Although he thought of leaving Champagne in 1640 (he was seventeen years old), it was only to enter the ecclesiastic life in the Paris Oratory, where he was a novice for nearly two years, until October 1641.[9] It may be an overstatement to say that, under the guidance of priests rightly renowned for their devout faith and great knowledge, he immediately restricted himself to reading and rereading the famous novel, full of love stories, *L'Astrée*. A vocation for divine matters had called him there; it would prove to be more in tune with poetry than with religion. Even upon his conversion at the very end of his life, the Epicurean poet remained faithful in his way to this first call to light, innocence, and meditation. But there is no doubt that he quickly escaped the exercises of piety and theological studies through other, more profane readings: they convinced him that he did not have the priestly vocation. Paradoxically, for this long-intimidated candidate to Parnassus, the Oratory was an excellent prelude: he found a rich library there and could meet the members of high society who frequented the illustrious motherhouse on rue Saint-Honoré, founded by Cardinal de Bérulle. The contemplative La Fontaine (would a monastic order have been better equipped to hold onto him?) nevertheless lived in Arcadia in his own mind. An imaginary landscape connected him to the province where he had first read *L'Astrée*. He wrote in 1665:

Etant petit garçon, je lisais son roman,
Et je le lis encore, ayant la barbe grise.[10]

As a little boy, I read his novel,
And I read it still, now that my beard is gray.

For him, that pastoral and provincial green world was inseparable from the raptures of love and the troubling connections that that enchantment maintained with poetic language. In 1691 he was seventy years old, and still drawing upon *L'Astrée* for his opera libretto, which was set to mediocre music by Colasse, Lully's son-in-law:

> Quand il plaît à l'amour, tout objet est à craindre.
> Ce dieu met bien souvent sa gloire à nous atteindre
> Du trait le plus commun et le moins redouté:
> Une première ardeur n'est bientôt plus qu'un songe:
>   La vérité devient mensonge,
>   Et le mensonge, vérité.[11]

> When Love so pleases, every object is to be feared.
> That god often glories in capturing us
> With the most common and least dreaded trait:
> Soon a first crush is no more than a dream:
>   Truth becomes lies,
>   And the lie, verity.

Hence, although there is some truth to Taine's famous passage on La Fontaine regarding the poet's roots in the Champagne region, it must be added that only a young reader of poetry and novels could feel these sensations and this early contemplative experience in a manner so extreme as to recognize his poet's vocation in them.

There is evidence in his works—not abundant, but it can be found—that the places of his provincial childhood lay deep at the root, not of his poetry, which is a literary discipline of higher learning, but of the wholly inner poetic disposition that made him a born poet, perhaps the highest born in the French language: confidences hinted at, then immediately cut short and veiled, as if one were approaching a secret and sacred door that the uninitiated would be wrong to try to force with the geographical and zoological imagination. The least elliptical of these allusions is also the one that was wrested from him in a moment of peril, in 1662, when he found himself open simultaneously to two threats from Olympus: Colbert's police suspected him of being an accomplice of Foucquet's defenders, who had rallied around his uncle Jannart; and he was dragged before the king's justice for usurpation of a noble title on notarized deeds. During a stay in Château-Thierry, he petitioned the duc de Bouillon, suzerain of the duchy since 1652, in a letter in which deep emotion surfaces through the banter. He describes himself to the duke as he sees himself, a stranger to the world that wants to find him guilty:

Que me sert-il de vivre innocemment,
D'être sans faste et cultiver les Muses?
Hélas! qu'un jour elles seront confuses,
Quand on viendra leur dire en soupirant:
Ce nourrisson que vous chérissiez tant,
Moins pour ses vers que pour ses moeurs faciles,
Qui préférait à la pompe des villes
Vos antres cois, vos chants simples et doux,
Qui dès l'enfance a vécu parmi vous,
Est succombé sous une injuste peine.[12]

What use does it serve me to live in innocence,
To be unassuming and cultivate the Muses?
Alas! how abashed they will be one day
When someone comes to tell them with a sigh:
This nursling whom you cherished so,
Less for his verses than his simple ways,
Who favored, over the great pomp of towns,
Your quiet caves, your songs, easy and sweet,
Who, from his childhood, has lived with you,
Has fallen to an unjust punishment.

Here the *Elegie aux Nymphes de Vaux* is applied to himself. But, this time, it is not the unhappy patron but the poet who is interrogated and forced to state his true identity. It was certainly in the provinces, in Champagne, that he was born a poet, but in a Champagne of poetry, an Arcadia of shepherds, whose "easy and sweet" songs liked to haunt the "quiet caves," and who, "from childhood," on the slopes of a Parnassus where they were not yet concerned to chase after Apollo's laurels, "cultivated" the Muses who had "nursed" them. It was not poems that made this shepherd of the *Eclogues* a poet: his true titles lie in his poetic way of life, his "innocence, his simple, unassuming ways," his inborn penchant for a contemplative life of love.

La Fontaine was well aware that this identity, which was meaningless for his judges, had a great deal of meaning for the great lord whose help he was anticipating. In 1641 the father of the young duke had agreed to be the dedicatee of one of Tristan L'Hermite's finest collections: *La lyre*.[13] But, at a deeper level, La Fontaine could count on the old affinities in France, and especially in his native Champagne, between princes by birth and poets by birth. A same natural election isolated nobles and poets from other men and placed them together above the common herd. Sometimes, as in the case of the trouvère Thibaut de Champagne, a prince by birth was also a poet by birth. Usually, however, the civil identity of the born poet concealed him from the eyes of the common people (but not from princes). The duc de Bouillon was thus perfectly capable of understanding that the apparent "usurpation of a noble title" by a born poet was so only in legal terms. In the natural order, which is not the order of law, though a poet/shepherd may be attached socially to a commoner's family, he is noble neverthless, of purer blood than the rest of his tribe, with an illustrious bloodline dating back to Orpheus and Virgil. He has a natural right to call himself a squire.[14] The poet was, in fact, understood implicitly by the duke: two years later, La Fontaine received a *brevet de gentilhomme*, putting an end to all equivocation, from the dowager duchesse d'Orléans, an old political ally of the La Tour d'Auvergne family.[15]

The poet also knew that the Arcadia of Champagne where he was "nursed by the Muses," and which was now a fiefdom of the House of Bouillon, had everything required to touch the young duke, who had recently married the very pretty Marie-Anne Mancini. For the French aristocracy, Arcadia had, since the Renaissance, encapsulated the world of its leisure activities, its festivals, its châteaux, and its grounds, which were enchanted by the art of its poets and artists. It was the land where nature reasserted its rights, far from the court, the army, and the church. From that Arcadia, one could set off for Cythera, enjoying the leisure most favorable for love.

In fact, the Champagne of La Fontaine's childhood and youth was also the secret land where he first experienced not only contemplation and poetic language, but also the feeling of love. The only love affairs of the discreet La Fontaine that Tallemant was able to report in his *Historiettes* were those set in Château-Thierry and its environs.[16] And, on two occasions, the poet himself provided a glimpse of the "green paradise of childhood loves," his own very youthful journeys to Cythera, which made his native province both the land of shepherds and the Muses and the island of Venus where "quiet caves" were plentiful:

> J'ai quelquefois aimé: je n'aurais pas alors
>   Contre le Louvre et ses trésors,
> Contre le firmament et sa voûte céleste,
>   Changé les bois, changé les lieux

Honorés par les pas, éclairés par les yeux
   De l'aimable et jeune bergère
   Pour qui, sous le fils de Cythère,
Je servis, engagé par mes premiers serments.
Hélas! quand reviendront de semblables moments?
            ("The Two Doves," 9.2)

I have sometimes been in love, and when I was,
   For the Louvre and its treasures,
For the heavens and its starry vault,
   I would not have traded the woods,
Or the places honored by the steps, lit by the eyes
   Of the lovable young shepherdess
   Whom, under the son of Cythera,
I served, true to my first vows.
Alas! When shall I see such moments again?

In a less lyrical mode, standing before the Académie Française in 1686, in his *[Second] Discours à Mme de La Sablière*, he confessed that he had experienced love early, that all his love affairs had been enjoyed in Arcadia, and that this natural gift, inseparable from his poetic election, still obliged him, even as a grizzled old man in Paris, to burn with renewed fervor, despite moral considerations:

Cent autres passions, des sages condamnées,
Ont pris comme à l'envi la fleur de mes années.
· ·
Je ne prétends ici que dire ingénument
L'effet, bon ou mauvais, de mon tempérament.
A peine la raison vint éclairer mon âme,
Que je sentis l'ardeur de ma première flamme.
Plus d'une passion a depuis dans mon coeur
Exercé tous les droits d'un superbe vainqueur.
Tel que fut mon printemps, je crains que l'on ne voie
Les plus chers de mes jours aux vains désirs en proie.
            (ll. 23–24 and 77–84)

A hundred other passions, condemned by the wise,
Have outdone each other to steal my life's bloom.
· ·

My only pretention is to say ingenuously
The effect, good or bad, of my temperament.
Hardly had reason enlightened my soul,
When I felt the ardor of my first flame.
More than one passion has since in my heart
Exerted all the rights of a superb conqueror,
Such was my springtime, and I fear that so too
Will my most precious days to vain desires fall prey.

These gilded verses allow us to imagine the unspeakable: the pho-
tographs of these rustic "scenes," the identification of the persons in
question, would be pornography, made impossible for the historian, fortunately, by the poet's vigilant discretion.

But to move away from the original poetic disposition, and the naive
songs that are part of it, on to verses capable of immortalizing essences, to
move from Corydon to Virgil, one must read Virgil and become capable of
rivaling his art. For La Fontaine, a born poet, but a French poet, reading
a French-language Virgil gave him the desire to be not only a virtual poet,
but an actual one.

L'Astrée, the Native Land of Poets

In Honoré d'Urfé's *L'Astrée*, dedicated to Henry IV, and in which the
gallant old king took delight, the awakening to love, in landscapes of
tall grasses, forests, and streams, was accompanied, for the most precocious and gifted young seventeenth-century readers of both sexes, with a
discovery of their own language, its possibilities for betrayal and for
trust. It was possible to transpose d'Urfé's Arcadian Forez to Champagne,
Brittany, or even Ile-de-France; it made the translation of Virgil's *Eclogues*,
Ovid's *The Metamorphoses*, and Latin elegies—in short, the ancient imagination as it was also being taught in school by "pedants"—into an intimate French experience.[17]

D'Urfé himself was as much a poet as a prose writer. In *L'Astrée*, stories
and lovers' conversations in prose alternate with lyric poetry improvised,
during moments of emotional intensity, by shepherds, shepherdesses, and
nymphs. In its poetry and its prose, the rhythm of *L'Astrée* is rich and
sweet, and this regular movement calms the passions even as it evokes

them. It is like the French courtly tunes accompanied on the lute at which
Pierre Guédron, whom d'Urfé knew at Henry IV's court, was a great master: under Louis XIII, his disciples trained the king's ear and that of the
young poets of La Fontaine's generation.[18]

For them, *L'Astrée* was also the musical and poetic horn of plenty they
could share, more easily than the ancient masterpieces studied in school,
with the shepherdesses and nymphs who played the leading roles in
d'Urfé's French Arcadia. These female creatures were the obligatory partners in the great word games and emotional trials of love. The Château-
Thierry and Champagne of the young La Fontaine, though often tested by
war and its troubles, were for him enchanted by a golden age, an age of
love; and *L'Astrée* had revealed to him its freedom and sweetness, but also
the sorrow and menace that weighed heavy upon it.

It is not by chance that the amazement he felt upon discovering
Malherbe's "heroic" ode *Que direz-vous, races futures?* recited in front of
him by an officer in 1643, took place in Château-Thierry, in Arcadia. The
abbé d'Olivet, who reported this little event, got it from the most reliable
of sources, François Maucroix, the poet's childhood friend.[19] That ode by
Malherbe, *On the assassination attempt committed on the person of Henry IV,
on 19 December 1606*, abruptly awakened the young ex-seminarian to the
tragic side of the state (from which he would later have to suffer) and to a
grand style he would undoubtedly attempt, but for which he was not at all
made. For him, poetry was always rooted in a prepolitical and premodern
condition, where the church and the state did not yet have jurisdiction.

The specifically French literature of the seventeenth century found
its two rival "classics," one "sweet," the other "great," in d'Urfé and Malherbe. The two poets offered a choice of existence, even a political choice,
as much as a choice of musical mode. For La Fontaine, Château-Thierry
remained for a long time, perhaps forever, on the d'Urfé side, and the court
on the Malherbe side. Throughout his life, he struggled to draw Paris closer
to *L'Astrée*.

In Paris he was able to find many allies in that Arcadian loyalism. The
"master" he respectfully invoked at the beginning of his first book of *Fables*,
the lawyer Olivier Patru, was born in 1604, a generation before La Fontaine, and became a member of the Académie Française in 1640: he
recounted his own initiation, through *L'Astrée*, into the French language.
He did so in a gallant epistle addressed to an anonymous lady, but which
circulated among the young Parisian men of letters whom La Fontaine frequented between 1642 and 1656. It was published only in 1680, under the
title *Eclaircissements sur l'histoire de L'Astrée*.[20]

Patru revealed to his correspondent, and to his young literary protégés, that the main plot of the novel, the long-thwarted love between the shepherd Céladon and the lovely Astrée, was an account veiled by fiction of the true-life adventure of the novelist himself, who was infatuated with Diane de Chateaumorand, and whom he finally managed to marry, despite apparently insurmountable obstacles. What prestige the unveiling of that mystery must have earned Patru among young men initiated into French belles lettres by L'Astrée! The "key" was especially valuable and reliable in that Patru had it from d'Urfé himself. In fact, Eclaircissements invented the very French commonplace of "the encounter with a great writer." The poet Racan gave another version in his Vie de Malherbe, published in 1671, but known in manuscript form much earlier. It was the public counterpart to Patru's private story.

"During my travels in Italy," writes Patru,

I passed through Piedmont and saw the illustrious d'Urfé. I saw him with so much joy that, even today, I cannot think of those happy hours without pleasure. He was fifty-odd years old; I was only nineteen. But the difference in our ages did not frighten me. Far from it: I sought him out as one seeks out a mistress, and the time I spent with him hardly lasted longer than the time I spent with you. He loved me as a father loves his son. Whenever he had any free time, he took me on walks. He made me see everything I wanted from high society, from the court of Savoie, but with so many expressions of affection and kindness that I would be an ingrate if I did not remember them forever. So I saw him very often during the three weeks I spent in Turin. In our conversations, he spoke to me of various things, but, as for me, I spoke only of his L'Astrée. At the time, there were only three volumes printed [this was 1623], and I knew them almost by heart, because I was reading them even at school. Since, apart . . . from the fact that this subject could not help but be very agreeable to our hero, I confess that, in matters of love, the temperament of that divine girl is also altogether to my taste, and, if you ask me why, it is because her heart is truly difficult to conquer, but from the moment it is yours, it is yours entirely.

Giving one's word, having the fidelity to keep it, and having the mutual trust it makes possible between two individuals who have chosen each other, constitute in fact the holy grail of L'Astrée, achieved in the midst of the forest of lies, betrayal, and deception where the quest for love stumbles. That French "frankness," whose ideal of happiness has its roots in the medieval chivalric romance, is also at issue in Corneille's theater, which transports it from Arcadia to the city, from the phratry of shepherds to political society. That frankness stood at the center of the Foucquet affair, and nothing would do more damage to Louis XIV in 1661–64 than the suspicion that, like a disciple of Machiavelli or a vulgar bourgeois, he had betrayed the loyal and noble faith the *surintendant* had placed in his protests of friendship.

Although a whole body of "great" state panegyric poetry was able to thrive under Richelieu, in the "heroic" school of Malherbe (La Fontaine saw it all in a flash as he listened to the 1643 recitation of *Ode à Henri IV*), a completely different family of poets, attached to princes poorly regarded by the cardinal or even, like Henry, duc de Montmorency, sentenced to die on Richelieu's orders, made *L'Astrée*'s gardens of love bloom in their lyric collections.

An Older Kindred Soul: Tristan L'Hermite

In 1642 (La Fontaine had just left the Oratory, whose patron was the king's brother, Gaston d'Orléans) the famous poet Tristan L'Hermite, still in the service of Gaston, published a fictionalized autobiography, *Le page disgracié*.[21] Among the Oratorians themselves, in Paris or Juilly, La Fontaine had already been able to devour the collections of lyric poetry that had made the prince's poet laureate famous: the *Plaintes d'Acante* (1633) and *La lyre* (1641). The Oratory was faithful to Marie de Médicis and grateful for the protection of the queen's favorite son, Gaston, which was very compromising in the eyes of the court. *La lyre* was inspired by a collection by the same name published by the queen mother's Italian poet, Giambattista Marino (1608).[22] Among the pleasures La Fontaine enumerates in his "Hymne à la Volupté," which concludes *Les amours de Psyché* (1669), one finds all those preferred by the very refined Italian poet, pensioned by the queen mother:

J'aime le jeu, l'amour, les livres, la musique.
(line 25)

I like games, love, books, and music.

But La Fontaine adds the pleasures that the tender Tristan preferred:

Les forêts, les eaux, les prairies,
Mères des douces rêveries.
(lines 23–24)

Forests, waters, prairies,
Mothers of sweet daydreams.

Finally, he sums up all these sensual delights in a single line, one of the most beautiful in the French language, which pays a wonderful tribute to the lyricism of the author of *Plaintes d'Acante:*

Jusqu'au sombre plaisir d'un coeur mélancolique.
(line 38)

Even the somber pleasure of a melancholic heart.

For the Arcadian shepherd reading *L'Astrée* at the Oratory, nothing must have seemed more *heroic* than the lines from *La lyre* that, in 1641, Tristan devoted to the poet and musician Blaise Berthod (then music teacher of the Sainte-Chapelle) under the title *L'Orphée:*

Berthod personne illustre en cet âge barbare
Où l'ami véritable est un trésor si rare,
Ami discret, fidèle, et digne de mon choix,
De qui l'esprit éclate aussi bien que la voix,
Et dont la merveilleuse et divine harmonie
A d'un feu tout céleste échauffé mon Génie.
Cesse de réveiller avec tant de beaux airs
Echo qui se retire au fond de ces déserts,
Et qui plaignant encor le trépas de Narcisse,
A besoin de repos plutôt que d'exercice.
Laisse dormir en paix les Nymphes de ces eaux
Qui, couronnant leurs fronts de joncs et de roseaux,
Sous le liquide argent de leurs robes superbes,
Dansent à tes chansons dessus l'émail des herbes
. . . .
Suspends cet art divin qui peut tout enchanter,
Et tiens la bouche close afin de m'écouter.[23]

Berthod, illustrious man in this barbarous age
When true friends are such a rare treasure,
A discreet, faithful friend, worthy of my choice,
Whose wit bursts forth as well as his voice,
And whose wondrous and divine harmonies
Have warmed my genius with a heavenly fire.
Cease to awaken, with your beautiful tunes,
Echo, who flees to the remotest of deserts,
And who, still lamenting the death of Narcissus,
Stands in need of rest rather than exercise.
Let the nymphs of these waters sleep in peace,
They who, crowning their heads with rushes and reeds,
Under the liquid silver of their superb robes,
Dance to your songs on the sheen of grasses.
. . . .
Suspend that divine art that enchants everything,
And keep your mouth closed while you listen to me.

Friendship, melancholy, rest, sleep, and song, the harmony of the voice and reflections on the water: were it not for the absence of the imperceptible touch of a detached and voluptuous irony, auspicious for La Fontaine, we would already be transported by that music of the soul to *Le songe de Vaux* or *Les amours de Psyché*.

The next year, 1642, Tristan published *Le page disgracié*. All in all, the effect of that autobiography on the young Oratory novice must have been as strong as the initial books of Chateaubriand's *Mémoires d'outre-tombe* on Baudelaire when he read them for the first time.[24] In his novel Tristan disguises memories of his own childhood and youth, whose picaresque comedy, shot through with lyric emotion, is transfigured into humor of an exquisite humanity.

Born a gentleman, and, like Chateaubriand, a provincial gentlemen with no fortune, Tristan did not initially go to secondary school. Like the young page and hero of his novel, he did not submit to the rule of "pedants" until late in life, when he was already no longer a child, and his pride, as a gentleman and a poet, rebelled against it. Later, under the humanist Scévole de Sainte-Marthe, he developed a taste for Latin letters. He was thus able to rival Corneille on the tragic stage: in 1636 his *Marianne* was as great a success as *Le Cid*. He joined the Académie Française in 1649. He had for several years been a regular visitor at the home of its secretary for life, Valentin Conrart, where La Fontaine made his acquaintance. For the younger generation, Tristan symbolized not only poetry but French "freedom" and "frankness": for a long time, he had loyally followed the revolts, exiles, and disgraces of his own "patron," Gaston d'Orléans, even though his loyalty had hardly been rewarded by the prince.

Le page disgracié is one of the jewels of French narrative prose. If we read or reread it with the eyes of the young La Fontaine, who held it in his hands when the ink was still fresh, we rediscover the profound similarities and differences, in manner and in fate, between the elder poet and the younger. They had the same saturnine nature, the same contemplative childhood in the provinces, the same early discovery, before secondary school, of a unique vocation. But Tristan was born a gentleman, brought up in a château, and, as a young prince of wit, was bold enough to declare his preferences immediately. He had humor; La Fontaine had an unfailing gaiety.

This gentleman poet, who dared to be himself very early, was the first writer of French and modern literature bold enough to commit to writing, after the age of forty, the sensations, emotions, and minute events of his own childhood and adolescence, under a veil of modest and detached fiction that knew how to make readers "smile through their tears." Montaigne had sketched his self-portrait as a mature moralist, and French memoirists never lingered on the childish trifles of their early lives. Tristan's *Le page disgracié* is made up of "confessions," but the confessions of a future poet who makes the charm of what will never return again comply to his own adult tastes, which are neither too severe nor too indulgent toward the boy he had been. One cannot overstate the transfusion of elegance in language and feeling that took place between this gentleman poet and the young bourgeois from Château-Thierry, the born poet that La Fontaine was at the time of his reading. For him, Tristan was both Chrétien de Troyes, the teller, and Lancelot of the Lake, the young hero of the chivalric romance.

After a "wild and free" childhood in a château in La Marche (now Creuse), before trying his luck at the court of several princes, the page, the stand-in for the adolescent Tristan, takes stock of his literary resources. "Let me tell you," he writes,

> that I was barely more than four years old, I knew how to read, and I was beginning to take pleasure in reading novels, which I recited pleasantly to my grandmother and grandfather; when, to divert me from that useless reading, they sent me to school to learn the elements of the

Latin language. I spent my time at it, but I did not apply my heart; I learned a great deal, but with such distaste for such insipid fare that it did me little good. I had been left too free to taste agreeable things, and when someone tried to force me to discuss more useful, but more difficult matters, I did not find myself well disposed to do it. I was learning because I feared the rod, but I hardly retained the things I had learned. I lost in a moment the treasures people had made me grasp by force, and I recovered them again only by force, because I had no fondness for them.

Study had made me so melancholic that I could not bear it, but then good fortune befell me and made me change my way of life. [His father sent him to be a page to a blood prince, the marquis de Verneuil, illegitimate son of Henry IV and his own age, who conspired with him against the "pedant" responsible for making them study.] I found pleasures everywhere except in study, and, instead of saying my lessons, I applied myself only to reading and reciting frivolous stories. My memory was phenomenal, but it was an arsenal equipped only with very useless pieces. I was a living catalog of fabulous novels and tales; I was able to charm all idle ears; I had in my repertoire conversations for all sorts of different people and amusements for all ages. I could agreeably and easily recite all the fables known to us, from Homer and Ovid to Aesop and *Peau d'âne*.[25]

Few seventeenth-century texts (apart from Charles Sorel's *Francion*) give us such a keen sense of the resistance, shared by gentlemen, women, and the common people—especially in the provinces—of a living oral tradition going back to the fabliaux and medieval romances, in opposition to the Latin discipline of the schools, the rule for young men destined for the king's service or the church. That resistance of an old fount of "naive" fictions is combined with that of French mores, noble or lower-class, in opposition to clerical discipline and to the state courts or tax system. Seventeenth-century French literature, in the interlude of the Regency and the Fronde, eagerly returned to that lively and autochthonous vegetation of fables and tales, which was its own childhood in a sense; it also shook up the bookish, learned, and serious framework of the schools and their pedants. It was all the more agitated in that it was combined with a concern to preserve its freedom against the political servitude of the past, its joie de vivre against Shrovetide. The Arcadia of French poets was not a neoclassical myth: it owed as much to the nostalgia for the "good old days" of French language, imagination, and mores, which still had a hold on Molière's Alceste, as it did to Virgil's *Eclogues*. Under the Regency, the resistance to Richelieu's "tyranny," but also to the Tridentine moral order, awakened the pungent aromas of a lost paradise that lingered around readers of the "old romances."

A FRENCH MEDIEVAL RENAISSANCE

So it was that, in 1642, the year the cardinal died, the "disgraced page," a Lancelot "coming too late to a world too old," could be the hero of a novel in vogue, which arrived at just the right moment. The vogue for the "old poets" and the "old romances," begun by Voiture under Louis XIII at the Rambouillet mansion, assumed such proportions under the Regency that even scholars could not ignore it. In 1647, on the eve of the Fronde, Jean Chapelain (who was writing his neomedieval epic, *La pucelle, ou la France délivrée*, for the duc and duchesse de Longueville) wrote a dialogue that would be published only in 1728: *De la lecture des vieux romans* (On the reading of the old romances). It was a presentation of conversations between the author, the philologist Gilles Ménage, and the poet Jean-François Sarasin, secretary to the prince de Conti. The book was dedicated to Paul de Gondi, the future Cardinal de Retz and Ménage's patron, who may have witnessed the conversation.[26]

Chapelain, with the idea of giving substance to his epic prose, had just read *Lancelot*; he suggested to Ménage, who was then preparing his *Origines* (1650), which later became the *Dictionnaire étymologique de la langue française* (Etymological dictionary of the French language) that these old texts were a treasure for his own undertaking. Ménage protested: his cult of Latinity was extremely intransigent. Chapelain pointed out the energy and vigor of the old forgotten turns of phrase, the economical syntax, and the word order, which still made the state of that French language a living Latin. He emphasized the noble naïveté of these men and women of yore, who had invented French courtesy. Even so, though Chapelain sought to understand the reasons for the recent vogue, he remained reserved and cautious, if not secretly hostile. That courtesy of the past was still very rudimentary; it was idolized by hearsay evidence; it was only the beginning of the refinement of gallantry and urbanity that French moderns possessed.

At about the same time, Jean-François Sarasin was composing his own dialogue, in which he depicted himself with Ménage, debating the topic

Whether a young man must be in love. That book was published by Ménage and Pellisson in 1658.[27] It was an exegesis in two voices of the romance *Perceforest*, which Sarasin, in opposition to the humanist Ménage, wanted to see as a wonderful manual of French courtly manners: it was love that, in the heart of the hero of this "old romance," inspired his fidelity to the word he had given his lord, and his generous desire to surpass himself to win his lady. Sarasin, Armand de Conti's secretary and a poet revered by the duchesse de Longueville, his patron's splendid sister, was the classic example of the writer coddled by a princely family, hostile on principle to the "public service" of belles lettres imposed by Richelieu and soon restructured by Colbert.

THE POET'S CONTEMPLATIVE COMMITMENT

To read *L'Astrée* (which is set in pagan Gaul during the fifth century) is also to summon all the French "days of yore," a French Arcadia that had since been damaged and half-abolished by Machiavellian ministers, by pedants, and by their ally, Time. When Tristan L'Hermite's page discovers *L'Astrée*, he feels at home in a book that, as "learned" as it is, speaks the same fabulous language as his own folklore and teaches the same magic, the power to deceive the bad fairies and protect the complicitous young people eager to love each other:

> I set about to relate to my mistress everything I had read in *L'Astrée*. Everyone knows it is one of the most learned and agreeable novels to come to light, and that its illustrious author acquired a marvelous reputation through it. I discussed it with my mistress for five or six hours every day, and her ears never tired of it, nor did those of her best friend, and I used it as a charm to put the mother and one of her confidantes to sleep, so that they did not notice the meaningful glances we exchanged and the sweet nothings we often whispered in each other's ears.[28]

This already displays the "natural" charm of the best of La Fontaine's *Contes*, or of Molière's *Le Sicilien ou l'Amour peintre*.

In 1642, the year *Le page disgracié* appeared, Tristan also published a collection called *Lettres mêlées*, dedicated to Elisabeth de Choiseul-Praslin. After the Fronde, in her Nevers mansion in Paris and her château in Fresnes, this young woman, who later became Mme de Plessis-Guénégaud, would prove to be one of the most brilliant heirs to the marquise de Rambouillet. A friend to Port-Royal, a friend to Foucquet, a friend to Mme de Sévigné, she welcomed La Fontaine in her home during the Foucquet years. The fall of the *surintendant* condemned her to semiretirement, which her friend the marquise de Sévigné often shared.

Tristan's *Lettres* is more like a series of essays verging on prose poems. They represent a number of variations on melancholy—melancholy in general and, in the first place, that of the poet himself, who is receptive to that of his correspondents, men and women who form a select saturnine family around him. This melancholy is not so much the bodily humor and temperament diagnosed by doctors, as an orientation toward a place beyond, a painful luxury of the soul, which nothing can truly cure but which seeks relief in rare and noble remedies: love, the most delicious of torments, and its gentle reflection in the liquid medium of music, namely, lyric poetry. Missing from that saturnine pharmacy is laughter, gaiety, which Scarron, at that very moment, was about to put into circulation with the violent emetic of the burlesque.

In one of these epistolary essays,[29] Tristan gives a memorable definition of poetry, daughter and consoler of melancholy, one that would earn him in the romantic century the admiration of Théophile Gautier, and which could have been that of the future author of *Adonis*. Apologizing for his long epistolary silence, he writes:

I am guilty only of the vice natural to all those who get involved in writing. In fact, Sir, it seems that the same planet [Saturn] that disposes us to write verses also imposes laziness on us. Poetry is a gift of heaven, but one might say it is only fostered well by idleness; it is a swift and abrupt fire drawn from stagnant waters. Just as it is difficult to embrace the active life and the contemplative life at the same time, it is not easy to be both a courtier and a great writer. The art of the Muses demands too much rest, and that of the court too many reverences. Anyone who gets up in the early morning to go out and see a large number of people, who pretends to take up many interests, and to get involved in many intrigues, will hardly succeed as a great poet; and anyone who nearly always keeps his eyes on a book, and does almost nothing but think of representing the great passions, or the beauties of the universe, will amass little wealth. These are two champions who do not run in the same race, and who are not eligible for the same prize. They follow two very diverse paths, and one is more traveled than the other. One leads to the temple of Fortune, the other to the temple of Glory. For myself, born too free to do the work of slaves, and who would rather live with the sorrow of being disappointed than with the malice of disappointing, I have until now followed the court without taking my lessons from it. I never made a plan to acquire wealth, because I never based happiness on it. I have always considered ambition a demon with the power to make me lose my real advantage by offering imaginary prosperity. Thank God, its warm vapors [unknown to melancholiacs, whose temperament is wet and cold] have not dulled my senses and obstructed the free exercise of my soul. I still consider dust what is nothing but dust, and do not consider precious those things that contain elements of Fortune or that result from it. I am well aware that this sort of simplicity is not to everyone's liking, but it is condemned only by people whose lives I would not approve of. At least I have had the honor of receiving praise and favor from the most worthy people on earth, and from these great princes, who, on their own, know how to give to merit what others let importunity wrest from them. I continue to hope, however little attention I pay to amassing property, that I will not be reduced to extreme need, or, at least, that I will have the consolation of being pitied by honorable people who can respect my poverty because of my virtue, the way the common people dissimulate the faults of the great, on account of their wealth. Such are my thoughts and my imaginings, my strength or my weakness.

For Tristan, "a life in poetry," a contemplative and less-than-lucrative life, is the last refuge of "noble life" against the slavery and base passions of courtly society. The literary "merit" of princes of wit awaits unsolicited recognition only in the form of the favor spontaneously granted by blood princes, who, in this letter, are very different from the royal court, and from the courtiers who make their career there. Even though La Fontaine, a commoner from the provinces, accused of usurpation of a noble title in 1662, never used such lofty Cornellian language, he was more sensitive than anyone to the loyalty the poet by birth owed to the life of contemplative leisure and the rejection of any form of "servitude," whether a mercenary profession, marriage, or, above all, domestic service at court. The dialogue between Tristan and Gaston d'Orléans (which had ended poorly because of the prince) was nonetheless the model—less haughty and more nuanced with playful irony—for the free contract that La Fontaine would sign with his patron Foucquet.

A Society of Knights and Shepherds

The young La Fontaine, who in 1641 left behind eighteen months of a voluntary novitiate at the Paris Oratory, knew very well that he was not fit for the vow of chastity. He was still far from knowing how his vocation as a poet would fit into the "condition" he would have to assume in civil society. Would he one day be his father's successor as head of the family in Château-Thierry? Would he become a lawyer in Paris? Would he get married?

He was lucky, as he got his start in life, that his good provincial and bourgeois parents were comfortably well off, and that he was therefore able to extend the time of his studies and delay, until 1652–53, the choices he would allow his family to impose on him.

The nature of his studies in Paris is not well known, but one thing is clear: the poet, attracted to Paris for a time by the severe and learned priests of the Oratory, drawn away from his novitiate by a poetic vocation awakened by the reading of d'Urfé and Tristan, was, during his later stays in Paris, associated with a group of young men "of letters" who suited his own tastes.

Nor is it known exactly how that little society of aspiring poets, which La Fontaine joined in 1642, came into being. At this point, we are groping our way through the mist of origins. In Paris, La Fontaine had a childhood friend from Champagne, François Maucroix, and very early on, even before 1640, on the benches of some Parisian college, he had been friends with Antoine Furetière, a native of the Latin Quarter. Higher studies, or rather, an interest in getting away from them, united this initial trio with other young Parisians: Gédéon Tallemant des Réaux; two of Tallemant's cousins, Antoine Rambouillet de La Sablière and his brother; François Cassandre, future translator of Aristotle's *Rhetoric* in 1654; and François Charpentier, future translator of Xenophon in 1650 and future secretary for life of the Académie Française.

These associations among young men gifted for letters, and thus aspiring to something other than the usual professional life, could only come together in Paris. This is rather paradoxical in appearance, since these aspiring poets lived in an Arcadia or a Bocage of their imaginations. But that Arcadia (or Bocage) sought to have regular transport services linking it to the island of Cythera, which was even more accessible from Paris than from the provinces; its literary aspirations with respect to Parnassus required bookstores stocked with new titles, encounters with great predecessors. Bookstores and great predecessors were found only in Paris.

From generation to generation, such associations had reconstituted themselves anew, ever since the legendary "Brigade" of Baïf, Du Bellay, and Ronsard. We know of several others from the seventeenth century: for example, the "academy" of Michel de Marolles in the 1610s and Antoine Godeau's and Nicolas Frénicle's "illustrious shepherds" in the 1620s. Beyond all question, the most famous was the one that, in the 1630s, a generation before La Fontaine, had formed around a young secretary to the king, Valentin Conrart. In 1635 it became the Académie Française, thanks to the favor and will of Cardinal de Richelieu.

Undoubtedly, under the rule of Richelieu as prime minister, it was begun along more serious lines than the group that La Fontaine and his friends formed under the "good regency" of Anne of Austria. Among themselves, La Fontaine and his friends jokingly called themselves by the names of "knights-errant" of the Round Table. But in the end, the temple of glory that Conrart and his first friends had entered left these young poets with great hopes, even though they were satisfied, for the time being, with frequenting the more or less literary cabarets, writing rhymes for their lady friends, and inviting lutenists and singers to add feeling to their meetings.[30]

Music and musicians, in fact, figured prominently in the amusements of these "knights," gallant by definition, and of these "shepherds," in love by definition. From Conrart, Antoine Rambouillet de La Sablière (the future unfaithful husband of La Fontaine's major protectress under Louis XIV) received the nickname "great madrigalist" because he was so prolific in the writing of occasional poetry ready-made for music and song. Pierre de Nyert, Etienne Moulinié, Blaise Berthod, and especially their young students, Michel Lambert and Mlle Hilaire, willingly agreed to "chamber concerts" for that audience of passionate music lovers. In his *Historiettes*, Tallemant portrays Lambert and his sister-in-law Mlle Hilaire, in the Bel Air cabaret close to the Luxembourg Palace, accompanying the famous mathematician (and libertine) Le Pailleur, an amateur but talented singer, in front of an audience of young people that included the poet Isaac de Benserade.[31] It took place at the end of Louis XIII's reign, but "meetings among friends" of this kind (the painter Eustache Le Sueur left behind an admirable group portrait of one, which is today in the Louvre) continued under the Regency and after the Fronde.[32]

La Fontaine, accompanied by his new comrades, was a regular there when he spent time in Paris. In 1677, in his *Epître à M. de Nyert* (which remained unpublished during his lifetime), he fervently recalled the *melo-dious songs, sung to a few selected tunes* that Lambert and Hilaire had once performed for intimate and rapt audiences. In 1677 he was fifty-six years old, and M. de Nyert, who remained an honorary gentlemen of the king's chamber under Louis XIV, was eighty. What a contrast between the private and unassuming feasts of the good old days, the inebriating music of the heart, and the pompous fanfares preferred by Louis XIV in 1677:

> Grand en tout, il veut mettre en tout de la grandeur.
> La guerre fait sa joie et sa plus forte ardeur;
> Ses divertissements ressentent tous la guerre:
> Ses concerts d'instruments ont le bruit du tonnerre,
> Et ses concerts de voix ressemblent aux éclats
> Qu'en un jour de combat font les cris des soldats.
> Les danseurs, par leur nombre, éblouissent la vue,
> Et le ballet paraît exercice, revue,
> Jeux de gladiateurs, et tel qu'au Champ de Mars,
> En leurs jours de triomphe en donnaient les Césars.
> (*A M. de Nyert sur l'Opéra*, ll. 49–58)

> Great in every thing, he wants greatness in all.
> War is his joy and his deepest passion;
> His amusements all feel like war:
> His concerts of instruments roll like thunder,
> And his concerts of voices resemble the shouts
> From the mouths of soldiers on battle day.
> The dancers, by their number, are dazzling to view,
> And the ballet resembles an exercise, a review,
> Gladiator games, like those of the great Caesars
> In their days of triumph on the Campus Martius.

What a contrast with the tastes of Louis XIII himself (which Saint-Simon rated far above those of his son)! Louis the Just, in fact, was a talented composer of court tunes, and, as soon as the cardinal had left, and when he himself was not going out to hunt, he had his own compositions performed at the Louvre, in intimate groups by the amateur Le Pailleur, and by his chamber musicians led by Pierre de Nyert.

Tallemant writes of the king's tunes: "We sang there to the end. Le Pailleur, to curry his favor, said half aloud: 'Oh, that last tune certainly deserves to be sung again!' The king said: 'Someone finds that tune beautiful, let's play it again.' It was sung another three times. The king beat time."[33]

These pleasures of the château, intimate and among friends, put Louis XIII and his melancholy in harmony with his subjects, and with their own reasons for joy or discontent. That chamber music made them all forget Richelieu for a moment, his reason of state, his police, and his war. The true kingdom, even for the king, lay elsewhere.

A First Group Leader: Tallemant des Réaux

In 1642–45, the group of the "Round Table" was in no sense an academy. On average, these candidates to Parnassus were about twenty years old. In the beginning, the life and soul of the group seems to have been Gédéon Tallemant des Réaux, the eldest of them all. It was he who bestowed his own nickname on the group: he recalls incidentally in his *Historiettes* that, in his youth, he had been nicknamed "the knight" because everyone knew how mad he was about *Amadis,* a madness that put him on the leading edge of the fashion for troubadours introduced by the "Blue Room."[34] He was also the one, among the associates of "the Round Table," who had the best access to high society at that time. He was received in the salon of the marquise de Rambouillet in 1637. He collaborated on *La guirlande de Julie.* At the home of the marquise, he could rub shoulders with the true inventor of the "troubadour style," the famous poet Vincent Voiture, oracle of the lady of the house, secretary to Gaston d'Orléans, and his emissary at the court of Madrid. It was also Tallemant who formed the first link between the "Round Table" of young people and the Académie Française. He invited to his family table illustrious literary elders, the academy's secretary for life, Valentin Conrart (who came as a neighbor, since he also lived in Saint-Eustache, on rue des Petites-Etuves), and other members of the academy: the poet Jean Ogier de Gombauld, the translator Nicolas Perrot d'Ablancourt, and his friend Olivier Patru. Tallemant, Huguenot that he was, was nevertheless on friendly terms with the young and brilliant abbot Paul Gondi de Retz, Richelieu's bête noire.

The "knights-errant" amused themselves in Arcadia, but, thanks to Tallemant, they already stood on the doorstep of the Académie Française and, with the academy, of high society, both social and literary. For the moment, however, they found much easier and more pleasant access, especially for the provincials La Fontaine and Maucroix, in the most recently built, most luxurious mansions of Paris, finely decorated and furnished by the artists in fashion. These homes were open to them, with their gardens and their bevies of not-so-prudish young beauties. They were the homes of Tallemant's tribe and La Sablière's family, rich Calvinist bankers who came to Paris after the Edict of Nantes and who thrived there, financing the military campaigns of Richelieu. The Rambouillets and the Tallemants, whose male offspring belonged to the "knights-errant," were connected by marriages and commercial and banking operations. Along with other wealthy Calvinists—the Bigots, the Hervarts, and the Hesseins—they formed a Protestant high society that in no way resembled the one in the Geneva mold that would later form in nineteenth-century Paris, on the ruins left by Necker.[35]

Once we understand that the author of *Fables,* whose youth as a "knight-errant" was coddled by the Huguenot bank, whose old age and death were made easier by the Hervarts' heirs—Catholic converts but faithful to the patronage of their parents—and who, above all, was for twenty years the guest of Marguerite Hessein—the separated wife of the comrade from his youth Antoine Rambouillet, herself a daughter of Calvinist bankers—we get an idea of La Fontaine's debt—and of our own—to the Protestants, who later would be persecuted, dispersed, or converted by force under Louis XIV. The former Oratory novice, the friend of Port-Royal, of the *surintendant* Foucquet, of the duc de La Rochefoucauld, and of the marquise de Sévigné, but also of the "roué" Vendôme, was, via his old ties to the Huguenots, closer to the center of all the true colors—intellectual, social, and literary—of the country than any other French person of his time. Compared to La Fontaine's Paris, the court of Louis XIV seems "unrepresentative" of the kingdom.

La Fontaine loved his Huguenots, and they loved him. Like "good king Henry," who had given them freedom in the city of Paris (they had their church and cemetery in Charenton), they were children of the Renaissance more than anything, as much or perhaps more the descendants of Rabelais and Marot than of Calvin. Their antipopery was based primarily on a principle of freedom: the freedom to reject the condemnation of commerce and lending at interest, the freedom to lift the yoke of the Catholic clergy, which would have liked gradually to extend to laypeople the constraints proper to their own condition. Thus they were easily the allies, in marriage, business associations, and artistic tastes, of the Montaigne-style Catholics who, braving the censure of their own clergy, and at the risk of being called "libertines," also remained faithful to "belles lettres," the *gaya scienza* of the Renaissance.

There was a bit of Pantagruel in these businessmen, as gifted at making money as at spending it with pleasure and taste. Antoine Rambouillet's father, Nicolas, had a veritable palace built in the Fossés-Montmartre district, and the grounds of his country house, "La Folie-Rambouillet" (Rambouillet's Folly) in Reuilly, rivaled those of the king in Saint-Cloud and those of Cardinal de Richelieu in Rueil.[36]

His neighbor in Fossés-Montmartre, Gédéon II Tallemant, the cousin of Tallemant des Réaux, was also not intimidated by Shrovetide. Tallemant des Réaux writes that, in Gédéon II's mansion on rue de l'Angoumois, decorated with commissioned masterpieces by the painter Laurent de La Hyre, entitled *Les sept arts libéraux,* "he had paintings, crystal, jewels, copper-plate engravings, books, horses, birds, dogs, pretty girls, and so on. He bought a house for one hundred thousand livres, then had it almost completely rebuilt, and this in a terrible neighborhood, the remotest section of the Marais, along the rampart."[37]

This lover of luxury and pleasure married the daughter (Marie) of a rich Catholic businessman, Pierre Puget de Montauron. The father-in-law also surrounded himself with a princely luxury in his mansion on rue Vieille-du-Temple. There he kept an open table. The French painters of the new school were not the only ones to benefit from that rich clientele: in spite of envious people, who played on deep-seated prejudices against money and the financiers, in 1643 Corneille accepted a generous gift in exchange for dedicating *Cinna* to Montauron.[38] François Maynard did the same in 1646. The Huguenot family by marriage of this Catholic banker was no less welcoming of writers and poets. Tallemant's father received the Huguenot members of the Académie Française, but also their friends, at his home. His son was warmly welcomed early on in the home of the marquise de Rambouillet, because she was grateful to that family of influential bankers for the support she had received from them in her "good works" toward penniless writers.

La Fontaine, in the footsteps of the "knights-errant of the Round Table" Rambouillet and Tallemant des Réaux, frequented these lovely homes, where he could converse with members of the Académie Française and take pleasure in the company of the young sisters and cousins of his friends, well-read but not prudish or affected: no confessor or director of conscience watched over their virtue. Along with his friends, he developed a taste not only for music and theater, but also for painting, sculpture, and the fine arts, which his hosts lavishly supported. In 1642–43, he witnessed the rise in Paris of a generation of artists, the pupils of Simon Vouet, who were no longer slavishly following Italy's lead, and who were creating a specifically Parisian "correspondence among the arts," an artistic Atticism in harmony with the urbanity of mores in which the capital could take pride, thanks to the influence of the marquise de Rambouillet.[39] When the time of Saint-Mandé and Vaux came, La Fontaine was better able than anyone to understand the *surintendant* Foucquet's plan: to assemble around him all the talents that had ripened since the beginning of the Regency, and to finally form a complete French "academy": architects and gardeners, painters and sculptors, interior decorators and haberdashers, instrumentalists and singers, actors and poets, a full workshop of sincere and original French art.[40]

It was under the Regency, when La Fontaine was received at the homes of the Rambouillets, the Tallemants, the Hervarts, and the Bigots, that these families joined the "Foucquet syndicate," which guaranteed the future *surintendant* the credit necessary to supply the royal treasury, always short of funds, with fresh money. Foucquet's fall would also signal the decline of the Haute Société Protestante (the Calvinist aristocracy of bankers, as they were called), which was brought down and, from 1661 to 1685, called upon to convert to Catholicism or go into exile.[41]

Tallemant des Réaux, then, played a key role in Maucroix's and La Fontaine's initiation into Paris, even though, in his *Historiettes* (written beginning in 1657), he pretended to make light of this "boy of belles lettres, and who writes verse," whom he had known at his obscure debut and who, in the meantime, had become Nicolas Foucquet's poet laureate. Of the two friends, the great man for him was Maucroix.[42]

THE RENAISSANCE GAIETY OF PARIS

Tallemant des Réaux was not himself a Parisian by birth, but he had lived in the capital with his family after his father moved there in 1634 to run the main branch of the family bank. He was fourteen years old at the time. Very quickly, he had become what Henry James calls a "success." He had little interest in joining the family business, and, from his father's house in the heart of the capital, the Saint-Eustache district, he burned the candle at both ends; at the same time, he was an excellent student and, very early on, earned an enviable reputation as a poet in the "Blue Room." Tallemant was the antithesis of Tristan. This son of a well-to-do bourgeois radiated vitality, wit, and gaiety. By the time he was seventeen, he had already become the life and spark of his generation in Paris.

He describes himself as he was when La Fontaine and Maucroix became associated with him in 1642: "For myself, I was cheerful, restless, jumpy, and again made more noise than anyone. Yes, my temperament tended toward the melancholic, but it was a sweet melancholy, and never prevented me from being merry when necessary."[43]

Could this not also be the portrait of the author of *Le voyage en Limousin?* Although La Fontaine's profoundly poetic nature had more affinities with the author of *Le page disgracié*, as a man and a poet he had learned and retained a great deal from the beneficent "Pantagruelism" that burst forth from the young Tallemant. The scattershot autobiography that Tallemant fit into his *Historiettes* was a training school for La Fontaine's *Contes:* it had the same bantering and greedy vivacity, wary of the snares of passion.

For a time, the precocious (and fickle) student of love came close to a lasting emotional attachment with a thirty-year-old mistress, Marie Le Goust: "I was there for every walk, every diversion, and the lovely lady could do nothing without me; thus I was rarely away from her; I studied all morning, and gave the evenings wholly to her. I never spent my time better, since I was well loved and very much in love: we had complete freedom to talk and embrace."

He left for Italy, where he did the "grand tour" in the company of the abbé de Retz, who put some distance between him and Richelieu. He was unfaithful to Marie Le Goust countless times; a few of the affairs were sentimental and painful, most ended bitterly. If the verb "amuse oneself," which La Fontaine was still using in his last letter to Maucroix a few weeks before his death, ever assumed a Rabelaisian meaning, it was truly in the society of the young Tallemant des Réaux and his pretty cousins:

> I will not mention all the outings we went on with Lolo [his cousin Charlotte Bigot, who later became Mme de Gondran] and her sisters. Several times, we spent three or four days in the country together, and I always enjoyed myself more than anyone; for I was always involved with the pretty lady, and that occupied my mind agreeably: I was only the better company. When those who were in the group remember all the follies they saw me commit, they still laugh about them, and she [Lolo] has spoken to me about them more than a hundred times since then.[44]

La Fontaine probably had only a walk-on part in Tallemant des Réaux's theater. But he was part of the troupe. In the young Tallemant, the future author of *Contes* could admire the precocious Parisian, his freedom, his ease in society, and his appetite for life, but he also felt the secret *taedium vitae* that his jokes tried to overtake. For La Fontaine, more inward-looking, slow, and contemplative, Tallemant was, in his own way, a master of ironic and comic verve, an exuberantly healthy Scarron.

Historiettes, written by Tallemant "when the mood struck" him, has long been considered a suspect archive collection, to be used cautiously by scholars. In reality, it is a literary masterpiece, whose fragmented form, dense language, and comic and unusual manner depart, more violently than Scarron's *Roman comique*, from the traditional narrative mold of the story and from academic prose. It is a "comic novel" of Louis XIII's Paris, written the way the author spoke, by a Léautaut who endured the reign of Louis XIV. Its veracity is all the more reliable in that Tallemant recorded not only his own memories and the firsthand accounts his friends—de Retz, for example—had given him, but also and especially the confidences of the marquise de Rambouillet. The former ebullient golden boy of his generation became her confidante in 1648, when the lights of the "Blue Room" went out and the brilliant queen of Paris accepted the fact that she was now only a lonely old lady, poking at the embers of her memory. The memoirist himself, now more somber, resigned himself to converting to Catholicism in 1685 and put all his energy into evoking a vanished, almost untamed world, where people dared be themselves.

Tallemant's magnum opus, along with Furetière's first books, Antoine Rambouillet's madrigals, Maucroix's early poetry, François Cassandre's translations, and La Fontaine's *L'eunuque* are also part of the sparse archives of a single literary group, united first for pleasure around Tallemant des Réaux, but which soon became a little academy where they worked in common, in a workshop, like painters and other artists of a generation rich in talents.[45] That workshop counted a great deal to La Fontaine, who found a second literary education there, and who borrowed numerous ingredients from it, which were later blended in his own poet's, painter's, and virtuoso musician's still.

A Mentor for the "Knights-errant": Paul Pellisson

What was missing from the "knights-errant" was the equivalent of what Valentin Conrart had been for his own society of friends before it became the Académie Française, a more mature group leader, but of their own generation, and a host who could assemble them together on a regular basis. He appeared in 1645: Paul Pellisson.[46] The son of a large family of Huguenot lawyers from Castres, recommended to his coreligionist Valentin Conrart, he was twenty-one when he first arrived in Paris. Handsome at the time, brilliant and gifted, an excellent jurist and serious writer, he immediately came to dominate the society of the Round Table, which he probably joined through Tallemant, a friend of Conrart's and of the French Huguenot members of the Académie Française. Pellisson was a southerner, imaginative and emotional, but with great inner discipline, and with the habit of exercising his mind.

Under his influence, his new friends willingly set to work, but the provincial Pellisson no less willingly allowed them to initiate him into the pleasures of the capital, its spectacles, its arts, its luxury, its bracing diversity.

In an epistle in octosyallables from Pellisson to Maucroix, written between 1645 and 1648, a real inebriation bursts forth:

Paris est un séjour charmant,
Les jours n'y durent qu'un moment,
Les mois et même les années
Y semblent de courtes journées.
L'étranger, en toute saison,
Quittant sa ville, sa maison,
Et ses affaires plus pressées,
Porte ici toutes ses pensées.
Ses jours passent, ses ans s'en vont,
Les rides lui naissent au front,
Son visage devient plus blême,
Il sent au-dedans de lui-même
La mort à grands pas s'avancer,
Et ne peut pourtant se lasser
D'être un spectateur inutile
De cette incomparable ville.[47]

Paris is a lovely place,
The days go by at a fearsome pace,
Every month and every year
Seems but a few short days here.
In every season the stranger comes,
Leaving behind his city and home
Setting aside more pressing affairs,
Directing all of his thoughts here.

His days pass away, his years go by,
His forehead now marred by lines,
His face grown pale and wan,
He begins to feel within,
Death advancing at great strides,
And yet he will never be tired
Of being an idle spectator
To this city beyond compare.

Montaigne said: "I am a Frenchman only by virtue of Paris." That was especially the feeling of the provincials of the Round Table, to whom Pellisson became very close. The art of "amusing oneself," which Tallemant taught to his companions, could enjoy free rein among the "diversities" of the capital. Pellisson describes, for perhaps the first time in French literature, a "character" destined for a long life, the "stroller" or *flâneur* (Fargue would say "pedestrian") of Paris, which he himself was not ashamed to become, and which La Fontaine was as well:

Tel voit-on un nouveau venu
Qui dans la Foire retenu,
Par l'éclat de mille merveilles,
Devient tout yeux et tout oreilles,
Et sans vendre et sans acheter,
Ne fait que voir et qu'écouter:
Tantôt la peinture l'arrête,
Tantôt il contemple sa tête
Dans la glace d'un grand miroir,
Tantôt son oeil se plaît à voir
Ou la fragile verrerie
Ou l'éclatante argenterie,
Les dames jouant sur le banc
Lui découvrent un bras plus blanc
Qui l'ivoire qu'elles empoignent,
Ici ceux qui perdent rougnonnent,
Là les filous font un bon tour,
Cependant il ne fait plus jour
Et ce badaud qui tout contemple
Loge peut-être auprès du Temple!

A new arrival you may have glimpsed
At the fair, standing transfixed,

By the gleam of a thousand wonders,
Frozen in place, all eyes and all ears,
He doesn't buy and he doesn't sell,
He simply watches and listens well:
Sometimes a painting stops him dead,
Sometimes he contemplates his head
In a great mirror catching the light,
Sometimes he sees to his eye's delight
Fragile figures made of glass
Or gleaming wares of silver or brass.
Ladies gambling on the lawn
Uncover their arms whiter than
The ivory dice they handle,
There, the losers grumble,
Here, the swindlers pull a fast one,
And yet daylight is almost gone
And the stroller watches it all
Far from his lodgings near the Temple!

Paris offers an ever-new and all-encompassing theater of the human comedy, and its "amusements" are, at bottom, a many-faceted mirror in which the stroller/contemplator can practice the precept "know thyself" with a greedy curiosity characteristic of Montaigne, and which La Fontaine still manifests in "The Cobbler and the Financier" (8.2).

But, in Pellisson's eyes, Paris is also a French and living Parnassus, where one can rub elbows with "our Virgils," Patru, Chapelain, Gombauld, Conrart, and can associate with "great souls" full of promise, such as Maucroix or Tallemant. For all the young writers who received and understood the lesson of Paris, the hope of becoming another "Virgil" was no longer impossible.

Pellisson's epistle, for private use only, is something of the first, still weak, manifesto of a literary generation. His interlocutor (Maucroix, always inseparable from his friend La Fontaine) was waiting like himself for "fortune" to pull him away from the provinces, or from the chicanery that threatened them. The great stroke of luck in their young lives was this society of friends they formed in Paris, and the exercises in a continuing "literary education," which Pellisson invited them to undertake together or by correspondence. Pellisson sent Maucroix his translation of the Greek romance *Daphnis and Chloe*, attributed at the time to "Longinus." In his thank-you note, Maucroix, with an entirely "modern" freedom, jokingly gave his "critique":

Or dans mes heures de loisir,
J'ai lu ton livre avec plaisir.
Mais pour dire ce que j'en pense,
J'y trouve peu de vraisemblance,
Et Daphnis est par trop lourdaud.
Car où trouverait-on Pitaut
Qui n'enseignât à sa Bergère
Tout ce qu'il faut pour être mère?
Des gens auraient été si fats
Que de serrer entre leurs bras
Pucelles fraîches et jolies,
Jeunes, grasses, blanches, polies,
Et qui ne demandaient pas mieux,
Et n'auraient baisé que les yeux,
Un peu la bouche, un peu la joue,
And puis se seraient fait la moue?
N'en déplaise à M. Longin,
En cet endroit, c'est un badin.[48]

So in my hours of leisure,
I read your book with pleasure.
But, to give you my honest view,
I find it lacks verisimilitude,
And Daphnis is a bit of a lout.
For where could you found a Pitaut
Who did not teach his shepherd girl
Every subject in maternity school?
People of such a conceited race
As to take in their arms and embrace
Fresh and pretty maids, polite,
Young, plump, and ever so white,
And to ask for no other favor,
Than a kiss on their eyes to savor,
Or a bit of cheek, a taste of mouth,
And who would then go off and pout?
No disrespect to Mr. Longinus,
But I think he's having a joke on us.

The freedom and carnal pleasures of love, and the irony directed against pedantry and prudery, were articles of faith among the "knights-errant." They remained faithful to them: Maucroix, in the erotic poetry he sent to his young provincial lady friends, the composition of which, under Louis XIV, brightened the forced idleness of his life as canon of Reims; Tallemant, in his spicy *Historiettes*; and, of course, La Fontaine in his *Contes*. Under the regency of Anne of Austria, the opportunity that Paris—impervious to the policing of parochial mores—offered them to pursue their love affairs in the streets, at fairs, and in cabarets was not one of the lesser attractions of the capital. They were not militant "libertines," however: the religious or antireligious controversy had no more effect upon them than religious feeling itself. They set aside theology, Catholic as well as Protestant. Belles lettres, the practice of poetry and critical readings, excited them as it did only because they sketched out an independent territory—Parnassus, Arcadia, and Cythera—which gave a second and intense meaning to the things of life, in Paris and in the provinces.

In another epistle, sent by François Cassandre to Maucroix, who could not get to Paris, the Parisian "knight-errant" let his colleague participate at a distance in the work the new company had undertaken in his absence, after a good dinner.

> Primo donc, le sieur Furetière
> A lu satire presque entière
> Contre nos saigneurs Médecins
> Qui font mourir des gens bien sains.
> Plus cette même après-dîner,
> La Lettre écrite contre Enée
> Reçut tout l'applaudissement
> Que mérite un style charmant . . .
> Item, épigrammes nombreuses
> Avec rencontres très heureuses,
> Qu'en latin, mais non de pédant,
> Nous fit voir Maynard, Président.[49]

> First, then, Sir Furetière
> Read almost a complete satire
> Against our butchering physicians
> Who put to death quite healthy men.
> At that same meeting, after the feast,
> The letter written against Aeneas
> Received all the applause
> That its charming style deserved . . .

Item, epigrams by the score
With felicitous encounters
Were read in Latin, but not pedantic,
By Maynard, our dear president.

Poetic essays and translations (the "letter written against Aeneas" was
a *Heroid* Ovid wrote in the voice of the abandoned Dido, the model for
the future *Lettres de la religieuse portugaise* by Guilleragues) were thus open
to the judgment of the group and that of their noble elder, François Maynard, a member of the Académie Française. This epistle makes it clear
that, by 1645, the "Round Table" had taken the form of an academy holding regular sessions for conversation and work.

THE POLITICS OF WRITERS

Cassandre also enthusiastically mentions (and this allows us to date
the epistle) the immediately famous *Ode héroïque* Pellisson wrote as a tribute to Mme de Rambouillet's only son, the marquis de Pisani, killed in the
battle of Nördlingen on 23 August 1645. But the session (and the epistle)
moved on to a subject that might seem to be alien to poets:

Après quoi la troupe savante,
D'une façon fort éloquente,
Disputa si le Potentat
Doit donner borne à son Etat.[50]

After which the learned band,
In a manner eloquent,
Discussed whether the Potentate,
Ought to put limits on his state.

It was late 1645 or 1646. Richelieu had been dead for three years.
Tallemant, who was very close to de Retz, was able to inform his friends of
what was happening at court. But anyone who was quick-witted and lived
in Paris could feel the air of freedom circulating in the "good regency."
These young men of letters may have dreamed they were on Parnassus,
writing in Arcadia, and traveling to Cythera, but they did not hesitate to

consider the major problem that Paris had been openly raising since the death of Richelieu: what is the state, and how far can and should its authority extend?[51]

The question naturally came up among them, especially since, for their literary future, they needed a Maecenas, and they wondered quite simply what his political nature would be, when the Italian cardinal who had governed them made way for a king who was still a minor. The fears and polemics that had accompanied the founding of the Académie Française by the terrible Richelieu were well known to them, through their elder Conrart and through Pellisson, who was already preparing his *Relations sur l'histoire de l'Académie*, in which Richelieu did not play the hero.

In fact, in the same epistle from Cassandre to Maucroix, the writers' debate on the state—which others were pursuing at the same moment more effectively and by more vigorous means, as heads of princely families or magistrates at the Parlement—had to do with the relation between the "potentate" and the republic of letters:

> Et puis ensuite fut traitée
> La question tant agitée
> Si le savoir absolument
> Nuit au sage gouvernement,
> Ou s'il veut peu de gens d'étude.[52]

> And then, the next thing treated
> The question so long debated,
> Was whether, absolutely, knowledge
> Does harm to wise government,
> And whether it wishes few men of study.

The writer of occasional "tales" confined himself to an elliptical remark; he knew very well that his interlocutor, Maucroix, would easily reconstruct the substance of the debate, which was obviously one of the major preoccupations of the "knights-errant." These budding "men of study," who were interested in preserving the freedom of their behavior from ecclesiastic censure, were no less interested in preserving their freedom of thought from political tyranny. They wondered whether it was desirable to move into the "potentate's" circle, to give his authority direction rather than submit to it, or whether it was preferable to remain under cover. These were not the questions of naive men. It was the problem of the century. These were also not the preoccupations of just any ambitious men.

The regular meetings that took place at the home of Pellisson were often led by members of the Académie Française—Gombauld, d'Ablancourt, and even François Maynard, one of the most famous of Malherbe's disciples, who came from his native Languedoc in 1646 to present his *Oeuvres* to the Académie Française. He agreed to be elected "president" of the Round Table for a few weeks. This was no longer a mere "brigade," but a true "youth academy," which, under Valentin Conrart's attentive eye, prepared to succeed the generation of 1630. This was the first outline of a French republic of letters, with two coordinated "chambers": the official one, which met at the home of Chancellor Séguier, and the other one, *in pectore Conrartii*, which met at Pellisson's home. It took shape at the joint initiative of Conrart and the young Pellisson, at a time when the long-organized "European republic of letters," of Latin and Italian origin, had prestigious private academies in Paris: the more erudite "cabinet" of the Dupuy brothers, and the more scientific circle of Mersenne, who belonged to the order of Minims.[53]

PELLISSON AND THE RENAISSANCE OF CLASSICAL LETTERS

The "youth academy" headed by Pellisson lasted a little more than ten years, ending with the Fronde and the young magistrate's return to Castres (where, indefatigable, he founded a local academy among his young colleagues). The second era of the Round Table began in 1650, with the definitive return of Pellisson to Paris (his face disfigured by smallpox), and ended, at least in appearance, in 1656, when the young magistrate became Foucquet's right-hand man. With two other "knights-errant," Maucroix and La Fontaine, Pellisson then formed a great encyclopedic academy around Foucquet, one altogether equal to those of the Italian Renaissance or that of the Valois. Pellisson also struggled, not without encountering resistance—even from Conrart—to play prematurely at being the secretary for life of the Académie Française, and to arrange the elections to better attach the society created by Richelieu to the Foucquet academy. In 1652 he purchased a post as secretary to the king, and, the next year, close on the heels of another "knight-errant," François Charpentier, he himself was accepted into the Académie Française, as a reward for his *Relation sur l'histoire de l'Académie*, which had just been published by Conrart. The destiny of the "knights of the Round Table" had already diverged into two branches when Foucquet's ascension began in 1656, and the knights dispersed during and after the Foucquet affair. Pellisson's political ambition was the origin of that parting of ways. But it was a noble ambition: to provide the young French republic of letters, whose foundations he had built with Conrart, a Maecenas who would be entirely favorable toward it.

In 1650, after Pellisson's return to Paris, the work of the young members of the academy of the Round Table began again in earnest, and even took a new turn. Impelled by a superior master, but one who was also a friend and peer, they did exercises and debated with a zeal that many of them had lacked under the yoke of the "pedants" at school. For Pellisson himself, this was undoubtedly a "comprehensive exam" that concluded his solid classical studies and brought them up to date with what was being done and thought in Paris, at the center of things. For Furetière, who, at the beginning of his *Poésies diverses* (1655), a book dedicated to "his friends," confessed to a true "longing to be an author," they were the qualifying courses for a future member of the Académie Française. But whatever the great social and literary hopes of each of them, the feeling, stirred up by Pellisson, of belonging to a French republic of letters— gifted, free, independent, superior to vulgar prejudices and even to the social conventions among which they had to make their way—united them more than ever in a wholly "Arcadian" solidarity. Expressions of passionate friendship, in the style of Montaigne and La Boétie, were already frequent in their correspondence between 1645 and 1648, especially in the epistles exchanged by the three provincials, Pellisson, Maucroix, and La Fontaine.[54]

In the letters of 1650–62 addressed to Donneville, one of his fellow "academicians" from Castres, Pellisson gave a sample of the maieutic method he was implementing at the time among his Parisian friends, and of the subjects with which it dealt.[55] It was a veritable "free faculty" program of European literature, and it is not surprising that La Fontaine, having taken it, could become the "miracle of culture" Gide called him. In 1687 La Fontaine could write: "I am reading books by those from the north and by those from the Midi," at a time when Perrault no longer wanted to know any "illustrious men" unless they were French and contemporary.[56]

Lettres à Donneville contains admirable critical insights on the Italian poets, notably Berni, author of *Orlando innamorato*, and Ariosto, author of *Orlando furioso*, two great ironists, models for the burlesque, which served very well to counterbalance *Amadis* and *L'Astrée*, with which several "knights-errant" were still a bit too exclusively captivated. These

Renaissance poets, however, also made love the great motivating force of valor, of inventive and subtle wit, and of the wise literary magic that makes one see the world with a worldly-wise, vivacious, and ironic eye.

But, as a humanist, Pellisson insisted on the incomparable lesson of the poets of antiquity, often ruined for his friends by the pedagogy of colleges. He reminded his correspondent of Montaigne's taste for Lucretius and the great Epicurean poem *De rerum natura*. He cited and commented on the "Hymn to Venus" at the beginning of that poem: "Lucretius's Venus, the source of love that combines with all things, . . . is God!"[57]

Since the Renaissance, people had been burned at the stake, in Rome and Geneva, but also in Paris and Toulouse, for propositions more innocuous than that one. This was not a theological thesis but a literary act of faith: the goddess of beauty and love, the principle of "sympathies" that make Nature into a Cosmos, is inseparable from the god of Parnassus. She communicates her magnetism to poetry and belles lettres; she gives them the power to soothe people and to lead the best of them to true wisdom. With learning and infinite caution, Pierre Gassendi, a canon in Digne, was having success at that same moment in his attempt to rehabilitate among scholars, if not Aphrodite, then at least Epicurus, the philosopher of pleasure, and to reconcile him with Augustinian spirituality. Pellisson was a literary and Huguenot Gassendi among his own friends.

Hence, Pellisson, La Fontaine, and his friends of the Round Table did not wait for Gassendi's disciple François Bernier to popularize his master's doctrine under Louis XIV.[58] Their rhetoric, poetics, and politics presupposed that French belles lettres could combat violence, discord, and prejudice with the illuminating principle of love celebrated by Socrates in *The Symposium* and by Lucretius in *De rerum natura*, and that, through poetry, such beneficent persuasion could insinuate itself into the kingdom. When, twenty years later, in the peroration to *Les amours de Psyché*, La Fontaine himself composed a "Hymn to Pleasure," he was the faithful interpreter, under Colbert, of the literary faith that animated the "knights-errant" at the end of the Fronde:

> O douce Volupté, sans qui, dès notre enfance,
> e vivre et le mourir nous deviendraient égaux;
> Aimant universel de tous les animaux,
> Que tu sais attirer avecque violence!
>   Par toi tout se meut ici bas.
>   C'est pour toi, c'est pour tes appas,

Que nous courons après la peine:
Il n'est soldat, ni capitaine,
Ni ministre d'Etat, ni prince, ni sujet,
Qui ne t'ait pour unique object.
                    (*Les amours de*
                Psyché et de Cupidon)

O sweet pleasure, without you, even in childhood
Living and dying would be all the same to us;
Universal magnet to every animal,
Which you know how to attract with violence!
    By you everything moves here below.
    It is for you, for your charms,
    That we go looking for pain:
    There is no soldier, no captain,
No state minister, no prince, no subject,
    Who does not have you for his sole object.

This is much less a doctrinal manifesto of Epicurean cosmology than the program for an art capable of creating harmony, sweetness, and an appetite for true happiness in the soul of its readers, and perhaps, of transforming the soul of the leaders of the state.

It is not surprising, then, that another Epicurean poet of antiquity, Horace, a friend to Augustus and Maecenas, had Pellisson's full approval. He offers a striking portrait of the author of *Epistulae* and *Satirae* in his thirteenth letter to Donneville in 1650–52. Written thirty years before the *[Second] Discours à Mme de La Sablière*, which was read before the Académie Française in 1684, it looks like a premonitory first draft of the self-portrait La Fontaine would sketch for his colleagues the day he was accepted to the academy.

Pellisson writes: "Horace is always great, always amiable, and never repels or bores his reader; but what I admire most in him is the freedom of his poetry, which, unlike ours, is not subject to a thousand scrupulous maxims. He introduces his material . . . moves from one subject to the next, elevates and lowers himself at whim, always in control of himself, with a truth so great and a manner so agreeable that no one can reproach him for it."[59]

Through his *Fables*, La Fontaine, the bee and butterfly of Parnassus, became a French Horace, far more faithful in spirit and far more original than Boileau in his *Epîtres* and in his *Satires*, which, by comparison, seem stiff and monotonous. La Fontaine, in his *Fables*, addressed neither

Maecenas nor Augustus. He was even freer than Horace. The starting point for that singular and solitary poetic success must be located in 1650–52, when he reread Horace through Pellisson's eyes.

The Apollo that appears in *Clymène* (1660) makes Horace the "well-tempered clavier" of poetry. In his *Epitre à Huet* (1687), in which he provides another brief literary autobiography, La Fontaine speaks of that long-ago encounter with Horace as a kind of conversion. For him, there was a "before" and an "after" Horace. Before Horace, he was fascinated by modern, incomplete masters; after Horace, he learned to "follow nature":

> A la fin, grâce aux Cieux,
> Horace, par bonheur, me dessilla les yeux.
> (*Epitre à Huet*, ll. 47–48)

> In the end, thanks to heaven,
> Horace, in a stroke of luck, opened my eyes.

The discovery of Horace's art was at the same time a shift from melancholic daydreams to the courage of a poetic wisdom.

Horace was not only dependent on a Greek philosophy, Epicureanism, he was also indebted to a Greek, Athenian, and Alexandrian poetics. The anthology of classical poets who had the favor of Pellisson and his friends was selected on the basis of how closely they resonated with Parisian literary tastes, as defined by the witty Voiture. In his fourteenth letter to Donneville, for example, Pellisson read Terence, the "Menander of the Romans," as if he were a contemporary, and even as if the comic Latin poet had outdone the French playwrights of the time, in giving theater the grace of form and the human truth that Parisians until then had found only in the literature and occasional poetry of the Rambouillet mansion. Terence was the mirror in which French comedy, purged of Scarron's broad burlesque, could find itself and come to life.

Pellisson writes to Donneville:

> I agree completely with your judgment of the purity and elegance of his style, and also with what you say, that his manner of speaking is closely related to our own; and, for myself, one of the greatest pleasures I find in his comedies and in Cicero's epistle is to see that the pure air of every century and every nation, along with the many small differences, always has something fundamentally very similar. In my opinion, you will be confirmed in this same feeling when you have

studied *Eunuchus* and the *Adelphi,* which are, in my view, the two masterpieces of this author.[60]

Once more, we have the feeling that we are witnessing the birth of one of
La Fontaine's works, in this case the first one he published, his translation/
adaptation of Terence's *Eunuchus* and *Adelphi* in 1654. In his preface La
Fontaine echoes Pellisson's enthusiasm and even his language from a few
years or a months earlier: fluidity, simplicity, naturalness, life itself, but in
the "marvelous" gleam of art. He does not even fail to speak of the *uninterrupted unanimity* "of every century and every nation," which Pellisson
assumed about Terence's art, and which now had to be rediscovered for
French dramatic poetry, on the basis of that Latin model, itself imitated
from the Greek Menander. "Few people are unaware," La Fontaine writes,
fairly mysteriously, "of the many charms that fill the Latin *Eunuchus.*"

Lucretius, Horace, Terence, the Greek romances of Longus and Heliodorus, and Homer, of whose works Pellisson produced an admirable translation: such were the many superior models for the refined taste that was
returning to Paris; such were the many practicing masters who could
improve that taste and deliver it from the mannerism, on the right and on
the left, that still infested French literature.

Pellisson writes to Donneville:

> You will notice, in fact, that the ancients, even in the heroic poems,
> had very little interest in having a very rich subject matter, since they
> were certain that they would enrich it sufficiently by the form they
> gave it. The subject of the *Iliad* amounts to almost nothing, and that of
> the *Aeneid* would not fill half a mediocre novel in our time. Hence one
> must not blame Terence, since he followed the style of his century,
> which was more natural and more simple, for remaining within the
> limits of the comic and for not writing in a genre [tragicomedy] that
> was still unknown.[61]

In 1650–54, the ancient Terence was an avant-garde author, as Poussin
would be for Cézanne in 1890. He pointed the way to a purification of
modern tastes and a feeling for form among the French poets. La Fontaine's 1654 *L'eunuque* was a premonitory effort. With good grace, in a
1661 letter to Maucroix telling of the festival of Vaux, La Fontaine would
celebrate Molière as the one who had succeeded at what he himself had
attempted in vain, making the comedy of Menander and Terence come to
life for contemporary Paris:

Te souvient-il bien qu'autrefois
Nous avons conclu d'une voix
Qu'il allait ramener en France
Le bon goût et l'air de Térence?
. . . .
Nous avons changé de méthode:
Jodelet n'est plus à la mode,
Et maintenant il ne faut pas
Quitter la Nature d'un pas.
      (*Relation à* M. *de Maucroix*)

Do you recall that in the past
We concluded with a single voice
That he was going to bring back to France
The good taste and manner of Terence?
. . . .
We have changed our method:
Jodelet is not longer in fashion,
And now one must not
Depart from Nature by one jot.

A good number of La Fontaine's fables would be so many comic scenes
in the manner of Terence and Molière, but performed in the "pocket theater" where the poet recounted the Aesop's apologues that he had "brightened up."

Pellisson and French Hellenism

In that anthology of ancients, chosen to improve modern French tastes
and arts, the Latins were honored, but only the Hellenized Latins, the
translators of Atticism and Greek Alexandrianism in Rome. The third and
most intense period of the Academy of the Round Table was in reality a
"return to Greece," though via Latin mediation. Pellisson was a Hellenist,
and one of the initiators, with the Messieurs of Port-Royal, of a "Hellenic
renaissance" in the Paris of the Fronde and of Mazarin.[62] In the little
troupe of "knights-errant," the only Hellenist besides Pellisson, Maucroix,

and Cassandre[63] was François Charpentier. In 1650 he published a translation of Xenophon's *Memorabilia*, preceded by a "Life of Socrates," which was published separately in 1657. The Xenophon translation immediately earned him his place in the Académie Française. He was the first of the "knights-errant" to enter the mother house of French letters. This success is revealing: the academy's secretary for life, Valentin Conrart, did not know Latin or Greek, but was an exquisite connoisseur of the language of the realm and of modern French literature, and was in favor of the Hellenist cure via translation and imitation. Pellisson (who had made Maucroix read *Daphnis and Chloe* in 1645–48), but also Perrot d'Ablancourt, the great translation specialist at the Académie Française, had persuaded him. In 1654 d'Ablancourt published a translation of Lucian's *Dialogi*. In his preface he revealed that it was requested by Conrart, and that the secretary for life himself had taken it upon himself to revise the French style. Then d'Ablancourt praised the Greek writer, in terms that made Lucian a Voiture—writing in prose—of classical Atticism, and hence an ideal model for the new "Attic" writers that language and taste were demanding.

D'Ablancourt writes of Lucian: "One cannot deny that he was one of the finest wits of his century, always charming and agreeable, with a bright and playful mood, and with the Attic urbanity that we would call, in our own language, banter. Not to mention the clarity and purity of his style, combined with its elegance and good manners."[64]

From the Academy to the Republic of Letters

The youth academy, led with true Socratic genius by Pellisson, thus placed itself, in the midst of the rage for the burlesque, in the school of the Italian Renaissance and the most Attic literature of the ancients. All the same, the political concerns it had before 1648 did not disappear from conversation after 1650, when the defeat of the Fronde was anticipated, then realized, and when the configuration of the new regime became the object of general speculation. The concern of the true Huguenots Conrart and Pellisson, interpreters of Parisian Protestant high society, was less to take the side of Mazarin or of the Fronde than to save the Edict of Nantes, which the Bourbon dynasty served to guarantee. Loyalty to Henry IV's grandson was their golden rule. Unable to act directly in the political arena, in 1648–52 the Parisian Huguenots supported the king's wavering authority with their financial capital (with Foucquet as their intermediary); their coreligionist members of the Académie Française, Conrart and Pellisson, prepared a literary generation that, by its talent, personal independence, and measured style, could be useful to a king who was finally master of the game, and could turn public opinion toward his Augustan arbitration. The matters of poetic and literary technique to which Pellisson had alerted the "knights-errant of the Round Table" were inseparable from ulterior political motives, whose aim was to rally everyone around the king. They were also inseparable from an education in the freedom of the writer, his moral autonomy. The French republic of letters, heir to the ideals of the Renaissance, had to be able to pursue its work, even if things took a turn for the worse.

An attenuated reflection of these preoccupations, which were sharpest in the Huguenot Pellisson, but shared with varying degrees of insight by his Catholic friends in his youth academy, can be seen in the books they were beginning to publish.

Antoine Furetière's *Poésies diverses* was published in 1655, but it dates from a much earlier time, as attested to in the dedication "to his friends"; it contained pieces composed for the Academy of the Round Table and now dedicated to François Maucroix, Paul Pellisson, François Cassandre, and Valentin Conrart. An epistle, *Les poètes*, appeared in it, written in alexandrines and addressed to the abbé Ménage. Gilles Ménage, literary mentor to Mme de Sévigné and Mme de La Fayette, had been de Retz's secretary. He maintained excellent relations with Tallemant, with the "youth academy" to which he belonged, and with Furetière. Ménage, a great philologist, had distinguished himself in 1649 with his *Requête des dictionnaires*, in which he attacked Richelieu's authoritative program for the Académie Française to establish the rules of the French language, without the independence or seriousness of true scholars.

Furetière, a mouthpiece at this stage in his career for the sentiments shared by the "knights-errant," took Ménage's polemic a step further. He sharply attacked the "mercenary" writers who "profaned Parnassus" and betrayed the "noble foundations" of poetry: the integrity of the word, without which the "Fortune" of any writer is an abjuration. "Writing verses" presupposes "the art of governing one's life." Furetière concluded by imploring Ménage to pursue his battle for the dignity of literature:

De notre Mont sacré, rends les ondes plus pures.

Of our sacred mountain, make the waves more pure.

These "pure waves" would become one of the motifs recurring throughout the twelve books of La Fontaine's *Fables*. These waves reflect, albeit mysteriously, the truth that only poets see. They all originate on the slopes of Parnassus. According to Furetière himself, who developed the consequences at length in the dedication to his friends, they make it imperative that one does not give in to the temptation of servile and self-interested panegyrics or to the wicked and libelous slant of satire. In this case, it was not Horace—dear to Pellisson and La Fontaine—but Lucian, who had just been published in Nicolas Perrot d'Ablancourt's translation, who was the touchstone of Attic irony, open to truth, intransigent toward error and evil, but with a superior smile that did no harm to anyone in particular. During this same period, François Charpentier was publishing Xenophon's *Memorabilia*, followed by a Life of Socrates, another master of Attic irony, a figure of thought granted to a republic of letters that was neither servile nor rebellious. The time would come when La Fontaine, leaning by nature toward lyric and "heroic" poetry, would become wholly faithful to that doctrine, which Furetière and Charpentier espoused only superficially and in easy times.

Thus, in the years before and during the Fronde, in that "youth academy" whose unanimity of opinion still concealed the extreme diversity of talents and vocations, a common philosophy took shape having to do both with the tradition and vocation proper to a man of letters, and with the form most likely to give them influence in the language of the realm. Within the framework of that philosophy, the destiny of Paul Pellisson can be glimpsed in the making: he would become Foucquet's main collaborator; he believed he had found in Foucquet the ideal Maecenas of belles lettres and the best Mentor for the king. In his post as "chief assistant" to the *surintendant*, he attracted Maucroix, who was given a mission to Rome, and La Fontaine, who became poet laureate. After 1661 the paths of the three provincials diverged: Pellisson, without ever forgetting Foucquet, served Louis XIV and abjured the Calvinist religion in 1668. Who can plumb the ulterior motives of that permanent adviser to princes? The two childhood friends, on the contrary, after their brief time with Foucquet, embraced the other possible course of conduct for a man of letters in difficult times: ironic freedom in Paris for La Fontaine; obscurity and the independence of a canonicate in the provinces for Maucroix.

The "Years of Obscurity" of a Born Poet

The Academy of the Round Table was the primary nurturing environment for La Fontaine's genius in his youthful "years of obscurity," between Paris and Château-Thierry. And yet, he seems to have played only a bit part in that "academy." The other "knights-errant" have left greater or lesser written traces of their participation at the Academy of the Round Table. They mention La Fontaine. We know little more about it than that. Tallemant, who devotes an exceptionally warm portrait to Maucroix in his *Historiettes*,[65] and who recounts the romantic misadventures of his friend with an emotion that is rare for him, gives La Fontaine barely a passing mention. He is "a boy of belles lettres" and he "writes verses." What verses? Apart from *L'eunuque*, published in 1654, and which corresponds perfectly to the "Attic" tastes that prevailed among the "knights-errant" as a result of Pellisson's influence, nothing remains. That silence is astonishing. The anecdotes reported by Tallemant have contributed a great deal to the legend of a somewhat bewildered poet, whose life was elsewhere, who was absentminded to the point of blatant and ridiculous eccentricity. A young *bonhomme*:

Once, when his father, master of the waters and forests of Château-Thierry in Champagne, was in Paris for a trial, he told his son: "Now, go take care of such-and-such, it's urgent." La Fontaine went out, and was no sooner away from the house than he forgot what his father had told him. He ran into some of his pals, who asked him if he had any business to tend to: "No," he told them, and he went to a show with them. Another time, on his way to Paris, he attached a large pouch of important papers to his saddle bow. The pouch was poorly secured and fell off: the [postal] agent came by, picked up the pouch, found La Fontaine, and asked him if he hadn't lost something. The boy looked all around: "No," he said, "I haven't lost anything."

"Here's a pouch I found," the other said.

"Oh! That's my pouch!" cried La Fontaine. "Everything I own is in it." He carried it in his arms all the way to his lodgings.[66]

Maucroix himself seems to confirm that portrait of the "distrait" in an epistle in verse, difficult to date, which is always quoted in truncated form. He sent it from Paris to his friend, who had suddenly returned to Château-Thierry without alerting the "knights-errant":

Epitre, va chanter injure,
Mais grosse injure, à ce parjure
Qui, par un étrange hourvari,
S'en est fui à Château-Thierry.
Que la belle fièvre quartaine
Vous sangle, sieur La Fontaine,
Qui si vite quittez ce lieu
Sans avoir daigné dire adieu . . .
Mais, Damoiselle Courtoisie,
N'en soyez pas si fort saisie,
La Fontaine est un bon garçon
Qui n'y a fait point tant de façon;
Il ne l'a point fait par malice:
Belle paresse est tout son vice,
Et peut-être quand il partit,
A peine était-il hors du lit.
Vraiment, la troupe fait un livre
Qui va bien vous apprendre à vivre
Et quand vous oirrez sa leçon,
Vous serez bien mauvais garçon.
. . . .
Mais Damoiselle Courtoisie
D'un tel départ s'est fort saisie,
Et s'en va dans Château-Thierry
Vous faire un beau Charivari.
Pour moi, lorsqu'elle vous accuse,
Tant que je puis, je vous excuse.
Mais elle repart aigrement:
Monsieur, c'est vivre en Allemand,
Et très mal entendre son monde,
Que de quitter la Table Ronde,
Sans dire aux nobles Chevaliers:
Adieu, braves aventuriers.
Mais Damoiselle Courtoisie,
N'en soyez pas si fort saisie.[67]

Go, epistle, and sing your insult,
A big fat insult to that cheat
Who, in a curious clamor,
Ran off to Château-Thierry.
May the great quartan fever
Get hold of you, Sir La Fontaine,
Who left this place so quickly
Without bothering to say good-bye . . .
But Mistress Courtesy,
Be not so taken aback,
La Fontaine is a good boy
Who didn't stand on ceremony;
He didn't do it out of malice:
Sweet laziness is his only vice,
And perhaps when he fled,
He'd only just got out of bed.
It's true, the troupe is writing a book
That will teach you how to live
And when you have heard its lesson,
You'll see what a bad boy you've been.
. . . .
But Mistress Courtesy
Of his departure was taken aback
And went off to Château-Thierry
To stir up quite a fuss.
But I, when she accuses you,
As far as I can, I excuse you.
But she leaves again bitterly:
Sir, you're acting like a German,
With little understanding of the world,
To leave the Round Table,
Without telling the noble knights
Farewell, brave adventurers,
But Mistress Courtesy,
Be not so taken aback.

La Fontaine's abrupt departure did not go unnoticed, then, and did not leave anyone "in the troupe" indifferent. Maucroix makes himself the advocate of his friend before the shocked "knights-errant." What is his main argument, which met with general assent? "Sweet laziness": in other words, the inner rhythms particular to the young poet, a rebel—in spite of himself as it were—against the conventions of the little society, and a fortiori against those of society in general. He comes and goes without warning, like a cat. He sleeps when he likes, like a cat. He is not impolite, he is bewildering and independent, even for his writer friends who pride themselves on their jealous independence. To so generously bestow language on animals, he must have preferred their silence for a long time.

The very form of this epistle by Maucroix, very different from the accustomed style of the "knights-errant" in the exchanges within their little society, reveals Maucroix's deepest feelings: it pastiches the fixed form of the medieval ballade, it abounds in archaisms and "Gothic" allegory, it is addressed to a minstrel in the language of a minstrel. What forces Maucroix and the briefly bewildered "troupe" to forgive La Fontaine is that he is recognized among the "knights" as the born poet, whereas they all know they are gifted, of course, but only as prose writers and versifiers. One can trust a saturnine nature and forgive everything of it; it must be allowed to set its own pace.

Maucroix, who was very popular among the "knights-errant," guaranteed that they would see his friend that way. His view was shared by Pellisson but left Tallemant skeptical. It is true, however, that La Fontaine must have submitted written exercises to the "academy of knights-errant" at one time or another; yet all trace of them has vanished, probably with the complicity of the faithful Maucroix. The reason for that auto-da-fé? We have only to read *Clymène,* written in 1658, when the poet was still working on his technique, his instrument, and his personal style. The melancholic Apollo of *Clymène* is a critic of poetry so harsh, a musician so intelligent and demanding, that he makes Boileau, the churlish regent of Parnassus, appear fundamentally easy to satisfy. Such a critic must have been ruthless toward the attempts of his own youth when, under the Regency, privately meditating and trying things out in a France still teeming with poets and happily contradictory literary pursuits, he sought to find his own voice.

Whatever absentmindedness the circle of the Round Table attributed to La Fontaine, there can be no doubt that he was very attentive. Through Maucroix, the possibly silent and certainly evasive La Fontaine immersed himself in the same views, asked himself the same questions, sought out the same experiences as his comrades. He was even Pellisson's best disciple. With more indifference, perhaps, in a backward sort of way, but with more detachment, he discovered Paris with his friends; he was, like them, initiated into a universe where several worlds intersected, and where the chord of the arts and the heart of the kingdom played together. In a more private manner than that of his "academy" brothers, who matured more quickly—too quickly—than he, he put his inner Arcadia—his readings, his emotions, and his language—to the test in that diverse Paris. Even as he accompanied the "knights-errant" in their shared adventures, he gradually metamorphosed himself, better than any of them, not only into a Parisian, which several of them were by birth and habit, but into a poet of Paris, that is, a poet with a universal vocation. In the end, he was the one who most faithfully kept all the promises of the youth they shared. His genius was also a long-term patience.

Paris made him an "Attic" poet, even an Alexandrian poet. Very early on, the capital also taught him something he had the opportunity to put to the test during and after the Foucquet affair, namely, that the rigorous practice of poetry requires a political conscience higher than that deemed satisfactory by the ordinary literary and social ambition. Even after he had moved to Paris, La Fontaine did not miss the chance to return to Château-Thierry, where he had his inner "green world," and where he could rediscover the origins of his poetic vocation, which he himself said dated back to his childhood.

In *Stances*, which was read before the assembly of the "knights-errant" in 1650–51, during the Fronde, the faithful Maucroix gives a portrait of a "sensible melancholiac," which seems to be a portrait of his best friend's inner life at the time, a portrait of the Jean de La Fontaine whom Tallemant, with more absentmindedness than he believed he was attributing to the poet, would later describe from the outside:

> Heureux qui, sans souci d'augmenter son domaine,
>   Erre sans y penser où son désir le mène,
>   Loin des lieux fréquentés.
> Il marche par les champs, sur les vertes prairies,
> Et de si doux pensers nourrit ses rêveries
> Que pour lui les soleils sont toujours trop hâtés.
> Souvent, auprès d'un arbre, il se repose à l'ombre,
>   Et couché mollement sous son feuillage sombre,
>   Délivré de tout soin,
>   Il jouit des beautés dont son âme est parée,
>   Il admire les cieux, la campagne azurée,
>   Et son secret bonheur n'a que lui pour témoin.
> Il se remet aux Grands des soins du Ministère,
>   Et laisse au Parlement à se plaindre ou se taire,
>   De nos malheurs divers,

Son coeur est à l'abri des tempêtes civiles
Et ne s'alarme point, quand pour piller nos villes,
D'escadrons ennemis il voit nos champs couverts.
Il rit de ces prudents qui par trop de sagesse,
S'en vont dans l'avenir chercher de la tristesse
   Et des soucis cuisants,
Le futur incertain jamais ne l'inquiète,
Et son esprit constant, toujours en même assiette,
Ne peut être ébranlé, même des maux présents.
Cependant vers la fin s'envolent ses années,
   Mais il attend sans peur, des fières Destinées
     Le funèbre décret:
Et quand l'heure est venue, et que la mort l'appelle,
Sans vouloir reculer et sans se plaindre d'elle,
Voyant qu'il faut partir, il s'en va sans regret.[68]

With no concern to expand his domain, blessed is he who
   Roams without thinking where his desire takes him,
     Far from inhabited places.
He walks through the fields and over green prairies,
And such sweet thoughts feed his daydreams
That always the suns rush too quickly by him.
Often, by a tree, he rests in the shade,
   And lying lethargic under its dark leaves,
     Delivered from every care,
   He savors the beauties that embellish his soul,
   He admires the skies, the blue-tinged countryside,
   And is his sole witness to his secret happiness.
He leaves to great men the cares of the ministry,
   And lets the Parlement complain or be still
     About our various ills,
His heart is sheltered from civil storms
And is not alarmed, when, to pillage our cities,
He sees our fields covered with enemy squadrons.
He laughs at the cautious who, from too much wisdom,
Look to the future to seek out sadness
     And burning concerns,
The uncertain future never bothers him,
And his steady mind, always on even keel,
Cannot be shaken, even by present ills.

And yet toward their end his years fly away
  But he awaits without fear, from proud Destiny
    The fatal decree:
When the hour is come, and death calls to him,
With no desire to shirk and no complaint to make,
Seeing he must leave, he leaves without regret.

This poetic attitude toward politics, if not this "sweet laziness," is akin to that of Nicolas Poussin, a voluntary exile to Rome during the Fronde, but one who was very attentive to the French political drama. While working on *Le ravissement de Saint Paul* and *Le paysage avec Pyrame et Thisbé*, the painter wrote to Chantelou:

> We are here, God knows how. Yet it is a great pleasure to live in a century where so many great things are happening, provided one can find cover in some little corner and be able to watch the comedy in comfort. . . .
> The future we consider the least is more to be feared than the present. But let those most affected by it consider it, let us escape if we can and hide under the sheepskin, let us avoid the bleeding hands of the rabid and furious Cyclops.[69]

CHAPTER 3

Friendship and Fear

I am guilty of making myself beloved.
> —Blaise Pascal

I want to reign by fear.
> —Louis XIV

On the Parnassus of Vaux

"*T*he whole court went to Vaux, and M. Foucquet combined the magnificence of his home with everything imaginable regarding the beauty of the entertainment and the grandeur of the reception. . . . The festival was the most perfect there ever was."[1]

Probably written in the 1670s, the above lines from Mme de La Fayette's *Histoire de Madame Henriette d'Angleterre* are unkind toward the festivals Louis XIV had given at Versailles in 1664 and 1668, to efface the memory of 17 August 1661. Never before had the conditions of grace (the *poïkilia*, or precious variegation, of the ancient Greeks) been so fully brought together as they were that night at the festival of Vaux. The spectacle was all the more marvelous in retrospect, given that it became unrepeatable after the sudden disaster that befell its magician. La Fontaine was one of the spectators most moved by this masterpiece produced by his own generation of artists and poets, offered to Louis XIV the way Ronsard had offered his odes to Henry II, as gages of the alliance between the king and the "science of the Muses," tutelary powers of "that happy reign so fortunate, / Under which happy destiny / Had sung lo many a year / That a prince so great would come."[2]

At dawn on 17 August, La Fontaine sought to share with his friend Maucroix, in Rome at the time, the enchantment that the complete success of that magical night had infused in him, a night when all the talents of the Foucquet academy, the most distinguished to have been assembled in France since the remote times of the Valois, had conspired together. Even in 1678, in the first line of *La princesse de Clèves*, Mme de La Fayette remained unforgiving toward the pomp of Louis XIV's court: "Never had magnificence and gallantry appeared with such splendor as in the last years of the reign of Henry the Second."

That judgment, in both what it says and what it does not say, falls like the blade of a guillotine.

In his letter to Maucroix, La Fontaine celebrates the banquet prepared by Vatel and the comedy *Les fâcheux* performed by Molière and his troupe. His enthusiasm leads him to abandon prose as he describes the fireworks that preceded the ball:

> Je voudrais bien t'écrire en vers
> Tous les artifices divers
> De ce feu le plus beau du monde,
> Et son combat avecque l'onde,
> Et le plaisir des assistants.
> Figure-toi qu'en même temps
> On vit partir mille fusées,
> Qui par des routes embrasées
> Se firent toutes dans les airs
> Un chemin tout remplie d'éclairs,
> Chassant la nuit, brisant ses voiles.
> As-tu vu tomber des étoiles?
> Tel est le sillon enflammé,
> Ou le trait qui lors est formé.

> . . . Adieu. Charge ta mémoire de toutes les belles choses que tu verras au lieu où tu es.

> *(Relation à M. de Maucroix)*

> Allow me, then, to write in verse
> Of all the fireworks diverse,
> The most beautiful ever seen,
> Battling with the water's gleam,
> And feel the pleasure of the crowd.
> Imagine too the sound

Of a thousand rockets taking flight,
Blazing trails in the night,
Lightning flashes in the air,
Artifice beyond compare,
Ripping the veils off the dark.
Have you ever seen shooting stars?
Such is the glowing streak
Left behind in their wake.

. . . Farewell. May your mind be filled with all the beautiful things you will see where you are.

A few weeks later, on 7 September, the poet learned of Foucquet's arrest in Nantes. The *surintendant* was charged with high treason and faced the death penalty. La Fontaine, just before falling ill, wrote to Maucroix:

He has been arrested, and the king is violently opposed to him, even saying he has documents in his hands that will hang him. Oh, if he does that, he will be even crueler than his enemies, since, unlike them, it is not in his interest to be unjust. Mme de B. [Mme de Bruce, marquise du Plessis-Bellière] received a letter in which she was informed that M. Pellisson is also being harassed: if that is the case, then the misfortune is all the greater. Farewell, my dear friend: I would tell you much more if my mind were at peace at present. But I will make up for today next time. (*Lettre à M. de Maucroix,* 10 September 1661)

La Fontaine's euphoria in his description of the festival of Vaux sprang from the same source of joyful love for the king and the kingdom that, the previous year, had led the young Racine, La Fontaine's friend and distant relation, to write *Ode de la Nymphe de la Seine à la reine,* in honor of the wedding of Louis XIV and the infanta of Spain:

Que le repos est doux après de longs travaux!
Qu'on aime le plaisir après beaucoup de maux!
Qu'après un long hiver le printemps a de charmes! . . .
   J'avais perdu toute espérance
   Tant chacun croyait malaisé
     Que jamais le ciel apaisé
   Dût rendre le calme à la France.[3]

How sweet is repose after long labors!
How lovely pleasure after many ills!
How, after a long winter, springtime has its charms! . . .
   I had lost every hope, so hard
Was it for all to believe
    That heaven, appeased,
Should ever return calm to France.

Following Foucquet's arrest, Saint-Evremond was forced into permanent exile from France, first in Holland and then in England, and his friends were constantly attacked or threatened. La Rochefoucauld and Mme de Sévigné had reason to be afraid. Mme du Plessis-Bellière was arrested, Pellisson thrown into the Conciergerie. Gourville, at first hidden in the La Rochefoucaulds' château in Angoulême, eventually had to flee abroad. Searches, often without a warrant, rained down on all the homes where La Fontaine had been received and entertained: Vaux and Saint-Mandé, the château of Mme du Plessis-Bellière in Charenton, the château of the Du Plessis-Guénégauds in Fresnes, their mansion of Nevers in Paris, which was the sparkling successor to the Rambouillet mansion, and the meeting place for everyone who mattered in the world of society and culture in Paris.[4] Even Racine, who, on the heels of La Fontaine, had probably made only a few cautious steps toward being sponsored by Foucquet and Pellisson, wrote his friend that his stay in Uzès (where he was reduced to currying the favor of an old uncle who was a canon) was not untouched by the coup d'état of September 1661. He seems to have divided time into a "before" and an "after":

Avant qu'une fièvre importune
Nous fît courir même fortune
Et nous mît chacun en danger
De ne plus jamais voyager.

Before an importunate fever
Made us brave even fortune
And put us in danger, every one,
Of never traveling again.

Two years later, La Fontaine accompanied his uncle Jacques Jannart to his exile in Limoges. He was not actually being harassed, but he found himself sullied by the disgrace that surrounded everything closely related to Foucquet.[5] Since 1659 he had been publicly known as the *surintendant*'s poet laureate. Had Foucquet become prime minister, he would have been the royal poet. Of his two best friends, Pellisson and Maucroix, the first had been Foucquet's "chief assistant" since 1657, and the second had become his diplomatic agent in Rome. Of his former brothers at the Round Table, Tallemant des Réaux, along with his family of bankers, moved in the Parisian circles of the *surintendant*'s "clients"; and Antoine Rambouillet, with Marguerite Hessein, his wife since 1654, shone not only at the mansion of his father, Nicolas, one of the backers of Foucquet's financial policy, but also in the Parisian salons enamored with the *surintendant*. Although the Academy of the Round Table had not reconstituted itself around Louis XIV's minister of finances, several of its members, including some of the most important, had joined the academy of poets, scholars, and artists with whom Foucquet surrounded himself, and to which Pellisson had attracted the most promising talents of the younger generation. That academy would find a new master in 1661.

In the vast open conspiracy to have Foucquet succeed Mazarin, Pellisson played a central and determining role beginning in 1657. The *surintendant*'s confidant and collaborator in political and financial affairs, he also helped him perfect his role as a Maecenas, suggesting to him the timely and elegant generosity that earned him the favor of men of letters, scholars, and artists. Swelling the ranks of Foucquet's academy were Scarron, the lame prince of the burlesque; his young wife, Françoise d'Aubigné; the two Corneille brothers, Pierre and Thomas; their noble Norman friend Brébeuf (who died of a stroke after Foucquet's arrest); the philosophers La Mothe Le Vayer and Sorbière; and doctors and musicians. Pellisson, who was well versed in the Paris of arts and letters, brought them in.

How could the Mentor of the years of obscurity have forgotten his Telemachus? La Fontaine had first been introduced to Pellisson's good friend Madeleine de Scudéry, who hosted a brilliant salon in her modest apartment in the Marais every Saturday, and who, after 1657, became the most ardent of the *surintendant*'s publicists.[6] When Pellisson "gave" himself to Foucquet, one of his first concerns was to introduce La Fontaine to the *surintendant* and his beautiful lady friends, who immediately adopted him.

The privileged relationship that, for more than fifteen years (since 1645), had brought Pellisson, La Fontaine, and Maucroix together at the Academy of the Round Table, became a close collaboration in the Foucquet academy's "inner circle." This time, the gifted but "lazy" poet was to keep his promises. And the directives came to him from his friend, who knew Foucquet and how to please him. If we compare the *Remerciement*, which Pellisson sent to Foucquet in 1656, with the dedication to the *surintendant* that La Fontaine placed at the beginning of his *Adonis* two years later, it becomes very clear that, though the style may differ, the design is the same. The two friends were working in concert, with one, as usual, leading the other. Approved as poet laureate on Pellisson's nomination, La Fontaine finally displayed the delicate colors he was capable of, but after drawings proposed by his Mentor.

These, however, were not of a nature to burden a poet passionate about freedom and privacy. Pellisson was a kindred soul, a second self. Foucquet did not have the capricious indifference of princes, or the prudish pedantry of magistrates, or the humiliating, because undiscriminating, goodwill of parvenus: he admired friendship and loyalty; he was liberal minded, well read—an artist. On the advice of Pellisson, who knew his friend, the powerful patron graciously bowed to a novelistic fiction to overcome La Fontaine's reservations: La Fontaine would be under an obligation to pay his benefactor a "poetic pension" on a regular basis, four times a year.[7]

An atmosphere of good cheer and charm reigned around Pellisson, Foucquet, and the gallant *surintendant*'s lady friends, themselves the disciples of the marquise de Rambouillet; as in the "Blue Room," that atmosphere trifled with social conventions and added a virtual grace to human relationships, despite the actual inequalities. The origins of that grace were obvious: they were poetry, the novel, belles lettres. The Foucquet academy grafted itself onto the most brilliant Paris salons—won over by Foucquet—which themselves lived in a kind of symbiotic state. His poet laureate was their beneficiary. The *surintendant*'s and the court's "affairs," like the court itself—now reduced to the circle of the young king and that of the queen mother—were not involved in Parisian high society, which was somewhat avenging Arthénice: under Louis XIII, the mansion of the marquise de Rambouillet on rue Saint-Thomas-du-Louvre had been a refuge and a relaxation for titled men and women of wit, who fled the melancholic sovereign, the terrible Richelieu, and his state secretaries as soon as they were able.[8] Relaxation was triumphant in several locales in Paris and in the châteaux of the surrounding regions, federated around Foucquet and his young second wife, Madeleine Jeannin de Castille, the "Sylvie" of La Fontaine's *Le songe de Vaux*.[9]

Like Voiture's occasional poetry, that leisurely sociability, enjoying a delightfully amphibious life between fiction and reality, rested on the contract Coleridge later identified as at the root of all literature: the voluntary suspension of disbelief, the act of faith that makes what might be, but what *is* not altogether, take on a bit more reality. In essence, civilization is an art of living in literature: that is why a novelist such as Mlle de Scudéry, and a poet such as La Fontaine, considered a new Voiture by Foucquet's Paris, were the trouvères of that archipelago of urbanity and gallantry, all the more at home in the Parisian landscape in that they harked back not only to Anacreon's Greece but also to the very ancient utopia of the kingdom of *France la doulce.*

With Foucquet, Pellisson, and the ladies heir to Arthénice, La Fontaine, who had not known the golden age of the marquise's salon, now bowed to the game expected of him. The private life of salons, châteaux, and grounds, utterly permeated by femininity, readings, music, and love, was, in the aftermath of the Fronde, more than ever Arcadia in Paris. But it was also Parnassus.

During 1657 a delighted Foucquet showed his friend the marquise de Sévigné La Fontaine's *Lettre à l'abbesse de Mouzon,* a short poem whose flowing rhythm and "pretty" mood of desire and prudence, gallantry and sweet blasphemy, rivaled the sharpest and most iridescent things Voiture had produced in the genre for the Hôtel de Rambouillet public. This verse, which narrates the taking of vows by a Benedictine abbess, would have been impious had it not been presented as a literary game, where every facet of sexual desire, grappling with fear and shame at the sight of a beautiful woman taking the veil, glimmers and gleams:

Ce même jour, pour le certain,
Amour se fit bénédictin;
Et, sans trop faire la mutine,
Vénus se fit bénédictine;
Les Ris, ne bougeant d'avec vous,
Bénédictins se firent tous;
Et les Grâces, qui vous suivirent,
Bénédictines se rendirent:
Tous les dieux qu'en Chypre on connaît
Prirent l'habit de Saint Benoît.
            (ll. 69–78)

That same day, in fair exchange,
Cupid became a Benedictine;
And, hardly raising any fuss,

A Benedictine too was Venus;
And Mirth, not budging from your side,
Vowed also to be Benedictine;
And the Graces, following you,
Benedictines became too:
All the gods who in Greece are worshiped,
Took the habit of Saint Benedict.

An enchanted Mme de Sévigné sang the poet's praises everywhere, and he thanked her with a dizain, paid to Foucquet as part of his "pension":

De Sévigné, depuis deux jours en çà,
Ma lettre tient les trois parts de sa gloire.
   Elle lui plut; et cela se passa
Phébus tenant chez vous son consistoire.
         (*Pour Madame de Sévigné*)

To Sévigné, for the last two days,
My letter owes three-quarters of its fame.
   It pleased her; and this occurred
As Phoebus held his consistory with you.

The great hopes that sustained La Fontaine and his friends in 1654–65, in their ascent to Parnassus, were fulfilled. Phoebus and the Muses crowned the poet. His poetry found the proper balance of humor and seductiveness to reflect high society, in various ways, but also to give it courage and guide it, and even, through Foucquet's approbation, to return the kingdom to its natural state of love and generosity. Fortune could change. Like Socrates in *The Symposium* and *Phaedo*, La Fontaine never ceased to believe in the divine power of fables to awaken a sense of what had been lost.

ALEXANDRIA IN PARIS: *ADONIS*

In this atmosphere of trust and good feeling, Pellisson had the chance to finally get the emboldened poet to show what he was and what he knew how to do. He might have easily become another Voiture, and the terms of the poetic pension, though he was sometimes in arrears, quickly established that high-society reputation. But Pellisson wanted and expected something more. He cleared the way for the idyll *Adonis* and the ambitious *Le songe de Vaux*, which ought to have made La Fontaine what Ronsard often was for the last of the Valois and what Giambattista Marino was briefly for Marie de Médicis and the young Louis XIII: the lyric poet writing encomiums to the kingdom, the poet of peace and of the pleasures of private life—the anti-Malherbe.

In his *Remerciement* (1656) to Foucquet, which helped him to get a position in the *surintendant*'s service, Pellisson wonders how to praise a Maecenas too enlightened to tolerate ordinary panegyrics, and who had declared that, like the Renaissance princes, he preferred poetry to prose.[10] Pellisson, instead of responding personally, sets in place an ingenious allegorical fiction. He has a dream, during which Apollo, the god of poetry, appears to him and converses with him. The god assures the dreamer that Foucquet's virtues ("wondrous skill, calm nobility of spirit and equanimity, great and immortal actions," which have saved the state several times) are crowned by an abhorrence of flattery. To thank him, the indirect and mysterious language of poetry is more fitting than prose. In a superb purple passage, inspired by the "descent into Hell" of classical epics, Pellisson attributes to Apollo an evocation of the kingdom of Mnemosyne, mother of the Muses, where poets go to find their creations. There, the universals of the imagination—myths, fables, allegories, prosopopoeia, and fictive prophesies—await the judicious choice of the poet desired by Foucquet, in a theater of memory built by skillful Architecture and decorated by the Fine Arts. It is from this store of fictions, come down to us from time immemorial and detached from immediacy, that he must draw, if he wishes to compose "sincere thanks" for the *surintendant*.

The plan is set out for Foucquet's poet. The generating principle of the allegories in *Le songe de Vaux*, the "heroic" and mythological style of *Adonis*, were already suggested to La Fontaine by Pellisson. Among the desirable poetic forms for praising the *surintendant*, the Aesopian fable (which Pellisson defines as a "prosopopoeia that bestows language on plants and animals") has its assigned place. Pellisson himself very quickly devoted himself to business prose. It fell to the "lazy" La Fontaine, the born poet of the "knights-errant," to find in Mnemosyne the forms befitting a Maecenas as unique and superior as Foucquet.

Even before the "poetic pension" contract was signed with the *surintendant*, La Fontaine, guided by Pellisson, offered him the idyll *Adonis* in 1658. It was his first long poem since *L'eunuque*.[11] The intrigues and death of Adonis had inspired the "epic idyll," dedicated in 1623 to Louis XIII, by the Italian poet Giambattista Marino. The same subject was treated by La Fontaine in a lyric French style that had been very much in favor in the minor princely courts that opposed Richelieu. In 1623 Saint-Amant dedicated such a poem—*Arion*—to the duc de Montmorency. It begins as follows:

> Invincible héros, mon unique Mécène,
> Reçois ces nouveaux fruits qui naissent de ma veine.[12]

> Invincible hero, my only Maecenas,
> Receive these new fruits born of my vein.

In 1641 Gaston d'Orléans's poet, Tristan L'Hermite, disappointed by his princely patron, dedicated his *Orphée*, which belongs to the same genre, to the musician Berthod.[13]

La Fontaine's *Adonis* is not addressed to a prince of the sword, nor to a simple, though great, musician, but to the new, refined Maecenas, who proposed to bring back to France, and not merely to a small court, peace and the arts of peace. La Fontaine's *Adonis* aspires to be the poetic emblem of "Foucquet's taste," and of the society around the *surintendant*, which already prefigured what the kingdom would be under his governance.

The importance granted by Foucquet and Pellisson to *Adonis* can be measured by the luxuriousness of the poem's presentation. The sole copy of the manuscript, sumptuously bound, was entrusted to the king's calligrapher, Nicolas Jarry. It was decorated with a frontispiece by the king's miniaturist, Jacques Bailly, and with a painting in grisaille by François Chauveau, the regular illustrator of Mlle de Scudéry's novels and the future draftsman of the pictures engraved above the printed text of *Fables*. That gem would enrich the splendid, thirty-thousand volume library assembled by Foucquet at his château in Saint-Mandé. This was a solemn gesture. It elicited a response from Colbert. As soon as Foucquet disappeared into the trapdoor of Pignerol, and as if to efface the memory of *Adonis*, Charles Perrault ordered Jacques Bailly and Nicolas Jarry to produce the splendid manuscript of miniatures *Devises pour les tapisseries du roi*, whose verses he himself wrote, and the sole copy of which would be placed in the collections of the king's library, just as that of *Adonis* had been in Foucquet's.[14]

La Fontaine's 1658 dedication to Foucquet repeats and amplifies the praises of Apollo in Pellisson's 1656 *Remerciement*. It is a portrait of the new Maecenas of France, as his ardent supporters saw him:

> Your mind is gifted with such enlightenment, and shows a taste so exquisite and so refined for all our works, particularly for the fine art of celebrating, in the language of the gods, the men who resemble you, that few people would be capable of satisfying you. . . . Yes, when I say that the state cannot do without your attentions, and that the ministers of more than one reign have not acquired so consummate an experience as your own; when I say that you value our vigils, and that this is a mark by which great men have always been recognized; when I speak of the unparalleled generosity, the nobility of all your sentiments, of the modesty that charms us; finally, when I admit that your mind is infinitely elevated, and when, moreover, I also admit that your soul is even more so than your mind, these are truly a few of your traits, but not the great number of rare qualities that make you an object of admiration for all honorable people in France. And not only, your Lordship, do you attract their admiration, you even compel them, by gentle force, to love you. . . . As you well know, they look upon you as the hero destined to vanquish the callousness of our century and the contempt for all the fine arts. (*Adonis*, "A Monsieur Foucquet")

This was an extremely "sincere" thanks, as was proven by what followed. No less sincere was the dedication that Corneille placed the following year, 1659, at the beginning of the published version of his tragedy *Oedipe*, which marked his return after a long silence to the Parisian stage:

> Oui, généreux appui de tout notre Parnasse,
> Tu me rends ma vigueur, lorsque tu me fais grâce;
> Et je veux bien apprendre à tout notre avenir
> Que tes regard bénins ont su me rajeunir.
>   (ll. 25–28)

> J'ai déjà vu beaucoup: en ce moment heureux,
> Je t'ai vu magnanime, affable, généreux;

Et ce qu'on voit à peine après dix ans d'excuses,
Je t'ai vu tout d'un coup libéral pour les Muses.
    (Oedipe, "Vers présentés à Monseigneur
        le Procureur Général Foucquet,
    surintendant des finances," ll. 59–62)

Yes, generous supporter of our Parnassus,
You restore my vigor, when you show me favor;
And I want to inform all who come after me
That your kindly gaze has made me young again.

I have already seen a great deal: in this happy moment,
I have seen you magnanimous, affable, generous;
And something rarely seen after ten years of excuses,
I have seen you suddenly liberal toward the Muses.

The elderly poet, who had suffered under the imperious Richelieu and the miserly Mazarin, did not conceal this support for Foucquet's candidacy to the ministry:

Mais pour te voir entier, il faudrait un loisir
Que tes délassements daignassent me choisir:
C'est lors que je verrais la saine politique
Soutenir par tes soins la Fortune publique,
Ton zèle infatigable à servir ton Grand Roi,
Ta force et ta prudence à régir ton emploi;
C'est lors que je verrais ton courage intrépide
Unir la vigilance à la vertu solide;
Je verrais cet illustre et haut discernement
Qui te met au-dessus de tant d'accablement;
Et tout ce dont l'aspect d'un Astre salutaire,
Pour le bonheur des Lys t'a fait dépositaire.
           (Ibid., ll. 63–74)

But to see you in full, it would take leisure time,
Which your moments of repose deign choose for me:
It is then I would see a sane policy
Support public Fortune by virtue of your work,
Your indefatigable zeal to serve your great king,
Your strength and caution to manage your post;

It is then I would see your intrepid courage
Combine vigilance with solid virtue;
I would see the illustrious and lofty discernment
That places you above so much despondency;
And everything of which a salutary star
Has made you a depositary to the good fortune of France.

The older and younger generations were in agreement. For the first time since the Valois kings, a statesman dear to the hearts of men of letters was about to restore the proper direction to the monarchy—corrupted by Machiavelli—as Ronsard had defined it:

Toute royauté qui dédaigne
D'avoir la vertu pour compaigne
Et la loger en sa maison,
Toujours de l'heur outrecuidée
Court vague sans être guidée
Du frein qui pend à la raison.
        (First book of *Odes*, I,
    "Au roi Henri II," stanza 1)

Any monarchy that disdains
To have virtue as its lady,
And to lodge her in its home,
Ever insolent toward fortune,
Runs wild without the restraint
Of the bit attached by reason.

In 1642, to console the marquise de Rambouillet, Jean-Louis Guez de Balzac had been reduced to drawing the portrait of Maecenas, virtuous adviser to the prince and friend of the poets, in the past tense and the optative mode, now that Maecenas had finally appeared in France. Corneille and La Fontaine addressed Foucquet, even before Mazarin's death, as if Maecenas/Foucquet and Augustus/Louis XIV already formed a pair and were reigning over France.[15]

This was undoubtedly a dangerous illusion, which underestimated the young king's true character, still impenetrable and veiled under the appearance of his long docility toward Mazarin. But even more than an illusion, it was a wager: Foucquet's own high-stakes wager on the nature of the prince. Could the *surintendant* forget that Louis XIV, descendant of

Saint Louis, was also descended from Philip the Fair and Louis XI, Philip II and Cosimo de' Medici? The Cornellian Foucquet believed in rivalries of generosity, and he expected the king to defeat him in that arena. But he also knew very well that this young man was still an enigma. The French royal religion nonetheless made him accept the risk of erring nobly, rather than sinning through impious suspicion. Foucquet's anguish, and that of those around him, who had an eye out for the king's hostile maneuvers in their direction, and who were constructing backup plans in case of failure, show that they did not rule out the worst outcome. Foucquet, Frenchman of a very old France, was at least sure that he had assumed the best about his king.

The objurgation he addressed to the young Louis XIV, in the name of the royal office itself, for departing from Richelieu's legacy, however silent and indirect that objurgation may have been, was nonetheless irritating, and even verged on usurpation. Foucquet, embodying the "virtue" of the monarchy, even if only to serve it well, cast a dangerous shadow on the king. He was guilty of endearing himself to the French people, as if he himself, born to the civil status of a minor member of the legal profession, could prefigure an ideal Louis XIV, a new Louis XII, a new Francis I, a new Henry IV.

In fact, Foucquet was loved the way Gaston d'Orléans had been loved, the way the ideal king—the one who has not yet reigned—could be loved in France. First, he was loved by the common people. They remembered he was the son of Marie de Maupeou, whose zeal in charitable works was recognized by Saint Vincent de Paul himself, father of the poor. His best ally, Mme du Plessis-Bellière, was also as famous among the common people for her works of charity as she was in the social world for her business skill and the superior taste she displayed in her various homes. Behind Foucquet, in the remote regions of France, lay a vast system of charitable support, built by the Compagnie du Saint-Sacrement and the large religious orders: Foucquet's financial skill played a role in nurturing it. There was a "social Christianity" in Foucquet, as there would be in Fénelon. Since that tended to make him popular, it did not garner him Louis XIV's good feelings. The battle (supported by Molière's *Tartuffe*) against "the religious cabal" in 1661–68 was the corollary of Foucquet's disgrace.[16]

For high society, which had suffered through the civil war and the war in Europe, Foucquet was just as beloved, though for different reasons. There was something miraculous about his surprising personality, which reconciled opposites. A magistrate, he knew how to be a great financier, a great politician, and a great lord, in ways that financiers, politicians, and lords by birth and occupation did not know how to be. He was ingenious and direct, modest and sure of his talents. Gifted for the finer things of the intellect, he was handsome, elegant, and very gallant, admired by men and adored by women.

After more than thirty years of cardinal-ministers hiding behind their capes and purple robes, this virtuoso "prince," who had appeared out of nowhere, had all the political and poetic "wonder" that Corneille attributed to his Nicomedes: the Apollo capable of defeating the Machiavellian Pythons, the great lover capable of the most surprising exploits, astonishing the ladies and saving kingdoms. In his very person, Foucquet, a literary statesman (the young Bonaparte would be one as well), crystallized all the hopes that the literature opposing the cardinals had fed. To top it all off, unlike a blood prince— Gaston d'Orléans, for example—he could not allow himself to be a political eccentric concealed behind a legend. Trained by the Parisian Jesuits, he had kept the best part of his teachers' humanism. The Society of Jesus was persuaded that, in order for the religion of love to be incarnated in human history, it had to seek and find allies everywhere that the natural genius of men had, unbeknownst to itself, already sought out and postulated it. From this missionary program, Foucquet had retained, in political matters, the obligation and method of synthesis, for which he was exceptionally gifted. From his mother, unanimously considered a "saint," Foucquet had the sweetness of a Francis of Sales and a Jeanne of Chantal, which corrected his dry Jesuitism and was endearing to Port-Royal. From his father, a cultivated magistrate and collector, he held the view of the French legal profession that the practice of law was inseparable from liberal high culture. From his own experience, he was trusted by the Huguenots and he sympathized with men of wit, even and especially libertines. The Christian Republic, like the republic of French letters, had hopes that Foucquet, as prime minister to the king of France, would govern at their center.[17] Paul Morand has portrayed him as a seventeenth-century Philippe Berthelot, a Maecenas who ought himself to have been Augustus.[18] But, too early on, that candidacy for the monarchy's government took on the appearance of a plebiscite in the eyes of a king who had all the trump cards up his sleeve. In France, Cicero's and Foucquet's fate seems to await the excellent politicians who claim to govern with the general approval of *all* good people, something Cicero called *consensus bonorum*. The young Bonaparte dared stage the coup d'état of 18 Brumaire. Foucquet endured that of 5 September 1661.

The Huguenot Pellisson seemed well suited to back a project that appeared to rise up from the remote regions of a kingdom weary of being conquered and divided. A great reader of Cicero, a great man of letters, the magistrate Pellisson recognized the *surintendant* as the hero capable of embodying his own liberal philosophy. With the support of his poet and artist friends, he was himself able to put another unifying principle on Foucquet's side: an idea of French beauty, style, and taste. He had given a great deal of thought to them since 1645. He was the theorist of French Atticism, or rather Alexandrianism, which, by eliminating all extremes of taste, could provide a poetic and musical key to the power of synthesis in the hoped-for regime.

In many respects, La Fontaine's *Adonis*, the only copy of which was placed in Foucquet's library, aspired to be the prelude to the harmonies of a century that was finally going to make France the kingdom of "grace even more beautiful than beauty."

The verse section of *Adonis*, itself preceded by a prose dedication, begins with an invocation to Foucquet: the essence of the poem and its meaning are joined to the person and destiny of the *surintendant*. The subject, a Greek myth, is treated in a brief epic form, the *epyllion* of Alexandrian poets. The advice of the Hellenist Pellisson can be discerned in this choice, and the selection of subject was a matter neither of chance nor of caprice. In France this myth of love and death had been linked since 1623 to the allegorical meaning the Italian poet Giambattista Marino had given it in his last poem, *Adone*, published in Paris and written for Marie de Médicis and Louis XIII.[19] Jean Chapelain, future critic of *Le Cid*, future compiler of the list of Colbert's pensioned writers, had given a long exegesis of Marino's epic in a preface written in French. Before leaving Paris for Rome, the Italian poet, in the language of myth, invited France, its king, and its nobility of the sword to convert to the arts of peace. Marino's *Adone*, a dazzling display of variations on Horace's *carpe diem*, evokes one by one Cythera's pleasures, the island of Venus where a Parnassus is being built, and the death of Adonis, loved by the goddess, who reveals to the Immortal the fleeting nature, but also the heart-breaking beauty, of happiness that, among mortals, does not return twice. In 1623, just before Richelieu joined the king's council, *Adone* invited Louis XIII and his mother finally to practice, in the uncivilized Frankish kingdom, the Epicureanism of Maecenas that had served Augustus's rule so well. After thirty years of a regime of exception, of wars and poverty, La Fontaine's new version of his myth in 1658, dedicated to Nicolas Foucquet, assumed an obvious political meaning for anyone with a sharp ear.

But the French poem owes nothing to the richly ornate form of the long Italian poem. In the purified language of Malherbe, Voiture, and

Tristan, but enhanced by the flowing melodies of the Regency's Parisian lutenists and singers, La Fontaine's *Adonis* offered the new Maecenas a cantata in which he was able to recognize both his own political magic and the store of terrible anguish that it wanted to ward off. Far from a flattering poem, *Adonis* is an enchanted but premonitory mirror. Nothing like a born poet—an inspired and hence dangerous poet—for mysteriously seeing and showing still-hidden truths.

In La Fontaine's flowing alexandrines, the specters of the sleeping Adonis and Venus—whose senses will soon be on fire—whom the handsome shepherd, upon awakening, first sees in the water's reflection, seem to bring back to life ancient marble bas-reliefs, but relieved of their great weight: sensible, but almost ineffable forms. For his first known lyric work, the poet showed an extraordinary mastery, not only of the music of the French language and French verse, but also of the power of emotional synthesis unknown until that time, and which, before Chénier, would be found again only in Racine. In La Fontaine's neo-Greek allusions, which owe as much to *Theagenes and Chariclea* as to Ovid and Virgil, the cosmic fervor of Lucretius and the modern languor and tenderness of Tristan L'Hermite and d'Urfé are made to vibrate in concert. In the modulations of the great aria *Adonis*, we seem to hear both Fénelon's Calypso longing song and the palpitations of Mme Guyon's *Torrents*:

> Tout ce qui naît de doux en l'amoureux empire,
> Quand d'une égale ardeur l'un pour l'autre on soupire,
> Et que, dans la contrainte ayant banni les lois,
> On se peut assurer au silence des bois,
> Jours devenus moments, moments filés de soie,
> Agréables soupirs, pleurs enfants de la joie,
> Voeux, serments et regards, transports, ravissements,
> Mélange dont se fait le bonheur des amants,
> Tout par ce couple heureux fut lors mis en usage.
>
> (ll. 127–35)

> All things sweet arising in the empire of love,
> When with equal ardor one for the other one sighs,
> And where, within the constraint of a lawless realm,
> One can be secure in the silence of the wood,
> Days turned into moments, moments spun from silk,
> Agreeable sighs, tears like children born of joy,
> Hopes, vows, and gazes, rapture, transport,

Combining to make the happiness of lovers,
All these things, with our happy couple, became the norm.

This marriage between an extraordinarily shameless autobiographical
confession and a phenomenally poetic, artistic, and literary tradition became a voluptuousness of language, reflected in a voluptuous myth, which
itself reflected the poet's personal experience transfigured by memory.
With *Adonis*, La Fontaine offered Foucquet, as a token of the alliance between poet and patron, the amethyst cameo ring that the priest Calisiris,
in Heliodorus's *Aethiopica*, offered in ransom for his adopted daughter, the
beautiful Charicleia, a sparkling magnet that encapsulated the joint powers of love and poetic language.[20]

The poem has another side, as raucous and dark as the first is melodious
and luminous. It is the narrative of the hunt during which Adonis, in
Venus's absence and to ward off his pain, flushes out a wild boar. A whiff of
the violence of medieval venery, in the deep of the forest, accompanies
the pack of bloodhounds and hunters. It is a modern French version of the
hunts in Euripides' *Hippolytus* and Ovid's *Actaeon*. It was bold and revealing to attribute to a shepherd, in a poem dedicated to Foucquet, who had
only just become a marquis, the type of hunt that had been reserved for
the king of France since the early Middle Ages, and which no other
European king engaged in. During the kill, Adonis falls victim to the wild
beast, which he nonetheless manages to strike dead. La Fontaine attributes a hero's valor to the handsome shepherd. He even compares him, in
his struggle against the boar, to the patron god of Cadmus:

> Tel Apollon marchait quand l'énorme Python
> L'obligea de quitter l'ombre de l'Hélicon.
> (ll. 313–14)

> So did Apollo walk when the enormous Python
> Obliged him to leave the shadow of Helicon.

The death of Adonis is also the defeat of Apollo. A crepuscular presentiment, in that idyll and the comedy *Clymène*, written about the same
time, set La Fontaine apart from the official euphoria prevailing around
Foucquet.

The poem ends with the lamento of the goddess, who is as eloquent as
Niobe or Dido:

Mon amour n'a donc pu te faire aimer la vie!
Tu me quittes, cruel! Au moins ouvre les yeux,
Montre-toi plus sensible à mes tristes adieux;
Vois de quelles douleurs ton amante est atteinte!
Hélas! j'ai beau crier: il est sourd à ma plainte.
Une éternelle nuit l'oblige à me quitter;
Mes pleurs ni mes soupirs ne peuvent l'arrêter.
Encor si je pouvais le suivre en ces lieux sombres!
Que ne m'est-il permis d'errer parmi les ombres!
Destins, si vous vouliez le voir si tôt périr,
Fallait-il m'obliger à ne jamais mourir?

(ll. 563–73)

My love, then, has not made you love this life!
You're leaving me, cruel one! At least open your eyes,
Be more sensitive to my sad farewells;
See the sorrows that afflict your lover!
Alas! I cry out in vain: he is deaf to my pleas.
A night without end obliges him to leave me;
My tears and my sighs cannot keep him here.
If only I could follow him to that dark place!
Why am I not allowed to wander among shadows!
Destiny, if you wished to see him perish so soon,
Did you have to require that I should never die?

Well before Racine's *Phèdre*,[21] *Adonis* was one of the two boldest attempts in seventeenth-century France to recapture, in its own language, the strangeness of the Greek myth: beauty and savagery, carnal pleasure and violence, gods, beasts, and men attacking one another, with the same rage to escape their condition or to defend it. The insertion *en abyme* of the violent episode of the hunt (which Paul Valéry would have chosen to leave out) between two other neo-Greek visions—happiness and grief—provides the key for that attempt to reforge the alliance between French royal art and Greek lyric sentiment. This private poem, reserved for Foucquet's exclusive use, is also the mirror of the subterranean emotions underlying and haunting the *surintendant* in his progress toward the center of royal power. It gives his political adventure a Shakespearean pathos. Shakespeare himself wrote and published a sumptuous *Venus and Adonis*. A rare folio of his works appeared in the collections of the Saint-Mandé library.[22]

Two-Headed Friendship: *Le songe de Vaux*

Pellisson was not satisfied with this esoteric masterpiece, reserved for the minister's personal enjoyment, or with the delicious occasional bagatelles required by the "poetic pension." Happy to have "discovered" an original poet, and one who dedicated all the first fruits of his genius to him, Foucquet approved Pellisson's suggestion to commission a long allegorical poem from La Fontaine, written to the glory of Vaux-le-Vicomte and its gardens.

In 1659 construction was well under way. Pellisson had asked André Félibien, a friend of Conrart who had recently returned from a long stay in Rome where he had been on intimate terms with Nicolas Poussin, to write a description in prose (parts of it have not been published until recently) of the wonders of the château and its gardens. But it fell to La Fontaine to reveal its true meaning, in the mysterious language of poets preferred by Foucquet. He would be the Ronsard of this modern Fontaine-bleau. After the festival, the *surintendant,* keys in hand, proposed to offer Vaux to the king, along with its mirror image, *Le songe de Vaux,* as a sign of submission, love, and alliance.[23] It was important that the poetic mirror of the gift that was to seal the union of Augustus and Maecenas, called upon jointly to bring back Astraea to reign over France, should make Vaux shine with all its fire and all its concealed intentions. In the prefatory note to the fragments he published in 1671, La Fontaine summed up the plot of the poem as a whole:[24] the dream was to begin like a novel, with the discovery, in Vaux, of an extraordinary "diamond," carved in the shape of a heart and accompanied by the motto: "I am constant, though I love two," in a jewel case decorated with the king's portrait. This mysterious token of friendship (in the extraordinary sense that this virtue assumed among Foucquet's entourage) gives significance to the entire correspondence of the different arts displayed at Vaux. Louis XIV, who had not got his education through novels, and who saw friendship as a Fronde-like rival to service of the state, could hardly have appreciated that ingenious enigma: he despised the alliance Foucquet was urging him to join.

To conceive and execute Foucquet's gift to the king, Pellisson had assembled a new academy of Fontainebleau: this time, the Italians—theater set designers, water engineers, or fireworks manufacturers—played only a minor role. The architect Le Vau, the painter Le Brun, the sculptors Anguier and Puget, the landscape gardener Le Nôtre, the master vegetable gardener La Quintinie, and even, off in Rome, Nicolas Poussin, from whom one of Foucquet's brothers, the ecclesiastic Louis, had obtained a design for a series of classical-style termini, were to make Vaux the first manifesto of a France reconciled with itself, and finally the perfect mother and mistress of its own arts. Vaux, far from being an end in itself, was supposed to offer Louis XIV the model for what royal art would be under his reign, if Foucquet were to be approved.[25]

The king perfectly understood this other message. But he preferred to execute the design himself, by annexing all Foucquet's collaborators to the Crown. He had gotten a good view of Foucquet's talent, but also of the tutelage that such a talent would impose on him, just as his father had suffered Richelieu's tutelage and his mother, Mazarin's. To follow Foucquet without Foucquet, he even rescued Pellisson, after freeing him from La Bastille in 1666—but at the cost of disavowals and humiliations, which may have been crueler than the cell at Pignerol was for Foucquet! To become the king's historiographer, Pellisson had to abjure his Huguenot faith. His duties to the king obliged him to brush up on the style of *Mémoires pour l'instruction du Dauphin*, in which Louis XIV gave his own account of the year 1661, and where the king called Foucquet (whom Pellisson had so eloquently defended against that accusation, from his cell in La Bastille) a vulgar *thief*.[26] In 1677 the king coldly dismissed him from his post, only to name two younger literary luminaries, Boileau and Racine. Having taken orders so that he could receive church prebends, Pellisson had to go so far as to maintain the "conversion coffers," which purchased the abjurations of his former coreligionists, well before the Revocation of 1686 and in anticipation of it.[27]

La Fontaine was not included in the general transfer of the talents of Vaux to the Louvre and Versailles. In September 1661 he had to break off his ambitious *Le songe de Vaux*, which had become pointless. But he published a first fragment of it in 1665, in the collection *Contes et nouvelles en vers*, along with a note: "This work has remained incomplete for secret reasons." The other fragments appeared in 1671, at the end of a collection of fables. He wrote in the foreword: "In the meantime, things have occurred that prevented me from continuing." Nevertheless, through the juxtaposition of the ruins of *Le songe de Vaux* and of his *Contes* and *Fables*, he affirmed the continuity of his body of work and showed he had remained true to himself. In 1669 he even dared publish *Adonis*, though of course without the dedication and initial invocation to the man who had become the living corpse of Pignerol. But, through that combination of speaking out and remaining silent, he reminded the seventeenth century that it had not begun in 1661.[28]

Adonis, in fact, was continued and strangely replicated in *Le songe de Vaux*, except that, in the first case, the death of Adonis is recounted within the poem itself, after the lyric account of his love affair with Venus. The catastrophe of *Le songe de Vaux* is found not within its fabulous edifice but in the harshest of extrapoetic realities. If ever there was an "open work," it is that incomplete poem, shattered by a lightning bolt.

The germinating principle of the poem is an encomium in the form of a dream, an encomium to the power of love and to the leisure during which that sweet mistress of the heart manifests her beneficent effects of beauty and happiness. Among the many inventions the poet draws from the theater of Mnemosyne, described by Pellisson in 1656, and which make Vaux a Cythera, an Arcadia, and a Parnassus, the joint kingdom of Venus and Cupid, Apollo and the Muses, there are the painting of the Cavern of Sleep, which the poet asks to show him his beloved in a dream, and which transports him to Vaux-le-Vicomte; the Quarrel of the Arts, responsible for constructing the château and its grounds in a heated competition; the description of the Chamber of Muses, painted on the ceiling by Charles Le Brun; the evocation of the gardens and grounds, enlivened by the rivalry between the songs of the musician Lambert and the voice of a dying swan, and by the adventure (already almost a fable) of the salmon and the sturgeon that converse in the pond; or again, the dance of the Cupids and Graces around Venus, "in a meadow bordered by willow trees." Mars is present at the mythological feast only through his love affair with Venus, full of Vulcan's fire. Jupiter and Olympus remain absent from that homeland of poetic fiction, which Foucquet and his academy made visible at Vaux.

Central to all the pathways of Vaux, and to all the apparitions to which they lead, La Fontaine places an account of the ecstasy of love, comparable to that which forms the voluptuous center of the poem *Adonis*. The poet is placed in the presence of his beloved Aminte, a sleeping neo-Greek nymph. All his inner senses come alive in contemplating her visible charms, which are both offered and protected by sleep:

> The lovely nymph lay upon violets, her head half resting on one arm, the other arm stretched out the length of her skirt. Her sleeves, which had rolled up somewhat because of the position she had assumed while sleeping, half revealed those gleaming arms to me. I did not know which of their beauties had the advantage, their shape or their whiteness, though the latter put alabaster to shame. . . . I shall not attempt to describe either the whiteness or the other wonders of her beautiful

breast, or the admirable proportions of her bosom, which was easy to see despite her linen, and which her soft breathing sometimes compelled to swell. Nor will I give a description of her face, for what could I say that would come near to the delicacy of its features, the freshness of its complexion and its luminescence? Though I might use all the lilies and roses, might seek comparisons in the stars themselves, it would be no use: all that is but feeble and can represent only imperfectly the charms of that divine beauty. I considered them for a long time with a rapture than can be imagined only by those who love. And even the word "rapture" is too little: if it was not truly enchantment, it was at least something resembling it. It seemed that my whole soul had rushed to my eyes. I no longer dreamt of waterfalls or fountains; and just as at the beginning of my dream I had forgotten Aminte for Vaux, in that moment, I forgot Vaux for Aminte. (*Le songe de Vaux*, 7, "Acante se promène à la cascade")

Vaux-le-Vicomte, symbolized by a young French Ariana, which Sleep reveals to the poet's senses, was not just a "villa" designed to entertain a minister; it was the capital of contemplation, leisure, and voluptuous repose, erected in the middle of the kingdom. It inspired detachment and gentleness in the governance of the kingdom. In the symbology of *Le songe de Vaux*, that beneficent influence is multiplied by the arts and poetry, and by the fecundity of Nature, earth and sea, forests and rivers, which agriculture and commerce promote. In *Le songe de Vaux*, the allusions to Flora and Pan, the evocation of Neptune and Oceanus, associate the *surintendant*'s literary and artistic patronage with the vast projects of seaborne commerce and the agricultural prosperity of a long reign of peace.

In a harangue in prose that the poet did not suppress in 1671, Neptune declares: "You all know of the alliance between Oronte [Foucquet] and your monarch" (*Le songe de Vaux*, 8, "Neptune et ses tritons").

In 1664 the Versailles festival known as "The Pleasures of the Enchanted Isle" served as the framework for an allegorically veiled declaration of a threatening foreign policy, preparing Europe for the rearmament of France and for war. In 1660–61, *Le songe de Vaux*, an exegesis of Foucquet's masterpiece, took it upon itself to give the king the message of political wisdom that the *surintendant* wished to have him approve: repose at the center of action, the appeal of beauty at the heart of virtue. It is rather astonishing to find, despite the Epicurean coloring of that program, the seeds of Fénelon's pedagogy for the duc de

Bourgogne, the spirit of good government as Mentor made his young student Telemachus desire it.

On 17 August 1661, when the festival of Vaux was in full swing, someone gave the *surintendant* a letter from his most ardent ally, Mme du Plessis-Bellière, warning him of rumors that the king was going to have him arrested that night. The *surintendant* knew he was walking a tightrope. But the declaration of his nomination and his gift to seal the alliance were ready, he was untroubled, and the flawless success of the festival further confirmed him in the illusion that the king was going to accept a friendship that would join the two men, like Augustus and Maecenas, and become the cornerstone of a state reconciled with the kingdom.[29]

Well before that disappointing night, the gentle civilization the *surintendant* had promised himself he would establish in France in a lasting manner shone brilliantly in the Parisian mansions and the country châteaux joined to his star. Madeleine de Scudéry was linked to Pellisson in 1647 by a "tenderness combined with respect"; she had met him in Conrart's home and came to love him even more ardently in 1650 when he returned to Paris, disfigured but all hers. She was the best "reporter" for that new Paris, which was excited about the patron to whom Pellisson "gave himself" in 1657, and which regarded Foucquet's ascension as that of the kingdom's child prodigy destined to civilize the state.[30]

ASTRÉE IN PARIS: CLÉLIE

Just as Tallemant des Réaux was beginning to compile his retrospective *Historiettes*, Mlle de Scudéry provided an idealized image, colored by a conventional notion of Greco-Roman antiquity, of what Paris had become, and what it ought to become, under the favorable constellation where the *surintendant* shone as its north star. *Clélie*, her serial novel begun in 1656, took a more politically committed turn after Pellisson became Foucquet's "chief assistant" in 1657. In the three final volumes of *Clélie*, the depiction of Vaux-le-Vicomte, under the name "Valterre," and the portrait of the *surintendant* himself, under the name "Cléonime," occupy a place of choice. There is a perfect harmony between the allegorical château of Foucquet/Cléonime and the high society and literary culture of Paris, which Mlle de Scudéry depicts in her fictional chronicle and roman à clef. It celebrates the triumph of manners in Paris (a Roman *and* Arcadian Paris), of gallant and literate conversation, and of the urbanity that the Rome of Cicero and Augustus had learned from Athens and Alexandria, and which now Foucquet's Paris was reinstating in France.[31]

Among the many reasons for Foucquet's disgrace, apart from that "power of amour propre" that his friend La Rochefoucauld later analyzed, and which led the king to do by himself and for himself what Foucquet had proposed to do with him, we must include Louis XIV's feelings about Paris. During the Fronde the king had learned to dread and fear the capital, which had insolently rebelled against his mother and Mazarin, that is, against himself, the king of France. The Parisians, in revolt at the bidding of Parlement and the princes, had even compelled him to flee, whereas, in the court's travels to the provinces, he always received the traditional welcome that the French people reserved for their king: faithful and fervent. How could he have accepted the fact that the guilty city had so quickly recovered its self-assurance, its diversity, and its joie de vivre? Everything about that happiness, and about the man who did not conceal the fact that he shared and even embodied it, was designed to displease the elderly Mazarin, and a fortiori his student, the young king.

In the last three books of *Clélie*, which focus on Foucquet/Cléonime and Pellisson/Herminius, Louis XIV appears only in a minor role. Under the pseudonym "Alcandre," he is certainly praised in superlative terms: he is young, handsome, in love, a great hunter. But he does not have any standing or role in intrigues, not even a moral physiognomy. And, although it is true that the king was neither a writer or a reader, he could not have failed to know, at least by hearsay, the substance of the last episodes of *Clélie*, which had its finger on the pulse of Parisian high society, somewhat like *L'Illustration* in the past or *Le Nouvel Observateur* today. His minister of finances, darling of the salons, might very well have promised the king that, if he were made in charge of business affairs, the king would have Paris at his feet. In his heart of hearts, Louis XIV aspired to be the focus of all his subjects' encomiums. He preferred to be feared by Paris than to be loved by proxy, in another man's name. Colbert did not frequent the Parisian salons, and poems were not yet dedicated to him, but that capable majordomo, who owed everything to the king, had already long been chosen in petto. Colbert was clearly an ambitious man, but a reasonable one, who had no intention of harming himself by standing between the royal glory of the Sun King and the state, in exchange for the kingdom's love.

At Vaux on 17 August 1661, Louis XIV not only saw Foucquet everywhere—as Apollo in the Salon of the Muses, as Alcide in the Salon of Hercules, as Neptune in the ponds of the Vaux gardens, as the Maecenas of French arts and theater—he also saw all the luminaries of Paris—more numerous than his own court—whom Foucquet had invited en masse, and who had eyes only for the hero of the day. He found this Paris under Foucquet's spell more insolent and intolerable than even the Paris of the barricades. This urban high society radiated an air of joy and freedom which, if it did not slight the love and respect due the king, was at least suspect in his eyes. Versailles would be Jupiter's response to the Parisian frogs that had embraced Broussel, acclaimed Condé, and which were now electing Foucquet by a large majority.

The similarity in the inspiration behind La Fontaine's Le songe de Vaux and Madeleine de Scudéry's Clélie was equal to the symbiosis that had been established between Foucquet's château and Parisian high society. Le songe de Vaux is a mysterious mirror of the château, Clélie (in its last three books) a fictional and idealized representation of the Paris that had rallied behind the château. Similar political issues are thus at stake in the poem and the novel, which make the guiding thread of the two books even more surprising: love, friendship, empathy, elective affinities, the entire gamut of the mutual and private attraction between men and women. The "Map of Tenderness" is more voluptuous in La Fontaine, more rational and prudish in Mlle de Scudéry: for Foucquet's two supporters, it is still the only program of internal policy that suited the kingdom of France and the vocation of its kings. Internal policy, in Saint-Mandé and Vaux, as in Parisian salons, had to be based on a philosophy and a poetics of the magnetic field formed by social relationships.[32]

Between the Mlle de Scudéry of Clélie and the La Fontaine of Le songe de Vaux on one hand, and the architects of the coup d'état of 5 September 1661 on the other, there was already the total misunderstanding about the governance of the kingdom, which, of late, has once more put the French "left" and the "right" at odds with each other. The left, linked to social Christianity, aspires to have the monopoly on feelings. It no longer reads L'Astrée, but it sees France as the Arcadia of the rights of man. The right no longer reads Machiavelli and Hobbes, but it feels more or less keenly that even French political society, perhaps it above all, cannot be governed like Marie Antoinette's dairy. The size of the state makes both sentimentalism and humanitarianism ridiculous. Compassion and social justice make the state authoritarianism on which they live odious. The resemblance ends there, however: in the seventeenth century, the question was infinitely more complex, since the elites were still supersaturated with very ancient traditions and symbolic mediations, which prevented the debate from being reduced to a mere demagogic and electoral antithesis.

To confine ourselves to one example, but one that is very pertinent to both La Fontaine and Madeleine de Scudéry, both the right and the left in France are now currying the favor of an official feminism that imagines no social and political progress for women other than an entirely virile and essentially Machiavellian self-interested ambition. The idea that a happy moral diversity distinguishes femininity from virility, and that that diversity, if only poetry and literature can make it truly perceptible and fruitful, can exert beneficent effects in political society and on mores, has become almost alien to us. We are lagging behind with respect to the possibility, developed in the seventeenth century by poets like d'Urfé, or by Christian moralists of the grand style like Francis of Sales, of a superior and more fluid synthesis between a masculinity made up entirely of action and ruse, and a femininity composed entirely of futility and dupery. Seventeenth-century France, the heir to the France of *Roman de la rose* and *Lancelot*, had, in the meantime, borrowed a language of myths, allegories, and symbols from the Italian Renaissance. That language allowed it to insinuate a search for more promising attitudes toward love and affective attachments into fixed sexual roles—more promising, because more faithful to the unique truth and extreme diversity of human "composites," and less harmful than the mutual intimidation or deception to which fixed social and sexual roles condemn themselves.

In that search, whose roots in France go back to the courtly ideal, d'Urfé's *L'Astrée*—a book of initiation for La Fontaine, Madeleine de Scudéry, and their friends—looked at the time like the fifth, secular gospel.[33] The aim of the entire moral alchemy distilled by that long novel is to guide readers, both men and women, toward social attitudes—private at first, then flowing out into the political order—that bestow on men some of the feminine qualities they lack and obtain from women some of the masculine qualities of which they are perfectly capable. That mutual transmutation, which leaves the differences and diversity of the sexes intact, modulates and nuances them in such a way that their union, rather than being a cruel misunderstanding and a battle between wolves and she-wolves, can be filled with empathy and intelligence. In *L'Astrée* it is women who, finding support in the desire that attracts men to them, rather than rejecting it or giving in to it without compensation, make it more suitable to their own desire; and, in that reciprocal education, which has its ordeals and failures along the way, they discover they are reflective and free, capable of bringing out in men a gentleness, patience, and intelligence of the heart, which hardly come spontaneously within the roles their sex is supposedly assigned to play.

In that mutual metamorphosis, the point where all roads converge is conversation, which gives freedom of speech equally to the different characters of men and women: in that school of tolerance and courtesy, both sexes, in confiding in each other through language, gently learn not to resemble each other, but to modify each other and make each other morally complementary.[34] The fruit of that alchemy in the crucible of conversation is "honorable love," which reconciles the traits of love, blind passion, with those of friendship, the virtue that the ancient sages wished to see as wholly masculine, but which, after centuries of Christianity and *fin' amor*, now made its entrance into the love relationship between a man and a woman. Eros had learned to resemble Agape.[35]

L'Astrée, the summit of that new moral ideal unknown to the ancients, makes it emerge in the strange episode wholly instigated by the pagan high priest Adamas, during which Céladon, disguised as a young woman and controlling his passion, shares, in the same gynaeceum, the life and bed of the shepherdess Astrée, who also loves him, but who takes him for a girl friend who resembles the man she loves. In that long ordeal, which trains the sex drive and adds to it the lasting form of friendship, Céladon and Astrée learn to respect each other, to harmonize their moods, before uniting and knowing the carnal pleasure of Venus and Adonis, which in their case is not followed by estrangement and tragic misunderstandings.

There have been learned discussions about the "gallantry" and "preciosity"—ridiculous or not—cultivated in the circles of Mme de Rambouillet and Mlle de Scudéry. In any case, it was a true moral revolution, which had been fermenting since the Renaissance in Italy, France, and England, and which Paris appropriated under the reign of Louis XIII and the regent Anne of Austria. It adopted intricate methods, whose ingenious casuistry would later be reborn in the Marivaux dialogues despised by Voltaire. Even the French Jesuits Pierre Le Moyne and Dominique Bouhours, because they were pedagogues by profession, were obliged to intervene in that moral revolution, or risk seeing their young students, trained on the Latin classics and the cult of the Virgin Mary, slip away from them. Father Le Moyne's *Les peintures morales* (1641–43) and *Galerie des femmes fortes* (1648) made every effort to take the lead in the movement and to become, if possible, its directors of conscience. Let us call that moral revolution gallant romanticism.[36]

The true vectors of that shift in mores are to be found in the secular novel and in poetry which, in the wake of *L'Astrée*, propagated the ideals of "honorable love" and proposed a language to describe it. After the Fronde, the fate of that literary and secular gospel crystallized around the person of Nicolas Foucquet.

A Literary Statesman: Nicolas Foucquet

The statesman Foucquet's political, financial, and diplomatic capacities, despite the later slander spread by Colbert, were acknowledged by Mazarin and by all of Europe. Yet the two finest portraits of the *surintendant*, one engraved by Robert Nanteuil, the other by Claude Mellan, reveal a very unusual luxury for someone in his profession: melancholic eyes and fine, sensitive features, which made him an irresistible kindred soul, not only for writers and poets, but for women. All women: those most naively feminine, like the very beautiful Mlle de Menneville (the Brigitte Bardot of the queen mother's daughters), those most intelligent and well informed in business matters, like Mme du Plessis-Bellière, and those most witty, vibrant, and alive, like the marquise de Sévigné. The extraordinary devotion that he attracted from both sexes, the close-knit friendships and inviolable loyalty he wove around him in the most hostile of environments, owed something to the gold he knew how to throw about with elegant generosity; but gold would not have been adequate to earn him that invincible affinity with the cream of French society. This minister, this Maecenas, was, as the abbé de Fénelon would later be, a mutant made possible by several centuries of literary refinement of the heart and senses.

Old families sometimes create masterpieces of humanity: the Renaissance and the seventeenth century offer numerous examples of this phenomenon, from Balthazar Castiglione to La Rochefoucauld, from Philip Sidney to Charles I. Foucquet, unlike Fénelon, did not come from a very ancient family, but his natural gifts, perfected by his religious and literary education, made him a prince. A prince not by birth, but by his level of civilization. He despised the particle *de* indicating nobility and, even in his elevated condition, kept the bourgeois name of his ancestors. He could be recognized as a prince, however, only in a hothouse environment, where the titles of a great man of civilization had currency, and where literature dictated the criteria for admiration. Neither Colbert nor the king, who weighed men in the balance of *The Prince*, could have supported this sort of chimerical superiority, which only an alerted and enlightened empathy can sense, as opposed to analyze.

A persistent rumor circulated in Paris and at the court after his arrest, that Foucquet had dared court Mlle de La Vallière, who had already received the king's favors, and that Louis XIV's anger at the *surintendant* came primarily from that crime of romantic high treason.[37] With or without La Vallière, there was certainly an incompatibility of temperament between the young king, whose sexual appetites were robust, and this *surintendant*, who was past forty, but who radiated a peculiar power of universal attraction. Foucquet, too sure of his personal magic, did not sense that incompatibility, or did not sense it enough. As courteous as Louis XIV was in his manners, he stood tall in the boots of a king and virile male of the dynasty. The shimmering quality of Foucquet and his entourage inspired contempt and even fear in the king. The most curious paradox of the reign was that Françoise d'Aubigné, the most accomplished précieuse ever known in the Parisian society of the Scudérys, Pellissons, and Foucquets, should, much later, marry Louis the Great and, with the help of Racine and even, for a time, of Fénelon, should wear herself out, but in vain, trying to awaken the tenderness under the potentate's outer carapace, already tough and leathery in 1661.[38]

LA FONTAINE/ANACRÉON

In the "Paris tableau" of *Clélie*, Mlle de Scudéry interlinks all the city's conversation societies, but, in the last three books of this novelistic new report, the constellation begins to reflect the light emanating from Cléonime, the *surintendant*, to whom the genius of Herminius, alias Pellisson, is drawn.[39] A few women, superior in business matters and in the art of living, now increase the power of their political idol through their own powers of empathy. Their Parisian mansions and their châteaux on Ile-de-France serve as the successors to the power of attraction of Saint-Mandé and Vaux. Valentin Conrart/Cléodamas (a pseudonym borrowed intact from *L'Astrée*), protector of Pellisson and of his "knights-errant," sees his country house and gardens of Athis/Mons figure, and with good reason, in the topography of Foucquet's Paris. The Solitaries of Port-Royal, whom Robert Arnauld d'Andilly, through his old alliances with high society, was able to link to the brilliant salon of Mme du Plessis-

Guénégaud at the Nevers mansion and her splendid château in Fresnes (a vanished masterpiece by François Mansart), themselves benefited from unexpected publicity thanks to that high-society gazette that had rallied behind the *surintendant*. The intrigues and love affairs recounted by Madeleine de Scudéry, the conversations that comment on them and draw a moral from them, are so many pre-Marivaudian variations on the theme of love and friendship, and on the capacity of both sexes to improve such social attachments. Friendship is glorified everywhere as the higher form of love, free of jealousy, lies, and inconstancy, and which gives one the strength to keep one's vows, one's word. In this novel, friendship, for both women and men, is a shared secret inviolably sealed by a communion of hearts: as in Corneille's plays, this higher contract is able to spiritualize sexual impulses even while exalting them. And if love is the generating principle of glory, in other words, of a public and political life deserving of admiration, friendship is even more powerful: the glory it leads one to desire is not public approbation, but the approval of those who are truly privy to one's inner life—friends, and oneself in one's friends' eyes.

Even though Mlle de Scudéry was wholly lacking in La Fontaine's lyric genius (which allows the poet of *Adonis*, as in a prophetic dream, to see the Machiavellian boar awaiting his victim in the kingdom's forest), her novel—apparently never dark and with the unfailingly euphoric prose of the encomium—implies an opposing view, which she leaves to her reader to flesh out. Secrecy, inviolable loyalty, the conjugal bond of love and friendship: to whom must all these feverish feelings stand opposed? Internalized glory, recognized by only intimate friends: what sort of public disgrace and usurpation of glory does that solution of retreat portend? A pervasive atmosphere of ardent conspiracy and extreme risk secretly runs through the last books of the novel. There is a certain Couéism in that perpetual enthusiasm, and a terrible compensatory anxiety. When the novelist wrote to her dear Pellisson a few days before Foucquet's arrest, "They're still saying that the *surintendant* is about to become prime minister, and even the people who fear him are beginning to say that might very well be," she was trying to fool herself, as she had fooled her readers for the duration of a novel.[40] She had lived and written in that semiconscious state since 1657, just after she and Pellisson joined Foucquet's ingenious—or infernal—game, and she placed her talent as a famous writer in the service of the *surintendant*. At least she believed she was serving him. As a matter of fact, if the king had the last episodes of *Clélie* read out loud to him, as he may very well have done, he would have been able to decipher at a glance the scope of the entirely Cornellian conspiracy developing in Paris and the surrounding châteaux in favor of his minister of finances. He could have caught a glimpse of the terror inspired in these countless conspirators, not so much by himself, whom they considered docile and easily influenced, but by the close-knit team of heartless high officials kept in power by Mazarin, and who possessed via Richelieu the true arcana of the state. In spite of the opinion polls, the short-lived Foucquet represented only intrigue in the king's eyes. Mlle de Scudéry's very long life (she died in 1701 at age ninety-three, rehabilitated by the efforts of her friend Françoise Scarron) would be just long enough to repair the appalling gaffe of Clélie, through panegyrics of Louis the Great.

In the last books of Clélie, La Fontaine, under the pseudonym "Ana-créon," replaces Jean-François Sarasin as the new Voiture (Sarasin plays that role earlier in the novel under the pseudonym "Amilcar," but he died in 1654).[41] The curious superimposition of times and places, which makes Clélie at once a Greek Parnassus, a Latin Arcadia, and a Parisian Map of Tenderness, allows Anacréon/La Fontaine to encounter the wise Aesop in the wholly fictional present of the novel. Was he already moving in the direction of Fables? In any case, the society he frequented during the Foucquet years was very familiar with the ancient Greek apologues, which had for many centuries been adapted by the French. Aesop, thanks to the illustrated edition published in 1660 by Raphaël Trichet Du Fresne, a friend of Nicolas Poussin and André Félibien, himself well received by Foucquet in Saint-Mandé, had a new relevance in the conversations of high society, and Mlle de Scudéry therefore invited the Phrygian slave to participate.[42] She had already depicted him in her previous voluminous novel Le grand Cyrus. Before choosing to become his companion in disgrace after 1661, La Fontaine was thus already his colleague on the cheery Parnassus of Clélie. The author of Adonis, the dispenser of a "poetic pension" to Foucquet, was himself received as a poet laureate in the most exclusive society of Paris: as a new Voiture or a new Sarasin, he participated with Pellisson/Herminius in the brilliance of the general conversation. At the homes of Mme du Plessis-Bellière, Mme du Plessis-Guénégaud, Mme Foucquet, Conrart, and of course at Mlle de Scudéry's every Saturday, La Fontaine now made his debut in Parisian high society. He moved about it with ease. The portrait Mlle de Scudéry gives of him, the words she attributes to him, are firsthand accounts that La Fontaine's biographers are wrong to neglect. Emerging from the silence and obscurity where he had remained until that time, he suddenly appeared in the bright light of chandeliers in the salons and on the most elegant garden paths of Foucquet's *belle époque:* "He is a pleasant-looking man," writes Mlle de Scudéry, "with a noble and playful manner."

"The man from Champagne" (and who remained one) cut a fine figure as a poet in Paris. Using a refined technique of superimpression, the novelist shows him as he appeared to his lady admirers in 1660, and at the same time transfigured into a fifth-century Greek poet on Parnassus, crowned with roses, enveloped in a chlamys. Among his works, she cites the titles of poems that had been attributed to Anacreon—dear to Jean Dorat and Ronsard—since the sixteenth century: "The Dove," "The Swallow," "The Lyre." But the mood and words she attributes to him are those with which La Fontaine delighted Paris in the Foucquet years, in conversations in salons or châteaux.[43]

Joy is the mistress of his heart, and he loves it everywhere he finds it. But should joy be lacking, La Fontaine/Anacréon risks "being bored to death." This playful poet, who knows how to "amuse himself," is also a melancholiac not satisfied by the world, and who tends to be indifferent toward its chatter. He knows it; he is his own best doctor and has a vast array of remedies for melancholia. As Mlle de Scudéry writes somewhat mysteriously, "he is atune to all pleasures, without exception." That tallies with the "hundred passions condemned by the wise," to which the poet would half-admit in his 1684 *Discours* in verse. But of these various personal pleasures, those he places above everything have nothing to do with high society: they are the feasts shared by "five or six friends without concerns, without sorrows," with whom "conversation is free, playful, and even droll," friends who know how to please with "agreeable songs, music, and a bit of a stroll." This poet, celebrated by high society, and who was open to its receptions and conversations, was in reality entirely devoted to his own hidden feasts, as he was when he deserted the academy of knights-errant without warning.

Nevertheless, the occasions set in the lovely homes of grandes dames, Foucquet's friends, or even in the country house of the illustrious Conrart had the charms of private and civilized life, and nothing of the poisonous politeness of courtly life. That is why the poet could be happy there. But he preferred less social delights, and the purely leisurely get-togethers of more intimate and intense friends. Even when he had made a name for himself in Parisian high society, he remained faithful to the caverns of his native Champagne and to the friendly games among his fellow writers and musicians, which had made his adolescence happy. Even after Foucquet's fall, it was always in such company, roving and unpretentious, that he would find consolation: the travelers in the coach that took him and Jannart to Limoges, and which transformed the exile order into a discovery of the "garden of France"; the four friends in *Les amours de Psyché*, who observe with him that Versailles is truly faithful to Vaux in all things, and who, in spite of Colbert, take an extreme pleasure in listening and commenting on a love romance together.

Friendship above the Nation

I place friendship first. I would love a friend even if he were a murderer, a traitor, a thief. The idea that politics ought to come ahead of friendship seems absolutely comical to me. Committed friendship, friendship as it is in the convent: a religion first.

—Paul Morand

Where friendship is, there too is the nation.

—Voltaire

The subject to which La Fontaine/Anacréon is most likely to return in the conversations reported by Mlle de Scudéry in *Clélie* is once again friendship. It is even the true subject of the novel. All her characters, in their various facets, contribute toward highlighting that shared moral ideal. The venerable Arnauld d'Andilly, ambassador of Port-Royal in the Parisian societies described by the novelist, prided himself on being a "professor of friendship."

In a letter he wrote to Mme de Sablé on 28 January 1661, and which was approved by his brother, the Great Arnauld, Arnauld d'Andilly wrote these sentences, anathema to both Louis XIV and Robespierre:

What is called love of the nation is, in fact, only the love we have for ourselves. We love it because it is advantageous for us to love it. In serving it, we serve our ambition or our fortune, and Rome would not have had so many martyrs for the republic if these great men had not labored much more for their own glory than for its grandeur. . . . That is not true for the love that unites friends by ties stronger and more excellent than those of need and self-interest. This means that, without the person one loves, one feels lonely within one's country; one believes one can love only inasmuch as one lives in that person; contrary to the opinion of the Stoics, the sage can love something more than himself, something that trains the will in such a way that it submerges it entirely in that of his friend; and finally, that the two souls find themselves intermingled in a manner so universal that, to paraphrase Montaigne, they do not perceive the seam that joins them. . . . We owe a great deal, no doubt, to our nation, we cannot work too hard for its preservation or be too jealous of its glory. But how could we owe it as much as we do our friends, since we owe our friends more than we owe ourselves? . . . Hence I believe I can say that friendship, considered in all its purity, must be unadulterated by self-interest or glory or particular pleasure, and that the love we have for the state is never of that sort, and is found wholly pure only within a very small number of friends; and that, for them, it is no crime to hold something dearer than the salvation of the nation which, apart from that obligation, we must find preferable in all things.[44]

The no-less-venerable secretary for life of the Académie Française, Conrart/Cléodamas, who Tallemant tells us was "starved" for friendships, appears in *Clélie* in this loving and obliging light. Madeleine de Scudéry introduces into her novel a complete rainbow of all the colors of intense feeling. What singles out the poet La Fontaine/Anacréon, what makes him so attractive and impossible to grasp, is that he is himself the shimmering synthesis of all those colors, distilled to a sweet incandescence that shapes his life and inspires his art. Eros and Agape dictate to him a life of love in poetry, and a poetry that attracts life to it. Mlle de Scudéry has him say that he wants to "remove the harsh and dry aspects of ethics, and give it something so natural, and so agreeable, that it amuses those to whom it gives lessons."

This is truly an alliance between an art of living and an art of writing, giving precedence to the pleasant over the useful, the two aspects that Horace recommended be joined together. Like his poetry, La Fontaine's friendship presumes a heart and imagination capable of embodying beautiful fictions and beautiful songs. But it is not Plato's Ion, who knows nothing of his divine gift. La Fontaine, following the views on love expressed by Socrates and Diotima in *The Symposium*, is also a philosopher and moralist on the art of living and singing. To Herminius/Pellisson, who professes his abhorrence of lies, which are contrary to the good faith required by friendship, La Fontaine/Anacréon responds by moving beyond this overly dry ethical principle: "As for pleasant lies, you do not condemn them either, and when I want to tell an agreeable tale, you allow me to add something to the story, since, ordinarily, there is always something serious about truth, which is not as entertaining as lies."[45]

And the learned Herminius, who has taught La Fontaine/Anacréon so much, also proves to be the poet's disciple. He replies without offering any resistance: "Oh, as far as that is concerned, I believe it can be allowed . . . I leave your imagination the liberty to invent what you like, and it's up to you to exercise the privilege of lying innocently. . . . The only innocent lies are the ones offered as lies, that is, all the ingenious fables of poets; and yet they too must have the appearance of truth."

This is already the poetics of the fable "The Faithless Depository," written a full ten years later:

Le doux charme de maint songe
Par leur bel art inventé,
Sous les habits du mensonge
Nous offre la vérité.
(9.1, ll. 32–35)

The sweet charm of many a dream
By their fine art invented,
Under the costume of a lie
Offers us verity.

For Pellisson, Conrart, Arnauld d'Andilly, and the other characters of Clélie, friendship is agape that has become second nature, a masterpiece of reason and will in the service of the loftiest regions of the heart. For La Fontaine/Anacréon, it is a way of being inventive and imaginative, the extension of a way of speaking to the concerns of life, and this way of being is to the ordinary human comedy what poetry is to prose. Such a continuity between poetry and "friendship" presupposes a keener and more closely allied intelligence, fancy, and taste: that alliance does not easily prostitute either its friendship or its poetry among the ordinary, needy historions of the world.

Even if he rose above and escaped the Parisian society assembled and narrated by Madeleine de Scudéry, La Fontaine shared and served the cult of "honorable friendship," itself greatly superior to vulgar roles and

passions. The merit of friendship, for this high society, which in turn recognized the unusual merit of a born poet, was that it created a universe
of intuitive and enlightened empathy, where fixed roles and rigid ideas
lost their hard, sharp boundaries, and invented particular concessions
and compromises. It is not by chance that the author of *Clélie* attributes
La Fontaine/Anacréon, whose thinking—and not only his verses and
life—were decidedly "not those of everyone else," with giving a philosophical and even a political meaning to the shared ideal. In fact, she attributes to the Epicurean lover of "beautiful lies" a resolute skepticism in the
face of doctrinaire—and a fortiori sectarian and partisan—dogmas and
fanaticism:

> There is no preoccupation so strong as that which has some appear-
> ance of religion and piety. In fact, when Damon [another character
> in the novel, a convert to Pythagoras's *Golden Verses*] found Pythago-
> ras's ethics pleasing, because it was full of humanity and sweetness, he
> then easily lent his mind to believing everything taught by a man
> whose virtue had charmed him. When a person for whom you have
> very great respect wants to persuade you to follow his opinion blindly, it
> must undoubtedly entail one of the things no one can ever know per-
> fectly, something that is known only when the gods reveal it. That
> being the case, it should come as no surprise that a person who cannot
> penetrate the truth with his own reason believes that a man for whom
> he has infinite respect has discovered what he was unable to discover,
> and, in the end, blindly believes what he thinks the other came to
> believe only after being convinced of it by a thousand reasons.[46]

The style is Mlle de Scudéry's, but the idea belongs to La Fontaine,
who, in this instance, is the interpreter of the environment in which he
has been received. These extremely tolerant and lofty words are not surprising in a society where the Jansenist Arnauld d'Andilly, under the
pseudonym "Timante," speaks with the Pyrrhonian philosopher François
La Mothe Le Vayer, disguised in Madeleine de Scudéry's novel under the
name "Cléante" (a name Molière used a great deal in his comedies). The
novelistic myth created by Mlle de Scudéry, though in many respects an
idealization, also has its truth, a truth loftier than any journalistic realism:
thanks to the language of allegory, which plays on several registers at
once, it shows from the inside the sort of vast academy in Paris that was
forming in concentric circles around the Foucquet academy.

THE DIPLOMACY OF WIT

In this climate of polite, tolerant, and gallant equality, men and women of the most various ranks and temperaments, the most divergent opinions, the most diverse vocations, and, in appearance, the least harmonious talents, all conversed together. François La Mothe Le Vayer was from the learned Dupuy cabinet, Robert Arnauld d'Andilly from the circle of Port-Royal-des-Champs Solitaries; Valentin Conrart was the founder of the Académie Française; Pellisson and La Fontaine came from the "youth academy" of the Round Table; Madeleine de Scudéry herself was one of the heirs to the "Blue Room": the partitions dividing these societies fell away. Different in their orientations, they all cultivated letters at leisure and with a friendship that was both skeptical and Epicurean in coloring. Foucquet's Paris created a synthesis of these diverse literary societies and set in place a republic of letters never seen before, which included in its ranks scholars and philosophers, poets and scientists, Calvinists and Catholics, men and women from a cultured high society. Foucquet's personal academy, which met in the library of his home in Saint-Mandé, had in 1657 been coordinated by Pellisson with the Parisian republic of letters; Pellisson thus found, in the person of Foucquet, an essential link by which to join the very governance of the state to that aristocracy of wits, which was in fact the best the kingdom had to offer.

The views Pellisson and his friends held about Foucquet did not fundamentally contradict the charitable empire of the secret Compagnie du Saint-Sacrement, to which the family of the *surintendant* was closely tied. They were cheerier, and linked Foucquet's fate to the most brilliant and innovative elements in Paris. In the absence of an English-style parliament, Paris had found a substitute: a republic of letters *sui generis*, both worldly and scholarly, an encyclopedic crossroads, a crucible of mutual tolerance, a forum of universal conversation, a fluid and conductive medium, liberal by definition, where the most unlikely syntheses could come about, where the most insurmountable contradictions could find a middle ground, a conspiracy of talents that dreamed of drawing the government of the kingdom over to the side of its own diplomacy of wit.

Louis XIV wanted as little to do with such an unpredictable republic of letters and self-proclaimed guardian of the state, as with the underground "religious cabal." As his future statecraft would prove, he hated and fought any group of would-be dissenters. And yet, kept on the shelf at Mme de La Sablière's home during his reign, that very same republic of letters would reappear in the eighteenth century, exercising an authority in Paris over which Versailles had definitively lost control after 1748, when Maurepas was disgraced and his protégé Voltaire left the service of the king of France in favor of the king of Prussia. Turgot, a new Enlightenment Foucquet, then became Voltaire's candidate to govern the kingdom.

La Fontaine did not share the king's reasons for fearing the rise, in Foucquet's wake, of this literary "power of wit." Even though he preferred more intimate encounters and private retreats, he felt at ease and in his place in that diverse academy, which, in its conversations, was like himself open to the diversity of ideas, tastes, and nuances of humanity. Like him, his lovely hostesses knew the distance that separated private life from the intimate life of the salon or the château, and the abyss that separated the latter from courtly life.

They knew how to distinguish between the life of literary leisure and the life of action. The first was the remedy for the second. Literary leisure nourished the heart and mind, which action wore down and dried out. Mme du Plessis-Bellière, Foucquet's friend and collaborator, Mme du Plessis-Guénégaud, and later Mme de La Sablière, their disciple and direct descendant, had keen intelligence as well as big hearts. They spoke as equals with the scholars, scientists, philosophers, and diplomats they received, as well as with the poets or cultured great lords. The Parisian academy of Foucquet's *belle époque*, of which some have chosen to see only the dregs of *bouts-rimés* and love letters—also destined for a great future in the eighteenth century—was a great studio of intellects, where the modern division between "the two cultures," literary pursuits and scientific inquiry, was still unknown. Nicolas Foucquet, in his academy in Saint-Mandé, himself assembled the most diverse group of scholars. He was happy in the company of the excellent physician and anatomist Jean Pecquet, the French disciple of William Harvey, or that of Marin Cureau de La Chambre, who in 1660 dedicated his *Art de connaître les hommes*, one of the keys to the moral anatomy of *Fables*, to Foucquet.[47] The *surintendant* was happy to converse with philosophers such as François La Mothe Le Vayer, the modern Sextus Empiricus, or Samuel Sorbière, translator of Hobbes and Gassendi's publisher.[48] He chose a Huguenot, Pellisson, as his principal collaborator. At the time, Pellisson was the spiritual son of the Huguenot Conrart and crown prince of the French republic of letters.[49]

On the forum of Parisian conversation, bankers, businessmen, and diplomats, engaged in difficult intrigues, also found détente, a palaestra where they could exercise their minds on more disinterested subjects.

Conversely, philosophers and scholars—persecuted by the university, distrusted by the church, and ignored by the court—found an attentive ear and a warm welcome in that informal academy of Paris, which did not lack the discernment necessary to distinguish true talents or the taste required to celebrate novelty. Between 1657 and 1661 La Fontaine combined philosophy and poetry in the high society that stood behind Foucquet, having increased his literary erudition within Pellisson's and Conrart's entourage.

The two poets who preceded him in high society may be just as misleading to the distracted historian as La Fontaine. Voiture was secretly erudite. That was not discovered until the nineteenth century,[50] when his correspondence with the learned Costar was published. Sarasin frequented the academy of the Dupuy brothers as often as the Rambouillet mansion; between 1617 and 1656 the Dupuy academy was the daily meeting place for all the great philologists, historians, and jurists in Paris (and, via travel and correspondence, in Europe). That learned "republic of letters" had found a Maecenas in Stockholm, in the person of Christina of Sweden. Now, linked to high society's "republic of wits," it could hope to find one in Paris as well, in the person of Foucquet. La Fontaine, the heir to Voiture and Sarasin, who became a poet/scholar under Pellisson and a poet/philosopher in that fusion of Parisian academies, stood at the center of the great movement of ideas and of the great hopes of Foucquet's Paris.

In the *surintendant*'s world, Cartesianism (despite its connections, indirect to be sure, to the Solitaries of Port-Royal, who were infatuated with the new philosophy) had no influence.[51] Paris had Cartesian salons, but they were located on the margins of the high society that conspired with the Maecenas of Vaux. That society had two bedside readings, which it sought to reconcile and which provided the framework for its eclectic tastes in ethics, philosophy, politics, and the sciences: *L'Astrée* and *Essays*. Montaigne's skepticism and Epicureanism and d'Urfé's Platonist philosophy taught, by different paths, that freedom and happiness depend upon a critique of appearances, and a reflection on the extreme difficulty of seeing clearly into oneself, others, and nature. The motto "know thyself," like Eros according to Socrates and Diotima, provides a lesson for the alert intellect, which despises dogma: it welcomes the most various and boldest pursuits. Pascal's Augustinianism could itself rely on this keen "spirit of refinement" to eventually pull these *honnestes gens* away from their shifting and unsettled positions and lead them to the *credo quia absurdum* of faith. The magnetic field of worldly "curiosity" suited even better a poet who did not want to sacrifice any of reality's richness, and a politician who wanted to stay the course while taking into account the changing facets of the situations he had to sort out. For La Fontaine, Foucquet, and their friends, the straightforward method Descartes had introduced into France was no more attractive than Colbert's administrative authority and central planning.

THE STATE AND THE KINGDOM, HOBBES AND GASSENDI

An excellent example of the diplomacy of wit favored by the Foucquet academy is given in the treatise *De l'amitié* (On friendship), published by Samuel Sorbière in 1660.[52] The theme of the treatise was central to the preoccupations of the *surintendant's* Parisian circles, which Sorbière frequented after his return from Stockholm. He was not alone in knowing that this subject fascinated the minister and his entourage. Charles Perrault, who, along with his brother Claude, also frequented the society of Saint-Mandé and Fresnes, wrote a dialogue in 1660 entitled *De l'amour et de l'amitié* (On love and friendship), which he allowed to be published only in 1672.[53] In it, Friendship, the daughter of Desire and Kindness, embraces generosity to overcome the power of self-interested *amour propre* and performs moral "miracles," necessarily reserved for rare creatures. Love, daughter of Desire and Beauty, has a more vast empire, at war with Reason, but which, with the complicity of Empathy and the "glimpses of understanding it has of the heart," *moves the whole earth*. However different they may be, these two cousins of gentle birth share one thing: they escape and allow one to escape the calculation of self-interest and coldly ethical virtues. The young Perrault, even in Foucquet's time, was already the moralist of *Contes de fées*. Between these two incarnations, he was one of the people who played a role in transporting the trappings of Foucquet's "civilization" to the king.

Saint-Evremond, another moralist with flexible affinities, was one of the *surintendant's* closest confidants, and one of the victims of his fall. Although his own essay *Sur l'amitié* (On Friendship) is difficult to date, in it the exile, faithful to his youth, reflects and continues in London a line of thinking dating to the Foucquet years in Paris.[54] In this essay Saint-Evremond wonders whether "the prince" can have "a friend." A court is a system of interests. The prince wants to "open his heart," he dreams of tasting "the sweetness that familiarity and freedom of conversation can give to best friends." The leader of political society also wants to enjoy the happiness of natural society. But woe to the favorite who would allow himself to be ensnared in that trap! His generosity will do him in, the ingenuity of court hypocrites will crush him. "But," adds Saint-Evremond, "let us not be envious of all those who make themselves feared: they lose the sweetness of loving and of being loved." That is his last word on Louis XIV, a word of retrospective admiration for Foucquet, a "Cornellian hero" because of his heart.

Sorbière's treatise *De l'amitié* stems from a philosopher's attempt to adapt himself and his knowledge to the wit reigning in the *surintendant*'s entourage.[55] It was easy for him to succeed at that attempt. A few years earlier, he had sent a confidant a skeptical profession of faith that could have been initialed by Anacréon, as described by Madeleine de Scudéry in 1660:

> If there is one thing that honorable people approve of in me, it is that I know how to recognize and revere those who possess to a preeminent degree the qualities I myself lack. I do not despise anyone, I praise everyone's gifts, I even admire reveries, which seem ingenious to me, and, because I have a universal taste for everything that men and women of wit present to us, I have reservations only about those who want to compel me to adopt their particular opinions, as if it were necessary that, having tasted their dish, I should renounce all other fare. I want them to leave me alone, so that, as at a banquet, I am allowed to eat everything that appeals to me. If a sauce is not to my liking, I do not blame the cook, and I know very well that different ones are needed to satisfy everyone. It is from that diversity that the excellence and sumptuousness of feasts come.[56]

Born a Huguenot, Sorbière quarreled with the Calvinist theologians, converted to Catholicism, and was rewarded with good ecclesiastical benefits. Along with others, including Descartes, he made the journey to Stockholm to enjoy the patronage of Queen Christina, "the Semiramis of the North." Sorbière was the French interpreter of Hobbes, whom he met in Paris, and the publisher and biographer of Gassendi, whom he took for his master. In *De l'amitié*, he engages in a bold and infinitely seductive synthesis of Hobbes's political philosophy and Epicurus's and Gassendi's wisdom of the hidden life. The classical idea of friendship is that it is a natural virtue, predating political societies. The famous treatise on the subject by Cicero shows how the superior forms of friendship are the reminiscence of an original and generative social bond of humanity, a reminiscence that rises above political calculations of self-interest, interest groups, and favor-trading. The Ciceronian theory of conversation is derived from the theory of friendship: leisurely exchange takes place on the fringes of the political forum and its eloquence, which is moved by the selfish desire to conquer. Conversation is the reemergence of a natural, contemplative, disinterested, confiding bond within the very heart of political society.

Sorbière's treatise begins with a diametrically opposed concept of friendship: men are by nature wicked, hateful, violent, drawn toward mutual destruction. Only political societies, and the authority that imposes respect through fear, create the conditions favorable for the appearance of civil humanity. Friendship, unlike love, which is a natural and violent passion, is one of the happy fruits of the art of politics. Nonetheless, Hobbes's philosophy, which Sorbière at first follows, allows us to think of friendship only in the terms of well-understood interests. But Gassendi's disciple also wants to conceive of a higher friendship, the sort that Aristotle, even before Cicero, proposed as the ideal, and which Corneille in his tragedies, and Madeleine de Scudéry in her novels, make the unbreakable bond between noble souls. For Epicurus and Gassendi it is also the philosophical bond par excellence. Sorbière thus adds another story to the edifice of the Leviathan. Political societies, through the iron rule they rightly impose on the natural violence of men, control it only crudely and imperfectly. Public authority, however vigilant it might be, cannot prevent many men subject to its jurisdiction from behaving, unbeknownst to itself, as they do in the state of nature, as wolves, devouring their fellows. To "live in peace and security" it is therefore necessary, within the public and overall order imposed by the sovereign, to form small, private alliances, which lead us to "lay down the weapons" with which nature has provided us, to create a "good faith" bond between individuals and, since there is strength in numbers, to effectively resist the archaic "wolves" with which even the best-policed society remains infested. These associations of private interests and defenses, through the pleasure they give to those who put their trust in them, create sweet habits: they then become the "pleasure of conversation and the communication of thoughts," in a felicitous synthesis of Hobbesian self-interest and Epicurean pleasure.

But that level of humanization of *Homo politicus* is not the final one. Self-interested friendship prepares the way for friendship enjoyed for itself. It then becomes an admirable moral masterpiece. Sorbière quotes

Horace: *Nihil ego contulerim jucundo sanus amico* (If I have any sense at all, there is nothing I place above a playful friend).

The private golden age within the iron age of political society, the company of friends, and the bond of trust that unites them, are rare things, which earn their merit through long ordeals. "To acquire a true friend," writes Sorbière, "and to draw this treasure away from the corrupt majority of men, one must correct with great skill the natural ferocity of the human spirit." And Sorbière, who has read the same classics as La Fontaine, cites Boccaccio's tale of the two friends who fight over a mule. The moral of the fable: the "exquisite" social bond of friendship must be constantly reestablished and clarified, because natural violence tends to make violence arise from even the smallest misunderstanding. To assess that moral miracle of friendship, its birth and its perpetuation, which is irreducible to any method or plan, Sorbière quotes a saying from the Augustinian Petrarch: *Si vis amari, ama, quanquam et hoc ipsum saepe frustra est* (If you want to be loved, then love, though even that path is often disappointing).[57]

Only "men and women of wit and the most learned people" have access to that higher level of political societies, where friendship becomes a mode of being together, and which is unknown to ordinary people and even to ordinary friendships. It is a perilous level, since is it is suspended above the rest of the edifice, as the penthouse so to speak: at any moment, political societies can do without that penthouse, which remains incomprehensible for the vast majority of uncouth men who compose society. That aristocracy of the mind and heart can even attract their hatred: "Since [these elites] are in some ways more human than other men," Sorbière writes superbly,

> through the faculty of thought that is aroused in them, they find nothing sweeter than to produce it and exercise it with a few of their fellows. They therefore need friends, to whom they communicate their thoughts, and with whom they argue, refine, and polish them: of all life's occupations, that is the most spiritual, the most noble, and the most worthy of the origin we rightly attribute to the soul, and to the immortality that we promise for it with such certainty and such solid demonstrations.[58]

Sorbière, tracing a complete circle of the diplomacy of wit beginning with Hobbes, arrives where Robert Arnauld d'Andilly and, later, Fénelon begin. Both men are successors to Saint Francis of Sales, and the theorists, respectively, of "pure friendship" and "pure love." Sorbière's treatise, halfway between moral theology and political philosophy, takes us in a few pages through the entire gamut of the classic French moralists, from the analysis of the calculation of interests to the search for disinterested generosity, from the reign of fear to the reign of love.[59] That circular argument, which puts the most diverse doctrines to the test, is in reality an ardent, imaginative, and inventive meditation on the kingdom, its political and moral future, on the chance its writers, philosophers, wits, and poets have to guide it toward its true and unique vocation. Nicolas Foucquet was at the center of all these projects, all these contradictory aspirations, and wished to embody their synthesis. Sorbière's treatise shows that, even for those who did not share Pellisson's faith in Foucquet's genius, the hour had come in France for the power of the civilizing state to coincide with the most "exquisite" conquest of nature by civilization, the friendship that establishes and moves the republic of letters, the secular sister of the religious *caritas* that presumably moves the Christian republic.

On 5 September 1661, the king settled the matter once and for all. In a 1663 speech entitled *Au roi* (To the king), Sorbière took note of it and assured Louis XIV of the republic of scholarly letters' respect. La Fontaine remained faithful to his private lyricism and to the friendship that had joined him to his vanquished Maecenas.

CHAPTER 4

Nicolas Foucquet, or How Not to Become Louis XIV's Favorite

The king and Colbert, those two raving madmen after absolute power, were agreed in their exemplary hatred for that cheery personality, who loved power only as a dilettante. Fouquet had the simplicity of those who did not take themselves too seriously; but Louis XIV and Colbert took themselves terribly seriously. . . . Reason often regrets having gotten the better of the heart. And perhaps, in hating Fouquet, the king was rather giving in to a certain nostalgia, a yearning for freedom as it had reigned before the despotism of Versailles, where art itself would be fully involved in politics, the politics of furniture, tapestries, tragedy, decoration manufactures, the politics of painting, the politics of gardens. Did Louis XIV, an athlete with an iron will, look with silent envy upon the *surintendant* Fouquet's casualness, the gracious negligence of the last Renaissance man, an alchemist of fiduciary currency? Did not the France of Louis XIV sometimes yearn for the France of Louis XIII?
— Paul Morand, *Fouquet ou le Soleil offusqué* (1961)

$\mathcal{O}$n 5 September 1661, after a meeting with the king in Nantes, the *surintendant* Nicolas Foucquet's post chaise was stopped by d'Artagnan and fifteen musketeers. D'Artagnan handed the minister the order under the king's private seal, signed by the king's own hand. Foucquet read it and said only "that he believed he was better in tune with the king than anyone in the kingdom."[1]

In La Fontaine's *Elégie aux Nymphes de Vaux*, which the friends of the *surintendant*, imprisoned on the accusation of high treason, began to circulate early the next year, the poet, in an effort to save Foucquet, melodiously develops the commonplace of the surprises of Fortune, pleading for the king's clemency:

> Voilà le précipice où l'ont enfin jeté
> Les attraits enchanteurs de la prospérité.
> Dans les palais des rois, cette plainte est commune,
> On n'y connaît que trop les jeux de la Fortune
> Ses trompeuses faveurs, ses appas inconstants;
> Mais on ne les connaît que lorsqu'il n'est plus temps.
> ·
> Jamais un favori ne borne sa carrière;
> Il ne regarde point ce qu'il laisse en arrière;
> Et tout ce vain amour des grandeurs et du bruit
> Ne le saurait quitter qu'après l'avoir détruit.[2]

> Behold the chasm where he has finally been cast
> By the bewitching charms of prosperity.
> In the palaces of kings, this lament is not rare,
> The games of Fortune are known only too well,
> Her misleading favors, her fickle charms;
> But they are known only too late.
> · · · · · · · · · · · · · · · ·
> Never has a favorite set limits on his career;
> He does not look back at what he leaves behind;
> And all the vain love of grandeur and acclaim,
> Will not let go of him until he's been destroyed.

This commonplace, designed to inspire leniency and sympathy, has Foucquet, who wanted to become Louis XIV's prime minister, join the long procession of figures most vulnerable to the political games of monarchies: "favorites."

What was a favorite in the seventeenth century? How did he differ from a "minister"? In the vocabulary of the Tuscan Academy of *Crusca*, a passage from Firenzuola is used to illustrate the definition of *favorito*: "Abbiti cura dalla invidia, la quale, come palla di sapone, si mette sotto i piedi de' favoriti" (Watch out for jealousy, which slips, like a piece of soap, under the foot of favorites).[3]

In Furetière's French *Dictionnaire*, to illustrate the definition of the favor of kings and great men, there is a passage from La Bruyère: "One sees men whom the winds of favor at first propel in full sail, and which make them lose sight of land in a moment's time."[4]

Misleading spells, vanity of vanities, slippery soap, the inconstancy of marine winds: in the seventeenth century, all the metaphors of tragic irony made the disgraced favorite, in Italian and in French, the quintessential object of the caprices of fortune, the subject most sensitive to political dramas, the mirror par excellence of human frailty. With his fall, Nicolas Foucquet, himself a highly literate man, adored in his time of splendor by the greatest writers and poets of his generation, had an even keener impact on the literary imagination. His charm and misfortunes cast a distressing shadow on the beginnings of Louis XIV's reign, a shadow that never went away, and that even today clouds the glory of Louis the Great at least as much the prophetic rumbling of Saint-Simon's *Mémoires* burdened the end of his reign. La Fontaine played a significant role in Foucquet's transfiguration into a hero of the "tragedy of the favorite."

The "favorite," emblem of the ephemeral and the illusory, is thus the opposite of a stable political institution. The dismissal of a minister is a public and normal event; the fall of a favorite is a tragedy as human as it is political. It sets in play not only state interests but, to an equal degree, the most intense personal passions and emotions. In France at least, the word "favorite" never appears in the official vocabulary. It designates someone on the fringe, with something close to the rank of a royal mistress. Furetière's *Dictionnaire* cites a very telling passage from Father Bouhours: "Favorites have no direct relationship with the public. All their duties deal solely with the prince's private life."[5]

ARISTIPPUS THE PHILOSOPHER: KINGS AND THEIR FAVORITES

In 1658, just when the *surintendant*'s ascent seemed at its zenith, a magnificent posthumous essay appeared by Jean-Louis Guez de Balzac, the supreme French literary authority at the time. It defined the terms of a true dramaturgy of the "minister" and the "favorite" in France.

The essay is dedicated to Queen Christina of Sweden and is entitled *Aristippe ou de la Cour* (Aristippus, or, On the court). Aristippus was the name of an ancient Greek philosopher, often quoted by Horace in his *Epistulae*: he was able to remain a meditative and contemplative spectator at the very heart of affairs of state. Under that classical name, Guez de Balzac depicts, gives voice to, and comments on a "learned sage" he claims to have met through the Landgrave of Hessen. The sage occupied the prince's "leisure time" and "intervals of illness" with "clever conversation" that closely examined the political affairs of Europe, diplomatic and military, through disinterested meditation. This "distant gaze" on the world of action is, according to Balzac, a higher form of happiness. "Public affairs," he writes boldly, "are sometimes dirty and strewn with filth; you hardly need touch them to begin to rot. But speculation is more honest than action: it is done with innocence and purity. The paintings of dragons and crocodiles, having no venom to harm the eyes, may have colors that delight them. And I admit to you that even the world, which displeases me so much in itself, seemed agreeable and entertaining to me in the conversations of Aristippus."[6]

Aristippus is a philosopher and spectator of the world. But he is not a Stoic. He stands with men, even if, within himself, he stands apart from their cruelty and follies. The dogma of the Portico, that "the sage does not need anyone," is an error in his view: *Only God is wholly content by himself.* Men, even philosophers, and a fortiori princes, cannot do without "society" and "company." To deliberate, they cannot be satisfied with consulting only themselves: they need advisers and friends. "The princes who have accomplished the most are those who have had the best support. . . . How blessed is the prince, and how heaven loves him, if, in his time, there happen to be minds of the first order, and souls equal to their intelligence in insight, strength, and sublimity. . . . They are the guardian angels of the kingdom."

Two political conclusions seem unavoidable to the sage: first, that it is an "established truth that kings cannot reign without ministers"; and second, that "it is nearly as true that they cannot live without favorites." Kings are men, both heads of state and private individuals, and one cannot require of them, in the exercise of their "work" and their affairs or in the discharge of their leisure time and rest, the divine autarky to which even Christ himself—God become man—did not restrict himself on earth, since he took his apostles as confidants and even preferred one of them, namely, Saint John. A king cannot do without ministers, "the first tier of servants, who all have a place in the administration of the state," or without favorites.[7]

But he must avoid the "misunderstandings" from which his century may suffer, and must not confuse "the people who please" and "those who are useful," by putting on the council those who "might have been agreeable to him in conversation." Although both are necessary and unavoidable, the "minister," who assists the king in his public life, and the "favorite," who establishes a foothold in his private life, are not interchangeable. It would be monstrous if a choice based on passion, and usually a blind passion (like that of Pasiphaë for his bull, or Caligula for his horse), pulled the favorite away from the private sphere where he belongs and propelled him onto the public stage where he is out of place. Such a thing would be accompanied by violence and disorder. "Amour propre and natural arrogance (which swells the hearts of kings in particular, when they cling to a mistake they have made, and do not admit that they can err)" are the only things that can impose a favorite, chosen for personal and private reasons, as a minister at the head of the state for a long period of time. Such a transferal is at the root of dreadful political tragedies, and of a world that has come unhinged. When favorites claim "to act like Phaëthon in this world," favorites, Balzac declares, "are in constant danger of being their own downfall and that of their country, especially when they have refined their ignorance through the practices of the court, and two or three good successes, stemming purely from the liberality of God, have given them a good opinion of themselves and have made them believe they are doing the good that they are, in fact, receiving."[8]

Hence, apart from the sense of pathos he can elicit after the fact, that is, after he has fallen, in France the "favorite" is designated as a political monster in the making: the object of the king's personal favor, something wholly natural, but which can spill over into public life and then become wholly unnatural. That favor makes the *mignon* a minister who is tyrannical by definition, who abuses the authority proper to the king. Yet, in that sense, Nicolas Foucquet was never a favorite, though he suffered the favorite's tragic fate. Even though, after the fact, La Fontaine used the word and the fiction of the "disgraced favorite" to make Foucquet's fate more touching, the state secretary who aspired to the powers of a prime minister never enjoyed Louis XIV's *private* favoritism.

Louis XIII, His State Minister, and His Favorites

Louis XIII had a "favorite" before 1624, and he made him a minister and a duke: Luynes. After 1624 he had others: Chalais, Saint-Simon, Cinq-Mars. They were never ministers (though one or another of them did dream of being one); Richelieu made sure of that. With Richelieu, the duties of "state minister" and the role of "favorite" seem to have been kept quite separate in the French court. Richelieu embodied reason of state, he was a sort of Minerva in cardinal's robes; under his rule, the king yielded, usually against his personal feelings and religious leanings, which he confided in secret to his favorites or his confessor. Closely watched by the cardinal's spies, these favorites, sometimes champing at the bit, caught, in Louis's "asides," his torments, laments, doubts, and remorse.

Irritated and bewildered by that incomprehensible split within the king, the princely and parliamentary opposition to Richelieu nevertheless attempted on several occasions to use Louis XIII's favorites or confessors to shake Richelieu's hold over the king and obtain the disgrace of the head of his council. Several times, Louis XIII himself was sorely tempted to side with his favorite of the moment, the mouthpiece of the political opposition to Richelieu, against his prime minister. But in the end, Richelieu always managed to convince the king that he needed to choose the state, and the duty the state dictated to the king through Richelieu, over his personal preferences as a man. Richelieu succeeded in literally training Louis XIII, by accustoming him to separating within himself the head of state from the man, reason of state from his personal feelings. Therefore, Richelieu was not at all a "favorite" in the sense of the Spanish *privado*, who officially combines the king's private preference with the trusted role of head of state, someone who is both the king's best friend and the prime minister of his kingdom.

Under the Richelieu ministry, the royal French state thus became an idea "clear and distinct" from the king's human tenderness. The sort of impersonal transcendence that Richelieu gave the state radically modified the exercise of monarchical power: unlike in the past, it was no longer the normal outcome of endless negotiations between the sovereign, the princes, the Parlements, and the estates-general and estates-provincial. In that balance of power, the affective element—personal friendships, mutual obligations, *amicitia, caritas*, local alliances—had played a determining role. With Richelieu, the higher interest of the state, defined by the state minister, had to prevail over every other consideration, even if, along the way, one had to destroy the most respectable interests and traditions, the most legitimate loyalties and sentiments. Louis XIII submitted to that cold-monster logic, but he did not yield to it without anxiety, hesitations, and fits of melancholia. The duc de Saint-Simon, son of a "favorite," was very grateful to Louis XIII for his qualms, which linked him to Old France. He did not forgive Louis XIV for having a soul that belonged entirely to the state.[9]

But words can be misleading. In spite of everything, Richelieu was called the "favorite" by the opposition, in the sense that, as the imperious depositary of royal authority, the minister, according to his adversaries, used that authority like a Machiavellian prince, a tyrant. Even though that excessive power was not rooted in Louis XIII's affection for Richelieu, for his adversaries it could be explained only by a weakness in the character of the king, powerless to govern himself, and who had abandoned the reins of the state to a dominating will. Under Henry IV, neither Villeroy nor a fortiori Sully had ever been called a "favorite"; they were quite simply ministers. They served the "good" king who governed on his own; they did not take advantage of the ambiguous favor that, stemming from a private disorder, affection, or weakness, could overflow into the public sphere. Louis XIII's "timidity" made Richelieu an omnipotent "minister/favorite," whereas the king's desires made his "favorites" the chosen of his heart, but without any political power.

That fascinating triad of king, minister, and favorite had long been the object of French reflection and political passion. As early as 1515, at the dawn of the reign of Francis I, Guillaume Budé, the father of French legal humanism, undertook a violent critique of the administration of Charles VIII's "favorite," Cardinal d'Amboise, who preferred to employ Italians, and who had dragged the king into a ruinous adventure in Italy. In his *De Asse,* Budé complains that a disastrous habit led the kings of France away from exerting their own authority with love for their people, a love of which only they were capable; instead, they handed it over to ambitious and greedy men. For Budé, the "minister" is the one who helps the king to exercise fully, but with moderation, his legitimate power. The "favorite" is the one who takes advantage of the king's weakness—the inauspicious root of his elevation to the rank of prime minister—in order to abuse royal power, overstep its proper use, and twist the state's entire orientation.[10]

When, under the regency of Anne of Austria a century and a half later, Pierre Dupuy, another giant of French legal humanism, wanted to make Richelieu retrospectively despicable, he made him a "minister/favorite" and attributed this dreadful maxim to him: "A favorite, a minister, never perished for doing too much evil, but only for not doing enough."

In Pierre Dupuy's *Histoire des Favoris anciens et modernes,* published posthumously in Leiden in 1660, there are no French examples, except, in the appendix, the maréchal d'Ancre, Marie de Médicis's Italian minister and favorite, whom Louis XIII had murdered in 1617 at the instigation of his own favorite, Luynes.[11] The intention of the book is to establish, against Richelieu's memory, that "minister/favorites," whose unregulated power makes a mockery of the laws of the kingdom and arbitrarily abuses the prince's favor, are in reality tyrants, and contrary to the spirit of French institutions. Their authority has always been founded on the king's "weakness" and not on his reasoned choice; it is exerted irrationally, outside legal norms and legitimate limits. Apart from the maréchal d'Ancre, the only contemporary example offered by Pierre Dupuy is that of Rodrigo Calderón, the favorite and short-lived minister of Philip III of Spain. During the Fronde, the *Mazarinades* credited Mazarin with the title "favorite" in order to discredit him. According to the Frondeurs, he owed his election to the caprice of a woman's heart, that of Anne of Austria.[12]

FOUCQUET, CANDIDATE FOR THE KING'S FRIENDSHIP, NOT HIS FAVOR

Nicolas Foucquet, *procureur général* of the Parlement de Paris since 1650, superintendent of finances along with Abel Servien since 1653, openly harbored the ambition of succeeding Cardinal Mazarin in the duties of prime minister of the kingdom. During the period when he was a candidate, he was never called the "favorite" and, in fact, never was one. He was not Mazarin's favorite, since the cardinal took great care to provide rivals to oppose him (Servien, then Colbert); nor was he Louis XIV's favorite, since the king, in the months following the cardinal's death, even while keeping Foucquet in the position of *surintendant*, secretly planned his fall, in close collaboration with Colbert.[13] If La Fontaine called him the "favorite" in *Elégie aux Nymphes de Vaux*, it was almost by antiphrasis: he was "disgraced" as a favorite might have been, even though he had never been one (which, in France, was a sign of merit). But the public—and even Foucquet himself perhaps—had attributed its own "reasonable" preference to the king, and it was only fair that the poet/advocate should play on that retrospective illusion: long dissimulated, it brought out all the more clearly the abomination of the king's long-dissimulated preference for Colbert, the "favorite" hated by the public, whose political power, founded on the sacrifice of Foucquet, seemed to owe everything to the "favor" finally demonstrated by Louis XIV.

Foucquet owed his position as *surintendant* and state minister not to the "favor" of Mazarin, who feared him, but to the enormous services he had rendered the queen mother and to her prime minister and favorite at the height of the Fronde of the princes. While the unanimously execrated Mazarin fled abroad or stayed away from the court between August 1652 and February 1653, Nicolas Foucquet, the head of the loyalist Parlement that had taken refuge in Pontoise at his suggestion, demonstrated all the intelligence, authority, and diplomacy of a statesman, often dictating from a distance what Mazarin ought to do, and sometimes standing in for his bewildered ministers. Even at the time, Foucquet's personal financial credit and that of his family had made it possible to finance the royal armies within the country and on its borders. The debt the Crown and Cardinal Mazarin contracted with Foucquet, who, with his brother's help, prepared for the minister's triumphant return to Paris in February 1653, was a matter of public knowledge. Upon his return, Mazarin named Foucquet superintendent of the finances of the kingdom; he could hardly have done otherwise. But his duties were to be combined with those of Abel Servien, the signatory of the treaties of Westphalia.[14]

As for Colbert, administrator of the cardinal's personal fortune since 1651, he was truly the cardinal's "favorite"; he lived for him and expected everything from him. Foucquet lived and asserted himself on his own, by means of the important political role he had played in the Parlement during the final crisis of the Fronde, and the financial credit that made him irreplaceable in the financing of the state. Colbert, administrator of Mazarin's private affairs, was the close accomplice of his master. That complicity gave him the means to work against the *surintendant* and to feed the jealousy and irritation Mazarin felt for an all-too-indispensable man. Spurred on by Colbert, the cardinal required that the new *surintendant* regularly provide for the financial needs of the state, and that, from time to time, he see to the reconstitution of his personal fortune at the state's expense. Foucquet was forced into displays of the utmost virtuosity. In 1659 Colbert sent the cardinal a scathing report attacking Foucquet's "irregularities." Mazarin did not dare follow Colbert's advice: he even urged the two men to reconcile.[15]

Everything was left hanging when Mazarin died in March 1661. Now it was the king's decision that had to be obtained. Perhaps Foucquet had not heretofore concerned himself enough with it. In contrast, Colbert, recommended by Mazarin, had long since earned the personal trust of Louis XIV, who had been a docile disciple of the Italian cardinal since his childhood. The young king would prove even more sensitive than his master to the difference in position between Foucquet and Colbert: Foucquet was an autonomous power; he enjoyed an authority and a popularity (or unpopularity, depending on the moment) that he owed above all to his personal talents and the services rendered to the state; and he aspired to win the king's friendship; Colbert was an obscure administrator who could succeed—as he was well aware—only by effacing himself before his masters and becoming more important through their favor. Mazarin already leaned toward Colbert, and Louis XIV could only confirm that preference. That was the blind spot of Foucquet's ministerial plans.[16]

The Rivalry between the Serpent and the Squirrel

A great deal was at stake morally and politically in the choice the young king was about to make, and which he delayed from 9 March 1661, the date of the cardinal's death, until 5 September of the same year, the date of Foucquet's arrest.

First, the king had to free his reign from the odor of financial corruption that had made Mazarin's ministry so despised. Among the other minor scandals, the huge fortune amassed by the prime minister beginning in 1653 implied a management of public funds that was injurious to the state and appalling to taxpayers.

As Mazarin's administrator, Colbert was better placed than anyone to know in what way and to what degree the cardinal had plundered the state. He was also better placed than anyone to see in what way and to what degree the reformation of that kind of abuse, ardently demanded by the Fronde, was one of the great state causes in which it was important to drape himself to please the young king. Yet, paradoxically, it was Colbert's role in the prime minister's misappropriation of funds that made for his strength and allowed him to play the role of Cato with impunity: reasons of state prohibited the accounts of the cardinal, the queen mother's "favorite" and official architect of the victory of the monarchy over the two Frondes, from becoming the object of public scrutiny. Colbert, in contrast, could lead the king to believe that his great rival Foucquet, much more in the public eye than he was and a great virtuoso of a traditional financial system in which misappropriation and peculation had become natural, so to speak, would make an ideal scapegoat for the financial management of the cardinal-minister. In sacrificing the person of the too-brilliant superintendent of Mazarin's finances, it was possible both to spare the cardinal's memory and to give enormous moral satisfaction to the public: Foucquet's punishment would show that the king was thoroughly resolved to break with the felonious financial practices that, under Mazarin, had outraged public opinion. The sacrifice of the *surintendant* had its origin in Colbert's ambition and, as a corollary, in his political ascent, wrapped in the garb of financial virtue.[17]

Nicolas Foucquet was defenseless against that strategy: he had, in fact, been responsible for public finances since 1653 and could therefore be charged with all their sins in the place of his deceased master. He was wealthy, of course: on his own, and by virtue of his second marriage into the family of Président Jeannin de Castille, superintendent of finances for Marie de Médicis. But the magnificence of his lifestyle, the generosity of his patronage of poets and artists, might lead some to believe that he had been the primary beneficiary of the plundering of the state, which the cardinal himself had supported, and from which he had by far most greedily profited, but of which, for reasons of state, he had to be absolved. It was considered normal in the seventeenth century, as it is today, for an individual to refrain from enriching himself at the state's expense. But at the time, it was no less normal for a high servant of the state to build a private fortune, which had to be immense, in order to maintain his rank through a magnificent lifestyle. There is a striking, unresolved contradiction between these two "norms." Mazarin extricated himself admirably under cover of reasons of state. Foucquet allowed himself to get caught in the middle.

In addition to the moral and financial stakes of the debate, linked to the memory of Cardinal Mazarin, much was at stake politically in 1661, this time with respect to the legacy of Cardinal de Richelieu: namely, the absolutism he had imposed during his ministry in the conduct of affairs of state. For Louis XIV, about to begin his personal reign, Colbert and Foucquet represented two diametrically opposed options, and Mazarin did not care before dying to choose between them publicly. He left the choice to his royal pupil.

Along with the public stabilization of the financial system, Colbert could promise the king the completion, under his authority, of the work of the two cardinal-ministers. It satisfied the king's will to crush the seeds of the Fronde once and for all and to resume the construction of an absolute state, which had had to pull back and even compromise under the regency of Anne of Austria. It was already a miracle that the administrative and military staff trained by Richelieu had not been dispersed and had served continuously between 1648 and 1654, in spite of the assaults of Parlement, the princes, and the raging mob. The time had come to permanently prevent, through an iron rule, the return of such disorder. Sooner or later, as under Richelieu, its glorious justification would be war.

Foucquet, in contrast, allowed the French public to look forward to a regime of reconciliation, synthesis, and compromise between the restored state authority and the political forces that had tenaciously combated its absolutist excesses since 1625, and with renewed vigor during the Fronde. In addition, there would be diplomacy and peace abroad.

How could Foucquet, who so glaringly belonged to the winning camp of the Fronde, have surfaced in 1657–61 as the prime minister ardently desired both by former Frondeurs, such as the duc de La Rochefoucauld, and, to an equal degree, by the moderate loyalists? The reconciliatory approach he championed at the time corresponded to a personal tendency already perceptible in his former career, and a tradition true to his background. His father, François Foucquet, a magistrate, then a state adviser, had served Richelieu well, but without excess of zeal and with a few reservations of conscience. Nicolas himself, adviser to the Parlement de Metz in 1633, at age eighteen, had probably been appreciated by Richelieu and his successor Mazarin. However, as intendant of Dauphiné in 1645, he had stood up to a tax riot with a personal courage and humanity that marked a radical departure from the brutality of the repression in Richelieu's manner. As general intendant of Paris in 1648, then *procureur général* of the Parlement de Pontoise in 1650, he had always displayed complete loyalty to the cause of monarchy, but with a freedom of style and an originality of perspective that implied a conception of the kingdom that was very different from that of Mazarin and his ministers. His marriage in 1651 to Marie-Madeleine Jeannin de Castille did not just bring him into a very wealthy family: his wife was the cousin of Chalais's widow (Chalais had been Louis XIII's favorite and was the first victim of Richelieu's arbitrariness). François Foucquet, Nicolas's father, had had a seat in the special court that had hastily sentenced Chalais to death. The deeply religious magistrate must have retained a bitter memory of it, and perhaps remorse as well, which he may have secretly confided to his family. Foucquet, then, knew firsthand the level of arbitrariness and violence Richelieu's domestic policy had reached. In 1657 he married his eldest daughter to Armand de Béthune, marquis de Charost, great-nephew of Sully, whose legend, associated with that of "good King Henry," was more popular than ever.[18] These details agree with the letter he sent to Mazarin in 1652, in which a political program fundamentally opposed to absolutism is very clearly outlined.

"I am very displeased," he wrote, "to see the servants of Your Excellency give up the hope they once had to see him presently exercise authority with the pleasure and satisfaction of all peoples, with the consent of the princes and of the Parlement, and in the celebration of a peace so universally desired."[19]

At the height of the Fronde, he was working for a victory by the king, to be sure, but without vengeance, and without a return to the authoritarian excesses that had outraged France against the minister/favorites. He had chosen Cicero over Caesar, Sully over Richelieu, concord over state violence. The most intelligent of the defeated Frondeurs naturally turned to him. His candidacy to succeed Mazarin corresponded to the general wish to be done with extremes. He took care to organize this "consensus" around his candidacy.

Winning the Public's Trust

That campaign, which Pellisson spearheaded in 1657, was a political revolution in itself. It presupposed that the king's prime minister, prior to being named by the sovereign, had to win the trust of the public at large, be a prisoner to no single faction, and enjoy the respect of all. That call for public confidence went against the practices of the monarchy. The choice of ministers was by definition the act of the king, who was supremely free to impose an unpopular man.

Far from anticipating Louis XIV's decision and encroaching on his freedom, Foucquet, for his part, assumed that the king would come down on the side of the kingdom's common good and, like him, would want to put an end to institutional practices that had divided and appalled the French people. The *surintendant* proposed to place the capital of political trust he had accumulated by virtue of his name at the king's disposal, just as, since the Fronde, he had placed the irreplaceable capital of financial trust at his service. A royalist and loyalist in his heart, the *surintendant* wanted to return to Louis XIV "the love of his subjects," which Louis's father had lost through Richelieu's violence, and make Louis-Gift-of-God another Louis the Well-Beloved, reawakening the memory of his grandfather Henry IV and, like Corneille's Augustus, basking in a conciliatory glory. That generous exchange between a minister and the king who approved him would have based their alliance at the head of the state on the understanding between friends, of which Sorbière, Arnauld d'Andilly, and Mlle de Scudéry's La Fontaine/Anacréon spoke. A political happy end would have been the outcome of the tragedy of the Fronde.[20]

The imagination was on the *surintendant's* side.

From 1653 to 1659, when Abel Servien's death made him the sole superintendent of finances, Foucquet cultivated around his person a close network of family alliances, special interests, and friendships from the most various circles. It was both a true political party and a financial breeding ground. That faction fooled itself into believing that, should Foucquet become Louis XIV's prime minister, he would know how to govern the restored monarchical state with the same combination of authority, diplomacy, and humanity he had demonstrated in 1651–53, at the height of the state's crisis.[21]

That faction had so many branches that, in case of his disgrace, Foucquet could even imagine "going underground" and negotiating a compromise with the court from a position of strength. This was truly the traditional conception of the monarchy, from which Richelieu, in his conflicts and compromises with the princes or the Protestants entrenched in their strongholds, had wanted to break away, but with which, willy-nilly, he often had to come to terms. The notorious "defense plan" written in Foucquet's hand, discovered in 1661 behind a mirror in the Saint-Mandé château but dating to 1658–59, played by the rules of the game in the many-sided politics of monarchy.[22] Mazarin, "disgraced" by the king (though against the king's will) at the height of the Fronde of the princes, had himself been a model for Foucquet when he negotiated his return from a position of strength from the fortress city of Sedan, and then from the German city of Brühl. In France this was a very old and normal custom after a rift between important men or Parlement and the king. Louis XIV was determined to put that worry to rest.

The King's First Appearance on the Political Stage

On 9 March 1661, the Italian prime minister's death raised the question of succession. It was at that point that the young Louis XIV, age twenty-two, first came onto the political stage. He was known primarily for his docility toward the prime minister chosen by his mother, for his youthful and virile good looks, his talent as a dancer and a hunter, and his

214 THE POET AND THE KING

robust sexual appetites. He was credited with all the royal virtues, but had not yet had the opportunity to show how he intended to exercise them: Mazarin cast a shadow over him. On 10 March 1661 at the Louvre, the young king assembled around him Chancellor Séguier, the *surinten-dant* Foucquet, state secretaries Le Tellier, Lyonne, Loménie de Brienne, Brienne's son, Duplessis-Guénégaud, and Phélypeaux de la Vrillière. According to the younger Brienne's *Mémoires*, to the surprise of all, the king declared:

> Monsieur le Chancelier, I have brought you together with my ministers and my state secretaries to tell you that, up to this time, I wanted very much to have my affairs governed by the late cardinal: it is now time for me to govern them myself. You will help me with your advice when I ask for it. . . . And you, sirs [turning to his state secretaries], I forbid you to sign anything, even a safe-conduct or a passport, without my command; [I order you] to report to me personally every day, and to favor no one in your monthly registers. And you, Monsieur le Surintendant, I have explained my will to you, I beg of you to use Colbert, whom the late cardinal recommended to me.[23]

That proud declaration seemed to correspond to the age-old wish to see the king of France exert his sovereign power on his own, without relying on the self-interested services of a "minister/favorite." That wish had always come from the most enlightened minds, who expected from their king an exercise of power that was at once moderate and vigorous, the antithesis of the "Machiavellian" excesses for which "favorites," arbitrarily promoted to ministers, appeared destined. For the first time since Henry IV's reign, Louis XIV seemed to want to do without the "favorite" and to "govern by himself." Naturally, that did not rule out the use of one or more ministers as *servants* of his royal will, and not as *usurpers* of that will. Therefore, Foucquet still had reason for hope. All the same, the last words of the royal declaration gave a first nudge to Colbert, who became Foucquet's supervisor. That minor measure gave some indication that, under the pomp of the affirmation of principle, there might be the seeds of a "minister/favorite." Nonetheless, no one at the time imagined that, under the declared intention to "govern alone," Louis XIV was concealing a plan to restore, with the participation of the devoted Colbert, the absolutist state, which had made Richelieu so despised and which the Fronde had prevented Mazarin from consolidating. Foucquet and his friends even had reason to believe that the declaration of intent marked the young king's desired break from absolutism and, hence, from the regime of

Machiavellian "favorites." They could even imagine that the king, "governing by himself," in a spirit of clemency and moderation, could find no better servant and mouthpiece than Foucquet, a minister/friend and not a minister/favorite.

No one, in fact, interpreted the victory of the regent and Mazarin over the two Frondes as the prelude to a reappearance of the dictatorship Richelieu had imposed between 1624 and 1641. That dictatorship passed unanimously for a temporary perversion of the state, and not a normal regime. It had created the general exasperation on which the Fronde had fed. The return to civil order could be attributed to the public's weariness and to Mazarin's political skill, with good support from Foucquet. The signing of the peace of the Pyrenees in 1659, accompanied by Louis XIV's marriage to Marie-Thérèse, the infanta of Spain, also put an end to the Thirty Years' War into which Richelieu had dragged France against its will in 1635, and which had been the excuse for the regime of exception imposed by the cardinal. Peace in Europe had been accompanied in France by a general amnesty, beginning with the pardon granted Condé himself, the insolent leader of the Fronde of the princes, who then went over, with bag and baggage, to the Spanish enemy. Now that peace had returned, both within the country and abroad, there was reason to hope that a regime inaugurated by clemency would safeguard the state's legitimate authority, even while reconciling the no-less-legitimate aspirations of magistrates, princes, and the public. That was the political golden age retrospectively attributed to Henry IV, the magnanimous victor of the civil wars.[24]

Nicolas Foucquet's candidacy to succeed Mazarin embodied that hope and enjoyed the general favor of men of letters and high society, who had chosen in Paris the side of peace abroad and reconciliation at home. The religious faction persecuted by Richelieu, repentant former Frondeurs, and gentlemen (*honnestes gens*) on all sides identified with Foucquet, an accomplished "honorable man" himself, a diplomat, a man of culture, gallant, witty, a virtuoso, and a great patron of all the arts of peace. Having admirably served and even saved the court in its dark years, he embodied in his way the victory of royal authority and civil order over the aberrations of the two Frondes. But his personality, both strong and flexible, his gift of charm and his thoughtful generosity, also guaranteed that, if he were to become prime minister, the court's victory would not take on the character of revenge or restoration. In his musician's hands, one could anticipate that the exercise of royal authority would never regain the brusque arbitrariness or cold cynicism that had turned France against Richelieu and Mazarin.

Although a friend of pleasures and erudite libertines, Nicolas Foucquet, thanks to his "sainted" mother (cofounder, along with Saint Vincent de

Paul, of the Ladies of Charity) and to his bishop brothers, had powerful sympathies in the church of the Counter-Reformation. He was equally trusted by the Protestants. The Huguenot Turenne was one of his admirers. The Calvinist Pellisson became his right-hand man in 1657. His genius at synthesis made Foucquet the heir to the Edict of Nantes. He was in every respect the candidate of civil peace and moderation. He had the "kingdom," in most of its nuances, on his side; in addition, his Breton roots made him the pride and joy of a particular region.[25]

Foucquet, who had the favor of people of "gentle birth" and of the "good French people," still had to obtain the essential thing, the young king's friendship. Nothing appeared more natural at first sight. Until Cardinal Mazarin's death, the young and handsome Louis XIV symbolized the return to normal of the kingdom's institutions and the promise of a long, peaceful, and prosperous reign.

For the hypothetical prime minister Foucquet, the king would have been, to speak the language of the time, the Augustus of this new Maecenas, the Henry IV of this new Sully. That was how Foucquet and his supporters saw it. But they had not plumbed the depths of the young king's amour propre. Louis XIV did not have the moderation of old Augustus or King Henry, or the heartfelt enthusiasm or sincere repentance of Louis XIII. Foucquet's personal talents, popularity, and support, even the debt that, as everyone knew, the Crown had incurred toward him, were so many reasons for the aversion of "self-love and love of all things for oneself," which, "hidden from the most penetrating eyes," attached Louis XIV to the state his ancestors had bequeathed to him, and which Richelieu and Mazarin had fortified against the kingdom, which had grown impatient with its yoke. The *surintendant's* close friend the duc de La Rochefoucauld dedicated no less than an entire book of maxims to an analysis of the coils of that dragon lurking in the human heart, and which prevented the king from accepting Foucquet's friendship. The king's choice turned the "seventeenth-century ethic" on its head.

THE MORT

By June 1661 Foucquet had lost his best advocate with the king, the queen mother, whom the duchesse de Chevreuse, a key figure in the revolts against Richelieu and the Fronde of the princes, had managed to turn against him during a long meeting between the two old friends at the château of Dampierre. The dark irony of that scheme was striking to everyone in the know: an adventuress, Richelieu's worst enemy in her youth and mistress of the ill-fated Chalais, had become Colbert's best ally (and soon the mother-in-law of his daughter). To thwart that dangerous maneuver, the well-informed Foucquet did not hesitate to ask Louis XIV for forgiveness for his "past faults" (which amounted to reminding him, in polite terms, of the role Mazarin had played in the financial disarray). At the end of that conversation, the chivalrous Foucquet could still imagine that the new Henry IV would ask him to be his Sully. He wanted to believe in the words of forgiveness and the protests of friendship that the king lavished on him.[26]

On 14 August 1661, Foucquet, increasingly confident in that "friendship" of which he was so warmly reassured, committed a fatal error: he resigned his position as *procureur général* of Parlement and was replaced by Président Achille de Harlay. That position had guaranteed him that, in case of arrest, he could not be judged by anyone but his peers, sheltered from the pressures of the court by the procedures of the Parlement de Paris. He believed that, in ridding himself of that legal post, which was, moreover, associated with bad memories of the Fronde, he could remove the last technical and affective obstacle to his being named by the king to head his council. He even believed—and the king let him believe—that Louis XIV would be touched to receive the considerable sum he received from the sale of his post as *procureur général*, as a political "wedding present." He zealously had that pile of gold taken to Vincennes and put in the royal treasury.[27]

He was undoubtedly warned by his spies as of June 1661 that his downfall was decided. But it was too late. Characteristically, he still wanted to believe in the king's *good faith*. That was the cornerstone of his own political plans. He could not suspect how much the very favor that Paris—and especially, the Paris of the former Frondeurs—showed for him would irritate Louis XIV: the king did not forgive, would never forgive, the rebels who had dared rattle his adolescence and challenge his nascent authority. The alliances, friendships, loyalties, and sympathies that made Foucquet a social and political magnet for the "good French people" must have looked to him like an abominable metamorphosis of the Fronde.

Except in his nightmares, Foucquet did not suspect he was the least desirable candidate for a king whose amour propre was tied up with a state free of debt. Louis XIV wanted to be (according to an old Gallican formula now fraught with a new meaning) "the emperor in his kingdom," not only with respect to the pope and the Holy Empire, but also to all the "intermediate powers" that the long history of the kingdom had produced outside his own. Foucquet's dream and that of his friends revived the Ciceronian idea of the *optimus princeps*, adopted by Augustus, set in place by Maecenas, and celebrated by Horace and Virgil. It was the dream of literary people. Colbert, zealous administrator of the private fortune of Mazarin, the shadow man little known to the public but well known to the king, had the stuff of a great minister, which, for Louis XIV, meant practically a gifted and experienced domestic servant. Unlike his father Louis XIII, the young king felt no uneasiness—moral or affective—in embodying reason of state in his person. Unlike Richelieu, Colbert never claimed to dictate reason of state to the king, but he knew how to apply it without qualms. That *vir marmoreus*, that "North" in Mme de Sévigné's expression, was even ready to take *upon himself* the aspects of Louis XIV's government, as absolute and contrary to the customs of the kingdom as Richelieu's had been, which were most hateful to all the "good French people," regardless of whether they had been Frondeurs or loyalists during the regency.[28]

THE REACTION OF FOUCQUET AND HIS FRIENDS TO THE COUP D'ETAT

In the first months following the *surintendant*'s arrest, the trap skillfully set by the king and Colbert worked remarkably well. As foreseen, the scapegoat became the focus of taxpayers' exasperation, which had grown throughout the years of war. The memory of Mazarin was preserved, especially since, on 23 September 1661, violating all legal standards, and without even a mandate from the king, Colbert had letters and documents that could attest to the less-than-glorious role the cardinal-minister had played in the administration of public finances removed from the Saint-Mandé château.[29] Foucquet, placed in solitary confinement, universally execrated, accused not only of embezzlement but of the crime of high treason, seemed destined for an imminent and ignominious death.

But his most fervent circle of friends, convinced of his innocence and knowing full well what was really afoot, would not be intimidated. Gradually, as the "Chamber of Justice" responsible for the Foucquet trial revealed the blatant arbitrariness of the new regime, public opinion shifted. The Paris of high culture, which had celebrated Foucquet as a Maecenas, and which had hoped Louis XIV would be an Augustus, secretly placed its talent and influence in the service of the *surintendant*'s family and loyalists.[30]

On the whole, the Parisian republic of letters had hated Richelieu as a "new Tiberius." It watched with revulsion or trembling as, under the new "favorite" Colbert, the regime of writers for hire resurfaced. That republic of letters played an essential role in triggering and pushing forward a true "Foucquet affair," to the king's and Colbert's great annoyance. Gilles Ménage and Guy Patin, for example, were only too happy to support the campaign of Foucquet's family and friends on his behalf, especially since they saw that what was at stake in the *surintendant*'s trial was something close to their hearts, something that had at times made them sympathetic toward the Fronde: freedom of thought and expression.

The Shadow of François-Auguste de Thou

The "pope" of the Parisian republic of letters, Pierre Dupuy, had left a last will and testament that established before the fact the significance of the fight for Foucquet.[31] Pierre Dupuy died in 1651, in the middle of the parliamentary Fronde, surrounded by the veneration of cultivated magistrates, academics of renown, and erudite men of letters. He embodied the great tradition of French "Politiques," that of Michel de L'Hospital and Jacques-Auguste de Thou. That tradition of political wisdom, inaugurated by Guillaume Budé, created the intellectual conditions favoring Henry IV's victory and the magnanimity of that victory. The academy of philologists for which Pierre Dupuy had served as "prince" continued to meet after his death, until 1657, in the Bibliothèque du Roi, under the leadership of his inseparable brother, Jacques. It was well known that Pierre Dupuy, a historian and jurist with a reputation throughout Europe, had devoted his last years, but in vain, to obtaining the posthumous rehabilitation of his cousin, François-Auguste de Thou. Along with his friend Cinq-Mars, Louis XIII's unfortunate "favorite," de Thou was executed in Lyons in 1642 as an accomplice in state crimes, after what was a mockery of a trial. The documents in the rehabilitation brief were widely circulated by the academy of the Dupuy brothers, also called the "Adelphes," which was very influential in parliamentary circles.

In this series of erudite and eloquent *Mémoires*, Pierre Dupuy analyzes every facet of the special procedure that led to the conviction and execution of the young magistrate, the pressures to which the parliamentary commissioners named to convict him had given in, and the tricks Laubardemont— Richelieu's instrument—had used to make Cinq-Mars and his friend de Thou condemn each other. In that affair, friendship played an essential role on all sides, a role in conflict with the service of the state that Richelieu required of the king himself. Pierre Dupuy's analysis is not only an implacable indictment of the tyrannical and arbitrary ferocity Richelieu had imposed on France: it is also a plea for the reestablishment of a "state of law" in the kingdom. The de Thou affair, removed from the scrutiny of Parlement, marked by irregularities, which allowed Louis XIII's prime minister to wreak his revenge on the king's "favorite" and to shed a bit more blood in his own reign, faithfully reflected the state of violence in which France, according to the scholarly historian of the monarchy, had been plunged under the cardinal's ministry.

On the basis of a long series of historical precedents, notably Louis XI's abuses, Pierre Dupuy establishes that the special jurisdictions or justice commissions named by the kings or their ministers, beyond the scrutiny of Parlement and usually under the authority of the chancellor of France, an agent of power, had on several occasions hastily condemned innocent people who, under subsequent reigns, had to be boldly—but usually, alas! posthumously—rehabilitated. It was precisely that rehabilitation on principle that, in his *Mémoires*, Pierre Dupuy demands for François-Auguste de Thou, sentenced to die as an active accomplice in a plot against the state, even though he had done no more than *not* denounce his best friend like a coward.

The issue at stake in that demand was very similar to that underlying the entire political debate under Louis XIII, and even during the Regency and the Fronde: is the state everything, or does it leave intact the legitimacy and morality, in their own realm, of private attachments, personal alliances, and elective affinities, which form the *natural* and *native* ties of any *human* community or society? The old French medieval order, united by mutual allegiances charged with feeling, was moving to the shadows of private life, but not without a protest against the heartless obedience and flattery that the modern state now demanded. King Louis XIII was the first to have suffered from that calamity.

In Pierre Dupuy's view, François-Auguste de Thou's silence, his refusal to betray his close friend, but without collaborating in the plot that this friend formed against Richelieu, had served the state well enough. This sublime silence did not betray any of his obligations toward the state and did not go against any of his private feelings. And yet, in the cardinal's eyes, that silence was his crime.

In the accounts of the execution of de Thou and Cinq-Mars that Dupuy attached to his *Mémoires*, the two young victims died like the martyrs of the early Christian era, heroic victims of a dictatorship of the pagan kind. Cinq-Mars had dared defy that dictatorship; de Thou had been content to tacitly despise it. Pierre Dupuy establishes a striking contrast between their nobility of soul and the servility of the writers for hire with whom Richelieu surrounded himself.

"The cardinal's head," he writes, "swollen with such supreme and absolute authority, joyously received the foul flattery of so many hungry little poets, so many venal quills, so many poverty-stricken panegyrists, who elevated him above all mortals, made him the equal of God and everything most holy and venerable among men. In his mind, so corrupted and distorted by this continual flattery, he did not know that only bad princes and tyrants take pleasure in this vain and false praise."[32]

THE REVOLT OF CONSCIENCE

Even though such moral intransigence characteristic of an old Cato was no longer in tune with the elegant and delicate style of the new generation, its authority was still intact in 1661 for every truly lettered mind and for every heart that was a little bit French or Christian. It was the voice of conscience itself for magistrates such as Lamoignon, Pontchartrain, d'Ormesson, and Roquesante, who were called to sit in the special chamber named by the king but were not eager to appear, in the eyes of history and of their peers, as accomplices of a new Laubardemont, reincarnated as Pussort, Colbert's relation and agent, maneuvering the special chamber.

That voice of conscience had a powerful resonance for writers such as Pellisson, Maucroix, and La Fontaine, whose affection for Foucquet was illuminated by the great lights of history and the law. The disgraced *surintendant* had himself been born in the seraglio of Parlement, and had

even quite recently been one of its high magistrates: his status as a sena-
tor and Maecenas was almost ideally suited to point out the arbitrariness
of his own trial. As soon as he was in a position to write and reply to his
judges, he pleaded his case as a great legal professional, notably in the
matter of police searches of one's home and in financial procedures.
Beneath the surface of this man of courtly society, salons, and elegant
conversation, a French Cicero, the worthy son of the "senate" of the
monarchy, revealed himself fully.

His *substitut* at the Parlement, La Fontaine's uncle by marriage, Jacques
Jannart, was the driving force in Foucquet's defense, along with Pellisson,
imprisoned in La Bastille. He had moved to the Quai des Orfèvres in
1659, in the Enclos du Palais, probably to connect his home to his duties,
and perhaps also, in case of misfortune, to be better protected from Colbert's searches. This was where La Fontaine stayed when he spent time
in Paris in 1661–63, deep in the hive where people were working on
Foucquet's defense. It was there, at his uncle's home, within the shadow
and shelter of the parliamentary citadel, that the poet composed *Elégie
aux Nymphes de Vaux* and *Ode au roi*.[33]

The *surintendant* and his family also benefited from the support of Port-
Royal, a well-known victim of Richelieu's and Mazarin's tyranny. Antoine
Le Maistre de Sacy, one of the most illustrious Solitaires, had been
Foucquet's colleague in Parlement. Another of the Solitaires, Robert
Arnauld d'Andilly, the theorist of a friendship higher than one's duty to
the state, and his son Simon Arnauld de Pomponne were so closely associated with Foucquet that Pomponne was exiled to Metz in September 1661.
For the Solitaires, as for the cultivated Parisian public, a retrospective link
was established between Foucquet, victim of Colbert's arbitrariness, and
the Great Arnauld, theologian of Port-Royal and the object of condemnation by the Sorbonne in 1656. That condemnation was upheld by the
Parlement at Foucquet's request; under the circumstances, the *procureur
général* representing the king had to bow to Mazarin's orders.[34] The campaign waged in Pascal's *Petites lettres*, printed clandestinely and distributed
to enormous success in 1656–58, had rallied the opinion of enlightened
people to the cause of Antoine Arnauld and restored his honor. Like Pierre
Dupuy's *Mémoires pour justifier M. de Thou*, Pascal's *Provinciales* provided
Jacques Jannart, Paul Pellisson, and Foucquet's loyal friends with a model,
a precedent, and a method. The rule of reason of state, which concealed
vindictive passions and altogether personal ambitions under its pretension
to serve the common interest, thus found itself facing an entire world of
private alliances, inaccessible in the remote regions to which they had been

relegated: the sacred sense of good faith violated and of nature offended once more inspired a true genius of resistance.

A Voice from Deep within the Prison

Beginning in the first weeks of 1662, Foucquet's friends had rallied. *Premier président* Lamoignon, who, since 3 December 1661, had led the work of the chamber of justice named by the king to judge him, was a magistrate of integrity. He owed his office to the *surintendant*, even though there had been discord between them. From his cell deep in La Bastille, Paul Pellisson managed to get Jannart to publish, on underground presses, his *Discours au roi par un de ses fidèles sujets sur le procès de M. Foucquet*.[35] With an eloquence both ardent and moderate, which Voltaire (an expert on the matter) would compare to that of Cicero, Pellisson challenged the special commission charged with judging Foucquet, demanded the case be returned to the ordinary rules of justice in the kingdom, and reminded everyone that the *surintendant*'s entire administration was the responsibility of the deceased Cardinal Mazarin. The effect of *Discours*, which went through at least three editions, was very strong. It was supported by La Fontaine's admirable *Elégie*, also published clandestinely and anonymously on loose sheets, as the *Mazarinades* and *Provinciales* had been.

In July Pellisson launched a second plea, *Considérations sommaires sur le procès de M. Foucquet*, while Foucquet's mother, wife, and daughter, the marquise de Charost, had the audacity to appear before the upper chamber of the Parlement to demand its protection. *Premier président* Lamoignon, with a delegation from the Parlement, believed it his duty to present the demand to the king, who did not conceal his anger. The following December, Lamoignon was invited to give up his seat in the special chamber to Chancellor Séguier, the former accomplice of Richelieu's extortion.[36]

On 30 July Foucquet's wife sent the king a letter indicting his "favorite" Colbert, a letter as scathing as Pierre Dupuy's *Mémoires* must have been, but only in retrospect, against the "favorite" Richelieu. She wrote:

While the king unburdens his conscience via the judges, the judges declare they are obeying the king's orders. But what will astonish Paris, France, and Europe is that Colbert has been bold enough to attend the council, as the judge of my husband: he, who is publicly known to be his truest opponent; who everyone knows has been his declared adversary for six years; who has inspired every chimerical and false thing he could against him, first, in His Eminence, whose unending jealousy and mistrust he saw, then in Your Majesty, whose position gave him the means to be at His side at every moment; who took all the papers from Saint-Mandé that could serve to vindicate my husband; the very one, Sire, who is known to have conspired and made appeals against my husband's life, as no one in Paris is unaware; who expressed the view, not once, but more than a hundred times, as I propose to prove and verify for Your Majesty . . . that my husband deserved to die, and did so in very abusive terms, which indicate quite well the particular interest he believes he has in destroying my husband, and removing a witness so informed of his actions, the knowledge of which he has reason to hide so diligently from Your Majesty.[37]

The preliminary investigation for the trial, which claimed to examine the state's accounts for the *surintendant*'s entire administration, dragged on and on. Beginning in January 1662, the prisoner managed to write his own *Défenses* in invisible ink and successfully passed it on to his loyalists; it was printed clandestinely and enjoyed the same success as Pellisson's pleas. Foucquet, a first-rate lawyer and writer, skillfully justified his difficult management of state finances in times of war and rebellion; he reminded readers of the irregularities of the investigation, especially Colbert's seizure in Saint-Mandé of sixteen hundred letters from Mazarin, which would have been more than adequate to exonerate him. He made repeated demands that his primary accuser, Colbert, be disqualified, and that those judges who were connected to the minister or too obviously his creatures be removed. His *Lettre au roi* (October–December 1662) implored Louis XIV, in an outburst of love, not to damage his image in France and Europe by failing to show his compassion for a zealous servant overwhelmed by the trickery of his enemies.[38]

On 23 August 1663, Jacques Jannart, the key to Foucquet's defense and La Fontaine's uncle by marriage, was sent into exile in Limoges.[39] The most blatant pressures were exerted on the judges who manifested impartiality, especially Olivier Lefèvre d'Ormesson, who was related to Mme de Sévigné. Beginning on 14 November 1664, the accused was finally prosecuted before the Chamber, which met at the Arsenal, not at the Palais de Justice. Mme de Sévigné, who got her information firsthand from Olivier d'Ormesson, followed the ups and downs of the sessions and reported them in her letters to Simon Arnauld de Pomponne, who was exiled in Metz. On 3 December she wrote to her correspondent: "Our dear unfortunate friend spoke for two hours this morning, but so admirably well that several could not keep from admiring him. Among others, M. Renard said: 'One must admit that this man is incomparable; he never spoke so well in Parlement; he controls his temper better than he has ever done.'"[40]

Foucquet, with perfect oratorical control, was even able to attenuate the effect of the Saint-Mandé plan, read out loud by Chancellor Séguier, the key piece of evidence for the prosecution in the accusation of state crimes. He reminded Pierre Séguier that he himself, at the height of the Fronde of the princes, had not been content to *imagine* his safeguard in a moment of anxiety, as the accused had done: he had actually betrayed the king at the time and shielded the entry of foreign troops into France.

THE KING'S PECULIAR PRACTICE OF PARDON

On 20 December, after hearing the two judges, d'Ormesson and Sainte-Hélène, the majority of the Chamber voted in favor of d'Ormesson's conclusions: banishment for life.

"All of Paris was impatiently awaiting the news," the magistrate recounted in his *Journal*,

> It spread everywhere at once and was received with extreme joy, even among the little shopkeepers, each blessing my name a thousand times without even knowing me. Thus, M. Foucquet, who had been abhorred during his imprisonment, and whom all of Paris would have seen executed with unbridled joy after his trial had begun, has become an object of public suffering and commiseration because of the hatred everyone harbors in his heart for the present government, and that is the true reason for the general approval.[41]

The king, exercising his pardon in reverse, commuted the sentence to life imprisonment in the fortress of Pignerol, where Foucquet died eighteen years later, in 1680. Some of the judges who had shown leniency toward

Foucquet, such as Roquesante and Bailly, were exiled, while others, such as Pontchartrain and d'Ormesson, were forced to retire. D'Ormesson, to whom the maréchal de Turenne paid a visit of congratulations after the sentencing, was, in his disgrace, surrounded by public consideration throughout his life.

It had cost Nicolas Foucquet dearly to have aspired to become Louis XIV's prime minister, to have naively believed, like Cicero, that the best qualification for governing was to have saved the state, to have had the confidence of "honorable people," and to have given evidence of his great talents and devotion to the public good.

The Annihilation of Foucquet

A sermon by Bossuet on ambition, delivered on 19 March 1662 at the Louvre, shows how the commonplaces of devotion, taken in hand by a great orator, can be placed in the service of the most extravagant flattery. Bossuet did not hesitate to deify the king, and to make Foucquet, whose trial was under way, a monster crushed by the vengeance of the biblical God:

> The Assyrian has risen up . . . like the cedars of Lebanon; heaven has nurtured him with its dew, the earth has fattened him with its substance; the powers have lavished their benefits on him, and he, for his part, has sucked the people's blood. That is why he has risen up, superb in his height, his branches broad, his shoots fertile . . . : a great number of his creatures, both great and small, have been linked to his fortunes; neither the cedars nor the pines—that is, the greatest people of the court—were equal to him.[42]

That vehemence of the altar, standing as guarantor of the acts of the Crown, triumphantly filled, without the shadow of a doubt, the space of the royal chapel. But Bossuet's eloquence, as sacred and public as it was, was far from coinciding with the sentiments, equally sacred in their private and personal domain, felt at the time by the most experienced and devoted of the king's subjects; in many respects, they were also very Christian souls. We now have the opportunity to hear once more these silent feelings, which the harsh words of the court's preacher attempted to intimidate and dissipate, whispered by the author of *Ode au roi* under his breath:

Accorde-nous les faibles restes
De ses jours tristes et funestes,
Jours qui se passent en soupirs.
(ll. 75–77)

Grant us the feeble remains
Of his sad and sorrowful days,
Days spent heaving great sighs.

La Fontaine was outlining a *Pietà*, which would grant Foucquet, struck down but then pardoned by the king, the consolation of his family and friends in an obscure retreat devoted entirely to prayer. The king's only response was to place the cell of faraway Pignerol under heavy guard.

A tragicomedy by Mme de Villedieu, performed by Molière and his troupe before the king in 1665, shows how the court, during the first year of Foucquet's imprisonment, found entertainment in the misfortunes and memory of the defeated man.

The action of that tragicomedy, entitled *Le favori*, takes place in an imaginary Spain. The king of Spain's favorite, Moncado, is tormented by melancholia, which spoils even the wonders of his château and gardens for him. He tells his prince, who reproaches him for his coldness:

Je suis jaloux de ma propre fortune,
Ce n'est pas moi qu'on aime, on aime vos faveurs,
Et vos bienfaits, Seigneur, m'enlèvent tous les coeurs,
    Ce serait pour mon âme un sujet d'allégresse,
    Si le sort me laissait le coeur de ma maîtresse;
Je sens bien qu'il est doux et glorieux pour moi
De devoir mes amis aux bontés de mon roi.
Je voudrais dans l'ardeur du zèle qui m'inspire
Que je vous dusse aussi tout l'air que je respire;
Que je ne puisse agir ni vivre que par vous,
Tant d'un devoir si cher les noeuds me semblent doux.[43]

    I am jealous of my own good fortune,
It is not me they love, but only your favors,

And your benefits, my Lord, turn every heart against me,
   Indeed, my soul would rejoice,
   If fate left me my mistress's heart;
How well I know it is a sweet and glorious thing
To owe my friends to the kindness of my king.
I would like, in the ardor of the zeal that inspires me,
To owe you as well the very air I breathe;
That I might act and live only through you,
The very dearness of such a duty makes its bonds sweet.

As it turns out, despite these niceties of servility, Moncado is bold enough to love the beautiful Lindamira, with whom the king is in love. Moncado is exiled. All his friends abandon him like cowards. Lindamira, however, confesses to Moncado that she loves him, and consoles him. The king finds out about everything. In his anger, he decides at first to seek revenge on Moncado. But he regains his self-control, gives up Lindamira, punishes Moncado's false friends, and unites the two lovers.

In this pleasant diversion, which the king found charming, everything was designed to disguise, as a sentimental fairy tale, the coup d'état that had allowed Louis XIV to become an "absolute" ruler. The ultimate cruelty to be done to Foucquet, in his remote cell in Pignerol, was that his fate was reduced to advice for the lovelorn.

THE KINGDOM SPLIT BY THE STATE

Ovid's *The Metamorphoses* attributes the melodious voice of the nightingale to a crime. Entrusted in good faith (*fides*) by her father to her brother-in-law King Tereus, Philomela is raped by the man who ought to have been her most trustworthy protector. Her despair and threats annoy the tyrant, who cuts out her tongue with his sword and again violates her, before leaving her a prisoner in the forest. He announces to his wife Procne, Philomela's sister, that the girl died on the way. But Philomela manages to get a tapestry to her sister, which she has woven in purple letters. Procne, mad for revenge, kills the son she had by Tereus and has him served up during a banquet. The tyrant, as he is feasting on his son's body, sees Philomela appear before him and throw the child's bloody head at him. The tragedy, having reached the height of horror, is resolved by the gods in a metamorphosis: Tereus becomes a hoopoe, Procne a swallow, and Philomela a nightingale.

In his own fable "Philomela and Procne" (3.15), La Fontaine casts that appalling history of sex, fury, and blood (which sharply highlights by contrast the exorcizing and liberating charm of his *Contes*) back into the distant past. After a thousand years, the only thing remaining of the tragedy is the song of the lonely nightingale, which transfigures the sorrow of memory. Procne asks her sister: why squander the sumptuous beauty of that song in solitude rather than let the crowds in the cities benefit from it?

> Le désert est-il fait pour des talents si beaux? . . .
> Aussi bien, en voyant les bois,
> Sans cesse il vous souvient que Térée autrefois
>   Parmi des demeures pareilles
> Exerça sa fureur sur vos divins appas.
> —Et c'est le souvenir d'un si cruel outrage
> Qui fait, reprit sa soeur, que je ne vous suis pas:
>   En voyant les hommes, hélas!
>   Il m'en souvient bien davantage.
>   (ll. 15, 17–24)

"Is the desert made for talents so fine?
    And what is more, the woods you see
Must keep Tereus endlessly on your mind,
    Who, among similar dwellings, once
Acted out his fury on your divine charms."
"And the memory of such a cruel outrage,"
Her sister replied, "is the reason I will not follow you:
    When I see men, alas!
    I am reminded of it all the more."

The translation of the tragic myth, and of Ovid's expressionistic violence, into a comedic dialogue, which, in La Fontaine's rendering, culminates in a brief, elegiac reply, protects the delicate reader from any contact with horror. But the infinite suffering and the judgment it passes on human barbarism are no less striking in this poem, inlaid, along with the others, in the mosaic of *Fables*, than they are in Ovid's text. The moral La Fontaine silently leaves his reader to draw is the same as Ovid's: "Pro Superi, quantum mortalia pectora caecae / Noctis habent!" (O Gods! what black darkness lurks in mortals' hearts).[44]

The Foucquet affair did not entail the terror that had accompanied the bloody execution of the comte de Chalais, the duc de Montmorency, and his two friends Cinq-Mars and de Thou. Why, then, did it resonate so deeply, incomparably more than the even more cynical and ferocious punishments exacted by Cardinal de Richelieu, which no poet (and there were many in the cardinal's opposition) dared to echo?

The affair was a revelation, and not only for La Fontaine. As has been pointed out a thousand times, it was a revelation of the victory in the kingdom of the modern state, assumed by the most legitimate and the least contested of kings. In addition, and perhaps above all, it was the revelation of one effect, uncontrolled by the king, of that total victory. An invisible wall now separated public and private life in the kingdom, even though the unanimous loyalty toward the king prevented it from reaching consciousness and from being expressed, except as a change of literary register.

Well before the court left Paris for Versailles, this moral distance between the court and the city pushed courtiers to the center of the royal spectacle and sent everyone else into the shadows, where they watched that spectacle but where they also had all the leisure time needed to look into themselves.

For a great number of educated French people during the Foucquet affair, that "precipitated," all of a sudden, a profound internalization of the modern split, foreseen by Montaigne during the civil wars of the sixteenth century and taken to the extreme by the Solitaries of Port-Royal during the Richelieu ministry, between private life, the inner life of the king's subjects, and the public life of the kingdom to which they belonged, now confined to the busy stage of the court.[45]

The Fronde of the princes had been a mixture of public and private life, a festive experience of the kingdom when the excesses of revolt humbled the excesses of the state. Corneille's tragedies, with their conflicting duties, catch their characters in a dramatic space, both unified and open, where the public and private interfere, as in the Paris of the Fronde. Mlle de Scudéry's Clélie was the last literary attempt to represent, in a single harmonious fiction, the public and private lives of the kingdom, in an ideal city that included the court. The kingdom as Foucquet and Pellisson foresaw it would have reconciled the state inherited from Richelieu and the flavor and virtues proper to private life.[46]

After 1661 Mme de La Fayette's novels focused on the private lives of her characters and on their interiority; Racine's tragedies relegated state concerns to the background and highlighted the inner drama suffered by solitary heroines and heroes; even Molière's comedies, when they involved the state, made it the sublime but distant guarantor of the autonomy of private lives. The kingdom was still intact, the shared space of all the king's subjects, but a thin fracture split it and each of the king's subjects in two, everyone but the king himself: the king's empire, having contracted into the omnipotent state, broke off from the realm of the heart.

At least in appearance, Foucquet's defeat was the defeat of friendship, the essentially private moral utopia where religious men such as Robert Arnauld d'Andilly, erudite libertines such as Sorbière and Chapelle, friends from Port-Royal-des-Champs, and those who belonged to the republic of letters and to the Académie Française all communed around the *surintendant*. Foucquet and his friends of various allegiances dreamed of introducing that higher and personal social bond, which overcame self-interest, amour propre, and religious and doctrinal differences, into the very government of the realm, as was already the case in the administration of finances: an alliance, a loyalty, an election, a mediation that extended to women and which, in the conversations in Paris mansions, also overcame distinctions of birth, rank, and profession.

The numerous academies, high-society salons, and small courts of culture that formed around the princes and that were easily transformed into political plots, thrived among Richelieu's opposition and multiplied during the Fronde. Their peaceful and loyal federation around Foucquet gave them a new opportunity to attract the king himself into that conspiracy of friends.

Friendship was the result: it grew up around Foucquet within the much less disinterested network of special interests and vassals, which the *surintendant,* imitating the cardinal-ministers and the princes of the opposition, had formed around himself to guarantee his financial credit and found his political power. When the Foucquet contingent was brought down and dispersed by the king, friendship survived.

It became internal and clandestine. It reflected on its defeat and closely examined the enemy that had defeated it: amour propre, with its own procession of passions, interests, blind spots, ferocity. It did not abandon the hope, first, of saving the *surintendant,* and second, quite simply, of adapting to its own internal exile, creating in Paris circles where, behind closed doors, one could speak openly, read letters written covertly, and find in this secrecy—corresponding to the king's own secrecy—a contemplative and inventive freedom unknown during the Foucquet years, which were so tormented by hope and fear. Defeat and oppression can be put to good use, and that use was discovered in Louis XIV's Paris.[47]

"The Heart's Empire Is Not of Your Empire"

One sometimes catches a brief glimpse of some of these personal and unexpected alliances in the seventeenth century, which spoke a language both coded and sincere, and which flourished unbeknownst to the court, even as they observed the court with very sharp antennae. In La Fontaine's *Oeuvres posthumes*, published in 1696 by his friend Mme Ulrich, there is a delicious epistle in verse sent by the poet to Mme de La Fayette, the friend (in Robert Arnauld d'Andilly's sense of the word) of the duc de La Rochefoucauld. That epistle gives an idea of the degree of affective complicity and intelligence that attached the poet to this extraordinary couple, whose children were the *Maximes* and *La Princesse de Clèves*. The epistle accompanies a little game of billiards sent to Mme de La Fayette, which the poet, without taking himself too seriously, wants to see as an allegory of the surprises of love at which the novelist is an expert. But the poet adds:

> Que vous dirai-je donc pour vous plaire, Uranie?
> Le Faste et l'Amitié sont deux divinités
> Enclines, comme on sait, aux liberalités;
> Discerner leurs présents n'est pas petite affaire;
> L'Amitié donne peu, le Faste beaucoup plus;
> Beaucoup plus aux yeux du vulgaire.
> Vous jugez autrement de ses dons superflus;
> Mon billard est succinct, mon billet ne l'est guère.
> Je n'ajouterai donc à tout ce long discours
> Que ceci seulement, qui part d'un coeur sincère:
> Je vous aime, aimez-moi toujours.[48]

> What shall I say to please you, Urania?
> Pomp and Friendship are two deities,
> Inclined, as we all know, to liberalities;
> Discerning their presents is no simple matter:
> Friendship gives little, Pomp a good deal more;
> A good deal more in the common people's eyes.
> You take a different view of its superfluous gifts;
> My billiard game is succinct, my letter hardly so.
> Let me therefore add to this long discourse

Only one thing more, which comes from a sincere heart:
I love you—love me forever.

The antithesis between disappointing love and indestructible friendship is intertwined with the antithesis between official Pomp, which dazzles
the common people, and private Friendship, which is happy with a lesser
gift. This supremely refined and personal letter is the predecessor of those
that Mallarmé sent to Berthe Morisot.

In this drama, where, as in Corneille's tragedies, the gravest political
issues are combined with the most tremulous emotions and feeling, the
poet Jean de La Fontaine makes his choice. His words, which might have
seemed designed for protected salons and gardens, are not swayed by a
storm where so many interests and perils came together to reduce him to
silence and timid conformity. They burst forth with an extraordinary
courage and find a new resonance in that ordeal. It is as if, during the
Foucquet affair, La Fontaine's voice, more alien than ever to force and
authority, found in its very gentleness its profundity and the secret to its
sonority. Neither *Elegie aux Nymphes de Vaux* nor *Ode au roi* claims to dispute royal omnipotence or the solid foundation of his coup d'état. But, in
many respects, the two poems are more terrible than the many vengeful
sonnets attacking Colbert that circulated underground. They hold up a
mirror to the king himself—to his triumph, his majesty, his legitimacy—
the mirror of personal feelings, sacred because they are personal. It would
have taken no more than a gesture of clemency to rally these feelings as
well behind his glory, but, without them, that glory, omnipotent in actual
fact, would never be anything but political, and deprived of the thing that
inspires love.

Without raising his voice, without transgressing the harshest and most
delicate proprieties, La Fontaine discovered in this ordeal the sort of hidden royalty—but equal to the visible royalty that believes itself master of
all language—in which the defenseless integrity of poetry can drape itself.

CHAPTER 5

Rest and Movement

In France, the century of the arts was that of Francis I and Louis XIII, not
at all that of Louis XIV. In the matter of taste, the little palace of the
Tuileries, the old Louvre, part of Fontainebleau and Anet, the chapel of
the Valois in Saint-Denis, and the Luxembourg Palace are or were
far above the works of Louis the Great. The race of the Valois was a
cultivated, witty race, a patron of the arts, for which it had a good sense.
Louis XIV looked upon artists as laborers, Francis I saw them as friends.
        —Chateaubriand, *Analyse raisonnée de l'histoire de France*

*W*ith Nicolas Foucquet's disgrace, a half century of "grandeur"
began in France. Louis XIV's subjects shouldered the weight of it and even,
already, the legend. After the brief purgatory following the king's death
in 1715, that legend, under Louis XV, took on the stability of history. It
now became the constant, the touchstone, of the French political imagination. Compared to Louis the Great and his century, the last two Louis
cut a pale figure. Even Fontenoy for Louis XV and the war in America
for Louis XVI, even the return, under both kings, to a neo-Versailles "grand
style" that was to become neoclassical were not enough to elevate the disappointing humanness of the Sun King's heirs. The Terror under the
Committee of Public Safety and the Napoleonic Empire were the first to
prove equal to the glory and wars of the central reign in the history of
France. The Napoleon of the battle of Austerlitz was finally able to rival
in splendor the king who had crossed the Rhine. The Bourbons of the
Restoration looked like flaccid pastiches of their great ancestor. Louis-
Philippe organized the return of the emperor's ashes and dedicated Versailles to all the glories of France, but to no avail; Louis XIV, as portrayed
by Rigaud, in league with the Napoleon of Ingres, crushed the peaceful
Louis-Philippe with his majesty.

In the French collective imagination, the dark legend of the "ancien régime" has done battle with that of the "great revolution." Today, these are less legends than specters, one on the right, the other on the left. They incite one portion of the French people to rise up against the other. The heirs to the Revolution are always ready to guillotine Louis XVI a second time, but, even in their dreams, they would hesitate to brandish so much as a penknife against the august person of Louis XIV. What is the source of this secret fascination of modern and French republicans, liberals, and socialists with the Sun King? The great century of absolute monarchy, the archetype of the "right-wing power" loathed in the person of the excellent Louis XVI, passes for the true Platonic Idea of the republican and modern welfare state and cultural state when presented under the haughty traits of Louis XIV. At the same time, the Third Republic tends to become confused in the national memory with the ancien régime. The Versailles of Louis the Great has become the sacred shrine of the French exception — in terms of its society, its culture, and its citizenry.

What an ironic posthumous revenge for Charles Maurras! For a half century during the Third Republic, Maurras and his literary and historical school lauded the possible grandeur of a monarchy in the style of Louis XIV to better ridicule a corrupt and listless regime of warring factions. The golden legend of the great king, in that school of opposition that the most gifted minds found attractive, was combined in the 1930s with the utopia of technocratic modernity. The century of Louis XIV was no longer simply a matter of nostalgia, but a program for national recovery. For Action Française, the Louis XIV of moderns — the king of engineers and artists, of great festivals and great public works projects — had become the nationalist project.

So much for the right. How did the heirs of the 1789 revolution come to make Louis the Great one of their idols? Voltaire, Lavisse, and even Maurras cannot explain everything.

The half century that followed the fall of the Third Republic witnessed the implementation, in several successive performances and under several different circumstances, of the neo-Louis XIV dramaturgy invented by Maurras to play a nasty trick on the Third Republic. The Gaullism of General de Gaulle himself and the anti-Gaullism of François Mitterrand (which one was on the right, and which on the left?) competed to see who would execute this project of grandeur more successfully. De Gaulle, with the genius of Richelieu, created a Maurassian monarchy under the colors of the republic; his principal adversary, François Mitterrand, with the talents of Mazarin, went on to popularize it. The other actors playing the reestablished role of monarch may have sought out a Louis XV, a Louis XVI, or an Orleanist style; it was no use. Louis XIV was still the norm that, in the end, made such deviations look ridiculous.

In 1927, to cast a slur on the Maurassian commonwealth (but the analysis applies just as well to the Marxist, Fascist, National Socialist, and even, in the end, Sartrian commonwealth), Jacques Maritain wrote:

> Nothing is more important to the soul's freedom and the good of the human race than the distinction between the two powers; to use the modern language, nothing has so great a *cultural* value. Everyone knows that this distinction has been the work of the Christian centuries, and it is their honor. The pagan commonwealth, which claimed to be the sole *totality* of the human being, absorbed the spiritual power into the temporal, even as it deified the state. It was by virtue of a very sure internal logic that it finally came to worship the emperors. . . . Lord Jesus said: "Render to Caesar the things that are Caesar's, and to God the things that are God's." He thus distinguished between the two powers, and, in so doing, emancipated souls. . . .
>
> Since the commonwealth is the most perfect (that is, the most capable of being self-sufficient) of the natural communities that men can constitute here on earth, it is supremely important to trace that distinction, and to mark the relation of subordination between politics, governed by the totality of the earthly commonwealth and its immediate and specified end, and ethics, governed by the divine transcendent Totality. . . . The subordination of the political to the ethical is complete and even infinite, since it is itself founded on the subordination of ends.[1]

Whether or not one accepts Maritain's Thomist language and faith, the twentieth-century experiment has taught us that, for all minds that embrace freedom, the imprisonment of the intelligence in the economic, social, and political realm to which modern ideologies on the right or left condemn us empties the word "culture" of its liberating breath and inspiration. "Culture" in the Hobbesian sense, integrated into the organic and material totality of the commonwealth, either withers and dries up or turns against its own purpose, which is to make man capable of the divine. Even under Louis XIV, the republic of letters did not renounce the task of exercising its vocation of irony and inner freedom. Where is that counterweight today?

A modernized and modernizing age of Louis XIV as Maurras wanted it inhabits the legal landscape in France, and the real country accommodates itself as it can. The bronze horseman on the Place des Victoires can finally look upon Paris with satisfaction: he sees on all sides the monumental proof that Versailles has retaken the city of the Fronde, has become its administrative extension, and that the château again controls the economy and the arts. Bernini's statue of Louis XIV, which the king had defaced and sunk in Suisses basin on the grounds of Versailles, now cast in lead, stands in the center of Paris. The king's avenue, itself transported to the capital, now stretches out toward the point of infinity under the Grande Arche of La Défense.

Is King Louis the Great responsible for what the French imagination and political history has finally made of him in the late twentieth century? The choice he foreclosed by disgracing Nicolas Foucquet, a minister who, with the king's consent, might have given his reign a moderate turn, is one of those apparently circumstantial decisions whose long-term consequences, in accord with a chain of events extending out to the universe— *Nec pluribus impar* (he is not unworthy to reign over several worlds) was the king's motto—precipitated what we still sometimes call, but less and less confidently, "the sense of history" and "progress."

The modernizing state in Richelieu's sense, as Louis XIV restored and magnified it on the altar on which he had sacrificed Foucquet, and as the Revolution and the Empire perfected it, was in France—and indirectly, in Europe and elsewhere—the fate of moderns. The very idea of modernity took root in 1687, during a famous quarrel, to the glory of the "century of Louis the Great," in a European consciousness that the reign of Louis XIV had contributed not a little toward leading into crisis. In a curious paradox, this reign, which, more than any other, made France a closed structure, a centralized *mandala* encircled by its seacoasts, its mountain chains, and the fortresses of Vauban, nevertheless introduced to the world the idea of the enlightened despot, overcoming nature and custom and roughly pushing forward, in a movement without precedent and without end. That curious contradiction between the principle of rest and moderation, inherent in the oldest European monarchy, and the principle of unlimited movement placed in the service of Louis's arrogance by an administration bent on conquest, introduced a crack in Old France that was much deeper than the peril of civil war that had heretofore racked, but not toppled, its profound structures and temperament.

In the first pages of *L'Ancien Régime et la Révolution*, Alexis de Tocqueville quotes a letter from Mirabeau to Louis XVI, written in 1790, which interprets the revolution as an unhoped-for opportunity for his state to realize Louis XIV's dream and encourages the monarch to act as Bonaparte would in 1799: "Is it nothing, then, to be without a parliament, without a country of estates, without a clergy, without people with noble privileges? The idea of forming a single class of citizens would have pleased Richelieu: that smooth surface facilitates the exercise of power. Several absolutist regimes would not have done so much for royal authority as that single year of Revolution."[2]

The absolute state, Richelieu's and Louis XIV's remedy during the civil wars, was in reality a rejection of the "wise middle ground" of which de Retz spoke (de Retz was himself a moderate driven to extremes), an absolute civil war and a permanent revolution led by the royal state against the received customs and against the bodies that had traditionally overseen them. That internal tension between the conservative genius of the monarchy and the will to power of a bureaucratic and technocratic monarch finally shattered the monarchy and, by a sort of general contagion, corrupted the wisdom of nations, which the oldest kingdom of Europe could and should have taken in hand. The misfortune (and the mad generosity) of Old France was to trust entirely in the good faith of its kings to safeguard this "happy medium"; unlike England, no written law constrained kings not to make immoderate use of their divine authority. The venerable royal religion concealed that chimerical generosity.

Louis XIII inaugurated his personal reign with an assassination, that of the maréchal d'Ancre, committed in the Louvre under his eyes and orders, outside any legal process, the same way Henry III had had the duc de Guise assassinated.

What was new—and fortunately so—in 1661 was, first, Louis XIV's refusal to imitate these barbarous examples to rid himself of Foucquet; and second, the profound emotion that accompanied the vicissitudes of the *surintendant*'s investigation and trial for the public of the politically well-informed city, and which the literature associated with spirituality had, since Henry IV's reign, gradually converted or led back to gentler mores, to urbanity, humanity, gallantry. Richelieu's state violence lagged behind the evolution of minds and the maturation of hearts. In 1661 the king learned at what point going too far was far enough, at least in terms of procedures. This was progress imposed on the king by his subjects, but it was a real progress: a very intense struggle, a great, silent struggle, began between the king and his ministers, who wanted state progress in Richelieu's sense, and the kingdom and city, which, after the upheaval of the Fronde, and in the absence of the lasting "happy medium" they had wished for, submitted to a harsh regime of law and order. Nevertheless, they took the innocent liberty, and even adopted the habit, of thinking and feeling on their own and among themselves.

Far from driving to extremes the public, which proved itself politically astute during the Foucquet affair, the king and Colbert, by dividing up the roles, finessed a quite skillful transition from the ministerial and conciliatory monarchy that their victim Foucquet had allowed people to hope for, and the total administrative and military monarchy that the great cardinal had set in motion. They themselves intended to modernize the machine and increase its effectiveness. As the work proceeded, a scaffolding of spectacles and high culture would keep the gawkers occupied.

The transferral of that patronage of the arts of peace, which had constituted much of Foucquet's attractiveness, to benefit the king and his service was part of this altogether superficial concession to the public that had applauded the *surintendant* at Porte Saint-Antoine, the day when, having heard his sentence at La Bastille, he was immediately taken in safe custody to Pignerol.

The Glory Machine

With the talents of the private academy Pellisson had assembled around Foucquet, and which had been formed in the effervescent Paris of the Regency and the Fronde, Colbert, taking up the projects that illness and death had prevented Richelieu from completing, within a few years built and set in operation an administrative system of arts and letters closely dependent on the court. Eloquence, as the great cardinal had foreseen, became a state industry in the service of the royal Olympus.

In November 1662 Colbert asked one of the "illustrious members" of the Académie Française, Jean Chapelain (chosen over the secretary for life, Conrart, who was too compromised by Pellisson) to compile, in order of merit, the infamous "list" of authors destined to receive an annual pension from the king.[3] The patron of the academy, Chancellor Séguier, who was also Foucquet's principal judge, must have counseled Colbert on that takeover of the French republic of arts and letters, which, on the whole, had yielded to the *surintendant's* seductiveness. At the same moment, most of the private fortunes that had aided Foucquet's patronage were themselves subject to an investigation by the Chamber of Justice.

It was time to link, by golden threads, the disoriented writers and artists to the state. Chapelain's list circulated in Paris in the first four months of 1663, and it did not take the capital long to understand what would be required of the king's pensioners. The king fell ill, then recovered, his health more robust than ever. Chapelain let the pensioners know that it was desirable to celebrate the event in verse. Many complied. It was a return to the age of Richelieu, when the abbé de Boisrobert had men of letters collaborate on collections in French and Latin to the glory of the cardinal and the king. The fears and scruples that had greeted the beginnings of the Académie Française were reawakened.

On 17 August 1663, the erudite Pierre-Daniel Huet, alarmed, wrote to Gilles Ménage, de Retz's former secretary. Both appeared on Chapelain's list: "There is a sort of shame in writing verses for money, as you rightly say."[4]

Ménage, a friend of Mme de Sévigné's and Mme de La Fayette's, refused to obey Colbert's orders. The new minister, however, had supported Chapelain's act by making it known that "due notice will be taken of anyone who is remiss [in his duty]." Even as he lamented the "shame" and "baseness" of the procedure in the letter to his prestigious correspondent (and elder), Huet complied, arguing for the obedience due the king's orders.

Poets who did not appear on the infamous list took the initiative, hoping to appear on it later. The abbé Cotin celebrated the miracle of the monarch's recovery, and Racine took care to write an ode on this required subject, which he submitted to Chapelain for correction.

In 1667 Colbert had the Académie Française placed under Louis XIV's personal protection; henceforth it was part of the Maison du Roi, one of his ministerial departments. Two years after Séguier's death in 1672, the king granted the academy, which until then had met in the chancellor's home, lodgings in the palace of the Louvre. It was a great honor. Now, every year, on the feast day of Saint Louis, the academy celebrated mass in the chapel of the royal palace, punctuated by a panegyric to the monarch. The welcoming and acceptance speeches now added an encomium of the king to that of the founder Richelieu, and the public sessions included a reading of poems addressed to the king and celebrating his most recent deeds of valor. Under the vigilant eye of Colbert, himself elected to the Académie Française in 1667, the company quickly became a very productive workshop of panegyrics for the king, offered as an example to all French men of letters.[5] The prize for eloquence (founded by Guez de Balzac before his death in 1654) and the prize for poetry (founded by the comte de Clermont-Tonnerre in 1674) were awarded for pieces praising the king. The first winner of the prize for eloquence was, in 1670, Madeleine de Scudéry, who rivaled her friend Pellisson, now the king's historiographer, in the official cult of Louis XIV.

Through the use of pensions, a regular "machine de Marly" of panegyrics was set in place by Colbert, transforming official French letters into the fountains of Versailles. Their organ music swelled together and always at the right moment to give all the king's public acts the appearance of a miracle. The fifteen or so foreign writers or scientists on the pension list received instructions for raising their own expressions of thanks to the level of those by the kingdom's own.

The pension list disappeared after Chapelain's death in 1675 and the beginning of the major works projects at Versailles. But the habit was well entrenched. What we call the "masterpieces" of Louis XIV's reign were actually deviations, whose originality and secret independence we underestimate, in relation to the official norm of praise, set by the uniform grandeur that, dictated by convention and not by contract, defined the style and commonplaces befitting the "greatest monarch in the world."

The arts followed the path determined for belles lettres from above. Like its modern enthusiasts, we can only admire the method with which Colbert perfected the powerful clockwork mechanism that made the various professional guilds cooperate in the permanent glorification of the prince. The fireworks at Vaux had lasted only one night. The organization and coordination created by Colbert were able to install the king at the center of a permanent polyphonic and audiovisual *Te Deum*. Architecture, painting, sculpture, goldsmithery, tapestry making, cabinet work, mirror manufacture, haberdashery: each was provided with its own state factories and worked together to give the royal person a magnificence and majesty worthy of a hero unique in his field and of his "unparalleled" actions. The sciences of optics and perspective and the techniques of engineering also contributed to the "machines" that produced the most modern effects of illusion in state "theaters." Their descriptions and illustrations, books and engravings, for which Paris had become the European capital, multiplied the effect of praise and extended its influence. The portrait of the monarch, drawn, painted, sculpted, and engraved by a large number of artists, went up everywhere, even in the most modest homes and on street signs.

In 1663 Colbert created the organization that would assure the general harmonization of production, would compose its subtitles, and, on his own political directives, would gradually conceive the plot developments and details of the action. From the Académie Française he extracted a committee, first called the "Petite Académie," which assembled three, then four members of the academy in Colbert's library and sometimes in the minister's very presence: Jean Chapelain, the abbé de Bourzeis, the

abbé Cassagnes, and François Charpentier. The office of secretary was occupied by Colbert's "chief assistant," Charles Perrault, Foucquet's former
client, who joined the Académie Française in 1671. Since the minister
had chosen those of the king's deeds that it was important to praise, the
Petite Académie determined the mottoes and inscriptions appropriate for
highlighting, in the language of symbol, allegory, and heroic commonplaces, the new merits revealed by the prince's virtue. Colbert and the
Petite Académie (which even revised Quinault's opera librettis) became
the collegial author of a glorifying epic, running parallel to the history of
the reign. Each new episode of this epic was mirrored in step by the king's
various academies and factories, each using its own means of expression.
That evolving epic gradually transformed history into legend, and gave
that legend the authority of history itself, imperturbably in motion and on
the march.[6]

Such a glory machine relegated all its predecessors to familial and
provincial craftsmanship: the Academy of the Valois, the Academies of
the Grand Dukes of Florence, to say nothing of the recent Foucquet academy. To get an idea of the impression it produced on contemporaries, one
must compare it—all other things being equal, of course—to Hollywood,
queen of the global imagination in the twentieth century and glorifier of
a Grand America. It was a Hollywood with only one "star," the Sun, and
with a single genre, the epic adventure film. At the time, the only somewhat serious rival of Colbert's cultural industry was the Holy See: but, in
1661, Rome was no longer the captivating capital of images it had been
since Julius II, and which had had a brilliant late season under Gregory
XV and Urban VIII. Since the death of the latter in 1645, the glory of
Papa-Rè had been supported only by the singular and extraordinary genius
of Giovanni Bernini, the new Michelangelo. Louis XIV summoned him
to Paris in 1665. Colbert, after some discussion, very politely sent him back
to Rome. The great Italian artist did not know how to measure his words
and could not adapt to the administrative mores of the new reign.

For the first time in Europe on that scale and with that degree of narrative coherence, the arts and letters emerging from the Renaissance were
mobilized by a state to translate the successive acts of its leader, in accor-
dance with the logic of a single grandiose and invasive fiction, visible
even in the remote provinces of the kingdom and throughout Europe.
From the choice of a motto designed to be struck by the royal mint or an
inscription destined for the pedestal of a statue or triumphal arch, to blue-
prints for royal palaces and châteaux, subjects for the history paintings
and Gobelin tapestries destined to decorate them, miniatures for the king's

library, and ballets, festivals, and operas performed in front of the court, each fragment of the uninterrupted narration of the reign was automatically refracted, at every level of official communication, into spectacles, images, and texts. The coordination and integration of the system was extraordinary.

An anonymous and central agency, attributing the voice of France to the ruler and bringing to life his public image as an Olympian, now held the French and European public in suspense, and, above the heads of that public, it pronounced the oracle of posterity in advance.

A sublime dialogue took place in the temple of glory between the voice of France, which celebrated its king's forward progress, and the eternal echo that recorded it. We might wonder, however, without taking anything away from that glorious semiological success, what guilty silence and passivity the admirable sense- and emotion-producing machine might have been pursuing. What void so terrorized this official art of praise that it sought to methodically fill space and imperiously annex time to such a degree?

The State's Grand Style

The Colbertist art of the royal elogium, in verse and prose, Latin and French, combined the enthusiastic excesses of hyperbole with the cold formality of state protocol. "Baroque" eloquence, which had had its center in pontifical Rome, was just as hyperbolic, but it was charged with a religious affectivity; it sought to persuade via the religious emotion shared by men and women, the learned and the ignorant, the great and the common. Panegyrics to Louis XIV, whether prose or poetry, did not seek to move: their abstract sublimity was addressed to no one but the eternal, universal, and rational ideas the king embodied on earth, whose grandeur it was fitting to admire and whose obviousness it was appropriate to point out.[7] On 26 November 1671, the acceptance speech of Colbert's chief assistant, Charles Perrault, upon his election to the Académie Française, provided the impersonal key to that state sublime. He declared before his colleagues:

But one cannot begin too early to polish and perfect a language that, apparently, must some day be the language of all of Europe, and perhaps of the entire world, and especially, a language that must speak of Louis

XIV. One cannot begin too early to train orators, poets, and historians to celebrate his great actions. . . . Therefore, Gentlemen, I look upon this great monarch as a perfect and accomplished model, whose every aspect is admirable, and who is placed in the midst of us so that we may draw from him faithful images that never perish, so that the actions of this prince, which have produced the present happiness of his people, will become even more useful to posterity through the great example they will give to princes in the centuries to come. That is the worthy object of our work and attention.[8]

One must keep in mind the conventional monotony of that neo-Platonic glory machine (entirely infiltrated by the idea of "improvement," however) to appreciate, by contrast, the lively strangeness of Racine's pathos and Molière's laughter, rare birds in that Psaphon's aviary singing, in chorus and in cadence, "The king is great." A fortiori, against this background noise, the inwardness and meditative humanity of Mme de Sévigné's letters or Mme de La Fayette's novels assumes the full value of a shared haven of silence and affective truth. These different literary flavors, confined to the stage or to private readings, slip away without warning from the imperious duty of dedicating the language of the kingdom to the exclusive praise of a model, both Byzantine in its timeless perfection and part of the ultramodern avant-garde in its ability to cleave time in two.

The day La Fontaine was accepted into the Académie Française, the abbé de La Chambre harshly reminded the poet how lazy and absent-minded he had been up to that time in fulfilling his duty.[9] And Racine, who felt guilty both in Port-Royal's eyes and in those of the prince, even though, at that time, he had given up theater to devote himself to the king's history, declared at the end of the speech given to welcome the abbé Colbert: "All the words of language, all the syllables, appear precious to us, because we look at them as so many instruments to serve the glory of our august protector."[10]

On the Proper Use of Disgrace: The Travels of La Fontaine

In 1663, the very year when, during the investigation for Foucquet's trial, Colbert set in motion King Louis the Great's glory machine, La

Fontaine (who had already published *Elégie aux Nymphes de Vaux* and per-haps also *Ode au roi*) accompanied his uncle Jannart, the key to the *sur-intendant*'s defense in Paris, to his house arrest in Limoges, which the king had ordered for Foucquet's defender. Was he himself included in that exile order, or did he choose to compromise himself even more by demonstrat-ing his solidarity with Jannart? During that journey, hasty for that era (less than two weeks) and in the safe custody of an agent of the king, the poet sent his wife in Château-Thierry a series of letters, undoubtedly made to circulate among their trusted friends.

He probably got the idea for that travel narrative via letters from a little masterpiece published in Holland the same year (1663), but which he surely knew already in manuscript form: *Voyage de Chapelle et Bachaumont en Languedoc et en Provence*.[11] This narrative adopts the form and tone of a personal letter, in a combination of prose and verse, written by two men and sent to a pair of friends who had remained in Paris, the Du Broussin brothers.

Theoretically, that discovery of "heartland France" by two erudite Parisian libertines dates from 1656. It was published in Holland at the right moment, in 1663. In fact, it demonstrates a freedom entirely private in its appeal, and a joyful force of will greater than the caprices of politi-cal fortune, which it had become essential to reassert at a time when men of letters were quickly being brought into line.

In the company of François Bernier, Claude Emmanuel Lhuillier—called "Chapelle"—had received Gassendi's lessons at a very young age.[12] Rich and idle, this son of a libertine and erudite magistrate frequented elegant salons and literary cabarets in Paris, where, during the Foucquet years, he had been closely associated with Boileau, Racine, Molière, and La Fontaine. By his birth and talent, he belonged to the republic of let-ters. As a refined enthusiast of leisure time spent cultivating the arts, he wrote:

> Que j'aime la douce incurie
> Où je laisse couler mes jours!
> Qu'ai-je à faire de l'industrie
> De l'intrigue, des faux détours.
> Quelques contes d'hôtellerie
> Des lettres de galanterie,
> Du vin et des folles amours,
> Ont fait jusqu'ici toujours
> Ma plus heureuse rêverie.

How I love the sweet negligence
With which I let my days slip by!
What have I to do with industry,
Intrigues, or wandering off course.
A few tales of hostelry,
Letters of gallantry,
Wine and mad love affairs,
Have always been till now
My happiest dream.

Chapelle's traveling companion, François de Bachaumont, had been an ardent Frondeur. He shared all his friend's tastes (and also his opulent fortune). Along the path that would lead the two friends to Bordeaux (a cousin of Tallemant des Réaux received them there), then to Toulouse and Marseilles, the two Parisians made fun of the judgment of the provincial précieuses, who knew no better than to stupidly run down Voiture, and who preferred the pedant Ménage over the shrewd Pellisson. One of the most significant episodes of the travel narrative, for the glimpse of ulterior motives it allows us to see, was a stop the two friends made at the home of the comte d'Aubijoux, near Toulouse. Aubijoux was one of the veterans of the plots against Richelieu and the Fronde of the princes. Chapelle and Bachaumont, who knew him well, admired the ancient wisdom of his rural retreat as much as his courageous career as an enemy of the cardinals:

We found him in a little palace, which he had had built in the middle of his gardens, between fountains and woods, and which was composed of only three bedrooms, but well painted and altogether suitable. He designed this place as a personal retreat for him and two or three friends [including his cousin Fontraille, author of the vengeful *Mémoires*, on Cinq-Mars], or, when he was alone, as a place to converse with his books, not to say with his mistress:

Malgré l'injustice des cours,
Dans cet agréable ermitage
Il coule doucement ses jours,
Et vit en véritable sage.[13]

Despite the injustice of the courts,
In this agreeable hermitage

He sweetly passes his days,
And lives like a veritable sage.

The vast hinterland of Paris that the two friends traveled, with apparently no other goal than to amuse themselves, was through and through a true paradise for Epicureans, whose delicious diversity, good wines, excellent fare, pretty girls, and, in general, gentle mores amply compensated for the ridiculousness of its bluestockings and the rare disappointments endured by the travelers, especially in Narbonne. "Heartland France," impervious to the revolutions in Paris, already lent itself to Voltaire's maxim, "Let us cultivate our garden."

The very Parisian Molière, Chapelle's close friend, had already made a similar discovery with his "Illustre Théâtre" during his long tour of the southwest—Provence, Languedoc, Burgundy, and Normandy—between 1646 and 1658.

All the same, despite all their wit, there is something of the arrogant city dweller in these two sons of Parisian families seeking in the provinces one more diversion from Parisian politics. If La Fontaine was inspired by their example for his own travel letters, he was so as a secretly aggrieved poet (among other places, his pain burst forth in Amboise, before the prison where Foucquet had been confined for a time) and as a man who was not traveling freely and at his own rhythm, but in safe custody and following "the king's orders." If, in spite of everything, he remained entirely open and sensitive to the succulent things and delicious creatures that the hinterland held in store, he owed this less to Chapelle and Bachaumont's philosophical framework than to his extraordinary poetic antennae, which allowed him to perceive, wherever he went, the echoes and traces of a great and ancient French drama to which he, better than anyone, had been initiated.

These letters are addressed to his wife, Marie Héricart, Jannart's niece.[14] She was fourteen years old when he married her in 1653, by arrangement of the two families. He had since made her his friend. He gently chides her about the limits of her literary tastes, but proves perfectly well aware of her sexual preferences, and very indulgent regarding them. "Admit the truth," he writes her, regarding a Venus Anadyomene exhibited in the Richelieu château, "that's not the sort of woman you'd mind seeing step out of her bath!"

Already turning a true story that had been told him along the way into a Boccaccio tale, he attributes Marie Héricart's features, as they appear to us in a fine portrait by Rigaud, to the lovely heroine (poetic gallantry). He writes: "It was as if he knew intimately the girl from Poitou in the story—a light brunette with a lovely waist, an admirable bust, plump where she needed to be plump, all her facial features well formed, beautiful eyes, so that, all in all, there was little to wish for, though not exactly nothing. . . . In addition, she knew novels and was not lacking in wit" (letter of 12 September 1663, from Limoges).

It is possible that La Fontaine was not a good father. He was surely not the "bad husband" of legend. He transformed a family duty into gallant companionship. As Jannart's good niece, who could understand things at the slightest hint, Marie also shared the poet's attachment to Foucquet and to everything in France that opposed Richelieu and Colbert.

The pungency of "muscat vines" perfumes these pages written by a "man of Champagne," introduced since his childhood to the charms of the French provinces, and who knew from the inside its past and its resources, invisible to self-satisfied city dwellers. From the first letter, La Fontaine's entire being, far from Olympus, breathes the air of these old and real Arcadias and Cytheras, strangers to modern progress ("beautés simples et divines / Vous contentiez nos aïeux"; beauties simply and divine / You satisfied our forebears) and sacred because they dated from time immemorial ("Souvenez vous de ce bois qui paraît en l'enfoncement, avec la noirceur d'une forêt de dix siècles . . . je ne crois pas qu'il y en ait de plus vénérable sur la terre"; Remember these woods that appear in the hollow, with the blackness of a forest ten centuries old . . . I believe there is nothing more venerable on earth). Having left Paris for these "very rustic places, which he loved above all things," the poet, like Antaeus, immediately regained his strength after the final vicissitudes of the Foucquet affair, with which he was intimately involved at his uncle Jannart's side. That hasty trip was transformed for him from an exile and punishment inflicted by Colbert to a meandering return to his roots and a general verification of his close attachments as a man, a Frenchman, and a poet.

In the post chaise that took him, his uncle, and the king's agent, he became close to the traveling companions of both sexes who adopted him: in particular, there was an excellent Huguenot countess from Poitou, as savvy about the theological controversy as about the delightful things of life. Along the way, in Châtellerault, he ran into male cousins and pretty female cousins on his mother's (the Pidoux) side. He was delighted to meet the Huguenot patriarch of that branch of the family, a Frenchman of the old school. He was eighty years old, "stayed on horseback for eleven hours without discomfort," liked hunting and tennis, knew Scripture, and wrote controversial books: he was, "moreover, the most cheerful man you have ever seen, and the one who thinks least of business, except the business of his pleasure." He very quickly felt at home in that France of the Edict of Nantes, as if on familiar ground, sampling carp and melon, and judging that people made love there "as happily as anyplace on earth." The regions in Montlhéry he passed through still bore the scars of the Hundred Years' War, or the civil wars of the sixteenth century, but they had healed on their own, without asking anything of the court, and had recovered the naturalness of a land of plenty: "You would not believe how excellent the butter we eat is: twenty times, I have wished for such cattle, such grass, such waters, all but the thresher, which is a little old."

It is as if he had returned to these provinces after a Parisian odyssey where he had also refined his senses, and had become more sharply aware of the true riches, but also of the true perils. This rediscovery of Old France (in the Orléans of Joan of Arc, the Notre-Dame-de-Cléry of Louis XI) reverberated with recent literary and political events. The unattractive features attributed to Joan of Arc on her statue in Orléans reminded him of the failure of Chapelain's epic *La pucelle*. The statue of Louis XI, where Louis XIV had come to gather his thoughts before having Foucquet arrested, inspired verses about the reigning king in the style of Commynes, verses that are indiscreet to say the least:

Je lui trouvai la mine d'un matois;
Aussi l'était ce prince, dont la vie
Doit rarement servir d'exemple aux rois
Et pourrait être en quelques points suivie.

I found he looked like a sly devil,
Such was this prince, whose life
Should rarely serve as an example to kings
And might in several points be followed.

If he was sensitive to medieval and fifteenth-century France, he was truly happy in the France of the Renaissance. The Loire Valley spoke to him in the language of Rabelais and reminded him of Ronsard: he imagined "sacrifices" of heifers and oxen offered to the ancient gods, which the poets of La Pléiade made the reigning spirits of the place. In Blois, whose *cheerful and pleasant* mood he admired, he suddenly came to worship Gaston d'Orléans, the Bourbon prince worthy of the Valois who reigned only in his duchy, the Loire Valley; the poet, like a great number of French people, obviously saw Foucquet as the prince's successor. He was a true prince: his stay in Blois brought gentle mores to the countryside, already blessed by the gods in its climate and the beauty of its women: "The people of these regions rightly mourn him still; never was a reign more sweet, more calm, or more happy than his reign." He had previously said: "There is no one who should not have great veneration for this prince."

Gaston's château, a legacy of the Valois, was for the poet an emblem of his own idea of "grace even more beautiful than beauty": "All three of these rooms, thank God, have no symmetry, and no relation or affinity with one another. The architect avoided that as much as he could. In looking from the outside at what Francis I had had done, I was more satisfied with it than with all the rest: there are a great many small galleries, small windows, small balconies, small ornaments, without regularity and without order; that makes for something grand, which was rather pleasing."

A true harmony emerging from an ingenious diversity and not from a regularity obtained without thought by virtue of a preconceived plan: that was the poetics of Chambord and Blois and it would also be that of Fables. It was also a mode of politics for the kingdom, the politics de Retz had dreamed of and for which Foucquet had vainly stood as a candidate.

Touraine and Blesae were preferred by the Valois:

> . . . coteaux enchantés,
> Belles maisons, beaux parcs, et bien plantés,
> Prés verdoyants dont ce pays abonde,
> Vignes et bois, tant de diversité
> Qu'on croit d'abord être en un autre monde.

> . . . Enchanted hillsides
> Lovely homes, lovely grounds well planted,
> Verdant meadows in which this land abounds,
> Vineyards and woods, such diversity
> That at first you believe you're in another world.

They inspired the poet to write a fable before Fables: "The Citizens of Orleans Complaining to Fate." His spirits were revived along with his good humor in this "garden of France," which he recognized as if he had always lived there in his mind (letter of 3 September 1663, in Richelieu).

This was a striking antithesis to the impressions recorded at Richelieu.[15] The château and the city ordered by the cardinal exude the same sense of peril that looms from the Louvre, where Richelieu's heirs had renewed his power. But the poet's voice and subtle mockery overcome all fear. This château and this "artificial city" on "infertile" soil, created by an all-powerful cardinal of humble birth "simply to have it built around the room where he was born," reveals to the visitor a strong-willed hero, but one with an abstract will enslaved to a predatory amour propre, and under whose feet the grass would not grow back. This would also be Saint-Simon's feeling about Versailles. Richelieu's monumental, utterly symmetrical château looks like a mausoleum. The perfectly aligned city ("straight street, square plaza") was itself the sterile result of the "self-satisfaction" of financiers and high officials, who had built on that spot "to curry favor with the cardinal," and who fled as soon as he died.

Between the living and gracious naturalness of the Loire Valley of the Valois and Gaston d'Orléans, and the sinister modernity of Richelieu, the poet experienced the gap that separates two ways of being a prince, two forms of politics, two poetics, two entirely contrary attitudes toward the genius and the vocation of the kingdom. La Fontaine's choice was as startling as the subtlety and precision of his diagnosis. Marie Héricart and their friends drew the implicit, dark conclusions of this relationship for themselves: Colbert was Richelieu's successor; one could expect from him, as one had from the cardinal, only a mechanical, sharply drawn geometry and a violence against nature.

The visit to the inside of the château, and to the fabulous art collections accumulated there by the cardinal (who never had the time to come and see them), was just as implicitly mocking of this gloomy museum, guarded by effigies of Mars and Hercules, and whose dome was topped by a statue of Renown in a running posture:

Telle enfin qu'elle devait être
Pour bien servir un si bon maître:
Car tant moins elle a de loisir,
Tant plus on lui fait plaisir.

Just as she ought to be, indeed,
To serve so good a master:
For the less free time she has,
The happier she makes him.

In addition to vanity, the willfulness directed against nature, geometrism, the appetite for war, violence, and propaganda—Richelieu's traits as La Fontaine deciphered them at the cardinal's château—he includes the most pathological of all, the modern trait par excellence: an incapacity for rest and leisure, a lethal haste. This deserted château, built to the glory of a deceased dictator of sorts, was the cenotaph for a French Sulla. La Fontaine carried a copy of Livy in his pocket and read it during his journey.

But his judgment of the container in no way prevented the poet from taking pleasure in the content. He was an amateur, without pretensions or pedantry, but more expert than he gallantly wanted his wife to believe. He was able to appreciate, with his own sense of taste, the splendid antiques, Poussin's *Bacchanales*, and the masterpieces of the early Italian Renaissance that the cardinal had assembled in his lair, and which the poet, because of the royal schedule, was forced to rush through. He was very sensitive to the beauty of the incomplete (*non finito*) character of Michelangelo's *Bound Slave* and *Dying Slave*:

> Qu'on ne se plaigne pas que la chose ait été
>   Imparfaite trouvée:
> Le prix en est plus grand, l'auteur plus regretté
>   Que s'il l'eût achevée.

> Do not complain that the thing
>   Was found to be imperfect:
> Its worth is all the greater,
>   Its author more sorely missed,
>   Than had he completed it.

The comparison with the interrupted *Le songe de Vaux* and with *Fables*, left without a conclusion, is unavoidable. The *non finito* is the share of silence the artist leaves for the inexpressible. But La Fontaine already bore within himself other works besides these epistles in prose and verse. The château of Francis I in Blois was like a prophetic dream, an apparition in the form of architecture of the diverse and living universe of *Contes* and *Fables*. This dream, which was also a creative spark, was revived in Richelieu, in front of a table inlaid with a mosaic of semiprecious stones, a masterpiece of the fine craftsmanship of sixteenth-century Florence, which today adorns the Apollo Gallery in the Louvre. The poet was stopped in his tracks in front of that fabulous table:

> Elle est de pièces de rapport,
> Et chaque pièce est un trésor;
> Car ce sont toutes pierre fines,
> Agates, jaspe, et cornalines,

Pierres de prix, pierres de nom,
Pierres d'éclat et de renom:
Considérez que de ma vie
Je n'ai trouvé d'objet qui fût si précieux.
Ce qu'on prise aux tapis de Perse et de Turquie,
Fleurons, compartiments, animaux, broderie,
Tout cela s'y présente aux yeux;
L'aiguille et le pinceau ne rencontrent pas mieux.
J'en admirai chaque figure;
Et qui n'admirerait ce qui naît sous les cieux?
Le savoir de Pallas, aidé de la teinture,
Cède au caprice heureux de la simple nature;
Le hasard produit des morceaux
Que l'art n'a plus qu'à joindre, et qui font sans peinture
Des modèles parfaits de fleurons et d'oiseaux.
(Letter of 12 September 1663, from Limoges)

It is made of reassembled pieces,
And every piece a treasure;
For all are precious stones,
Agate, jasper, carnelian,
Stones of great price and great name,
Stones of splendor and renown:
Just think that in my life
I have found no object so precious.
What is valued in carpets from Persia and Turkey,
Fleurons, squares, animals, embroidery,
All appeal to the eye;
A needle or paintbrush could do no better.
I admired its every shape;
And who should not admire what is born under heaven?
The craft of Pallas, aided by dyes,
Yields to the happy caprice of mere nature;
Chance produces fragments that
Art has only to unite, and which, without paint,
Gives perfect shape to fleurons and to birds.

With such a degree of conviction and coherence, playing on several registers at once, La Fontaine's political and poetic thought implies what must in spite of everything be called a philosophy of nature, heir to the naturalism of the Renaissance and free from the intellectualism of theologians such as Mersenne or philosophers such as Descartes. In that magical table, the poet saw the artist following the genius of nature, satisfied to pursue its fertile suggestions to their logical end. The artist's mind proves all the more fertile when he knows how to remain modest and attentive, observing and bringing to maturity these marvelous silent operations, whose loving and mysterious secret, in which chance plays a role, is superior to all the concepts that intellectual arrogance wishes to impose on matter by doing violence to it. A science, a philosophy, a politics, and a poetics of ingenious and living diversity were encapsulated in that table gleaming with shapes and colors.[16]

What is true for the plastic arts is also true for the political arts of governance and construction. Gaston d'Orléans had governed the Blesae well; his architect, François Mansart, produced the "modern," but in the spirit of his predecessors. Francis I realized his châteaux and Michelangelo and the Florentine jewelers made masterpieces because they followed nature and observed its profound laws regarding the development of things, instead of imposing a preconceived and abstract design on it. The art of governance, the art of construction, and the poetic arts are all encapsulated in an art of love. For all his genius, Cardinal de Richelieu was only a pedant, a terrible spoiler of French naturalness, silently refuted by the treasures he collected without even looking at them.

These letters to Marie Héricart, neglected by biographers and critics, are in reality the most personal and direct account we have of the deepest thoughts, in a decisive moment of crisis, of a poet very prone to silence and concealment. They are a masterpiece polished with consummate and nonchalant skill, but only for friends in the know. Clearly, it is not surprising that they were never published during La Fontaine's lifetime. Under Louis XIV, they were a firebrand. The reason they were not destroyed by the poet, as was undoubtedly the case for most of his correspondence with Maucroix, is that, thanks to the independent Marie Héricart, longhand copies were put into limited circulation in 1663–64 within the circle of the *surintendant* Foucquet's most trusted supporters.

THE SPECTACLE SOCIETY

There is a striking gap between these epistles written for private ends, a luxury all the more delightful in that it was aimed at an audience of connoisseurs and accomplices, and the din of official eloquence that began at that time to fill the ears and eyes of the French people. The gap must and should have been glaring between this lowly but varied, capricious, witty, and gallant style, to which the French had become accustomed through Voiture and even Scarron, and the sublimity of royal panegyrics, which corresponded, in the art of construction, to the cold symmetry of the Louvre colonnade designed by Claude Perrault to replace Bernini's plan. But Colbert and his administration could do no better than commission works of eloquence, in writing or the visual arts, determined by a scale of grandeur measurable and measured by a plumb line and level.

The young king had another ambition for himself, the ambition to be a star. At first, that ambition was mysterious to Colbert, who resisted the expense of Versailles, and who preferred the Grand Louvre. Louis XIV was jealous of Foucquet, just as Louis XIII had been jealous of Gaston d'Orléans, for reasons that Colbert's practical mind, on its own, had difficulty discerning. The king was too much the *grand seigneur* not to have suspected that the French people, in matters regarding the noble luxury of taste, placed the Valois far above the Bourbons. In that respect, "good King Henry" himself, who had been so generous toward Paris, did not carry as much weight—or carried too much—compared to his cousins and predecessors from the older branch. After the somber couple of Richelieu and Louis XIII, after the baroque, Italo-Spanish alliance between Anne of Austria and Mazarin, a gallant *roturier* like Nicolas Foucquet could pass in Paris for another Francis I.

Colbert, a shrewd organizer, skilled politician, and expert publicity agent, saw the advantages to be had from eliminating Foucquet. The king saw them as well, but he relished in advance the sole opportunity it gave him (and that delight escaped Colbert) to stand on Foucquet's ruins as the arbiter of modern French taste. It now fell to him to avenge the Bourbons of the tenacious French cult for Valois Maecenases. He could certainly count on Colbert, Chapelain, and the other heirs to Richelieu for mechanisms that worked, for the garish mishmash of publicity, propaganda, and glory. But if he did not want to pass for a pedant in Paris, as Richelieu had at the Rambouillet mansion, he had to give himself the touch of gallantry, good cheer, and spark that had made Vaux a success. The public, out of sorts, skeptical, and very difficult to please, still had to be convinced. The education of Louis XIV's tastes was beginning.

The king began awkwardly. In 1662 he appeared before the Parisians, at the head of a "race for heads and rings," surrounded by the greatest names of France, including the prince de Condé. Here is what the crowd saw from afar, as described by Charles Perrault:

The king was in Roman dress: the body of the garment was made of silver brocade, accented with gold embroidery, with the shoulders and the bottom of the plate finished with gold brocade mail accented with silver thread and large diamonds incrusted in the embroidery, and further bordered by a row of diamonds. On either end of the ruff, with the same trimming as on the body of the garment, and composed of forty-four rose diamonds attached by diamond clasps, were the epaulières, made of the same fabric and embroidery as the body, and with a diamond bell filled with diamond pendants hanging from the ends. In the middle of the stomach hung another large bell of the same kind. Three bands of the same fabric and embroidery as the rest, covered with one hundred and twenty extraordinarily large rose diamonds, and joined together on the inside by three large diamond clasps, circled that magnificent breastplate at the waist. At the bottom of the skirt of tasses, made of the same material and embroidery as the body, were chains of mail like the other, each with a bell at the end. The lambrequins at the shoulders and bottom of the plate, which fell over this skirt of tasses, were of gold brocade embroidered with silver, with large diamonds incrusted in the embroidery, and bells. The sleeves, of the same fabric and embroidery as the body, were decorated with fifty-two links of chain; at the top, twenty-four diamond roses on the gold brocade encircled the edge of the sleeve, and this ring was also adorned with mail like the other. From that sleeve emerged a puff sleeve of silver fabric, which ended in a cuff of the same material embroidered in gold, and attached at the wrist by a diamond bracelet. The belt that set off the body of the garment was composed of fifty-four extraordinarily large links of diamond chains. He wore a silver helmet with gold leaf adorned with two large diamonds, twelve rose diamonds on the sides, and a string of twelve other roses. That helmet was shaded by a crest of plumes the color of fire, from which four herons emerged.[17]

The Lord's anointed has disguised himself as Rostand's cock, Chantecler. Unfortunately, it was old hat, a return (but with the crown jewels) to the baroque pomp of Venetian opera costumes, introduced to Paris by Mazarin in 1646, and which reappeared in 1660. From the first, it turned the stomachs of the Paris public.

The king was very fond of the cock, an animal phenomenally decked out from head to toe. He sought inspiration from it long after he had learned not to display himself in its plumage. Even as a child in 1648, he had read this stirring symbolic gloss, in a large illustrated collection (which, under the circumstances, also charmed the queen mother of the court), *Le vrai théâtre d'honneur et de chevalerie*, dedicated to the king by Marc de Vulson de la Colombière, an eccentric country squire mad about heraldry:

> The most excellent astrologers and mathematicians of antiquity taught us that Mars is the dominant planet over France, and that its influence makes the French bolder and more courageous than any people on earth. . . . That same influence and natural inclination is the reason they were given the name *Galli,* because of the resemblance they have to the bellicose temperament of cocks, who often fight in duels, and who, like the French, are very bold and courageous . . . and because cocks have the natural virtue of intimidating by their presence and their crow the bravest of lions, and of making them flee: hence, the French, of which cocks are the truest emblem, have often chased off the Lions of Spain and the Leopards of England with their invincible blows.[18]

In the sixteenth century, the cock, which medieval bestiaries made a solar bird, intimidating even the proud lion with its "cock-a-doodle-do," had been added to the gospel lilies as symbols for the French kingdom.[19] The play on words between *Gallus* (Latin for "Gallic," but also "cock") facilitated that unfortunate adoption. For centuries, lilies had symbolized the very Christian kingdom; the cock came to symbolize the character of the nation and its gentlemen. Henry IV, reviving a still-dubious tradition forgotten somewhat since Francis I, introduced it with great fanfare into the Bourbon patrimony: at the birth of the future Louis XIII, the happy father had a medal struck representing the Dauphin holding the lily and scepter, below a cock crowing itself hoarse while standing on a globe of the world. The motto on that coin was *Regnis natura et orbi* (Nature has made him for his kingdom and for the world).

When, in 1662, Louis XIV adopted as his official device a sun illuminating the world, with the motto *Nec pluribus impar,* he gave the declaration of pride attributed to his father by his grandfather a hyperbolic slant. On that coin, the sublime figure of the sun conceals, but does not obliterate, the barnyard animal that announces its rising. The sun veils the cock in a dazzling light. All the same, the heraldic cock dear to Louis XIV was well represented and visible among the cartouches of *Devises pour les tapisseries du roi,* painted by the miniaturist Jacques Bailly in 1664.[20] In 1659 Charles Le Brun invented a new architectural array that combined on the same capital the sun, lilies, and the cock: the king, the monarchy, and the kingdom. That very heterogeneous array did not win large approval: nevertheless, the king's first painter and decorator placed it later on the columns and pilasters of the Galerie des Glaces at Versailles.

La Fontaine was never a Cartesian. Nonetheless, he had a very fine mind, and, in one of his letters to Marie Héricart, he adopted the maxim "In all things, it is good to avoid confusion" (12 September 1663, from Limoges).

This man who loved diversity shared with Pascal a taste for distinguishing among orders. For him, there were animals, and then there were animals, even though he defended all of them together against Descartes's and Hobbes's mechanization; and, for him, the cock as a symbol was not a bird appropriate for the France he loved. In his *Fables*, the young cock is often the most ridiculous and vain figure in the barnyard:

> Il aiguisait son bec, battait l'air et ses flancs,
>   Et s'exerçant contre les vents
>   S'armait d'une jalouse rage.
> . . . .
> Tout vainqueur insolent à sa perte travaille.
> Défions-nous du Sort, and prenons garde à nous
>   Après le gain d'une bataille.
>   ("The Two Cocks," 7.13)

> He sharpened his beak, beat the air and his flanks,
>   And, doing battle against the winds,
>   Summoned up a jealous rage.
> . . . .
> Every insolent victor works toward his own downfall.
> Let us beware of Fate, and be wary of ourselves
>   After we win a battle.

If the poet attended the Carrousel Royal in 1662, the king decked out as a cock certainly did not strike him as being in good taste or auspicious, and the ostentatious luxury with which the disguise was laden elicited the same judgment he made of the king's apartments in the Richelieu château: "wondrously superb," but with so much gold "that, in the end, I tired of it" (letter of 12 September 1663, from Limoges).

For him, the political clash with Colbert was exacerbated, as far as the king was concerned, by ethical differences and an incompatibility in matters of taste. The 1676 *Epître à M. de Nyert* would be the critical assessment of Louis XIV's ear for music, and it would be devastating.

For Parisians of the time, who had been invited en masse by Foucquet, the festival of Vaux-le-Vicomte the previous year had been what Diaghilev's Ballets Russes would later be for the Paris of Robert de Montesquiou and the comtesse Greffulhe: a miracle of poetry and enchantment. The gaudy and provocative exaggeration of Venetian opera costumes for the benefit of the gallery, imposed as absurd getups even on the Great Condé, could therefore not efface that very recent joy to the eyes. As a historical actor, Louis XIV could count on Colbert, but the dancer king had to find something different if he was to become, without Foucquet and in the eyes of Paris, the arbiter of elegance he wanted to be.

The princes of wit were not on his side. Neither La Rochefoucauld's *Maximes* nor Pascal's *Pensées* nor Mme de La Fayette's *Mémoires pour servir à l'histoire d'Henriette d'Angleterre* nor her novels nor Cardinal de Retz's *Mémoires* nor Mme de Sévigné's *Lettres* nor, above all, La Fontaine's *Fables* owed anything to the king or to Colbert. All these masterpieces of French literature, conceived far from the court, in semidarkness, in the repose of internal exile and private life, had another thing in common: they were all closely linked to what the king hated most, Port-Royal in some cases, Foucquet in the others. Apart from the panegyrists on Colbert's payroll, the only ones left to glorify the king were image-producers and men of the theater. The first absolute state, which invented propaganda on a grand scale, also owed it to itself to perfect the spectacle society. Colbert and Chapelain took upon themselves the epic of the reign. The king himself saw to his own image. He learned to polish it to a shine.

In that more delicate game, the king, without having to look any further, had a tested and favorite card up his sleeve, Isaac de Benserade. At the birth of Louis XIV, that very witty gentleman poet—related to Cardinal de Richelieu, something that had improved his fortunes—a regular at the literary and musical cabarets in Paris but persona non grata at the Rambouillet mansion, was already a favorite of the court's "inner circle."

His birth, wrote the abbé Paul Tallemant in 1697, in the preface to Benserade's *Oeuvres*, published after the author's death, "had given him a bold manner of behavior, which led him to treat the people of the highest rank with informality, so that you had to overlook, without daring to contradict him, everything it pleased him to propose, and he even seems to have dominated the people of the greatest substance."[21]

Thus, the court had long ago found its own Voiture in Benserade: brilliant, formidable, indispensable. After Richelieu, he knew how to cheer up Mazarin and the regent Anne of Austria. His biting wit—though he knew when "going too far was far enough"—allowed a bit of Parisian spiciness to circulate in the cramped and anxious circle of royal power. No one could resist his bagatelles, like this very irregular sonnet with an odd number of syllables to each line, dedicated to Grisette, Mlle Deshoulières's cat, under Louis XIV's reign:

> Vainement à miauler
> Vous passez des nuits entières,
> Vous qu'on voyait égaler
> Les Chattes les plus altières.
>
> Hélas! pour vous consoler,
> Rien ne vient par les chatières.
> Où vous pourriez donc aller?
> Désertes sont les gouttières.
>
> Bien d'autres chattes que vous
> Se plaignent de ces Matous,
> L'un avec l'autre se joue.
>
> Mortifiez vos désirs:
> En vogue sont les plaisirs
> Que Nature désavoue![22]

> Vainly mewing
> You spend entire nights,
> You who once equaled
> The haughtiest she cats.
>
> Alas! to console you,
> Nothing comes through the cat door.
> Where could you go, then?
> The alleys are deserted.
>
> Many cats besides you
> Complain about those toms
> Playing with each other.
>
> Mortify your desires:
> The fashionable pleasures
> Are those Nature disavows!

The king grew up on intimate terms with Benserade, which was not the case for Colbert. Quite naturally, when, at the end of the Fronde, the time came to give the young man the opportunity to display his "merit," it fell to Benserade to custom-fit ballet libretti for the king and the younger generation of the court. Having tried out every genre, the clever Benserade had found his vocation.

"It could be said," wrote the abbé Tallemant, "that he was the delight of the court, and what sealed his reputation were the king's ballets, in which, with remarkable genius, he described the character of the one dancing, and confused it with the role being played, performed in a manner so subtle and fine that there was not a soul at the time who did not read his verses with extreme pleasure, and who does not read them still."[23]

Charles Perrault analyzed the stratagem of the witty publicity agent this way: "Before him [the stanzas recited by the dancers] spoke only of the characters, not of the actors performing the role. M. de Benserade shaped his verses in such a way that they could be understood as being about both. . . . The first blow struck the character and ricocheted back on the person, which gave a double pleasure."[24]

These double-edged libretti belatedly brought to the court the principle of gallant wit, fond of riddles and hidden meanings, which had provided the charm of the parlor games introduced to the Rambouillet mansion by Voiture in 1624. But now, these games took on an entirely new dimension and weight: a young king under observation, whose character traits were still being sought out, could conceal himself onstage even as he exhibited himself. After the Fronde, Foucquet's marked taste, and that of his own high-society "court," for the magic of masks, double entendres, and the euphoria they produced among those in the know regarding secrets of the boudoir and affinities of the heart, created another tacit rivalry between the "wit" of Foucquet's Paris (the successor to the Rambouillet mansion), where La Fontaine became an oracle in 1658, and that of the young court, for which the old hand Benserade was able to become the official supplier.

Foucquet's fall gave even more prominence to Benserade, whose ballets, depicting a now-absolute king, became wholly an affair of state.[25] Benserade had to accept rivals, especially Molière, and, to a certain extent, Président de Périgny, the Dauphin's tutor and author of occasional poetry. He also had to collaborate with Perrault and Quinault. But he remained at the center of the small, gallant academy assembled by the king and for the king.

Until 1670, when Louis XIV stopped dancing (according to Louis Racine, he was stung by the harsh lines of Burrhus judging Nero in Jean

Racine's *Britannicus*),[26] Benserade produced an abundance of royal ballet libretti, and his occasional poetry, subtly slanderous and risqué, continued to fill the king and his court with joy, sensitizing them to Parisian wit and saving them from the chill of the official sublime orchestrated by Colbert. In 1674 the librettist was elected to the Académie Française. He published a translation of Ovid's *The Metamorphoses* as rondeaux and spent the end of his life in quiet retirement, enjoying the prestige of having known the "good times" of the Regency, the Foucquet years, and the king's youth. The verses he composed for Michel Lambert and Mlle Hilaire were still being sung at the end of the century, in Paris and in the provinces. In 1693 when he, along with La Fontaine, Mme de Sévigné, and her cousin Bussy, was maliciously attacked by Furetière, he openly defended them against the "pedant." By that time, La Fontaine and Benserade had together become "living treasures" of gallant wit, two French Ovids.

Before the 1661 coup d'état, Benserade and the choreographer Beauchamp highlighted the seductiveness of the adolescent king, an object and a promise of love. In 1656, for example, in the *Ballet royal de Psyché*, the king performed the role, first of Springtime, then of Sprite, whose movements on the stage were glossed musically in the following sonnet:

> Est-ce chose réelle? Est-ce sorcellerie?
> Ne sauriez-vous, mes yeux, éclaircir ce soupçon?
> Adonis était beau; pourtant sans flatterie,
> L'Esprit qui m'apparaît a meilleure façon.
>
> Cela marche de l'air d'un grand jeune garçon
> Où la Nature a mis toute son industrie,
> Et dont toute la Cour pourrait prendre leçon,
> En fait de bonne grâce et de galanterie.
>
> Comme sont les Amants, cela fait tout ainsi,
> Cela n'aura vingt ans que dans deux ans d'ici,
> Cela fait mieux danser que tout la gent blonde,
>
> Et n'est femme à choisir dans ce grand nombre-là
> A qui cela ne fit la plus grand peur du monde,
> Et qui ne se rendît volontiers à cela.[27]
>
> Is this something real? Is this sorcery?
> O eyes, can't you elucidate this suspicion?

Adonis was handsome, and yet, without flattery,
The Sprite appearing before me is finer still.

It has the gait of a tall young boy
In whom Nature has put all her skill
And from whom the whole court could take its lesson,
In the matter of good grace and gallantry.

As lovers conduct themselves, so it does everything,
It will not be twenty for another two years,
It dances better than all the blonde folk,

And there is not a woman among us
To whom it does not give the greatest fright,
And who would not be happy to surrender to it.

The royal Adonis, with all the merits of the perfect young romantic lead with his beautiful olive Italo-Spanish complexion, was still a callow youth. There was nothing to suggest the "nascent monster" Racine dared speak of in retrospect in 1669. But within that hall of mirrors constantly constructed around the attractive and youthful star by the hand-picked artists and spectators, Louis XIV matured; and, except in his frequent nightmares, Foucquet did not suspect that he would mature into a dangerous master, and not a friend and ally.

In 1658, in *Ballet d'Acidiane*, the king played a Moor, whom Benserade called a "dark and mysterious beauty" (*Beau ténébreux*). In 1659, in *Ballet de la raillerie*, he played Mirth:

Il est charmant et doux, et sa manière touche
Infinité de coeurs qui n'en témoignent rien:
    Que ce *Ris*-là serait bien
    Le fait d'une belle bouche!

Amour qui tant qu'il peut pousse les traits qu'il forge,
N'attend plus rien, sinon, que le temps soit venu,
    Où ce *Ris* moins retenu
    Passe le noeud de la gorge.[28]

He is sweet and charming, and his manner touches
An infinite number of hearts that say not a word:

How fine that Mirth would be
For a pretty mouth!

Love, who promotes his creatures as much as he can,
Has nothing to do but wait for the time to come,
    When this Mirth, less restrained,
    Pulls the noose from around its throat.

In 1661, in Benserade's ballets, the prince charming became a fully virile king, a husband, a lover, a father: still a seducer, but with authority. The mythological and allegorical productions were transformed into regular bedroom scenes, in which the king and his mistresses, virtual or already in favor, paraded about under the complicitous eyes of the young court. The king's sexual vitality, now displayed openly, took on the comforting sense of the plenty and fertility promised to France under a prince reigning on his own. The year of the coup d'état, in *Ballet des saisons*, the king played Ceres, and Benserade gave him the following lines:

Non, je ne veux plus voir les peuples accablés,
Moi-même, je ferai le partage des blés,
Et je prétends qu'à moi s'adresse tout le monde:
Qui prend d'autres chemins ne saurait faire pis,
Ma seule volonté libérale et féconde,
Dispensera les grains qui sortent des épis.[29]

No, I do not want to see the people in distress,
I myself will divide up the wheat,
And I demand that everyone come to me:
Anyone going elsewhere could hardly do worse,
My liberal and fertile will alone
Will dispense the grain that comes from the staff.

From year to year, with the true talent of a medium, Benserade was able to wittily retouch and nuance the king's portrait in a way that did not belie his political majesty, but which added to it the virtue of the great god Pan. Thanks to the ingenious fertility rites thought up by Benserade, the metamorphosis of the Adonis of 1656 into the Mars of the Dutch War, which began in 1671, was masked on the court's stage by the endless promise of general peace and prosperity.

Also in *Ballet des saisons*, Louis XIV played Springtime, and, the same year, in *Ballet royal de l'impertinence*, he played the Great Lover. The next year, in 1662, in the twelfth entrée of the ballet *Hercule amoureux*, Venus and the Pleasures danced, celebrating the conjugal bliss of the royal couple, and, in the seventeenth entrée, the king appeared as the Sun. He was welcomed by an aria which abounded in intimidating allusions to Foucquet's fall. The lover king was also a vigilant and jealous king:

> Des secrets Phaétons les grands et vastes soins,
> Pourraient bien s'attirer la foudre et le naufrage;
> Si pour la chose même il faut tant de courage,
> Pour la seule pensée il n'en faut guère moins,
>
> Voyant plus par ses yeux que par les yeux d'autrui,
> Il empêchera bien ces petits feux de luire;
> Par sa propre lumière il songe à se conduire,
> Tout brillant des clartés qui s'échappent de lui.[30]

> The great and vast displays of secret Phaethons
> Might well attract thunderbolts and disaster;
> If doing the thing takes so much courage,
> Even thinking it requires hardly less,
>
> Seeing more through his own eyes than those of others,
> He will prevent those little fires from gleaming;
> He dreams of being guided by his own light,
> Shining with the rays that emanate from him.

Even in 1665, when Benserade had the king appear as Alexander in *Ballet de la naissance de Vénus*, opposite Henrietta of England as Roxana, he gave her the following lines:

> Et ce jeune héros doit être satisfait
> Qui sur ce jeune coeur emporte la victoire:
> C'est où l'Ambition termine son désir,
> On ne va pas plus loin du côté de la gloire,
> Moins encore plus loin du côté du plaisir.

> And this young hero must be satisfied
> Who over this young heart has won his victory:

It is there that Ambition reaches its last desire,
One cannot go any farther in the matter of glory,
Still less in the matter of pleasure.

In the roles of a Shepherd (1661), of Pleasure (1668), and once again
of the Sun (also 1668), the king's first victories, more diplomatic than military, were, in the fluid verses of the librettist, mere efflorescences of his
sexual vitality, heartening for all his beloved subjects and threatening for
the kingdom's enemies. In 1670 the king stopped dancing. In 1673
Molière died. The happiest phase of the kingdom, the phase that most
resembled what a Foucquet ministry might have been, came to an end. It
was then that the "king of war" appeared on the European stage. The
Colbertist state placed at his service his finances in order, his navy and
army in good operating condition, and his propaganda machine thoroughly broken in. *Cedat toga armis.*[31]

Benserade's acceptance speech to the Académie Française in 1671, like
Racine's in 1673, the year Molière died, was a telling symptom of the end
of that late spring. The courtly poet who had survived the Voiture years,
the Foucquet years, and the Molière years became part of the collective
glory machine controlled by Colbert.

"I admit one weakness," Benserade declared to his fellows, "and the
real reason that led me aspire to belong to this body: I am unable to sustain
any longer the idea I have of our monarch, and, feeling overwhelmed by
the weight of his glory, I thought how advantageous it would be for me to
join with you, and to add my feeble voice to your concerts, and your
songs of triumph, especially after His Majesty has put the finishing
touches on the things he is considering, and which will give you so much
to consider."[32]

Two Geniuses in the Spectacle Society

The king could thus trust Benserade, but that man of wit dated from
before Foucquet's time. He had to be made to forget Foucquet. At just the
right moment, the Providence of potentates and the tastes of his brother,
Monsieur, and of Nicolas Foucquet himself placed a long-anticipated
genius of the stage in Louis XIV's path: Molière. And it was through
Molière that the king also acquired another genius, Jean Racine.

Foucquet and Pellisson had borrowed Molière for the festival of Vaux from Monsieur, patron of the "Illustre Théâtre" since 1658. The king stole him away from his brother in 1661 and made him his personal Diaghilev.

It was a stroke of luck for Molière as well, a fair exchange. For the king, hardly eager to identify with the stature of the Byzantine basileus that the pensioned panegyrists were already attributing to him, the great poet invented a genre never before seen, suitable to highlight his physical advantages, his talents as a dancer, and his robust temperament, all in the register of the gallant good cheer dear to Paris. In addition to its internal variety, the advantage of that formula was its capacity to appeal directly to both the court and Paris. In the interludes of the comedy ballets, the king could appear in the "original language" version in front of the courtly public, as he had done with Benserade since 1656; but Molière could then offer the Parisian public, on the stage of the former Palais Cardinal, which the king had given him, the same spectacle, but "dubbed" as it were with one of the king's professional dancers playing the king's role in the interludes.

Molière's comedies imported to the court the risqué and vivacious laughter of which the Italians were the masters, and their interludes in song and dance returned to Paris a bit of the king's real presence, his Jovian authority, the heady *odor di femmina* that surrounded his reputation as a Don Juan. In 1664 *Le mariage forcé*, shuttling between the court and the city, put to the test that collaboration between the king and his choreographer and made it a lasting success.

The previous year Molière, who, despite being excommunicated as an actor, was placed on the pension list by Chapelain, published *Remerciement au roi*, which, in its charming tone, was altogether reminiscent of the confidential "poetic pension" La Fontaine had paid Foucquet:

Votre paresse enfin me scandalise,
Ma Muse; obéissez-moi:
   Il faut ce matin, sans remise,
   Aller au lever du Roi.
   Vous savez bien pourquoi:
   Et ce vous est une honte
De n'avoir pas été plus prompte
A le remercier de ces fameux bienfaits;
Mais il vaut mieux tard que jamais.
   Faites donc votre compte
D'aller au Louvre accomplir mes souhaits.
· · · · · · · · · · · · · · · · · · · ·

Mais les grands princes n'aiment guère
Que les compliments qui sont courts;
Et le nôtre surtout a bien d'autres affaires
　　Que d'écouter tous vos discours.
La louange et l'encens n'est pas ce qui le touche;
　　Dès que vous ouvrirez la bouche
　　Pour lui parler de grâce et de bienfait,
Il comprendra d'abord ce que vous voudrez dire,
　　Et se mettant doucement à sourire
D'un air qui sur les coeurs fait un charmant effet,
　　Il passera comme un trait,
　　Et cela vous doit suffire:
　　Voilà votre compliment fait.[33]

Your laziness is a scandal to me,
O my Muse; obey me now:
　　This morning, without fail, we must
　　Go to the king's bedside.
　　You know very well why:
　　And it is a shameful thing
That you were not more prompt
To thank him for his famous benefits;
But better late than never.
　　Make it your business, then,
To go to the Louvre and fulfill my wishes.
. . . .
But great princes hardly like
Compliments unless they are short;
And ours, especially, has many other things to do
　　Than to listen to all your speeches.
Praise and flattery are not the things that touch him;
　　As soon as you open your mouth
　　To speak of grace and good deeds,
He will understand what you mean to say,
　　And, putting on a gentle smile,
The kind that has a charming effect on the heart,
　　He will be gone in a flash,
　　And that must suffice for you:
　　Your compliment has been given.

This is La Fontaine at Saint-Mandé and Vaux, except that Foucquet's poet, less subject to the extreme "haste" that the king imposed on Molière, was bold enough to advise his Maecenas to have a better sense of repose:

Bon Dieu! Que l'on est malheureux
Quand on est si grand personnage!
Seigneur, vous êtes bon et sage,
Et je serais trop familier
Si je faisais le conseiller.
A jouir pourtant de vous-même
Vous auriez un plaisir extrême.
    (To Monsieur le Surintendant)

Good God! How unhappy one is
When one is a great personality!
My lord, you are kind and wise,
And I would be too forward
If I played the role of adviser.
But enjoying yourself
Would give you extreme pleasure.

The nuance might seem insignificant. But it reveals the gap that separates an imperial patronage from a patronage based on friendship.

The same year as *Le mariage forcé*, Molière was called upon to conceive and direct, along with the duc de Saint-Aignan (also a Vaux survivor), "The Pleasures of the Enchanted Isle." In the heat of the Foucquet trial, in the natural setting of Versailles redesigned by Le Nôtre, it was the very pointed revenge the king wanted to seek for the festival of 17 August 1661. Unlike the comedy ballets, it was impossible to repeat in Paris these seven almost uninterrupted days. Only the court was invited, whereas at Vaux, for its single evening, Foucquet had generously welcomed Parisian high society. To make up for that lack of communication while awaiting the publication of books that, in their descriptions and illustrations, would make the details of the monumental festival known to the world, the king invited one of the most visible and gifted Parisian personalities to recount what she saw. Mme de Sévigné, a notorious friend of the *surintendant,* and who never really belonged to the court, was nevertheless one of the witnesses to those days and nights of triumph for the king.[34] A refusal was out of the question: the king was the king, the marquise's weakness was snobbery, and, after all, she had her daughter to marry off.

The collaboration and rivalry between Molière and Benserade in the service of the loving (and beneficent for France) image of Louis XIV reached their apogee in 1666–68. In 1666 Molière collaborated with the librettist on *Ballet des Muses*, a royal diversion destined to ward off, via a few entrechats, the last memories of Foucquet's Parnassus, which La Fontaine had so melodiously evoked in a fragment of *Le songe de Vaux*, and which Le Brun had immortalized on the ceiling of the Salon des Muses.

In 1668 *Amphitryon*, a superb dramatic adaptation of the dry Benserade ballet, was performed at the Palais-Royal for the Paris public, then at the Tuileries before the king and the court. The Jupiter of the play is obviously the king, who at one point sets down his thunderbolt to indulge in a love affair with Alcmène/the marquise de Montespan. The god is gallant, no doubt, but only as a man in a rush, and one who does not conceal that fact, since much more important matters are consuming his time. Molière has him say to Alcmène:

> Mon amour, que gênaient tous ces soins éclatants
> Où me tenait lié la gloire de nos armes,
> Au devoir de ma charge a volé les instants
> Qu'il vient de donner à vos charmes.
> (Amphitryon, act 1, scene 3)

> My love, troubled by all the distracting cares
> To which the glory of our weaponry has kept me bound,
> From my obligation to my duties has stolen the moments
> That it has just given to your charms.

This god, who has no time and who rushes even the lovely object of his desire, is at first impatient for military glory. The images of the king in love and that of the chief of state, commander-in-chief of the armies, were now visible and distinct.

They were already superimposed in the portrait Robert Nanteuil did of the king at twenty, enjoying virile authority under his mane, and resolved to impose it without resistance in every area. There was a sharp contrast between it and the portrait of Foucquet, also by Nanteuil, done during the same period: the *surintendant* appeared self-assured in his intelligence and power of seduction, but a *L'Astrée*-style seduction where a secret melancholia and almost feminine sweetness seemed to put his interlocutors of both sexes on guard against any presumption or abuse of authority.

The political contrast between the two men was also a clash of temperament and taste. The king, who had already annihilated Foucquet politically, also wanted to defeat him in the field of taste. Molière was valuable to him in his conquest of the Parisian, bourgeois, and lower-class public. Racine was even more valuable to him in his conquest of the elite public, the most difficult for him to win over.

Amphitryon, the comedy ballets, and "The Pleasures of the Enchanted Isle," admirable as they were (like everything the playwright touched), were the ransom that Molière the writer had to pay the court in the currency of spectacles so that, in the city, he could perform his disturbing comedies of "inner laughter," which were not always a success (*Le misanthrope*, for example) or which were banned (*Tartuffe* and *Dom Juan*). These latter plays were not part of the gargantuan "poetic pension" he had to produce, at an exhausting pace, to satisfy the king's appetite. His real richness as a poet and observer lay elsewhere. The glimmer of his "back thought" was for a later time.

Racine won over Louis XIV by betraying Molière and his troupe, to whom he owed his first jobs in the theater. His tragedy *Alexandre*, treacherously transported from the Palais-Royal to the Bourgogne mansion, where the king's official troupe was performing, delighted the king. The sovereign, then, was not only capable of laughing, he could also be moved.

By 1667 the "tender" Racine (such is the Homeric epithet by which Racine's son Louis best defined his father), the child who secretly read the Greek novel *Theagenes and Charicleia* at Port-Royal, just as his friend La Fontaine had read *L'Astrée* at the Oratory, had become the official poet of tragic tenderness, striking the chord in the king's heart that La Fontaine had vainly sought to touch in his *Ode* and *Elegie*. It was a tenderness refused, rejected, held back, ignored, ridiculed, turned inside out, stifled, reduced to silence, and sentenced to death, yet irrepressible under the torments inflicted on it by amour propre and the masks of language, with which it had to be muzzled. Such was the feast fit for a king that the poet offered Louis XIV, from *Andromaque* to *Phèdre*, with the consummate skill of a musician and a moralist, with the unfathomable irony of a great lyric poet disguised as a court playwright. And, in fact, the king condescended to be moved. Sometimes he even shed tears, like the queen in La Fontaine's "The Funeral of the Lioness" (8.14), who asked for that miracle from the stag's bag of tricks:

Laisse agir quelque temps le désespoir du roi.
   J'y prends plaisir.

Let the king's despair work for a time.
   It gives me pleasure.

If the adjective "cruel" is the key word in Racine's tragedies, it is easy to believe that he did produce a "somber pleasure" in the king's heart that had nothing in common with that of the "melancholic hearts" of "Hymne à la Volupté" in *Les amours de Psyché*.

AWAY FROM THE CHÂTEAU

With respect to the court and the royal spectacle reigning there, La Fontaine's situation when he returned to Paris and Château-Thierry in 1664 was that of the ideal observer: he was neither too close nor too far away.

He was not too close because, imperceptibly and resolutely, he was kept away. When the courtly spectacle coveted the riches of the poet in disgrace, it did so through an intermediary, indirectly, as if he did not exist. It was Charles Perrault who provided the official version of *Fables* in the labyrinth of Versailles, several years after the publication of the first collection.[35] It was Molière, backed by Corneille, who provided the official version of *Les amours de Psyché* (published in 1669) in a tragicomic ballet performed before His Majesty in 1671.

When the poet spent time in Paris, he continued to stay with his uncle Jannart, who was loyal to Foucquet and the *surintendant*'s family. He fulfilled his duties — which were hardly engrossing, in any case — as gentleman to the dowager duchesse d'Orléans, in a forsaken and deserted Luxembourg Palace, which had become a shrine to Gaston. He frequented the Nevers mansion, where Mme du Plessis-Guénégaud received in private the cream of the Parisian friends of Port-Royal and the *surintendant*'s faithful. There he renewed his acquaintance with the duc de La Rochefoucauld, his friend Mme de La Fayette, and the friend of that friend, the marquise de Sévigné. Naturally, he was received and even celebrated at the Bouillon mansion, where the suzerains of Château-Thierry, the duke and his wife Marie-Anne Mancini, freely made fun of the Louvre even while currying its favor, as their name, rank, and youth required them to do. At the Oratory, where he still had contacts, he often saw the "young Brienne," who had sought refuge there, and who was seeking some balance between belles lettres, the fine arts, and the piety that evaded him. Brienne, a dismissed state secretary and the son of a state secretary was able to inform La Fontaine on the arcana of the court before and during the Foucquet affair.

The poet was also not too far from the official scene. Several writers and artists of the old Foucquet academy, who were now in the service of the new administration, remained his friends: André Félibien, historiographer of the "Bâtiments du roi," François Girardon, now the main sculptor for Versailles's fountains and grottoes, Charles Le Brun, now the *premier peintre* working exclusively for the king, and André Le Nôtre, now the landscape gardener of the royal château. He was able to follow their work from within. Figures as official as the duc de Saint-Aignan, master of ceremonies at court festivals, Charles Perrault, Colbert's chief assistant, and even Jean Chapelain, though this shrewd man refrained from putting the poet on his "list," maintained very friendly and courteous relations with La Fontaine.

Above all, Foucquet's poet laureate, whom *Contes* (1664) and *Fables* (1668) had allowed the wider public to enjoy, had a distinguished place in the French republic of letters, even though he was not part of the Académie Française. He was at home within a group of writers, some of whom, like Molière and Racine, were successful at court spectacles, while others, such as Furetière and Boileau, aspired to be successful, or, like Chapelle, remained fiercely independent. His peers may have freely called him a *bonhomme*, since at times his mind seemed to be elsewhere, just as the "knights of the Round Table" had once scolded him about his absences: even though he did not always participate, he was nevertheless on the *inside*, in the "back shop," where he had access to their conversations, their ambitions, their disappointments, their worries, and their plans. They met in literary cabarets or at Molière's home in Auteuil. They had fun together and composed *Chapelain décoiffé*, then *Les plaideurs* with Racine. Together they worshiped at the altar of Bacchus and Venus. They also sometimes had peculiar fits of melancholia, unknown in the Paris of Tallemant des Réaux, as, for example, in the episode recounted by Grimarest and Louis Racine, in which Chapelle, Boileau, and Racine would have been driven to throw themselves into the Seine in Auteuil after a bout of drinking if Molière had not gently taken them back to his home, where they got even drunker.

A Distrait Observer of the Spectacle Society

Les amours de Psyché et de Cupidon, which La Fontaine published in 1669 along with *Adonis* (with his two dedications to Foucquet lopped off), is, like the 1663 *Lettres à Marie Héricart*, a travel narrative. The collective and fictive journey of four friends leads them to Versailles, which has meanwhile become Louis XIV's Vaux-le-Vicomte. Unlike *Lettres*, it was not a balance sheet of French arts from the past, misunderstood or condemned by Richelieu's tyranny, then rediscovered with the Regency and given new life by the ill-fated Foucquet. Rather, it was a spectral analysis of the court spectacle as it was taking shape according to Foucquet's legacy, both faithful and unfaithful to the spirit of Vaux. Versailles was not Richelieu. Vaux had left its mark. But, in certain respects—and what was to follow did not prove La Fontaine wrong—it was still and always Richelieu. Beginning in 1683 (when the king and court definitively moved in), this site, still innocuous in 1669, was to become the El Escorial of the absolute state and the headquarters of its armies.

Who was better qualified than Foucquet's poet laureate, and the author of *Adonis*, to do justice to the French art that, after Vaux, was triumphing a second time in Versailles, and to formulate his personal reservations in the veiled language of fiction? *Les amours de Psyché*, it seems, had no success at court, which is understandable; nor did it have success at the Liancourt mansion, which was increasingly tinged with Jansenism, and where *Le songe de Vaux*, faithful to the lyricism of the previous reign, was called "provincial." But true connoisseurs were not fooled. Charles Perrault advised Molière to compose, with all due haste, a tragicomic ballet on the same subject for the king. And Pierre-Daniel Huet, who in 1670 published, along with Mme de La Fayette's *Zayde*, his own essay *De l'origine des romans*, could only admire that other attempt to sum up the essence of novelistic gallantry or, in other words, of gallant romanticism. Above all, when in 1671 the Jesuit Dominique Bouhours, in his praise of the king in *Entretiens d'Ariste et d'Eugène*, wanted to depart from the administrative sublime which, in the end, bored men of wit, he ingeniously diluted it in a familiar and cheerful conversation among friends, whose "temperament" was borrowed from the dialogue in *Les amours de Psyché*, but extended to a slightly higher register to befit better, albeit indirectly, the majesty of the royal Olympus. The transfers from Vaux to Versailles continued indefinitely, well after Foucquet's death.

La Fontaine's phenomenally self-reflexive novel, which, according to his own preface, gave the poet a broader tablature than any other of his works, could only be truly understood by himself and his friends in the know, especially the king's new historiographer, Paul Pellisson. At almost the same moment as La Fontaine, Pellisson's lady friend Mlle de Scudéry also published a novel, *La promenade de Versailles*, in which she gave public approval, by the former friends of Vaux, to the château and gardens that had supplanted it. Her approval was without reservations, but her gratitude made her enthusiasm a bit forced.

Apparently in La Fontaine's *Les amours de Psyché*, and with glaring obviousness in *La promenade de Versailles*, the seal separating poetics and politics, which had originated during the Fronde, was broken. The beauties of Versailles belonged to the sovereign's leisure time and the Olympian taste he imposed on their design. Unlike Blois or Richelieu or Vaux, they did not symbolize a political choice. They reflected the king's omnipotence in a beauty commensurate with it, and he was the only one to determine its use. The age stood on the threshold of modern aesthetics, which broke the connection that until then had joined, in self-evident sequences, moral and political philosophy to poetics and rhetoric. Beauty, isolated within its specific order, had became a mirror for the absolute prince, himself insulated within his secrecy and sacredness.

But it was not as true of La Fontaine as it was of Madeleine de Scudéry, who devoted an entire chapter of *Conversations sur divers sujets* (1680) to excluding politics (Stendhal's "pistol shot at a concert") from any truly polite, honorable, and gallant conversation. Although La Fontaine had given up the hope—and for good reason—that the king would refrain from his urge to absolute self-assertion, he did not stop observing the ruler and man of action's evolution toward military power. The choice now was no longer between two general political modes in times of peace, Foucquet or Colbert: it narrowed to a choice between peace and war, between the monarch's pleasures and his military grandeur.

La Fontaine's visitors to Versailles, praising the king's virtue in action, as is fitting, insist on adding this reservation in favor of leisure and pleasure: "Only Jupiter can apply himself continually to ruling the universe: men need some relaxation."

The respectful admonishment hit its mark in the dedication of *Les amours de Psyché* to the duchesse de Bouillon. Evoking the duke, a hero of action, the contemplative poet attributes these words to him: "Of course, it is an extraordinary piece of good fortune for me, that a prince who has so much passion for war, who is so opposed to rest and weakness, sees me with a somewhat favorable eye, and shows me signs of benevolence, as if I had risked my life in his service."

Could the arts of peace and rest, along with the nonchalance and carnal pleasure they invited, keep Louis XIV off the path leading not only to incessant reform actions but also to the most consuming form of action, military conquests? In that sense, the critical evaluation of the Vaux legacy in the lion king's lair had a poignant and ulterior political motive, characteristic of a lyric poet true to himself: the only way remaining to turn off the machine of absolute power was to call and recall Louis to pleasure and leisure, which poets and artists, through their skillful spells, could get the king of France to enjoy. In the preface he wrote for his *Adonis* in 1669, La Fontaine, in the banter of a kingfisher, rejoiced that the sexuality of Jupiter the king, which Molière had carried to the point of apotheosis in *Amphitryon*, was able to respond to that beneficent appeal. He saw a continuity with Vaux, even though Venus and Cupid were now disarming Mars instead of honoring Apollo as an Adonis. He wrote: "How many people are there who close off their chambers to the gods in whom it is my habit to delight? No need for me to name these gods: everyone knows they are Cupid and Venus. These powers have fewer enemies today than they have ever had. We live in a century when people listen with some favor to that family."[36]

The four main characters who travel and visit Versailles in *Les amours de Psyché* are fictive and symbolic. Three of them incarnate a moral "temperament," a mode of being, and a certain taste.[37] Acante is a gentle phlegmatic, a lover of gardens, flowers, and shade. Gélaste is a sanguine, lover of laughter and good cheer. Ariste is a melancholiac, gifted with a lively and emotional imagination. The fourth, Poliphile, combines all the temperaments and tastes of the other three. He is the artist: he composed the novel *Amour et Psyché*, which he is about to read to his companions, and it falls to him to sum things up and to symbolically dedicate Versailles to Venus with his "Hymne à la Volupté."

The four friends, who have made themselves known "to Parnassus," together constitute a portrait of La Fontaine himself, of the ever-changing facets of his inner life and the poetic power of synthesis that made him creative. Their mode of being together and the tolerant vivacity of their conversation reflect the climate of contemplation and the meandering way of thinking, in the manner of Montaigne, characteristic of the poet's "self," in contrast to an "ego" that gathers together all its strength to compel itself to produce and act:

The first thing they did was banish all well-ordered conversation and everything with a hint of the academic lecture. When they found themselves together, and had spoken at length of their diversions, if they happened upon some aspect of science or belles lettres, they took advantage of the opportunity, but did so without pausing too long on a single subject, flitting from one topic to another, like bees who encounter various kinds of flowers along their way. Envy, spitefulness, and scheming had no voice among them.[38]

That good company (which does not fit the fourth temperament of ancient medicine, the violent or choleric) lives, moves, and converses at a rhythm and by a principle of pleasure that is diametrically opposed to the perpetual and willful movement of the state according to Richelieu and Colbert. When the four friends visit Versailles, it is a day of relaxation.

But these contemplative souls without a purpose have a vast memory. Their hastiness in passing over the description of the château (which was still Louis XIII's) suggests a concern to silence any impertinent comparison to Vaux. Of the recent modernization of the interior, they note only the "fabric from China" that covers the walls of the king's chamber, with exotic figures containing "all the religions of those lands." What they admire in the gardens are the lovely patterns of Le Nôtre, which surpassed even his own masterpiece of Vaux. They also admire the menagerie, which, in the magical variety of species unknown to Europe, encapsulates "the artifice and diverse inventions of nature." And they admire the Grotto of Thetis, with its "caprices" of water and shells, which provides a living decoration for *Apollon au repos chez Thétis* (still uncompleted in the sculptor François Girardon's studio in 1669). That neo-Greek marvel, which, in the grace and harmonious gestures of its statues, corresponds so well to the forms La Fontaine attributed to Venus and Adonis for Foucquet, is the subject of an enthusiastic description in alexandrines. Through Girardon as well, Vaux lived on at Versailles. The four friends stop at the Orangery, filled with trees stripped from Foucquet's gardens, and La Fontaine has Acante recite the fragment from *Le songe de Vaux* that he himself wrote in 1660–61 to celebrate the *surintendant*'s greenhouses:

> Sommes-nous, dit-il, en Provence?
> Quel amas d'arbres toujours verts
> Triomphe ici de l'inclémence
> Des aquilons et des hivers?

Are we in Provence? he said,
What mass of trees, ever green,
Prevails over the inclemency
Of north winds and harsh winters?

On the royal grounds where they are at once strangely at home and intruders, taking great care not to be overheard, and where they speak in paraleipsis even among themselves, Poliphile begins to read his version of the fable *Les amours de Psyché et de Cupidon*.[39]

It is not the description of a work of art decorating the château of Louis XIII and renovated by Louis XIV. It is the beneficent and magical evocation, on the Bourbon estate, of a subject of poetry and art stemming from a long and noble tradition dear to the Valois kings. It goes back to antiquity, to the neo-Platonic romance by Apuleius, *The Golden Ass*. But, above all, it is associated with the Renaissance of belles lettres to which La Fontaine was attached with every fiber of his poetic self. Through Conrart's and Tallemant's friend André Félibien, and through François Maucroix, who was well acquainted with Rome, he knew that one of the jewels of the Roman Renaissance, one of the models of Francis I's Fontainebleau and Foucquet's Vaux was the villa of Farnesina, built by the banker Agostino Chigi under the reign of Pope Leo X. The walls and ceilings of the villa were painted in fresco by Raphael and his students Guilio Romano and Giovanni da Udine: Chigi gave them the subject *The Loves of Psyche*. At the time, it was certainly not a manifesto in favor of Luther's excommunication.

In his poem *Adone* a century later, the poet Marino has Venus's lover Adonis hear the *novelletta* of *The Loves of Psyche*. Along with Francesco de Colonna's *The Strife of Love in a Dream*,[40] which also inspired Marino in his poem, this was the most secret message of the Italian Renaissance that Marie de Médicis's poet could leave to Louis XIII's France in 1623: "Make love, not war"; "Eat, drink, and be merry, for tomorrow we die." It was that same message that Rabelais had translated into French a century earlier. To restate it in 1669 at Versailles, a few months before Louis XIV's army invaded Holland without warning, was as significant as Ernst Jünger's *On the Marble Cliffs*, published in 1937, two years before German troops invaded Poland without warning.

The fable of Psyche recounted by Poliphile is not only a marvel of "humanist" art in the true sense, which knows how to "follow nature" to awaken in itself the best of human nature. It also recounts its own birth; it reflects and illuminates the mystery at the origin of all human things of good birth. But at first sight, it is the story of a beautiful and touching love affair between the god of love himself and a mortal woman, Psyche. The beauty of this mortal masterpiece of nature elicits the hostility of the immortal Venus on Olympus and the jealousy of Psyche's sisters on earth. Cupid has to hide from his mother, Venus, in order to love Psyche, and he wants to remain invisible to Psyche herself so that her attraction for him, spurred by the unknown, will always remain fresh. For this loving but wise and clever god, secrets, veils, and silence must conspire to protect the most sacred thing among men and gods, the principle and very embodiment of the spirit of nature, and the mutual desire that summons two different beings to meld together in the same union that holds the cosmos together.

This sacred mystery that animates the world, as well as fables, poetry, and works of art, is the most fragile, the most vulnerable to profanation or destruction by rage, jealousy, hatred of all who discover it and who believe they are, or wish to be, excluded from it. This love story is also a very dark novel. The harmony of the golden age, the friendship between a god and a mortal woman, is depicted as embattled by the ferocity and ruses of the iron age. The god of love feels the blind and jealous violence that works against his reign and produces human unhappiness: the young Psyche, even beloved and in love, even happy, and because she is naively happy, does not suspect it at all. She subjects herself to the abuse of her sisters, who are envious of her happiness. Partly because of her own impatient curiosity, she breaks the vow she made to Cupid never to seek to look at him. Being true to one's word is the equivalent of fidelity in love, when love is worthy of friendship. Psyche, who has gone against her word, is banished by the god as an unfaithful woman who has profaned their shared mystery.

Ariste's narration is punctuated by the exclamations or remarks of his listeners and friends, who react with emotion and irony to the vicissitudes of the story. They reflect upon their own reactions, which leads them to measure against themselves the natural life that fills this artful fiction, and the degree of poetic success of its author, against themselves.

But when Psyche is banished by Cupid (she awakened him from his sleep by letting a hot drop of wax fall on his sexual parts), Ariste interrupts his story, and a general conversation begins among the four friends. The ordeals of the lovely and touching Psyche are about to begin. Will Poliphile be able to keep the proper balance in his story between deep emotion and lightheartedness, as he has skillfully done until now? In which direction is it better to lean? Must one really lean in one direction or the other?

For the friends assembled at Versailles, the choice between the "somber pleasure" of sadness and the cheerful pleasure of gaiety is not only a narrator's decision or a reader's wish, not purely a matter of poetics. It is related to the experience of the things of life, the intermingling of misfortunes and joys, and especially to what remains constantly and implicitly between the lines, in a place where everything speaks of it: the triumphant Louis XIV on the surface and the plundered and destitute Foucquet beneath the surface. Acante is the interpreter both of the narrator and of his friends when he declares: "If the Sun should see us cry, it will be no great misfortune: he sees many others do the same throughout the universe, not for the misfortunes of others, but for their own."

Tears (the daughters of pity, "the reaction to discourse that we consider the most noble, the most excellent, and the most agreeable"), these tears that the fiction of *Les amours de Psyché* will be able to elicit, silently join the four visitors' hearts to the "unfortunate" Oronte, on whose behalf the author of *Les amours de Psyché* had invoked the aid of the Nymphs of Vaux and the king's compassion, but in vain. Of the various facets of meaning that the fable told by Poliphile suggests, the application to Nicolas Foucquet and his fate is unavoidable: like the god Cupid, he too transported the soul of his prince to an enchanted palace, where he deployed all the fictions of poetry and art to awaken him to the truth of his fondness for him and, above all, to the royal truth of love, which surpasses fear as a method for ruling men. The rejection of that offer of friendship by the prince, who, like Psyche, received poor advice, made the enchanted castle disappear, the hope of happiness flee, and night fall once more upon the world. In reality, *Les amours de Psyché* is a rewriting of *Le songe de Vaux* in the darkness that began on 5 September 1661.[41] Such was the inner tenacity of which that distrait *bonhomme* was capable.

The question that stops the four friends halfway through the story is the same as the one the author of *Elegie* and *Ode* must have asked himself when he wrote and published his early *Contes*, lighthearted masterpieces, even before the end of the *surintendant*'s trial: was it still possible, was it not more desirable than ever, to smile and make good people smile when the political tragedy was already under way? "I did not know," the poet wrote in the preface to *Les amours de Psyché*, "what character [style] to choose."

That particular question of narrative poetics took on a wider scope in 1664. In the court theater that replaced Vaux, two of La Fontaine's friends became Louis XIV's favorite playwrights. First, there was a great comic poet, Molière, the "new Terence," celebrated by La Fontaine beginning in

1661, and in tune with one of the tendencies that the author of *L'eunuque* recognized in himself. In his story, the narrator of *Les amours de Psyché* represents the comic genre, of which Molière was the master, through Gélaste, a "sanguine" character who loves to laugh. Second, there was a great poet of tragic tenderness, Racine, the "new Euripides." He too was very close to La Fontaine and recognized his own profound poetic affinities with his elder: the tragic genre at which Racine (a frustrated lyric poet) excelled is represented in the novel by a "melancholic" character who loves tears: Ariste. The tragedy *Andromaque* (created in 1667) is expressly cited in the conversation between Gélaste and Ariste.

But lyric poetry, for which La Fontaine, a passionate reader of Tristan L'Hermite, was also gifted, no longer had a place within the royal spectacle. It too was suffocated, and for a very long time, under the profusion of panegyrics in verse ordered by Chapelain: Malherbe, but a made-to-order Malherbe, replaced Saint-Amant and Tristan L'Hermite. In his novel, the character Acante (a "Parnassus name" associated, in the mind of any seventeenth-century reader, with Tristan's most famous lyric poem, "Les plaintes d'Acante," published in 1663) corresponds to that lyric postulation of his own poetic nature, which was no longer reflected around him. Yet, throughout the entire conversation on laughter and tears, Acante remains silent. Nor does Poliphile participate very much. In these other two characters, La Fontaine maintains the reserve and vocation befitting a poet, which have no chance of finding favor with Jupiter, unlike Molière's laughter and Racine's tragic tears.

The judgment on Versailles, the unavowed heir to Vaux, is thus echoed in a judgment on the theater personally supported by Louis XIV, a no-less-unavowed heir to Foucquet. An heir, or a usurper? The king happily abandoned himself to great outbursts of laughter. Louis Racine wrote, regarding the performance of *Les plaideurs* in 1668: "The king was greatly affected by it, and believed it no dishonor to his seriousness or his taste to indulge in outbursts of laughter so great that they astonished the court."[42]

Moreover, when Gélaste declares, in support of laughter, that for Homer it was the "inextinguishable" privilege of the gods, "who are exempt from evil, and live on high at their ease, without suffering," La Fontaine has Ariste dryly respond: "Plato criticizes him for giving the gods excessive laughter, which would be unworthy of even much less important persons."

The appearance, shortly thereafter in the conversation, of "amour propre constantly acting in such a way that all eyes turn toward it" sheds light on that display of arms: an excess of laughter in the spectator of a comedy is one symptom of the "self-love and love of all things for oneself," by which one makes an idol of oneself as the Immortals do, and exempts oneself from frail humanity, which is destined for ridicule. It is an appalling lack of heart, but it is also a fatal flaw of taste. Molière and even the Racine of *Les plaideurs* are not at issue, any more than the literary genre of comedy. On the contrary. The entire subtle debate between Gélaste and Ariste on the profound reasons for laughter and tears at the theater is in reality an homage to the knowledge these two great playwrights have of their art, and was very likely inspired by conversations they themselves may have had with and in the presence of La Fontaine.

In contrast, the attitude of the spectator king, incapable of escaping his "ego," is cruelly analyzed between the lines of the dialogue between Ariste and Gélaste. After all, what is true for comedy is also true for tragedy.

According to Ariste, nothing prevents a spectator hardened in his amour propre from "remaining cold" before the misfortune of others represented on the stage and from not "participating" in it. Even if the work is excellent, even if the tragic poet "transforms us" and makes us "become different men," still we must "not put ourselves in the place of some king." Is it so difficult to identify that "some king," who takes himself to be a god, who believes himself above the human condition of the kings of tragedy, in the figure of negation and silence where La Fontaine pointed him out by not mentioning him?

The indirect praise of Molière's art of comedy (which is able to touch us "while using only ordinary adventures that could happen to us") and Racine's art of tragedy ("which makes us happy to shed tears for the misfortunes of others that we would hold back for our own"), far from being extended to a king who loves to display himself at the theater, actually attests to the gap between the humanity that his own poets know how to awaken in the common mortal, and to the deified amour propre that shields the king himself, and which, in these masterpieces of the stage, shows Jupiter new trophies to add to his own triumphs, new ornaments to add to his pomp.

Louis XIV's support of Molière and Racine thus displays a phenomenal misunderstanding between the king and belles lettres, a misunderstanding whose dark irony is ingeniously suggested by the author of *Fables*. That irony even leads Ariste to say, regarding the "tenderness of the heart" awakened by tragedy, that it places us "above kings in the pity we have for them" and makes us become "gods with respect to them, contemplating their troubles, their afflictions, and their misfortunes from a quiet place, neither more nor less than the gods esteem the wretched mortals from Olympus."[43] The art of Corneille, the "new Sophocles"—little appreciated by the king—along with that of Racine must also be included in this appraisal.

The Parnassus of great poets might well be servile to the god of the Olympus, who does not understand their profound songs; but it also offers the feasts of the gods to the subjects of Olympus. In the secret recesses of the heart, the art of true poets, even when chained to Olympus, royally compensates the loss its subjects have suffered by singing for a proprietary Jupiter, blind and deaf to the song of the Muses.

The four friends, especially when they are in the busiest parts of the garden, judge it wise to voice praises in the official style to the lord of the estate and to Colbert ("the intellect which is the soul of these marvels and which makes so many skilled hands work to satisfy the monarch"). For the hasty reader, these praises further veil the profound, soft-spoken analysis of the essential misunderstanding between even the most official poets and the king himself, lion or cock. The king boasts of the very things in their works that ought precisely to cure him of his boasting. The poets are faithful to the golden age; the king is a bit player from the iron age.

The conversation between Ariste and Gélaste has no conclusion, even though Ariste's praise of tears seems to prevail. How can we not think of the effect La Fontaine himself was once able to hope his *Elegy* and *Ode au roi* would have, when we read Ariste's admirable commentary on the final scenes of *The Iliad:* "When [Homer] has Achilles and Priam cry, one at the memory of Patroclus, the other at the death of the last of his children, he says that they were drunk on this pleasure; he has them take joy in crying, as if it were something delicious."[44]

In reality, the solution to the problem of poetics (laughter or tears?) raised at the beginning by Poliphile finds its response not in the theory but in what follows his narrative. The tone of Poliphile's narration, in fact, does not confine itself to measuring out the delicate comedy dear to Gélaste and the true pleasure of tears enjoyed by Ariste; in some sense, it avenges Acante by making the lyricism of "Hymne à la Volupté" the grand finale and profound lesson of the novel. The poetic key to that second part of the fable is the smile, which reconciles pleasure and sadness, and which shines through tears like lyric truth intact in the poet's heart of hearts, in a kingdom a heartless sovereign has devoted to spectacle before leading it into war.

But the fable *Les amours de Psyché,* even though it is an opportunity for La Fontaine to meditate in indirect language on the nature of the prince and on Foucquet's tragic failure, also has a universal meaning, which encompasses but surpasses on every side the direct and particular experience that France and La Fontaine personally, through their king's "poor choice," were enduring. It is not partisan passion or nostalgia or bitterness or personal resentment that governs the thinking of the author of *Les amours de Psyché*, but rather a serene vision of the human drama in its essence, as serene, painful, and cheerful as that of Socrates in *The Symposium*, midway between Aristophanes and Agathon, comedy and tragedy. The rare individuals faithful to the golden age, in a world of men consumed by amour propre, jealousy, and cruelty, who seek to ignore their own heart of hearts, are undoubtedly vulnerable to error, failure, ruin, torture, and death. But love itself, the principle of attraction and compassion common to Renaissance cosmology and the Gospel, continues its labor. Love writes straight via curved lines, as Claudel said. Progress, the true progress of hearts that awaken to themselves, proceeds through the ordeal inflicted by the apparent progress and blinding triumphs of the *power of darkness*, which Ovid had already recognized in the breasts of mortals.

The god of love may have suffered a burn in the most sensitive part of his body, and, after Psyche's betrayal, may have experienced the dark night of the heart. One Psyche was destroyed. Another was reborn in misfortune. The charm of that beautiful girl is that she is living, suffering, touching, capable of error, capable of opening her eyes. She first considers suicide, which Epicureanism and Christianity both condemn. She recovers and continues on her way through the desert, staggering from one ordeal to the next, lonely, abandoned by her family, persecuted by Venus. Her sin itself and her ruin are the beginning of her inner enlightenment. Once she thought only of herself; as a true coquette, she believed she was the center of the universe, even the god of love was her due. Now, in poverty, loss, and tears, she cruelly feels the absence of love and discovers her heart of hearts:

> Que nos plaisirs passés augmentent nos supplices!
> Qu'il est dur d'éprouver, après tant de délices,
>   Les cruautés du Sort!
> Fallait-il être heureuse avant qu'être coupable?
> Et si de me haïr, Amour, tu fus capable,
>   Pourquoi m'aimer d'abord?
>
> Que ne punissais-tu mon crime par avance!
> Il est bien temps d'ôter à mes yeux ta présence,
>   Quand tu luis dans mon coeur!

Encor si j'ignorais la moitié de tes charmes!
Mais je les ai tous vus: j'ai vu toutes les armes
   Qui te rendent vainqueur![45]

How our bygone pleasure amplify our torments!
How hard it is to endure, after so much delight,
   The cruel blows of Fate!
Did I have to be happy before being guilty?
And if, Cupid, you were capable of hatred,
   Why did you first love me?

If only you had punished my crime in advance!
It is high time to take your presence from my eyes,
   When you shine already in my heart!
If only I had not known half of your charms!
But I have seen them all: I have seen all the weapons
   That have made you the victor!

Is it a tragedy? Is it a comedy? It is both combined, and something more: the dream, paradise and hell, delicious dream and painful nightmare, from whose fabric the entire human adventure is cut out, incomprehensible for the conceptual and dogmatic intelligence, but an open book for the poet's sweet and lucid irony and for the reader of his tale, to whom he generously offers the luxury of smiling like an Epicurean god while reading it. Cupid smiles as well when he discovers the new Psyche, who begins to be cured of her amour propre in the desert and in solitude. Without yet showing himself—like the wise characters in Marivaux's comedies and Mozart's operas—the god in love always comes to help Psyche, who is being born to her own humanity. Is La Fontaine wagering on the new maturity of the king himself? Or is this rather a universal act of faith in the divine labor of love? With the help of the god, the young woman is able victoriously to get through the superhuman ordeals to which the jealous Venus subjects her from Mount Olympus.[46] She must nevertheless overcome the worst ordeal of all on her own: her metamorphosis into a Moor, which she believes is the loss of her beauty and hence of her attractiveness to Cupid. When she finally sees the god of love again, she has achieved the degree of humility that is the beginning of all wisdom, all happiness, and all beauty:

"Alas!" said Psyche. "I do not flee you; I simply take from before your eyes an object that I fear you yourself would flee."

That voice, so sweet, so agreeable, and once familiar to the son of Venus, was immediately recognized by him. He ran to the spot where his wife had taken refuge.

"So! It's you!" he said. "So! My dear Psyche, it's you!"

Immediately, he threw himself at the lovely girl's feet.

"I erred," he continued, kissing her feet. "Because of my impulsiveness, an innocent person, a person born to know only pleasure, had to suffer punishments that the guilty do not suffer; and I have not turned heaven and earth upside down to prevent it! I did not bring Chaos back to the world! I did not take my own life, for all the god that I am! Oh, Psyche, you have so many reasons to hate me! I must die, I must find the way, however impossible the thing might be."

Psyche sought out one of his hands to kiss it. Cupid sensed it, and, standing up, cried:

"Oh! You have added sweetness to your other charms! I know the feelings you have had; all nature told me of them: not a single word of complaint has escaped you against this monster, who was unworthy of your love."

And, because she had found his hand, he continued:

"No. Do not grant me such favors; I am not worthy of them; the only grace I ask is for some punishment that you yourself will impose. My Psyche, my dear Psyche, tell me, to what do you condemn me?"

"I condemn you to be loved by your Psyche for eternity," said our heroine, "for she would be wrong to beg you to love her: she is no longer beautiful."

These words were pronounced in a tone of voice so moving that Cupid could not hold back his sobs. He drowned one of Psyche's hands with his tears, and, pressing that hand between his own, was quiet for a long time, and by that silence expressed himself better than if he had spoken: the torrent of tears did what a torrent of words would not have done. Psyche, charmed by that eloquence, responded as a person who knew all about it. And consider, I beg you, what love is: the best-suited and most passionate couple there may be in the world used the opportunity to shed tears and to sigh. O happy lovers, you are the only ones to know pleasure![47]

That illumination of the heart blooms into a state of consciousness completely different from the deceitful bliss the lovers enjoyed in the enchanted palace. Mingled with silence and painful memories, it had to destroy the darkness of the iron age to better deserve the light and joy of the golden age. As an alliance between the divine and the human, the happiness of Cupid and Psyche, renewed and sealed by ordeals, now recognizes it is the son of Time: it is permeated by the poignant awareness given it by Time that it is a fragile, improbable, and singular miracle. The two lovers have also become friends. This happiness, mirroring Psyche's beauty, is more divine than that of the goddess Venus because it is incarnate,[48] subject to disappearance, and all the more alive in that it knows it is short-lived.

Just as La Fontaine's lyricism agrees to drape itself in the ass's skin of *Fables*, it deploys, in this "novel of novels," its profound poetics: it is not the elimination of troubles but rather the sensation of them that makes mortals enviable and desirable to the gods.

Jean Dutourd has linked *Les amours de Psyché* to Laforgue's *Moralités légendaires*.[49] This masterpiece must, in fact, be placed at just such an altitude of lyric irony. Not the least of its merits is that it provides us with the keys for reading *Fables* and for discovering the play of mirrors among the divine, the animal, and the human. Foucquet's poet truly resisted the century of Louis XIV.

CHAPTER 6

Sublimity and Smiles

*L*a Fontaine was a poet, but not—at least not entirely—in the modern, altogether subjective, not to say sentimental sense we too easily give that title of literary nobility.

The manner in which La Fontaine was a poet is surprising to us, and obliges us, if we truly wish to understand it, to take long journeys and marvelous detours through poetry and other texts prior to his own, as if his poetry barely belonged to him and stemmed more from the pastiche. But is that manner and that obligation as distant as we imagine them from the modern way of being a poet and of understanding poets?

The "lazy" La Fontaine was an indefatigable translator. For his writer friends, he translated all the poetic quotations dispersed throughout long works such as Saint Augustine's *City of God* or Seneca's *Letters to Lucilius*, which these friends had themselves undertaken to translate. He teamed up with his friend Maucroix via correspondence between Paris and Reims, revising his friend's translations for style, with the original texts in hand.[1] That exacting work, whose results, for the most part, were published only after both men's deaths, dealt with large sections of Plato's and Cicero's works and attests to the poet's familiarity with ancient forms and modes of thought.

Even his most original works—*Adonis, Contes, Fables*—are ornate translations, expanded to give off a vivacious charm of novelty that surprises and pleases. The lightheartedness of "this virgin, vivacious, and lovely day of today" veils the transferral to a brand-new public of the cream of the ancient texts, classical or humanistic, Greek, Latin, Italian, or Spanish, threatened with oblivion and yet charged with a vivid meaning, which the poet has awakened by translating it. La Fontaine's vocation was as a lyric poet. Like all lyric poetry, ancient and modern, his was addressed to the emotions, the feelings, but, to touch those emotions, it relied on forms, fables, and commonplaces (common to his readers and to himself) that had already come from far away and long ago: this is known as "the tradition." Tradition and translation are cousins. That in no way prevented La Fontaine's poetry from rejuvenating everything it touched, as if the tradition from which it proceeded had been born with him, as if the translation it proposed were an act of rebirth.

The great modern poets, from Baudelaire to Bonnefoy, have also been translators; their original lyricism is a meditation on all the lyricism that has preceded them. "Translator" means ferryman, carrier. That ferrying or carrying can take place between one contemporary universe of language and another, such as Baudelaire's translation of Edgar Allan Poe, Valery Larbaud's of James Joyce, Bonnefoy's of Yeats. It can also transpose the fragments and emotion of classical poets into our modern languages, as Verlaine and Rimbaud, both expert Latinists, often did.

When this act of transferral is the work of a poet, it eradicates not only space but time as well. It is a victory over the amour propre of contemporaries. Valery Larbaud makes Saint Jerome—the Latin translator of the Bible from the Hebrew text and from the Greek version done by the Septuagint in Alexandria—the patron saint of the self-effacement that allows a translator-poet to facilitate the journey, even of Holy Scripture, to a foreign land and modern times.[2]

The collective amour propre of contemporaries imprisons and suffocates them. It leads them to believe that humanity begins with them and is encapsulated in them. This is the prison of the iron age. Poets, who by definition wish to liberate others and themselves from that imprisonment, become a nuisance. La Fontaine saw that peremptory vanity appearing on the horizon. In 1687, in his epistle to Pierre-Daniel Huet, he protested the doctrine of the "moderns," who wanted the generation born with Louis XIV to believe that it and its king were self-sufficient: they believed they were the only past to which the future had a right.[3]

La Fontaine had too much a sense of the instant, of its fleetingness but also of its latent plenitude that can break through time, to accept without protest any desire to deprive his contemporaries of the very thing that gave the instant its supreme and singular intensity, what made it a shared instant: the reflection and coincidence, in a single drop of time, of limpid instants fixed since antiquity in the forms and mnemonic fables of poetry. These forms come alive again in that moment of coincidence and give it their resonance. Poetry's power to liberate immediately is all the greater the further it has come and the more memory it brings with it. It has emerged from time but within time. It is the "air of antiquity" of which the epistle to Huet speaks.

Translation is one of the surest means poets have to congeal in the present the aspects of poetry—the witness to the golden age—that have been scattered long ago and far away. The poetic practice of translation is thus related to letter writing: letters eradicate distance and make absent friends present; they keep their interrupted dialogue alive. These messages on paper were in antiquity inscriptions engraved in stone: La Fontaine, like Horace, prolifically produced epistles in verse; like Voiture, he also produced epistles in verse and prose combined. And he composed inscriptions and epigrams.[4] These "letters" gave their name to literature itself; the part stands in for the whole. Letters are a conspiracy of friendship within the threatening darkness brought on by the iron guard of amour propre. The Oriental fable "The Gazelle, the Tortoise, the Crow, and the Rat" (12.15) sums up that clandestine solidarity, which allows friends separated by centuries, nations, and misfortunes to escape the blind cruelty of the world.

There are levels of translation. The "beautiful but unfaithful" ones, to which La Fontaine's Huguenot friend Nicolas Perrot d'Ablancourt, the translator of Lucian, Tacitus, and Thucydides, owed his influence in the seventeenth century, were already poetry: they tailored the form and message of the great classical texts, full of experience but in danger of remaining or once more becoming inaudible, to contemporary concerns and tastes.[5] La Fontaine's epistles in verse are not translations of Horace; unlike those of Boileau, they are not even imitations:

Je ne prends que l'idée, et les tours, et les lois,
Que nos maîtres suivaient eux-mêmes autrefois.
(Epître à Huet, ll. 27–28)

I take only the idea, the tropes, and the laws,
That our own masters followed in times bygone.

But they recapture the Horatian variety, melancholic and ironic flavor, and urbanity and reintroduce them into the most immediate and contemporary reality, put them back in circulation in a meandering conversation. That conversation sometimes veers close to Loret's journalism in verse,[6] which people were so fond of in the Foucquet years, but it immediately flies off again. From journalism to "beautiful but unfaithful" translation, from tradition revived for present times to passing times touched upon and held onto by memory, La Fontaine's poetry tried out an array of forms and "temperaments." That always required that he hold onto both ends of the long chain, both to his roots in the poetic tradition, his familiar homeland, and to his acute sense of contemporary reality, his curiosity about the fleeting, his antennae for opportunity, changing fashions, different tastes. It would be difficult to be simultaneously more ancient or more modern than this poet of crossings.

A Pocket Theater under Louis the Great

Opportunity plays a decisive role in the wisdom of love in *Contes*:

Mais ce que vaut l'occasion,
Vous l'ignorez, allez l'apprendre.
> (*Contes et nouvelles* 3,
> *Nicaise*, last line)

But the value of opportunity,
You do not know, go find out.

So says a pretty maid to the inexperienced Nicaise, who has not been able to seize "the shepherd's hour."

La Fontaine did not let the auspicious hour of *Contes* go by, either for himself or for the Parisian public. He had published nothing since *L'eunuque* in 1654 (except the two anonymous poems in 1662–63 petitioning for his condemned Maecenas). Now, in December 1664, he addressed himself to a new Maecenas: not the king, who was deaf to his complaint, but "the reader." The reader too had remained deaf to La Fontaine's entreaties in 1654. But that reader had excuses: at the time, Scarron was prevailing over Terence. Ten years later, tastes had changed. The festival of Vaux had sealed Terence's victory over Scarron.

In the preface to his first two books of *Contes et nouvelles en vers* (1664), the poet wrote: "It is up to the reader to . . . make up" the author's mind about the choice he made of irregular meter and "old language" in setting his "tales" to verse. He was not finished and, in fact, was already looking at other novels with the intent of putting them into verse. But first, he had to be sure of the success of his first tales and of the tastes of most of the people who would read them. In that respect, as in others, Terence was to serve as his model. Terence did not write solely to satisfy himself or a select group: *Populo ut placerent quas fecisset fabulas* (so that the fables he had written should be enjoyed by the common people).

Was it the journey to Limousin that first inspired him? Along the way, he had invented a fable and a tale for Marie Héricart. The epistles he sent to his wife, like those written by Horace and like Montaigne's *Essays*, were open and generative forms. Was it at readings in Paris or Château-Thierry, for friends who, like him, were anxious about Foucquet's fate, that he confirmed the beneficent effect of his licentious fables? In any case, he now wanted to test them on a large scale; and clearly, if the experiment was a success, he was already prepared to press forward, since the public's desire made him prolific. A month later, with Foucquet already buried for life in his dungeon in Pignerol, the success of the first booklet was followed by the publication of a second collection, which was equally well received by the general public. "The reader" was again asking for what his pen was producing. And this lazy, silent man suddenly revealed himself to be an ingenuous and ingenious strategist, who explained his scheme with more ease than an old hand at publication.

In the preface to his first collection, he wrote: "A few people advised me that I should provide the remainder of these bagatelles right away, so that the curiosity to see them, which is now enjoying its first flame, will not cool. I came around to that view without great difficulty, and thought I could take advantage of the opportunity."[7]

Cool, flame, opportunity: This is the language of sexual pursuit, applied to the relationship between the author and the public. La Fontaine was so thoroughly aware of this that, in the same preface, he immediately contrasted this "natural" success, which he had obtained so quickly but on the basis of mutual affinities, to the artifices of the "pensioned" Arnolphes, who appealed to higher, external authorities to extract by force the "favor" spontaneously refused their works by the naive Agneses. In the same preface he wrote: "It would be vanity on my part to spurn such an advantage. My only wish is that no one be imposed upon on my behalf, and that I follow a path opposite to that of certain people, who acquire friends only to acquire approval through them: creatures of the cabal, very different from the Spaniard who prided himself on being the son of his own works."

In preference to that violence, which wishes to "impose" via the "cabal," the poet calmly and publicly delighted in being able to choose the cordial approval of the "common people."

This is the prose equivalent of the notorious *Excuse à Ariste*, which Corneille published a quarter of a century earlier in 1637 during the quarrel over *Le Cid*, in reply to his jealous rivals, who, seeking to damage the success of his tragicomedy, had appealed to Cardinal de Richelieu, to his Académie Française, and to Chapelain, who was already acting under his orders:

J'ai peu de voix pour moi, mais je les ai sans brigue,
. . . .
Mon travail sans appui monte sur le Théâtre,
Chacun en liberté l'y blâme ou l'idolâtre,
Là sans que mes amis prêchent leurs sentiments
J'arrache quelquefois trop d'applaudissements;
Là content du succès que le mérite donne
Par d'illustres avis je n'éblouis personne;
Je satisfais ensemble et peuple et courtisans,
Et mes vers en tous lieux sont mes seuls partisans;
Par leur seule beauté ma plume est estimée:
Je ne dois qu'à moi seul toute ma Renommée.

(ll. 38 and 41–50)

I have few votes, but those I have I have without intrigue,
. . . .
My work is performed on the stage without backing,
Everyone is free to criticize or idolize it,
There, without my friends propounding their feelings,
I sometimes draw too much applause;
There, happy with the success that merit brings,
I dazzle no one with illustrious opinions;
I satisfy the common people along with courtiers,
And, in every place, my verses are my only champions;
Solely through their beauty is my quill respected:
I owe all my renown to myself alone.

Now, in 1664, it was no longer a theater audience at issue, but rather readers (though La Fontaine invoked Terence at the beginning of his first collection). A great theatrical genre— tragedy—was no longer in question, but rather, at least in appearance, "bagatelles," written in the old language and imparting joy. The poet saw the difference quite well, and justified himself without arrogance or false modesty. To please the public, to treat official backing with disdain, implies that an author has an art of pleasing that public. Corneille was the very first to have made that pleasure—the only guarantor of his poetic independence, beginning with his first comedies—the supreme law of his art. For La Fontaine, a great reader of L'Astrée, "to please" meant to gallantly fit the form and mode of poetry to the public's current expectations. Corneille shifted from comedy to tragedy when the emotional tenor of the circumstances required it.

Similarly, La Fontaine had to shift from the *heroic* to the *comic* mode if he wanted to please that collective patron, which remained impassive toward the official sublime, and whose tastes favored "gallantry and jest" (preface to *Les amours de Psyché*, 1669). For him, as for Corneille, to please was to place poetry in a position to achieve the beneficent effect expected of it. And it takes two to achieve it. There must be a mutual desire. La Fontaine himself spoke of the "caution" which compelled him to change his mode, to adapt to a fashion that was also an expectation, an appetite, a taste:

> Even though I need these artifices as much as any other [pensioner], I cannot resolve to use them: I will simply accommodate myself, if that is possible for me, to the tastes of my century, informed as I am by my own experience that there is nothing more necessary. In fact, it cannot be said that every season is favorable for every sort of book. We have seen rondeaux, metamorphoses, and bouts rimés prevail by turns: now such gallantries are out of fashion, and no one is concerned with them. Hence it is clear that what pleases in one era can fail to please in another.

All the same, like Corneille, he did not abandon the "supreme beauty" that is "well received by every soul and in every century," and which he wanted to make the subject of his *Fables*. But if the poet wanted to be free and rely only on the public's spontaneous affection, the law of opportunity—which is the law of love and pleasure—required that he please immediately, in the "here and now," through improvisation and occasional pieces. More probing work would come later. If you extend your hand, it must be taken on the spot. This was the spontaneity of a child following in his father's footsteps, in this case, Molière's: "The ancients are the ancients, and we are people of the here and now." Could *Contes et nouvelles en vers*, placed from the beginning under the sign of Terence and the "fable," a term common to narrative fiction and drama, be theatrical in some way? It was in theater, and in particular in a comedy, that La Fontaine first attempted to please, but without success. It was too early. During the Foucquet years he wrote (but did not publish) *Clymène*, and, in the uncompleted *Le songe de Vaux*, he sketched episodes in dialogue form among several characters. This was still theater for Valéry's Monsieur Teste.

During the same period, he wrote *Les rieurs du Beau-Richard* for an actual performance among friends at Château-Thierry; it is a "tale" in the style of Boccaccio, but with dialogue and constructed like the "Farce of

Master Pathelin."[8] With delightful imagination, the first five entrées of this comic impromptu capture the lower-class life of the Château-Thierry marketplace, as in a Callot etching. It could be a Tuscan *piazza*, where a merchant, wheat sifters, a miller and his ass, a debt-ridden cobbler, and a notary go about their business.

The last three entrées make quick work of the plot of this tale in dialogue form. The merchant, something of a usurer, wants to extract his payment in kind from the wife of the debt-ridden cobbler:

Ce logis m'est hypothéqué;
L'homme me doit, la femme est belle,
Nous ferions quelque marché
Non avec lui, mais avec elle.[9]

This house is mortgaged to me;
The man owes me, the wife is pretty,
We might make some deal,
Not he and I, but I and she.

But the friendly cobbler's wife, without discouraging the sordid gallant at first, begins by asking for the "paper," the acknowledgment of her husband's debt. She then warns her husband by coughing, just as Elmire in *Tartuffe* warns Orgon, who watches himself be cuckolded from under her table. The merchant, caught more quickly than Tartuffe and less sure of how things stand, is only too happy to get away so easily.

In *Les rieurs*, which dates from 1659 to 1660, the tale and the comedy, the narrative fable and the dramatic fable, are interchangeable. It is "pocket theater": sharp, spicy, colorful. It should be seen as a first rehearsal for *Contes et nouvelles*. With the first two collections of 1664 (published in duodecimo, the paperback format of the time—inexpensive, very portable, accessible to every audience), La Fontaine opened a kind of Théâtre de la Huchette (Breadbox theater) in Paris, and to resounding success. Despite its rudimentary equipment, this little theater was able to rival the Théâtre du Palais-Royal where Molière was performing, the Théâtre Italien where Scaramouch reigned, and the king's players, who, to stand their ground against Molière, had to stage little comedies at the Bourgogne mansion.

The "poor man's" theater of *Contes*, sparkling with talent, was similar to the little scenes performed outside shops and street stalls on the grounds of the seasonal Foire Saint-Germain and Foire Saint-Laurent, frequented by the common people by day and the upper crust by night. La

Fontaine published the repertoire of this theater, made to delight readers of both sexes, in collections that came out at irregular but unflagging intervals from one season to the next, in 1664, 1666, 1671, and 1674. Finally, in 1675, this little "theater in the wild" had to close its doors, by order of the police lieutenant La Reynie, preceding by twenty years the closing of the Théâtre Italien. The director, author, and sole actor of that seventeenth-century Huchette then decided (even though he had many other plays in stock) to try his luck at the Opéra and the Académie Française, since the times had again changed for the worse.

In his own estimation, La Fontaine had "practiced, all his life, the genre of poetry we call heroic, the most beautiful of all . . . the language of the gods" (preface to Adonis, 1669); he did not have force himself to "encounter" (a word he shared with Montaigne) the public's appetite for merriment, which now celebrated Molière. Les rieurs (1659–60) and Lettres à Marie Héricart (1663) had already given free rein to his Tallemant des Réaux side; that tendency spawned a verve of language in him, the very same that had served to make Rabelais, Beroalde de Verville, and Brantôme—weaned on the Italian storytellers and actors of the commedia dell'arte—so prolific. The poet's access to this Renaissance mother lode of joy also armed him with health—and in a manner true to nature, which longs for the golden age—against the anxiety of the new regime and its political pressures. La Fontaine, the Voiture of Vaux, in adopting the verve, "old language," and therapeutic laughter of the burlesque, also became the heir to Scarron (who died in 1660), or the last Scarron: humorous and gallant, less well known than the Fronde original, but one who, before his death, was the delight of the surintendant, Madeleine de Scudéry, the chevalier de Méré, and the marquise de Sévigné.

The creation and publication of Contes was not the result of a calculation but of a profound impulse. The Italians have a word to describe it, the word of a poet, an actor, or an improvisational musician: estro.[10] The French translate it as feu (fire). Estro or fire, which in 1663–64 counterbalanced the poet's grief and suffering, produced and deployed not only the storyteller in him, who knew how to make these plot-driven comic scenarios desirable and who wittily commented on them, but a playwright, who could make each of his characters speak in his or her own language, and especially a protean actor, capable of cloning himself once or many times, of incarnating himself on the entirely imaginary stage, whose set he had himself built, whose costumes he had designed, whose lighting he had set up, and of using the most various tones of voice and postures of a fauna-and-fairy actor, playing all the roles that the storyteller-playwright required of him.

In these *scenarii*, taken from the same literary sources and with the same genius for variation as the plots of Molière and the Italians (Ariosto, Boccaccio, Machiavelli, Rabelais, Marguerite de Navarre, *Cent nouvelles nouvelles*),[11] everything turns on the physical joy of love. This can be attributed to the very logic of that theater designed to delight the imagination, to cure it of melancholia and restore the body and mind to health.[12] The storyteller's banter and the tale's *burle*, the comic conceit of the actor playing several different characters, come together especially in the dialogue, where the vitality of the love rhetoric plays on the social, moral, and clerical obstacles and finally achieves the natural celebration of carnal pleasure, which is anticipated by laughter and always left to the imagination.

The sharp and brilliant theatricality of the La Fontainian tale makes its prose models appear listless and long-winded. That theatricality manifests itself not only in the frequency with which dialogues spring up naturally outside the narrative frame and bring characters to life on an imaginary stage, but within the narrative itself, in the quickness and sharpness of actions and gestures. The presence of the poet—soloist and one-man band—gives the entire spectacle a second meaning and a heightened pitch. Rarely has the victory of fiction, its hold on the imagination, its power to liberate readers from the weight of nightmares, been more delightful and accomplished. And what a comeback to Colbert's monotonous glory machine!

A very old tradition of therapeutic literature, wonderfully revived by Scarron during the Fronde, found an original successor under Louis the Great, on the brink of modernity: La Fontaine knew how to temper and modulate the comic with gallant refinement and to brighten up gallantry with irony and joy. Beyond the masters of the burlesque, Scarron and d'Assoucy, La Fontaine reconnected with the alluring "mode" of the fable that had been in favor during the Renaissance. (In his *Contes et nouvelles* [1665], he did not hesitate to include the section of *Le songe de Vaux* recounting the ardent embraces of Venus and Mars, caught in the act by Vulcan.) And just as he brought both Scarron and Voiture back to life, he also reconciled Plautus and Terence, Apuleius and Petronius. Without the slightest trace of remorse, he justified his decision to circulate a drink of old literary liquor, as delicious as it was intoxicating.

In the 1665 preface he declared: "I believe there should be no doubt that I be allowed to write of these things, as so many others have done, and with success; one cannot condemn me without also condemning Ariosto before me, and the ancients before Arisoto."[13]

To tone down, take the edge off, or attenuate that erotic "mode" of the poetic imagination out of some inopportune scruple would have been to diminish or eradicate the beneficent effect that his readers—his audience—of both sexes had the right to expect. Either one revived this mode (and La Fontaine was well aware that it provided him with an entirely new theatrical coup and comic verve) because the moment had come to do it, in which case one had to respect all the conventions inherent in this "mode," or "one spoiled everything." If the beneficent effect was—had to be—achieved, it lay first and foremost in an easing of the oppressed soul in the body, a sort of vicarious and imaginary carnal pleasure that the literary fiction (or fable) instilled with its pleasure, smiles, and laughter, dissipating the poet's dark mood and that of his readers. It was not an incitement to debauchery, since debauchery is the fruit of the dark moods that the tale proposed to cure. The melancholia that sentimental novels inspire in young girls, the poet added mischievously, with a Lucian-style irony, is much more dangerous for mores.

The tale "The Sick Abbess" (in the collection *Nouveaux contes*, seized by La Reynie in 1675) introduced into the narrative reflections on its own therapeutic purpose, which the 1665 preface did no more than suggest. The storyteller, standing in front of the lowered curtain, begins by creating the atmosphere and placing the reader in a mood to enjoy the spectacle: he recounts the delicious fable, taken from Rabelais's *Quart livre*, of Panurge, Dindenaut, and the flock of sheep that throws itself into the sea. He thus suggests that the "substantial marrow" of the wisdom of sages can be made out under the pleasant surface of the tale.

The setting for the spectacle proper is a women's convent, and its protagonist is the abbess of the "flock of nuns." "Flock" can have an evangelical sense, but it also suggests a sheeplike foolishness. The shepherdess of this flock is suffering from "vapors," the feminine version of melancholia. She is thus afflicted, in her own way, with the worst evil that can befall a monk or nun: *acedia*, the carnal sadness that, in medieval theology and according to Saint Francis of Sales, makes those struck by it heretics and madmen, when it does not kill them.[14] The contemplative spirituality of the convent (which did not shine very bright) is extinguished by these vapors that have overwhelmed the abbess. The doctor is consulted and gives his verdict. For the abbess to recover her physical health (the prerequisite, no doubt, for any spiritual health), there is only one remedy: physical love with a man. Otherwise, she will slowly die. The indignant abbess prefers to succumb. The nuns who are attached to her resolve to serve as examples to rid her of that scruple. They *go at it* with contagious enthusiasm: the abbess yields.

> Un jouvenceau fait l'opération
> Sur la malade. Elle redevient rose,
> Oeillet, aurore, et si quelque autre chose
> De plus riant se peut imaginer.
> O doux remède, ô remède à donner,
> Remède ami de mainte créature,
> Ami des gens, ami de la nature,
> Ami de tout, point d'honneur excepté.
> Point d'honneur est une autre maladie:
> Dans ses écrits Madame Faculté
> N'en parle point. Que de maux en la vie!
>
> (ll. 133–43)

> A youth performs the operation
> On the patient. She turns rosy again,
> Pink, golden, or any other thing
> More cheerful that you can imagine.
> O sweet remedy, o remedy to be given,
> Remedy the friend of many a creature,
> The friend of humans, the friend of nature,
> The friend of everyone, except of honor.
> That point of honor is another malady:
> In her writings Madam Faculty
> Does not speak of it. How many evils in life!

Jeanne de Chantal's granddaughter, the marquise de Sévigné, who sampled the very first effort in these *Contes*, the "Letter to Madame de Coucy, abbess of Mouzon," did not easily give up praising the "pretty" (*jolie*) appeal of La Fontaine's novels in verse to her daughter, who resisted that appeal. In the word *jolie* is the word *joie* (joy). Like Molière's Elmire and Toinette, Jeanne de Chantal, a Renaissance Christian, knew from Francis of Sales that there is no true devotion without joy and without knowledge of the "things of life." Mme de Sévigné certainly did not rank *Contes* with treatises on spirituality or ethics, but she was one of its readers who knew how to enjoy the health and joyful spirit that La Fontaine's poetry shone over the "evils in life."

AN ART OF GALLANT LOVE

The other thing about these *Contes*—often dismissed as "bawdy," and which delighted the eighteenth century as a whole after consoling the seventeenth—that might have touched Mme de Sévigné was the way La Fontaine the storyteller carefully balanced joking and gallantry. The poet produced a synthesis of Voiture and Scarron—who, for seventeenth-century French readers, "spiced up" Renaissance storytellers and the Ovid of *Ars amatoria*—and infused it with charm. *Contes*, far from clinging to tradition, was extraordinary progress in the literary and imaginary domestication of what might be the most somber and ferocious aspect of human beings, the predatory sexual instinct. In this instance, La Fontaine was the anti-Sade. He made sex lighthearted, delicious, and spicy. Sade's overpowering seriousness located Burke's sublime and terror in the boudoir.

Even the last volumes of Tales (*Nouveaux contes*), published without royal privilege and seized by the police lieutenant in 1675, had an extraordinary lucidity about their own means and ends and were more elegant than the compulsive frenzy manifested, since the early part of the century, in a "satyric" poetry in the same "mode," with a virility of the barracks, or later, in often brutal burlesque parodies.

Even the tale "The Picture," modeled on one of Pietro Aretino's *Ragionamenti*, the *Kamasutra* of the Italian Renaissance, is a victory of art and tactfulness over the raging senses. Rather than explain, as his cynical model had done, the scabrous posture that is the true subject of the tale, the poet sets himself the task of allowing readers to imagine it without ever describing it.

> On m'engage à conter d'une manière honnête
> Le sujet d'un de ces tableaux
> Sur lesquels on met des rideaux.
> Il me faut tirer de ma tête
> Nombre de traits nouveaux, piquants et délicats,
> Qui disent et ne disent pas,
> Et qui soient entendus sans notes
> Des Agnès même les plus sottes:
> Ce n'est pas coucher gros, ces extrêmes Agnès
> Sont oiseaux qu'on ne vit jamais!
>
> (ll. 1–10)

I am assigned to give a decent account
    Of the subject of one of those pictures

Across which curtains are drawn.
I must extract from my mind
A number of new traits, spicy and delicate,
Which say and do not say,
And are understood without the aid of notes
By even the dimmest Agnes:
That's no hard task, such an extreme Agnes
Is a rare bird indeed!

This concern for women readers and their delicate ears, even and especially on subjects hypocritically kept quiet, but which the poet feels
it is important to bring to light and laugh about, was a novelty in this
genre and mode. It obliged the gallant poet to combine speaking with
keeping quiet, showing with concealing, which was less a tribute to the
true feminine sensibility than a public sacrifice to male impudence, a
symbolic recognition of the female point of view, and an implicit lesson, addressed to men, in decency with respect to the (so-called) physical things of life:

Qui pense finement et s'exprime avec grâce
Fait tout passer, car tout passe:
Je l'ai cent fois éprouvé:
Quand le mot est bien trouvé,
Le sexe, en sa faveur, à la chose pardonne:
Ce n'est plus elle, alors, c'est elle encor pourtant:
Vous ne faites rougir personne
Et tout le monde vous entend.

(ll. 22–29)

Anyone with subtle thoughts and eloquent expression,
Gets away with anything, since everything passes:
I have seen it a hundred times:
When the word is well chosen,
The fair sex, in its favor, forgives the thing:
It is no longer itself, yet it is it still:
You embarrass no one
And everyone understands.

As a poet, La Fontaine the fabulist and storyteller adopts the female
point of view on the "physical" side of love; women are attentive to its
moral issues, whereas men, even storytellers, are more likely to see it as

sport. The misogyny that is not absent from the poet's classical and humanistic sources is dissipated in the gallant metamorphosis he has them un-
dergo. That misogyny is even turned against men to satirize them, as in
the opening lines of the fable "How Women Kept a Secret" (8.6):

> Rien ne pèse tant qu'un secret:
> Le porter loin est difficile aux dames;
>   Et je sais même sur ce fait
> Bon nombres d'hommes qui sont femmes!
> (ll. 1–4)

> Nothing weighs so heavy as a secret:
> To carry it very far is hard for the ladies;
>   And I even know, on this score,
> A good number of men who are women!

The author of *Fables*, in perfect harmony with that of *Contes*, though
on a register more affective than sexual, goes even further. His constant sympathy, which makes the reader feel for the fate of animals,
treated as slaves by men, becomes true compassion when he puts on
display men's brutality toward women. In the first collection, the heroine of "Philomela and Procne" (3.15), forever wounded by the violence
to which she was subjected by Tereus, moves away from the comic register: she is lyricism itself, using the melody of her song to console herself over her tragic fate. In the second collection, the heroine of "The
Partridge and the Cocks" (10.7) is described with the same melancholy,
even though, in that fable, it is concealed behind a smile. Penned in
with the cocks "a people drawn to love but uncivil, ungallant," the partridge, a seventeenth-century Madame Bovary, dreams of nobility. She
receives only "horrible pecks." But the poet generously shares his own
wisdom with that unfortunate bird and makes her superior to her fate
and her tormentors:

> S'il dépendait de moi, je passerais ma vie
>   En plus honnête compagnie.
> Le maître de ces lieux en ordonne autrement.
>   Il nous prend avec des tonnelles,
> Nous loge avec des coqs, et nous coupe nos ailes,
> C'est de l'homme qu'il faut se plaindre seulement.
> (ll. 19–24)

If it were up to me, I would spend my life
  In more honorable company.
The master of this place commands otherwise.
  He captures us with tunnel-nets,
Puts us with the cocks, and clips our wings:
It is only of mankind we must complain.

The pocket theater opened by La Fontaine in 1664, and enriched in 1668 with a royal repertoire of fables, was designed to delight and instruct both men and women about a realm of their experience that had remained in shadow. In the "jests" and "farces" of *Contes*, the poet's gallantry wants to make even pillow talk, which drops the mask of salon good manners, more "honorable"—in other words, felicitous and reciprocal. For La Fontaine, love is not limited to the social comedy. The poet takes the gospel of gallant poetry down to the nether regions of sexual intimacy. He does not confine the "things of life" to things above the waist.

Is it by chance that, for what is considered his most scandalous tale, "The Picture," he chose the sexual position from Aretino's *Ragionamenti* that is the most "humiliating" for the male and the most gratifying for his female partner? The nuns of this "convent of Cythera" use a well-built youth as a passive instrument for their own pleasure. The poet is bold enough to offer his female readers revenge for their everyday experience. Nor does he conceal the perilous bitterness and reckless folly into which that revenge drags its female agents. The women were grateful to the poet for understanding without idealizing them, eighteenth-century women even more overtly than those of the seventeenth.

With the very first Tales, thanks to the spicy comments with which the narrator intervenes in his own narrative, this interest in civilizing male desire, in suggesting that men be less hasty and less blind in their vanity, that they use more preliminaries, more tact, more attentive and shrewd gentleness, is revealed as the poet's most tenacious goal. The tale, with its arousing subject matter and its lively depiction, catches the reader's interest and holds him or her within the storyteller's plot: the poet takes advantage of this to become the mouthpiece for his female readers and to hint at the true art of love for the benefit of their male partners:

Il fit l'époux; mais il le fit trop bien.
Trop bien? je faux: et c'est tout le contraire:

Il le fit mal, car qui le veut bien faire
Doit en besogne aller plus doucement.
                    ("The Cradle," ll. 112–15)

He played the husband; but he played it too well.
Too well? Not true: it's just the opposite, in fact:
He played it badly, for if you wish to play it well,
You must more slowly undertake the task.

L'Astrée has evolved from a school of feelings to lessons in physical
love. The generating principle of that gallantry in the act is articulated
by the narrator at the very center of the tale "The Muleteer" (Contes et
nouvelles 2):

Maître ne sais meilleur pour enseigner
Que Cupidon: l'âme la moins subtile
Sous sa férule apprend plus en un jour
Qu'un maître ès arts en dix ans aux écoles.
Aux plus grossiers, par un chemin bien court,
Il sait montrer les tours et les paroles.
Le présent conte en est un bon témoin.
                    (ll. 28–34)

I know no better master at teaching
Than Cupid: the least subtle soul
Under his sway learns more in one day
Than a master of arts in ten years at school.
To the coarsest minds, in very short order,
He knows how to show the right tricks and words.
The present tale is good evidence of that.

The "trouvère" of Contes (the poet who knows how to find the words
that will let anything get by, who has subtle thoughts and expresses himself with grace) is thus not only a master of joy within a regime of dark
compulsion; he also initiates men to gallant gentleness within a realm of
violence. Part of that school of sexual mores is a retrospective tribute to
Nicolas Foucquet, the gallant adored by women; and part is an indirect
satire, understood implicitly, of the Bourbons' expeditious manner, from
which Louis XIV, the cock king, was far from free. Success was assured
among those who yearned for Vaux and the Abbey of Thélème. But suc-

cess was no less assured among the intelligent women who, it was well known, held sway over public opinion in Paris and even at court. It is no accident that, very early on, La Fontaine found a favorable ear with the royal mistress, the marquise de Montespan. But she was not the only one. All things considered, *Contes,* going against the so-called Gallic tradition, grants women a better role and listens to them more attentively than to men (what a heartening succession of female victories can be found in "The Princess Betrothed to the King of Garba"!). Its audience was such that even Chapelain, who in his youth had written the preface to Marino's *Adone* and who was well acquainted with Renaissance Italy, had to yield to its success. In February 1666 he wrote the poet:

> You have outdone Boccaccio, who would be jealous of you if he were alive, and who would consider himself honored to have you as his stylistic companion. I have not found in any other novelist so much naïveté, purity, gaiety, so many good choices of subject matter or so much judgment in handling ancient or popular expressions, which are the only sharp and natural colors in that sort of composition. Your preface gives a good sense of your erudition and your experience of society.[15]

That Parisian "society," in fact, had to have celebrated the first collections of *Contes* if Colbert's scholarly agent, always quick to give good or bad grades, was to rally behind the fashion in that manner. Chapelain interpreted that fashion in terms of national vanity, which was quite alien to the poet: *to outdo Boccaccio* was to further establish the superiority of Louis XIV's France over Italy! The literary event was of such magnitude that Nicolas Boileau, the future regent of Parnassus, relatively friendly with La Fontaine at the time, judged it wise to approve of it as well. In 1669 he arranged to have printed, but anonymously, his *Dissertation sur Joconde* on the first tale in verse published by La Fontaine.[16] In it Boileau celebrates an art of laughing and playing with the reader worthy of Ariosto, which he had enjoyed in this translation of a canto from *Orlando furioso*. He ranks it far above the flat prose translation of the same canto that one of Gaston d'Orléans's officers had done, and which had been published in 1663. Boileau too thought he was hailing a new victory of the Gallic cock over foreigners. La Fontaine did not even contradict him. Boileau would later change his tune: in his *Satire X, Contre les femmes* (1694), he calls "Joconde" an "odious tale."

Even though he was excluded from the list of pensioners, even though he was openly ignored by the king, in 1664–65 Foucquet's poet laureate rallied readers and connoisseurs of both sexes to his side. His little pocket theater with its Cupid sign had won the victory for him. All that was left for him to do was to display the sign of Aesop on the marquee.

Irony and Tenderness: Gallant Romanticism

Once La Fontaine caught the public's ear in 1664, his proteanism as a poet revealed itself and developed. Within a single decade, between 1664 and 1674, he published not only his "novel of novels," *Les amours de Psyché*, but also four of his elegies,[17] the swan song of lyric poetry, of which he had rightly said in his preface to *Adonis* that it was now, under Louis the Great, marked by "general disgrace." Above all, in 1668 and 1671 he published the first two "seasons" of his *Fables*. Was this diversity or dispersion? In fact, we must always return to this central point: the poet's "I" is not an "ego"; it is an open and metamorphic multiplicity, like the language of his poetry, but a multiplicity that guards against all "confusion" and is able to play on several registers without confounding them, even as it seeks the synthesis that will reveal their profound unity.

A link can be drawn between *Contes* and *Fables*. The same is true for *Elégies*, even though the two genres, fable and elegy, are opposed in principle. One of these links is the gallant wisdom that reorients La Fontaine's *Contes* and entirely subverts the headstrong misogyny of most of its sources. It reappears in the four elegies and makes them a true comedy — *The School for the Languorous* — without, in appearance, detracting from their lyric purpose. The poet pretends to adopt the first-person point of view of a man who desires, speaks, and laments; it is himself no doubt, but a self at whom he imperceptibly smiles:

> Me voici rembarqué sur la mer amoureuse
> Moi pour qui tant de fois elle fut malheureuse.
> (*Elégie deuxième*, ll. 1–2)

> Here I am, setting off once more on the sea of love
> I who so many times have been unhappy there.

This secret playfulness alerts the reader that the poet himself, behind the poetic scenes, has also adopted, to an equal degree, the point of view of Clymène, the silent character, object of this desire, these words, and these laments. And Clymène has excellent reasons for not taking her suitor at his word, since the first elegy has shown us that he is fickle and, moreover, has always been unsuccessful. As in *Contes*, the poet and play-wright is very different from his main character; he hints, via the lyric monologue and a fragment of dialogue with Clymène, cited by her bashful lover, that she is testing him and awaits in vain something else or some-thing better than melodious moans.

The commonplaces of elegiac lyric poetry are all there: sorrow, doubt, despair, death, jealousy. But they seem to be permeated by a subtle parodic irony, comparable to that invented by Corneille in his first comedies. The entire plot of the brief comedy in four "lyric" cantos is driven, unbe-knownst to the speaker, who believes he occupies the entire stage, by the superior instincts of a woman resolved not to sacrifice the fine melancholy of a widow who was once loved to a man gifted at moaning, but hardly gifted for making a woman forget her sweet and cruel memories. In this masterpiece of gallant wit and romanticism, the true lyric subject is the woman of Arles, who prefers her loneliness and somber pleasures to a lan-guorous suitor who is first and foremost a nuisance to her.

Mme de La Fayette, with her friends the duc de La Rochefoucauld and the marquise de Sévigné, paid very close attention to everything La Fontaine's pen produced, and especially to his *Contes*, to which, in fact, *Elégies* is a supplement or sequel. The author of *Contes* was, for initiates and noninitiates alike, an unparalleled master of gallant wit, which, from *L'Astrée* to *Télémaque*, was the romanticism of the seventeenth century. And so much the worse for the court and the king, if they received only indirectly and faintly the light from this "national treasure" in full verve, in the full maturity of his genius. The slight distance between *Contes* and *Elégies*, the affinities they share with gallant romanticism, is further di-minished (love is the reason for everything) if one thinks of the vast reso-nance of "Joconde," the very first of the poet's "novels in verse."

That story, written down by Ariosto in *Orlando furioso* (canto 28), had already been reinterpreted by Cervantes in one of the stories included in his *Don Quixote*, "The Ill-advised Curiosity." From the time of *L'Astrée*, the fortunes of that novel, in translation and on the stage, were extra-ordinary in France. In its two versions, the Italian and the Spanish, "Joconde" then became part of the common French store of gallant roman-ticism. The hero of Ariosto's fable is a handsome Roman, Giocondo. His friend Astolfo, king of Lombardy, is no less handsome. Both men's wives cheat on them and they, outraged by that unworthy betrayal, set out to console each other by playing the role of Don Juan, whom no woman can resist. All that boasting leads to the discovery that the same woman, Fiammetta, whom they believed they shared, is cheating on both of them at the same time, in their own bed, while they are sleeping, with her favorite lover, a Greek servant. They have the good grace to laugh at the trick Fiammetta has played on them. They return home, resolved to never again disrupt their marriages with their jealous amour propre.

Inspired by this model and by another episode in *Orlando furioso* (the tale of Anselmo and Adonio, in canto 43), Cervantes' novel reshapes it in the tragic mode. The friendship between two young men, Lothario, who is still single, and the married Anselmo, becomes indistinguishable from the jealousy that torments Anselmo, for no reason whatsoever, with regard to his loving and faithful wife. Anselmo is led to ask his single friend, Lothario, to personally test his wife's fidelity. Besieged by the formidable sophistry of the jealous husband, Lothario finally pretends to woo his friend's wife. He is gradually caught up in the game, as is the young woman. Anselmo, who is watching them, discovers that his jealousy is finally justified and kills himself.

Cervantes' genius was to turn Ariosto's droll tales on their heads, by turning them inside out to reveal the somber and anxious depths, verging on madness and anticipating death, which the ironic and comic mode adopted by the Italian poet veiled and intentionally warded off. Like La Fontaine, Ariosto thought that the "evils of life" were so cruel that art had to magnanimously help us look at them from afar, transfigured by a smile. In his novel Cervantes shows these same things, also from afar, but this time from a dizzying height. For him, male amour propre destroys others and itself if it blindly pursues its tendency to the end. Man's heart can be his own worst tyrant and tormentor.

In the stories of all three authors, the women are unfaithful, but the orientation of the plot is far from misogynous. In their vanity, their false sense of honor, and their virile narcissism, the men are far more guilty. In Ariosto's "Giocondo," the reader is invited to discern implicitly to what extent the two young men are thinking of no one but themselves. The Italian poet depicts both of them as incapable of being happy or of making others happy, literally interdicted from any complicity of heart and body with a woman, mistress, or wife: they thus leave every woman unsatisfied and tempted to seek better elsewhere. The wisdom they finally achieve is the ability to laugh at themselves and at their wives.

Cervantes' "The Ill-Advised Curiosity" obliges the reader to delve a little deeper. The friendship between the two men and the irrational anxiety of the married friend make the wife, without her suspecting it, the outsider in this infernal trio. Despite all the appearances of a happy and faithful marriage in the peacefulness of a private and serene life under the Tuscan sun, an opaque partition, at first invisible to the wife but an object of obsession for the husband from the outset, separates them from each other. Poisonous jealousy is the melancholic and tragic secretion of the male's impossible affinity for the female. In contrast the aim of *L'Astrée's* moral alchemy and of gallant romanticism as a whole, which is derived from it, was precisely to dissipate that mutual opacity between the sexes, the underlying and threatening silence. In France gallant poetry, gallant novels, and gallant moral analysis sought to create the conductive poetic medium in which these poisons and demons of amour propre and the ruling sex could yield to the smiling sweetness of friendship and physical pleasure between two different but complementary beings, who can know and recognize each other without illusions but also without bitterness or aggressiveness: the return of the golden age in private life.

In many respects, Mme de La Fayette's *La princesse de Clèves* (1672) is a very original variation on Cervantes' "The Ill-Advised Curiosity," which was also the source of the key episode in another of her novels, *Zayde* (1670). One could rightly call the heroine, and the novelist herself, "Jansenist," which gives us some notion of the symbiosis created in Parisian high society between Port-Royal and gallant romanticism. That symbiosis was facilitated by women of the stature of Mme du Plessis-Guénégaud, Mme de Sablé, and Mme de La Fayette, and by Solitaires as intentionally worldly as Robert Arnauld d'Andilly. The author of *Contes*, a friend of Arnauld d'Andilly, La Rochefoucauld, and Mme de La Fayette, who had many other facets and connections, also moved in that intermediate circle between Jansenist Augustinianism, a Salesian religious life, and the neo-Platonic gospel of *L'Astrée*. This ironic and tender poet stood at the center where all the avenues of gallant romanticism intersected. His tale "Joconde" is one of the links that joins "The Ill-Advised Curiosity" to *La princesse de Clèves*.

In Mme de La Fayette's novel the princess cannot respond to the bashful love of a husband, M. de Clèves, whom she respects but did not wish for, and she dreads the narcissistic and fickle moodiness of the man she loves and who loves her, the duc de Nemours. Not deigning to hide her inclination from her husband, powerless to contain the mortal jealousy she incites in him, and which kills him, she refuses, even though she is free and a widow, to marry the handsome Nemours, who she has good reason to believe would love her less if she was ever his. She is faithful to a golden age, which, she has discovered, was a utopia for the lonely heart. She prefers to withdraw into her own sorrowful femininity, like Clymène in La Fontaine's *Elégies*, but at least she is free from a burdensome male amour propre, with, at the end of the day, the consolations of religion and thoughts of death. This is less the twilight of gallant romanticism (which still has its brightest days ahead, with Mme de Lambert and Marivaux) than one of the modulations—the most tragic one—of the great groundswell of French literary sensibility that permeated the seventeenth century. Its only equivalent, after the Revolution, would be romanticism in the narrow sense, that of *René* and *Atala*, *Mademoiselle de Maupin* and *Volupté*. Their common kernel is the "unquiet heart" of Saint Augustine's *Confessions*, which Epicurus also experienced. Pascal encapsulates its oscillations when he contrasts the heart, "whose desires are infinite," to the mind, "whose capacity is limited."[18] That surging can as easily seek a cure in carnal pleasure as in repose or in love of the hidden God. But whatever its preference, it requires too much profundity, via the inner experience of which it is the root, to be satisfied with courtly spectacle, however magnificent.

Since the forms, fables, and modes of the imagination communicate with one another, it is not surprising that the author of *Contes* was also the author of a narrative poem, *La captivité de saint Malc* (1673), which has many points in common with *Atala*: first, the "desert," and, in the desert, a couple whom the Christian faith prohibits from being happy. The two heroes will find peace only separately, in prayer, each in his own cloister.[19]

La Fontaine's "Joconde" remains faithful to Ariosto's comic mode; it refrains from touching on the sorrowful profundity that Cervantes and Mme de La Fayette reveal to their readers. Nevertheless, the first tale published by the French poet is a masterpiece of gallant romanticism. Like Mérimée's and Gautier's best tales, it combines humor, irony, and a true understanding of the surprises of love. The male amour propre of the two friends in La Fontaine's tale, thanks to the inflexions of irony that the poet impresses on his narrative, is the object of an imperceptible but ruthless derision that goes even beyond Ariosto. The French poet thus depicts King Astolphe strutting about in front of his court:

> Un jour, en se mirant: Je fais, dit-il, gageure
> Qu'il n'est mortel dans la nature
> Qui me soit égal en appas.
>
> (ll. 6–8)

One day, while gazing at himself: "I wager," he said,
"That there is not a mortal in nature
Who is equal to me in charm."

Only the light mood of the tale keeps that level of vanity in a king, worthy of a coquette, from causing more than simply private tragedies. As for Joconde, the other hero, is it surprising that his wife cheats on him? Let us pay heed to what the French poet insinuates:

Sa femme avait de la jeunesse,
De la beauté, de la délicatesse;
Il ne tenait qu'à lui qu'il ne s'en trouvât bien.
(ll. 40–42)

His wife had youth,
Beauty and delicateness;
It was his own fault that he was not happy with it.

A narcissistic friendship (in La Fontaine's tale, Astolphe himself naively calls the handsome Joconde "Narcissus") is quickly established between the two heroes of the tale: that friendship further hardens the male amour propre they share, which sees women only as prisoners or traitors, as strangers you have had, or who have had you. The criticism and parody of Petrarchian commonplaces, excuses for indifference toward the love object, are touched on everywhere in the narrative.

These two Narcissuses-turned-Don-Juans come to share the same mistress, for whom they draw lots as if she were a domestic animal, and who cheats on them both in a humiliating act of revenge. They laugh about it. But they have not learned very much. Unlike Ariosto, La Fontaine points out the conventionality of the tale's "happy ending." Astolphe and Joconde become bourgeois upon returning home, their amour propre having lost its youthful virulence. But they have failed to plumb the mystery of the human heart and will remain forever exiled from it. Only the lighthearted perspective of Contes spares the reader—whether male or female—from the unconscious cruelty of their naive or callous egotism.

The profound cohesiveness of La Fontaine's gallant romanticism, though deployed in several modes—the comic tales, the elegiac tale, the novel Les amours de Psyché, and the "religious" novel La captivité de saint Malc—can be understood only from the perspective of the plural but central "I" of the poet, at times playwright, at other times storyteller or novelist, but always a moralist who depicts and animates his characters but does not identify with any of them or with the comedy. At every stage, from the physical to the moral, in every container, from the most comic to the most pedantic, from the many angles he adopts to show the shortsighted cunning of desire, the poet tirelessly suggests the same love gospel but without ever forcing the reader or spectator to embrace it. That gospel cheerfully works to remove one by one the bandages in which amour propre—especially its male form—has wrapped up and held fast the gnarled and predatory "ego." He seeks to have a "self" rise in its place, a self akin to his own—open, fluid, attentive to its own diversity, to the uniqueness of others, and to this delicate and delicious mystery of elective affinities, which are so rarely glimpsed and even more rarely captured. Although it is true that the Corneille of *Mélite* and *La veuve* infiltrated the comic and gallant genius of the La Fontaine of *Elégies* and *Contes*, all Marivaux's moral subtlety and profound humanity is already found, and not just in germ, in *Les amours de Psyché*. The unity of that poetic "I," the ambition of that butterfly of the golden age, depends on his extraordinary flexibility and diversity. Now La Fontaine had only to find the poetic genre where that multiplicity could not be used as an argument against its unity, and where the flimsy veils of the tale and novel would no longer be used as an objection to the universal greatness of the design, it too evangelical in its way.

Aesop, from Foucquet to Louis XIV

Even amid this proliferation of writings between 1664 and 1669—the comedy of *Contes*, the lyric irony of *Elégies*, and the sparkling wit of the novel *Les amours de Psyché*—La Fontaine was still able to produce the masterstroke of *Fables* (1668). From the outset, and in spite of official indifference, it was *Fables* that made him the only classic writer of the seventeenth century indifferent to his century's grandeur.

With the foundation laid by the success of *Contes*, the first collection of *Fables* received a triumphant welcome by the public. It was immediately and copiously imitated,[20] but in vain, especially by the poet's very old friend Antoine Furetière. Supplemented by later collections, it became, from one new edition to the next, in France and in Holland, from one translation to another into several European languages, one of the bestsellers of the seventeenth century and of following centuries, with no interruption in popularity.

It was in *Fables* that the poet (and he wrote Mme de Montespan in 1678 that it was "the favorite book by which I dare to hope of a second life") wanted to keep the implicit promise he had made at the beginning of *Contes* (1665): "Only truly solid works, and those of supreme beauty, can be well received by every mind and every century."[21]

La Fontaine knew full well that "bagatelles" such as "Joconde" condemned him to Ovid's fate. They excluded him from the "supreme beauty" that, by definition, was the privilege of everything relating to the king. The mode of that official beauty was grandeur, grandeur for eternity, the sublimity—so often cold and bombastic—of encomiums to the reigning king.

Such were the facts. If the author of *Contes* did not want to be dismissed forever as one of the "risqué Muses" of which Chapelain spoke condescendingly in 1666,[22] his "art of loving," without betraying or repudiating itself, had to prove it could rise to the level of human experience as a whole, had to manifest its own sovereignty on a Parnassus that could stand on its own against state art.

To be sure, *Fables* was published in 1668 in duodecimo, in the same small format as *Contes*. To be sure, with its one-act comedies, it increased the repertoire of the private little theater La Fontaine had opened in Paris (with branches in Holland and in the Spanish Netherlands). They were to La Fontaine's marquee what Molière's grave comedies were to the repertoire of the Palais-Royal theater: a profound, universal smile that extended to all levels the insight that farces and comedy ballets shed solely on the lower levels of the human comedy. But, in addition to the paperback edition, the first collection of *Fables* (and this was not true of *Contes*) was also published in a quarto edition with a more noble format and typography, in keeping with the dedication to the Dauphin.[23] In 1668 La Fontaine's pocket theater placed the coat of arms of the future king of France on its marquee, adding, in 1678, those of the king's acknowledged mistress and, in 1694, just before it was closed down, the arms of the duc de Bourgogne, the young hope of Old France, Fénelon's pupil.

Of all the genres of fables (or, as we would now say, of fiction), there were few available in 1661–64 to a poet disheartened by the most sought-after great genres of the time (epic and tragedy) and aware that the lyric genres were being snuffed out. If he wanted to avoid the frank, outmoded burlesque, there was only comedy, but that was the privilege of Molière; the epistle and satire, but Boileau had already got hold of them; and the tale and the novel, which La Fontaine happily took up. Finally, there was the Cinderella nobody wanted, even though Horace had sprinkled his own epistles and satires with them: the Aesopian apologue.

One of the thorniest questions raised by La Fontaine's poetic biography is the choice he made, and the moment he made it, to demand of the Aesopian apologue "set to verse" the *supreme beauty*, victorious over time and fashion, of which he spoke in the 1664 preface to his *Contes*.

He did not expect these "evergreen laurels" from the tale, from the novel *Les amours de Psyché*, or from lyric poetry, genres the royal spectacle looked down on after 1661. Yet, in 1668, the Aesopian apologue may have been a form of literary expression even more incompatible with "supreme beauty" as understood by Chapelain and Colbert. In his 1668 preface to *Fables*, La Fontaine recalled that Olivier Patru, a member of the Académie Française, advised against "setting to verse" Aesop's prose fables. Boileau provides us with even more decisive proof of the great impropriety surrounding the fable at the time. In 1668, in an epistle addressed to the king ("Grand roi, c'est vainement qu'abjurant la Satire / Pour Toi seul désormais j'avis fait voeu d'écrire"; Great king, it is in vain that swearing off satire / For you alone I have vowed to write henceforth), he introduces an apologue, "The Oyster and the Litigants," to vary somewhat the formal tone but also to imitate his Latin model Horace. In later editions the apologue was suppressed: the highest authorities at court, perhaps the prince de Condé himself (according to Boileau), let the author know that the king required poets to respect a sustained sublime poetics, incompatible with the hoard "of oysters and litigants."[24]

This downgrading of the Aesopian apologue was a new event. It was the logical consequence of the redistribution of literary values by the scale of pensions, at once scholastic and administrative, which now hierarchized authors on the basis of the degree of sublimity due the king of which each author proved himself capable.

Before 1661, contrary to what is often imagined, Aesop and his animals were honored on Parnassus, which was not yet regulated by Olympus. The Phrygian slave and even his beasts had full rights of citizenship in the French republic of letters.

After 1661 the Aesopian apologue became a literary Cinderella. It now required a remarkable audacity on the part of a poet to wave his magic wand and claim to reveal the charms of a princess of Parnassus in that slovenly servant!

La Fontaine's *Fables*, which triumphantly resisted the disgrace of that "lowly genre" under King Louis the Great, perpetuated undisturbed the favor Aesop had known not only in classical and Renaissance poetry but also, and more than ever, during the Regency and the Foucquet years. Even the Indian Aesop known as "Bidpai," who gave an Oriental coloring to the last books of *Fables*, had his day in Paris in 1644 with a French translation published under the title *Le livre des Lumières*.[25] Writing fables under Louis XIV, claiming "supreme beauty" for this disgraced genre, was to run resolutely against the grain. Just like *Elégie* and *Ode au roi*, this decision attests to the poet's fidelity to his own youth, to his Maecenas, Foucquet, and to a former literary age.

To gamble with *Fables* in spite of Aesop's official banishment was to take a great risk; it was to play for double or nothing but to play very well. In fact, unlike *Contes* or the novel *Les amours de Psyché*, modern genres traditionally lacking in prestige, the verse apologue, which La Fontaine had the audacity to take for his poetic medium, could lay claim—if not in Colbert's mind, then at least in the public's—not only to a vast and universal popularity but to a perfectly well-documented classical authority and to the favor of modern and gallant Paris. All the pressures and blackmail of the official poetics had no power against a poet who had the audacity and the talent to seek his salvation in what was a barnyard on Olympus, and nothing but the bestiary of Orpheus on Parnassus and for the public.

Aesop and Orpheus

The Orphic stature gallant romanticism had recognized in Aesop and his beasts in Foucquet's time[26] revived a poetic tradition of the apologue dating back to classical antiquity, but which the Italian and French Renaissance had honored even more generously. *Fables* was able to draw on a very noble and very ancient poetic genealogy.

The Renaissance mattered more to La Fontaine than did classical antiquity, to which Boileau and Racine laid claim, just as it mattered to all his Huguenot friends. He wrote cavalierly in the 1668 preface to his first collection: "The example of the ancients is of little consequence to me."

He was more willing to embrace the example of the "moderns" (by which we should understand fifteenth- and sixteenth-century authors) to legitimate the undertaking of the "fables set to verse." It is true that the moderns he claimed were humanists. They were weaned on antiquity.

Horace was one of the literary heroes of the Renaissance, and that poet, friend to Augustus and Maecenas, did not have Boileau's scruples: he used all the poetic power of his *Satirae* and *Epistulae* to compose many Aesopian apologues.[27] The French—and especially La Fontaine, whose roots were in Champagne—were particularly proud that one of their own, Pierre Pithou from Troyes, had revealed the fables of Phaedrus, a contemporary of Horace, to the cultivated European public. These fables in verse from the Augustan era, like Horace's *Epistulae*, elevated the Aesopian apologue to the rank of a classic masterpiece of poetry. The century of Augustus and Maecenas, which La Fontaine's generation dreamed of reestablishing in the kingdom, as had occurred in Italy during the Medici era and in France during the Valois period, had thus given Aesop a warm welcome on its Parnassus. But La Fontaine was right: the essential thing lay elsewhere; the literary fortunes of the Aesopian apologue, redis- covered by humanist philology in the original Greek and Latin texts, prospered and developed a new ambition in the Renaissance,[28] the effect of which was felt more than ever in France between 1643 and 1661.

The Italian humanists, in order to break away from these academic specialists, whom Rabelais called "theologasters," and their "Parisian way" of arguing in the abstract among themselves, in accord with a purely logi- cal protocol about being and its modes, turned back to Greek and Latin rhetoric. They were seeking from it a "more human" mode of thought and expression or, in any case, one more in keeping with nature and the lim- its of language and universal human experience.

Under the rule of rhetoric, speech became "eloquent" and ceased to be addressed to experts on "universals"; it put into play the intervals of silence and the symbolic resources of language with a liberating joy and prolificacy of which Rabelais is the best example. Hence it could produce an effect on the carnal and "natural" man in his entirety and not only on his intellect, trained in the schools. Its fabrications touched the reason, the passions, the imagination, and the senses all at once; it could per- suade them of the greater good and divert them from the worst evils by putting things before their eyes.

That art of showing well in order better to persuade was thus inseparable from an "experimental science" of man, based on a direct knowledge of the paradoxes within his nature, but also on the precedents, constants, and variations in that nature, depending on place, time, age, rank, and talent, over which literature stood as presiding judge. The poetry of Orpheus, with its metaphors, its fictions, and its music, far from being alien to that plan to reincarnate Cicero's "eloquent" language in the present and in the somber reality, were in reality its highest goal: the knowledge of human nature, the joy of the imagination, and the enchantment of the senses.

The oratory genres revived by the Renaissance regained their place in the active life of the political commonwealth.[29] Along with civil conversation, they introduced all the diplomacy of the "urbane" art of persuasion in conflicts of interest and opinion, in the battles of passions. But poetry, the superior fruit of the useful and delightful knowledge of contemplators, destined to nourish other contemplators, readers, and spectators on leave from the active life (Boccaccio called it *poetic theology*), was, in fact, the brightest moment of eloquent speech, the moment when it truly became the vehicle of detachment and disinterested knowledge.

During the Renaissance, the highest merit recognized in a man of action—a prince, cardinal, military leader, banker, or merchant—was that he did not remain confined within the utilitarian circle of language that his public profession required. He was never so "noble" as when he left it behind to protect and listen to the contemplative language of writers and poets, the only ones able to reconcile pleasure and knowledge for the benefit of important personalities and the public. These writers and poets wrested their audience from the hasty and ephemeral time of action and converted them, during their leisure time, to gentle mores and a knowledge of the things of life. The friendship between Olympus and Parnassus, between Augustus and Maecenas, between the princes of action and the princes of contemplation, was the program of the Renaissance of "belles lettres," that of the Medicis and the Valois.[30] In sixteenth-century France, that political and poetic program was identified with nationalist feeling and remained one of the most ardent and widely shared French ambitions in the seventeenth century, shored up by a true romanticism that operated on several registers.

Of all the forms, fables, and metaphors of poetry elevated by the humanists to the supreme rank of their "science of man," the beast apologues, whose invention was attributed to the mythical Aesop, were not the least relished. In the "fable" *Dindenaut et ses moutons*, Rabelais himself demonstrates the great value attached to them: like a comedy or tale, it is a fable that illustrates and makes us laugh, but it also contains an experimental hypothesis on "sheeplike" human nature, which is useful to know for anyone who wants to conduct himself with wit. Both the spiciness and the usefulness of Rabelais's fable are derived from the same principle: the "sheeplike" character of humans is reflected in the magnifying glass—both amusing and salutary—of animal behavior, a metaphor for human behavior.

The beast apologue, akin to comedy but encompassing it as well, is thus not the poor relation of the rhetorical and poetic humanities. In fact, it is the hard kernel of their "science of man," an exact algebra of human nature contemplating and knowing itself in its weaknesses and excesses. The Italians were the first to have granted the coarse and spicy Aesopian apologue a preeminent stature in the poetic science of man, which they expected from "belles lettres."

In 1495 Leonardo Abstemio, librarian to Guidolbaldo, duke of Urbino, did not believe it unworthy of his princely patron to dedicate a collection of one hundred Latin beast apologues set to verse to him; published in Venice, they were ultimately translated into French in 1572, under the title *Hecatonmythium*.[31]

In his dedication, Abstemio takes issue with the ignorant prejudice that the beast apologue is a weak genre: on the contrary, its comic and metaphorical models offer the poet a chance to inspire an incredible pleasure (*incredibilis voluptas*) and joy (*jucunditas*) in his readers, so that he makes them willing to hear and accept the bitterest truths of philosophers, which are otherwise unbearable. Even those who resist all persuasion allow themselves to be captivated by the urbanity of these narratives, which transport the human comedy to the animal world, and which know how to make readers smile even as they awaken them to the maxim "know thyself." As an example, Abstemio reports the story of Demosthenes, who explained to the Athenians, eloquently but in vain, why they should resist Philip II of Macedon: but when, out of desperation, he began to paint for them their own situation as a colorful narrative, the curiosity and suspense stirred up his listeners again (Plutarch, *Life of Demosthenes*). Abstemio also cites the story of Aesop, who dissuaded the Samians from rebelling against their tyrant: he told them the fable of the fox, the fly, and the hedgehog, and through this concrete and funny narrative led them to understand that a tyrant already satiated on blood is preferable to a new, bloodthirsty one (Aristotle, *Rhetorica* 2.20). The humanist also invokes the story of the poet Stesichorus: the citizens of Himera, who had to avenge themselves on an insolent neighbor, wanted to appeal to the formidable tyrant Phalaris to lead their army to certain victory. The poet dissuades them by telling them the fable of the horse which, to avenge itself on the stag, appealed to man and became forever his slave (Aristotle, *Rhetorica* 2.20).

Abstemio recalls that the poets, including the greatest among them, the Greek Hesiod and the Latin Horace, sprinkled these fables throughout their works, and that philosophers of the stature of Plato, Aristotle,

and Plutarch considered them indispensable for moral and civil education. He adds that, with the Renaissance of belles lettres, the great philologist Lorenzo Valla did not look down on translating Aesop's fables
from the Greek into Latin.

The essential principles of the poetics of the apologue, articulated by
La Fontaine in his 1668 preface, but also in "The Power of Fable," a jewel
in the 1678 collection, were already fully developed in that Latin dedication of 1495. The examples Abstemio draws from Aristotle and Plutarch
are repeated by the French poet. They are all dread-inspiring examples,
which portray the philosopher/fabulist as one who reveals human foolishness and wickedness: the political blindness of the common people in
Plutarch's example ("The Power of Fable," 8.4); the ferocity of princes
("The Hedgehog, the Fox, and the Flies," 12.13); the predatory callous-
ness of men ("The Stag and the Horse Who Would Be Revenged," 4.13).
The comic urbanity of these ingenious fictions is thus not out of place;
it veils the realism of the warnings they generously want to give their listeners, readers, or spectators. That combination of detached gaiety, cold
and contemplative lucidity, and a concern to delight the readers with
such poetic insights made the beast apologue, akin to comedy, one of the
most characteristic forms of what we, in a deceptivly "goody goody" term,
call "humanism." It was one of Erasmus's and Rabelais's favorite forms.
Montaigne begins his most ambitious essay, his "Apology for Raymond
Sebond," with a stunning parallel between man and animals, in which
mankind does not come off looking the better. La Rochefoucauld imitates
him in one of his "Réflexions," a true companion piece to *Fables*.

Another great Italian philologist, Gabriel Faërne, who enjoyed the
affection and patronage of Pope Pius IV, also composed a collection of one
hundred Aesopian fables in Latin verse, published in Rome after his death
in 1565 by the humanist cardinal Silvio Antoniano.[32] That sumptuous
edition, illustrated with superb engravings by Pirro Ligorio, came off
the presses of the pontifical printer. It is an admirable example of friendship between Olympus and Parnassus, the pontifical Olympus and the
Aesopian Parnassus. Faërne was also someone who, in the sixteenth century, contributed toward establishing the correct text of Terence's comedies. For him the Aesop's fables he himself set to verse and the scenarii of
Menander set to Latin verse by Terence were cousins. This was what La
Fontaine, translator of Terence, meant when he wrote that his own *Fables*
was a "vast comedy in one hundred different acts."

One may wonder how the French poet, who boasted of his own laziness, was able to become as erudite as Abstemio and Faërne. But he was a

poet in the Renaissance sense of the word, the interpreter par excellence of contemplative language, and thus, by definition, had access to the goddess of memory Mnemosyne, mother of the ancient Muses. In reality, his contemplator's laziness presupposed a poetic memory far superior to that of the scholar and the philologist, because for him it went all the way back to the sources, an indispensable prelude to the rejuvenation in the present of the beneficent song of the ancient Muses. The language of Orpheus (for La Fontaine, Aesop was the mask Orpheus put on when he was banished from Olympus), the language with the most powerful effect on souls, had to sink its roots in an ancient tradition, not because it was the tradition, but because it was self-knowledge (*connaissance*) of man by man, well attested by the experience of centuries. The current effects of that contemplative language were irresistible, especially since, for the public, they were both a *re-connaissance*, a re-cognition, and a *co-naissance* a co-birth, at once exhilarating and humbling.

The Fables, which enchanted their age, surpassed it precisely because they welled up from a very ancient store of literary knowledge, and because they were, first and foremost, a recognizable translation of the irrefutable text latent in everyone's heart of hearts. Abstemio and Faërne were the sixteenth-century relays of a tradition dating back to the century of Maecenas, to the time of Hesiod. These Italian philologists and poets were contemporaries of both Ariosto and Rabelais. La Fontaine had enough scholar friends to provide an erudite foundation to support his re-creative approach. Of these scholars, the philologist Gilles Ménage, former secretary to de Retz, a friend of Mme de Sévigné and Mme de La Fayette, published his own fables in Latin verse in 1652, in imitation of Faërne.[33] But like every true poet, he was also a voracious reader.

In seventeenth-century France every educated person worthy of the name knew that Gabriel Faërne had competed to establish the definitive text of Terence with a French philologist, Marc Antoine Muret, illustrious friend and commentator of Ronsard. Faërne's name and his fables were particularly familiar to French readers since, in Jacques-Auguste de Thou's *Mémoires*, the famous Gallican magistrate, to avenge Muret, accused the Italian humanist of having plundered the text of Phaedrus of unpublished fables known to him, while refraining from publishing them to dissimulate his plagiarism. (Faërne's most inexpiable crime, in de Thou's eyes, was to have been a "protégé" of Pius IV, the pope who presided over the last sessions of the Council of Trent.)

Faërne, in fact, did not know the fables of Phaedrus, and Jacques-Auguste de Thou's accusations against the Italian philologist and poet were primarily designed to advance the cause of his friend Pierre Pithou, the first publisher, in 1596, of the Latin fabulist. Indeed, several of the fables set to verse by Faërne were based on a model of his own invention: La Fontaine imitated a few of them, just as he borrowed from Abstemio. In his wit, he was the contemporary of these Renaissance writers, who had become moderns by bringing the ancients up to date.

The readings and literary memory of the author of *Fables* were far from a rarity. Even among the gallant poets, who concealed their libraries, Faërne and his collection were known. Charles Perrault was very close to La Fontaine, whom he had met at Nicolas Foucquet's home, and whom he ran into on a regular basis, after 1661, in Mme de La Sablière's salon. In 1699 Perrault published Faërne's Latin fables in French verse. He was well aware that these Renaissance poems were among the ancestors of La Fontaine's *Fables*. They were thus able to enjoy a second life in France, following the enormous popularity of their French heirs. Already in 1693 one of the king's historiographers, Guyonnet de Vertron, had published *Fables diverses de Jean-Baptiste Alberti*, dedicated to the duc de Bourgogne, another indirect homage paid to La Fontaine and his fidelity to the Renaissance wits.

In a famous epistle, *A mon ami Lyon*, Clément Marot, upon leaving prison in 1526, set the Aesopian apologue "The Lion and the Rat" to verse (recorded in book 2.11 of *Fables*); this must have convinced La Fontaine that Aesop's animals, depicted somewhat later by Rabelais, were common to the French and Italian Renaissances. His friend the poet Guillaume Colletet, a true archivist of sixteenth-century French literature, may have had him read the fabulists of the Valois such as the Huguenot Guillaume Haudent.[34]

At the time, far from being limited to schoolboys' training, Aesopian apologues were also not the monopoly of Latin libraries for philologists and scholars, either French or Italian. In the early decades of the sixteenth century, Abbot Agnolo Firenzuola—an Italian Rabelais, protégé of Leo X and Clement VII Medici, translator of Apuleius's *The Golden Ass*, a great admirer of Boccaccio, and an author of comedies—composed his *Discorso degli animali* in the vernacular and dedicated it "to the gentle and valorous ladies of Prato." This was not an Aesopian collection haphazardly juxtaposing apologues: it was a very free Italian adaptation (combined with licentious tales) of the Indian *Panchatantra* (translated several centuries before into Pahlavi, Persian, and Arabic), which La Fontaine came to know under the title *Le livre des Lumières*, translated by the Orientalist Gilbert Gaulmin and published in 1644.[35] That story from the Orient, like Firenzuola's imitation of it, weaves the beast apologues into a continuous novel of education.

Firenzuola's main story tells how a future king has been trained by a philosopher (an *altro Esopo*, or new Aesop), who is without stoic austerity and sloppy cynicism—an "honorable man," a friend of *gaya scienza*. Firenzuola writes: "Dolce aspetto, urbane parole, abiti usati, tenuto buono, savo e costumato con fatti, e non colle demostrazioni" (sweet in his appearance, polite in his language, dressed in style, and passing for wise and honest not by his reasoning but by his conduct). Instead of assailing his young princely pupil with abstract precepts, the lovable Mentor walks him through the "hundred different acts" of an animal comedy, so many lessons filled with diversions, but which also give food for thought. With Firenzuola's *Discorso degli animali*, which initiates readers to politics and mores but without tears, we are not very far from Rabelais's *Pantagruel*, on a journey to learn the ways of the world; and the program shared by the three collections of La Fontaine's *Fables* is already spelled out. Like Firenzuola (but in verse, and without overtly replicating the narrative thread of the prince's education), the French poet, in his little poems, combines comedy in the style of Terence, the tale in the style of Boccaccio, the Milesian fable in the style of Apuleius, the Aesopian fable, and the Oriental fable of the Indian Bidpai. In addition, La Fontaine may have already found in Firenzuola (whose famous *Discorso* was reprinted in Venice in 1620), as in Ariosto, the gallant concern to have women, the "second half of humanity," benefit from the human science that many humanists wanted to jealously reserve for male writers, as was still the case for Boileau in Louis XIV's France.

Marot, the author of the epistle *A mon ami Lyon*, was also the author of rhymed French Psalms, which La Fontaine's many Huguenot friends sang every Sunday at the church in Charenton. But he was also a model in *gaya scienza* and poetic eloquence for one of La Fontaine's masters: Vincent Voiture, the short-sized Orpheus of the Rambouillet mansion, author of a letter sparkling with wit addressed to the duc d'Enghiem: *Epître de la carpe au brochet*.[36] In the animal comedy, apart from a noble classical and humanist genealogy, La Fontaine's generation could also breathe in a delicious aroma of Old France, an aroma of gardens and châteaux going back to before La Pléiade, to before Marot, to the "old authors" of the Middle Ages whom Marot loved and published, and of which the gallant romanticism of the Rambouillet mansion was fond. Nicolas Foucquet's splendid library in Vaux included an entire cabinet filled with ancient manuscripts and modern editions of these "old authors."

In the Foucquet years, Aesop found a valuable bonus of prestige in Paris: in 1647, one of the most illustrious Solitaries of Port-Royal (the Port-Royal which, since 1643 and the resounding success of Antoine Arnauld's *La fréquente communion*, was able to combine the most severe moral doctrine and the persuasive "gentleness" of the best French style), Louis-Isaac Le Maistre de Sacy, published *Les Fables de Phèdre affranchi d'Auguste traduites en français, avec le latin à côté*. This volume, which was well received in elegant circles, like everything from Port-Royal, was reprinted in 1669 following the success of the first of La Fontaine's collections. At the time, Le Maistre, wearing a martyr's halo, was just being released from La Bastille, where he had been imprisoned for nearly three years, which he spent translating the Bible. In his preface, reprinted in the second edition, the illustrious Solitary, nephew to the three great figures of Port-Royal, Mère Angélique, Antoine Arnauld, and Robert Arnauld d'Andilly, did not hesitate to link the Aesopian teaching method to that of Jesus in the Gospel:

> It is clear that this sort of fable must not pass for a lowly and puerile thing, since, in the past, it was believed that Aesop was inspired by God to compose his, and even that Socrates, the wisest of men in the judgment of the pagans and the father of all the philosophers, was the author of those attributed to him. This sort of writing is almost the same as the hieroglyphs, so full of mysteries, which were once in use among the sages of Egypt. And Holy Scripture itself did not fear to use a few fables, in which it is not just beasts who speak but trees as well.[37]

La Fontaine borrowed this passage almost word for word for the preface to the first collection, thereby suggesting an "evangelical" reading of his Fables, and, at the very least, acquiring for them the favor of the Jansenist and Jansenist-leaning public. Le Maistre de Sacy's readers were able to recognize an echo of the words of the Solitary in the poet's verses, suggesting, in his animal symbols, the hieroglyphs and parables of a forgotten wisdom:

> Tout parle en mon ouvrage, et même les poissons.
> ("To His Royal Highness the Dauphin,"
> 1668, l. 4)

Everything speaks in my book, even the fish.

J'ai fait parler le loup et répondre l'agneau.
J'ai passé plus avant: les arbres et les plantes
Sont devenus chez moi créatures parlantes.
("For Those Impossible to Please,"
2.1., ll. 10–12)

I gave the wolf speech and made the lamb reply.
I went further yet: every plant and tree
Has become a speaking creature for me.

Neither in his prose nor in his verse did La Fontaine have to force his thinking to conform to that of Le Maistre de Sacy. In *De l'origine des romans* (1670), Pierre-Daniel Huet, another of the poet's friends, also defends the idea, already familiar to the Erasmus of *Adagia*, that apologues and fables stem from the same "mysterious language" as gospel parables. This was the doctrine of the entire Renaissance, which sought to incarnate the gospel's "good news" within the human, via "belles lettres," more faithful to the bittersweet truth of the ancient knowledge of the sages and saints than to the modern intellectual arrogance of "theologasters."

Antoine Furetière, La Fontaine's childhood friend, who became very jealous of his success but was only all the more careful to gather up the crumbs, published *Fables morales et nouvelles* in 1671, and, the next year, *Les paraboles de l'Evangile. Traduites en vers. Avec une explication morale et allégorique tirée des Saints Pères* (The parables of the Gospel. Translated into verse. With a moral and allegorical explanation drawn from the Holy Fathers). Furetière, a member of the Académie Française since 1662, was provided with rich abbeys; in his dedication to the king, with a treacherous allusion and garish flattery, he put forward his own advantages over the poor libertine poets living away from court:

If I had applied myself only to the translation of a profane book [so much for his friend La Fontaine], I would not have been so rash as to offer it to Your Majesty; and I would not have nurtured the hope that He would wish to honor me with His gaze. But its title makes me bold and leads me to believe that He will receive it favorably. For I cannot doubt that He has a particular veneration for the most beautiful part of the Gospel, and that, in spite of the feeble expressions I have used to facilitate understanding among His peoples, He may consider these parables as the most beautiful instructions by which Wisdom incarnate has chosen to teach the way to Heaven.[38]

Nevertheless, this refined writer, who in 1642 had been at the poet's side in the Academy of the Round Table, understood very well that one of the facets of *Fables* was, in the midst of Louis XIV's reign, the evangelism of Rabelais and Marguerite de Navarre.

AESOP AT THE LOUVRE, AT VAUX-LE-VICOMTE, AND AT VERSAILLES

Through Voiture and Port-Royal, through other authors as well, such as Jean Baudoin of the Académie Française, who in 1649 successfully re-issued his *Fables d'Esope illustrées de discours moraux, philosophiques et politiques*, Aesop became so acclimatized to the Parisian Parnassus that, in 1660–61, Madeleine de Scudéry, the George Sand of gallant romanticism, made him a character in her *Clélie* next to La Fontaine/Anacréon, Pellisson/Herminius, and Foucquet/Cléonime.

The Foucquet academy itself adopted Aesop to such a degree that, among the projects for embellishing the gardens of Vaux, Pellisson and his friends, it seems, came up with the idea of a labyrinth strewn with fountains and illustrating Aesop's fables.[39]

By 1659–61, had Charles Perrault, well situated in Foucquet's entourage, already collaborated with Pellisson and La Fontaine in the conception of the future Aesopian labyrinth at Vaux? Might he at the very least have been informed about it? When he became Colbert's chief assistant, he set about realizing the project, but this time in the gardens of Versailles, where the Aesopian fountains designed by Charles Le Brun, sculpted by artists from Vaux within a labyrinth grove conceived by Le Nôtre, were set in place between 1674 and 1686.[40] Like the orange grove, it may have been a true trophy of Vaux. Only La Fontaine was not included on the royal team: the legends for the fountains were requested from Benserade, and it was Perrault himself who introduced the booklet, printed and engraved in 1677, to let the world know of this masterpiece of the art of gardening.[41]

The Aesopian labyrinth at Versailles was destroyed in 1774 under Louis XVI but is still familiar to us through Jacques Bailly's miniatures (about 1675), Sébastien Leclerc's engravings for the booklet (1677), and Cotelle's paintings for the Grand Trianon (1688). At the entrance a statue of Aesop, the work of the sculptor Tuby, faced a statue of the god of love, the work of the sculptor Le Franc. Both were painted by the miniaturist Jacques Bailly. Under the statue of Love, who held the thread to the labyrinth, one could read:

Oui, je puis désormais fermer les yeux et rire:
Avec ce peloton je saurai me conduire.

Yes, now I can close my eyes and laugh:
With this ball of string I will know which way to go.

To which Aesop, a scroll of paper in hand, replied:

Amour, ce faible fil pourrait bien t'égarer:
Au moindre choc il peut casser.[42]

Love, that thin thread might well lead you astray:
At the slightest jolt it may break.

Aesop versus Love: the moral progress presented to visitors checked gallant progress. It is possible that the projects of *Fables* and of *Les amours de Psyché* were born together on the ruins of a labyrinth project for Vaux, while Foucquet's Aesop had to adjust himself to Louis XIV's gardens. La Fontaine gave him a completely different resonance for Parisian ears.

A more reliable indication that Aesop's fables, far from being looked down upon within Foucquet's entourage, as they would later be by Boileau, were a language enjoyed by the *surintendant* and his people, was the 1659 publication by Raphaël Trichet du Fresne, a regular at Saint-Mandé and Vaux (prior to that time, he was a protégé of Gaston d'Orléans and Christina of Sweden), of a fine illustrated and glossed collection of Aesopian apologues.[43]

This collection is far removed from the Map of Tenderness. But, according to the poetic Renaissance, it was the task of mysterious languages to reflect all the multiple and contradictory aspects—heroic and comic, bizarre and troubling, sinister and graceful—of fleeting human truth, by ingeniously veiling it. Trichet du Fresne, like other members of Foucquet's entourage who had spent time in Rome (the *surintendant*'s brother, the abbé Louis Foucquet, André Félibien, François Maucroix, and Charles Le Brun), was an admirer and friend of Nicolas Poussin, himself an expert if ever there was one in mysterious languages. In 1651 Trichet du Fresne published, in its original Italian text, the fragments of *Trattato della pittura* by Leonardo da Vinci, which had been the pride of the library of Cassiano dal Pozzo, Poussin's Roman patron, and for which the French painter had drawn illustrations.[44]

With Trichet du Fresne, then, we are entirely on the republic-of-scholarly-letters side of the Foucquet academy. A political and moral realism without illusion is wrapped up in these *Fables d'Esope*. It is wholly directed against tyrants who oppress the mind—against their violence and their ruses. It wants to provide the candidate to wisdom with the lucidity and strength required to live among wild animals, that is, among men. After Foucquet's arrest, La Fontaine was no longer able to peruse this collection without melancholia. In fact, from the first fable, "On Birds and Four-legged Animals," Trichet du Fresne comments on the engraving with this inscription: "It is the custom of cowardly minds to follow the side of fortune, without any regard for honor or their duty." The inscription that comments another fable, "On the Lion Going on a Hunt with Other Animals," is no less harsh: "Force has in all times given the law to reason; it is force that corrupts monarchy when it is poorly used, and most often makes it degenerate into tyranny."[45]

This is in fact one of the facets, in the dark style of Tacitus, of La Fontaine's fables. Their candid humor is merely another facet.

A concern for the autonomy of literary conscience bursts forth from Trichet du Fresne's Aesop; it is all the more striking in that it is a complete antithesis to the Aesop of Prior Audin, for the king's private use, dedicated, also in 1660, to Chancellor Séguier (the royal privilege dates to November 1659) under the title: *Fables héroïques comprenant les véritables maximes de la politique et de la morale*. The engraved frontispiece represents Aesop as Orpheus charming wild animals with his lyre.

The work's dedicatee was one of the most determined allies of Cardinal de Richelieu: he supported him well in the last two terrible years of his ministry. Séguier was also one of those who, in concert with the king and Colbert, planned the coup d'état of 5 September 1661. As a last resort, he presided over the Chamber of Justice named to condemn Foucquet. Prior Audin composed and published his own collection of fables in 1648, to contribute to the education of the young king, ten years old at the time.[46] The new edition and the dedication to Séguier in 1660 ("Apollo and the Muses are wholly indebted to your greatness for elevating the arts and letters of this kingdom") were part of the resistance by Richelieu's heirs to Nicolas Foucquet's ascension. Audin's *Fables héroïques* was again reissued in 1669: at that date, it was a futile attempt to inflict damage on the irritating success of La Fontaine's *Fables*.

Prior Audin prefaced his collection with a pedantic apologia for the fable, where all the ancient authorities were reassembled who, since the Renaissance, had attested to the dignity and power of these animal tales: Demosthenes, the Plato of *Laws*, Menenius Agrippa ("The Members and the Limbs," "The Fox and the Leeches"), Stesichorus, Cyrus and the Ionians ("The Fisherman Playing the Flageolet"), Gregory of Tours ("The Snake Gorged on Wine Who Cannot Get Out of the Flask"), Caesar and the Cnidians, whom the Roman conqueror spared because one of their compatriots was the fabulist Theopompus. These illustrative fabulists had left their mark upon the genre: for Prior Audin, they could now be used again to "depict in full color the prince's responsibility, the people's duty, the republic's happiness."

The royal tutor also added the Bible to these pagan authorities: the fable of the embassy of Thistle at the Cedar of Lebanon appears in 1 Kings 4; and the rich farmer who steals a poor shepherd's sheep and mistreats him, in the Book of Judges. They are "mysterious words" dictated by the Holy Spirit to the prophets to obtain the repentance of the adulterer and murderer David. Prior Audin, following Silvestre de Sacy, the publisher of Phaedrus, adds that the Gospel itself is filled with parables, "that is, with fables wisely invented to win over the infidel." "Since all these things are full of mysteries," adds the prior, "and since Jesus Christ is truth itself, it must be maintained that the fables he used had the character of truth."

Unfortunately, this exhaustive discourse ends somewhat like Sganarelle's in Molière's *Dom Juan*, with a self-denial: the prior, risking ridicule without suspecting it, writes that this "food for the wise is more salutary to the heart when it is disagreeable to the ear." This is very anti–La Fontaine.

They must have had a good laugh at his expense in 1660, at Saint-Mandé, Vaux, and the Nevers mansion. They were wrong: Audin was deadly serious. The king, whose name had been officially associated with this collection since 1648, approved the reissue of this book that had shaped his principles of conduct. The politics and ethics Prior Audin had extracted for him from Aesop's animal hieroglyphs guided Louis XIV more than ever during the planning of the plot against Foucquet. The lord of Vaux should have read these *Fables héroïques* more carefully. They had shaped the mind of the king.

To confine ourselves to one example, Audin extracted the following maxims from the fable "On the Eyrie of the Eagle and the Birds":

1. It is shameful for a subject to be better accommodated than his prince.

2. The subject must display his affection, and the prince acknowledge it.

3. Nothing must prevent the prince from always having his eye on his state.

4. All subjects must work to elevate the prince's majesty.

For men of wit in the *surintendant*'s entourage, this was undoubtedly something to smile at. It should have been something to worry about. Prior Audin, who, for his part, never smiled, had taught Louis XIV reason of state through fables. Thus, he commented on his first maxim:

Everything belonging to sovereigns must have something that rises far above the common lot, whether that be his dress, his officers, or his table. But, most of all, his buildings, which must excel in symmetry, mass, size, and the material used for them. All masters employed for royal buildings must see that those who look at their art admire it and judge that their labor ends [sic] in the work of a great prince.[47]

Colbert's idea of the Louvre ("the model for all of Europe," wrote Audin) and Louis XIV's own idea of royal buildings—their symmetry, their mass, and their size—were part of the program of conduct articulated in *Fables héroïques*. The principles Prior Audin had inculcated in the king were hardly reassuring for the "generous," and Foucquet ought to have read these fables better, even if they were totally alien to the gallant romanticism of which he was the hero.

"It is expedient," wrote the court's Aesop,

that he win over [the subjects] through beautiful appearances; hence, for the passions that occupy them, they are hardly capable of other charms. That is why they would more willingly give their hearts and affections to fine-looking princes and would revere them more if these princes lavished beautiful words on them, even if they had to deceive them and break all their promises.[48]

The Aesop and Socrates of La Fontaine's *Fables*, enlightened by bitter experience, are not unaware of that cold politics which Machiavelli himself perfectly summed up in his advice to his prince: be at once a lion and a fox.

The realism of *Fables* deploys all the art of a great poet to show its readers, beginning with the Dauphin, the future king, sophistry and tyranny in action—but it does not do so to encourage these traits.

Foucquet, Pellisson, and La Fontaine did not pay attention in time to *Fables héroïques*, written by one of Louis XIV's tutors, but they also did not understand the wisdom of Trichet du Fresne's *Fables*. Aesop was nevertheless involved on both sides in the struggle for Mazarin's succession, of which Louis XIV was the long-silent adjudicator. Too late, but for good, La Fontaine discovered how ambiguous, oracular, and insightful the Aesopian language of animal fables could be.

AESOP, SOCRATES, AND EPICURUS

Far from being an impromptu and therapeutic inspiration (as *Contes* may have been in 1663–64) that came to the poet in a time of great sorrow, *Fables*, even more than *Les amours de Psyché*, emerged from the deepest part of himself and had its bitter roots in the long Foucquet affair.

The two figures who open the first collection of 1668 are Aesop and the Socrates of Plato's *Phaedo*, preparing for death in his prison cell and transforming Aesop's prosaic apologues into poetry. Unlike Aesop and the god of love at Versailles, the figures are not opposed to each other but are superimposed, even confused. The figure of the philosopher of love, condemned to death in Athens, just as Aesop had been centuries earlier in Delphi, had become a symbol of resistance and freedom under the Regency and the Fronde. He took on a clearly subversive character in the post-Foucquet era, in the new light that the fate reserved for the *surintendant* cast on the king and the tyrannical orientation of his regime.

In 1647, one year before the parliamentary Fronde was set off, Le Maistre de Sacy, in his preface to Phaedrus's *Fables*, gave heartfelt praise to Socrates, "the father of all philosophers." Thus, Plato's and Aristotle's teacher was held up as a master and a model among the "Solitary" friends of Port-Royal persecuted by Richelieu and Mazarin. Like Aesop before the populace of Delphi, Socrates before Athenian reason of state, and Christ himself before Caesar's representative or the Pharisees, they bore witness to the rights of conscience in the face of the force and ruse of earthly powers.

Three years later, in 1650, in the midst of the Fronde, François Charpentier, one of La Fontaine's and Pellisson's companions from the Academy of the Round Table, published a *Life of Socrates* with the Académie Française publisher Jean Camusat, to accompany his translation of

Xenophon's *Memorabilia*. This work must have very much pleased the secretary for life, the Huguenot Valentin Conrart: its author was elected to the academy on the spot.

This *Life of Socrates* is rather curious. Like many seventeenth-century texts, it must be read candle in hand to make out its characters in invisible ink.

"The corruption of mores [in Athens]," writes Charpentier, "was so great that young people were almost not allowed to be chaste. Everyone knows what the criminal flame was that burned Greece as a whole and which, in the language of our saints, changed the order of nature."[49] It lay beyond the moral strength of Hercules or Theseus to battle head-on that incoercible appetite for sinful pleasure:

> [Socrates] thought of another means, which was to behave like everyone else in appearance, in order to more effectively introduce his philosophy into the minds of young men, and to gradually lead them away from such an unspeakable practice. Hence he loftily professed to love beautiful boys, regularly frequented the places where they exercised, ardently pursued them, and did everything to make them virtuous that the others did to corrupt them.

This apparently libertine ruse is that of a philosophy of love.

"It is pointless," writes Charpentier,

> to justify conversations, of which fathers feared their children would be deprived; one must not seek excuses for an affection as chaste and innocent as that of pure minds, whose only goal is the true good of the beloved and which, far from being the unspeakable ardor of profane love that soils and blackens the objects to which it becomes attached, is a celestial flame that purifies and illuminates everything it comes near.[50]

That philosophical love is the principle of a "true study of man," which includes knowledge of oneself, and which puts one on guard against "the temerity and foolishness of those who are happy to be ignorant of themselves in order to seek things outside and above themselves." It is like the wisdom of Ecclesiastes, according to which any knowledge that does not consider mores "is full of vanity and afflictions of spirit, and which tells us that God has left the world to be argued over by men, not wishing them to recognize the secret of his works."[51]

To radiate that philosophy of love, friendship, rest, and the maxim "know thyself," and to awaken others to it, Socrates had all the charms of the true gentleman (*honneste homme*): equanimity in all sorts of company, an unaffected but neat manner of dress, conversation no less charming than useful.

> He had an utterly extraordinary power to attract the attention and benevolence of everyone who listened to him. . . . Alcibiades compared these speeches to certain boxes then in vogue, which bore the figure of some Satyr on the outside, and in which, upon opening them, one found the images of gods and goddesses; because Socrates' speeches, which sometimes appeared frivolous, to judge by the outward appearance, when considered in depth were found to be full of an admirable wisdom and to bear the living image of virtue in each of their parts.[52]

There are many similarities between this Socrates and La Fontaine's Aesop, whose "Life," written by Planudes, is placed at the beginning of *Fables*, following Baudoin's example. One of Socrates' lines quoted by Charpentier might have been pronounced by Planudes' Aesop, who is full of irony for the self-importance of the powerful: "Questioned as to whether the king of Persia, whom the Greeks called the great king par excellence, was happy, he replied that he did not know what to say, because he did not know whether he was virtuous."

Charpentier's Socrates took most of his characteristics from Xenophon and Plato, but, above all, he had a living model in Paris. This was the canon Pierre Gassendi, the great seventeenth-century interpreter of Epicurus's doctrine, the French heir to the first modern apologist of Epicureanism, the Roman philologist (and fabulist) Lorenzo Valla.[53] Gassendi moved to Paris in 1645, where he published, in Latin, *The Life and Mores of Epicurus* (1647). He taught mathematics at the Collège Royal. He fought against Descartes's physics and metaphysics within the scientific academy, which was assembled regularly by his host, Henri-Louis Habert de Montmor. The scientist Gassendi was considered an oracle within the very exclusive circle of the Dupuy brothers. He had no less influence on the younger literary generation. In particular Gassendi's students were La Fontaine's friends the young Claude-Emmanuel Lhuillier, known as "Chapelle"—whom the poet began to frequent again after 1664, in the company of Molière, Racine, and Boileau—and the young François Bernier, whom the poet would meet up with again, upon Bernier's return from a long journey in Persia, in the company gathered around her by Mme de La Sablière.

The philosophy that Charpentier attributes to Socrates is anti-Cartesian, antimechanistic, antimetaphysical, and, despite the extreme caution befitting a would-be member of the Académie Française, permeated with neo-Epicurean empirical science and wisdom. That enemy of dogma, master of a hidden art of living, did not so much teach as awaken.

That art of living, however, needs to be shared. Thus, in Socrates/Gassendi it governs both an art of persuasion and a style of being: the art of persuasion of a philosopher/diplomat who knows how to draw from evil (self-indulgent pleasure) its own remedy (the science of *voluptas*); and the style of a gentleman-philosopher, whose charming and cheerful behavior is able to extract the seeds of a critical knowledge of self and of men even from the appetites of his disciples.

The "substantial marrow" of the Fables, their "virtue," concealed under the envelope of the Silenus of which Alcibiades speaks in Plato's *Symposium*, was already, in the era of the Fronde, in gestation within that diffuse Epicureanism common to varying degrees to the "knights of the Round Table" and to some of their elders in the Académie Française, such as Olivier Patru. The spread of that philosophy in 1658–61 became obvious in the literary and scientific circles that rallied behind the *surintendant* Foucquet. Samuel Sorbière, who had free run of Foucquet's home, was received there less as Hobbes's friend and publisher than as Gassendi's disciple, whose *Life and Works* he published in 1658, dedicated to Habert de Montmor.[54]

THE SUBLIMITY CONTROVERSY

Was this a response to Charpentier's *Life of Socrates?* In 1652 the old and illustrious *académicien* Jean-Louis Guez de Balzac, from his remote retirement in Charente, where he followed what was happening in Paris from afar, but attentively, published *Socrate chrétien*, which was reprinted many times in the Dutch paperback edition under Louis XIV.

The prince of the French republic of letters, superseded in Paris by Voiture and preparing to die, converted to a sincere, quasi-monastic piety. In many respects his book is a confession and condemnation of his youthful errors and the culmination of a long development that now intersected the concerns and tastes of the rising generation. In his foreword he acknowledges, with François Charpentier and his "Socrates," that literary Epicureanism, which he himself could not embrace, was no more than was necessary to counterbalance the lofty eloquence enslaved to reason of state:

> What, I beg of you, was wrong with wanting to cure with delicious remedies? . . . As a last resort, it used charms to a good end. It used debauchery of style to correct the defects in mores . . . However cautious and wise [the ancient sages] may have been, they put on their theater masks and costumes, and were no less wise or cautious for it.[55]

Balzac, damning what he had worshiped rather too much in his youth, when he celebrated Richelieu's political genius as a virtuoso organist of prose, now declared he could no longer read without tedium the panegyrics and all the official literature of grandeur, both French and Italian. "Always to praise," he writes,

> always to admire, and to use sentences a mile long, exclamations that rise to heaven, vexes even those being praised and admired. The victorious complain of it in the midst of their triumphs. And I know on good authority that the late king [Louis XIII], looking at himself in a mirror one day, and astonished at the great number of gray hairs, blamed the complimenters of his kingdom and their long sentences.[56]

This was not kind to the "glory machine" that Richelieu had perfected to deify himself and, incidentally, the king. After 1630 Balzac was eliminated from the list of writers approved by the cardinal. To the cold and bombastic sublime, the eloquence of public rhetoric for which he had at first provided models, just as Malherbe had done for poetry, Balzac now opposed the sharp, brief style of private freedom preferred to it by the ancients and the great Renaissance writers:

> Our friends in Greece and Italy understood it much better. Just as their risqué style did not diminish its dignity, the expansiveness of their discourse did not enervate the vigor of their thought. These corpuses were not flabby for being long. . . . Their words were actions, but actions animated by strength and courage. And this courage was communicated to those who read their books, to the point of making them desire and seek death when they had read a treatise on life's ills or a dialogue on the immortality of the soul.[57]

Balzac now declared that the Romans' "pens were steeped in sense."

Therein lies the great literary secret of truly supreme beauty, which touches and persuades the inner self, and of which the industrialists of public praise, high-sounding and servile "foolish bovines," know nothing. And, to confound them, Balzac goes on to evoke the most curious rhetorical treatise of antiquity, *On the Sublime*, which at the time was attributed to the Greek rhetor Longinus. What is true sublimity, what is the "supreme beauty" capable of prevailing over the hollow bombast of court panegyrists? What is the lightning flash Longinus recognized in Demosthenes' vehemence? Is it the "great fire that extends on all sides," which he sees as the merit of Cicero's orations? The old prince of the republic of letters makes his choice: "On the contrary, it seems to me, to take the Greek critic's thinking a step further, that the sun does not have more power over the body than Cicero had over souls. It does not seem to be wreathed with any more rays."[58]

Sublimity is the act of a sharp and nonviolent light that is born within the soul, and not a borrowed brilliance that reflects the external rays of the sun in order to dazzle. Balzac, in the guise of his Christian Socrates, asks Cicero, the orator and philosopher, for the principle of a sincere art of touching the heart.

Although La Fontaine and his generation were no longer as sensitive to the oratory models invoked by Balzac (Demosthenes, Cicero, Seneca), the lesson of great art that the repentant old master gave could not leave them indifferent (and the poet listened and judged the sermonists as a connoisseur and an admirer). They shared their elder's abhorrence of "pieces of eloquence . . . without end" ("The Schoolboy, the Pedant, and the Man with a Garden," 9.5) and like him wished for an internalized literature that would resist glaciation by the "eloquence of pomp."

La Fontaine and his friends, without yielding to the bitterness of the old repentant master, may have also shared the realist attitude of Balzac (who was ironically called the *Unico Eloquente* in 1624) toward the narrowing of minds under the effect of the absolutist court regime and the biased language it postulates:

> I know the present world; I know its dislikes and its aversion to our sort of writing. Eloquence has less power than men have hardness. . . . They are now almost incapable of persuasion. The grandchildren make fun of what their grandparents admired. Philosophical discourses were oracles under the reign of Francis I. Now they are hallucinations. Art, science, prose, and verse are different species of a single genre, and that genre is called "bagatelle" in the language of the court.[59]

The ambition, which manifests itself with increasing vigor in La Fontaine's *Fables*, to hark back to the philosophical poetry of the century of the Valois, even while taking into account the taste for "bagatelles" that replaced the freedom and daring of the Renaissance humanists, was under Louis XIV the poet's response to the sadness and lucidity formulated by the elderly Balzac in 1652. La Fontaine called his own Tales "bagatelles": they responded to the "taste of the century," but they earned him its good will, and that good will allowed him to reaffirm a *gaya scienza*. They also paved the way for the public's reception of *Fables*.

The opposition established by Balzac, between true and false light, the living sublime and sterile grandeur, is a guiding thread that also allows us to understand the design of "supreme beauty" that inspired the entire undertaking of *Fables*.

Balzac was also an admirer of and fervent correspondent with the founder of Port-Royal, the abbé de Saint-Cyran. The discourse he attributed to his Christian Socrates in 1652 was one that might have been uttered by a Solitary of Port-Royal-des-Champs, with which La Fontaine had been associated since his novitiate at the Oratory of Paris. Balzac, in humbling human reason, its pride and self-sufficiency, and in exalting the wit of minds sensitive to mystery simultaneously defined a properly Christian poetics of the sublime, attributed to the biblical sublime: the inner word that illuminates and does not seek to dazzle is the retort of true writers to the overpowering sublime of deified reason and reason of state:

> Listen to an oracle from the mouth of Cardinal du Perron. . . . Two things, he said, which are separate everywhere else, come together and unite in Holy Scripture: *simplicity and majesty*. Only Scripture knows how to harmonize two such different characteristics. But [they] are conserved only in the original, and not in copies. They are found only in the mother tongue of Scripture, or, at least, in translations so faithful (the politeness of this century would have difficulty tolerating this) . . . so literal, and which so closely approximate the Hebrew text, that it is still Hebrew, in Latin or French.[60]

Le Maistre de Sacy's entire project to translate the Bible (in 1652, he was already the translator of Phaedrus's *Fables*) is here given official approval by the Mentor of French literature. La Fontaine himself continued to follow attentively the gradual publication of that enormous labor of translation, which went on after Le Maistre de Sacy's death in 1683.[61] Under Louis XIV, La Fontaine's *Fables*, "translated and set to verse," remained a subtle counterpoint to this masterpiece of Port-Royal piety, science, and taste, albeit in a different modal register. In *Recueil de poésies chrétiennes et diverses* (Collection of Christian and diverse poetry), published in 1671 with a preface by the "Solitary" Pierre Nicole, La Fontaine, who prepared the anthology, had a large selection of his own fables appear in it, with the entire approval of Port-Royal.[62]

Balzac's *Socrate chrétien*—and this trait too links it to Port-Royal—tirelessly contrasts the true sublime, humble and daring, the sublime of the Bible, the Church Fathers, and Tacitus, to the servile pomp of imperial literature. The former is both true and free, the latter, turgid and base flattery.

That contrast is also found in Charpentier, who exalts Socrates' language and attacks that of the Sophists. This dialogue between a Christian Socrates and an Epicurean Socrates took on its full scope in the encounter between Pascal and the libertines Méré and Mitton. What unites the two versions of Socrates is a concern for an idiom that awakens readers to inner truth, and that will not be intimidated or disoriented by the authority of the state and its flatterers. What divides them is the conclusion that must be drawn from inner experience, worldly wisdom in one case, Christian salvation in the other. Nevertheless, Pascal's art of persuasion has more than one point in common with Méré's art of conversation. Until 1661 there were many bridges between Port-Royal and worldly people, even Epicureans. Until his death La Fontaine often crossed them.

The gap that, according to Balzac, separates the spiritual sublime from temporal bombast in the linguistic order is reflected in the political order. It is no accident that the Christian Socrates praises the abbé de Retz, who, in the midst of the Fronde, was as famous for his authority as a preacher as for his role as head of Mazarin's opposition. Balzac confers the title of "the new Chrysostom" on the coadjutor to the archbishop of Paris. Since the Day of Dupes in 1630, Balzac had become fiercely opposed to the dictatorship of Richelieu, which had delivered itself that year from its last yoke in the king's council: Cardinal de Bérulle and Chancellor Marillac. He now became the mouthpiece of a republic of letters resistant to Mazarin and in league with Port-Royal, the Oratory, and de Retz. A literary and a Christian conscience joins together in his Socrates to protest against a state that, in literature as in religion, wants to know only slaves and flatterers.

Balzac also devotes an entire chapter to the translation of Tacitus's *Annales* by the Huguenot member of the Académie Française, Nicolas Perrot d'Ablancourt, and argues that the restrained indignation of the great Latin historian of the reigns of Tiberius and Nero was part of the *praeparatio evangelica*: the sublime and sharp brevity of his style in the depiction of tyrants was a model for the modern literary and Christian resistance to the violence of reason of state and the servile pomp of flatterers.

A true political romanticism, like that which incited the Fronde and the plots against Richelieu, crops up in this book, with the same Stoic coloring as in Vigny's *Cinq-Mars*. It was common to the best-educated pious Catholics, to Gassendi's libertine disciples, to "honorable" and "gallant" people of the world, but also to the Huguenots, whose "evangelical" faith was primarily a protest of conscience against all Caesars, beginning with their pontifical heir. In Balzac's *Socrate chrétien* one finds many well-educated Huguenots engaging in conversation with the author's stand-in, who listens sympathetically to their arguments; he dreams less of converting them than of proving to them by his judgment and actions that the Catholics, as much as the Protestants, were consciences expert in the Gospel's injunction "Render unto Caesar." In his conversations with the Huguenots and with the libertines, the later Balzac was, in his own way, an advocate of diversity: he wanted to federate all free minds.

The sublimity controversy began with *Les sentiments de l'Académie française sur le Cid*.[63] At the time, Balzac loftily stood up for Corneille's interiority against Richelieu's exteriority. He remained consistent in his *Socrate chrétien*. That controversy took a new turn under Louis XIV. In 1674 Boileau supplemented his *Art poétique*, which was an application for candidacy to the magistrature of French letters, with a translation of Longinus's treatise *On the Sublime*.

That translation is a supreme attempt by the author of *Art poétique* to dissociate himself and his friend Racine from the common lot of pensioned authors, who confused the "grand style" (that of panegyrics and official flattery) with the truly "wondrous in discourse." "The sublime style," writes Boileau, "always seeks big words; but the sublime can be found in a single thought, in a single figure, in a single turn of phrase." Boileau's republic of letters renounced neither its duty toward reserve nor its tacit vocation for truth.

On 1 January 1675 Mme de Thianges offered her nephew (the illegitimate son of the king and of her sister Mme de Montespan) a sumptuous little theater where the young duc du Maine was depicted on Parnassus, surrounded by his governess Mme Scarron, his aunt Mme de Thianges, Bossuet, La Rochefoucauld, Mme de La Fayette, Boileau, and Racine. Boileau was beckoning to La Fontaine, too timid to join that "chamber of the sublime."[64] The patronage of the royal mistress and her family thus corrected Olympus's ostracism of the author of *Fables*. With the help of *On the Sublime*, he was taken from the soft ground of the pensioners and elevated halfway up Olympus, among the elite of the Rochechouart-Mortemart coterie, itself very separate from the court as a whole. In the view of this audience in the highest circle of society, the Fables (one of which was dedicated to the duc du Maine in the second collection of 1678) also seemed to belong to the "wondrous in discourse" devoid of "big words." Under Boileau's leadership they brought a higher degree of excellence even to official literature and, for those who were knowing and feeling, distanced themselves from the state glory machine. Boileau's silence in *Art poétique* regarding *Fables* was primarily respect for the king's personal prejudice. Even under extreme constraints, each great writer had to play his own game.

In fact, one of the major concerns of *Fables* was to set forth, against the forced version of official and external grandeur, a living and natural idea of the sublime, continuing the most "supreme" literary tradition stretching from Homer to Ariosto, Lucretius to Ronsard, Ecclesiastes to Le Maistre de Sacy. La Fontaine, going against the current, never "depart[ed] from Nature by one jot," and in 1676 the renown of his Fables was such that, even within the court, a private coterie that could afford the luxury recognized their "supreme beauty," which persuaded from within.

That controversy, of which the "chamber of the sublime" was a secondary episode, and in which *Fables* played a prominent role, was determinant in both the political history and the religious and literary history of France. Theology, poetic philosophy, and poetics intersected at this point to form a Gordian knot of formidable complexity.

Old France as a whole, with the wealth of its extreme diversity, with its fondness for freedom, grave or lighthearted, philosophical or religious, even at the center of Louis the Great's court, stood opposed to that monumental abstraction of the state, which *Contes* and *Fables* lampooned under Louis XIV, and which they would lampoon more than ever in the eighteenth century, with the full assistance of rococo art. The grandeur imposed by Louis XIV's glory machine already bore the seeds of the Jacobin sublime that would lead the architect Ledoux to say: "Art without eloquence is love without virility." And a Demosthenesian David, painting *Le serment du Jeu de Paume*, added: "Present and future peoples of the world, I have a great lesson to impart to you."

In 1793 the apotheosis of reason of state was victorious in the battle for grandeur. In 1801 Chateaubriand's *Atala, René*, and *Le génie du christianisme* made hope change its allegiance. But the war began with Richelieu's ministry, and La Fontaine gave the side of the resistance one of its better assets: the power of *Fables*.

AESOP AND HORACE: BEES AND THEIR BARBS

Aesop, Socrates, and Orpheus represent a knowledge that disturbs and moves, rather than a lesson that inspires awe. But poetry is not only an orientation of the soul. It is fable and form. To understand *Fables* is first to understand a unique, supreme, and generous form, which provided Aesop and Socrates with Orpheus's lyre.

In 1661, in the still-intact legacy of the Renaissance, La Fontaine found, next to the theater of the fable of gods and heroes—Homer, Virgil, and Ovid—that of the Aesopian fable, akin to the comedies of Aristophanes, Terence, and Plautus, akin as well to the Milesian fable, of which Apuleius's *The Golden Ass* is the Latin masterpiece and Boccaccio's *Decameron* the Italian and modern one. The "realm of the fable" was thus vast: it had its provinces, but each in its own order had its uncontested function as a symbolic reservoir, reflecting the "back thought" common to poets and sages. None did damage to the others; all contributed to a sort of "ingenious science of man," under the diversity of human conditions and from varying points of view. Pellisson drew a map of this liberal realm of fables in his *Remerciement à Foucquet* (1656). All the provinces, according to him, were open to the poet who would praise the *surintendant* and please him with wit, without flattering him.

The comic and animal province of the poetic imagination, far from being quarantined, found a renewed vitality in the outburst of parody and so-called burlesque irony that had preceded, anticipated, and accompanied the Fronde. The return to civil peace led to a search for a balance between that exclusively comic imagination and the necessary return to less polemical, more moderate modes of speech. La Fontaine's styles between 1654 and 1661 took the direction of a synthesis without sacrifice. They ran the gamut from Terence in *L'eunuque* to a Champagne-born Boccaccio in *Les rieurs de Beau-Richard*, from the little neo-Greek epic *Adonis* to the mythological theater of *Clymène* and *Le songe de Vaux*.

It is therefore understandable why, after the Foucquet tragedy and the triumph of a jealous Olympus that monopolized the fable of gods and heroes, the poet had to renounce heroic fables and heroic poetry. *Les amours de Psyché*, written in prose, was a farewell to that province where he had wished to settle. He sought the salvation of his poetry and a counterweight to official art in the province of comic fables and tales.

Although well known and appreciated before 1661, and recognized as a legitimate province of the fable, Aesop and his beast tales were not considered a major poetic form. Aesopian fables came in the most various forms, in prose, verse, prose and verse combined, and often with illustrations: that pairing made them a subgenre of the emblem, with a "body" that spoke to the eyes and a "soul" that addressed the ears. Authors of emblems, like authors of fables, subjected that two-tiered oracle to their often prolix commentaries and exegeses. The great variety of forms that the Aesopian apologue could take had to have been appealing to a poet fond of the Horatian dictum: *Pictoribus atque poetis / Quidlibet audendi semper fuit aequa potestas* (Painters and poets always had the legitimate power to dare anything).

But if he wanted to put his own mark on these fables with their very unstable form, he had to impose an overall plan, a guiding idea. This plan had to transcend the host of disparate forms, but without confining the Aesopian fable within a constrictive mold. The aim of poetic unity and "supreme beauty" had to be reconciled with diversity, the mother of naturalness and pleasure and the symbol of freedom.

In 1658 the poet Guillaume Colletet (who would die the following year) published a collection of historical and theoretical essays that might have shown La Fontaine the way. He was well acquainted with Colletet, who joined the Académie Française in 1635. All of cultured Paris, with Valentin Conrart and Paul Pellisson in the lead, respected and loved the excellent Colletet. He was the elder statesman of French poetry. He had been the secretary of Ronsard's last companion, Amadis Jamyn. He had been a disciple of Théophile de Viau and an admirer of Malherbe, a collaborator with Richelieu in the "Compagnie des cinq auteurs," and a friend of Voiture and Sarasin. The high esteem Colletet enjoyed in France and Holland was due less to his talents as a versifier than to his poetic erudition, which made him the living memory of French poetry. His Lives of French poets (most of them, still unpublished, were consumed in the fire of the Louvre library set by the Commune in 1871) sealed his glory among all true connoisseurs.

The essays in *Art poétique*, published in 1658, were of a remarkable originality.[65] It is true that Colletet used the same method as the great Renaissance philologists such as Scaliger, a liberal method totally alien to Boileau's pretension in his own *Art poétique* to "rule Parnassus," mirroring

King Jupiter on his Olympus, by authoritatively fixing, in the abstract and for all eternity, a hierarchy of norms, models, and prohibitions.

Colletet deduced the shape of every poetic form from the historical judgment made of it. Every form has its own genius, which cannot be reduced to rules, but whose constants can be observed in the sequence of original interpretations that the best poets have given it. A poetic form, from that historical and philological perspective, cannot be closed or fixed: as a vehicle and path of invention, it leaves the poet not only latitude for innovation in accord with his own genius but also a broad gamut of variants and even bold exceptions, already tested over time, which can in turn inspire him and authorize his own boldness. Sixteenth-century philologists limited themselves to Greek and Latin authors. Colletet extended his survey and method to the entire French tradition, and, since it was a living tradition, he did not confine himself to an inventory of past phenomena but suggested, for the forms he studied, other developments instigated by the tradition, but which remained to be explored. For him the philologist was at one with the poet, concerned with a knowledge of the secrets of his art, but especially of the unlimited and free power to invent, as affirmed by Horace.

Of these essays the most original is certainly the one he devoted to the epigram. That poetic form fascinated Colletet, as it had fascinated the Renaissance as a whole. In its concentrated brevity, its bold relief, and its capacity to become deeply engraved on the memory, the epigram (very short and dense in principle, like an inscription on marble, and not exceeding the length of a distich) could pass for the verbal atom most similar to the iconic hieroglyph of the ancient Egyptians: the primary element of a mysterious language whose persuasive power was robust and whose mnemonic capacity was very strong. In combination with a symbolic image, it could be part of the composition of an emblem and thus become the quasi-hieroglyphic vehicle of the poetic and moral "human science" that the humanists wanted to substitute for the abstract language and sterile knowledge of the scholastics. In a famous essay Montaigne characterizes the epigram as the very cipher of poetic language at its most sublime, as the science of man (*Essays* 3.5). Commenting on the art of Lucretius, who, in *De natura rerum* (1.33), describes the coupling of Venus with Mars, he writes of the ancient poets: "They are all epigram, not only the tail but the head, stomach, and feet. . . . When I see these brave forms of expression, so alive, so profound, I do not say 'This is well said,' I say, 'This is well thought.'"

This lesson was not lost on Malherbe or, above all, on his disciple François Maynard, famous for his genius for the epigram and well known to the young La Fontaine and his friends at the Round Table, since he had agreed to preside over sessions of their academy in 1646.[66] La Fontaine had practiced the epigram in the strict sense, and its cousin the epitaph, during the Foucquet years. His *Epitaphe d'un paresseux* (Epitaph for a lazy man), in which the barbs are aimed at himself, and which became indelibly fixed in the memory of his biographers, is one of his most famous works.[67] His epigram *Sur la mort de Scarron* (On the death of Scarron) contains the seeds for three of his best-known fables: "Death and the Poor Wretch" (1.15), "Death and the Woodman" (1.16), and "Death and the Dying" (8.1).

Scarron, sentant approcher son trépas,
Dit à la Parque: Attendez, je n'ai pas
Encore fait de tout point ma satire.
—Ah! dit Clothon, vous la ferez là-bas:
Marchons, marchons; il n'est pas temps de rire.[68]

Scarron, sensing the approach of death,
Said to the Fate: "Hold on, I have not yet
Put the final touches on my satire."
"Oh!" said Clotho, "You'll do it over there:
March, march; this is no time for laughter."

Critics have often pointed out, and rightly so, the kinship between La Fontaine's *Fables* and Alciati's *Emblemata:* the Fables too are inseparable from the vignettes above the text of each one, rendered by François Chauveau, illustrator of Mlle de Scudéry's novels.

In his *Traité de l'épigramme* (1658), Guillaume Colletet opens horizons far vaster for the epigram than the pointed distich or the brief "soul" of the emblem, to which Boileau, the sworn enemy of "barbs," wanted to condemn this little genre in his *Art poétique:*

L'épigramme plus libre, en son tour plus borné,
N'est souvent qu'un bon mot de deux rimes orné.
(2, ll. 105–6)

The freest epigram, in its turn more confined
Is often just a jest adorned with two rhymes.

Colletet, infinitely more perspicacious and liberal, certainly begins by insisting on the "bare" origins of the form, whose essence is extreme brevity, sometimes concentrated in a single word. It was first engraved in the hard material of statue pedestals, temple columns, and tombstones, and its aim was to praise a god or hero, but it could also forever sully the memory of a villain. As we know, brevity and praise were subjects for reflection dear to La Fontaine, especially after 1661, when the expansive sublimity of the royal panegyric besieged the peaks of the royal Olympus with incense.

But Colletet comes very quickly to observe that poets, over time, even while remaining faithful to the guiding idea, brought it to fruition in very broad and diverse ways, sometimes "in gay matters, sometimes in serious ones."

Thus the epigram, a brief and pointed form, was transformed into a universal form, and its object since then has become "everything that can fall under our senses and even beyond our senses: gods and goddesses, the intellectual, moral, and Christian virtues." Without deviating from the vocation proper to it, it came to embrace all human experience. In that respect it resembles the elegy, which was at first reserved for sad and lugubrious subjects, but later, as Horace notes, extended to cheerful and playful matters. La Fontaine made use of that poetic license in his 1671 Elégies.[69]

The epigram, even as it extended and nuanced its subject matter, nevertheless remained faithful to its original genius as an engraved inscription deeply etched in the memory, heart, and mind. It was simply that, printed separately by the poet, isolated from the statue or bas-relief whose meaning it had at first powerfully encapsulated, it reversed the relationship between the two orders of representation: it was now the sculptor's work that was minimized and relegated to the rank of legend, and the poet's inscription that became the aesthetic work requiring all one's attention and emotion. This was how La Fontaine had his *Fables* assembled: Chauveau's illustrations are only subscripts supporting the fable's *title*. It is the fable that is the work of art: brief, visual, lively in its shape, etching itself in the memory. This vigorous little vehicle that thinks was designed to travel far.

Two fables reveal how much La Fontaine, Colletet's disciple, reflected and gave subject for reflection on the epigrammatic essence of the form he adopted for the Aesopian apologue, and on the critical orientation he gave it. In "The Man and the Idol" (4.8), the satire of foolish praise ("vows, offerings, sacrifices, garlands, rich foods"), offered in overabundance to "gods who are dead, even though they have ears," makes a devout man angry; he destroys the idol and finds it "filled with gold." This is a fierce barb against earthly gods and their blind worshipers. In "The Fox and the Bust" (4.14), the satire of "important men, theater masks" that inspire awe only in the "vulgar idolater," is etched with a burin in the reader's imagination, thanks to the epigram (in the strictest sense) engraved by a fox on the pedestal of a "hero's bust," wrongly erected in his praise:

Belle tête, dit-il, mais de cervelle point.
(l. 11)

Fine head, it said, but no brain.

Guillaume Colletet was the first to foresee that "vast" extension of the epigram, also anticipated and authorized by the "long" examples—up to forty lines—given in the Greek anthology or by the Roman poet Catullus. He speaks of *epigrammatic libertinage*, or of *epigrammatic style*, tensions and extensions of which, still incompletely explored, would leave hope for the poet who took the risk of "reaching the supreme degree of perfection in the noble productions of the mind."[70]

The "character" proper to the epigrammatic style is the antithesis of the panegyric style, but not of the style of lyric and heroic poetry. All genres and modes can sparkle with brevity in the epigram's "naive and natural" language, which is not unrelated to bucolic language, but whose aim, like Horace's language, is as much to instruct as to please. The epigram as Colletet describes it is a universal genre, an all-terrain weapon of resistance and an "all-audience" force of seduction. The republic of letters also has its arsenals and, for lack of armies, its foot soldiers.

Colletet calls the epigram "capable of everything," even of encompassing Aesop.[71] That assertion is so prophetic that it might seem astonishing. In reality, the humanist scholar Colletet knew very well that the Renaissance, in its quest for a symbolic language for the science of man, had very early on linked the Aesopian apologue and the epigram. The first edition of the Greek text of Aesop's fables was published by Aldo Mannucci in 1508, in the same volume as the anthology of Greek epigrams by the Byzantine Maximus Planudes, the author, as mentioned earlier, of a "Life of Aesop," translated by La Fontaine at the beginning of his own *Fables*. It is thus quite easy for Colletet to assert that this form of writing is "the most difficult," the most subtle, by virtue of "the wit and life"[72] it asks of the poet, the exquisite and elegant choice of words it requires, and its "clean fluidity of language"[73] that postulates "metric variety."[74] Ten years before *Fables*, the ideal example for that analysis of the various facets of an "open" form was obviously Maecenas's friend, that is, the Horace of the *Satirae* and *Epistulae*. Therein lies the best Latin key to the secret of the French form of *Fables*.

It is in the swift and sharp barb (which can extend to the entire body of the poem) that the epigrammatic style's capacity to "move and elevate the reader's mind" resides, thus intersecting the effects of the veritable sublime as Pseudo-Longinus defined it. Colletet is perfectly sensitive to the dangerous power of a political strike that lurks within that form. He advises the poet to observe the greatest caution, not to openly launch ad hominem attacks. But he advises princes to be very attentive, not to underestimate the terrible contagious irony of which annoyed and gifted poets may be capable. He writes:

> Bees are gentle and peaceful by nature; but when they are annoyed, they have barbs to make those who have annoyed them soon repent of it. The minds of good poets are generally the same: there is nothing easier or gentler, nothing more innocent, so long as no one persecutes them or disturbs the gentle repose they like. But once they are attacked without reason, the fine blood that animates them heats up and boils in their veins; and it is to be feared that their sharp-pointed verses will avenge them and reduce their cowardly adversaries to a shameful and listless life, and to suffering even unto death.[75]

The Manifesto of the Generation of 1660

In 1656, on the eve of the Foucquet years, Paul Pellisson, who was close to Colletet, even closer than La Fontaine—in age, Epicurean affinities, and the friendship that had united them since 1645—formulated a version of the sublime in accord with the wishes of his generation but in tune with a historical conjuncture full of promise. The occasion for this poetic and literary manifesto was Pellisson's tribute, in the form of a preface to his collected works, to the poet Jean-François Sarasin, who had died two years earlier, at almost the same time as Balzac, who held him in high esteem.

In spite of everything, Balzac had remained a man of prose and eloquence. La Fontaine's friend Pellisson made poetry the main subject of his manifesto qua preface. A translator of Homer and an admirable commentator on Horace, Pellisson was well aware that the fates of French poetry and French liberty were linked.

As soon as Pellisson addressed the status of poetry in his preface, the question of the sublime was immediately raised. And it was raised from the perspective of constraint and freedom, already adopted by Balzac to discuss prose. Prose, according to Pellisson, has difficulty wresting itself from the "general view" and keeps words from attaining the elevation of the most profound and intuitive sentiments. Poetry is a voluntary constraint to which language bows, in order to liberate thought from its chains. He writes:

> It is a great and marvelous thing that, in a language as constrained as that, one can express the most subtle and delicate, the most lofty and sublime thoughts with such freedom. . . . These admirable poets, these men who seem truly inspired, having imposed upon themselves the requirement of employing only certain ways of speaking, and of scorning all others as too vulgar, of confining all their words within a certain, unvarying meter; add to that, if you like, of always ending in rhymes; after, I say, subjecting themselves to so many laws, so harsh and difficult to observe: despite all these obstacles, they give us to understand everything they choose in a more noble and easy manner than one could do in ordinary language. One would think they could not have said what they said in any other way, even if they had wished to do so, so fluid is the expression. These words have fallen from their pens without design, and each one has taken its place naturally. Amphion's lyre, it seems, did not produce greater miracles when the stones attracted by its music came and piled themselves one on top of another to build the famous walls of Thebes.[76]

In this admirable passage of literary criticism, in which he set out the idea of poetry, the Hellenist Pellisson was thinking not of his friend Sarasin, whose collected works he was prefacing, but of Homer. But he was then about to introduce La Fontaine to the *surintendant* Foucquet, and it is possible that the Château-Thierry poet, who had been his friend since 1645 and from whom he was expecting miracles, fully shared with him a notion of the poetic sublime, which was for La Fontaine an ambition, a vocation. The architectural metaphor Pellisson uses is the same one La Fontaine would employ in his 1663 letters to Marie Héricart to indicate, through the contrast between the château of Blois and the château of Richelieu, his own preference: ease, naturalness, diversity, given as free improvisation by the Muses, and which produce only the better a sense of harmony and wonder in the style: "There are a great many small galleries, small windows, small balconies, small ornaments, without regularity and without order; that makes for something grand, which was rather pleasing" (letter of 3 September 1663, from Richelieu).

In keeping with that parallel between architecture and poetry, which La Fontaine would make one of the ornaments of *Le songe de Vaux*, Pellisson describes the long efforts, will, and violence that a "powerful and inquisitive master," but one down to earth and closed to higher inspirations, can deploy to force nature (how can we fail to think of the cardinal's château?). He contrasts them to the world the great poet can make spring up in the imagination in an instant, "in that vast expanse of air, where nothing arrested our gaze a moment before": palaces, countrysides, hills, forests, rivers, and seas, "as if by a kind of creation that seemingly surpasses human powers."

That admirable poetic program, based entirely on the productivity, ease, and freedom of a genius attuned to Nature, ultimately would be realized not in *Le songe de Vaux* but in the *De natura rerum* of *Fables*.

Paul Pellisson's 1656 manifesto called for a poetry both "heroic" and "natural," whose first masterpiece would undoubtedly have been La Fontaine's *Adonis*. The Nicolas Foucquet tragedy obliged the poet to seek, within the kingdom of Mnemosyne, other fables, other forms, another style less "heroic" in appearance but still natural to respond to a state sublime whose triumph—and the role of slave that triumph reserved for him—Pellisson had not foreseen. The project of *Fables* was precipitated by the events of 1661–64. But its roots lay deep in the years of obscurity preceding the *surintendant's* fall. These roots fed on everything germinal and vital in the literature of Old France: Roman poetry, medieval romances and fables, the Renaissance of Rome and Touraine, the cultured Catholicism of Francis of Sales and Port-Royal, liberal and humanistic Calvinism, Cornellian generosity, the libertinage of skeptical and Epicurean scholars, the poets' lyricism and science of form, in short, everything that could nurture man's knowledge of himself and free him from the power of darkness within himself.

Lyricism Pursued by Other Means

The first collection of *Fables* (the first six books, published all at once in 1668) is the most disconcerting for modern readers, as soon as we try to

conceive of it as a totality, as the poet wished. It was from the first collection, a few isolated fables of which had already entered the common store
of French memory by the eighteenth century, that Rousseau chose the
examples of immorality of which he accused La Fontaine.

It is not so much the immorality of "The Wolf and the Lamb" that
gives us pause today (we sense its dark irony better than Rousseau did) as
the very form of the collection (capricious anthology or ingeniously composed mosaic?) and the meaning of that discontinuous poetry. The charm,
spice, colorfulness, vivacity, and topicality of these first fables give a bold
aesthetic (and mnemonic) relief to the old "Aesopian" models. They are
more or less comic, more or less tragic, but, in the choices the poet has
made, they draw a multifaceted portrait of contemporary society: comic,
tender, but most often curiously sad.

The uneven, lively rhythm of "The Grasshopper and the Ant" (1.1), in
which the lack of concern of the hard-pressed artist is shattered by the
hard-heartedness of the miserly ant, makes the ferocity of that little comedy all the more terrible (and unforgettable). Similarly, in another little
comedy, the careless clay pot exposes itself to the fatal impact of its hard
and frivolous friend, the iron pot (5.2).

The dramatic and visual vitality of the narration fixes in the mind the
disastrous encounter between the humble innocence of the gardener and
the thievery of his squire, whom the rural artist believed he could call to
help him against the hare that was nibbling his lettuce and wild thyme
("The Gardener and the Squire," 4.4). Human arrogance is thus the equal
of animal appetites and is incomparably more odious.

One fable or another may surprise by the contrast between the serene
art of the fabulist, the rich flavor of his language, his virtuosity as a
metrist, and the disheartening misfortunes his narrative has us witness.

In fact, the storyteller's serenity is not as detached as the pleasure of
reading or reciting isolated fables might lead us to believe. La Fontaine's
lyricism has gone underground, but it has not disappeared. Under the
lively, animated surface of the narration, which seems to suffice in itself,
gestures of sympathy or antipathy can be discerned; they send a signal to
the reader able to grasp and connect them. There is sympathy for the reed
"that bends and does not break" ("The Oak and the Reed," 1.22), for
"poor Philomela" and her lonesome song ("Philomela and Procne," 3.15),
for the "sweet idiom" of the swan that stops the cook's knife (3.12), for the
rat's loyalty to the lion ("The Lion and the Rat," 2.11), for the ant's loyalty to the dove ("The Dove and the Ant," 2.12), and for the destitute, of
whom one must "never make fun" ("The Hare and the Partridge," 5.17).
The antipathy is toward the flatterers, deceivers, cheaters, and pedants, all

those who "use their tongue" inconsiderately or in cruel collaboration with misfortune. Even "the wicked" are at issue ("Bitch and Friend," 2.7) against whom one must always be on guard.

These sympathies and antipathies, which give us a glimpse of the lyric poet under the dazzling and calm storyteller, become perceptible and decipherable only in relation to one another. Their subterranean orientation imposes itself only on the attentive reader of the entire collection. If one considers only isolated fables, each of these emotional notes may pass for only another fleeting color in the service of the narration's vivacity. In the first collection, pathos is not only restrained, it is hidden as if it were a temptation, as if the poet, in highlighting the visual power of his art as a storyteller, wanted to present the irrefutable evidence of a world of savage beasts and prey, where irrepressible and contradictory propensities are at work, where the comic does not make up for the tragic, and where naïveté is unforgivable. The urgency of disillusionment takes precedence over any indignation or tenderness that might delay or weaken it.

Thus, everything suggests that the voracious reader of *L'Astrée* and *love romances*, the poet who created *Adonis* and *Le songe de Vaux*, had, in that exercise of setting selected fables to verse, undertaken a course of treatment in sober and harsh reality. The lyric poet uses all his gifts and the grace of his art to battle his own inclination and properly serve Aseop, the wise expert in the "things of life." From one apologue to the next, he cures himself, and he cures his readers of their shepherd's penchant to dream naively of the golden age and of imminent joy. In "The Shepherd and the Lion" (6.1), the poet takes care to warn his reader: the enchantment he lends to the storyteller/fabulist must not veil the hard lesson of wisdom that this delightful art conveys:

> En ces sortes de feintes, il faut instruire et plaire,
> Et conter pour conter ne semble pas d'affaire.
>
> (ll. 5–6)

> In these sorts of fictions, one must instruct and please,
> And telling just to tell does not seem too germane.

Hence, the fables in the first collection awaken readers from the fascination exerted by the "theater masks" of official praise ("The Fox and the Bust," 4.14), from the grand appearances one is deceptively led to attribute to "sticks floating on the waves" at a distance ("The Camel and the Flotsam," 4.10). They disabuse readers of the trust of which assiduous but fundamentally malevolent friends take advantage ("Socrates' Answer," 4.17), of the illusory security that being in the right provides ("Bitch and Friend," 2.7), and of the first childish impulse that prevents one from distinguishing between true and false dangers ("Mousie, the Cat, and the Cockerel," 6.5). The hare may well have ears and not horns; it is no use; the cricket is wrong to invite him to trust his ears, since the ukase of the tyrant lion might well apply to him ("The Ears of the Hare," 5.4). At every turn mortal dangers lurk behind error and delusion, and anyone who allows himself to be caught is annihilated without a word.

The first collection is certainly something other than an anti-Colbertist polemic or a virtuoso performance of Aesop's commonplaces. La Fontaine engages in a profound criticism of his own illusions, those that led Foucquet's advocates to confuse the reality of the iron age with the memory of and desire for the golden age.

All the same, the author of the first collection does not repudiate any part of his lyric point of view, even though he subjects it to the test of realism. He rediscovers all its tenderness and good cheer in "The Young Widow," which brightens book 6. But he has learned to tune his lyre to the pitch of a new awareness, which has shown him the cruelty as well as the sweetness of things, and which weighs reality against the heart's desire.

If the Tales were a burst of vitality within misfortune, the first Fables were the poet's meditation on that misfortune, the literary internalization and appropriation of the lessons it entailed for him and his fellows.

That ordeal found its meaning in the practice of an unexpected form. La Fontaine had the good luck to live in a world still teeming with forms, and, when the time came, in order to "remunerate the shortcomings" of his lyricism that events had revealed, he employed one of the least lyric of all of them, the collection of Aesopian emblems.[77] La Fontaine undoubtedly altered that form in profound ways, made it completely his own, adapted it to the tastes of his public: all the same, he found the model for it and its main lines in the literary tradition he inherited from the Renaissance.

The palace of the magician Alcina vanished into thin air in 1661, even if the king's Isle of Pleasures reconstituted it in 1668 as a state spectacle in the gardens of Versailles. It took extraordinary courage to admit the entire scope of this disenchantment of the world and to draw all its conclusions with such calm. One cannot imagine Ronsard, Malherbe, or Tristan L'Hermite capable of such a change in tone, style, and "vision of the world." But Horace was a better master. Maecenas's friend, the author of Pindaric odes as well as familiar epistles adorned with Aesopian fables, knew how to shift easily from lyricism to irony, from the ideal to reality, from the mind's desires to acquiescence to beings and things.[78] The example of Horace more than any other favored La Fontaine's "conversion" to Aesop and inspired the proper moral and literary use the author of *Fables* was able to draw from his own misfortune.

Since the Italian Renaissance, Aesopian emblems had reminded moderns of the ancient sages' ironic wisdom, akin to that of the biblical David and Solomon. The first six books of La Fontaine's *Fables* "brightened up" the genre and form of these emblems for the 1668 public and adapted them to its "demanding taste." Aesop, Anacréon's neighbor on the Parnassus of *Clélie* (1661), was waiting for La Fontaine. The author of *Le songe de Vaux* turned to the fables of the Phrygian slave when experience had revealed all their value to him.

In fact, since the sixteenth century, in France as in Italy, collections of Aesopian emblems, like a basso continuo of "belles lettres," brought to light the two registers of symbolic language elaborated during the Renaissance from material borrowed from Egyptian, Chaldean, Hebrew, Greek, and Latin antiquity.[79] Another register of this language was directed toward the divine, and it depicted, "in mirrors and in enigmas," the heroic ideas that men had originally received from heaven. The modest register of the apologue, maxim, adage, and moral emblem, though reflecting the same wisdom of divine origin, was oriented toward earth and toward fallen man in the society that fall had produced, filled with traps for both the wise man and the man aspiring to wisdom.

In the Bible, the Psalms combine, in a single gesture of prayer, the faithful man's appeal for his God's protection and the depiction of the perils that surround him on the human earth. The Proverbs teach the faithful man the discernment he must exercise to govern himself in a world filled with deceitful traps and seductions by the wicked, who are skilled at leading the careless man on the road to misfortune. In the Greek philosophical and literary tradition, Pythagoras's symbols, popular in appearance,[80] and the maxims reported by Plutarch in the *Convivium septem sapientium*, to which Aesop contributed with his apologues, played the same role as the biblical Proverbs: they deduced, via a contemplative wisdom of divine things, the practical knowledge that must guide the wise man in his actions among men, in the perilous and glimmering current of human things.

Heroic symbols speak of the divine even while veiling it from ordinary men. Familiar symbols, which speak of ordinary men to men who have a vocation for the divine, are also veiled. These veils protect a science of man among men, which is not made for the common people, but which is nevertheless addressed to everyone, awakening the curiosity, ingenuity, and intelligence of at least those who, deep within themselves, desire to be enlightened. In the case of Aesopian apologues, the most obvious veil is the animal metaphor. It lends itself to exegesis and even demands it.[81]

In La Fontaine, metaphor and, more generally, the beast allegory take on the flesh and sensible life of "things seen." They are adequate in themselves. They require no exegesis. Often they even do without an express moral, or they transcend the partial moral given them. Their naturalness contains within itself its own obviousness and its own lesson.

But other, more subtle veils are deployed by the poet, who does not disappear behind the storyteller. He turns to irony, which seems to say the opposite of what one intends, and to *emphasis*, which seems to say the least in order to signify the most.[82] A modulation of silences runs through the metaphorical narrative (the animal/man the storyteller shows in action) and makes it quiver with restrained emotion. This restraint, without attenuating any of the harshness of the moral "painting," allows the lyric poet to pour out his feelings within the circle of "good listeners" who, like him, are capable of suffering from what they see and know. A secret life of feeling animates from within these apologues transfigured into theater scenes, little paintings, little bas-reliefs, and brief epigrams, often heightened with a contemporary flavor. This is the wisdom of Aesop tested from time immemorial, but that wisdom is turned to advantage by a poet, who lends to it the lyricism of his own "self" as much as the learned refinement of his art. The disillusionment in the great lyricism, far from drying up emotion and discouraging imagination, has greatly intensified them and has taught them to see and suffer in silence. The realism of the early Fables has learned to smile, for fear of crying or protesting in vain.

These restrained emotions are even more contagious for readers who, not satisfied with simply being amused, sense that the science of *emphasis*, at which the author of the early Fables was already a past master, knows how to reserve the poet's secret for those capable of feeling his sorrow and lucidity themselves. *Emphasis* is a surprising word choice. It would appear to be the opposite of La Fontaine's modesty and naturalness. In fact, the current meaning of *emphase* (grandiloquence) is the opposite of what the classical and humanistic tradition meant by *emphasis*: for us, it is a ponderous and sentimental insistence by means of which a discourse poor in content believes it can redeem its vacuousness.

In the literary tradition, *emphasis*, as a figure of thought, is the exact opposite of what we understand by *emphase*. It is the art of understatement, of suggesting much more than what is said, of appearing all the more cheerful, or casual, or brief, insofar as one has every reason to be grave, alarmed, or prolix. That reserve of silence forming the background for what one says invites the listener to guess at what is not being said and to value that economy of words and emotion. The apparent retreat of lyricism in the early *Fables*, the "gaiety" of their narratives that allow things to speak, are masterpieces of *emphasis* in the most traditional sense.

The reversal of meaning among moderns, from *emphasis* to *emphase*, was possible only because, in oral presentations, that higher art of veiling in order to be better understood required dictions, gestures, expressions, or attitudes that could supplement the written reserve and help listeners to recognize the unexpressed thoughts behind a figurative discourse. Of that tradition of *emphasis*, moderns retained only the oral and gestural tone of insistence and supplementation that orators, especially official orators, added to the reserve of figures of *emphasis* they used or which permeated the texts they quoted. The redundant performance obliterated the spirit of that art of saying less than one knows and feels, an art that makes one desire the intimate meaning of silences, veiled and revealed by the modesty or gaiety of figures of thought.

One entire fable from the first collection, "Phoebus and Boreas" (6.3), encompasses and implicitly celebrates that art of saying without saying, which accounts for the restraint of the first collection and for its seductiveness. Nothing is more vibrant, concrete, and self-sufficient than that vast aerial view the storyteller evokes of a landscape and an autumn day with its alternation between squalls and calm spells, and of the lonely traveler, lost in that vast land, making his way wrapped in a warm and comfortable coat. Within that vision a second meaning secretly dawns, and then only for someone attentive to the poet's feelings. Above the traveler's head, Boreas, the north wind, tries to persuade Sun to make a wager on which one will be able to remove the traveler's coat. The sun, "without so many words," accepts the wager. The alternation between squalls and calm spells thus becomes a competition between two orators, one prolix, violent, and vehement, who seeks less to persuade than to extort with brute force. The other, without hammering away at his effects or using up so much energy, confines himself to radiating light and heat to "amuse" the traveler. He is the only one who manages to get him to "unburden himself" on his own initiative, and without Sun having to "use all his power." It is the victory of *emphasis* over *emphase*, natural persuasion over force, which has disdain for persuasion.

The sublimity of which rough force is capable, and which is exerted only on bodies, must yield to the sublimity of gentle calm which, with restraint, with its reserve of thought, touches hearts and "unburdens" them of their mistrust and resistance, solely by the power of the light it sheds on things and creatures.

That art of silence and gentleness, which allows things to speak, but which is no less thinking for that, confers poetic unity on the first collection. It is in perfect harmony with the moral design governing the first six books, whose key is to be found in the fable "The Man and His Reflection" (1.11), dedicated to La Rochefoucauld:

> Notre âme, c'est cet homme amoureux de lui-même;
> Tant de miroirs, ce sont les sottises d'autrui,
> Miroirs, de nos défauts les peintres légitimes;
>> Et quant au canal, c'est celui
>> Que chacun sait, le livre des *Maximes*.
>
> (ll. 24–28)

> Our soul is that man in love with himself;
> The foolish acts of others are the many mirrors,
> Mirrors of our faults, the legitimate painters;
>> And, as for the canal, it's the one
>> Everyone knows, the book of *Maxims*.

If La Rochefoucauld's *Maximes* is at once a critique of amour propre and an initiation to honesty toward oneself and others, the first collection of *Fables*, by its own figurative and colorful path, has in view the same object, sublime in the true sense; that is its great ambition, despite its reserve and modesty.

That is because amour propre, according to La Rochefoucauld and La Fontaine, is much more than self-love. It is an ignorance of the divine from which wisdom wells forth, a fall into the blindness of the "ego" and its brutality; it contains the seeds for all the metamorphoses, tiny or gargantuan, of man's idolization of himself, next to which the unsophisticated appetites of savage beasts seem excusable. That greedy perversion of the gaze directed toward itself, and of the perception of others, is the Pandora's box from which political tyranny and cold egotism stem forth: this optical deflection allows cynicism, greed, and ferocity to prey on the innocent and the naive, who are unaware of their own blindness.

To warn those aspiring to wisdom of this monster of the iron age, which metamorphoses men into the wild boars of *Adonis*; to learn to perceive it in oneself and fear it in others, for lack of the ability to overcome it: that is as much the vocation of a poet as of a sage. But poetry can also allow one to discern, outside that chain of violence and vanity, the miracles of naturalness and humanity that calm and delight the heart:

> —Où est donc ce jeune mari
> Que vous m'avez promis, dit-elle.
> ("The Young Widow,"
> 6.21, ll. 47–48)

> "Where, then, is this young groom
> Whom you promised me," she said.

The natural movement that leads this young woman to happiness, like that which spontaneously dictates to a satyr that he offer a passerby the hospitality of his home, but then warns him in time that the passerby is not a friend ("The Satyr and the Visitor," 5.7), participates in an entirely intimate and familiar wonder. That wonder is wholly reserved for private life, which the classical "science of man," whose humble and venerable symbols the poet reinterprets and rejuvenates, can help to protect and foster, safe from the wolves and lions looking for someone to devour (*quaereus quem devoret*) in the city/jungle.

CHAPTER 7

The Living versus
the Mechanical

Memories of the wrath of the League and the clashes of the Fronde had
favored the establishment of absolute monarchy; the governments of
Louis XIV's despotism, when that great prince went to relax among his
ancestors in Saint-Denis, made the yearning for freedom more bitter.
The old monarchy had lasted six and a half centuries with its feudal and
aristocratic liberties. How long had the state formed by Louis XIV lasted?
One hundred and forty years. After that monarch's tomb, there were only
two monuments of monarchy: the pillow of Louis XV's debauchery
and Louis XVI's executioner's block.

—Chateaubriand, *Etudes historiques*

*T*he coup d'état of 5 September 1661 echoed cruelly deep within
the poet. The response was a series of creative outbursts: the Tales, the
early Fables, *Les amours de Psyché*. It is tempting to say that the best of his
work was wrested from him in response to Foucquet's grief and to accommodate his poet's vision to the challenge and scandal of the brutal victory
of reason of state, in the person of a king in whom so many hopes had
been placed.

There was a precedent to that internal poetic revolution in response to
a political cataclysm. But it would not be until the nineteenth century
and the failure of the Second Republic in 1848 that the same phenomenon, sharper and more striking, could be observed in operation for an
entire generation of poets. At that time, Hugo became the Juvenal and
Baudelaire the Ovid of political modernity.

The seventeenth-century precedent is to be found at the moment when,
after Richelieu and Louis XIII died a year apart, one in 1642, the other in

1643, the dictatorship of public safety set in place by the cardinal—seriously ill, burned by intelligence and will—abruptly came to an end. In 1643 Paul Scarron published *Recueil de quelques vers burlesques*, which inaugurated with a flourish the prolific work of that poet of digressions: it ended when Scarron died in 1660, early enough to avoid witnessing the fall of Foucquet, his generous patron since 1652.[1]

Scarron himself had been seriously ill since 1640. The extraordinary verve with which he reacted to the ruin of his body and to suffering burst forth alongside the general euphoria at the end of the "dark years" of the kingdom and the beginning of the "good regency." A true poet reflects not only his inner climate but also that of the language community for which he serves as interpreter. Scarron suffered an unfair posthumous "downgrading" on Louis XIV's and Boileau's authority. The romantics, from Gautier to Flaubert, rehabilitated him.

Even before Scarron, the burlesque was active in Italy and latent in French poetry.[2] Saint-Amant, a great lyric poet, practiced it in a heroicomic register between 1629 and 1661: his poetic "caprices" did so little harm to his success that he was elected to the Académie Française in 1634. But it was Scarron who isolated and perfected the formula in 1643, and who gave it its name. The circumstances (La Fontaine would say "opportunity") supported him.

The circumstances in 1643, so favorable to Scarron's inventiveness, were exactly the reverse of those in which La Fontaine found himself in 1661. In 1643 there was relief after a period of oppression. In 1661 it was oppression after eighteen years of unrest and catastrophe, to be sure, but unrest and catastrophe within recaptured and squandered freedom, followed, since 1654, by the great hope of peace abroad and harmony at home. The rise of the burlesque and Scarron's literary career were precisely circumscribed within that interlude, between 1643 and 1661, of the long seventeenth century. The year 1661, which witnessed Foucquet's fall, was also marked by the deaths of Saint-Amant and Scarron.

What is the burlesque? It is the poetic version of a freedom with few illusions. To practice this genre of writing, which has no respect for any norm and takes an ironic posture toward itself, seventeenth-century poets had to summon "fire," and that fire was the foremost woundwort that saved Scarron from sinking into despair. It also fascinated contemporaries. Burlesque poetics is the world turned upside down: the gods and heroes who people the lofty genres are metamorphosed into a humanity akin to the animal world, and the grand style, which in principle ought to have suited them by rights, is replaced by the low style and a general derision. That precipitous fall of the great models and great examples, ordinarily protected by convention and propriety, into the troubled, acidic, and sarcastic waters of comic life was the poetic method Scarron set in place with dazzling verbal and metrical inventiveness, and in several different genres (a parody of *The Aeneid*, a parody of the lyric and encomiastic genres, caricatural comedy, the comic novel). The fall of the great to the lowly creates a reality effect that dismantles all illusion and an illusion effect that nullifies all reality: it triggers harsh and liberating laughter in the style of Samuel Beckett, laughter that assured Scarron's success for the duration of Richelieu's and Colbert's interregnum.

In the burlesque, however, there is an all-too-conspicuous method and, beneath its gaiety, an all-too-deliberate skepticism: Scarron himself altered and toned down his technique during his final years, the Foucquet years. He moved closer to Pellisson, his advocate with Foucquet: in effect, the entire pedagogy deployed by Pellisson with his friends of the Round Table between 1645 and 1657 tended to act as a counterweight to the burlesque flood, through the study of the classical and Italian models of "naturalness"—Homer, Horace, Ariosto—who were able to smile even in the sublime register and bring grace down even to the lowly register.[3] Vaux and its poets (Molière, La Fontaine) had to be able to reconcile freedom and monarchy, intelligence and harmony.

After Foucquet's fall, its grief and sorrow, the "heroic" author of *Adonis* turned quite naturally toward the burlesque, Scarron's strong medicine, but a burlesque purified of its mechanical aspects and harsh violence, a gallant and smiling burlesque, that of *Contes*. In the new context of the Colbertist "glory machine," that gaiety and irony, however elegant it might have been, took on the sense of an antidote to the official conformity of grandeur. Their success with the public made matters worse for the poet. La Fontaine, without having sought it, found himself in the position of an ironist toward the new regime in the minds of the educated public who celebrated him, but he also became the most valiant critic of the daydreams that had accompanied Foucquet's rise.

Fables, which integrates many of the elements of Scarron and the burlesque into the lessons of Terence, Horace, and Lucian, was the most reflective and serene response to the catastrophe of 1661. It was not only addressed to the public; it was aimed—under the banner of the Dauphin's education—at the king himself. It interpreted the general disillusionment and sought to warn the king of his own blindness. Unlike *Contes*, it was not simply a remedy to private melancholia; it sought to dissipate the kingdom's melancholia; it competed with the courtly spectacle.

The triumph of absolutism in 1661 had the effect, paradoxical in appearance, of spurring on the function of counterweight and remedy that French literature had learned to exercise under Richelieu. La Fontaine found himself on the side of literary vigilance and found in himself the "fire" necessary to exercise it with formidable ingenuity and ingenuousness. Since 1636 one poet more than any other had been the depositary of that literary vigilance: Pierre Corneille.

THEATER, THE CRITIQUE OF REASON OF STATE

In that domain, it might seem strange to link Corneille and La Fontaine, Sophocles and Anacreon. But in 1671, the seventeenth-century Sophocles proved himself capable of collaborating with Molière on the libretto for *Psyché*, inspired by La Fontaine's novel, and of introducing a lyricism of love worthy of the Champagne-born Anacréon into that tragicomedy ballet. The confessions Corneille attributes to Psyche are altogether equal to the final duet of *Les amours de Psyché et de Cupidon*:

A peine je vous vois, que mes frayeurs cessées
Laissent évanouir l'image du trépas,
Et que je sens couler dans mes veines glacées
Un je ne sais quel feu que je ne connais pas.
J'ai senti de l'estime, et de la complaisance,
    De l'amitié, de la reconnaissance,
De la compassion les chagrins innocents
    M'en ont fait sentir la puissance,
Mais je n'ai point encor senti ce que je sens.
Je ne sais ce que c'est, mais je sais qu'il me charme,
    Que je n'en conçois point d'alarme;
Plus j'ai les yeux sur vous, plus je m'en sens charmer:
Tout ce que j'ai senti n'agissait point de même,
    Et je dirais que je vous aime,
Seigneur, si je savais ce que c'est que d'aimer.
Ne les détournez point, ces yeux qui m'empoisonnent,
Ces yeux tendres, ces yeux perçants, mais amoureux,

Qui semblent partager le trouble qu'ils me donnent.
Hélas! Plus ils sont dangereux,
Plus je me plais à m'attacher sur eux.
                    (act 3, scene 3, ll. 1050–69)

Hardly have I seen you when my fears abated
Let the image of death fade away,
And I feel running through my frozen veins
Some sort of fire I do not know.
I have felt respect and kindness,
     Friendship and gratitude,
Compassion's innocent sorrows
     Have let me feel their power,
But I have never felt what I now feel.
I do not know what it is, but I know I am charmed,
     That the feeling does not cause alarm;
The more my eyes gaze upon you, the more charm I feel:
Everything I have felt did not affect me this way,
     And I would say I love you,
My lord, if I knew what loving meant.
Do not turn away your eyes that poison me,
Those tender eyes, those piercing eyes of love,
Which seem to share the trouble they give me.
     Alas! The more dangerous they are,
     The happier I am to hold to them.

La Fontaine, a year before the publication of his most risqué tales inspired by Pietro Aretino, was capable of offering his devout poem *La captivité de saint Malc* as an homage to Port-Royal; in the same way, a year before composing Psyché's confession, worthy of the best Marivaux, Corneille was able to publish his sumptuous translation of *The Office of the Holy Virgin* into French verse, dedicated to the poor cuckolded and devout Queen Marie-Thérèse and accompanied by very necessary prayers for the king.

Both poets were drawing from the diverse resources of their own tradition to hold back the kingdom—and first of all the king—on its path toward the imperious military state: hagiography, liturgical poetry and fables, poetic sanctity and poetic humanity were able to remind by turns that invasive and leveling power of the right to a free inner life and to transcendence. Corneille and La Fontaine had a friend and admirer in common, an exile in England: Saint-Evremond. Both had close ties to the great ancient families of the kingdom who had conspired in their own way for the "freedom of moderns" and had courageously resisted Richelieu. Both had been enthusiasts of the *surintendant* Foucquet. Both, in very different tones, were interpreters of the gallant romanticism that took Louis XIV twenty years of reign to suppress. Both, in different generations, were born to French poetry by reading *L'Astrée*.

In 1637 the *Le Cid* controversy seems to have dealt solely with questions of poetics: it revealed indirectly, but publicly, the incompatibility between Cornellian poetry and politics and the eloquence of reason of state backed by Richelieu. At first (in 1635), Corneille agreed to collaborate with four other authors (Rotrou, L'Estoile, Colletet, and Boisrobert) in a team for composing dramas, led by the cardinal and designed to supply the theater hall in his Parisian palace. Corneille fairly quickly shirked that collective labor, which had obliterated his autonomy as an author. With the success of *Le Cid*, followed by his resistance to the attacks against the tragicomedy, attacks secretly encouraged by Richelieu, he assumed the stature of a secular director of conscience, whose poetic authority dared stand up to the political authority of the all-powerful minister.

In his first comedies and in *Le Cid*, he presented onstage the profundity and moral potential of the feeling of love, which outstrips the obligations due fathers and spouses, and the freedom of individuals, which itself cannot be reduced to the obligations due the state. In *Le Cid* he showed that the vocation of the true modern and Christian king was precisely to understand and reconcile the order of law with that of love and freedom: that is what made the king a king rather than a tyrant who, like the gods and pagan emperors, crushed the natural and spiritual nobility within the heart under his caprice erected into law, giving free rein to the wickedness lurking within enslaved souls.

It was that "nonalignment" that Richelieu had suspected in *Le Cid*, and for which he did not forgive its author, so wildly appreciated by the public. Far from giving in, the poet, educated by his own experience, further extended his public meditation on freedom and monarchy in an original dramatic language whose syntax he had made more muscular, even as he borrowed his symbolic vocabulary from ancient history. Between 1641 and 1651 this coded language, well protected from censorship but well understood by the public, allowed him to interpret out loud and onstage the crisis of the absolutist state and the early symptoms of the Fronde. In reality, the Bourgogne mansion and the Théâtre du Marais, where Corneille's plays were performed, became true academies of political and moral science in "mysterious language," whose public meetings bore the names of his tragedies: *Horace, Cinna, Polyeucte, Rodogune, Nicomède*.

In *Rodogune* (1644–45), his favorite tragedy, Corneille put on stage a Cleopatra who, symbolically, had all Richelieu's implacable traits (the cardinal had died two years earlier): the usurping queen does not hesitate to sacrifice the most sacred feelings, and even a mother's love for her sons, to her thirst for absolute power: "Away from my heart, Nature!" The blueprint for dictatorship and terror conceived by that intelligent Eastern Fury fails only because of a miracle, thanks to the bonds of solidarity, friendship, and love formed between her two sons and her prisoner, Rodogune, with whom both young men are in love. Cleopatra seeks skillfully, but in vain, to break that bond of the heart: at the end of the nightmare, the loyalty that Antiochus and Seleucus never abandon between themselves and the sacrifice that Seleucus imposes on himself give birth to the hope for a monarchy that has returned to its vocation and is finally exercised with humanity. In *Rodogune* the language of deception and servitude, despite violence and trickery, runs aground on the rock of the inviolable words exchanged between friends, whose kinship with his own art the tragic poet reveals and celebrates. In 1658 Nicolas Foucquet, on Pellisson's good advice, asked Corneille (who had retired in 1651) to return to the theater to take on, in his own language, the subject of Sophocles' *Oedipus*. The tragedy was performed in 1659 at the Hôtel de Bourgogne theater and was a great success. Formulated in the mysterious language of the classical fable, it may have been the most profound and complete analysis of what the *surintendant*'s supporters expected from him on the eve of a new reign. As Corneille depicts him, Oedipus is a tyrant: "I am king, I can do anything." He sees others only as the passive political instruments of his intrigues and power: "Politics everywhere," says his daughter-in-law Dirce, regarding with contempt a reign in which the spiritual is suffocating under the temporal. Corneille's Oedipus symbolizes the absolutist program of Richelieu's heirs, which the tragic poet shows to be an archaic resurgence of pagan religious fatality and the ancient commonwealth in the midst of the Christian era.

The original couple Dirce and Theseus, whom Corneille introduces into the classical myth, is a modern couple whose private freedom and mutual love is finally victorious over the "infernal machine" imposed on Thebes by the boundless appetite for power that devours Oedipus. The pre-Christian Dirce can say of the earthly tyrant:

Le Roi, tout roi qu'il est, Seigneur, n'est pas mon maître.
                    (act 1, scene 1, l. 105)

The king, for all the king he is, Lord, is not my master.

Corneille has Theseus, Dirce's "lover," utter the most stirring protest against any moral determinism which could legitimize tyranny, ancient and modern. Theological free will is inseparable from political freedom:

L'âme est donc toute esclave: une loi souveraine
Vers le bien, ou le mal, incessamment l'entraîne,
Et nous ne recevons ni crainte ni désir
De cette liberté qui n'a rien à choisir,
Attachés sans relâche à cet ordre sublime,
Vertueux sans mérite, et vicieux sans crime.
                    (act 3, scene 5, ll. 1153–58)

The soul, then, is completely a slave: a sovereign law
Unceasingly leads it toward good or ill,
And we have neither fear nor desire
From that freedom, which has nothing to choose,
Unrelentingly attached to that sublime order,
Virtuous without merit, and depraved without fault.

That iron order, imposed on the supposedly servile human will by the whim of the gods, and on men's political liberty by the oppression of tyrants, is disrupted by the freedom to love and choice of love that unite Dirce and Theseus against Oedipus. That freedom and choice of the heart are two vocations proper and natural to man, which every truly legitimate king, as the vicar of a God of love, owes it to himself to recognize in himself and to deal with it in his art of governance. Never before had gallant romanticism found a poetic and political expression so vigorous as in that Cornellian revision of the Greek myth of Oedipus.

After 1661 Corneille, along with his younger brother Thomas, himself a successful playwright, remained independent literary and moral authorities on the Parisian stage. With a very sure sense for strategy, Pierre Corneille gave the king the "sublime" tributes due him, but, through theater, publications, and journalism (Donneau de Visé, the director of Le Mercure Galant, was entirely won over), he maintained a firm grasp on the public. He headed a veritable "faction" in the republic of letters and Parisian high society.

His reflection, in the language of drama, on the fate of the monarchy became increasingly marked by a haughty disgust in the style of Tacitus. The public did not always follow him on that treacherous path. And his younger brother (and pupil) did not hide the fact that he had to borrow from Racine, the rival author of tragedy acclaimed by the court. In his last tragedy, *Suréna, général des Parthes*, performed in 1675 and quickly removed from the bill, the elderly Corneille, who still had ten years left to live, wrote his poetic last will and testament and displayed his heart of hearts in plain view. Far from being able to make a tyranny evolve toward liberal monarchy, as Antiochus and Seleucus or Dirce and Theseus had succeeded in doing, the two heroes of *Suréna* are prisoners condemned to die by the infernal machine of political Machiavellianism. Their freedom, their mutual love, are pledged to secrecy and private interiority, but even the inviolable restraint they impose on themselves is a mortal offense for the royal jailer who finds them out: he has Suréna murdered and leads Eurydice to die of despair. In itself, the name of the heroine of that tragedy and testament suggests that, with the death of freedom and the triumph of unbridled power in political society, poetry is condemned to hell.

In that tragedy, Corneille did not hesitate to suggest the two escape routes offered "individuals" crushed externally by the iron order of the absolute state: quietist mysticism (Suréna borrows his motto from Teresa of Ávila: "Love always, suffer always, die always" [act 1, scene 3, l. 165]) and Epicurean *voluptas* (the hero declares to Eurydice, from whom he is about to be forever separated: "A single moment of happiness desired / Is better than such a cold and vain eternity").

The Cast of Characters on Olympus: Minerva, Jupiter/Mars, and Venus

Fables no more dreamed of converting the king's heavily armored "ego," reflected in the monumental mirror of the absolute state, than did La Rochefoucauld's *Maximes*, published anonymously in 1664, or Pascal's *Pensées*, published in 1671 by Port-Royal. And yet, the first collection embraced the monarchy, absent the king: it was dedicated to the Dauphin, heir to the throne. The second collection of *Fables*, published in 1678, opens with a splendid dedicatory epistle in verse addressed to the royal mistress, Françoise-Athénaïs de Rochechouart-Mortemart, who was then at the zenith of her official liaison with the king. Already in 1675 the "chamber of the sublime" offered the duc du Maine, the morganatic "Dauphin of France," had elevated La Fontaine among the elect of the royal Venus's personal Parnassus.[4] Mme de Montespan, closely backed by her brother the comte de Vivonne and her sister Mme de Thianges, both well-educated people, and by her other sister, the very beautiful and very learned abbess of Fontevrault, had her own sponsored writers and artists, quite distinct from those of her lover the king, to compensate for her inability to exert the slightest influence over affairs of state.

As a mirror of human blindness, *Fables*, like the Indian *Panchatantra* and the Iranian *Kalilah and Dimnah,* claimed to be "advice for the conduct of kings." It was a royal poem, even though the king wanted nothing to do with it. The author of *Fables* dedicated the first collection to the Dauphin. He dedicated the second collection to the royal mistress. The comte de Vivonne, Mme de Montespan's brother, was very close to Boileau and, according to Voltaire—well informed by the abbé d'Olivet—lived with Molière "like Lelius with Terence." The Mortemart coterie was, by family tradition, well trained in letters and friendly with writers.[5] Through the Mortemarts the king again became accessible, via the sole chink in his armor: pleasure. The dedication of the second collection to Mme de Montespan brought a new version, befitting the circumstances, of the dedication of *Adonis* to Nicolas Foucquet, or even better, of "Hymne à la Volupté" in *Les amours de Psyché,* into the vicinity of the throne. The poet portrayed the king's mistress as Venus:

> Tout auteur qui voudra vivre encore après lui
>   Doit s'acquérir votre suffrage.
> C'est de vous que mes vers attendent tout leur prix.
>   Il n'est beauté dans nos écrits
> Dont vous ne connaissiez jusques aux moindres traces.
> Eh! qui connaît que vous les beautés et les grâces?
> Paroles et regards, tout est charme dans vous.
>   (A *Madame de Montespan*, ll. 17–23)

> Every author who wants to live on after his death
>   Must acquire your approval.
> It is you who will give my verses all their value.
>   There is no beauty in our writings
> Of which you do not know even the slightest trace.
> Oh! Who but you knows beauty and grace?
> Words and glances, all is charm in you.

Spontaneous affinities and unspoken sympathies led Françoise de Rochechouart-Mortemart to understand the author of *Contes* and *Fables* at a glance and to take him under her protection, despite the hostile indifference of her royal lover ("Under your auspices alone these lines / Will be judged regardless of envy"). La Fontaine, a gentleman of the house of Orléans, friend to the duc de La Rochefoucauld and the duc de Guise, appreciated by the entire La Tour d'Auvergne family, especially by the maréchal de Turenne, who, like him, knew his Marot by heart, exerted a peculiar attraction on the heirs to the most ancient lineages of the kingdom. The Rochechouart-Mortemarts were foremost among them, and recognized only the La Rochefoucaulds as their French equals with respect to genealogy and illustriousness. Mme de Montespan did not forego treating her Bourbon lover as a member of the provincial nobility of recent eminence. And when the king asked her brother, the comte de Vivonne, "But what is the point of reading?" the latter was not afraid to respond: "Reading does to the mind what your partridges do to my cheeks."[6] The comte de Vivonne had a practiced flair for recognizing the best products that, like himself, came from the most ancient French soil, poets as well as wines and partridges.

La Fontaine found himself in good company among these rare experts in freedom, leisure, and pleasure, who, moreover, had a familial oral tradition of language as old and delightful as that of Champagne peasants. The Mortemarts were famous for their "wit," which Saint-Simon adored. Voltaire wrote that it was "a curious turn of conversation combined with banter, naïveté, and refinement."[7] That formulation suits *Fables* and *Contes* to an equal degree: Vivonne, the marquise, and their sisters did not fail to stand among the readers who immediately assured the success of this poetry rooted as their own names and language, in a deep genealogy of a very ancient tradition.

In La Fontaine's case, then, the appetite for the great names of France was not at all the intellectual snobbery that impelled Descartes in Holland to cultivate the illustrious but listless friendship of Princess Elisabeth, daughter of the Palatin elector, or, in Stockholm, to join the academy of Queen Christina of Sweden, for whom the philosopher composed a ballet libretto before he caught a bad chill and died. Something more personal, a natural, quasi-Nervalian solidarity, linked the poet of Old France to these great lords and ladies who, far from being inclined to a dry and nasty intellectual arrogance like Proust's duchesse de Guermantes, experienced their well-born condition like the poet, that is, "naively."

The elder Rochechouart-Mortemart branch was not involved in the Fronde, and the comte de Vivonne, who became maréchal-duc de Mortemart, adapted very gallantly to the condition of political capon to which he was reduced in Louis XIV's court. Nevertheless, this adventurous and cultured soldier was a free mind, like his sisters. The commandeur de Jars, one of the good heroes of the resistance to Richelieu, jailed between 1633 and 1639, and who stood up under torture to his tormentor Laffemas, was a close relative of theirs. The subterranean current of the Fronde and loyalty to Foucquet, which runs beneath the smiling surface of *Fables*, would not have scared away the Mortemarts. In 1676, at the waters of Bourbon, Mme de Montespan took it upon herself to grant an audience to the plague-stricken wife of the *surintendant*. Touched by this elegant gesture, Mme de Sévigné wrote to her daughter: "Madame Foucquet [went to see her], and Mme de Montespan received her very honorably; she listened to her sympathetically and with a look of admirable compassion. God prompted Mme Foucquet to say the best things imaginable."[8] The art of painting precisely the inner truth of beings without commentary was common to Mme de Sévigné and La Fontaine.

Even as topflight courtiers, the Mortemarts, like the poet himself, knew full well that the absolute monarchy under Louis XIV, despite the king's ministers and administrations, was beholden to people of their quality for remaining a French-style monarchy in spite of everything, radiating if not political moderation and the riches of the heart, then at least the spark of wit and the leisure arts.

After the Revolution, Napoleon was able to reconstitute and perfect the absolutist state machinery, and was even able to create by statute the etiquette of an ancien régime court. But, in his effort to hark back to the Louvre and Versailles, he was lacking the living fables that thrived around Louis XIV like a still-medieval heraldic bestiary peopled with superb, strange, and curious animals, rich in luxury and often in folly, with which the oldest and largest aristocracy of Europe was teeming for the last time. If there had been only Colbert, Le Tellier, Lionne, and Louvois in Louis XIV's entourage, his reign would have left the unappealing impression of the regime of Robespierre or Fouché. Paradoxically, the first modern head of state owed his legend to the still-fabulous court assembled around him. Saint-Simon's *Mémoires*, which was unkind to Louis XIV, would have been as devastating as Tacitus without the superb humanity the memoirist angrily described rearing up and champing at the king's bit.

Among these heraldic hircocervuses and unicorns that competed to entertain the bureaucrat king and to adorn his court, the marquise de Montespan, like the Amazons of the Fronde, was certainly a masterpiece of nature and history, whose value was sensed by La Fontaine, a poet and connoisseur.

As a marginal patron of the arts and letters (the only power allowed to her by her royal lover), the marquise played the role of Venus, queen of Cythera. She had the goddess's great and proud beauty: "Her height was imposing and majestic, her bearing full of the dignity that is accompanied by grace. Her complexion, her eyes, the shape of her face, her whole person incarnated the works we owe to the imagination and the studies of painters and poets."[9] She also had the exacting and refined tastes of Venus. So long as she was in favor, the king, whose education was to be completely redone, wanted to "appear" before her and show himself equal to a goddess not satisfied with facile and gaudy display.

The tribute paid her by La Fontaine in 1678 was thus justified, even in political terms: the magnificence and elegance of the Montespan years (1668–78) somewhat attenuated or veiled in true splendor Louis the Great's appetites for sex, war, and power. The expenses the king incurred for his difficult mistress meant that much less in taxes spent for the horrors of war, of which the king was so fond.

There is a further argument in favor of Venus and her personal taste. The château of Clagny, between Versailles and Saint-Germain, the first of Jules Hardouin-Mansart's masterpieces, which the king had built for her according to her directives between 1675 and 1685, was a temple of Cnidus as imagined in the eighteenth century.[10] A gallery of paintings depicted the story of Aeneas, son of Venus. The marquise laid the foundations for the private "rococo" architecture of the Regency and Louis XV's reign. The comte d'Angiviller, Louis XVI's director of buildings and a great patron of neoclassicism, had Clagny destroyed in 1774, along with the labyrinth of Versailles: a premonitory vandalism, even if practical necessities dictated it.

The royal Venus at the state's summit stood in for the Maecenas Foucquet ought to have been beside Augustus/Louis XIV. Foucquet had had himself depicted as Apollo on the ceilings of Vaux, and La Fontaine, in *Le songe de Vaux*, assigned him the role of the god of Parnassus. In reality, he was never replaced. In proper mythology, the Sun is not Apollo; they are too very distinct deities. The Sun frequents neither Parnassus nor the Muses. He is the Mithraic god of emperors and their soldiers. In *Phèdre* (1677), a ferocious struggle in pagan heaven sets the Sun against Venus, and it is Phaedra who pays the price for that terrible domestic scene between the two vindictive and "cruel" deities. Apollo appears nowhere in Racine's tragedy, except perhaps under the mortal guise of Hippolytus, crushed to death by his horses, which Neptune had spooked. The Racinian Parnassus was left unprotected from the lightning bolts of Olympus.

Venus/Montespan (Racine's future "haughty Vashti") may well have occupied the niche left empty by Apollo, but she did not reign on Parnassus: she herself was merely one of the parts played on Olympus. In spite of everything, it is understandable how La Fontaine could have been attracted to that substitute. He would have much preferred an alliance between Venus and Apollo. But he had no choice: since 1661, on the royal Olympus, Colbert had played the role of cold Minerva; the king proved by turns to be a thundering Father Jupiter and a Mars, lover of Venus, conqueror of Europe. The marquise de Montespan, by splendidly performing the role of Venus beginning in 1668, by giving her a voluptuous spark that would be recaptured under Louis XV, and in the same part, by Mme de Pompadour, at least had the merit of uniting her *mundus muliebris*, favorable to elegance and wit, with the reason, secrecy, and bombastic pomp of the absolute state.

Writers, artists, and musicians flocked to that goddess of pleasure and taste, even though she did not appeal to their hearts. With her, state libertinage replaced gallant romanticism at court.

THE MAP OF THE COURT

That "Dumézilian" tripartition of Minerva, Jupiter/Mars, and Venus (gradually replaced, after 1678, by the trinity of the devout Maintenon/Esther, Bossuet/Mardocai, and the king/Ahasuerus) was set in place in the days following the 1661 coup d'état.

In 1663, in an essay in "mysterious language" entitled *La carte de la cour* (The map of the court), Gabriel Guéret, a remarkable observer of political and literary Paris, presented allegorically this administrative compartmentalization of the new Olympus.

Allegory, that hide-and-seek game of discourse that ancien régime France had always practiced with a kind of delight, and more than ever in the Foucquet years, also has the dangerous property of being able to turn easily from praise to irony.[11] Used with tact, it can become a writing system with a double meaning, an official meaning on the front side and a secret, mocking sense on the reverse. Beginning in 1663, Guéret wrote under the shelter of this code, which Madeleine de Scudéry, for her part, was more likely to use to praise without flattery than to conceal her reservations. Hence the landscape whose map Guéret, a superior journalist, wanted to draw was very different from that which, four years earlier, Mme de Scudéry had joyfully described in *Clélie*. In the intervening years the secondary character Alcandre/Louis XIV had acquired the status of a sun god, and an earthquake had made a steep Olympus rise up beneath him and dominate Paris.

Guéret seized the moment to dedicate his *Carte de la cour* to Mme Colbert, whom he described in dithyrambic language as a sublime Minerva, which dispensed him of the need to name her inaccessible husband, Jean-Baptiste, the true Minerva of the state.

He suggested very well, with no great risk of being contradicted, that a jealous secret now kept every eye and every indiscreet word away from the state apparatus. He evoked this Kafkaesque seventeenth-century castle under the name *Harbor of Secrecy*, but postponed the veiled description of it until the end of his journey. In the offices and council rooms of the "harbor," forbidden to women (Esther/Maintenon had access to it only a quarter century later, to her everlasting glory), work proceeded "on the sly," under the protection of "the thick of night." At the entry to the roadstead stood a "reef of trust." It had to be avoided at all costs, since, if you fall into that trap of loyalty, "you can never get out again, any more than the unfortunate Oronte [Foucquet], whose dreary wreck one still sees floating in that place."

It is only from this "harbor," very difficult to reach on the dark side of Olympus, that one can hope to see "the sun that produces all our bright days, this great monarch to whom our fields owe the fertility they enjoy."

The cold insolence these apparently slavish and cunning pages exude is stupefying today. Guéret perfidiously sets up a coded language, whose tradition he inherits from the republic of letters, in opposition to the new secrecy of the state and its young idol.

The reality of the state and the deliberations of its ministers are thus circumscribed within the *Harbor of Secrecy*, in conference with the Sun. In contrast, the society of vanity and of the spectacle, the court in the narrow sense, spreads out across the visible and better-lit slopes of Olympus to amuse gawkers. Guéret spends his time describing, not without satirical ulterior motives, the various theaters open to full view but only from afar. Everything there is shining and enchanting. But everything is also mask, disguise, dissimulation, a comedy of self-interests, devious bodies of knowledge taught by Benserade, Cotin, and other court abbots specializing in the sophistry of display and pomp.

Guéret's allegorical journalism lingers with the greatest satisfaction on *The Isle of Pleasures*, led by Licidas (Monsieur, the king's brother) at the time, with the cooperation of his wife, the "divine Madonte" (Henrietta of England). On that island is found the Cavern of Passing Fancies, Venus's abode, and the Palace of Delights (Saint-Cloud), whose portico is adorned with a statue of the goddess. In these places everything is made for voluptuous relaxation. Among the regulars, next to the comte de Vivonne, are the "gallant Eraste," Bussy-Rabutin, who had not yet been sent away to the provinces for his indiscreet *Histoire amoureuse des Gaules* (1665), and "the clever Clarice" (Mlle de La Vallière), one of the most beautiful ornaments of the island. In 1668 Mme de Montespan, in the company of her brother and sisters, would authoritatively take over for Monsieur and Madame in that ready-made loge of the court, which specialized in the king's relaxation and pleasures. The "City of Comedy" and the "City of Ballets" are obviously dependencies of that *Isle of Pleasures*.

Contrasted to *The Isle of Pleasures* is *The Promontory of Employment*, by which we must understand military employment. This is the ministry of war, like the ministry of pleasures a spectacular organ of the bureaucratic and secret executive who works and makes his decisions offstage in the darkness. Guéret writes: "There one observes the Temple of Courage, dedicated to the god Mars. Belles lettres are, as it were, muffled under the heavy equipment of undercoats and corselets, and under a great store of weapons of several different kinds." Among the statues that decorate the temple is that of the "great Alcandre," the king, "who in his earliest days gave marks of the most consummate valor, and who every day proves the nobility of his soul through the excellence of his actions."

To be sure, Olympus and its various faces hold nothing reassuring for "Letters," strangers to Mars, treated as slaves in Minerva's home and as prostitutes on *The Isle of Pleasures*. Parnassus appears nowhere on the horizon, and this silence in itself says a great deal about the "back thought" of the young author of *La carte de la cour*.

Five years later, in 1668–69, the same Guéret wrote, but this time refrained from publishing (it would not be published until 1751), a dialogue entitled *La promenade de Saint-Cloud* (The stroll through Saint-Cloud), a weak but interesting prelude to the stroll through Versailles in *Les amours de Psyché*.[12] No allegories this time. It is a "map of Parnassus," in a direct style and for the internal use of the republic of letters. As Guéret describes it, that republic has no "central committee"; it is divided, but divided on the tactic to follow with respect to the new Olympus: Chapelain wants to rally behind it, the ambitious Boileau leads a battle for more dignity, and the most secret souls, such as Chapelle, practice "infiltration" from within. But all the writers, even Chapelain himself if one is to believe Guéret, have in view the higher interests of the republic of letters, in an entirely new situation where it had to increase its caution and wiles.

The setting for the dialogue is Saint-Cloud, on Monsieur's *Isle of Pleasures*. But what a difference from the picture given of it in *La carte de la cour!* In the absence of their masters, the deserted gardens have undoubtedly become an agreeable place for the group of writers who come to converse there, but above all, they have become a safe place. Guéret writes: "Here one has freedom of thought, one considers things in their full purity and their natural simplicity: nothing conceals the knowledge of them."

Among those in the know, one can evoke out loud and outdoors Boileau's determined battle to dethrone through ridicule the old prince of letters, Chapelain, whom the "approval of the court" has made master of "His Majesty's liberalities." There are comments on his satirical digs against Boyer, Boursault, and Quinault, the poetic dandies of the court. It is judged unfair that Boileau extends his criticism to the true masters of the previous generation, Voiture and Sarasin, on the pretext that these young mediocrities laid claim to them. But it is also discerned that he has his reasons. He wants to rule over belles lettres as the king rules over the kingdom. Guéret has one of his interlocutors say: "Do not be surprised, Despréaux belongs to a certain faction, apart from which, he is persuaded, there is no merit in France. He believes that all the glory of belles lettres belongs to it."

Guéret analyzes the satirical poet's strategy of reconstructing a Parnassus around himself: it includes the alliance with Molière. It is out of consideration for Molière that, in his satires, Boileau spares Chapelle, whom he fears and hates, since the latter "worked on all the plays" of the comic author, the king's favorite. That collaboration between the erudite libertine, whose sympathies for the Fronde had been keen, and the official playwright of Louis XIV and Monsieur was confirmed later and elsewhere by François de Callières: "It is to Chapelle . . . that one owes a great portion of the finest things in the comedies of Molière, who consulted him in everything he did, and with complete deference for the soundness and delicacy of his taste."[13]

Far from being shocked by the alliance between Molière and Chapelle, Guéret was impressed. In fact, the infernal game directed by Molière, indulging the king's and the court's taste for jokes and taking advantage of it to pass on to the audience the message of the most worldly-wise and anti-authoritarian libertines of the years 1640–60, was enough to amaze those in the know. Guéret admired the strategic virtuosity with which

Molière was able to transform the archbishop of Paris's mandate against *Tartuffe* in 1667 into a victory for his comedy, even though the sources of that comedy, according to him, were in Aretino.

Guéret's predilection was nevertheless for Chapelle, who refrained from publishing anything, and whose silence could not be interpreted, except perhaps indirectly through his contribution to Molière's masterpieces. The journalist's respect also went out to the abbé de Saint-Réal (who would soon become secretary to the wandering duchesse Hortense Mazarin; always at her side, he would join Saint-Evremond in England).[14] In 1668 the skeptical Saint-Réal had as yet published nothing, but that was not what mattered in the republic of letters. Through his political knowledge and wit, he exerted a great influence on Racine and Despréaux, who were publishing.

Guéret made the rounds of Parisian literary circles, which communicated with one another; he promoted the invisible literary authorities; he revealed tricks of the trade (especially the persistent subterranean prestige of burlesque poetics, repudiated in public, but silently adopted by Molière and La Fontaine).

La promenade de Saint-Cloud, an extraordinary witness, thus casts a bright light on a Parisian Parnassus that, in the shadows, was obliged to exercise extreme caution, and that manifested itself onstage or in bookstores only with great circumspection; but it was not at all intimidated by Louis the Great's Olympus. It had the long memory of classical literature in its favor and, above all, the experience of the battles waged by the previous generation (Voiture, Sarasin, Balzac, Corneille), often cited by Guéret, who were hardened to the various censors and had learned to engage in a battle of wits with the court. Guéret does not mention La Fontaine, except to praise his *Contes* in passing. But the critical detachment he demonstrates toward the poets of *The Isle of Pleasures* (with the exception of Molière) and toward the court in general gives some feeble idea of the ironical detachment of which the author of *Fables* was capable.

FRIENDSHIP IN THE LABYRINTH OF THE WORLD

Even though, in 1671, La Fontaine was represented in the "chamber of the sublime" as a last-minute guest, even though, in 1678, he placed his second collection of *Fables* under the invocation of the royal Venus, the king's *Isle of Pleasures* was certainly not his ordinary abode. The second collection (which appeared in two installments, in 1678 and 1679), much more than the first, was animated by a secretly vengeful comic power against the court of the lion king. In his little pocket theater, the Socrates of fables also became the Aristophanes of absolute monarchy.

In the first collection the poet, displaying extreme caution, confined himself to showing a human comedy in the style of Terence, its delights and its terrors, the natural play of passion and character, its living truth. That comedy was sufficient to contradict the enthusiasm for command and the spectacular affectations in which the new reign was wrapping itself. In the conclusion to book 1, however, and with a biblical authority, "The Oak and the Reed" (a very Pascalian "thinking reed") marked the poet's superiority, the flexible but faithful resistance of his language, compared to the swaggering but vain material force of earthly powers. Nor should the charm of the melody and the vivacity of the narrative dissimulate with what force, beginning in book 1 with "The Wolf and the Dog" (5) and "The Town Rat and the Country Rat" (9), freedom, which cannot be bought off or corrupted, and without which there is no true joy, lies at the foundation of any honorable art and life. There was also no sparing use of the art of indulging institutional powers.

But, from the beginning of the second collection, through a violent contrast with the dedicatory hymn to Athénaïs/Venus, the fable "The Animals Sick of the Plague" is animated by a virulent strain of humor in the style of Juvenal or Saint-Simon, contained but not restrained by the art of the theatrical narrative and the grace of the irregular meter. A new style has appeared: the satirical force becomes phenomenally concentrated, while the powers of tenderness and lyricism, as if to release that dark energy, themselves achieve new heights. The limits of the comedy/fable, already tested in the first six books, are now exceeded at every turn. In the pocket theater, tragedy, the epic, the pastoral poem, the lyric genres, the gravity of the Psalms and the Book of Wisdom, in counterpoint to the virtuoso celebrations Lully provided on the great court stage for Mme de Montespan, argue in favor of the truth of the heart and deploy their implacable epigrammatic irony against its tormentors.

In 1671 Mme de Sévigné criticized La Fontaine for not knowing how to be satisfied with the "talent he has for storytelling." On 20 July 1679 she, who had once called the Fables in the first collection "pretty," declared those of the second "divine." "No one," she added on 2 August, "knows or feels his merit better than I do."[15] One would like to bring to light that silent reading of the heart.

In the background of "The Animals Sick of the Plague," Mme de Sévigné could make out ("since it must be called by its name") the landscape of the plague of Thebes, as it had been described in *Oedipe* by Corneille, whose merit she also "felt" like no one else. In his tragedy, to introduce the redemptive principle that would free Thebes from the plague, that is, from Oedipus's tyranny, Corneille summons forth a pair of lovers, Dirce and Theseus. Mme de Sévigné knew by heart Dirce's lines in act 1, scene 1, which make Oedipus, and the plague he is spreading, the obstacle to their union (ll. 113–14).

> Pourra-t-il trouver bon qu'on parle d'hyménée
> Au milieu d'une ville à périr condamnée,
> Où le courroux du Ciel, changeant l'air en poison,
> Donne lieu de trembler pour toute sa maison?

> Can he find it wise to speak of marriage
> In the midst of a city condemned to perish,
> Where the wrath of heaven, changing the air into poison,
> Gives reason to tremble to all his house?

La Fontaine finds no better mirror for the horrors of the plague than the fear that separates even lovers and comes between natural affinities of the heart:

> Les tourterelles se fuyaient:
> Plus d'amour, partant plus de joie.
> (7.1, ll. 13–14)

> The turtledoves were fleeing:
> No more love, therefore no more joy.

Corneille's Oedipus, gradually discovering the entire scope of his crimes, comes face-to-face with his own truth: he blinds himself to efface his long egotistical blindness, and exiles himself to bring the plague to an end, leaving room in Thebes for Dirce and Theseus:

> Mais si les Dieux m'ont fait la vie abominable,
> Ils m'en font par pitié la sortie honorable,
> Puisqu'enfin leur faveur mêlée à leur courroux
> Me condamne à mourir pour le salut de tous.
> (*Oedipe*, act 5, scene 5, ll. 1833–36)

But if the gods have made my life abominable,
They have out of pity made my exit honorable,
Since finally their favor, combined with their rage,
Condemns me to die so everyone will be saved.

As the romantic illustrator Granville understood very well, the monstrous appearances assumed by the hierarchs of the plagued kingdom in "The Animals Sick of the Plague" prevent them from attaining Oedipus's final return to humanity. The banal "moral" drawn by the storyteller on *courtly judgments* only serves to deflect the pointed meaning of the fable. The true, unexpressed moral is not to be deduced from the unjust fate of the ass, which after all is also part of the small council assembled by the lion king. His ridiculous case is the same as the lamb's in "The Wolf and the Lamb," which, for all the expert in courtly compliments the lamb may be at his age ("Your Majesty, twenty steps below you"), is nevertheless devoured, according to the prevailing law, by a wolf, who has strength and hunger on his side. The hidden meaning of the fable lies elsewhere. It is revealed only in the often word-for-word similarity with Corneille's Sophoclean tragedy. In both poems, the plague, "an evil that spreads terror / An evil that heaven in its furor / Invented to punish earthly crimes," originates in the king's tyranny, whose pathological effects on the commonwealth it makes explicit. La Fontaine's lion king, like Corneille's Oedipus in act 5, knows the truth full well:

Je crois que le ciel a permis
Pour nos péchés cette infortune.
                 (7.1, ll. 16–17)

I believe that heaven allowed
This misfortune for our sins.

But his royal "our" avoids any personal responsibility in advance, and, in designating the plague as a *misfortune*, he fiercely minimizes the epidemic. The council the La Fontainian king has assembled—the fox, the tiger, the bear, and their flatterers—is there precisely to bury that responsibility. The sacrificed ass (the Aesopian Rosencrantz and Guildenstern), which, like the lamb of book 1, has no advantage other than his courtly rhetoric, is not the main subject of the drama. This sacrifice is only there to replace the sacrifice that the self-satisfied lion king, surrounded by slaves and flatterers, is resolved not to impose on himself. The true moral is thus not the final maxim, but rather lies in the king's implacable denial, whose implicit consequence is the indefinite continuation of the plague in the kingdom.

For all that, "The Animals Sick of the Plague" is not a burlesque parody of Corneille's *Oedipe*, any more than *Suréna* is a parody of *Rodogune*. Like *Suréna*, but concentrated in the barb of a brief form, this fable is a political tragedy under a "low and ponderous sky," a modern Flower of Evil that the poet lets us see and smell. For their part, *Oedipe* and *Rodogune* are romantic tragedies: before 1661 faith in a reconciliation between the art of governance and the imperatives of the heart, between action and dream, between the kingdom of poetry and the earthly kingdom, was still possible.

The absolute state, the *fatum* renewed from pagan tyrannies and empires that had crashed down upon the kingdom, kept a tight lid on freedom, happiness, and truth. Would the king, safe at the center of that overpowering state, awaken from the blindness and self-importance that made him a tyrant, contrary to his vocation and his office? Public life has been afflicted with the plague for a long time, perhaps always. La Fontaine's bee knew it, but it also knew how to sting cruelly.

Humanity, joy, and poetry died away. Everything exuded lies, perfidy, cruelty, fear, cold calculation. Where could one rediscover or transport what gave value to life? That was the question La Fontaine asked readers of both sexes from the beginning. He would go seek answers with them. The only real option lay elsewhere, in another order, in interiority, in private life, in affections untouched by the calculation, lies, and terror that emanated from the cold monster.

Mme de Sévigné had long ago reached these conclusions for herself. A fascinated and ironic observer of the court's games (like her friend Mme de La Fayette, the author of memoirs on the court of Henrietta of England), a bereaved witness to the cruelties of war, she made her daughter her reason for existence. The love that impelled her to live and write for Mme de Grignan was her true kingdom, shared only with her daughter and a few intimate friends: a kingdom in the world, but not of the world, and which, for that very reason, increasingly sought its light from Port-Royal. In fact, the marquise was truly capable of *feeling* that terrible fable *better than* anyone, a fable that raised the curtain to the second collection and set out the premises of the drama.

From one book to the next, a "lion cycle" echoes "The Animals Sick of the Plague," skillfully dispersed in a labyrinth opposed to all symmetry, and whose coherence and meaning can be recognized only by those who "feel" with and like the poet, by Mme de Sévigné or La Rochefoucauld: in book 7, "The Lion Holds Audience" (7); in book 8, "The Lion, the Wolf, and the Fox" (3) and "The Funeral of the Lioness" (14); in book 11, "The Lion" (1) and "King Lion, the Monkey, and the Two Asses" (5). None of these fables has the secretly tragic bitterness of the very first fable in the cycle. A loftier irony in relation to the details of court and its fierce vanities now takes precedence over any vehemence, even contained, in the style of Juvenal or Tacitus.

It was as if the poet, and his friends and readers, had other resources, other joys unknown "in that country," which allowed them to look at events in full knowledge of the facts and to deplore them, but also to laugh under their breath about them and to turn away toward the untouched provinces of the soul. The courtly realm, like Corneille's Oedipus in the first acts of his tragedy, might well obey the principle "Politics always, politics everywhere"; but the politics of poetry is not contained within that prison, which, according to Teresa of Ávila, is as foul smelling as hell ("Quel Louvre! un vrai charnier, dont l'odeur se porta / D'abord au nez des gens"; What a Louvre! A true charnel house, whose odor was carried / First to the noses of the people ["The Lion Holds Audience," 7.7, ll. 15–16]).[16]

Fables created another community—entirely private, entirely amicable— the true kingdom, linked by language of an entirely different order than the corrupted and corrupting language of the absolutist court. This circle of readers who saw into the shadows without being seen, who "felt" with and like the poet, shared other curiosities, other preoccupations, other pleasures, unsuspected by the great monarch's "political class" and "entourage":

> Je définis la Cour un pays où les gens,
>   Tristes, gais, prêts à tout, à tout indifférents,
> Sont ce qui plaît au prince, ou, s'ils ne peuvent l'être,
>   Tâchent au moins de le paraître,
>   Peuple caméléon, peuple singe du maître,
>   On dirait qu'un esprit anime mille corps;
> C'est bien là que les gens sont de simples ressorts.
>   (8.14, "The Funeral of the Lioness," ll. 17–23)

> I define the court as a land where folk,
>   Happy, sad, ready for anything, indifferent to it all,
> Are what pleases the prince, or, if they cannot be,
>   Try at least to appear so,

A chameleon people, a people aping the master,
As if one spirit animated a thousand bodies;
It is truly there that people are mere wind-up toys.

These predictable automatons, set to the king's watch, have thus left their humanity behind; in contrast, the internal quest for that humanity is the object (and the recourse) of the author of *Fables* and his friends and readers. The animals of Aesop and Bidpai, even the wild beasts, at least have life and naturalness in their favor. They have more affinities with the human than the mechanisms operated by vanity. The circle of understanding readers created around the poet's revelatory language is seeking a commonwealth, turned *the other way*: it is attentive to the diversity of creatures, to their naturalness, to their living comedy, amusing or disappointing, vain or cruel, which they at least perform naively, provided that the Medusa's gaze of the state does not petrify it.

In the second collection, death is not only the natural limit imposed on human life, which gives it intensity and meaning. Like Proust's M. de Charlus, the Parisian King Lear, wandering alone in a capital under curfew, lamenting over an entire generation of young men cut down in the springtime of their lives, the poet's meditation in "Death and the Dying" (8.1) shifts from the order of nature to that of the kingdom, which now moves from one deadly Great War to the next:

Tu murmures, vieillard; vois ces jeunes mourir,
    Vois-les marcher, vois-les courir
A des morts, il est vrai, glorieuses et belles,
Mais sûres cependant, et quelquefois cruelles.
                    (ll. 55–58)

You murmur, old man; see those young ones die,
    See them march, see them run
To deaths, glorious and fine, to be sure,
But certain nonetheless, and sometimes cruel.

After that sounding of the charge, the final touch is a litotes more troubling than a concealed tear or a stifled sob.

That community of "feeling," where Mme de Sévigné and the duc de La Rochefoucauld appear in the forefront (a fable in the first collection, "The Lion in Love" [4.1], is dedicated to Mme de Sévigne's daughter, and hence indirectly to her, and the second collection contains a discourse that is addressed to La Rochefoucauld [10.14] and a fable dedicated to his niece Mlle de Sillery [9.13]), is attached to the poet who summoned it through a set of bonds of mind and heart alien to the "springs" of the court's automatons or autocrats. These are not ideas, a doctrine, or a replacement program. The poet does not reply to abstraction with abstraction. The court of *Fables*, that "charnel house" of souls, is not a hell opposed to some conventional earthly paradise. "The Mogul's Dream" (11.4) goes so far as to suggest that even in the unbreathable atmosphere of the Louvre, honorable men can be saved from contagion. Whether he was thinking of Simon Arnauld de Pomponne (Foucquet's friend, who became Louis XIV's minister, and was then disgraced) or of his ambassador friends Barrillon and Bonrepaux, who were at ease at court, or whether he had a presentiment of Fénelon, La Fontaine attributed an almost miraculous power to the internal "retreat" of "solitude," meditation, and reading as a counterweight to the determinism of courtly society. Even in the *Harbor of Secrecy*, La Fontaine knew that he could count upon concealed readers and friends.

What unites the friends of *Fables* is above all affinities of taste: the taste for gardens, light, trees, flowers, fruit, but also for books, for true scholars, adventurous dreamers, for lovers, and for intimate conversation in leisure and relaxation. It is also affinities of distaste: distaste for pedants, people who are rushed, vain, or brutal, oafs and bunglers. In the darkness of an iron age, the friends reconstitute within and among themselves a priceless but fragile and fleeting golden age.

The storyteller, impartial in his painting of creatures, now does not hesitate to set aside his reserve and to take his reader friends as witnesses, most often by hints, but sometimes openly as well, against the enemies of "true feelings." His anger against the schoolmaster and his vain and harmful lectures is not feigned. This pedant is at once rushed, vain, brutal, oafish, and a bungler. On his own, along with his little sheeplike apes, he could destroy an entire garden whose art, fostering nature with love, has gradually made a masterpiece ("The Schoolboy, the Pedant, and the Man with a Garden," 9.5). The pedant of the fable, secure in his abstract knowledge, is not even jealous of the master gardener; he is himself the tyrant in miniature, confined within his "ego," exiled from "true feelings" and ignorant of just how exiled he may be, but slyly bent on annihilating everything that his infirmity does not understand and see. The idiotic plunder, which encapsulates so many others, is all the more poignant in that, to a seventeenth-century reader, it is reminiscent of one of the most famous episodes of *Daphnis and Chloe:* the destruction by a jealous man of the marvelous garden, lovingly planted by Daphnis's adoptive father, the slave Lamont, on the eve of the dreaded master's visit.

Fables and its readers, to see and sense things and beings in their true light and color, are linked not only by their tastes and distastes, but by a common vocation, that of imaginative and tender people trained by poetry and novels for the heart's paradise: friendship. Their perfect lucidity with regard to the wickedness in the world is the exact opposite of their capacity to love and to suffer for what they love. In the labyrinth of the second collection, the counterpoint to the lion cycle is the cycle of friends and lovers.

More secret than the first cycle (it is the secrecy and sacredness proper to the poet and to his sister and brother souls, the flip side of the secrecy and terror of the lion and his court), this initiatory cycle takes shape late in book 8. A sort of first ordeal shows a friendship stupidly destroyed side by side with an ardent friendship, as if the two fables were companion pieces. "The Bear and the Garden-Lover" (10) describes the encounter between two hermits separated by everything, except by the weight of loneliness and the secret desire for sympathetic company. The bear kills what he loves in a quasi-maternal excess of protective tenderness toward the sleep of his friend, "the garden-lover." This is the tragedy of friendship in its pure state, all the more heart-wrenching because it explodes suddenly in an Arcadian landscape and an Arcadian light. The following fable, "The Two Friends," repeats the same model: the more sensitive of the two friends, disturbed by a dream, goes to awaken the other in the middle of the night. But this time he confines himself to verifying that his foreboding has deceived him. These are two fables that temper each other: the first burlesque, tender, and dreadful, the second almost a fairy tale, set in the improbably named Monomotapa. But the link between these two similar, yet so different, cases of friendship, one deprived of wit, the other sustained by wit, leads to a brief lyric improvisation:

Qu'un ami véritable est une douce chose.
Il cherche vos besoins au fond de votre coeur;
    Il vous épargne la pudeur
    De le lui découvrir vous-même.
    Un songe, un rien, tout lui fait peur,
    Quand il s'agit de ce qu'il aime.
        ("The Two Friends," 8.11, ll. 26–31)

How sweet a thing is a true friend.
He seeks your needs in your heart of hearts;
  He spares you the shame
  Of revealing it to him yourself.
A dream, a trifle, everything frightens him,
When the one he loves is in question.

These lines sum up the same almost ecstatic state of fusion between hearts defined by Arnauld d'Andilly, which was also the aspiration of Cornellian friends. In *Rodogune* Seleucus invites his twin, Antiochus, to desert both the ambitious mother who persecutes them and the redoubtable woman they both love, and to withdraw from that familial and political hell into the kingdom of their friendship:

> Dérobons-nous, mon frère, à ces âmes cruelles
> Et laissons-les sans nous achever leurs querelles.
> (Corneille, Rodogune,
act 2, scene 5, ll. 1091–92)

Let us escape, my brother, from these cruel souls
And without us let them conclude their quarrels.

The feeling of love, in its native freshness and in its torments, in its *L'Astrée*-like springtime, is not absent from the second collection of *Fables*. In book 8 the eclogue "Thyrsis and Amaranth" (13) offers the reader an idyllic pause, colored with humor, before being exposed to the dark court comedy of "The Funeral of the Lioness." But, in the 1678 *Fables*, friendship is not a naive flower of nature, however moving it may be to experience and admire it, the way nascent desire and the feeling of love can be. La Fontainian friendship presupposes, or portends, the entire completed circle of the cruel human experience. It is born and endures as the tender flip side to a lucid and shared despair. It is the poetry of the difficulties of life, a luxury of the soul whose open possibility within the heart of hearts cannot be imagined by the clumsy or the blind, eternal collaborators in misfortune. "The Two Doves" (9.2)—turtledoves whose sex it is impossible to determine, inasmuch as this fable is both at the center and at the high point of the labyrinth, beyond the realm of purely sexual attraction, beyond the threshold of passion—occupies the opposite pole from "The Animals Sick of the Plague": it is the fable of initiates, in counterpoint to the fable of tormentors.

It should not be surprising that its origin can be found in the French version of *Panchatantra* (the treatise of education for the prince, Persian in origin and written in fables, from the Latin translation of which La Fontaine borrowed a great deal for his second collection). The French sense for Oriental despotism (which Racine was the first to interpret in *Bajazet* [1672] and which in turn invaded *Fables*) also led La Fontaine to seek enlightenment from the wisdom and poetry of India and Persia.[17]

Seventeenth-century gallant romanticism, like its nineteenth-century revival, interpreted, surveyed, and desired the Orient with more intuitive sympathy than eighteenth-century philosophy. The permeation of still-Christian sensibilities with Epicureanism led them to sense the East as a motherland of religion and fable, the land of Epicurus himself, expert in the science of freeing people from pain and the discontent of living in "advanced" political societies. Louis XIV's court was not unfamiliar with Far Eastern exoticism, which the Jesuits had industriously introduced in Catholic Europe. In 1669–70, among the *fabriques* in the gardens of Versailles, the king had erected a Chinese-style "porcelain Trianon"; it was destroyed in 1687 to make way for Jules Hardouin-Mansart's "marble Trianon," the perfect companion piece to Clagny at Versailles.

But Pierre-Daniel Huet's Orient, in his essay *De l'origine des romans* (1671), and especially La Fontaine's version in the second collection of *Fables*, have nothing in common with that decorative exoticism. The great scholar Huet and the poet sensed a wisdom and intimate knowledge in the East, with a knack for getting through the entrenched Oriental despotism; this wisdom was in alliance with the imagination, emotions, and wit, forming a secret path to inner freedom and humanity.

For La Fontaine even Eastern merchants, like those in "The Faithless Depository" (9.1) who fight bitterly amongst themselves, do so with rich parables, whose ingenuity departs from harsh reality by only an eyelash, and then only to better carve out a nook of complicitous and comic détente. Even the powerful Turks know how to impose their advantage on their Greek subjects ("The Pasha and the Merchant," 8.18) through the invention of an apologue that allows them to put their finger on and accept the truth of their mutual situation, which remains moderate provided it is not pointlessly shaken up.

"The Two Adventurers and the Talisman" (10.13) (also borrowed from the *Panchatantra*) is the La Fontaine fable in which the pre-Stendhalian *espagnolisme* of a poet often accused of chilly caution is best revealed: through the fantastic adventures of its hero, it encapsulates "the land of novels" (by which we must understand quest novels) and awards the prize to the boldness of the imagination, which is more cautious than caution because it is more intuitive about the share of mystery and chance hidden within the folds of reality. Like Viriathus in Corneille's *Sertorius*, who cries, "It is wonderful to attempt unheard-of things," nothing is more alien to La Fontaine than the predicted and the predictable, the calculated and the centrally planned. La Fontaine's adventurous East combines the Renaissance of Erasmus's *Adagia* with that of Alciati's *Emblemata*, Poliphile with Pantagruel: the Orient and the Renaissance have an equally keen sense of the goddess Fortune, friend of imaginative people. Under the nose of despots, pedants, and professional evil-doers, the Oriental wisdom of *Fables* founds a submerged world that leaves chance to the freedom of creatures and the wonders of language. Far from clinging to the political disenchantment of the world, the poetry of *Fables* wants to guide men of wit and elevate men of heart to reach a "far-off land."

La Fontaine's two Indian doves appear again in the central fable of the second collection, but only after cruel ordeals to which the more "curious" and the less wise of this pair of friends is exposed. Its perilous journey, which it had to make in order to mature, recapitulates in action the experience that the reader of *Fables* has gone through within the imagination, under the poet's guidance. It has endured stupid human brutality, which is much more damaging than the unintentional assaults of nature; it has survived chaos and mutilation only in order to become fully conscious of the miracle of happiness it had left behind. It is the story of Psyché and Cupidon told again in the language of birds. Friendship's *Harbor of Secrecy* lies at the end point and high point of the journey of *Fables*, at the opposite pole from the court's *Harbor of Secrecy*.

"The Two Doves" continues with a lyric interlude. It picks up on the one that concludes "The Two Friends," an elixir of Cicero's treatise on friendship. The elegy that serves as the conclusion to "The Two Doves" sums up Plato's *Symposium*; its fragrance clings forever to our memories and our language.

> Amants, heureux amants, voulez-vous voyager?
>   Que ce soit aux rives prochaines.
> Soyez-vous l'un à l'autre un monde toujours beau,
>   Toujours divers, toujours nouveau.
> Tenez-vous lieu de tout: comptez pour rien le reste.
>   (9.2., ll. 65–69)

Lovers, happy lovers, do you want to travel?
  Let it be to nearby shores.
Be for each other an ever-beautiful world,
  Always varied, always new.
Be everything for each other; count the rest for naught.

That oracle of Socrates/Orpheus invites the reader to reconstitute the original androgyne. It is an impossible proposition on earth, but it is a star that can guide pilgrims of the heart even if they cannot humanly attain it in a lasting manner. Its distant rays illuminate memory and hope. In the absence of that paradise, the hours of shared love, as ephemeral as they may have been, as cruel as it is to feel them slipping away forever, are ineffable reflections of that distant star. They break the heart, yet they also awaken it and bring back the desire for the impossibility that makes it beat:

Ah! si mon coeur osait encor se renflammer!
Ne sentirai-je plus de charme qui m'arrête?
  Ai-je passé le temps d'aimer?
              (9.2., ll. 81–83)

Oh! If only my heart dared catch fire once more!
Will I never again feel a charm to make me pause?
  Am I past the time for loving?

Gallant romanticism, in this analysis of the inner oscillations of desire and regret, memory and hope, melancholia and its pleasures, anticipates by nearly two centuries Victor Hugo's *Tristesse d'Olympio*.

THE TWO BEES

In his second collection, La Fontaine presents another female figure equal to La Rochefoucauld and not outside and on the margins like the royal Venus: Marguerite Hessein Rambouillet de La Sablière.[18] Mme de Sévigné fondly called her "turtledove Sablière."
Beginning in 1673, when his income and capital from Champagne were exhausted, and when the death of the duchesse d'Orléans liberated

him from his obligations at the Luxembourg Palace, La Fontaine took room and board in Mme de La Sablière's home, in the mansion she was then living in on rue Neuve-des-Petits-Champs. She was a longtime friend: he may have met her on 15 March 1654, her wedding day, at the Huguenot church in Charenton, when she married the poet's former companion from the Academy of the Round Table, Antoine Rambouillet de La Sablière.

Through her father, Gilbert Hessein, she belonged to the same world of bankers as her husband and, through her mother, Marguerite Menjot, to a family from the good Champagne bourgeoisie, who had lived in Paris since the Edict of Nantes: three Huguenots, all very well trained in letters and sciences. Having lost her mother at age nine, Marguerite Hessein found tutors and protectors in the persons of her uncle, Antoine Menjot, like Rabelais a doctor in Montpellier, and her aunt, Anne, wife of the wealthy financier Samuel Gaudon de La Raillière. Antoine Menjot, a scholar in the encyclopedic, sixteenth-century sense, comfortable arguing theology and mathematics with Pascal at Mme de La Sablière's home, gave that very gifted child a higher education, in the modern sense of the expression, which set her apart and above every other Frenchwoman of her time. That fact later attracted the sarcasm of Molière, of whom she was a target in *Les femmes savantes*, and of Boileau, who nevertheless had the charity to wait until after she died before publishing his *Satire X contre les femmes*, in which she is dealt with cruelly.

Nonetheless, thanks to her aunt La Raillière and, above all, her young cousin Madeleine Goudon, given in marriage in 1646 to the comte de Saint-Aignan as a result of her beauty and the enormous fortune of her father, the pretty "college girl," both scientific- and literary-minded, from her childhood moved in the very high society of Paris and the court. She was able to acquire the most elegant manners, language, and tastes at the Hôtel de Clermont the home of the comte and comtesse de Saint-Aignan. Thus she became the joint masterpiece of nature, fortune, the republic of letters, and the court aristocracy. And it was this masterpiece (she was fourteen at the time) whom the younger son of the very wealthy Nicolas Rambouillet du Plessis married. This other banker's mansion "outside the walls" on Faubourg Saint-Antoine, and its magnificent gardens dropping down to the Seine, were, until the beginning of the eighteenth century (at which time everything was sold in parcels), one of the legends of Paris.

Antoine Rambouillet de La Sablière was thirty years old at the time of his marriage, which he entered three years after his friend Jean de

La Fontaine's marriage to Marie Héricart, a relative of Jean Racine. Seventeenth-century France impresses us today as a single family with somewhat complicated branches, but which all cling together or touch one another. Before the Revolution of 1789, the revocation of the Edict of Nantes in 1685 brought the ax down on that tree with luxuriant branches.

Antoine Rambouillet, a writer and gallant poet, urged by his father and protected by their coreligionist Valentin Conrart (who awarded the young rhymester the title "Great French Madrigalist"), pursued his education by taking a trip to Rome in 1647.[19] Guided by André Félibien, secretary of the French embassy and a good friend of Poussin's, and despite his preference for passing fancies, which all the same perfected his Italian, he extended somewhat the superficial knowledge of the arts he had acquired beside his father, a great builder and collector. Marguerite Hessein, while still a child, had married a formidable skirt-chaser. He was all the more formidable in that he excelled, in prose and verse, in the commonplaces of novel and song whose insincerity La Fontaine's Apollo in *Clymène* laments as deceptive for its victims and disappointing for its readers.

The Foucquet years had been happy ones for the young wife, who, with her husband, moved in the most sparkling society sympathetic to the *surintendant*. Between 1654 and 1658 Mme de La Sablière gave birth to three children. In 1661 her father died. He left a legacy in a state of disarray. While Antoine Rambouillet's business prospered—he had become secretary to the king in 1667—Gilbert Hessein's anticipated legacy amounted only to debts, which put a strain even on his daughter's considerable dowry. The "Great Madrigalist," who had been pleasantly cheating on his wife for a long time, began to mistreat her; he even confined her to a convent (the height of boorishness for a Huguenot) and managed to obtain a separation that deprived the young ridiculed wife of the custody of her children. Beginning in 1669 a battered Mme de La Sablière moved to rue Neuve-des-Petits-Champs. Her uncle Antoine Menjot and a whole group of friends formed a circle around "the beautiful Sablière" (as Mme de Sévigné called her, and as a portrait by Mignard attests) who sought a remedy to the wounds inflicted on her womanly, wifely, and maternal heart in conversation and the things of the mind, to which she had been initiated since childhood.

Boileau, who knew and respected her, nevertheless caricatured Mme de La Sablière, a dangerous example for her entire sex, as a "woman scientist . . . astrolabe in hand," flanked by the mathematician Roberval and the astronomer Cassini.[20] The marquise de Lambert, who also knew her well, provided a much more perspicacious portrait of her:

One of her friends, a man of wit, was asked one day what she was doing and thinking during her retirement. "She never thinks," he replied, "she only feels." All those who knew her agree that she was the most appealing person in the world, and that taste, or rather passion, became the master of her imagination and her reason, in such a way that her tastes were always justified by her reason and respected by her friends. No one who knew her dared condemn her except by no longer seeing her, because she was never wrong face to face. This proves that nothing is so absolute as the superiority of mind that comes from sensibility and the force of imagination, because persuasion always follows.[21]

La Fontaine gave Mme de La Sablière the Parnassus name "Iris." He remembered that, in the Platonic dialogue *Theatetus*, Socrates makes that goddess the daughter of the god Thaumas, or Astonishment, "who impelled the first thinkers toward philosophical speculations." To be astonished, to feel, to see reality in its surprising diversity were gifts common to that superior woman and to the author of *Fables*. The name "Iris" particularly encapsulates the spiritual kinship between La Fontaine and Mme de La Sablière, inasmuch as the goddess of the rainbow was, in the classical fable, the female version of Hermes: she too was a messenger between the gods and men, and she presided over language. Certain mythographers also make Eros the son of Iris and the god Zephyr. The brief symbolic portrait of the poet's friend provided in the name "Iris" matches that of Mme de Lambert: for Mme de La Sablière, to think and to know were, first of all, to feel and to know how to love.

Before 1661 Mme de La Sablière was already very close to Saint-Evremond and Madeleine de Scudéry. After 1669 she had no difficulty assembling at her home, along with her brother Pierre and her uncle Antoine Menjot, their writer and scholar friends: Molière, Racine, Chapelle, the chevalier de Méré, Pierre-Daniel Huet, Charles Perrault. Women as different as Mme de Sévigné and Ninon de Lenclos, and the best-educated people at court, especially the ambassadors Bonrepaux and Barillon, frequented this intelligent circle.[22] La Grande Mademoiselle (the haughty and aging daughter of Gaston d'Orléans), in love with the young lion Lauzun, who fled the court in favor of Mme de La Sablière's salon, was reassured after an inquiry: in her *Mémoires*, she notes that Mme de La Sablière was "some little 'bourgeoise,'" "a passion-filled peasant woman"—nothing to fear.

In reality that "little woman" became the Iris of the Parisian republic of letters. The only *femme savante* at court, the abbesse de Fontrevrault—sister of Mme de Montespan, who probably introduced her to Pierre-Daniel

Huet—from a distance exchanged letters with that "bourgeoise," on an equal footing. It was that female Maecenas who, in 1673, offered room, board, and good company in her mansion to a disgraced Ovid, who now had only very loose connections to his family and Château-Thierry. La Fontaine remained her guest—and in her debt—until the death of his friend and protectress in 1693.

Mme de Montespan earned the right to a very beautiful frontispiece at the beginning of the second collection of *Fables*. In the entire history of poetry, no king, queen, or prince had been thanked with more "immortal" inscriptions or more vibrant lyricism than Mme de La Sablière was by her guest and friend in the last two collections of his *Fables* (1678 and 1692) and in his *Discours en vers* to the Académie Française in 1684. She was nevertheless by court standards only a "little 'bourgeoise,'" great only through her gift for friendship and the grace she gave to private life.

This praise of a woman's heart and mind, equal to the poet who celebrated them, formed a counterpoint to the commissioned flattery addressed to the king. We need not venture very far to assess the gap that separated the language of the heart of hearts from the idiom of obligatory praise. We have only to compare La Fontaine with La Fontaine. In 1687, probably to be safe, the poet judged it wise to send Bonrepaux, Louis XIV's agent in London but a longtime close friend of Mme de La Sablière, a panegyric in verse for the king. He took care to have it published immediately in *Le Mercure Galant*, following his *Epître à Huet*, openly signing it "La Fontaine, of the Académie Française." The initiative was particularly timely in that the poet, in the preceding months, had been more or less initiated into the cabal of princes of blood, motivated by the hope that the surgery on the king's fistula would prove fatal, and that the throne would finally be left to the Grand Dauphin.[23]

These smoke-screen encomiums, very unlike the poet's natural style, are a parody of official language: their ironic flavor is imperceptible out of context. They assume their true meaning only within the subterranean flow of conversation behind closed doors that subtends the letters (too rarely saved) between the poet and his ambassador friend:

The king has recovered completely: you cannot imagine the joy his subjects displayed.

> Ils offriraient leurs jours pour prolonger les siens;
>   Ils font de sa santé le plus cher de leurs biens;
> Les preuves qu'à l'envi chaque jour ils en donnent,

Les voeux et les concerts dont leurs temples résonnent,
 Forcent le Ciel de l'accorder.
 On peut juger à cette marque,
Par la crainte qu'ils ont de perdre un tel monarque,
 Du bonheur de le posséder.

 De quelle sorte de mérite
 N'est-il pas aussi revêtu?
 Sa principale favorite
 Plus que jamais est la Vertu.

. . . .

 Les vaines passions chez lui sont étouffées;
 L'histoire a peu de rois, la fable point de dieux,
  Qui se vantent de ces trophées.
 Il pourrait se donner tout entier au repos:
  Quelqu'un trouverait-il étrange
 Que, digne en cent façons du titre de héros,
 Il en voulût goûter à loisir la louange?
Les deux mondes sont pleins de ses actes guerriers;
Cependant il poursuit encor d'autres lauriers:
Il veut vaincre l'Erreur; cet ouvrage s'avance,
Il est fait; et le fruit de ces succès divers
Est que la Vérité règne en toute la France,
 Et la France en tout l'univers.
  (*A Monsieur de Bonrepaux,* ll. 1–14, 19–31)

They would offer their days to prolong his own;
They consider his health the dearest thing they own;
The proof they rival one another to give every day,
The oaths and songs that echo in their churches,
 Force Heaven to grant it to him.
 One can judge by that mark,
By the fear that they have to lose such a monarch,
 The happiness they have to possess him.

 With what sort of merit
 Is he not imbued?
 His primary favorite,
 More than ever, is Virtue.

. . . .

Vain passions are muffled within him;
History has few kings, and fable no gods,
    Who boast of such trophies.
He could devote himself entirely to play:
    Would anyone find it strange
That, worthy a hundred times of the title of hero,
He wanted to enjoy such praise at leisure?
The two worlds are full of his bellicose acts;
In the meantime he chases still other rewards:
He wants to vanquish error; the work advances,
It is done; and the result of these many successes
Is that truth reigns in France,
    And France throughout the world.

Two poems, written in a cheerful, good-natured tone, congratulating
the Grand Dauphin, conqueror of Philipsburg, which La Fontaine published the next year, indirectly attest that he shared the hope of the
Condés and the Vendômes in a new, less-sublime reign; the letters seized
in 1685, belonging to the young prince de Conti and his brother La
Roche-sur-Yon, who was very close to the poet, shed light on the feelings
that La Fontaine himself was to feel for Mme Scarron ("Virtue," the king's
favorite). Furthermore, La Fontaine's entire oeuvre attests to his distance
from Louis XIV's war policy, the *Te Deums* that punctuated it and the
operas that celebrated it. Finally, his everlasting kinship with the French
Huguenots casts a chilling light on that "truth," whose reign Louvois's
dragoons were imposing throughout France. In his *Mémoires* (written after
1715), the marquis de La Fare, also very close to La Fontaine at the
time—and for a long time—like Saint-Simon bitterly lamented the
king's shocking blindness in the matter of the revocation of the Edict of
Nantes. The poet and member of the Académie Française, like all the
king's subjects, was speaking the official "Newspeak": only his closest
friends could detect the irony and parody under the obligatory incense.
The key to and justification for that fictive epistle of flattery are found in
the fable "The Funeral of the Lioness."
    The praise of Iris appears in book 9 of *Fables*, in a discourse that provides
the book with a magnificent peroration. It is an encomium that displays
and does not conceal, that wells forth and does not calculate. It begins by
distancing itself from any form of flattery: that self-serving mode of discourse does not please Iris any more than it pleased Oronte/Foucquet. Iris
"rejects incense, flattering noise," the "nectar" that suits the "humor common to gods, monarchs, and pretty ladies, and with which we inebriate all

earthly gods." It would be impossible to go further, and in fewer words, in the rejection of the practice to which the kingdom's official literature had been condemned for nearly twenty years. In this respect, the complicity between the poet and his lady friend is complete: both are unscathed by this "false environment," artificial and collective, created by the "common people of rhyme." This is already the finest praise, presented in negative terms, that La Fontaine could make of Mme de La Sablière: like Mme de La Fayette, she is *true*, to use Mme de Sévigné's expression. Iris does not enjoy hollow words but prefers another mode of speech, rooted in the heart and its primary preoccupation: intimate conversation between select friends in private life, where they do not show off or seek to dazzle each other. It is the very environment Iris created around her, the nurturing environment of the second collection of *Fables*:

> Propos, agréables commerces,
> Où le hasard fournit cent matières diverses,
> Jusque-là qu'en votre entretien
> La bagatelle a part: le monde n'en croit rien.
> Laissons le monde et sa croyance:
> La bagatelle, la science,
> Les chimères, le rien, tout est bon. Je soutiens
> Qu'il faut de tout aux entretiens:
> C'est un parterre où Flore épand ses biens;
> Sur différentes fleurs l'abeille s'y repose,
> Et fait du miel de toute chose.
> (9, [Premier] Discours à Mme de La Sablière,
> ll. 13–23)

> Words, agreeable exchange,
> Where chance provides a hundred different subjects,
> Until, in your conversation
> Trifles play a part: the world believes none of it.
> Let us leave the world and its beliefs:
> Trifles, knowledge,
> Chimera, nothing at all, everything is good. I maintain
> That a bit of everything is needed in conversation:
> It is a garden plot where Flora spreads her blessings;
> On different flowers the bee comes to rest,
> And makes honey from every thing.

In his *Traité de l'épigramme* (1658), Guillaume Colletet, borrowing a Platonic and Virgilian symbol, compares the poet to the bee, which, from the diversity of nectar it gathers, makes a delicious and nourishing honey, very different from the potion courtly Sophists offered the earthly gods. In a second discourse to Iris, presented before the Académie Française in 1684, La Fontaine borrowed that image but emphasized the contrast between his lady friend's inner concentration and his own love of variety:

> Papillon du Parnasse, et semblable aux abeilles
> A qui le bon Platon compare nos merveilles.
> Je suis chose légère, et vole à tout sujet;
> Je vais de fleur en fleur, et d'objet en objet.
> > *([Second] Discours à Mme de La Sablière,*
> > ll. 67–70)

> Butterfly of Parnassus, and, like the bees abuzz,
> To whom good Plato compares our wonders.
> I am a flighty thing, and flit to every subject;
> I go from flower to flower, and from object to object.

The symmetry persists: Iris the thoughtful bee and Acante the flighty butterfly—the Muse and the poet, two fertile minds, one with a conversation circle, the other presenting an epigrammatic bouquet—form a couple, an androgynous couple. This creative companionship that, according to the ancient tradition, La Fontaine expected from a princely Maecenas, he found in a friend in private life, anticipating what Mme Sabatier might have been for Baudelaire, and what Mme Bulteau was for Toulet.

Thus in book 12, like Céladon for Astrée, he builds a temple of fiction, an imaginary temple, an *as if* temple, but one with an inscription so enduring that it would make that temple survive all the great public works projects of kings. The description that *creates* this temple, both unreal and more real than any piece of architecture, is also an oratory of private life; it is decorated with a painting gallery very alien to Le Brun's "history painting." Above its altar is the portrait of Mme de La Sablière:

> Les murs auraient amplement contenu
> Toute sa vie: agréable matière,
> Mais peu féconde en ces événements
> Qui des Etats font les renversements.
> Au fond du temple eût été son image,
> Avec ses traits, son souris, ses appas,
> Son art de plaire et de n'y penser pas,
> Ses agréments à qui tout rend hommage.
>
> . . . .

J'eusse en ses yeux fait briller de son âme
Tous les trésors, quoique imparfaitement:
Car ce coeur vif et tendre infiniment,
Pour ses amis et non point autrement,
Car cet esprit qui, né du firmament,
A beauté d'homme avec grâces de femme,
Ne se peut pas, comme on veut, exprimer.
("The Gazelle, the Tortoise, the Crow, and
　　the Rat," 12.15, ll. 16–23 and 28–34)

The walls would have amply contained
Her entire life: agreeable subject,
But hardly rich in those events
That make for the overthrow of states.
In the heart of the temple her image would have been,
With its features, its smile, its charm,
Her art of pleasing and not thinking a thing of it,
Her grace to whom everything pays homage.
. . . .
I would have made every treasure of her soul
Shine in her eyes, albeit imperfectly:
For this heart, keen and tender eternally,
For her friends and in no other wise,
Since that spirit which, born of the firmament,
Has a male beauty and a woman's grace,
Cannot be expressed as one likes.

The fable itself—where that temple, that altar, that portrait, that inscription appears—is borrowed from the *Panchatantra*; it describes the inviolable and ingenious alliance among several friends who victoriously take turns wresting one another from the claws and fangs of political society's wolves.

Bees and Spiders

In her home, Mme de La Sablière was exposed to the arguments of the two advocates of Epicurean thought and science—her dear uncle Antoine Menjot and the "fine philosopher" François Bernier, back from Persia.[24]

Nevertheless she, like Fontenelle, was attracted to Cartesianism. An end-less debate divided the salons in Paris under Louis XIV. Under Louis XIII and during his regency, within the discreet circle of the Latin republic of letters and before it spread to the *femmes savantes* ridiculed by Molière and Boileau, this quarrel had already set two giant philosophers against each other: Pierre Gassendi and René Descartes.

As the author of beast apologues, La Fontaine could enliven his earlier homage to Mme de La Sablière in book 9 of *Fables* ("a male mind and a woman's grace") without appearing to be a pedant, by arguing in favor of the souls of animals, in a conversation with her written in verse and strewn with stories ("trifles, knowledge, chimera, nothing at all, every-thing is good"). The animal "soul" was recognized by the Gassendians and rejected by the Cartesians.[25] Was this simply a very minor aspect—one accessible to a poet—of the great modern dispute, both philosophical and scientific, between empiricism and metaphysics? That is how commenta-tors, even those most generous toward La Fontaine, have presented the first *Discours à Mme de La Sablière* in book 9 of *Fables*.

In reality, under the gleaming and nonchalant surface of *Fables*, an entire spiritual battle was joined against the behemoth of the absolute state, and this battle was quite naturally also directed at the best ally of political absolutism: idealist metaphysics. La Fontaine, a born poet, rec-ognized with a keen nose and keen intelligence which were the friends and which the enemies of his poetry and of the poetic Renaissance of which he was the heir. Since Mme de La Sablière was the best friend of his poetry, it went without saying that he would attempt to turn her away from the "fable of the world" as Descartes told it. Just like the "fable of the great king," though in a different order, the fable invented by the author of *Discours de la méthode* demanded that it be considered the only truth, and that all other fables, which the Renaissance had seen as receptacles of wisdom, be relegated to the rank of children's stories.

The consequences the Cartesian "fable" entailed for the intelligence of animals, which was admitted by common experience and confirmed by the entire literary tradition, in themselves merited a refutation. Descartes, in relegating animals, in the name of the metaphysical distinction between thought and matter, to the order of automatons and clockwork mecha-nisms, destroyed one of the most powerful safeguards against human vanity invented by ancient wisdom. According to the Cartesian fable, only men participate in divine thought and, provided they are able to reject the fables fashioned by poets, show themselves capable of conducting their reason according to the eternal truths freely dictated to matter by its Creator. The question of the intelligence of animals thus pertains to the essence and origin of Cartesian idealism. And La Fontaine perceived that perfectly well. An Epicurean, he had the same view as the Thomist Maritain, who wrote of Descartes: "An angel in iron gloves, extending his supreme action on the world of bodies through the countless arms of mechanical engineering! Poor angel, turning the grindstone, enslaved to the law of matter, and soon unconscious under the terrible wheels of the earth-and-water machine gone awry."[26] The poet had no trouble recognizing, at the origin of Descartes's metaphysical "fable of the world," that same peremptory hypertrophy of the "ego" ("I have the gift of thought, and I know that I think" is his translation of the Cartesian cogito) that all his poetry condemns as the very principle, in moral and political life, of a new iron age among mankind.

The consequence of that metaphysical hypertrophy of the "ego," now the principle of all circumscription of the diversity of reality and its reduction to the rational, is, in the first place, that abstraction takes hold of and freezes nature in its totality, and denies it as it is naively felt, experienced, suffered, tasted, and known by a humanity not yet reformed by Descartes. It is also the amputation of imagination, feelings, taste, tact, the evidence of the senses and of the body itself, to bring into being the intellectual hero of the Cartesian fable, the "master and possessor of nature," a cold monster like the absolute king, and who also considers himself the earthly substitute for the engineer God of the world. Swift's Laputa Island, which, from its place in the clouds, skillfully carves up and despoils the earth beneath it, is the allegory both for Cartesian thought and for Cartesian government.

In a letter to the duchesse de Bouillon (1687), La Fontaine again amused himself by contradicting Descartes's claim that he was the first inventor of his "fable of the world," a claim altogether analogous to that of Louis XIV, "the greatest king in the world." That same year the king's amour propre was flattered by Charles Perrault, when the latter presented his poem, *Le siècle de Louis le Grand*, before the Académie Française and made Louis XIV the inventor of the modern age, the titleholder of a reign without precedent, on the threshold of enlightenment and progress. In his readings of classical authors, La Fontaine rediscovered proof that this metaphysician's vanity, whose principle and system Descartes boasted of inventing, was in fact an old, even ancient, and unfortunate inclination of the human spirit, like tyranny itself.

He wrote to his protectress and friend:

Every day, then, I discover some opinion of Descartes's expounded everywhere in the works of the ancients, such as this one: that there is no color to the world; it is only the different effects of light on different surfaces. Farewell, lilies and roses of our Amintes. There is no white skin or black hair; the basis of our passion is simply a colorless body. And, after all that, I will write verses for the primary beauty of women![27]

"Colors" are not only sensorial data: they are also the sensible, emotional, and imaginative properties of discourse delineated by rhetoric and put to use by poetry. Descartes's "fable of the world" is not content to drain the color from the world; it also drains the color from language and ravages it in the name of a metaphysical system. It keeps it from describing the world as we experience it, in the sweet or terrible self-evidence of its beauty or tragic cruelty as fables present it, and from which poetry helps us to stand and understand. That metaphysical fable is like Attila, under whose feet the grass does not grow back; and it moves in the same direction as the fable of reason of state, which tends to reduce literature to the commonplaces of flattery and to kill poetry altogether. It oppresses and silences life itself, the universal life common to men, animals, gods, the life of desire, pain, pleasure, an uncertain battle, which the poet's language has the vocation to reflect and not to reform.

In a letter to Brossette on 14 July 1715, the poet Jean-Baptiste Rousseau wrote: "I have often heard M. Despréaux say that Descartes's philosophy had poetry by the throat."[28]

What matters most is not that La Fontaine more or less borrowed the wherewithal to feed his resistance to the Cartesian "fable of the world" from Gassendi and his Epicurean friends. Gassendi had predecessors in fifteenth-century Italy: Lorenzo Valla was the first to have written a treatise on pleasure rehabilitating Epicurus. La Fontaine's resistance drew its strength from the resources amassed by the Italian and French Renaissance, by a philology that is also a philosophy of love and a poetry of a world, to which only reminiscence gives meaning and joy. Before Gassendi and La Fontaine, the humanists contrasted the metaphysical universals of the "theologasters" to the intelligence of a language capable of rediscovering in the sensible and its ever-changing diversity the traces of divinity, which spoke to what might be divine in man. The Renaissance provided the background for gallant romanticism, and La Fontaine the bee had gathered pollen everywhere, so that the honey of the Renaissance could continue to feed the world. Jonathan Swift was thinking of the French poet when, in his *Battle of the Books* (1696), he made Aesop state the moral of his fable of the bee and the spider: "Instead of excrement and poison," say Aesop's bees, "we have chosen to fill our cupboards with honey and wax, thus providing humanity the most noble things that can be: sweetness and light."

The Poet and the Princes

In 1676, even before the publication of the second collection of *Fables*, Mme de La Sablière (she was thirty-six at the time) developed a burning passion for the marquis de La Fare, who was thirty-two. La Fare, of gentle birth, was a brilliant soldier and had hoped to make a fine career at court and in Louis XIV's armies: that hope was dashed by Louvois, who did not forgive the young gentleman for daring to be found pleasing by the maréchale de Rochefort, his own favorite. The marquis retreated to private life, which he at first filled with a "religious worship" of Mme de La Sablière.

Compiled after 1715, the uncompleted memoirs of the marquis de La Fare, an agreeable poet when he chose to be,[29] give no place to his private feelings and do not even mention Mme de La Sablière. Nevertheless, they begin with a quotation from Frère Jean des Entommeures ("'We monks, alas! have only our life in this world!' 'What!' replied Pantagruel, 'What more, in the devil's name, do kings and princes have?'"), which gives a glimpse of the Epicurean principles to which, with his friend the abbé de Chaulieu, he had long resigned himself. The portrait the memoirist gives of the French political developments since Henry IV, and through which he justifies his renunciation of the active life, even after Louvois's death, corresponds to a feeling already broadly shared in Paris and even at court from the early days of Louis XIV's reign. Richelieu's and Louis XIV's remedy to civil wars and anarchy was another extreme.

De La Fare writes: "I remember hearing it said by the duc de La Rochefoucauld, who played such a key role in the last civil war, that it was impossible for a man who had attempted such a thing to ever wish to do it again, so hard to endure were the pain and distress for a man who had waged war against his king."[30]

Another form of violence came in response to that violence against nature, which had led the opposition to Richelieu and Mazarin to conspire against their king: it manifested itself in the coup d'état of 1661. Since then, that violence had become an established disorder, an "absolute" disorder:

> So it was that [by virtue of Foucquet's disgrace] the king's phenomenal authority began, unheard-of before this century, which, having been the cause of great good and great evil, reached such excess that it became a burden to itself. It can thus be said that the spirit of the entire century was, on the part of the court and the ministers, a continual plan to elevate royal authority to the point of making it despotic; and, on the part of the people, perfect patience and submission, with the exception of a period during the Regency.[31]

This disabused aristocrat, converted to idleness, gambling, and ennui, could not respond for long to a "passion-filled peasant woman," as La Grande Mademoiselle called Mme de La Sablière. De La Fare is more explicit in his poetry, which, in its dry lucidity, rivals that of Chaulieu, than he is in *Mémoires:*

De Vénus Uranie, en ma verte jeunesse
    Avec respect j'encensai les Autels:
Et je donnai l'exemple au reste des Mortels
    De la plus parfaite tendresse.

Cette commune Loi, qui veut que notre coeur
    De son bonheur même s'ennuie,
    Me fit tomber dans la langueur
    Qu'apporte une insipide vie.

    Amour! viens, vole à mon secours,
    M'écriais-je dans ma souffrance;
    Prends pitié de mes derniers jours.
Il m'entendit, et par reconnaissance
    Pour mes services assidus

    Il m'envoya l'autre Vénus,
Et d'amours libertins une troupe volage,
    Qui me fit à son badinage.
Heureux! si de mes ans je puis finir le cours
    Avec ces folâtres amours.[32]

Of Venus Urania, in my greenest youth
  With respect I censed the altars:
And I gave an example to the rest of mortals
  Of the most perfect tenderness.

That common law, which wishes that our heart
  Grow bored with its own happiness,
  Made me fall into the languor
Brought on by an insipid life.

"Love! come, rush to my aid,"
I cried out in my suffering;
"Take pity on my final days."
He heard me, and in gratitude
For my assiduous service

He sent me the other Venus,
And of libertine loves a fickle band,
  Who accustomed me to their banter.
Happy I'll be if I can finish my years
  With these playful lovers.

In November 1679 Mme de Sévigné wrote to her daughter: "Mme de Coulanges . . . maintains that de La Fare has never been in love; it was laziness, laziness, laziness. And the bassette [a sort of baccarat game very much in vogue at the time] has shown he was seeking only good company at Mme de La Sablière's home."[33]

Mme de La Sablière's conversion to Catholicism, thanks to the diligence of the Jesuit Rapin in 1680, and her retreat to the Hôpital des Incurables closely followed her breakup with de La Fare. La Fontaine remained her guest, but at a distance, in a much more modest house she rented out on rue Saint-Honoré. From 1680 until the death of his protectress in 1693, the poet saw her less and less often. After his difficult election to the Académie Française in 1684, La Fontaine, in want of money, became one of the royal company's "regulars" (*jetonniers*) and had to turn to the marquis de La Fare and his coterie of great lords to avoid the fate of the old mud-caked poet.

In his *Mémoires*, de La Fare shows himself particularly well informed about the goings-on of the duc de Vendôme and his brother the Great Prior, whom he frequented regularly both in the Enclos du Temple and at the château in Anet, along with his inseparable Chaulieu and often La Fontaine as well. The memoirist describes the king, between the peace of Nijmegen in 1678 and the siege of Philipsburg in 1688, as the "imitator of the kings of Asia," enjoying general "enslavement" to Mme Scarron. When the news spread that the king was suffering from a life-threatening fistula and that the doctors hesitated to operate on it, hope was reborn in Chantilly at the prince de Condé's country castle, and in Anet at that of the duc de Vendôme. Extravagant parties were thrown in the two chateaux in honor of the Grand Dauphin ("reared," de La Fare said, "in servile dependency"). Monseigneur was soon going to become king.

But Louis XIV did have the operation, he recovered, and, despite the "great visions" that the princes of blood had had, "nothing of what, at the time, we imagined with some reason occurred."

In the years that followed Mme de La Sablière's retirement, La Fontaine, too, turned more than ever toward the duc and duchesse de Bouillon, who had already saved him after the *surintendant's* fall. It was among the Bouillons' clients that he encountered Mme Ulrich, a talented adventurer who published La Fontaine's *Oeuvres posthumes* in 1696, and the abbé de Chaulieu, the court poet and intendant to the duc de Vendôme, Bouillon's nephew. With the Bouillons and the Vendômes, the poet found the compassion, generosity, and gentle mores that suited a "nursling of the Muses."

It is true these princes were "roués," corrupted by thirty years of political idleness. They had made their choice more or less sincerely, pretending to follow the maxim of Epicurus: *Sapiens non accedat Rempublican* ("The wise man shall not meddle in politics"). They nevertheless schemed with the king's ministers to obtain military commands and to show their mettle under gunfire on the various front lines lit up by the series of "great wars" in Europe waged against Louis the Great. Did they lose all hope of recovering their former rank and role in the *Harbor of Secrecy?*

At the time La Fontaine was closest to these princes of blood, they were vying with the Grand Dauphin. La Fontaine could hardly have been unaware of that cabal. Even twenty years earlier, in 1668, he had dedicated the first collection of *Fables* to Monseigneur. In 1688 the old king did not forgive his indecisive eldest son for daring to appear as head of the opposition and as a candidate to succeed him. In 1711 Monseigneur died without having reigned, as an idle dauphin. The conclusion of the funeral oration by Saint-Simon (who, to be sure, had belonged to the rival cabal of the duc d'Orléans) is as devastating for the satrap of Versailles as for his eldest son, dulled by court slavery.

He wrote:

The result of this long and curious internal economy was that Monseigneur was without vice and without virtue, without enlightenment or knowledge of any kind, radically incapable of acquiring them, very lazy, unimaginative and unproductive, without taste, without selectiveness, without discernment, born for boredom, which he communicated to others, born to be a ball rolling randomly at the impetus of other people, stubborn and petty in everything to the point of excess, with an incredible proclivity toward informing himself and believing everything people had seen, falling into the most pernicious hands, incapable of getting away from them or of realizing it, consumed by his fat and his gloominess, and who, though he had no will to do evil, would have been a pernicious king.[34]

La Fontaine's biographers have criticized him for frequenting princes in his old age. But that same society of Chantilly, the Enclos du Temple, and Anet, which—in its mores, its irony, and its intrigues—privately rebelled through its words against the king, his ministers, and Mme de Maintenon, was in fact the same society that would later shape the young Voltaire's freedom of thought, if not his genius. The author of Fables lent himself but did not give himself to that society of great lords champing at the bit.

At least these roués on principle, which La Fontaine would never be, were very intelligent and amusing. If the old Anacréon did not feel like a stranger in their company, it was because several aspects of his character and literary talents corresponded to their moods, maxims, and tastes.

On principle, Foucquet's poet, constantly kept in a sort of internal exile and inducted into the Académie Française in 1684 under somewhat humiliating conditions, had their sympathy. The literary authority of Contes, whose "pretty" piquancy appreciated by Mme de Sévigné may have escaped them, was a cover for their loose morals, with which the poet's own were glad to be in harmony.

Above all, these princes could take pride in his epistles in verse,[35] which revived the "poetic pension" in their favor, which La Fontaine had once paid the surintendant, and which, in 1662, had earned the poet the favor of his suzerain in Château-Thierry, the duc de Bouillon. These conversational epistles, with a delightful charm and variety heightened by the fact that they were handwritten, were the envied privilege of a small society of friends and accomplices; and they did not confine themselves to reviving the spirit of gallant journalism that the gazetteer Loret, Nicolas Foucquet's protégé, had introduced in his versified covert and town newsletters parallel to the prose *feuilleton* of Mlle de Scudéry's *Clélie*. These small opposition courts, shut away, masked, sarcastic, were heirs under Louis the Great to the much more elaborate circles, on the fringe of the Louvre and the Palais-Cardinal, of Gaston d'Orléans, the duc de Montmorency, the duc de Liancourt, and the abbé de Retz. They appreciated the good cheer and playfulness in the style of Voiture that this poet of bygone times knew how to dispense to them. For La Fontaine and his princely friends, these nonchalant epistles were also a way to return modern life, fleetingly and on a small scale, to the pagan universe of Horace and Maecenas. In the verses of *Epistulae*, the Latin poet Horace, who also laid claim to Anacreon, echoed the Greek loves of Maecenas. La Fontaine did not push gratitude that far, although the "Greek" mores were extremely fashionable in the roués' castles. He was content to evoke the "Chlorises" and "Jeannetons." He owed much to the generosity of his hosts. But Horace and Anacreon lurk behind his French epistles, and the poet's very urban improvisations on a rural flute give an air of gay antiquity to the modern gardens of Epicurus, the Enclos du Temple, and Anet.

And then, La Fontaine, in these little courts that he kept in constant touch with the London circle of Saint-Evremond and the duchesse Mazarin, played the role of headmaster. The abbé de Chaulieu and the marquis de La Fare,[36] who belonged to the younger generation, considered themselves his disciples to a certain extent. That filiation rested on a profound misunderstanding, which La Fontaine's conversion in 1692 would shatter. In reality their true master in libertinage was the mysterious Chapelle, the least lyrical of men, and from La Fontaine they retained only a manner, an affability, devoid of the emotional resonance of the old master's gilded language and peculiar melody.

Chaulieu and de La Fare were the ones really at home in these little pleasure societies, which exactly circumscribed their limited talent as amateur poets, elegant and witty no doubt, but comfortable above all. Their verses were confined to the adornment of that comfort; they lacked literary memory and spiritual disquiet, but these were the least of their concerns. Their hymns to laziness, their epistles, notes, songs, and epigrams prefigured, under Louis the Great, the high-society assembly line of salon and château poetry in the eighteenth century. The monotonous frivolity of literary Epicureanism was in reality as alien to La Fontaine's lyricism as the panegyric drone of official poetry. In their turn, Chaulieu and de La Fare would play the role of headmasters in Sceaux for the duchesse du Maine, where Anthony Hamilton would join them, and where the young

Voltaire would learn the most sociable and conventional forms of his poetic talent from them.

Chaulieu gives a portrait of his inseparable friend, de La Fare, which attenuates somewhat the terrible colors Saint-Simon uses to depict the Vendômes and their society:

> He combined a great deal of simple and natural wit with everything that can be found pleasing in society, made up of feelings and pleasure, and above all replete with the amiable weakness and relaxed mores that made him full of indulgence for everything men did. Future centuries will have difficulty forming someone with such likable qualities and such great charms.[37]

This is already a picture of the famous "sweetness of life," as Talleyrand retrospectively defined the worldly eighteenth century: it is already incubating in the hothouse that escaped the rule and etiquette of Louis XIV's Versailles. These princes eased the poet's last years, when he was deprived of the former attentions of Mme de La Sablière (and of her money) through de La Fare's betrayal. It was owing to their friendly and generous patronage that the old Anacreon could describe, as he did it to Bonrepaux in a letter of 1687, this domestic scene, at once very modern and Alexandrian in its inspiration:

> Un clavecin chez moi! Ce meuble vous étonne,
> Que direz-vous si je vous donne
> Une Chloris de qui la voix
> Y joindra ses sons quelquefois?
> La Chloris est jolie, et jeune, et sa personne
> Pourrait bien ramener l'amour
> Au philosophique séjour.
> Je l'en avais banni; si Chloris le ramène,
> Elle aura chansons pour chansons:
> Mes vers exprimeront la douceur de ses sons.
> Qu'elle ait à mon égard le coeur d'une inhumaine
> Je ne m'en plaindrai point, n'étant bon désormais
> Qu'à chanter les Chloris et les laisser en paix.
> Vous autres chevaliers, tenterez l'aventure;
> Mais de la mettre à fin, fût-ce le beau berger
> Qu'Oenone eut autrefois le pouvoir d'engager,
> Ce n'est pas chose qui soit sûre.[38]

A harpsichord in my home! This instrument may surprise you,
　　What will you say if I give you
　　A Chloris, whose voice
　　Sometimes blends with its sounds?
This Chloris is pretty and young, and her person
　　Might well bring back love
　　To my philosophical abode.
I had banished it; and if Chloris brings it back
　　She will have songs in return for songs:
My verses will express the sweetness of her sounds.
Should she have the heart of a heartless woman for me,
Still I will not complain, since I am only good now
For singing of Chlorises and leaving them in peace.
You other cavaliers will attempt an intrigue;
But to succeed, even for the handsome shepherd
Whom Oenone once had the power to bind,
　　Is no sure thing.

In appearance, this is not far removed from Chaulieu's gallant writings ("My Iris comes to spend the evening with me / She comes here with simple and modest charm"). And yet, a subtle resonance with vanished worlds and reservations and shifts in the sentiment give this epistle a musicality and emotion on a completely different scale. As he had been among the "knights of the Round Table," La Fontaine was at home with the princes, but he was elsewhere too. His lyricism may have found refuge in the welcoming company of Conti, Vendôme, and de La Fare, may have even invented forms that were in agreement with that society of hardened Epicureans; it was no use: he was cramped for space. Even as he was writing these Anacreontic epistles, he composed the fable "The Companions of Ulysses," which became part of book 12 of *Fables*. He associated with Fénelon. Rather than consider as a moral weakness these years of "poetic pension," spent with princes who were already living, in anticipation, in the Paris of the duc d'Orléans's regency, we must recognize them as one of the aspects of the tragedy the last great lyric poet of the ancien régime went through, exiled from the royal court, exiled to the little opposition, seeking to breathe where he could, in an age more and more hostile to lyricism.

CHAPTER 8

Death of the Poet

Condition of man: inconstancy, boredom, worry.
—Blaise Pascal

The inconstancy and worry that are so natural to me.
—La Fontaine, preface to *Galatée* (1682)

*P*oetry originated as praise. La Fontaine indirectly reminds us of this in his fable "Simonides and the Gods" (1.14). The hero of the fable is a Greek poet, a contemporary of Pindar. The lyricism of Simonides, like that of the author of *Olympian Odes*, celebrates the victorious athletes of the Olympic Games. Homer, the father of poetry, makes *The Iliad*, which Alexander the Great found intoxicating, a celebration of Achilles. But above all, "Simonides and the Gods" demonstrates the gap that separates praise from flattery, and poetry, which reveals the divine, worthy of love, from sophistry, which deifies man incapable of the divine. Simonides receives a commission for a lyric ode in praise of a mediocre athlete, "a petty and sterile subject": he deals hastily with his "human, all too human" subject and reserves all the brilliance of his praise for the Dioscures, Castor and Pollux, two stars and the twin sons of Jupiter and Leda. That disproportion, which the athlete-patron does not fail to bitterly remark on, reveals the poet's personal feelings, which coincide with those of the gods. Praise thus has a higher veracity, which the poetic word cannot dodge without repudiating itself. It is the truth of Parnassus.

In the works of La Fontaine, there is a constant meditation on praise, which is indistinguishable from his sense of poetry. He praises—but with what a light touch—the divinity that deserves to be praised in the creatures and things he admires and loves. To Foucquet, to La Rochefoucauld, to Mme de La Sablière, to Mme de Montespan, to friendship, to wit, to pleasure, to belle lettres, he renders the nuance of fervor befitting each. To praise is to display and trumpet, to speak of what, in its splendor, deserves to be praised, what is essentially and universally divine (true, beautiful, and good) in the particular object being praised. To praise is to put creatures and things in their true place, in their proper light, participating more or less in the divinity that only poets know how to see with the eyes of the Muses, in the darkness where mortals declaim and perish.

But praise also has its flip side, or its extension by other means: vituperation or blame. That poetic anger at the absence or negation of the divine in creatures and things puts them in their place to an equal degree. It is the negative path of praise. The comic, satirical, epigrammatic La Fontaine is more than ever a poet of praise, turned inside out, following the poetic principle articulated by Hugo: "Love becomes hatred in the presence of evil." Sometimes La Fontaine even lets us hear his satirical restraint in the form of praise, when that praise has been imposed on him.

Flattery, the art of the Sophists, is not praise, but the reversal of the real order of creatures and things, the corruption of poetic language, which makes it the warped instrument of an exaltation alien or even contrary to its true object: to speak the divine, to speak the lovable, to speak the heart's truth. If the eloquence of panegyrics consists of making great in words what is small in actuality, it is not only sophistry, the opposite of philosophy, as Plato said, but also, as all true poets believe, the opposite of poetry, which is excited or annoyed only at what deserves to be praised or blamed. Flattery is to true praise what slander is to true blame. It is the poet's task to jealously watch over the fidelity of the language of love in relation to the reality of creatures and things. He expects a reward for his art, a reward all the more legitimate in that he has not betrayed his art. But he also knows he must not expect a reward.

In his lyric ode, then, Simonides praises a great deal what deserves to be praised a great deal—namely, the gods—and praises feebly what deserves to be praised feebly—a vain man. He respects the loftier proprieties of his art, of which his patron can only be unaware. He has cause to regret it: the athlete, whose amour propre is wounded, refuses to pay him the price expected for his poem and sends the poet to collect the balance from the gods he has praised with such fervor. Simonides is nevertheless invited to the banquet where the ode is to be recited. During the celebration, someone comes looking for him on behalf of two strangers. Simonides leaves the house, the Dioscures come forward and invite the poet to leave: at that very moment, the ceiling of the banquet hall col-lapses on the guests. It is on that occasion (the fable does not say so, but its seventeenth-century readers knew it) that the art of memory is in-vented.[1] For the crushed victims to be decently buried, they have to be identified: Simonides can do so by recalling the exact seat each occupied in the hall. The art of memory is thus of the same nature as the art of praise: it puts each thing in its true place and allows one to recapture it even when time, the destruction of appearances, and death have effaced the illusions that masked the reality of creatures and things. Mnemosyne is the mother of the Muses. "Music" is the word the Greeks used for edu-cation. Greek poetry was at the heart of that musical education. To edu-cate is to recall the true price of creatures and things, which ignorance does not see and which amour propre does not want to see.

Such were the Renaissance's ambitions for poetry. Chancellor Coluccio Salutati, a disciple of Petrarch, defined the poet this way: an excellent man, experienced in the art of praise and blame. Lorenzo di Medici wrote that poets were the authors of holy praise.[2] The tact of praise is the ulti-mate science, requiring both vision and critical judgment. It is the science of poets. Is it so far from the science of saints that Corneille encapsulates in an alexandrine spoken by Pauline in *Polyeucte:* "I see, I know, I believe, I am disabused"? La Fontaine had a gift for this sort of science, for which Socrates was beholden to Diotima and to his inner "demon." La Fontaine did not refuse the king the praises that were due his title as a king, partici-pating ex officio in the divine. The poet never granted him anything but the conventional praise befitting that office and the person who occupied it, which he assessed according to the occasion. The opaque man never stirred his ardor. But that man was the king of France.

In an epistle of 1684 to the prince de Conti, La Fontaine "essayed," in the manner of Montaigne, a comparison between Alexander, Caesar, and the prince:[3] it was this same Condé to whom Madeleine de Scudéry, in 1649–53, devoted a fervent elogium in her vast heroic novel, *Artamène ou le Grand Cyrus.* Although faithful to that ancient admiration, La Fon-taine did not hesitate to nuance it; what he most respected in the prince, the uncle of his young patron Conti, was his contempt for court flattery: "I will never tell him to his face: 'You are greater than Alexander,' and even less: 'Alexander must be placed below you.'"

This was an indirect manner, for people who knew how to read, to nuance the praise he himself must have given of a king insatiable for praise, idolized and an idol to himself. In a 1687 letter from Troyes to his friend M. Simon, the poet reported the new fervor of the cult of which the king was the object in Paris since the surgery on his fistula and his recovery. The letter was published by the Jesuit Bouhours in 1693, during the poet's lifetime. La Fontaine made an allusion to the great Protestant journalists of the Refuge, Pierre Bayle and Jean Leclerc, and he confessed that he regularly read *La Gazette de Hollande*. He also wrote, with an admiring gaiety that perfectly concealed his annoyance and irony:

> Nous revînmes au roi; l'on y revient toujours:
>   Quelque entretien qu'on se propose,
>   Sur Louis aussitôt retombe le discours;
> La déesse aux cent voix ne parle d'autre chose.
>   (*A Monsieur Simon*, from Troyes, ll. 49–52)

> We came back to the king; one always comes back to him:
>   Whatever subject is proposed,
>   The conversation immediately falls back on Louis;
> The goddess with a hundred voices speaks of nothing else.

That sheeplike Renown, which jabbers nonetheless, was the caricature of praise. The king was blind and deaf to that difference. He was a dupe of appearances and of himself. La Fontaine said so, but by antiphrasis.

In a 1689 epistle to the duc de Vendôme (published in 1696, along with the 1684 epistle to Conti, by the excellent Mme Ulrich, who waited until the poet died to make these compromising texts known),[4] the Revocation is described in frankly irreverent terms, then immediately retracted:

> Notre roi voyant quelques villes
> Sans peine à la foi se rangeant
> L'appétit lui vint en mangeant.
>   (ll. 55–57)

> Our king, when he saw a few cities
> Coming round to faith without trouble,
> Found his appetite whet once he'd begun to eat.

The lion of *Fables* displays his mane. The quickly muffled echo of the epistle lets us make out in a flash what had been said in conversation among trusted friends. But what centuries-old pressure and French sense of community did that almost silent protest have to elude?

PARNASSUS AND THE ACADÉMIE FRANÇAISE

We might wonder why, in 1683, La Fontaine began a campaign to be elected to the Académie Française.[5] At the time, this company, founded by Richelieu in 1635, was the kingdom's most productive forge of panegyrics to Louis XIV, who had become its personal protector in 1672. La Fontaine's campaign becomes even more astonishing when we learn that its target was the seat left by Colbert, who died on 6 September of that year, exactly twenty-two years and a day after Foucquet's arrest. And that astonishment becomes outright stupefaction when we realize that the poet was not only elected without difficulty by the academy, but was then approved, after some reservations, by Louis XIV.

The poet's deep feelings (and their coded expression) about the king and about his art of governance never changed. But the attachment he felt, as an ancien régime Frenchman, to the monarchy also had not changed. He would have been a royal poet if Foucquet had become prime minister. He was not able to be one after the coup d'état of 5 September 1661. But the tradition of Marot, Ronsard, and Malherbe invincibly pushed him to become one. For a French poet, even for young Voltaire himself, there was no object of praise on this earth more desirable than his king. La Fontaine could not imagine any political form for France other than the monarchy of divine right, any more than Foucquet, Fénelon, and Saint-Simon—all "good Frenchmen" if ever there were any—could have done; but he suffered (an admirable and strange suffering for an Epicurean) when the kingdom was not governed by a man of wit and heart. And his lofty notion of poetry—like Fénelon's of eloquence and religion and Saint-Simon's of the diplomacy of wit—impelled him to believe that, even then, these powers of persuasion had to work tenaciously, via the paths left available to them, to fill the gap opened by the king's blindness between the kingdom as it could and ought to be, between the idea, the image, the essential finality of the kingdom and the reality of the monarchy led astray by reason of state. The education of the Dauphins was one of these paths of public salvation for the future. For La Fontaine, poetic language's access to the center of the court and to the king himself (for Fénelon, it was the access of a true religious language), even in covered and veiled forms and by indirect channels, was another path for that public salvation over the long term. For these individuals of vision, the kingdom was not what carnal eyes observed with sadness, but what the language of the heart valiantly created and re-created.

In 1683, the year he was elected to the Académie Française, it had been at least ten years since La Fontaine was the utterly disgraced poet from the early years of Louis XIV's personal reign. The king himself was no longer the young Nero whom Racine convinced, in the 1669 *Britannicus*, not to appear in any more court ballets. To a certain degree, the conquered Greece had vanquished its fierce conqueror. In the end, the generation of the republic of letters that had witnessed Foucquet's fall gradually achieved, under Boileau's leadership and in Molière's wake, rights of citizenship at court, at the price of patient ruses and cruel sacrifices. That right was closely circumscribed. For Boileau and Racine, Pellisson's successors, it even resembled the condition of hostages. Their role and visibility were also very minor, compared to the extraordinary favor Lully enjoyed from the king, on *The Isle of Pleasures* that Monsieur, the duc d'Orléans, was now, after Molière's death in 1673, not the only one to inspire.[6] But finally, in 1677, Boileau and Racine became royal historiographers. That victory of belles lettres, though nominal and very costly to the victors, could not have been predicted in 1661. It was due less to Molière's and Racine's favor in Louis XIV's eyes than to the patronage of Mme de Montespan, her brother, the duc de Vivonne, and their sister Mme de Thianges.

The "chamber of the sublime" offered the duc du Maine in January 1675,[7] though it reserved a limited role for La Fontaine, had him share, in spite of it all and via the service door, a little of the ground captured for Boileau and Racine at court. In addition to the powerful Mortemart coterie, La Fontaine had excellent backing in his own right: his suzerain of Château-Thierry, the duchesse de Bouillon, her brother the duc de Nevers (Mme de Thianges's son-in-law), and their nephew the duc de Vendôme. The previous year (1674), Boileau had published his *Art poétique* and *Traité du sublime*, thus officially announcing his candidacy to succeed Jean Chapelain, who died that same year. Also in 1674, an auspicious year for the Mortemart patronage, Mme de Thianges invited La Fontaine to compose, in place of Quinault, Lully's official librettist, the libretto for the opera *Daphné*.[8]

For the author of *Fables*, this was the path, opened by the musical theater enjoyed by the king, toward Louis XIV's personal favor, and perhaps the end of the poet's disgrace. The place of literature within the court would increase remarkably as a result. Could a bit more light from it have enlightened the king's heart and mind?

In 1661 Gabriel Guéret included Quinault among the minor poets of *The Isle of Pleasures*, then patronized exclusively by Monsieur. The Mortemarts could not easily shun Lully, who relied on the immovable state monopoly that, since 1672, had conferred on him the title of superintendent of the royal academy of music. In addition, he was the underground king of a Sodom that included within its courtly ranks Monsieur himself, his officers, and a good number of great lords. Louis XIV suspected it but could not do without the wretched man, possessed of an *estro armonico* whose magic the king, as a young dancer, had already experienced in the music of the 1653 *Ballet de la nuit*.

As much as it was in their power, however, the Mortemarts backed a rival, the Italian Paolo Lorenzani, an excellent composer brought to France from Sicily by the duc de Vivonne, whose motets the duc managed to get the king to appreciate: at least the royal chapel escaped Lully's monopoly. The stunning success of Quinault and Lully's opera *Bellérophon* (1679) foiled the plot.[9]

The Mortemarts also tried to catch the king's ear on behalf of their protégé La Fontaine, by separating Lully from his beloved Quinault. That maneuver had no more success: Lully rejected the libretto for *Daphné*, after victoriously denigrating it before the king. The Mortemarts made another attempt in 1682–83: this time they obtained the disgrace of Quinault, who had prematurely mocked Mme de Montespan's jealous rage at a short-lived rival in his opera libretto *Isis* (1677). Racine and Boileau were urged to write the libretto for Lully's *Chute de Phaéton*.[10] They were soon obliged to break off, because the king had forgiven Lully's favorite poet in the meantime. All the same, in 1685 Racine wrote *Une idylle pour la paix*, graced by Lully's music (Mme de Montespan, now truly disgraced, was no longer a factor). That diversion was presented to the king at the château of Sceaux, during a festival put on by Colbert de Seignelay. A few days earlier, Mme de Coligny had written Bussy: "It is said that the festival of Vaux was not so magnificent as this one will be." Thus, a quarter century after the catastrophic festival, the shadow of Foucquet, who had died in 1680, continued to haunt Louis XIV's court.

In 1674–77, La Fontaine's irritation toward the superintendent of the royal academy of music—sustained, but also cautiously contained by Mme de Thianges—dictated three admirable satiric poems to him, which did not spare the king, military even in his musical tastes: *Le Floretin*, *Epître à Mme de Thianges*, and *Epître à M. de Nyert*. They remained carefully handwritten and had only a very limited distribution. The public was not able to read them until the eighteenth century.

But what in the world was the poet doing there? He was as little made for the devious intrigues of the court as Lully was trained for them since childhood. La Fontaine wrote to Mme de Thianges:

Il est homme de cour, je suis homme de vers.

He is a man of the court, I a man of verse.

In his verse epistle to Mme de Thianges, the poet, who knew how to please the Parisian public, asserted that, if Lully had not botched *Daphné*, it would have at least succeeded in Paris and may have made its way to the royal châteaux. He added:

> Qu'est-ce qu'un auteur de Paris?
> Paris a bien des voix, mais souvent, faute d'une,
>   Tout le bruit qu'il fait est fort vain.
> Chacun attend sa gloire autant que sa fortune
>   Du suffrage de Saint-Germain.
> Le maître y peut beaucoup, il sert de règles aux autres:
>   Comme maître premièrement,
> Puis comme ayant un sens meilleur que tous les nôtres.
>   Qui voudra l'éprouver obtienne seulement
>   Que le roi lui parle un moment.
>   (*Epître à Mme de Thianges*, ll. 45–54)

> What is an author of Paris?
> Paris has many voices, but often for lack of one,
>   All the noise it makes is in vain.
> Each awaits his glory as much as his fortune
>   On the approval of Saint-Germain.
> The master can do a great deal,
> He serves as a rule for the others:
>   First as master, and second,
> As someone with better sense than our own.
>   Anyone who wishes to test it,
>   Will have the king speak to him for but a moment.

La Fontaine had not obtained a favorable word from the king in 1662–63, in reply to his two poems on Foucquet's behalf. Ten years later, by a different channel, he sought to wrest it from him. That is the extent to which the "good Frenchman"'s faith in the monarchy and the poet's faith in poetry were indestructible in the author of *Les amours de Psyché*. One must read the libretto for *Daphné* to understand why he was so insistent upon making himself heard in high places, and why Lully refused to officially consecrate this wrong message through his music.[11]

On its own, the prologue is a full program that goes against the current of the king's doctrine and that of his ministers. La Fontaine depicts Jupiter, Minerva, and Venus, the "three functions" of the court. The three deities wonder what king to offer the unstable men with whom Prometheus has repeopled the earth after the flood. Minerva wants "reason," "virtue," "order," and "glory" for this king. Venus wants leisure, rest, pleasure, a "gift for love." The choir concludes:

Heureux qui par raison doit plaire!
Plus heureux qui plaît par amour!

Blessed is he who by reason must please!
More blessed still he who pleases by love!

Under the appearance of gallant commonplaces, La Fontaine reopened the debate on which Foucquet's fate and that of the kingdom had turned in 1661, and oriented it toward peace, the arts of peace, and government by moderation.

The final scene of that dramatic pastorale is even more audacious. It would have made Parnassus appear on the stage of the Olympus theater, and in front of King Jupiter; yet in 1661, Gabriel Guéret had not even perceived that Parnassus on "the map of the court." It would have symbolically put an end to the tragedy that had obliterated poetry and dried up sincere praise of the king. We read in the libretto:

Parnassus reveals itself in the background. A few Muses are seated in various places on its crest, and a few poets at its feet. At the summit, the palace of the god is visible. The two sides of the theater are two galleries that resemble those where curiosities are displayed on feast days and fair days. These are the archives of Destiny. The architecture is decorated with laurel leaves. Under each portico is a bust; there are nine conquerors, and the same number of poets. The conquerors are on one side, the poets on the other. The conquerors are Cyrus the Great, Alexander, and so on, and the poets are Homer, Anacreon, Pindar, Virgil, Horace, Ovid, Ariosto, Tasso, and Malherbe. Apollo wanted the future to be shown for the benefit of that celebration [the marriage of the god to Daphne, deified by love].

Hence, through the conclusive epiphany of a pastoral opera, La Fontaine would have presented, during the great century of the French monarchy, the allegory reinvented by the Italian Renaissance to signify "belles lettres" and their beneficent hints of "good government" and the "common good."[12] France would have witnessed, under the king's nose, the appearance of a scenic version of the most famous Raphael fresco in the *Stanze* of the Vatican, and from three paintings by Nicolas Poussin, including the dazzling *Inspiration du poète,* today in the Louvre. At the time it was part of the collections inherited from Mazarin by the duc and duchesse de La Meilleraye, the lovely Hortense Mancini, cherished by Saint-Evremond, Saint-Réal, and La Fontaine. Contrary to a deeply ingrained legend, the allegory of Parnassus, so dear to the Medicis, to the Italian princes of the Renaissance, to the Valois, and to Foucquet, was totally absent from Louis XIV's iconography and, in particular, from the gardens of Versailles. The military Sun of Louis the Great was not the god of poets, a contemplator playing the lyre among the Muses. It was to remedy that deficiency, disheartening for any writer, that, beginning in 1708, Titon du Tillet labored (but in vain) to have a sculpted group erected representing Apollo, the Muses, and the French poets (including Madeleine de Scudéry and La Fontaine) on Mount Parnassus, either in the gardens of Versailles or in Paris.[13]

To make *Clymène*'s Parnassus victorious over Louis XIV's Olympus, the poet made a concession to the king: on his *Daphné*'s Parnassus, he showed effigies of the "conquerors" with whom the potentate liked to identify. In a paroxysm of flattery that aroused Saint-Simon's ire, in 1687 the duc de La Feuillade erected, on the Place des Victoires, Desjardins's statue of Louis XIV as the "god Mars," embodying and effacing all other conquerors, trampling underfoot the nations of a Europa in chains. The king himself inaugurated the statue.

In 1674 La Fontaine, an awkward flatterer, did not even have a bust of the king appear on his Parnassus next to those of Alexander and Caesar! In exchange for what he may have nevertheless considered a personal sacrifice, the poet presented, among the nine busts of poets, two ancients with whose art he could identify: Anacreon (his own Parnassus name in *Clélie*) and Ovid, from whom he had borrowed the subject for *Daphné* and who was one of the primary classical sources of the allegory of Parnassus. Moreover, in the dialogue held on the holy mountain, the poet elaborated an entire manifesto of French poetry: the "sublime" (the classical treatise on the subject was translated by Boileau that same year) was sent away to "sleep" with epics and flattering panegyrics. Lyric and pastoral poetry, under the luminous Virgilian name of Daphnis, were rehabilitated; satirical poetry and its liberating laughter, redeemed by Molière and Boileau in 1661, were linked to it. The epiphany of Parnassus ended in the ballet: "Four lyric authors and as many Muses of the same sort came to dance, to bear witness to joy; then the fools mingled with them, forming different shapes with the laurel branches they were all carrying, and of which they made cradles of sorts. It is grand ballet."

Mingling the lyric interlude with the irony of satire, this allegorical ballet coincided with the poetical mood of *Fables*. If the prologue went against the grain of the king's war policy, the peroration of *Daphné* aimed at accelerating the evolution that the Mortemarts had introduced into court art, to such a degree that it radically inverted the meaning of that art, as if with a symbolic wave of the wand. On this French Parnassus in the optative mood, praise of the king ceased to be a pompous duty and once more became a pleasure; it put lyricism, comedy, and irony at the heart of the French court. It returned lively and delightful. If the libretto for *Daphné*, a true literary "Edict of Nantes," had prevailed over Lully's censorship, it would have reminded the king of that poetic wit and diversity (*poïkilia* in Greek, a key word for the poets of Alexandria) which *Fables* strove to assemble. The inclusion of Ariosto and Tasso on that Parnassus, next to the Greeks and Latins, would have closely linked French song to the Italian fantasia. It would have been a return to Vaux and even to the Fontainebleau of Francis I and Henry II, as if the entire intervening period had been just a bad dream. This wish presupposed that Louis XIV would have ceased to resemble himself.

It would be nice to know what Lully could have told the king to justify his refusal to set *Daphné* to music. All we know is that he pointed out to Louis XIV that the subject for the pastorale and the excessively fluid style were not heroic enough for his glory. That was quite enough to confirm the king's permanent aversion, despite the efforts of the Mortemarts, toward Foucquet's poet. But the superintendent of the academy of music must have found it strange that La Fontaine should dare ask him to submit his own notes and harmonic genius to the glorification of poetry. His own monopoly on pompous music and on favor at court was perfectly adequate to satisfy the king's appetite for diversion and exaltation.

In spite of that failure, La Fontaine's name, backed by the Mortemarts and the success of the second collection of *Fables*, dedicated to Mme de Montespan, was pronounced more often in Louis XIV's presence. Somehow, the poet had entered the familiar landscape of that man of habit. The stage was set from a great distance off for a possible nomination to the Académie Française.

Parnassus, an allegory for the "spiritual power" that Renaissance litera-ture intended to exert over temporal powers, did not have a place set aside in Louis XIV's spectacle society—spectacles of war or musical spectacles. On the fringes of the court, however, there was one institution to which La Fontaine had been closely linked between 1645 and 1661 (it was almost a family for him), thanks to Valentin Conrart and Paul Pellisson: the Académie Française. A number of friends from his youth had a seat there (Pellisson himself, Antoine Furetière, François Charpentier, the abbé Paul Tallemant, the duc de Saint-Aignan, Jean Racine, Charles Perrault, and Isaac de Benserade), and some of his masters in poetry had once had seats as well (Tristan L'Hermite, Saint-Amant, Pierre Corneille, François Maynard, Racan). Over time it had become a living allegory for the king-dom's belles lettres, a royal Parnassus above the successive reigns. On Colbert's suggestion, the king himself became its protector upon the death of Chancellor Séguier in 1672. The academy thanked him and would con-tinue to thank him through a rich proliferation of panegyrics. But it was not his creation, and this body of writers had its own memory, its own his-tory, offshore from *The Isle of Pleasures* and even the *Harbor of Secrecy*.

It was very natural, and very French, that La Fontaine should aspire to take his place on this actual Parnassus, meeting at the Louvre since 1672, inasmuch as the court deserted the old palace for Versailles in 1683. Now more than ever, the academy was a Parisian institution, filled with memories and friendships dating to the poet's youth. Despite the presence of minor court poets in its ranks—Cotin, Boyer, Quinault—the academy was not part of the spectacle society proper to the reigning king. The incense it dispensed to its patron protected its singularity as a literary body. In addition, Colbert's death relieved it of a relatively un-wanted colleague.

The only peril for La Fontaine came from a small group of clergy, including Bossuet, who saw the author of *Contes* as a corruptor of souls. In 1683 Mme de Maintenon's rising star gave the prelates and abbots of the academy a new authority at court, which threatened to do as much dam-age to the poet as Colbert's or Lully's influence had once done. The difficulty was always the same for La Fontaine: wrest the "word" from the king that had been refused him in 1662–63, and which was again taken back (under Lully's successful pressure) in 1674. That withheld word was all the more desirable now. The opportunity to obtain it would not be repeated.

The poet's election to Colbert's seat was accomplished on 15 September 1683, by a vote of sixteen to seven. Everyone knew that La Fontaine was

not fond of the late minister. He had greeted his death with a cruel epigram.[14] To succeed him at the Académie Française was an extraordinary
and ironic revenge. Nevertheless, La Fontaine made sure that Boileau,
well received at court and whom the king wanted for that chair, would
not be in competition with him. The court faction and the religious faction of the academy lashed out against the poet, but in vain. Under the
circumstances, the academy had somewhat lampooned its royal protector.
The king made his disapproval felt with a scowl, refused his approval to
the new member, and put it off until his historiographer Boileau was elected.
In spite of everything, this was a royal yes-vote, long, drawn out, and in
very bad grace.

Boileau was elected on 17 April 1684. In the interval La Fontaine published a ballade in *Le Mercure Galant*,[15] in which he embroidered his own
cause on the model of *Ode au roi*, written in 1662 on Foucquet's behalf.
He celebrated (but in a form resembling that of Marot and Voiture, with
nothing epic or sublime about it) the king, always conquering, solitary
victor over a Europe united against him. And he concluded that obligatory panegyric with an envoi/petition that minimized the misdeeds of his
unlucky *Contes*, denounced before the king by ecclesiastic academy members as a "hanging offense":

> Ce doux penser, depuis un mois ou deux,
> Console un peu mes Muses inquiètes.
> Quelques esprits ont blâmé certains jeux,
> Certains récits, qui ne sont que sornettes.
> Si je défère aux leçons qu'ils m'ont faites,
> Que veut-on plus? Soyez moins rigoureux,
> Plus indulgent, plus favorable qu'eux;
> Prince, en un mot, soyez ce que vous êtes:
> L'événement ne peut être qu'heureux.

> That sweet thought, for a month or two,
> Has consoled somewhat my troubled Muses.
> A few souls have criticized certain plays,
> Certain stories, which are nothing but rot.
> If I bestow the lessons they have taught me,
> What more do they want? Be less severe,
> More indulgent, more favorable than they;
> Prince, in a word, be what you are:
> The outcome can only be happy.

The outcome was happy, at least in appearance. The king finally gave his approval on 20 April 1684. But he added a note to the abbé Testu, chancellor of the Académie Française: "He has promised to be good."[16] The long-awaited word took the form of an order. The religious faction of the academy was very worried. The poet had in fact given the churchmen his word, as he acknowledged in his *Ballade au roi*.

He published no more licentious tales, but he did not prove to be as "good" as the master had ordered. His correspondence with the duc de Vendôme (the other king of Sodom in Louis the Great's court), the prince de Conti, Mme Ulrich, Marie Champmeslé, and his London friends (the duchesse Mazarin, her sister the duchesse de Bouillon, Lady Harvey, and Saint-Evremond) demonstrates that the new member of the Académie Française changed nothing at first, either in his daily habits or in his feelings.

A Healthy Mind in a Healthy Body

These daily habits were those of a writer who knew how to reward his labor polishing his words, his reading and writing in the library, and even the sorrow of seeing and knowing the truth, with long walks outdoors, the pleasures of food and conversation, daydreaming in the garden, and, as often as possible, the company of some young beauty. In 1687 he wrote to Saint-Evremond:

On peut goûter la joie en diverses façons:
Au sein de ses amis répandre mille choses,
Et, recherchant de tout les effets et les causes,
A table, au bord d'un bois, le long d'un clair ruisseau,
Raisonner avec eux sur le bon, sur le beau,
Pourvu que ce dernier se traite à la légère,
Et que la Nymphe ou la bergère
N'occupe notre esprit et nos yeux qu'en passant.[17]

One can taste joy in many ways:
Among one's friends pour out a thousand things,
And, seeking the causes and effects for every thing,
Over dinner, at the edge of a wood, along a clear stream,

Reason with them on the good and the beautiful,
Provided that the latter be treated with frivolity,
And that the nymph or shepherdess
Occupies our minds and eyes only in passing.

The writers of humanist ancestry, whatever their profession, clerics and laypersons alike, developed a sixth sense for maintaining their moral, humoral, and physical equilibrium, which was always threatened by the melancholia of their risky situation, the second sight that haunted them, and their labors among books.[18] Paradoxically, their life expectancy was often longer than that of most of their contemporaries. The health of the body, as much as the joy of the imagination on which it depends, was one of the major preoccupations of the Renaissance, as biased against medical pedantry as against theological pedantry. The health of the studious, officers in charge of belles lettres along the twists and turns of Time and Fortune, was a thing too serious to be entrusted to health professionals. It was thus part of their own discipline. Every writer became, in the tradition of Marsilio Ficini and Rabelais, his own best doctor, and learned how to internalize the energies of nature and social pleasures to compensate for the deficiencies in humor and to cure the ailments of his body. La Fontaine was the author of a poem on "cinchona" (the bark, powerful against certain fevers, brought back from the Americas by the Jesuits, but which the hidebound and jealous Faculty of Medicine in Paris fought against). As a writer, he sought the health of the body as much as that of the soul in his choice of the companions, places, food, and music that could keep him happy in spite of everything. Other poets battled melancholia with Bacchus, the god of wine. All of that was necessary, along with a cheery imagination, to counterbalance the proclivity of "a tender heart that hates the vast black void."

Several of his closest friends—Saint-Evremond, Huet, Maucroix, and Boileau—lived past eighty. Like him, they had a natural, relatively good temperament, but they refrained from ruining it by excess. Despite all his boasting about Chlorises and Jeannetons, designed to make the roués smile, we must not imagine La Fontaine at Anet, in the Enclos du Temple, or in the company of the very gallant Mme Ulrich, dissipating himself in the debauchery that consumed Lully, wore down Vendôme, and to which Saint-Simon angrily alluded. The poet could pass through the most diverse circles of well-wishers without being moved and could observe their mores without deviating from his own life course. To Saint-Evremond, to whom he cheerily complained of his rheumatism in 1687, even as he appealed to

Marot, Rabelais, and Voiture to watch over his robust old age as they had his youth, he wrote: "I am no less opposed than you are to the false witty manner a libertine assumes. I will give any one who affects it the prize for absurdity."

In his view, libertinage was less an error than a nervous twitch that distorted the free movement of "our mother nature," whose "eternal lessons" it suited him to graciously follow. That same year (1687), he was able to go from Bois-le-Vicomte to Paris on horseback, his imagination so occupied with the charms of the fifteen-year-old Mlle de Beaulieu, a guest of his friends the d'Hervarts ("her beautiful eyes, her delicate white skin, her infinitely charming features, mouth, and gaze"), that he lost his way. He had to stay in poor lodgings, and he transformed that misadventure of an extravagant shepherd in love with an "Amarante" from a pastorale into a delicious epistle that delighted his friends at his own expense. In it he produced a few verses reminiscent (minus the bitterness) of *Stances à Marquise* ("Marquise, if my face / Looks old in certain ways / Remember that when you're my age / You'll hardly look any better")[19] with which Corneille, a devout old man in 1658, ended a brief fit of passion for the ravishing Mlle Du Parc, the star of Molière's troupe. The love of beauty, the imagination of beauty, and the production of language in beauty were admirable cures, the secret of which was reserved for poets. These fleeting visitations were rays of light from the golden age.

His good health, interrupted late in life by cruel crises of rheumatism, was one of the points La Fontaine had in common with his king, who was more imperiled than he by the eagerness of his doctors. Louis XIV governed himself not so much by the hygiene of Renaissance writers as by tested recipes he knew from the oral tradition of the courts. For him, the discipline of the king's job, the meticulous work of his councils as well as his required performances, was even more regular and constraining than the exercises in a poet's library. It was also less satisfying for the mind. But it well suited a temperament such as that of Louis XIV, who had few gifts of imagination and was entirely incapable of disinterested contemplation. The king knew how to work. He also knew to entertain himself, but in his own way. Quinault and Lully had no trouble convincing him, in the prologue of the royal ballet *L'amour malade* (1676):

> Si tu veux conserver des jours si pleins d'attraits,
> Grand roi, laisse Hippocrate et sa vaine doctrine:
>   Nous avons de meilleurs secrets
>   Que tous ceux de la Médecine.

Donne un peu de relâche à tes nobles désirs,
Mêle un instant de joie aux soins qui te possèdent,
Goûte nos jeux, nos vins, nos chants et nos plaisirs,
    C'est la véritable remède.[20]

If you want to hold on to days so full of charm,
Great king, set aside Hippocrates and his vain doctrine:
    We have better secrets
    Than all those of medicine.
Give a little space to your noble desires,
Mingle a moment of joy with the worries that possess you,
Sample our games, our wines, our songs, our pleasures,
    That is the true remedy.

The diversions sampled by the king were not the kind that threatened to make him forget himself. He needed external jolts, big and small: hunts, as everyday an occurrence in peacetime as the ministerial councils; grand spectacles at the theater; music with high-intensity sounds; emotionally charged sermons; vast gardens and great buildings that could be taken in at a glance; military campaigns when they were very well advanced and worthy of his rare spectacular presence (until 1693, when he began to command the armies only from maps at his headquarters in Versailles, like Philip II at El Escorial); and finally, the hasty outings with his mistresses—official or short-lived—such as the overly pretty duchesse de Fontanges. The king's favor for her did not withstand her first miscarriage, which dangerously weakened her, took her away from the court, and made the poor girl pine away and die at Port-Royal in April 1682, at age twenty-two. In 1680 La Fontaine dedicated a beautiful homage in verse to that victim of the Minotaur.[21] He did it with the approval of Mme de Montespan, who was using every means she could to combat Mme Scarron's growing influence over the king.

Mme de Maintenon's matrimonial influence, old age, and the arguments of her Jesuit confessors were gradually able to overcome the king's carnal appetites; they did not in any way affect the sturdy Gargantuan edifice of egotism, built on bureaucratic labor and courtly leisure. Saint-Simon tells how, without heeding the remonstrance of the quasi queen and Dr. Fagon, he ordered that the duchesse de Bourgogne, who amused him a great deal, take a trip away from the court to Marly in 1708, despite her advanced state of pregnancy and her alarming weakness. The king, taking a walk near the carp pond in Marly, had to announce to his courtiers, including the duc de Saint-Simon: "The duchesse de Bourgogne is injured." The duc de La Rochefoucauld cried out that "this was the greatest misfortune in the world, and that, since she had already been injured other times, she might not have any more." "Be that as it may," the king suddenly interrupted in anger, "what would that mean for me? Doesn't she already have a son? . . . Thank god she is injured, since she had to be, and I will never again be thwarted in my travel plans and in everything I want to do by the ideas of doctors and the reasoning of matrons. I will come and go as I please, and I will be left in peace."[22] Saint-Simon, after reporting the long silence and terror of sorts that these words spread even among the gardeners of Marly, added: "I was right to have judged long ago that the king did not love or consider anyone but himself, and was in himself his ultimate end." Louis XIV's health and the smooth operation of his state came at that price.

FROM FOUCQUET TO FÉNELON

In 1693 La Fontaine published the last edition of *Fables* to appear in his lifetime. It included a new book (now book 12), many parts of which had been published separately since 1685. This last collection was preceded by a dedication to Louis XIV's grandson, the Grand Dauphin's eldest son, the duc de Bourgogne. A quivering excitement for the very young prince animates this prose epistle, which ends (like the one the poet wrote for the Grand Dauphin in 1668, nearly twenty years earlier) in coldly excessive and indirect praise directed at the king. Within book 12 there are no less than four fables (two with a particular dedicatory epistle in verse) addressed to the royal child.[23] Even Mme de La Sablière and the duc de La Rochefoucauld had not received such a generous welcome in the "favorite book."

That fervor was addressed to the young prince's tutor as much as to the prince himself: this was the abbé François de Salignac de la Mothe-Fénelon, charged by the king, since 16 August 1686, with the education of his grandson.[24] He was named to that post at the same time as the little prince's governor, the duc de Beauvilliers. The poet (who was sixty-five in 1686), whose biographers depict him as old, debauched, distracted, and filthy, thus found himself closely associated from the inside and late in his life with the most remarkable and secret political adventure of the seventeenth century, comparable only to the rise and fall of Nicolas Foucquet: the Fénelon adventure. In 1668 the dedication to the Dauphin was only a facade. In 1693 book 12 of *Fables* openly bore witness to the poet's close cooperation in the great work of the kingdom, the formation of the heart and mind of someone who would probably soon become king of France. For La Fontaine it was another way, inspite of his disgrace, of exercising the duties of royal poet.

When and how did Fénelon become connected to Foucquet's poet? The duc de Bourgogne's tutor was born into one of the oldest and most illustrious families in Languedoc. Several members of that family had been closely linked to the Compagnie du Saint-Sacrement: Fénelon was a late and splendid product of that "religious cabal" combated by Richelieu and then by Colbert. During his adolescence, he spent a long time at the Oratory of Paris where La Fontaine himself had once been a novice. Noticed by Bossuet in 1673, who immediately became fond of him, the abbé de Fénelon already held his secret views. He was very quickly able to lay claim to the post working with the duc de Bourgogne, which the bishop of Meaux had held in relation to the young prince's father, the Grand Dauphin. The noble ecclesiastic had a great deal of magnetism. Saint-Simon, fascinated by this miracle of intelligence and charm, left behind a portrait of Fénelon after he had become an archbishop; for once in *Mémoires*, praise wins out unreservedly over sarcasm:

> This prelate was a tall, thin man with a good build, pale with a large nose, eyes that blazed with fire and wit, and a physiognomy such as I had never seen, and which was unforgettable once one had seen it. It combined everything together, and yet the contraries did not clash. It had gravity and gallantry, seriousness and gaiety; it also had the look of a doctor, a bishop, and a great lord; what came to the surface on that face, as in his entire person, was refinement, wit, grace, decency, and, above all, nobility. It took some effort to stop looking at him.[25]

Saint-Simon thus gives a glimpse of several centuries of the kingdom's history, literature, and religion, concentrated and embodied in Fénelon — a true mutant — as second nature, as if it had emerged from ordinary human nature. In fact, the doctrine of "pure love" that Fénelon championed seems to have anticipated by several centuries the evolution of the human race and a final victory of spirit over matter. That doctrine describes him, and perhaps him alone. Gallant romanticism, in alliance with a devout knowledge of mystical ways, reached its summit in the person, thoughts, and actions of Fénelon.

In his early poems, the future author of *Télémaque* seems to have already sampled and imitated La Fontaine. The ecclesiastic had received the best literary education from the Jesuits of Cahors. Like the author of *Fables*, he was exceptionally gifted for friendship. Like him, he was weaned on Homer, Plato, Virgil, and Horace. His origins, his alliances, and his talents immediately earned him powerful supporters at court: none of these supporters were unknown to La Fontaine. Fénelon's primary backer, Paul de Saint-Aignan, duc de Beauvilliers (and the husband, like his friend the duc de Chevreuse, of one of Colbert's daughters), was in fact the son of the duc de Saint-Aignan, whom La Fontaine had known in Foucquet's entourage, and who had married a rich cousin of Mme de La Sablière. The duc de Beauvilliers's father nevertheless remained a favorite of Louis XIV after 1661; the king was beholden to that man of letters and wit for much of the splendor of the first festivals he held at Versailles to erase the memory of Vaux. The duc de Beauvilliers and the duc de Chevreuse were the first great lords since 1661 to join the king's council. They were united in the same highly devout circle with the duc de Béthune-Charost and his wife, Nicolas Foucquet's eldest daughter. The duchesse de Mortemart, another of Colbert's daughters, who had married the marquise de Montespan's brother, also belonged to that circle. In the second generation, at least on the women's side, Colbert's and Foucquet's families had thus been reconciled by heaven, in the same ardent piety and in accord with a political orientation that was secretly opposed to Colbertism in every way. Following Bossuet, this nest of devout halcyons poised at the top of the monarchy, and with which La Fontaine had more than one affinity, adopted, from his first appearance at court, the abbé Fénelon as its spiritual guide and political inspiration.

In 1688–89, the duchesse de Charost, in her country house of Beynes near Saint-Cyr, introduced Fénelon to her close friend Jeanne Guyon du Chesnay, whose mystic experiences and doctrine were, for the duc de Bourgogne's tutor, the starting point for his political tribulations but also for the elaboration of his doctrine as a theologian of "pure love." She was the widow of a rich financier once compromised by Foucquet's disgrace, and who had sought refuge in 1661–64 in the Paris mansion of the duchesse de Longueville; at the time, the Great Condé's sister was the protectress of Port-Royal. In these same tumultuous months, Mme Guyon's father gave shelter in his home in Montargis to the duchesse de Charost,

Foucquet's elder daughter. A quarter century later, in 1689, at the home of Mme de Miramion, lady of Saint-Cyr, Foucquet's elder son, the comte de Vaux, married Mme Guyon's daughter. Hence the hottest embers of the "religious faction," buried under ashes by Richelieu on the Day of Dupes in 1630 and apparently put out by Colbert in 1661 after they flamed up anew around Foucquet and his family, caught fire again in the very heart of Versailles, but this time with a glow of dawn in its flames that neither Bossuet nor Mme de Maintenon immediately perceived.[26]

As a poet disdained by the king, La Fontaine could easily identify with the libertinage of the Vendômes and Bouillons, his easygoing patrons: old and deep attachments to the Oratory, Port-Royal, the Saint-Aignans, and especially the Foucquet family familiarized him to an equal degree with the feelings and hopes of the "little flock" for which Fénelon had become the shepherd.

Mme de Sévigné always maintained affectionate ties with those whom she called "saints": Nicolas Foucquet's mother, Marie de Maupeou, his second wife, Madeleine Jeannin de Castille, his daughter by his first wife, the duchesse de Charost, and his eldest son, the comte de Vaux. We know nothing of the ties La Fontaine may have had with these unfortunate souls. But the poet and his closest friend, Maucroix, Foucquet's former agent in Rome, could not possibly have become indifferent to the fate of the prisoner of Pignerol and his family.

Foucquet, a writer and even a gifted versifier, did not stop writing and composing lines in La Bastille, and he continued to do so in Pignerol; a network of accomplices managed to get them to his friends. The illustrious prisoner's "conversion" preceded La Fontaine's by a long time and showed the way to all those who, in his family or associated with it, now sought to penetrate the nerve center of the monarchy through religious pathways, and no longer solely by those of arts and letters. It is very probable that La Fontaine's paraphrase of the Seventeenth Psalm in 1671[27] was a fervent response and emotional echo of Foucquet's translation of the One Hundred and Eighteenth Psalm, written in Pignerol and mysteriously transported to Paris. In 1667 another of Foucquet's poems was published anonymously in Paris under the title Le chrétien désabusé du monde (The Christian disabused of the world). Foucquet, recapturing the inspiration of the stanzas in Corneille's Polyeucte, wrote:

Trompeuses vanités où mon âme abusée
A vu de ses beaux jours la trame mal usée
Esclavage de cour, où tous les courtisans

Dissipent en fumée et leurs biens et leurs ans,
Vous ne me tenez plus: vos faux biens, vos faux charmes
Sont ici maintenant le sujet de mes larmes:
Je déplore le temps que j'ai perdu pour vous.
Vos favoris, vos rois qu'on adore à genoux,
Au-dessus du commun n'ont qu'un éclat de verre;
Ils sont faits comme nous de poussière et de terre.
Quand l'heure sonnera, malgré tous leurs efforts,
Leur pourpre et leur grandeur, leur trône et leurs trésors,
Leur haute majesté tombera dans la bière
Et quelques jours après ne sera que poussière.
. . . .
Un seul jour avec Dieu vaut mieux que mille jours
Passés avec vos rois dans vos superbes cours:
. . . .
Il n'en est pas ainsi du Dieu que nous servons.
Nous demandons sans cesse et toujours nous avons;
Toujours prêt d'écouter nos voeux et nos demandes
Plus nos désirs sont forts, plus ses grâces sont grandes.[28]

Deceitful vanities where my misled soul
Saw the thread of his best days poorly used,
Courtly slavery, where all the courtiers
Dissipate in smoke both their possessions and their years,
You no longer hold me: your false possessions, your false charms
Are here and now the reason for my tears:
I deplore the time that I lost for you.
Your favorites, your kings adored on bended knee,
Above the mob have only the sparkle of glass;
Like us, they are made of dust and dirt.
When the hour sounds, despite all their efforts,
Their purple and grandeur, their throne and treasures,
Their lofty majesty will fall in the bier
And a few days later will be nothing but dust.
. . . .
A single day with God is worth more than a thousand days
Spent with your kings in your superb courts:
. . . .
It is not so with the God we serve.
We ask unceasingly and always receive;

He is always ready to listen to our wishes and requests,
. The stronger our desires, the greater his grace.

Was not the repentant La Fontaine in his last days more faithful than
ever to Foucquet? A treatise on spiritual guidance, *Les conseils de la sagesse,*
compiled in Pignerol by the former *surintendant,* who had grown and
matured as a result of his long martyrdom, circulated in manuscript form
after his death in 1680 among the "little flock" of dukes and duchesses,
who were soon to be placed under Fénelon's spiritual guidance.

The parting of ways between Fénelon and Bossuet, the former's exile
to the archbishopric of Cambrail, and Rome's condemnation of his
Maximes des saints, occurred only in 1696–99, after La Fontaine's death.
Until 1695 the unity of the religious faction at court—its zeal for the
state, its ardent participation in the enormous work of conversion preceding and following the revocation of the Edict of Nantes, its growing
influence over the king and the court—seemed to be the handiwork of
Bossuet and the new "mother of the Church," the secret queen of France,
the marquise de Maintenon. Between 1689 and 1695 Fénelon, and even
Mme Guyon, who had more distant goals in view, could move in the
official wake of the quasi queen and the pontiff of the Gallican church
without inspiring distrust, and usually enjoyed trust and admiration. In
1693 Fénelon was elected to the Académie Française, where, providen-
tially, he succeeded Paul Pellisson, formerly chief assistant to Foucquet,
for whom he wrote a splendid eulogy. In 1695 Bossuet anointed Fénelon
archbishop of Saint-Cyr.

The *Map of the Court,* that *Isle of Prayers,* almost a royal abbey with
Mme de Maintenon as its founder and prioress, now erased the lustful
memory of *The Isle of Pleasures* that had made the court glow red during
the time of Monsieur and the marquise de Montespan. The chapel at
Versailles began to resonate with splendid sound frescoes by François
Couperin, Michel-Richard Delalande, and Marc-Antoine Charpentier,
on the words of Jeremiah, David, Venantius Fortunatus: the words of the
Latin liturgy.[29]

Twice, in 1688–89 with *Esther* and in 1690–91 with *Athalie,* Racine
triumphantly put on "devotion plays" in front of Louis XIV and James II
in exile, performed by Mme de Maintenon's young pensioners. To Mme
de Sévigné, admitted as one of the last spectators of *Esther,* the king said
of Racine: "He has a great deal of wit." The poet was even invited to
Marly. What a road the author of *Phèdre* had traveled since he had been
named historiographer in 1677! In his person, belles lettres had entered

the royal holy of holies; they could melodiously and mysteriously remind Louis XIV, through innocent mouths, of "the maxims of a truly royal heart." To achieve that difficult success at court, which had been refused La Fontaine and was of a completely different order than that of the histrion Molière, the symbolic language of Parnassus, Apollo, and the Muses had to give way to that of Zion, the God of armies, and the daughters of Jerusalem.[30] Foucquet's daughter also had to forget that her father had hoped to govern France with the Huguenots, the erudite libertines, and writers of every denomination: she was faithful to him by virtue of her piety and the solidarity of religious souls.

But that holy court was not untroubled for long. In 1695 the break between Bossuet, who professed the orthodox theology of absolutism, and Fénelon, whose entire education program for the duc de Bourgogne and whose spiritual doctrine actually had the aim of reversing the orientation the kingdom had taken since Richelieu, was a silent menace. With Fénelon, who made the mystical evangelism of Francis I's sister, Marguerite de Navarre, and the royal piety of Henry III's last days bloom again in the final years of the seventeenth century in the Bourbon king's court, Foucquet's program for the monarchy, brought to fruition by the thirty-year experiment of the absolute state, was also attempting once more to find an opening. The "little flock" of dukes and duchesses stirred up by Jeanne Guyon and guided by Fénelon had their eyes set on his masterpiece, the duc de Bourgogne, the new Daphnis of Virgil's Fourth Eclogue, called to restore the reign of Astrea, and a new biblical David, called to one day see to its end the kingdom of France's great piety.

Fénelon, along with the abbé Claude Fleury and Jean de La Bruyère, was undoubtedly part of the "little synod" meeting around Bossuet to advise on the reformation of the kingdom's morals. The two reformist and religious projects intersected on many points, but they diverged on the essential thing: the aim of the first was the moral rearmament of the state to better preserve it in the absolutist form Louis XIV had given it; the second sought to replace that harsh form by a regime that was both older, more faithful to the traditions of the kingdom, and newer, better in accord with the moral and spiritual aspirations that had developed since the Renaissance and the Council of Trent.[31]

La Bruyère's Les caractères, the first edition of which appeared anonymously in 1687, reflected the critical and reformist views stirred within the conservative "little synod" assembled around Bossuet. The comic and satirical vigor of the devout moralist, its epigrammatic turn, owed a great deal to La Fontaine's "human comedy." If proof were needed that the Fables of the first two collections were profoundly understood under Louis XIV, one would have to seek it in *Les caractères*, among other places.[32]

But La Bruyère was a morose prose writer, a preacher of the printed page. He knew nothing of the gaiety and fancy of the last poet of the Renaissance: La Fontaine was not simply a moralist. Fénelon himself, who had every gift to the supreme degree and even the best-stocked imagination, was a very great poet, but in prose: the first in the French language. La Fontaine, the musician of words much more than the painter of mores, found a deep resonance in Fénelon the writer and pedagogue. In addition to the sense for fables that they shared, a similar feeling about the true vocation of the kingdom and a common affiliation to Foucquet's memory and all its repercussions predestined them to travel part of the road together. For the poet this road was also, in the more or less long term, the road toward reforming his own mores: the road to conversion.

In 1686 the future king's tutor invited La Fontaine, whom he professed to admire, to add his charm to his own educational strategies. In the king's mind, it was the very success of that education—that initiation, one is tempted to say—of the duc de Bourgogne that sealed Fénelon's fate, even more than his alliance with Mme Guyon or his theological theses.

The reform projects for the kingdom outlined by Fénelon, along with the duc de Chevreuse, in November 1711 (the *Tables de Chaulnes*), at a time when Monseigneur's death made Fénelon's pupil the heir to Louis XIV, and his former teacher a future Richelieu, responded in advance (by nearly a century) to the 1798 list of grievances. They took the opposite tack of the regime built by Richelieu and Colbert. The history of Old France hung in the balance for several months, as it had done in 1658–61. Everything might have taken a different turn without the death of the duc de Bourgogne on 18 February 1712. In the years 1686–96, La Fontaine, the human lyre, vibrated with that secret hope. His poetry gradually gave way to prayer.

The written program for the *Tables de Chaulnes* (1711) took for granted what had been cruelly missing from Foucquet's elliptical "program" when Mazarin died: a king's heartfelt support.[33] Fénelon, taking into account the experience of 1661, put all his genius as an educator into overcoming the future king's amour propre; in Fénelon's view, it was the root of his grandfather's Machiavellianism. It was also the nook where the serpent Python had settled and coiled itself around the monarchy: it would take both the god of Parnassus, dear to La Fontaine, and the God of Fénelon to bring it down. Fénelon gave an irrefutable portrait, worthy of La Rochefoucauld, of Louis XIV's amour propre, the cornerstone of the absolutist edifice, in the famous anonymous *Lettre au roi* (1693), probably referred to Mme de Maintenon, but which the king never read:

> You were born, Sire, with an honest and equitable heart, but the only knowledge of governance that those who reared you gave you was mistrust, jealousy, alienation from virtue, fear of all outstanding merit, a taste for wishy-washy and groveling men, haughtiness, and attention to your own self-interest. For some thirty years, your chief ministers have shaken and overturned all the old maxims of the state, and supremely elevated your authority, which had become their own because it was in your hands. No one spoke of the state or of rules any longer; one spoke only of the king and his pleasure. . . .
>
> Your name has been made hateful and the entire French nation intolerable to all your neighbors. . . . For example, Sire, Your Majesty was made to undertake the Dutch War in 1672, for your glory and to punish the Dutch who had made some joke, in their sorrow caused by the disruption of the rules of commerce established by Cardinal de Richelieu. I cite that war in particular because it was the origin of all the others. It was justified solely on the grounds of glory and vengeance, which cannot make a war just; hence it follows that all the borders you have extended via that war were unjustly acquired from the beginning. . . . Therefore, Sire, one must return to the origin of the Durch War to examine before God all your conquests. It is pointless to say that they were necessary to your state. The possessions of others are never necessary to us.[34]

In this last paragraph, the prophetic vision and all the prophetic authority of "spiritual power" stands above temporal and carnal power. Through Fénelon's words, Golgotha, more intrepid than Parnassus, cast thunderbolts at Olympus. The vehemence of Bossuet's sermons and funeral orations was mere flattery compared to that sword of fire that sought to impose limits and modesty on the state.

The duc de Bourgogne/Telemachus, educated as his grandfather should have been, initiated to the "pure love" and the knowledge of evil it supposes, was to bring the virtues and lofty views of Saint Louis, ignored by Louis XIV, back to the throne of France, and to remedy a half century of errors. The advice of his mentor, a new Minerva for the kingdom, would guide the young king in that salutary task. In the last analysis, what was at stake in the formidable battle between Bossuet and Fénelon, which began in Issy in July 1694, was the keystone of the entire edifice of the

French monarchy: the king's heart. But for these theologians, it was also the Gordian knot of Christianity: the theology of freedom and grace.

For Bossuet, the king's heart was like that of all men, incurably occupied since the fall by amour propre, and it could not obey God's plan and do the kingdom's good without also following, even with the aid of grace, its own self-interested proclivity toward glory, passions, and pleasure. This was also the feeling of Pierre Nicole, the great moralist of Port-Royal. For Fénelon (in that respect, a pure writer as much as a pure religious man), education in cooperation with grace could make a king's heart move beyond the stage of amour propre. It was not the figurehead, but the person of the duc de Bourgogne that the teacher initiated to the state of indifference he demanded of himself, from which it was possible to see evil without being swayed and to do good without expecting glory or pleasure.

According to Bossuet's hypothesis, Louis XIV and his state were certainly what they ought and could be, even if reforms were desirable to bring them closer to the wishes of the Church. According to Fénelon's hypothesis, the lock of amour propre had been broken in his royal pupil's heart, and a profound transfiguration of the kingdom, purified from reason of state, was becoming possible. In 1695–97, in the duel between the eagle of Meaux and the swan of Cambrai, one entered the eye of the hurricane of "seventeenth-century morals."

All of a sudden, the very fables of La Fontaine that Louis XIV had always ignored could work, as part of the duc de Bourgogne's educational program, toward making the scales fall from the heart of the king's grandson.[35] This was certainly already the "useful" plan of *Fables*, enveloped in its "pleasures," as it was the plan of La Rochefoucauld's *Maximes*. In 1686 the nightingale of the kingdom finally found the swan that understood the ultimate, political, royal meaning of his "favorite book."

BOOK 12 OF *FABLES*

Love of language, the experience of the dispossession of the "ego," and the mysterious dictation by the Muses that poets call "inspiration" are not alien, in their own order, to the state of "pure love" that Fénelon made the threshold of spiritual progress outside the hog wallow of amour propre. La Fontaine, a "distrait" man but a peculiarly self-conscious poet, took for granted this wavering and the renunciation of the selfish "ego" that accompanies the vision and dictation of the poem, and that, far from extinguishing the powers of the mind, a witness to the operation of the Muses, actually spurs them on. A reader of d'Urfé, close in so many respects to Saint Francis of Sales,[36] he was also not unaware of the correspondences among that state of poetic inspiration, the most lyrical forms of the feeling of love—especially when remembered—and the most oblatory forms of the experience of "prayer." For his part Fénelon, a writer and poet weaned on the best of Greek and Latin literature, knew of his own personal knowledge the kinship that exists between prayer and poetry, between the divine inspiration which possesses itself of the poet and the internal divestment, the renunciation, the humility presupposed at the foundation and summit of the work of prayer, the disappropriated abandonment of the loving soul to God. Between the swan of the court's "family of love" and the nightingale of gallant romanticism, the affinities went deeper than the apparent differences between a church nobleman and a somewhat bohemian poet.

"The Companions of Ulysses," the first fable in book 12, preceded by a verse dedication (just as *Adonis* was preceded by a dedication to Foucquet), suggests that the poet had read in manuscript and in secret at least the first books of *Les aventures de Télémaque,* the allegorical novel by Fénelon, educator of the duc de Bourgogne (in 1699 the publication of this pedagogical novel without Fénelon's knowledge caused a scandal). La Fontaine's fable is a variation on the episode of Ulysses on the island of Circe. *Télémaque,* a series of free variations on themes from *The Odyssey,* begins with one of the most beautiful litotes in French literature: "Calypso ne pouvait se consoler du départ d'Ulysse" (Calypso could not be consoled of Ulysses' departure). Telemachus lands on an island where his father has left behind just such a passionate yearning. La Fontaine, in turn, has the duc de Bourgogne land on one of the islands from *The Odyssey,* namely, that of Circe, and has him symbolically hand over to Ulysses, Telemachus's father and model, the key to *Fables,* its hidden moral and spiritual meaning. There could be no more gracious way of sealing the contract that, in 1686, united the teacher of Louis XIV's grandson and the author of poems that now served the royal child as Latin themes and composition exercises.

Circe has metamorphosed the companions of Ulysses into animals, but the "wise and sharp" hero of *The Odyssey* with whom, like Calypso, Circe is in love, knew how to take precautions for himself. The philter the beautiful magician used guides the reader toward the overarching metaphor through which the poet himself transports the human comedy, and its conflicts of amour propre, to the register of animal life: as Circe (a figure for the author of *Fables*) announces it to Telemachus's father (a figure for his reader), the companions of Ulysses, far from accepting the reprieve of a return to humanity, declare they are happy and confirmed in their animal shells. The beast fable, the genre to which La Fontaine had devoted all his genius as a storyteller and musician since 1668, now revealed the root of its initiatory irony: looking into the mirror of his companions transformed into animals, Ulysses is disabused of the last of his naïveté and discovers all the terrible power of the "ego's" pull on the human "self," powerful as a magnet, a suction cup, or the fall of heavy bodies. This is, in fact, one of the essential lessons of *Fables*, and La Fontaine was in perfect agreement on this matter with Fénelon, who never had the slightest illusion about the iron laws of moral gravitation that the redemptive work of love is up against. The theater of "The Companions of Ulysses" uncovers the harsh truth of mortals all the more cruelly in that his animal men, from the deepest dungeon into which they have fallen and where they willingly take their pleasure, can also see the horrible and stupid spectacle they were involved in—but without understanding it—when they had human form. That gives them an apparently irrefutable excuse to continue to loll about in perfect freedom in their new zoological comfort, still "slaves to themselves," but now in full knowledge and by choice. Ulysses believes he can exhort his companion who has become a wolf:

> Quitte ces bois, et redeviens
> Au lieu de loup, homme de bien.
> —En est-il? dit le loup. Pour moi je n'en vois guère.
> Tu t'en viens me traiter de bête carnassière:
> Toi qui parles, qu'es-tu? N'auriez-vous pas sans moi
> Mangé ces animaux que plaint tout le village?
> Si j'étais homme, par ta foi,
> Aimerais-je moins le carnage?
> Pour un mot quelquefois vous vous étranglez tous.
> Ne vous êtes-vous pas l'un à l'autre des loups?

> Leave these woods, and become again,
> Instead of a wolf, an honorable man.
> "Are there any?" said the wolf.
> "For myself, I don't see many."

You come along and call me a carnivore:
Yet you who say this, what are you? If not for me,
Would you not have eaten these beasts, pitied by all the village?
    If I were a man, tell me true,
    Would I love carnage less than you?
For a word sometimes you all strangle one another
    Are you not also wolves toward each other?

The "cycle of the duc de Bourgogne" continues in book 12 with several fables that all warn their reader, with all the grace of lighthearted conversation, of the destructive and self-destructive monstrosity of human predators.[37] The old poet, with the consent of the prince's tutor and without excessive caution, prepared the new Saint Louis for the crown of thorns he would have to wear, in a labor to redeem the kingdom more back-breaking than those of Hercules. For Fénelon "pure love," like poetry in the iron age for La Fontaine, was the opposite of a bed of roses. It was the poignant grasp of contraries in a single glance, which coldly looked the devouring absolutism of amour propre and the desperate boldness of love in the face. Rousseau, who greatly admired Fénelon and hated La Fontaine, was incapable of that spiritual and moral oxymoron. The education of Emile leaves the disciple of the Savoyard vicar ignorant of the reign of evil and, in the first place, of the evil in his own heart.

Book 12, which makes generous allowances for the Fénelonian adventure (in book 8, the fable "The Torrent and the River" and, in book 10, "The Adventurers and the Talisman" had already glorified mad generosity, more prudent than the prudence of sages), is also a collection of personal essays, more directly in tune with the old poet's experience, and leaving to others the possibly happier future he will not see:

Je ne suis pas un grand prophète;
Cependant je lis dans les cieux
Que bientôt ses faits glorieux
Demanderont plusieurs Homères;
Et ce temps-ci n'en produit guères.
Laissant à part tous ces mystères
Essayons de conter la fable avec succès.
        ("The Wolf and the Fox," 12.9)

I am no great prophet;
Nevertheless I read in the heavens

That soon its glorious deeds
Will require several Homers;
And these times are producing few.
Leaving aside all these mysteries,
Let us try to tell the fable successfully.

The affinities between the great ecclesiastic and the poet ran deep. But between the heroic character of the theologian-prophet able to judge his king, to stand up to Bossuet, and aspiring, in a spirit of sacrifice and renunciation, to regenerate the state and the lay inspiration of the author of *Fables,* the differences and distances were still too great. The humility and humanity of the nightingale afflicted by old age, poverty, and weariness was only a distant echo of the swan's internal tension, the hardened steel of his will, the dry flame of his religious genius fed by the torrent of blessings flowing from the extraordinary sister-soul, Mme Guyon. There was not a shadow of the personal in Fénelon, any more than there was in Bossuet. They were sacred orators, born for the public pulpit. One was Greek, the other Latin. One was appealing, the other intimidating. La Fontaine was, if we dare say it, only a great poet. He sang and told stories. He never sang and told stories so purely as in the last decade of his life, when he tested the limits of the "power of fables" and turned once more to prayer. Thus he now gave the Muse a free hand. Fénelon and his little flock took over from him, in a manner that was essentially devout. It was as fatal to this late Renaissance poetry as Louis XIV's absolutism had been.

There was a consistent line, suggested more than spelled out, in the earlier books of *Fables.* Book 12 is a sort of open workshop in which La Fontaine, pushing the multiple meanings of the word "fable" to their extreme limits, sets out and juxtaposes his attempts in various genres, as so many entries in the personal journal of the poet at work, letting himself be carried this way and that by the four winds of wit, but without giving up any of his supreme craft. Opportunity reigns as mistress in these desperate and melodious exercises, which have no purpose beyond themselves, reflecting the colors of his sensibility and his lifelong way of thinking, but as if already settled around a central void, which he ceaselessly returned to contemplate. The dates of composition, omitted by the poet, are unnecessary: they are memoirs, the serendipity of the arrangement distances them from the opportunity that occasioned them.

Loyalty to a cause very dear to him led him to collaborate with Fénelon. Book 12 bears ample traces of that collaboration. But his gratitude toward the duc de Vendôme led him to dedicate the Ovidian fable "Philemon and Baucis" to his patron; in this fable, marriage, of which he had spoken so much ill, is reconciled with holy and inviolable friendship, which he had so celebrated. It was a private joke for everyone who knew the duke's life and manners. The poet's fondness for everything relating to Mme de La Sablière, and his enormous debt to *L'Astrée* (on which he based a lyrically tragic and luminescent libretto in 1691, unfortunately set to music by Lully's mediocre son-in-law, Colasse) produced an idyll: *Daphnis et Alcimadure*, dedicated to Mme de La Mésangère, Iris's daughter.[38] Regret over his *Contes*, which he disavowed when he was admitted to the Académie Française, and which he condemned in 1693, led him to translate Ovid's "The Daughters of Minea," Petronius's *The Matron of Ephesus*, and Machiavelli's *Belphegor* with his own inimitable variations and adornments but without the spiciness of Boccaccio. His resistance to Louis the Great was itself encapsulated in the delicious Oriental story "The Kite, the King, and the Hunter" (12.12), dedicated to the disgraced prince de Conti. Without bitterness, he amused himself with what was once his own wound and, in the final epigram of the fable, jabbed into the king's nose, he congratulated himself on having never gained anything from that major quarrel of a disappointed lover, except the perfection of his art.

The fable "The Two Goats" (12.4) is even more detached and visionary; it ought to serve as an epigraph for any impartial history of seventeenth-century Europe. The "key" to that apologue, which seems to wittily mock the mutually destructive caprice of two mountain goats, is concealed within an apparently ornamental simile at the center of the tale:

> Je m'imagine voir avec Louis le Grand
> Philippe Quatre qui s'avance
> Dans l'Ile de la Conférence.

> I imagine I see, with Louis the Great,
> Philip the Fourth advancing
> On the Isle of Conference.

Is this merely an amusing allusion to the long-ago Franco-Spanish wedding of 1660 on the Island of Bidassoa, in Saint-Jean-de-Luz? This little magic mirror reveals the true heroes of the fable/anamorphosis, which shows us two goats desperately fighting for precedence on a plank of wood over a pit, until both fall in. The La Fontainian art of the barb leaves no room for hesitation. "The Two Goats" is the encapsulation of a disabused spectator's experience of the European scene: he has always seen the Bourbon and the Habsburg arrogantly fighting over the rule of Europe, with the Bourbon always imagining he was definitively going to gain the ascendant; finally, in 1688, he found Europe in a nine-year war, completely united against France, which was increasingly overwhelmed by the grandiose "caprices" of its king. Book 12 even bears a trace (the dedication of "The English Fox" to Lady Harvey) of La Fontaine's whim, in about 1687, to leave the kingdom and join his French friends in exile in London.[39]

The fable "The Two Goats" undoubtedly also targets the bloody duels of amour propre and precedence, arbitrated by the king with relish, of which Saint-Simon reports so many examples from the ordinary life of Louis XIV's court. But its universal meaning lies first in the rivalries proper to "history on a grand scale," the pathetic mockery of which the poet brings out with a Buddhist humor. And yet he died soon enough not to have to witness Louis XIV start the "Great War" of Spanish succession in 1701 (the third of his reign and the most disastrous).

The recapitulative fable "The Companions of Ulysses" is nevertheless a companion piece to the fable and last will and testament that concludes the book: "The Judge, the Hospitaler, and the Hermit."[40] It would be difficult to push further the disillusionment with the world and the alienation from any form of action. The protagonists of this last fable are human beings and not animals. Of the three friends depicted, two have chosen not to discover the world, like the traveler in "The Two Doves," but rather to exercise justice and charity in it, with the honest intention of reforming abuses and relieving suffering. Life holds only disappointments and tribulations for them. The third friend, the "hermit," has chosen to retreat to a hermitage near a "pure spring" on the rocky flanks of Parnassus; of this trio "jealous of its salvation," he has the last word:

Apprendre à se connaître est le premier des soins
Qu'impose à tous mortels la majesté suprême.
Vous êtes-vous connus dans le monde habité?
L'on ne le peut qu'aux lieux pleins de tranquillité:
Chercher ailleurs ce bien est une erreur extrême.
    Troublez l'eau: vous y voyez-vous?
Agitez celle-ci.—Comment nous verrions-nous?
    La vase est un épais nuage
Qu'aux effets du cristal nous venons d'opposer.
—Mes frères, dit le saint, laissez-la reposer,
    Vous verrez alors votre image.
Pour vous mieux contemplez, demeurez au désert.

(12.29)

Learning to know oneself is the first concern
Imposed on all mortals by supreme majesty.
Did you get to know yourself in the inhabited world?
One can do so only in places of tranquility:
To seek this blessing elsewhere is a grave error.
  Disturb the water: do you see yourself in it?
Stir it up—How could you see yourself?
  Mud is a thick cloud
That we have contrasted to the effects of crystal.
"My brothers," said the saint, "let it be still,
  Then you will see your image.
To better contemplate yourself, remain in the desert."

The fable remains on the near side of Fénelon's or Bossuet's theological options. Its "lesson," which "ends" and sums up the lesson of *Fables*, in any case rediscovers the wisdom of Petrarch in his treatise *De vita solitaria*, today one of the less familiar Renaissance sources. The maxim "know thyself," with which La Fontaine, definitively and with dignity, says farewell to poetry, sets aside all noise, all illusion, all the vain wickedness of the world, but leaves intact the friendship, intimacy, and conversation in the desert of the "three saints" finally brought together near a spring that, with its "sharp rocks," might well be the Castaglia of the Ovidian myth, where all true poets come to drink before being swept up in the song of the Muses.

The poet has now made his farewells. The man now has slightly more than two years to prepare himself, like common mortals, for sweet death.

GOD OF MERCY OR GOD OF FEAR?

After four years of dreadful drought and deadly famine, the winter of 1695 was finally wet but still frigid. On 9 February of that year, the poet suddenly felt faint in the middle of the street. He wrote to François Maucroix in Reims:

You are surely wrong, my dear friend, if it is true, as M. de Soissons [Bishop Fabio Brulart de Sillery, friend of Maucroix] told me, that you believe me more ill of spirit than of body. He told me this in an attempt to give me courage, but that is not what I am lacking. I assure you that your best friend does not have fifteen days to live. It has been two months since I've been outside, except to go to the Académie a little, to have some amusement. Yesterday, as I was coming back, I became so weak all of a sudden in the middle of rue du Chantre [between the Louvre and rue Saint-Honoré] that I truly believed I was dying. O my dear friend, dying is nothing, but do you think I am going to appear before God? You know how I have lived. Before you receive this note, the gates of eternity may have opened for me.[41]

The same words that for centuries had come to the lips of every man "born Christian and French" at the approach of death came naively to the pen of this poet of Old France, words very close to the most simple prayers of contrition, learned, heard, and murmured since childhood.

It was in this same register of resorting to the old words of mercy that François Maucroix replied on 14 February:

My dear friend, the sorrow that your last letter has caused me is as you must imagine it. But, at the same time, I will tell you I have the consolation of the Christian frame of mind in which I see you. My very dear friend, even the most righteous need the mercy of God. Have full faith in it, therefore, and remember that he is called the father of mercies and the God of all consolation. Invoke him with all your heart. What can true contrition not obtain from that infinite goodness? If God blesses you with the return of your health, I hope you will come to spend the remainder of your life with me, and that we will often speak together of the mercies of God.[42]

No one knew La Fontaine better and more fondly than Maucroix. It was to him that the poet had written on 10 September 1661 a distressed letter after the news of Foucquet's arrest: "He has been arrested, and the king is violently opposed to him, even saying he has documents in his hands that will hang him. Oh, if he does that, he will be even crueler than his enemies, since, unlike them, it is not in his interest to be unjust." Maucroix knew the deep furrow that was plowed into the poet's soul by the king's "cruelty" toward Foucquet, the silence with which Louis XIV had met *Elégie* and *Ode*, written in support of the *surintendant*, and his refusal of any kind word for the poet of Vaux (not excepting "He has promised to be good" in 1684). Now that the "gates of eternity" were about to open, it was no longer Parnassus exiled by Olympus, but Paradise, from which the Almighty in heaven, as well as the Almighty on earth, could exile a poet who had never ceased to feel and live like a poet, "in innocence, to be unassuming and cultivate the Muse."

Mercy, consolation, trust, contrition. The canon Maucroix, who equaled his friend in every way on the question of libertine poetry and lax mores, now drew the words familiar to him from the text of the Roman ritual related to confession and the sacrament of Extreme Unction (*colestia medicina, non animae solum set etiam corpori salutaris*) and the Roman Office of the Requiem, words in which, he knew, his friend had now put his trust.

Nothing is more gripping than to reread today, over the shoulders of the two friends separated and united once more, but this time by prayer— either from the *Rituale romanum* revised by Urban VIII in 1645 or from its Paris version with a preface by Cardinal de Retz, published in 1654— these magnificent liturgical Latin compositions, accompanied by pastoral instructions for the use of priests in charge of the rites of "sweet death."[43] Everything in them is simple, strong, and infinitely touching, worthy of the "gates of eternity" that La Fontaine was now looking toward with dread. To get through the great ordeal, the poet, who had such a keen sense that all great literature is living tradition and translation, could not have entrusted himself to words both more anonymous and more august, whose salutary effects had been felt over the centuries. The king of France himself at the same time listened with more and more gravity to these syllables, set to music by the choirmasters in Versailles, at the Invalides, and at Notre-Dame.

Two years earlier, in December 1692, at the start of the four years when the French climate went awry, La Fontaine had already been gravely ill in the lodgings on rue Saint-Honoré where he was still the guest of Mme de La Sablière. At the time, she had moved to another house on rue Rousselet.

A young vicar, the abbé Pouget, fresh from his doctoral studies in theology, was sent to the ailing man by the priest of the Saint-Roch parish. He was the son of one of the poet's friends. That, and the fact that the young abbot, a Sorbonne graduate, was not Jansenist (he would enter the Oratory in 1699) facilitated the trust between the doctor of the soul and the ailing La Fontaine.[44]

The poet, in fact, who had himself established a close relationship with Port-Royal during the Foucquet years, broke off with the Solitaries after publishing, as if by way of farewell in 1673, his devout idyll *La captivité de saint Malc,* based on *La vie des pères du désert,* translated by his friend Robert Arnauld d'Andilly, who died the following year.[45] In 1687 he wrote to his "suzerain" Marie-Anne Mancini, duchesse de Bouillon, in exile in London at the time:

> Par Jupiter! je ne connais
> Rien pour nous de si favorable.
>   Parmi ceux qu'admet à sa cour
> Celle qui des Anglais embellit le séjour,
> Partageant avec vous tout l'empire d'Amour,
> Anacréon et les gens de sa sorte,
> Comme Waller, Saint-Evremond et moi,
> Ne se feront jamais fermer la porte.
> Qui n'admettrait Anacréon chez soi?
> Qui bannirait Waller et La Fontaine?
> Tous deux sont vieux, Saint-Evremond aussi;
> Mais verrez-vous au bord de l'Hippocrène
> Gens moins ridés dans leurs vers que ceux-ci?
>   Le mal est que l'on veut ici
>   De plus sévères moralistes:
> Anacréon s'y tait devant les jansénistes.
>   (A Madame la duchesse de Bouillon)

> By Jove! I know
> Nothing so favorable for us.
>   Among those admitted to her court
> By the one who embellishes the home of the English,
> Sharing with you the whole empire of Love,
> Anacreon and people of his kind,
> Like Waller, Saint-Evremond, and I,
> Will never have the door shut on us.
> Who would not admit Anacreon?
> Who would banish Waller and La Fontaine?
> Both are old, Saint-Evremond as well;
> But will you ever see on the bank of the Hippocrene
> People less wrinkled in their verses than these?
>   The trouble is that people want here
>   Moralists who are more severe:
> Anacreon falls silent before the Jansenists.

The poet had obviously reached the conclusion that "poetic license," which was his vocation, was incompatible with the severe morality and theology of effective grace at Port-Royal. After 1686 he had not only grown close to Fénelon, who had never wavered in his hostility toward Jansenist theology, but had also become associated with a Jesuit writer, Father Dominique Bouhours. In 1693 Bouhours took pleasure in publishing, in his *Recueil de vers choisis,* unpublished poems that La Fontaine had submitted to him. It was a long time since he had supported the persecuted Port-Royal with stanzas that mocked the "velvet path" opened to sinners by Jesuit casuists (1664).[46] It is likely that the experience of *Recueil de poésies chrétiennes et diverses,* which had such a painful genesis,[47] began to enlighten him on the distance that separated him from the rigorism of his increasingly doctrinaire Jansenist patrons. The Epicureanism of the second collection was much more pronounced and, from 1675 to 1686, La Fontaine came more and more to frequent libertine circles exclusively; these developments can be better understood if they are seen as the poet's vital reaction to what he found suffocating in the morality and theology of Port-Royal, which was withering away into a sectarian cult. His acquaintance with Fénelon in about 1686, his ties to Father Bouhours and Pierre-Daniel Huet, and the role that another Jesuit, Father René Rapin, had played in the conversion of his friend Mme de La Sablière show that he and his dear protectress were in contact with the most cultivated and least strict clergy. In 1687 Mme de La Sablière took the formidable abbé de Rancé as her director of conscience. In 1692 a gravely ill La Fontaine "converted" at the hands of the abbé Pouget, who was learned in theology, young, and severe.

The Death Knell of the Renaissance

The conversion of the author of *Fables* has always been interpreted in psychological terms. The aging poet, "a common-sense melancholiac," according to a diagnosis of the 1670s, troubled by worries of which he himself spoke more and more often, worries that were turned to anxiety about death and damnation by his grave illness, sought to calm them by asking the Church for the remedies at its disposal: the humility of the Apostle's Creed, penance, the sacraments, obedience to a director of conscience. That is how his Epicurean friends Ninon de Lenclos and Saint-Evremond understood his conversion: "His head is much weakened." The final "saintliness" that other contemporaries were surprised to observe in a poet reputed for "lax" mores has been considered an act of grace. In fact, at the deepest level of his religious soul, neither the man so inattentive to himself nor the poet so attentive to human beings' oscillation between the animal and the divine, brutality and grace, had ever truly departed from the first inclination of his youth, the monastery.

Ninon and Saint-Evremond lived as philosophers, following the maxims of Epicurus. That was not the case for La Fontaine, who was not a philosopher, even though he was curious about philosophy. He lived as a poet. A poet does not live and think within a system of ideas, laboring, like the philosopher, to make his ideas coincide with his life. He lives and feels and thinks within language, its figures, its fables, and its forms; this mode of knowledge is also his orientation and program of growth. There is every reason to imagine a literary biography of La Fontaine that would place itself within *L'Astrée* from the beginning and would show how, via magnetic attraction and accretion, that symbolic universe and its framework (an overview of the Renaissance, containing Virgil, Petrarch, Ficini, Francesco Colonna, and Castiglione) determined, from beginning to end, the poet's tastes, readings, friendships, and even social itinerary, taking him away from his roots and transporting him to a world for which *L'Astrée* was also an Abbey of Thélème.

When he had extracted the forms—diverse but truly his own—from that "primitive world," reinterpreted in the light of his readings and the ordeals of his experience (comedy, the heroic idyll, verse epistles, epistles in verse and prose, epigrams, tales, and fables), it was these very forms that, from 1654 to 1688, became the framework and orientation for his behavior. Received poetry and reinvented poetry were the principle of his knowledge and way of life.

In view of that degree of literary devotion, he was the last poet of the Renaissance. His life, like his work, was at first carried along on the still-vigorous currents from the sixteenth century; increasingly, it had to withstand opposing currents and adapt to them. Beginning in 1661 La Fontaine was compelled to write in order to create around him, via works that found him a public and attracted friends, a favorable microclimate within a hostile world. That creative struggle was in some ways the "last judgment" of the poetic project that surfaced in fourteenth-century Italy, was grafted in France, and which this remarkable poet made endure late into the season under Louis XIV. His final conversion was, in the first place, the result of a troubled conscience, all the more troubled because he heard the death knell sounding for the poetic Renaissance, which he himself had managed against the grain to keep alive in France.

The poetry of La Fontaine, a belated and French heir to Petrarch (the Latin Petrarch as much as the Italian), embraced Aesop, Plato, Terence, and Horace and was steeped in Epicurean philosophy and images. All the same, it never ceased to have a Christian horizon, even though the life of the poet "fickle in love"—his anticlerical and licentious *Contes*, his libertine friends and mores—made him a scandalous sinner from the Church's point of view. Nevertheless, La Fontaine continued a poetic tradition true to Augustinian Christianity, even when he took considerable license with dogma and clerical discipline.

La Fontaine's internal isolation was never so great as in the years 1680–90. Molière died in 1673. Racine and Boileau moved off to the slopes of the royal Olympus. Chapelle died in 1686. On 21 January 1670 Honorat de Bueil, lord of Racan, the last great lyric poet of the generation of Tristan, Saint-Amant, and Malleville, a generation rich in lyricism, died in Paris at age eighty. Racan's *Vie de Malherbe* would be published two years later, in 1672. La Fontaine could hardly feel profound affinities, except in terms of amusements and social milieu, with Chaulieu and La Fare, the most gifted poets of the new generation. Even Maucroix, the faithful companion of his youth, who always sensed and supported his poetic genius, was primarily an erudite humanist. That was a great deal, and it was becoming increasingly rare: but it was not everything. In addition, Maucroix lived in Reims, and the exchanges between the two friends were confined to correspondence.

In *Epître à Huet* (1687), La Fontaine, in his indirect way, suggests in a few lines the feeling of literary isolation he was having at the time:

Malherbe avec Racan, parmi les choeurs des anges,
Là-haut de l'Eternel célébrant les louanges,
Ont emporté leur lyre; et j'espère qu'un jour
J'entendrai leurs concerts au céleste séjour.
    (A Monseigneur l'évêque de Soissons, ll. 93–96)

Malherbe along with Racan, among the angel choirs,
In heaven above, praising the Almighty,
Have carried off their lyre; I hope one day
That I will hear their concerts in that heavenly home.

They *have carried off their lyre*: the paraleipsis is infinitely delicate and infinitely sad. Their lyre was the lyre of Apollo.[48] It no longer reverberates in the kingdom. It is now only otherworldly.

The worldly lyric genres were still practiced, and would be overabundantly so until the end of the ancien régime, with a craftsmanship Alexis Piron ridicules in his comedy *La métromanie*. But lyric genius had died out. La Fontaine was the first to have suffered from what was called the "French crisis in poetry," which began with the death of Scarron and Saint-Amant in 1660, and which the eighteenth century would discuss ad infinitum without being able to escape it.

The Renaissance had been good to lyricism: it was haunted by the barbarism and amnesia that had darkened the world, it was stirred by the desire to summon back "the Muses."

Erudition, philology, and poetry were able to soar in the wake of Petrarch, to dissipate the darkness and filth of an iron age, and to bring the nourishing honey of the golden age back down to earth from heaven, or back from antiquity to the moderns. The fables of Orpheus, the "golden verses" of Pythagoras, the oracles of Chaldea, the hieroglyphs of Memphis, and the "knowledge of the Muses" collected by the poets Homer, Hesiod, Pindar, and Anacreon were all seeds of a humanity restored to its dignity as an interlocutor with the divine. In the course of the fifteenth and sixteenth centuries, a whole symbolic and emblematic language, borrowed from Greco-Latin antiquity but systematized in a veritable encyclopedia of oracular wisdom, became the best nurturing environment for European lyric genius, which was also the genius of memory and mourning, the cutting edge of "humanistic literature."[49]

European melancholia, of which Dürer gave the most gripping image — desolation, loneliness, doubt, impotence, ennui, yearning, and sorrow — could find an outlet only in a "furious" aspiration to rediscover the lost light, either by violently reforming the Church or, within the old Church, by reconnecting, through the power of forms, fables, and symbolic figures, with the "divine knowledge" common to pagan and Christian antiquity, which the "dark ages" had ignored and obscured.

The France of the Valois was in its turn good to lyricism, spurred by the desire, shared by Budé and Ronsard, not to remain indebted to Italy, and to guide the kingdom threatened with decadence back toward the Greek golden age. This same desire, translated into theological language and directed toward Holy Scripture, led Calvin and his disciples to break off from the church of Rome.

In its vital capacities, Louis XIII's France, put to the test by the death of the "good king" of the Edict of Nantes, had not lost its desire, hope, and melancholia for the golden age. But it wanted to disarm the violence of that desire and to make it a principle of gentleness.

Louis-XIII lyricism still took for granted a keen feeling for the divine and grief over its loss. In many respects Nicolas Foucquet's political adventure was also the swan song of lyricism. It is no accident that the poets of Louis XIII's reign (rediscovered much later by romantic lyricism) rallied so fervently behind a statesman who said he preferred poetry to prose, and who had chosen a teacher of poetry, Paul Pellisson, as his "chief assistant." The lyricism of the Foucquet years was already out of steam. In *Clymène* and even in *Adonis*, La Fontaine sensed better than anyone that the late-season climate was under threat and already gone. Yet he was born for "the language of the gods."

What is much trickier to analyze but important to understand, if we are to grasp the profound meaning of La Fontaine's "conversion" in 1692, are the correspondences and dissonances between the "theology of the poets" he inherited from the Renaissance and theology in the strict sense; between the antique and humanist notion of the "divine," whose distance or loss lyric poetry laments and whose return it invokes, and the deity of the Bible and the Gospel, from which Christians have been separated by sin.

The myth of Ovid's *The Metamorphoses* was not called the *Bible of poets* for nothing: it too tells of a fall, and, in that tragedy of humanity returning to the iron age, gives poetry the fragile and tenacious function of making people recollect the lost happiness and the misfortunes that followed that disaster, one after another. The lyricism of poets, if one is to believe Ovid, tells the terrible truth of the dereliction and errors of men and also serves as consolation for it. It at least makes poets accede to a poignant awareness of the condition of mortals and of the power of the darkness that lurks within them. La Fontaine's *Fables*, with its power to evoke both the animality of men and what may still link them to the divine, are modern *Metamorphoses*.

The Bible also tells of divine anger and the fall of man: the lyricism of the Psalms of David is at once the painful account of that misfortune and a burst of confidence in the divine mercy that prayer alone is capable of obtaining. The Gospel gives that confidence a new fervency: a divine Redeemer has tramped the wretched earth of men and has preached a religion of love.

In the Renaissance, the grafting of the "universals" of the lyric imagination (the anger or friendship of the gods, the wretchedness or happiness of men) onto the categories of religious feeling (the anger or grace of God, the darkness of sin or the redemption of men) came about in the domain of the pastorale. After the tragedy of the religious wars, *L'Astrée* encapsulated for the French people these correspondences that Italy had invented between the theology of poets and Catholic theology. In the fable *L'Astrée*, the theology of the pastor/poets is not the opposite of the theology of the Church, even though their realms of influence are distinct—the life of the layperson in the world for the former, the life of the layperson facing death for the latter—and do not rule out conflicts of jurisdiction. That Catholic synthesis (to which Huet, Fénelon, and the Jesuits remained faithful under Louis XIV) brought lyric feeling into harmony with religious feeling, attenuated the latent violence to which both were susceptible, and oriented them both toward gentleness. The appeal of that syncretism among French Protestants is undeniable: they shared with Catholics the same worship of "belles lettres," even though their Calvinist faith presupposed a holy abhorrence for the corrupted dogmas and rites of the church of Rome, and a harsh fidelity to the original purity of the biblical and evangelical message.

Catholics and Protestants of the Edict of Nantes could share the melancholia of the shepherds of Arcadia, their contemplative life, their ordeals, their songs, their allegiance to Apollo and the Muses. That lyricism set aside religious controversies and promised a kingdom recovered from its iron age, if only a good government would return it to the golden age, its profound vocation. Neither the princes' revolts against Richelieu nor the Fronde had made them despair of that promise. The century of Louis XIV put an end to it once and for all.

The emergence of a "new science," breaking with the Aristotelianism and Platonism of the Renaissance, privileging a physics whose symbolic language was mathematics, no doubt led to the collapse of the entire edifice built by the poetry and general philology of the Italian Renaissance. But that "new science" would not have taken root with such force if the modern state, with its appetite for rationality, regularity, order, and control, had not sought an ally in that language without mystery, its method devoid of pathos, its immediate efficacy on men and things. What "thinking substance" was to "extensive substance" for Descartes, Louis XIV's imperious state was to the old kingdom, shaped by the centuries and gradually renovated by the slow and uneven alchemy of the humanists. The philology and lyricism of the humanists, attentive to the unique and the diverse, the Socratic mind and its flashes of insight on which Marot, Rabelais, Ronsard, and Montaigne had counted, were outpaced by this new project of mastery over society, contemporary with the Cartesian project of mastery over matter. For its part, the church of the Council of Trent, which resisted the "new science" and collided with the emerging modern states, had accommodated the legacy of the Renaissance only with reservations. In France above all, where anti-Italianism and anti-Jesuitism dominated within the Gallican church, the clerics worked to reduce that legacy, to make it more consistent with the details of dogma and the norms of discipline, which had to be set out in reply to the Calvinist challenge.

The absolute state, the "new science," and the "severe" Gallican church joined forces in France and often focused on keeping at bay the lyric project and symbolic language of the Renaissance, and on substituting a regularized language, transparent to censorship and reserved for rationality: "I call a cat a cat."

In the course of Louix XIV's reign, a cascade of *querelles*, in which La Fontaine was both a witness and an actor, attested to the growing difficulties encountered in France by the lyric genius of the Renaissance. Its oxygen was being depleted. The comfortable idea of progress was winning out. The *quarrel of inscriptions to the glory of the king* (should they be in French or Latin?) revealed the decline of the classical languages—the reservoir of symbolic language and the still-intact witnesses to the golden age. The *quarrel of the pagan supernatural* condemned even the advocates of the fable, including Boileau, to eviscerating it and reducing it to the role of an ornamental and allegorical system. The bridge the fable built between profane lyricism and religious feeling was broken: the "awesome mysteries" of faith were set apart in Boileau's *Art poétique* (1674), far from the "ornaments" that "enlivened" profane literature. The quarrel of the Epicureans, Gassendi's disciples, against the Cartesians, and Pierre-Daniel Huet's polemic against Descartes show that the heirs to the "learned knowledge" of the ancients, libertines or Christians, philosophers or mythologists, were being put on the defensive in the face of the swaggering ambitions of modern reason, which was growing impatient with memory and emotion. The *quarrel of the ancients and the moderns*, officially set off by Charles Perrault in 1687, fed the fires of an academic debate that, in reality, in the artificial euphoria of royal panegyrics, had long ago turned toward the triumph of reason and progress. The king, intrepid at the center of that revolution of the mind, understood nothing and perceived nothing. Bossuet and Mme de Maintenon served as his ramparts against the effects of his own reign on the general spirit of the kingdom. The revocation of the Edict of Nantes was the masterpiece of that placid blindness.

La Fontaine, the last poet of the French Renaissance, resisted the absolute state. He battled Cartesian idealism and its rationalist self-assurance. He made diversity his motto against the ennui born of uniformity. His

Epître à Huet (1687) shows him in alliance with the learned bishop Huet and his doctrine—faithful to the Renaissance—of two antiquities, the mythological and the biblical, mothers of all wisdom and all salvation. But it also reveals the depth of his uneasiness about the future of that knowledge and that symbolic art, which his poetry, with such valor and so much creative freedom, had kept alive against the current of his era:

> Je vois avec douleur ces routes méprisées:
> Art et guides, tout est dans les Champs-Elysées.
>
> . . . .
> Ne pas louer son siècle est parler à des sourds.
> Je le loue, et je sais qu'il n'est pas sans mérite;
> Mais près de ces grands noms notre gloire est petite:
>
> . . . .
>   Hélas! Qui sait encor
> Si la science à l'homme est un si grand trésor?
>   (*A Monseigneur l'évêque de Soissons*,
>   ll. 33–34, 40–42, 75–76)

> With sorrow I see those routes despised:
> In the Elysian Fields lie both art and guides.
>
> . . . .
> Not to praise one's century is to speak to the deaf,
> I praise it, and I know it is not without merit;
> But beside those great names our glory is small:
>
> . . . .
>   Alas! Who yet knows
> If science is such a great treasure to man?

In 1687 the "power of *Fables*" reached the limits that the Apollo of *Clymène* had feared in 1658:

> Nous vieillissons enfin, tout autant que nous sommes
>   De dieux nés de la fable et forgés par les hommes.
> Je prévois par mon art un temps où l'Univers
> Ne se souciera plus ni d'auteurs ni de vers,
> Où vos divinités périront, et la mienne.
> Jouons de notre reste, avant que ce temps vienne.

> We are growing old, in the end, even though we are
>   Gods born of fable and forged by men.

With my art I see a time when the universe
Will no longer care for authors or for verse,
Where your deities will perish, and my own.
Let us enjoy what remains before that time comes.

The time came in 1692. The "fine fire" that, since 1661, had sustained the poet's fidelity, inventiveness, and freedom lost its force and its sharpness. In 1693, in his dedication to the duc de Bourgogne, La Fontaine spoke of an "imagination that the years have weakened." The plasticity of his lyricism and his capacity to find different but still attentive audiences around him diminished. A desire for renunciation manifested itself. It had long ago been revealed in *Fables* through an altogether Epicurean penchant for relaxation in solitude. It had taken on a religious coloring in the poem *La captivité de saint Malc*:

Hélas! qui l'aurait cru que cette inquiétude
Nous chercherait au fond de cette solitude?

Alas! Who would have believed that that distress
Would come seek us out deep within this lonely recess?

The symbolic world on which the poet's lyricism thrived and within which it gave life may have long believed itself akin, in its own order, to the devotion of the Salesian heart, and even to that of Port-Royal in its early days. After 1674 and *Saint Malc,* La Fontaine must have realized that the seventeenth century also hinged on religion. Port-Royal had shrunk into itself. Bossuet and Mme de Maintenon had "converted" the court to a strict Gallican Catholicism, whose political theology manifested itself in the 1685 revocation. The premonitory symptoms of the quietist controversy, for anyone with a sixth sense, were perceptible well before the Conferences of Issy. Yet Fénelon's "pure love," which was to do battle with and defeat Bossuet, was precisely the "modern devotion" with which the Renaissance wanted to work, in preference to all the dogmatic and juridical forms of Catholicism. With Fénelon, it was not only mysticism that was directly excommunicated from the kingdom but, to an equal degree, the alliance formed since Petrarch between the theologies of poets and the theologies of saints.

In 1692 the poet's psychological insecurity increased, aggravated by powerful social and moral authorities around him. The very thing that constituted the merit of language, to which La Fontaine had devoted his life—its symbolism, its capacity to know and make known the divine within the diverse—now turned against him. He was condemned as "vain," "chimerical" (these were his own words in 1684 in [Second] Discours à Mme de La Sablière). The "fine fire" that had made him a born poet, and had made his songs and love affairs innocent, now revealed itself as a "fury that mocked laws," and fed in its wake "a hundred other passions, condemned by the wise." The enlightenment of the century had shifted. The power of Fables, the royal Venus, friendship with the Solitaries, the protection of Mme de La Sablière, all these supports were lacking. Health abandoned him. The kingdom, of which he was a lyre, now reverberated only with drumbeats and conversions more or less forced. Was the king of fear right, then? Was he not the image on earth of a God of fear?

"My Soul Is Weary of My Life"

The abbé Pouget, at the bedside of this famous, gravely ill poet, whose sulfurous reputation secretly inspired horror in him, conformed strictly to the instructions that the Parisian diocesan ritual dictated to him. Later, in 1717, he gave a written account to the abbé d'Olivet, the historian of the Académie Française, of the mission assigned to him by the parish priest.[50]

In place of the dangerous libertine he feared, the young vicar found a remarkable and engaging person: "a very clever and a very simple man, with a great deal of wit," but, in the matter of religious convictions, fairly vague: "an abstract man, who rarely thought methodically, who sometimes had very agreeable sallies, at other times had little wit, who was not embarrassed by anything and took nothing to heart." That portrait, by a doctor of theology, of a Renaissance wit who thought in epigrams, whose feelings were those of a skeptic, and who was in the world without being of the world, was not lacking in perspicacity.

In the bedroom of the ill bachelor cared for by a servant woman, who told the abbé Pouget, "God will not have the heart to damn him," a conversation began. It was very different from the Conferences of Issy, which would begin three years later among three of the most eminent theologians of the Gallican church— Bossuet, Tronson, and Noailles—to convince their young colleague Fénelon of his youthful error. La Fontaine, emaciated but as serene as Vélazquez's Aesop, continued "sacred conversations" with this intelligent young priest, twice a day for "ten or twelve days." The abbé Pouget, proceeding methodically and following the instructions of the *Ordo ministrandi Sacramentum Extremae Unctionis*, did not grant his penitent of sound mind access to the sacraments until he had persuaded him to make a general confession, to repent.

La Fontaine had already decided to rely on him in order to die properly in the hands of the Church. The greatest difficulty had to do with the penance demanded of him: the sacrifice of his *Contes*. The abbé Pouget, perhaps charged as well by the poet's ecclesiastic colleagues at the Académie Française, was inflexible. The author of the "infamous book" had to repudiate it, condemn it, renounce collecting all royalties for it, and do so publicly, making amends, at the assembly of the Académie Française.

"M. de La Fontaine," the abbé Pouget wrote in 1717,

> could not imagine that the book of his Tales could be a work so pernicious, though he did not look upon it as an irreproachable book, and did not justify it. He protested that this book had never made a bad impression on him when he was writing it, and he could not understand how it could be so harmful to the people who read it. . . . M. de La Fontaine was a simple and true man, who on a thousand matters thought differently than the rest of mankind, and who was as simple in evil as he was in good.

For a poet who had always believed that the irony of his *Contes* put carnal matters in their true comic light, the boundary between good and evil, and that between pure and impure, did not coincide with those of his confessor. The abbé Pouget emphasized to La Fontaine that in the ritual of Extreme Unction, for which he was preparing himself and which he had requested, the priest anointed in turn the dying man's eyes, ears, nostrils, lips, chest, and hands, making the sign of the cross, his thumb tinged with sacred oil, and pronouncing the sacred formula each time. When the poet's five senses were about to be purified and sanctified so that he could pass over, he could not carry *Contes* with him before God, since it taught people to use the five senses here on earth with an entirely sacrilegious intelligence. La Fontaine abandoned *Contes*.

On 12 February 1695, in front of a delegation of the Académie Française and "a great number of men of quality and wit" gathered in his home, La Fontaine made the public declaration repudiating *Contes* that the abbé Pouget had demanded of him. The same day, the duc de Bourgogne, Fénelon's pupil, to make up for the profits from his book, which the poet also renounced, had a purse of fifty louis taken to him.

Like Bossuet, like the Gallican church as a whole, the abbé Pouget took any representation of "contented" love, at the theater or in poetry, as an incitation to sins of the flesh. All the same, when he spoke of "simplicity" in reference to his ill penitent, the abbé Pouget was using a term of spiritual theology dear to Fénelon, and, in spite of everything, he recognized that the poet, despite his errors, had a "naturally Christian soul." "Simplicity," wrote Fénelon, "is a rectitude of soul that cuts off any pointless reflection on oneself." The poet was acquainted with that detached state, which frees one from the scruples with which amour propre torments itself, but only to better harden itself.

Just as Fénelon would submit with perfect obedience to the brief *Cum alias* wrested from Innocent XII by Louis XIV, which condemned his *Maximes des saints*, La Fontaine, with simplicity, agreed to distance himself from his *Contes*. At least he could depart with his *Fables*. He even agreed to destroy a comedy he had written, and which was going to be performed by the theater, "a notorious profession," according to the abbé Pouget. La Fontaine thus surrendered most of his identity as a poet. To complete his last journey, Jean wanted to return naked to the communion of the Church and benefit from its sacraments, its liturgy, and its prayers.

The former novice of the Oratory was no stranger to religious feeling or to prayer. Nothing human was alien to him. It was that same frame of mind that best distinguished him from the doctrinaire Epicureans he had often frequented: they conceived of the sage's private life, leisure, pleasure, friendship, and relaxation as a radical break from the customary communities of the kingdom and the church. They belonged to the tiny minority of the "worldly-wise," for whom there is no happiness shielded from vulgar errors except in philosophical secession. They could not be disconcerted by any sense of mystery, any sense of a divine being spying on men's external ploys and standing watch over their heart of hearts.

This internal sense of the divine, common to the lyricism of poets and the faith of Christians, to Virgil and Saint Paul, Saint-Amant and Pascal, La Fontaine and Fénelon, was already Petrarch's distinguishing trait in the early Renaissance. The ataraxia of the Epicurean sage was not the foundation on which the author of *Fables* established himself. Under his portraitist's reserve, under his storyteller's smile, there beat an "unquiet heart" tormented by the infinite distance between the human and the divine, and which wrote under a mysterious gaze. This gaze gave a second and secretly strange meaning to everything he said and everything he saw; it directed his oblique manner of speaking with the reserve of silence. The "language of the gods," which reveals and veils, which magnifies what claims to be small and diminishes what believes itself great, remained La Fontaine's language more than ever, even after he had abandoned openly heroic poetry and had put on the "ass's skin" of the Aesopian apologue.

One cannot imagine Chapelle, Saint-Evremond, Chaulieu, or La Fare, even in their youth, mistaking their vocation and aspiring, even for a short period of time, to the sacrificial priesthood, as Pierre de Bérulle, founder of the Oratory, defined it. Yet not only had La Fontaine wanted to become an Oratorian, but after he left the Oratory, far from rejecting the Church like many young men who left the priesthood, he always continued to move as happily within religious circles as within libertine circles. The Oratory led him to Port-Royal; from Port-Royal he moved on to high-society Jesuits, Bouhours and Rapin; from the Jesuits he went to Fénelon. Along the way he experienced no difficulty frequenting Molière and Chapelle, corresponding with Saint-Evremond, or covering the sensualist and secretly rebellious life of his princely patrons with his literary authority.

It was as if his criterion for empathy did not rely on dogma or doctrinal conviction or morality, but on a "sixth sense," a "taste," a discernment between minds prompt to recognize divinity in creatures in the most diverse, partial, contradictory, and fleeting forms, but always in affinity with the central feeling that moved his own heart of hearts. His friend Pierre-Daniel Huet thought that all peoples, either in their fables or in their beliefs, had glimpsed a facet of divine truth, which only Christ, in a glass darkly, as enigma and parable, revealed completely. La Fontaine, a lyric poet, lived in this mode familiar to the Renaissance, on a "divine knowledge," lost but living within the heart, whose scattered traces could be found and brought together anywhere they allowed themselves to be recognized: in the beauty of women, in the melancholy of music, in plays of light, in the movements of animals, in the emotions and ideas natural to men. These ephemeral, allusive traces, damaged by barbarians, became, in poetic language, fables, forms, and figures once more and connected men to the divine part of themselves.

This poet, steeped in Plato, Virgil, Ovid, and Horace, was also not insensitive to the biblical Psalms or the various forms of Christian religious feeling, when he encountered it sincere and ardent around him. In his *Voyage en Limousin* he sympathized with the Calvinists he ran into, people of robust faith and, at the same time, with a gift for the true riches of creation. He recognized something of himself in them.

LA FONTAINE AND RELIGIOUS LYRICISM

Outside *Fables*, it is even possible to follow a thread in his work that leads him, at the cost of sacrificing his particular paths, along the common path of piety to the royal office, and to the Church, which gave it its divine meaning.

In 1671 *Recueil de poésies chrétiennes et diverses* appeared under his name; several of his fables appeared in it. To sustain that effort of reconciliation between profane lyricism and religious lyricism, he even included within the collection a superb paraphrase of Psalm 17.

The form adopted by La Fontaine for his *Paraphrase*—grand lyricism in the tradition of Malherbe—is of a completely different order from that of *Fables*. It reveals a supplication in the lyric poet that had not found an opportunity to manifest itself around Foucquet or after 1661, when his hopes for becoming the royal poet were dashed. In *Odes sacrées* (1651 and 1660), that magnificent form had found an exemplary interpreter in Malherbe's best disciple: Racan.[51] On several occasions La Fontaine expressed his admiration for Racan and especially for his religious poetry. Racan's sacred odes were already paraphrases of the Psalms. It was to this grand lyric genre, established at the time of the Fronde, when Corneille himself was working on his paraphrase of *Imitation of Christ*, that La Fontaine applied himself in 1671. The form and character of the sacred ode were very close to the grand royal lyricism invented by Malherbe, which had experienced a magnificent blossoming during the Peace of the Pyrenees and the royal marriage in 1660: Racine's *Ode à la Nymphe de la Seine* was one of these royal songs. If, in Foucquet's wake, La Fontaine had become Louis XIV's poet, it is probable that he would have sounded that religious and royal chord of his lyre at an earlier date.

With the paraphrase of Psalm 17, he wrested that chord from silence for the first time under Louis XIV and made it vibrate with superb tones altogether worthy of Racan. Eight years later, in 1679, he published *Ode sur la paix* to the glory of the treaty of Nijmegen ("Déjà la déesse Astrée / Par toute cette contrée / Reconnaît ses derniers pas / Encore empreints sur la terre"; Already the goddess Astrea / Throughout that entire land / Recognizes her last steps / Still printed on the ground). It revealed his profound—and suppressed—aspiration to join the kingdom's choir singing praises of its king. Sacred odes and royal odes, bequeathed by Malherbe, were two sides of the same liturgy of the royal religion. La Fontaine thus attempted to let Louis XIV know that, on a word from the king, he could also excel in these two registers.

The author of *Adonis,* in applying himself to the French grand style of sacred poetry, set out the profound kinship between biblical lyricism and the Ovidian lyricism he seems to have preferred. The voice of the Psalmist rises from the depths of a world where evil and the wicked wreak havoc; it rises toward the light of a God who punishes, but who can also wrest his faithful from evil and misfortune. A similar laceration between the human and the divine lies at the origin of the lyric energy of *Adonis.* It was also the deep impulse behind Malherbe's earlier ode to Henry IV, the victim of an assassination attempt ("Que direz-vous, races futures?"; What will you say, future races?), an ode that over-powered the young La Fontaine when he first heard it declaimed in front of him in 1643.

In his *Discours de remerciement,* addressed to the Académie Française in 1684, Anacréon/La Fontaine did not hesitate to place Catholic and royal poetry above the profane art of Parnassus: "You, gentlemen, know the language of the gods just as well as the language of men. I would raise these two talents above all things, except for a third thing that surpasses them: that is the language of piety, which, excellent as it is, is nevertheless familiar to you."

In Psalm 17 it is King David who sings and prays, addressing himself to his Lord. For centuries the prayers of the biblical Orpheus had been linked to the French royal religion. In paraphrasing that royal prayer in 1671, as Racine would do much later in the choruses of *Esther* and *Athalie,* La Fontaine for the first time blended his singular voice as a lyric poet with that of the community of the kingdom, and with that of its church. Deep within himself, he aspired only to do it in communion with the king. If it had been up to him, he would have begun in 1661:

> De leur triste et sombre demeure
> Les démons, esprits malheureux,
> Venaient d'un poison dangereux
> Menacer mes jours à toute heure.
> Ils entraient jusqu'en mes sujets,
> Jusqu'en mon fils, dont les projets
> Me font encore frémir de leur cruelle envie;
> Jusqu'en moi-même enfin, par un secret effort;
> Et mon esprit, troublé des horreurs de ma vie,
> M'a plus causé de maux que l'Enfer ni la mort.

Les méchants, enflés de leurs ligues,
Contre moi couraient irrités,
Comme torrents précipités
Dont les eaux emportent les digues;
Lorsque Dieu, touché de mes pleurs,
De mes soupirs, de mes douleurs,
Arrêta cette troupe à me perdre obstinée.
Ma prière parvint aux temples étoilés,
Parut devant sa face, et fut entérinée
D'un mot qui fit trembler les citoyens ailés.

. . . .

Oui, Seigneur, ta bonté divine
Est toujours présente à mes yeux,
Soit que la nuit couvre les cieux,
Soit que le jour nous illumine:
Je ne sens d'amour que pour toi;
Je crains ton nom, je suis ta loi,
Ta loi pure et contraire aux lois des infidèles;
Je fuis des voluptés le charme décevant,
M'éloigne des méchants, prends les bons pour modèles,
Sachant qu'on devient tel que ceux qu'on voit souvent.
Non que je veuille en tirer gloire;
Par toi l'humble acquiert du renom,
Et peut des temps et de ton nom
Pénétrer l'ombre la plus noire.
A leurs erreurs par toi rendus,
Sages et forts sont confondus,
S'ils n'ont mis à tes pieds leur force et leur sagesse.
Ce que j'en puis avoir, je le sais rapporter
Au don que m'en a fait ton immense largesse,
Par qui je vois le mal, et peux lui résister.[52]

From their sad and somber home
The demons, wretched spirits,
Came with a dangerous poison
To threaten my days at all hours.
They entered even my subjects,
Even my son, whose plans
Still make me shudder with their cruel desire
And finally entered even me, through a secret effort;

And my mind, troubled by the horrors of my life,
Has caused me more ill than Hell or death.

    The wicked, puffed up by their leagues,
    Ran toward me in their rage,
    Like rushing torrents
    Whose waters carry off dams;
    When God, touched by my tears,
    My sighs, my sorrows,
Stopped that herd intent on doing me harm.
My prayer reached the starry temples,
Appeared before his face, and was ratified
With a word that made the winged citizens tremble.
. . . .
    Yes, Lord, your divine goodness
    Is always present to my eyes,
    Both when the night covers the heavens,
    And when day illuminates us:
    I feel love only for you;
    I fear your name, I follow your law,
Your pure law, contrary to the law of the infidel,
I flee the deceptive charm of pleasure,
Depart from the wicked, take the good as models,
Know that one becomes like those one sees often.

    Not that I wish to draw glory from it;
    By you the humble acquire renown,
    And can penetrate the darkest shadow
    Of time and in your name.
    Made by you to face their errors,
    The wise and the strong are confounded,
If they have not put their strength and wisdom at your feet.
Whatever part I may have of them I know to attribute
To the gift given by your great largesse,
Through whom I see evil, and am able to resist.

La Fontaine, Epicurean in many respects (but then, so was the biblical Ecclesiastes), a full-time profane poet, unique and independent in all things, reveals in this poem (as in his efforts to have his pastoral opera *Daphné* performed at court) to what extent, deep down, he never ceased to be a Frenchman of Old France, within its church, within its kingdom, disconcerted but not discouraged by the accident that distanced him from his king. In reality it was against his will, and by the act of the king, that he occupied a marginal position in the belles lettres of the monarchy. That marginality (which, in our view, makes him greater, a poet of the future) weighed on him, cost him. In imitating Malherbe and Racan in 1671, in imitating the Racine of *Ode à la Nymphe de la Seine* in 1679, he shed light on one of his most secret and personal aspirations as a lyric poet within the royal religion. For us, that is one of the strangest aspects of his sorrow at seeing Parnassus exiled from Olympus.

That yearning for grand Catholic and royal lyricism is inseparable from a dream of conversion. Racine, to become the king's historiographer, got married and converted from the theater to a devout family life. Before Racine and for the same reasons, Pellisson abjured Calvinism. *La captivité de saint Malc,* the devout idyll La Fontaine published in 1674, is in reality an autobiographical dream of conversion, veiled under a hagiographic fiction. Beginning with an invocation to the Virgin (in imitation of Tasso), this long poem was a churchman's version of the fable "The Two Doves." A young hermit leaves his companion in solitude; he is attracted by "temporal possessions." His journey teaches him the bitterness of the world, then that of his own heart: everything ends at the monastery, where "Malc keeps himself busy in silence."

The peroration of this poem, the most edifying La Fontaine ever composed, is also the most painstaking praise the poet had ever addressed to Louis XIV. And at issue is the most questionable Louis XIV, even and especially from the point of view of the irenic poet: the Gallican king/pontiff at the head of his troops, the invader of Holland in 1671. He prefigured the Revocation of 1685 by imposing Catholicism on the Dutch cities occupied by his soldiers. The same poet, who was already dreaming of abjuring the impiety of his mores, also dreamed of effacing his political impiety toward the king:

> Je la chante en un temps où sur tous les monarques
> Louis de sa valeur donne d'illustres marques,
> Cependant qu'à l'envi sa rare piété
> Fait au sein de l'erreur régner la vérité.
>   (*La captivité de saint Malc*)

> I sing it at a time when, over all monarchs,
> Louis gives illustrious signs of his valor,

Even as, vying with it, his extraordinary piety
Makes truth reign in the heart of error.

Thus, La Fontaine suffered from the impossible situation in which he
found himself, of making the traditional schema of royal religion, and the
role the lyric poet occupied within it, coincide with the reality of Louis
XIV and his state. Until then he had been able to overcome that tension,
but, in 1692, he no longer had the fire necessary to sustain it. All that
remained was for him to die with dignity, as a sinner who did not know his
eternal fate.

On the brink of death, La Fontaine the poet once more became Jean, a
humble Christian and docile Frenchman. The freedom of the Muses gave
way to a discipline of language that had for centuries been the armature
of the royal religion, and whose efficacy the abbé Pouget possessed: the
impersonal and choral Latin of the Catholic liturgy. *Dilexi, quoniam exaudiet
Dominus vocem orationis meae. Quia inclinavit aurem suam mihi: et in diebus
meis invocabo* (I rejoice, because the Lord will listen to the words of my
prayer. He has lent an ear to me, and I will invoke him all my remaining days).[53]

Mme de La Sablière Prevails over La Fare

Converting the poet was made easier for the abbé Pouget by the
indirect but powerful assistance of Mme de La Sablière, who had herself
converted to Catholicism in 1680 after her breakup with the marquis
de La Fare. Of the two separated lovers, both friends of the poet, it was
she who now prevailed. At first she retreated to the Hôpital des Incurables
and devoted herself to caring for the sick, but in 1687 she lost her director of conscience, the Jesuit Rapin. Afflicted with cancer, she turned to
the abbé de La Trappe. Like the Hospitaler in La Fontaine's last fable,
in her *Lettres à Rancé* she seems to have turned away from *works*. She
returned home and wrote to Rancé: "I am happier than I could tell you:
I am with God and my suffering, which I regard as signs of his goodness
for me."

Among these letters to Rancé, bits of another correspondence have
been preserved, addressed to an anonymous recipient who was very likely
La Fontaine. In one of these letters, dated 12 August 1692, three months

before the poet's illness and the abbé Pouget's visit, Mme de La Sablière wrote: "I believe that silence, suffering, and peace are all that is necessary to me. So then, Sir, I have shown you my heart of hearts and have produced in your own the peace I ask for. . . . I ask you again, Sir, to remember me before the Lord. It is only in that way that we must love each other, simply: all the rest is mere illusion, and only the greater when we believe we are practicing charity."

Had the poet begun a "sacred conversation" with his benefactress before he received the vicar of Saint-Roch at his home (and at hers)? Later, on 6 January 1693, when the poet's conversion was well under way, Mme de La Sablière wrote to this same correspondent: "I am very sensitive to your kindness, Sir. For the love of Our Lord, aim the hatchet at the base of the tree: there is nothing to be done from one branch to another. If you knew the aid and security that lie in renunciation, you would soon come to hate all your caution. I pray Our Lord with all my heart to penetrate your heart, so that all the enlightenment of your mind will disappear."

She died the same day.

The internal peace that accompanied La Fontaine's return to the church of his youth restored his health. On 26 October 1693 he wrote to Maucroix: "I continue to fare well and have an appetite and fierce vitality. Five or six days ago, I went to Bois-le-Vicomte on foot, having eaten almost nothing: it is a good five leagues from here." He then found refuge in the luxurious mansion of his friends the d'Hervarts on rue Plâtrière, Saint-Eustache parish. Via correspondence, he became passionately involved in the correction of the translations Maucroix had sent from Reims. He had sacred poetry in mind. It was in June of that year, 1693, that Ninon de Lenclos wrote to Saint-Evremond: "I have learned that you would like to have La Fontaine in England. He is hardly enjoyed in Paris. His head is much weakened."[54]

This Day, Day of Wrath

At the same moment, La Fontaine was having the abbé de Lavau read a verse paraphrase of the reply to the ninth reading of the Office of the Requiem before the Académie Française and in the poet's presence: *Libera me Domine, de morte aeterna, in die illa tremenda. Quando coeli movendi sunt et terra. Dies irae, dies illa, dies calamitatis et miseriae, dies magna et amara valde.*

Dieu détruira le siècle au jour de sa fureur.
Un vaste embrasement sera l'avant-coureur,
Des suites du péché long et juste salaire.
Le feu ravagera l'Univers à son tour.
Terre et cieux passeront, et ce temps de colère
Pour la dernière fois fera naître le jour.

Cette dernière aurore éveillera les morts:
L'Ange rassemblera les débris de nos corps;
Il les ira citer au fond de leur asile.
Au bruit de la trompette en tous lieux dispersé,
Toute gent accourra. David et la Sibylle
Ont prévu ce grand jour, et nous l'ont annoncé.

De quel frémisssement nous nous verrons saisis!
Qui se croira pour lors du nombre des choisis?
Le registre des coeurs, une exacte balance
Paraîtront aux côtés d'un Juge rigoureux.
Les tombeaux s'ouvriront, et leur triste silence
Aura bientôt fait place aux cris des malheureux.

. . . .

Tu pourrais aisément me perdre et te venger.
Ne le fais point, Seigneur; viens plutôt soulager
Le faix sous qui je sens que mon âme succombe
Assure mon salut dès ce monde incertain;
Empêche malgré moi que mon coeur ne retombe,
Et ne te force enfin de retirer ta main.[55]

God will destroy the world on the day of his wrath.
A vast conflagration will be the harbinger,
The long and just wages that follow from sin.
Fire will ravage the universe in turn.
The earth and the heavens will pass away, and this time
Of anger for the last time will bring forth day.

That last dawn will awaken the dead.
The angel will gather the debris of our bodies;
He will summon them deep where they lie.
At the sound of the trumpet dispersed everywhere

Everyone will come running. David and the Sibyll
Foresaw that great day, and prophesied of it.

How great shall be our quaking!
Who will believe he is one of the chosen?
The record book of hearts, a precise set of scales
Will appear beside a rigorous judge.
The graves will be opened, and their sad silence
Will soon give way to the wails of the wretched.
. . . .
You could easily damn me and take your revenge.
Do not do so, O Lord; come rather to relieve
The burden under which I feel my soul succumbing
Assure my salvation in this uncertain world;
In spite of me, keep my heart from falling again,
And, finally, do not force yourself to withdraw your hand.

The abbé Pouget, who had left for the provinces, was no longer attending La Fontaine. The last letter to Maucroix, in February 1695, attests that the poet's anguish at the idea of "appearing before God" was keener than ever. His words, "you know how I have lived," is a litotes that gives only a glimpse of what is passed over in silence. To expiate his poetic license, Jean then indulged in extraordinary acts of mortification, worthy of those Saint Louis inflicted on himself, and which astonished Boileau:

The unlikely things I have been told about M. de La Fontaine are more or less what you have guessed; I mean that they are the hair shirts and the scourges with which, I have been assured, he frequently afflicted his body, and which seemed all the more incredible to me with respect to our late friend, in that nothing was ever farther from his character than such mortifications. But what of that? God's grace does not confine itself to ordinary metamorphoses, and sometimes accomplishes true ones. That grace does not appear to have spread in the same way to M. Cassandre [La Fontaine's former comrade at the Academy of the Round Table] who died as he had lived, that is, very misanthropic, and not only hating men but even having a fair amount of trouble reconciling with God; and to whom, he said (if the report on him that was made to me is true), he had no obligation. Who would have believed that, of these two men, it would be M. de La Fontaine who was the chosen vessel?

The abbé d'Olivet, who had known François Maucroix well, said, even more strikingly: "I saw in the hands of his friend M. Maucroix the hair shirt he was found wearing when he was undressed and put on his death-bed." The director of conscience who oversaw the poet's last months was much more demanding than the abbé Pouget, who denied to the abbé d'Olivet (the ex-Jesuit) that he had prescribed such a harsh penance: "I do not believe it was necessary to do so with a man weighed down by the years and by bodily infirmities."

But, in his final months, La Fontaine, distancing himself from the daring and independence to which his poetry had led him, also became involved in other expiatory practices. The abbé Pouget justifiably wrote that he was "in penance as he was in all the rest of his conduct, and did not think to deceive God or men."[56] He put as much zeal into casting off the old man as he had put genius into telling human stories.

Having humbly returned to the communion of the Gallican church, he also wanted to return humbly to the communion of the kingdom and to correct the dissident aspects of his poetry. Apart from the paraphrase of the *Dies irae,* during the period between his conversion and his death, on 13 April 1695 he composed only *Inscriptions en vers* to the glory of Louis XIV the conqueror. He thus bowed without reservation to the dutiful place where Racine and Boileau—members of the "Petite Académie" devoted to royal mottoes and inscriptions, his other friend Charles Per-rault, and his colleagues at the Académie Française had long since pre-ceded him.

These inscriptions (a private and slavish imitation of the ones appended to Le Brun's painted ceiling in the Versailles Hall of Mirrors) were de-signed to comment on a gallery of "history paintings," which represented what the poet had always had the most difficulty praising in Louis XIV: his military victories and glory. That gallery had been assembled by Du Fresnoy, one of Louvois's assistants, at his country house in Glatigny, near Pontoise. It was part of the revival of the cult of royal personality that had followed the monarch's recovery in 1686. Perrault's extravagant poem *Le siècle de Louis le Grand* had been part of the revival. At the time, La Fontaine protested against this "modern" manifesto with an epistle in verse to their mutual colleague Pierre-Daniel Huet, but he published it accompanied by a prose panegyric of the king. The Desjardins equestrian statue of Louis le Grand, on Place des Victoires, commissioned by the duc de La Feuillade and inaugurated by the king himself on 30 January 1687, was the most hyperbolic gesture of that new fit of monarchical idolatry.

The inscriptions in French verse, for which Du Fresnoy commissioned La Fontaine, were a particularly sacrificial penance in that they were simply a translation of the very mediocre Latin subtitles already composed for Du Fresnoy's paintings by another of Louis XIV's admirers, Baron Michel-Ange de Voerden, a high magistrate in Lille. The work remained unfinished at the poet's death, and the patron, in a letter to Voerden, disdainfully called the old poet a "poor man" and a *bonhomme* unable to finish what he had undertaken. That, in any case, was the royal administration's feeling about Foucquet's poet.

It is worth quoting one of these translations, which was to appear on the cartouche of the painting *La conquête de Hollande* (The conquest of Holland, 1674), depicting a "military march" begun with enthusiasm, but which took a bad turn for the king's armies:

Triompher en courant d'un climat invincible,
Pénétrer un pays que de leurs propres mains
La Nature avec l'Art rendaient inaccessible
    Aux entreprises des humains;
Passer le Rhin, l'Issel, et lasser la victoire,
Faire à plus de cent forts son tonnerre éprouver,
C'est ce qui de cent rois pourrait remplir l'histoire:
En trois mois cependant un seul sut l'achever.

Defeat an invincible climate in a rush,
Penetrate a country which with their own hands
Nature and Art made inaccessible
    To human enterprise;
Cross the Rhine, the Issel, and wear down the victory,
Make more than a hundred forts feel one's thunder,
That could fill the history of a hundred kings:
Yet in three months a single one was able to accomplish it.

For the author of *Adonis* and "Joconde," that exercise in oblation was certainly equivalent to a hair shirt.

In his *Mémoires*, which is less memoirs than a "book of reason" as a medieval cleric might have written it, Maucroix notes:

On 13 April, my very dear and very faithful friend M. de La Fontaine died in Paris: we were friends for more than fifty years, and I thank God that I pursued the intense friendship I felt for him to such an advanced age, without any interruption or any cooling off, being able to say that I have always loved him tenderly, and as much on the last day as on the first. May God in his mercy grant him holy rest. He was the most sincere and naive soul I have ever known; never any dissimulation, I do not know if he ever lied in his life; in addition, he had a very fine mind, was capable of anything he wanted to undertake. His fables, in the view of the most capable people, will never die and will do him honor among all future generations.[57]

In its content, if not in the intensity of the feeling, the paradox on which Maucroix constructed the funerary portrait of his late friend—naive soul/very fine mind—is found in the Latin translation exercise Fénelon gave the duc de Bourgogne, in the days following the poet's funeral at Saint-Eustache:

Alas! He is gone, that playful man, the new Aesop, superior to Phaedrus in the art of jest, who gave a voice to the beasts so that they would impart to men the lessons of wisdom. With him, games full of mischief, playful Mirth, the elegant Graces, and the learned Muses have expired. Weep, you who love naive playfulness, unadorned and simple nature, elegance unvarnished and without affectation. To him and him alone did the scholars allow negligence. How far superior to a more polished style that golden negligence proved to be![58]

Fénelon emphasizes a coincidence of opposites in the late poet: "simple," "unvarnished" nature, like a relic of the golden age in the iron century, and a superior knowledge of art, as if this perspicacious naïf was the only one able to transpose into French, all at once and all equally well, Anacreon, "who performed," Terence, "who painted," and Virgil, who knew how to veil, in gentleness and elegance, the same knowledge as Ecclesiastes, and who wrote: *Sunt lacrymae rerum* (Things are steeped in tears).

Fables, reuniting the crowning accomplishments of the classical poets and reviving them in French, was certainly able to form the taste of a future king of France; La Fontaine, before and as much as Racine and Boileau, had been destined to become a royal poet. Disgraced by Louis XIV, he had to be satisfied—and he took it upon himself to be satisfied, with grace, ingenuity, and sorrow—with being the most remarkable and "private" poet of a reign in which nothing seemed to exist any longer except as a function of the king, his court, and his state. The last poet of the Renaissance was nevertheless the first modern poet: still far from being *maudit*, refusing to be so with all his might, but already warned of the dissonance, which he was the first to make heard—even as he covered it with gentleness and gaiety—between action and dream, between the state and the kingdom, between reason and poetry. In 1688 the abbé Vergier wrote to Mme Hervart, regarding La Fontaine: "You know, Madam, that he is bored everywhere." La Fontaine's boredom was the same as that of which Pascal spoke, and already that of Baudelaire. He nevertheless died as a man of Old France, who had humbly returned to the communion of his church and the religion of his king.

The sole grace of this poet was to have passed through the swells of his time and the mutations of history without ever losing his internal orientation, in a literary adventure always guided at a given moment by the words that cheat time and history: poets' words to get through the bitterness of life, prophets' words engraved in the liturgy to accompany him into the unknown, unto death. Even after his conversion, his letters to Maucroix show him engaged in patient literary exercises, in the intervals between his prayer exercises and his penance. At the time he was no more a poet than Rimbaud in his last days. The death of lyricism in ancien régime France was accomplished well before 13 April 1695, the day he closed his eyes for the last time.

· · ·

At another level, and in a completely different order, correspondences and harmony were finally established between this poet and his king. One had been the Ovid of the kingdom, the other had long danced figures taken from Ovid by another poet, La Fontaine's friend Isaac de Benserade. Both of them, the poet and the king, finally entrusted their souls to the care of the Gallican church.

Louis XIV was both the last prince of the Renaissance and the first modern head of state. The modern head of state, wresting France from the cyclical time of the ancients, set in motion and into action the progress of a mechanism destined to prevail over his kingdom, the oldest in Europe. He authorized that progress on the basis of his traditional and sacred authority. And yet, as the last prince of the Renaissance, Louis XIV knew how to move in harmony with the ancient sense of time, the cycle of the seasons: a springlike Pan with the shepherdess La Vallière, a summery Mars and an autumnal Jupiter with the majestic Montespan, he ended up as a wintery and devout Saturn, a French Philip II at his El Escorial, with Mme de Maintenon at his side, confronting misfortune, grief, old age, and death.

Notes

At the request of the publisher (Editions de Fallois), the notes have been reduced to the essential, as far as that was possible. I have thus given precedence to brief explanations, especially with respect to sources and concepts. For La Fontaine's bibliography in particular, the reader can easily consult the review *Le Fablier* (Revue des Amis de Jean de La Fontaine, Musée Jean de La Fontaine, 02400 Château-Thierry, France; telephone: 03 23 69 05 60), which regularly publishes studies and bibliographical precisions. General historians, historians of ideas, and literary historians will forgive me if I have not always referred to their works, classic or recent, to which I am quite obviously indebted.

PREAMBLE

The epigraph is taken from Marcel Proust, *Sodome et Gomorrhe* (Paris: Gallimard, 1988), p. 167. The narrator's target is Sainte-Beuve and the patronizing tone of his literary criticism.

1. Léon-Paul Fargue, the author of *Le Piéton de Paris* (Paris: Gallimard, 1939; repr. 1982 and 1993), wrote an essay entitled "La Fontaine," in *Tableau de la littérature française XVIIᵉ–XVIIIᵉ siècles. Préface par André Gide. De Corneille à Chénier* (Paris: Gallimard, 1939), pp. 65–77. See also Paul Valéry, "Au sujet d'Adonis," *Revue de Paris* (1921); repr. in *Variété 1* (1924).

2. Sébastien-Roch-Nicolas Chamfort, *Eloge de la Fontaine qui, au jugement de l'Académie de Marseille, a remporté le prix de l'année 1774*; reproduced in La Fontaine, *Oeuvres complètes*, vol. 1, *Fables, Contes et nouvelles*, edited by Jean-Pierre Collinet (Paris: Gallimard, 1991), pp. 953–95, passage quoted p. 964.

3. Pierre Cureau de La Chambre, *Discours prononcé au Louvre le 2 May 1684 par Mr l'abbé de La Chambre, Directeur de l'Académie Française à la réception du sieur de La Fontaine, en la place de feu Monsieur Colbert, Ministre et secrétaire d'Etat* (n.d., n.p.), p. 4. This welcoming speech was published independently from the acceptance speech given by La Fontaine, after the abbé de La Chambre obtained the academy's approval for that departure from custom. Cureau de La Chambre's "official" attitude invalidates very late sources, who mention two meetings between Louis XIV and La Fontaine. The first supposedly took place after the publication of *Fables* (1668) and was accompanied by a visit to Versailles and a purse of ten thousand livres. See Beauchamps, *Recherche sur les théâtres* (1735), quoted in Georges Mongrédien, *Recueil des textes et des documents du XVIIᵉ siècle relatifs à*

La Fontaine (Paris: Editions du Centre National de la Recherche Scientifique, 1973), pp. 216–17. The poet and the king are reported to have met again, through the mediation of Saint-Aignan, in January 1669, after *Les amours de Psyché* was published, to calm the king's irritation caused by certain allusions in that work. See Montenault, *Vie de La Fontaine* (1755), quoted in Mongrédien, *Recueil des textes*, p. 222. See also Roger Duchêne, *Jean de La Fontaine* (Paris: Fayard, 1990), pp. 265 ff.

4. Valery Larbaud, "Devoirs de vacances," in *Enfantines* (Paris: Gallimard, 1918).

5. Paul-Jean Toulet, *Les contrerimes* (Paris: Editions du Divan et Emile Paul frères, 1921; repr. Paris: Gallimard, 1979), poem 58, p. 70; and idem, *Capitales*, edited by Michel Décaudin (Paris, 1990).

6. Jules Barbey d'Aurevilly, in fact, wrote a eulogy of La Fontaine in *Les oeuvres et les hommes*, vol. 2: *Les poètes* (1889).

7. Barbey d'Aurevilly, letter to Guillaume Stanislas Trébutien, 2 February 1855, in *Oeuvres complètes de J. Barbey d'Aurevilly*, 17 vols. (Paris: François Bernouard, 1926–27); vols. 14–17, *Lettres à Trébutien*, repr. in two volumes (Geneva: Slatkine, 1979), passage quoted 2:198.

8. Michel de Montaigne, "A Consideration upon Cicero," book 1, in *The Complete Essays of Montaigne*, translated by Donald Frame (Stanford: Stanford University Press, 1958), p. 185.

9. Voltaire, *Le siècle de Louis XIV*, chap. 22, "Des Beaux-arts." Charles Augustin Sainte-Beuve, *Port-Royal*, edited by Maxime Leroy, book 2, chap. 14 (Paris: Gallimard, 1953), 1:687.

10. Voltaire, *Catalogue de la plupart des écrivains français qui ont paru dans le siècle de Louis XIV, pour servir à l'histoire littéraire de ce temps*, in Voltaire, *Oeuvres complètes*, edited by Louis Moland (Paris: Garnier frères, 1878), 14:32–144; passage quoted p. 83.

11. Voltaire to Vauvenargues, 7 January 1745, in Voltaire, *Correspondance*, edited by Theodore Besterman, letter 3062, 9:200.

12. Voltaire, *Connaissance des beautés et des défauts de la poésie et de l'éloquence dans la langue française*, s.v. "Fable," p. 1749.

13. Sainte-Beuve, *Causeries du lundi*, vol. 7, "La Fontaine."

14. Sainte-Beuve, *Port-Royal*, book 5, chap. 9.

15. On the meaning of that play, see Marc Fumaroli, *Héros et orateurs: Rhétorique et dramaturgie cornéliennes* (Geneva: Droz, 1990; 2d ed. 1996), chap. 1, "Pierre Corneille, fils de son oeuvre," pp. 59–61; and Pierre Corneille, *Suréna, général des Parthes, tragédie* (1675), edited by José Sanchez (Paris: Ducros, 1970), pp. 86–89. See also chap. 7 in the present volume.

16. Jean Giraudoux, "La tentation du monde," in *Les cinq tentations de la Fontaine* (Paris: Grasset, 1938). These lectures were given by Giraudoux at the Université des Annales on Wednesdays, 22 and 29 January, and 5, 12, and 19 February 1936. The best edition to consult is the reprint by Jacques Robichez (Livre de Poche), pp. 70–95; passage quoted p. 87.

17. Léon-Paul Fargue, "Jean de La Fontaine," *Nouvelle Revue Française* (1 April 1933):519–37; reprinted in idem, *Tableau de la littérature française*.

18. Chamfort, *Eloge de la Fontaine*.

19. Montaigne, "Of Repentance," book 3, chap. 2, in *The Complete Essays*, p. 611.

20. Odette de Mourgues, *O Muse fuyante proie . . . : Essai sur la poésie de La Fontaine* (Paris: José Corti, 1987). That is also Patrick Dandrey's approach in *La fabrique des Fables: Essai sur la poétique de La Fontaine* (Paris: Klincksieck, 1991).

21. Montaigne, "Of Cato the Younger," book 1, chap. 37, in *The Complete Essays*, p. 171.

22. See Marc Fumaroli, "Rhétorique d'école et rhétorique adulte: La réception européenne du *Traité du sublime* au XVIe et au XVIIe siècle," in *Héros et orateurs*, pp. 377–98.

23. Montaigne, "On Some Verses of Virgil," book 3, chap. 5, in *The Complete Essays*, p. 665.

24. See Jean Lesaulnier, *Port-Royal insolite: Edition critique du Recueil de choses diverses* (Paris: Klincksieck, 1992), p. 286.

25. Montaigne, "Of the Inequality That Is between Us," book 1, chap. 42, in *The Complete Essays*, p. 195.

26. Henri de Campion, *Mémoires*, edited by Marc Fumaroli (Paris: Mercure de France, 1967; new edition, 1981), p. 236.

27. René Jasinski, "Le Gassendisme dans le second recueil des Fables," in *A travers le XVIIe siècle*, 2 vols. (Paris: Nizet, 1981), 2:75–120.

28. Montaigne, "Of Solitude," book 1, chap. 39, in *The Complete Essays*, p. 177.

29. Idem, "The Useful and the Honorable," book 3, chap. 1, in ibid., p. 602.

30. Cureau de La Chambre, *Discours prononcé au Louvre*.

31. Giraudoux, "La tentation du monde," in *Les cinq tentations*, p. 87.

32. Sainte-Beuve, *Causeries du lundi*, vol. 7, "La Fontaine." In this passage, Sainte-Beuve quotes François-Louis Cizeron-Rival, *Récréations littéraires, ou anecdotes et remarques sur différents sujets*, collected by M.C.[izeron] R.[ival] (Paris: Dessaint, 1765), p. 111. Cizeron-Rival is reporting an account by Claude Brossette, who referred to a story Boileau had told him in person. The same text is reproduced in Mongrédien, *Recueil des textes*, p. 223.

33. Quoted in "Portrait de Monsieur de La Fontaine: Par M. ——," in *Oeuvres posthumes de Monsieur de La Fontaine* (Paris: Guillaume de Luyne, 1696), unpaginated; reproduced in Mongrédien, *Recueil des textes*, pp. 196–98.

34. On the portraits of La Fontaine, see Dominique Brême, "Mon portrait jusqu'ici ne m'a rien reproché," pp. 108–21 of *Jean de La Fontaine*, edited by Claire Lesage, published on the occasion of the exhibit held at the Bibliothèque Nationale de France for the tricentennial of the death of La Fontaine (Paris: Bibliothèque nationale de France/Seuil, 1995).

35. Hippolyte Taine, *Essai sur les Fables de La Fontaine* (Paris: Joubert, 1853); reprinted and expanded in *La Fontaine et ses Fables* (Paris: Hachette, 1861).

36. Idem, *Les origines de la France contemporaine*, 5 books in 3 volumes (1876–1894). Reprinted in 2 volumes (Paris: Laffont, Bouquins, 1986), with an introduction by François Léger.

CHAPTER 1

The second epigraph for this chapter is excerpted from the abbé Pouget's account to the abbé d'Olivet, reproduced in Mongrédien, *Recueil des textes*, p. 183. François-Aimé Pouget (1666–1723), with a doctorate from the Sorbonne, had been ordained a priest three years before the death of La Fontaine, whom he had "converted." He entered the Oratory in 1696. See *Dictionnaire de spiritualité*, vol. 12, s.v. "Pouget 1."

1. Mongrédien, *Recueil des textes*, p. 213. Text taken from Mathieu Marais, *Mémoires* (1725). This legend originated in the description of the republic of ants the poet gives in *La captivité de saint Malc* (1673). The hero of the poem admires "the love of the common good" in ant society, especially on the occasion of a well-organized funeral procession. This spectacle led him to bitterly regret that he had abandoned the orderly life for "temporal treasures," and to curse his own egotism. See La Fontaine, *Oeuvres complètes*, vol. 2, *Oeuvres diverses*, edited by Pierre Clarac (Paris: Gallimard, 1958), p. 57. This volume will henceforth be cited as *Oeuvres diverses*.

2. Jean-Jacques Rousseau, *Emile*, book 2 (1762).

3. Alphonse de Lamartine, *Méditations poétiques* (1849), "Préface."

4. Claude, duc de Saint-Simon, "Additions à Dangeau," no. 116, in Saint-Simon, *Mémoires*, edited by Yves Coirault (Paris: Gallimard, 1983), pp. 1024–25. This edition has eight volumes of memoirs plus one volume of political treatises.

5. Leo Strauss, *Persecution and the Art of Writing* (Glencoe, Ill.: Free Press, 1952).

6. Rainer Maria Rilke, "Mensonges, I, I," in *Sämtliche Werke, Zweiter Band* (Wiesbaden: Insel, 1956), p. 613.

7. Jean-Pierre Labatut, *Louis XIV roi de gloire* (Paris: Imprimerie nationale, 1984).

8. Marie de France, *Les Fables*, edited by Charles Brucker (Louvain: Peeters, 1991). On medieval poetry in La Fontaine's native province, see Marie-Geneviève Grossel, *Le milieu littéraire en Champagne sous les Thibaudiens*, 2 vols. (Orléans: Paradigme, 1995).

9. See Philippe Salvadori, *La chasse sous l'Ancien Régime* (Paris: Fayard, 1996). Saint-Simon has a harsh judgment of the level of Louis XIV's learning: he underscores his deficiencies regarding "the best-known matters of history and events," which led him to fall into "the grossest absurdities." See Saint-Simon, *Mémoires* 4 (1715):478 and 3:370. On Louis XIV's education, see Georges Lacour-Gayet, *L'éducation politique de Louis XIV* (Paris, 1923); and Henri Chérot, *La première jeunesse de Louis XIV (1649–1653)* (Lille, 1894).

10. On Oudry, see Hal Opperman, *J.-B. Oudry, 1686–1755*, exhibition catalog for the Galeries Nationales du Grand Palais, Paris, 1 October 1982–3 January 1983 (Paris: Editions de la Réunion des Musées nationaux, 1982); and idem, *Jean-Baptiste Oudry* (New York and London: Garland, 1977).

11. On the painter François Desportes, see *L'atelier de Desportes*, exhibition catalog of the Musée National du Louvre, edited by Lise Duclaux and Tamara Préaud (Paris: Editions de la Réunion des Musées nationaux, 1982).

12. See Marc Fumaroli, "La Fontaine et l'Académie Française," *Le Fablier* 8 (January 1997).

13. On the literature glorifying the king, see Nicole Ferrier-Caverivière, *L'image de Louis XIV dans la littérature française de 1660 à 1715* (Paris: Presses Universitaires de France, 1981).

14. See the official account: *Les plaisirs de l'Isle Enchantée . . . à Versailles, le VII May 1664 et continuées plusieurs autres jours* (Paris: Imprimerie royale, 1673). On the ballet genre under Louis XIV, see Marie-Françoise Christout, *Le Ballet de Cour de Louis XIV (1643–1672)* (Paris: Picard, 1967). See also the many recent studies by Philippe Hourcade, esp. his article "Ballet" in the *Dictionnaire du Grand Siècle*, edited by François Bluche (Paris: Fayard, 1989).

15. On the pictorial genre of "grotesques," see André Chastel, *La Grotesque* (Paris: Le Promeneur, 1988). Rococo art, which would find such appeal in *Fables* and *Contes*, has deep roots in the "grotesque," long a marginal genre, which owes its name to the "grottoes" (ruins of Roman homes) and their many whimsical fresco decorations, the source of inspiration for Raphaël's pupil Giovanni da Udine, for minor painters, and notably for Watteau's masters in Paris, for example, Claude Audran III.

16. See Alain-Marie Bassy, "Les Fables, La Fontaine et le Labyrinthe de Versailles," *Revue Française d'Histoire du Livre* 12 (1976):3–26. See also chap. 5, n. 35.

17. Louis XIV, *Manière de montrer les jardins de Versailles*, edited by Simone Hoog (Paris: Editions de la Réunion des Musées nationaux, 1982; rev. ed. 1992); translated by John F. Stewart as *The Way to Present the Gardens of Versailles* (Paris: Editions de la Réunion des Musées nationaux, 1992).

18. See Simone Blavier-Paquot, "Sur l'accueil que reçurent au XVIIe siècle les Fables de La Fontaine," *XVIIe Siècle* 73 (1966):49–57.

19. See above, "Preamble," n. 32.

20. On the success of *Fables*, secured by, among other things, the many pirated editions, see Claire Lesage, "Comment La Fontaine édita ses fables, 1668–1694," in *Jean de La Fontaine*, pp. 146–51. In addition to the duodecimo edition, the first collection by Barbin was published in a nobler and more sumptuous quarto edition.

21. See Marc Fumaroli, "Les Fables dans la tradition humaniste de l'apologue ésopique," in Jean de La Fontaine, *Fables*, edited by Marc Fumaroli (Paris: Imprimerie nationale, 1985; repr. Pochothèque, 1995), pp. lxix–ciii.

22. Marc Fumaroli, "Antoine Watteau et le comte de Caylus: Une amitié paradoxale," *Revue de l'Art* (January 1997).

23. Cited by René Jasinski, *La Fontaine et le premier recueil des Fables*, 2 vols. (Paris: Nizet, 1966), 1:274.

24. Ovid, *The Metamorphoses* book 1, ll. 316–17: *Mons ibi verticibus petit arduus astra duobus, / Nomine Parnassus, superantque cacumina nubes.* Translated by Horace Gregory (New York: Viking, 1958), p. 39. In "D'Ovide à La Fontaine: En lisant l'Adonis," (*Le Fablier* 1 (1989):23–32, Jules Brody provides a critical bibliography regarding the relation between La Fontaine and Ovid. For *The Metamorphoses* in European literature, there is a vast body of work. See, among others, Charles Martindale, ed., *Ovid Renewed: Ovidian Influences on Literature and Art from the Middle Ages to the Twentieth Century* (Cambridge, 1988).

25. Jean-Jacques Boissard, *Parnassus biceps: In cujus priore jugo Musarum Deorumque praesidum Hippocrenes, in altero Deorum fatidicorum phoebadum, et vatum illustriorum* . . . (Frankfurt, 1627), with forty engravings by Jean-Théodore de Bry. A copy bound with the coat of arms of Gaston d'Orléans is housed in the reserve collection of the Bibliothèque Nationale de France. This work is the reprint of an earlier edition, published in 1601, also in Frankfurt (accompanied, it appears, by the same engravings), under a slightly different title: *Parnassus cum imaginibus Musarum Deorumque praesidum Hippocrenes.* In this essay, Boissard (1528–1602) makes Apollo, the god who has descended among men, the founder and lawmaker of Arcadia and its shepherds. The same author published *Romanae urbis Topographiae et Antiquitatum* . . . *Figurae*, 6 parts in 3 folio volumes (Frankfurt, 1597–1602), from which *Parnassus* was excerpted. La Fontaine also found the text of a Latin inscription in it (vol. 2, part 4), which he saw during his trip to Limousin in 1663. He published a translation of it in 1685, in volume 1 of *Ouvrages de prose et de poésie*, which he published jointly with Maucroix the same year. This text, reprinted under the title "Inscription tirée de Boissard," appears in *Oeuvres diverses*, pp. 769–73 and notes pp. 1090–91.

26. François-René de Chateaubriand, *Essai sur les révolutions*, book 4, in *Essai sur les révolutions. Génie du christianisme*, edited by Maurice Regard (Paris: Gallimard, 1957), p. 60. For Chateaubriand, a reader of Ovid but also of Rousseau, the mythic fall back to the iron age recounted in *The Metamorphoses* is similar in gravity to the moral fall that, according to Rousseau, followed natural man's introduction into political societies.

27. See La Fontaine, *Oeuvres diverses*, pp. 20–46; and Jean-Charles Darmon, *L'ennui des Muses: La Fontaine et la fable du Parnasse (autour de Clymène)* (Paris: Hermann, 1997). The play, which had been forgotten since its publication in 1671, had its world premiere on 17 June 1991 at the Festival Jean de La Fontaine in Château-Thierry, in a production by J.-C. Darmon, and was performed again in Paris at the Théâtre 14 Jean-Marie Serreau, on 8 and 9 July 1991.

28. On Maurice de Guérin, see Barbey d'Aurevilly's judgment in his letter to Guillaume Stanislas Trébutien, 2 February 1855, in d'Aurevilly, *Lettres à Trébutien*, 2:198.

29. On this lifelong friend of La Fontaine's, see François Maucroix, *Lettres de Maucroix: Edition critique suivie de poésies inédites et de textes latins inédits extraits du Manuscrit de Reims* . . . , edited by Renée Kohn (Grenoble: Imprimerie Allier, 1962), esp. pp. 15–35, "Biographie de Maucroix."

30. On the notion of "heart" in the seventeenth century and the place that concept from mystical theology occupied in the secularized language of interiority, see Benedetta Papasogli, *Il "Fondo del cuore": Figure dello spazio interiore nel Seicento francese* (Pisa: Editrice Libreria Goliardica, 1991). See also *Dictionnaire de spiritualité*, s.v. "coeur."

31. See Léon Petit, "Autour du procès de Foucquet, La Fontaine et son oncle Jannart sous la griffe de Colbert," *Revue d'histoire littéraire de la France* 47 (1947):193–210. On *Relation d'un voyage de Paris en Limousin*, see chap. 5; and the chapter devoted to it in Roger Duchêne's biography, *Jean de La Fontaine*. La Fontaine kept Jannart company during this "forced journey" (L. Petit) to the land of Jean Dorat. Jannart had been Foucquet's *substitut* in the office of *procureur général* at the Parlement de Paris, an office purchased by the *surintendant* in 1650.

32. On the reversal of Parisian public opinion during the Foucquet trial, see chap. 4.

33. See Jasinski, *La Fontaine et le premier recueil* 1:274.

34. See Valéry, "Au sujet d'Adonis."

35. André Suarès, "La peste du mensonge," in *Vues sur l'Europe*, edited by Robert Parienté (Paris, 1939; repr. Paris: Grasset), p. 154.

36. Jean-Paul Sartre, "Qu'est-ce qu'écrire?" in *Qu'est-ce que la littérature?* (Paris, 1948; repr. Gallimard, 1985).

37. *The Divine Comedy of Dante Alighieri*, translated by Melville Best Anderson (New York: Heritage, 1944), p. 281.

38. On royal religion and the medieval ideology of monarchy, see Colette Beaune, *Naissance de la nation France* (Paris: Gallimard, 1985); and Jacques Krynen, *L'empire du roi, Idées et croyances politiques en France XIIIe–XVe siècle* (1993). See also Jacques le Goff, *Saint Louis* (Paris: Gallimard, 1996); the exhibition catalog *Le culte de Saint Louis au XVIIe siècle* (Paris: Musée de la Légion d'honneur, 1970–71); and Manfred Tietz, "Saint Louis roi chrétien: Un mythe de la mission intérieure du XVIIe siècle," in *La conversion au XVIIe siècle: Actes du colloque du CMR 17*, January 1982 (Marseilles, 1983), pp. 59–69. On the "rending" (de Retz) of the ancient kingdom, see Etienne Thuau, *Raison d'Etat et pensée politique à l'époque de Richelieu* (Paris: A. Colin, 1966); William F. Church, *Richelieu and Reason of State* (Princeton, 1972); and the recent collections *L'Etat baroque, 1610–1652*, edited by Henry Méchoulan (Paris: J. Vrin, 1985), and *L'Etat classique, 1652–1715*, edited by Henry Méchoulan and Joël Cornette (Paris: J. Vrin, 1996). On the clash between the two universes, the mythico-religious Christian kingdom and the political and administrative state, see Marcel Gauchet's essential "L'Etat au miroir de la raison d'Etat: La France et la chrétienté dans la raison et la déraison d'Etat," in *Théoriciens et théories de la Raison d'Etat au*

XVIe et XVIIe siècles, edited by Yves-Charles Zarka (Paris: Presses Universitaires de France, 1994), pp. 193–244.

39. See the proceedings of the colloquium held at the Sorbonne on 26–27 May 1986: *La monarchie absolutiste et l'Histoire de France: Théorie du pouvoir, propagandes monarchistes et mythologies nationales*, edited by François Laplanche and Chantal Grell (Paris, 1996). On the question of the Trojan origins of the kingdom, see Colette Beaune, "L'utilisation du mythe des origines troyennes en France à la fin du Moyen-Age," in *Lectures médiévales de Virgiles*, proceedings of the Colloque de Rome, 25–26 October 1982, Ecole Française de Rome (Paris: De Boccard, 1985).

40. Paul de Gondi, cardinal of Retz, *Oeuvres*, edited by Michèle Hipp and Michel Pernot (Paris: Gallimard, 1984), pp. 193–95.

41. Guillaume Postel has been the object of increasingly fine studies in recent years. See esp. Georges Weill and François Secret, *Vie et caractère de Guillaume Postel* (Milan: Archè, 1987); a key text by Postel himself, *Les paralipomènes de la vie de François Ier*, edited by François Secret (Milan: Archè, 1989); and Claude Postel, *Les écrits de Guillaume Postel publiés en France et leurs éditeurs: 1538-1579* (Geneva: Droz, 1992).

42. On d'Urfé and his works, see Maxime Gaume's studies, esp. *Les inspirations et les sources de l'oeuvre d'Honoré d'Urfé* (Centre d'Etudes Foréziennes, 1977).

43. See Bernard Beugnot, "La figure de Mecenas," in *La mémoire du texte: Essais de poétique classique* (Paris: Honoré Champion, 1994), pp. 53–66. On the influence of the example of the Roman Empire, beginning in the early part of Louis XIV's reign, see Ferrier-Caverivière, *L'image de Louis XIV*, p. 28.

44. Molière, *Le misanthrope*, act 5, scene 1, ll. 1501–4: "Il court parmi le monde un livre abominable, / Et de qui la lecture est même condamnable, / Un livre à mériter la dernière rigueur, / Dont le fourbe a le front de me faire l'auteur!" (Circulating about is an abominable book, / The very reading of which is to be condemned, / A book that merits the utmost severity, / And the rogue has the nerve to call me its author!). This manuscript from the Bibliothèque de l'Arsenal in Paris (ms. 3148), made up of 164 folios, bears the title *L'innocence persécutée*, and was "rediscovered" by G. Mongrédien. It had been previously published by Louis-Auguste Ménard under the sensational and misleading title *Le livre abominable de 1665 qui courait en manuscrit parmi le monde, sous le nom de Molière (Comédie politique en vers sur le procès de Fouquet)* (The abominable book of 1665, which circulated in society in manuscript form, under the name of Molière [political comedy in verse on the Fouquet trial]), 2 vols. (Paris: Firmin Didot, 1882). The publishers judged it necessary to explain, in their "Note to the Reader," that they distanced themselves "from any affirmation that might lead one to suppose" they were in agreement with L.-A. Ménard in attributing the text to Molière. See Antoine Adam, *Histoire de la littérature française au XVIIe siècle* (Paris: Domat, 1949–56), vol. 3, *L'apogée du siècle: Boileau, Molière*, pp. 307–9. Adam argues that the book might be seen as a collective work in which Molière "may have played some role," and which must have been composed within "a circle both hostile to the minister [Colbert] and devoted to the Solitaries [of Port-

Royal]." He alludes to "the salon of Mme du Plessis-Guénégaud." In *L'affaire Foucquet* (Paris: Hachette, 1956), pp. 155–68, Georges Mongrédien gives a good analysis of the text and adopts Adam's hypotheses, but also nuances them: "All that can be asserted today is that *L'innocence persécutée* comes from a milieu entirely devoted to Foucquet and very hostile to Colbert" (p. 157).

45. On La Fontaine as the friend of Port-Royal, see his own epigrams, "Le chemin de velours," "Ballade sur Escobar," and "Stance sur le même," in *Oeuvres diverses*, pp. 586–90; and the important article by Pierre Clarac, "La Fontaine et Port-Royal," *Revue d'histoire de la philosophie et d'histoire générale de la civilisation* (1943):1–31 and 147–71.

46. On Chapelain, see Georges Collas, *Jean Chapelain, (1595–1674), étude historique et littéraire: Un poète protecteur des lettres au XVIIe siècle* (Paris: Perrin, 1912); and R. Bray, *La formation de la doctrine classique en France* (Paris, 1927).

47. On the genre of the dedication in the seventeenth century, see Wolfgang Leiner, *Der Widmungsbrief in der französischen Literatur (1580–1715)* (Heidelberg: Winter 1965). Since then, the author has added to his analyses in several articles. Corneille (who on several occasions declared his aversion for the panegyric genre) wrote in that dedication: "It is with great restraint that I always suppress a quantity of glorious truths, in order not to make myself suspect of spreading the obliging lies that many of our moderns know how to produce so readily." On the social position of the writer in the seventeenth century, see Alain Viala, *Naissance de l'écrivain* (Paris: Edition de Minuit, 1985).

48. Many sources reveal the hostility at the time toward the authoritarian government of the young Louis XIV and Colbert. See esp. Olivier Lefèvre d'Ormesson, *Journal*, edited by Adolphe Chéruel, 2 vols. (Paris, 1860–61), 1:405.

49. On *Chapelain décoiffé*, which targets only a performer, a traitor to the profession, see Adam, *Histoire de la littérature française*, 3:11. In *La carrière de Jean Racine* (Paris: Gallimard, 1961), pp. 61–81, Raymond Picard clarifies the thorny question of the royal pension granted to the young Racine.

50. See Racine, *Oeuvres complètes*, edited by René Groos, Raymond Picard, and Raymond Pilon (Paris: Gallimard, 1956), 1:981–85, and variants given in the note pp. 1194–97.

51. See Picard, *La carrière de Jean Racine*, chap. 2: "Alexandre (1665–1666)," pp. 108–18, and the text of the dedication to the king, in Racine, *Oeuvres complètes*, 1:193–94.

52. On this play, see Picard, *La carrière de Jean Racine*, chap. 4: "Bérénice," pp. 154–67, and the text of the dedication to Colbert, in Racine, *Oeuvres complètes*, 1:481–82.

53. On Nicolas Boileau-Despréaux, see Bernard Beugnot and Roger Zuber, *Boileau, visages anciens, visages nouveaux* (Montreal: Presses de l'Université de Montréal, 1973); and Gordon Pocock, *Boileau and the Nature of Neo-classicism* (New York: Cambridge University Press, 1980).

54. See these texts in Fumaroli, ed., *Fables*, or in La Fontaine, *Oeuvres complètes*, 1:3–10.

CHAPTER 2

1. On Ariosto's influence in France, see Alexandre Cioranescu, *L'Arioste en France des origines à la fin du XVIIIe siècle* (Paris: Presses modernes, 1938); the supplement to *Studi francesi* 35 (May-August 1968), devoted to "Italianism in France in the Seventeenth Century"; and Marc Fumaroli, "La mélancolie et ses remèdes: Classicisme français et maladie de l'âme," in *La diplomatie de l'esprit: De Montaigne à La Fontaine* (Paris: Hermann, 1994), pp. 403–39.

2. Mongrédien, *Recueil des textes*, p. 197.

3. Ibid.

4. "Not only did he invent the genre of poetry to which he applied himself, but he polished it to absolute perfection; hence he was the first both to have invented it and to have excelled at it, to such an extent that no one could ever occupy second place in this genre of writing" (Charles Perrault, *Les hommes illustres qui ont paru en France pendant le siècle* [Paris: Derallier, 1696–1700; repr. Geneva: Slatkine, 1970), pp. 83–84; quoted by Mongrédien, *Recueil des textes*, p. 200. See also ibid., pp. 199–201.

5. On this salon and those who frequented it, see Menjot d'Elbenne, *Madame de la Sablière, ses pensées chrétiennes et ses lettres à l'abbé de Rancé* (Paris: Plon, 1923), chap. 5: "Le salon de la rue Neuve-des-petits-champs (1669–1680)," pp. 65–83. "It was about 1673 that Mme de la Sablière invited La Fontaine to come live at her home" (p. 84).

6. Fargue, *Le Piéton de Paris*; idem, "La Fontaine," pp. 65–77. See also Valéry, "Au sujet d'Adonis."

7. On the wit of that society, as the man of letters conceived it, see Beugnot, "La figure de Mecenas," in *La mémoire du texte*, pp. 53–66. The author presents two texts by Jean-Louis Guez de Balzac: "Suite d'un entretien de vive voix ou De la conversation des Romains," and "Mecenas, A Madame la Marquise de Rambouillet," which are found in Guez de Balzac, *Oeuvres diverses (1644)*, edited by Roger Zuber (Paris: Honoré Champion, 1995).

8. The passage from Léon Daudet is taken from *Salons et journaux* (Paris: Grasset, 1932), pp. 253–55, and quoted in Marc Fumaroli, *Trois institutions littéraires* (Paris: Gallimard), "La conversation," pp. 111–210, passage quoted p. 188.

9. The primary source on La Fontaine's presence at the Oratory is Father Louis Batterel, *Mémoires domestiques pour servir à l'histoire de l'Oratoire* (1729), edited by Augustin-Marie-Pierre Ingold and Emile Bonnardet, 4 vols. (Paris: Picard, 1902–1905). The article on La Fontaine is in vol. 2 (1903), pp. 599–613. On the spirit of the French Oratory (a very original creation on the model of the society of priests founded in the sixteenth century in Rome by Saint Filippo Neri), see Jean Orcibal's studies, esp. *Le cardinal de Bérulle: Evolution d'une spiritualité* (Paris, 1965); and Charles E. Williams, *The French Oratorians and Absolutism, 1611–1641* (New York: Peter Lang, 1989). Let us recall that Bérulle's successor to head the Oratory from 1629 to 1641, Father de Condren, was the

confessor of Gaston d'Orléans, the rebellious brother of Louis XIII, beloved by La Fontaine.

10. Lines 15–16 of "Ballade," published in *Contes et nouvelles en vers* (1665), in La Fontaine, *Oeuvres diverses*, pp. 585–86. Another account of La Fontaine's appreciation of *L'Astrée* at the Oratory, coming from La Fontaine himself, is provided in Le Verrier's comments, reproduced in Mongrédien, *Recueil des textes*, p. 35.

11. Honoré d'Urfé, *L'Astrée*, act 1, scene 2. See La Fontaine, *Oeuvres diverses*, p. 428.

12. Lines 86–95 of the epistle "A Monsieur le Duc de Bouillon," in La Fontaine, *Oeuvres diverses*, p. 571.

13. On Tristan L'Hermite's *La lyre*, see Françoise Graziani, "*La Lyre*: Tristan et le madrigal mariniste," *Cahiers Tristan L'Hermite* 5 (1983):18–24.

14. On this question, see La Fontaine, *Oeuvres diverses*, p. 919, note to p. 569.

15. On 14 July 1664, La Fontaine took an oath as a gentleman serving the dowager duchesse d'Orléans (Marguerite de Lorraine, widow of Gaston d'Orléans), who was living at the Luxembourg Palace. He occupied that post until the duchess's death on 3 February 1672. See Mongrédien, *Recueil des textes*, pp. 67 and 110.

16. Tallemant des Réaux, *Historiettes*, edited by Antoine Adam, 2 vols. (Paris: Gallimard, 1960), 1:391–92.

17. In addition to Maxime Gaume's *Les inspirations et les sources de l'oeuvre d'Honoré d'Urfé*, see Madeleine Bertaud, *L'Astrée et Polexandre: Du roman pastoral au roman heroïque* (Geneva: Droz, 1986); and Servais Kervorkian, *Thématique de l'Astrée* (Paris: H. Champion, 1991).

18. On Pierre Guédron, composer of *Airs de cour*, and Louis XIII as a musician, see *The New Grove Dictionary of Music and Musicians*, edited by Stanley Sadie, 20 vols. (1980), 7:784–85 (on Guédron) and 11:253–54 (on Louis XIII).

19. The abbé d'Olivet, *Histoire de l'Académie française* (1729; 1858), 2:303–304; cited in Mongrédien, *Recueil des textes*, p. 36 (line 1643).

20. Olivier Patru, *Eclaircissements sur l'histoire de l'Astrée*, first published in his *Oeuvres* (1680); see Maurice Magendie, *Du nouveau sur l'Astrée* (Paris: H. Champion, 1927), pp. 77–85; and Roger Zuber, *Les "belles infidèles" et la formation du goût classique* (Paris: A. Colin, 1968; new revised and augmented edition, Paris: Albin Michel, 1995), p. 216.

21. On Gaston d'Orléans and his court, see Claude K. Abraham, *Gaston d'Orléans et sa cour: Etude littéraire* (Chapel Hill: University of North Carolina Press, 1964); and Georges Dethan, "Tristan L'Hermite et Gaston d'Orléans, un appel à l'héroïsme," *Cahiers Tristan L'Hermite* 11 (1989):19–25. The poet remained in the prince's service from 1621 to 1646. For the text of *Le page disgracié*, see the edition by Marcel Arland (Paris: Stock, 1946), and the more recent one edited by Jean Serroy (Grenoble: Presses Universitaires de Grenoble, 1980). See also idem, "La folie du page," *Cahiers Tristan L'Hermite* 9 (1987); and idem, "Tristan et la mélancolie," *Cahiers Tristan L'Hermite* 2 (1980):26–34.

22. See Richard Crescenzo, "Une poétique de la Galerie? Sur quelques pièces de *La Lyre*," *Cahiers Tristan L'Hermite* 14 (1992):46–62. For the text of *La Lyre*, see the edition by Jean-Pierre Chauveau (Geneva: Droz, 1977).

23. François Tristan L'Hermite, *La Lyre*, p. 41.

24. On the effect the reading of *Mémoires d'outre-tombe* produced on Charles Baudelaire, see the thesis of Patrick Labarthe, *Poésie et "rhétorique profonde": Baudelaire et la tradition*, Paris, Univ. de Paris IV-Sorbonne, 1996, esp. chap. 1: "Baudelaire et la poétique du Christianisme: Le dialogue avec Chateaubriand."

25. See Tristan L'Hermite, *Le page disgracié* (Arland edition), chap. 3: "L'enfance et l'élévation du page disgracié," p. 34; chap. 4: "Comme le page disgracié entre au service d'un prince," pp. 34–35; and chap. 5: "L'affinité qu'eut le page disgracié avec un autre page de la maison, dont l'amitié lui fut préjudiciable," p. 37.

26. Chapelain's text can be found in *Lettre-traité sur l'origine des romans*, based on Pierre-Daniel Huet's edition, edited by Fabienne Gégou (Paris: Nizet, 1971).

27. Jean-François Sarasin, "S'il faut qu'un jeune homme soit amoureux," in *Oeuvres*, edited by Paul Festugière, 2 vols. (Paris: Champion, 1926), 2:146–232. See Ada Speranza Armani, "Jean-François Sarasin: Sull'amore," in *Eros in Francia nel Seicento*, edited by Paolo Carile (Bari and Paris: Nizet, 1987), pp. 213–43.

28. Tristan L'Hermite, *Le page disgracié*, chap. 34: "Les présents que le page disgracié reçut de la part de sa maîtresse, ainsi qu'ils faisaient voyage ensemble," p. 94. On the relations between Tristan and La Fontaine, see Jean-Pierre Collinet, "La Fontaine et Tristan," *Cahiers Tristan L'Hermite* 5 (1983):59–68.

29. François Tristan L'Hermite, "LXXXVIII, A Monsieur le C. de M. Il s'excuse de la négligence qui accompagne la poésie, et lui représente ses sentiments," in *Lettres meslées*, critical edition by Catherine Grisé (Geneva: Droz, and Paris: Minard, 1972), pp. 199–201. The addressee of this letter may have been Adrien de Montluc, comte de Cramail, Tristan's colleague at Gaston's literary court. He was imprisoned in La Bastille on the order of Richelieu from 1632 to 1642, following the failure of the armed rebellion of the duc de Montmorency, inspired by Gaston d'Orléans.

30. Several people who witnessed these "brigades" have left published recollections: for example, Marolles in his *Mémoires*, Tallemant des Réaux in his *Historiettes*, and Pellisson in his *Histoire de l'Académie*. All the same, it is in manuscripts that have only recently been published, such as that of Tallemant des Réaux, *Le ms. 673 (de la bibliothèque de La Rochelle)*, edited by Vincenette Maigne (Paris: Klincksieck, 1994), or that remain unpublished, such as ms. 19142 of the Bibl. nat. Fr. in Paris, that one finds the very lacunary "archives" of the academy of "knights-errant" and its intellectual exchanges. A good overview of that literary sociability has been done by A. Adam, "L'Ecole de 1650," *Revue d'histoire de la philosophie* (1939–42). It was made possible by the pioneering work of Josephine de Boer, "Men's Literary Circles in Paris, 1610–1660," *PMLA* 53 (September 1938): 730–80. See Marc Fumaroli, "Arcadie, Académie et Parnasse, trois lieux allégoriques du loisir lettré," in *L'Ecole du silence, le sentiment des images*

au XVIIᵉ siècle (Paris: Flammarion, 1995), pp. 19–36, which also refers to M. Cauchie, "Les églogues de Nicolas Frémicle et le groupe des 'Illustres bergers,'" *Revue d'histoire de la philosophie* (1942):115–33.

31. Tallemant des Réaux, "Madame de la Rocheguyon," in *Historiettes* 2:495.

32. See Alain Mérot, *Eustache Le Sueur (1616–1655)* (Paris: Arthéna, 1987), no. 21, p. 173; and idem, *La peinture française au XVIIᵉ siècle* (Paris: Gallimard/Electa, 1994), reproduction of *Réunion d'amis* (about 1640, now in the Louvre), pp. 32–33.

33. Tallemant des Réaux, "La maréchale de Temines," in *Historiettes* 2:97.

34. Idem, "Les amours de l'auteur," in ibid., 2:811.

35. See Claude Dulong, *Banquier du roi Barthélemy Hervart, 1606–1676* (Paris: Ségur, 1951), and, more generally, Michel-Edmond Richard, *La vie des protestants français de l'édit de Nantes à la Révolution (1598–1789)* (Paris: Les Editions de Paris, 1994), esp. chap. 4: "La vie sociale Noblesse de cour et classe dirigeante." On the stately mansions built in Paris during that era, see Jean-Pierre Babelon, *Demeures parisiennes sous Henri IV et Louis XIII* (Paris: Hazan, 1991).

36. Tallemant des Réaux, "M. des Yveteaux," in *Historiettes*, 1:143, and the note 2:828–29.

37. Idem, "Tallemant, le maître des requêtes," in ibid., 2:547. On the painted decorations in this mansion, esp. the series *Les sept arts libéraux*, see Pierre Rosenberg and Jacques Thuillier, *Laurent de La Hyre, 1606–1656: L'homme et l'oeuvre*, exhibit catalog (Geneva: Skira, 1988), pp. 292–302; and the Sotheby's sales catalog of 11 December 1996, pp. 126–27. On the art collections in Paris under Louis XIII and the Regency, see Antoine Schnapper, *Curieux du grand siècle, collections et collectioneurs dans la France du XVIIᵉ siècle* (Paris: Flammarion, 1994).

38. On Montmauron, see Tallemant des Réaux, "Montmauron," in *Historiettes* 2:537–42; and Mongrédien, "Le mécène de Corneille, M. de Montauron," *Revue de France*, 15 November 1928.

39. Although they lived side by side in Paris, the aristocratic family Vivonne de Rambouillet and that of the financiers Rambouillet had nothing in commmon except the name of the land taken by a branch of the former.

40. See U. V. Chatelain, *Le Surintendant Nicolas Foucquet, protecteur des lettres, des arts et des sciences* (Paris: Perrin, 1950; repr. 1980); and more generally, André Chastel, *L'art français: L'Ancien Régime, III, 1620–1775* (Paris: Flammarion, 1995).

41. On the ties between the Tallemants and Mazarin (and then Foucquet), see D. Dessert, *Fouquet* (Paris: Fayard, 1987), pp. 214–15 and p. 339. Dessert indicates that the financier Rambouillet testified against the *surintendant* (p. 250). See also M.-E. Richard, *La vie des protestants*, chap. 8: "Les choix décisifs, l'abjuration ou l'exil."

42. On Maucroix, see Kohn, ed., *Lettres de Maucroix*.

43. Tallemant des Réaux, "Les amours de l'auteur," in *Historiettes* 2:817.

44. Idem, "Madame de Launay," in ibid., pp. 833–34.

45. In her edition of *Le ms. 673*, Maigne nuances our knowledge of Tallemant des Réaux, until now limited to the writings of Emile Magne.

46. On Paul Pellisson, see F. L. Marcou, *Etude sur la vie et les oeuvres de Pellisson, suivie d'une correspondance inédite du même* (Paris: Didier and Auguste Durand, 1859); and Alain Niderst, *Madeleine de Scudéry, Paul Pellisson et leur monde* (Paris: Presses Universitaires de France, 1976). See Noémi Hepp, "Un jeune castrais pionnier du goût classique, Paul Pellisson," in *Castres et pays tarnais: Actes du XXVIᴱ Congrès d'études régionales organisé à Castres les 5–7 juin 1971 par la Société culturelle du Pays castrais et la Société des sciences, arts et Belles-lettres du Tarn* (Albi: Editions de la "Revue du Tarn," 1972), pp. 289–97. I have consulted French ms. 19142 a great deal.

47. French ms. 19142, folio 82.

48. Ibid., folio 92. An erotic epigram by François Maynard, president of the Academy of the Round Table in 1646, gives an idea of the freedom of language and imagination that reigned there:

> N'ois-je pas dire à la censure
> Des Esprits qui font les prudens,
> Que voici des vers impudens
> Au delà de toute mesure?
>
> Qu'ils mettent l'honneur à l'encan
> Et qu'il faut que le Vatican
> Contre moi ses foudres allume?
>
> L'humeur de ces gens me ravit:
> Ils veulent défendre à ma plume
> Ce qu'ils ont permis à leur vit.
>
> Have I not heard from the censors
> Of Wits who play it safe,
> That these verses are impudent
> Beyond all measure?
>
> That they put honor on the auction block,
> And that the Vatican
> Must strike me down?
>
> The humors of such people delight me:
> They want to forbid my pen
> What they have allowed their cock.

Maynard, "Epigramme," cited in the review *Le Pont de l'Epée* 67–68 (1979):36. La Fontaine is true to this spirit in *Contes*.

49. Ibid. Maynard was the author of Priapeans (published in anthologies) that his friend Conrart, the royal censor, did not want to include in the 1646 collection of his poetry.

50. Ibid.

51. See Roland Mousnier, *L'Homme rouge ou la vie du cardinal de Richelieu (1585–1642)* (Paris: Robert Laffont, 1992).

52. French ms. 19142, folio 13.

53. See "La République des Lettres," *Annuaire du Collège de France, résumé des cours et des travaux* 1 (1987–88):417–32; 2 (1988–89):383–400; and 3 (1989–90):461–77. On the political attitude of the Dupuy brothers, directors of the most influential private Parisian academy under Louis XIII and the Regency (see chap. 4), see the recent thesis of Giuliano Ferretti, *Fortin de La Hoguette ou le vertige de la politique: Lettres aux frères Dupuy et à leur entourage (1623–1662)*, Lausanne, 1996; forthcoming, Florence: Olschki. On Father Marin Mersenne and his academy, see the forthcoming biography by Armand Beaulieu, who has also completed a critical edition of the correspondence of this ecclesiastic scientist.

54. See chap. 3, the analysis of Samuel Sorbière's *Traité de l'amitié*.

55. See Marcou, *Etude sur la vie*, appendix.

56. See G. Hall, "Le siècle de Louis le Grand: L'évolution d'une idée," in *D'un siècle à l'autre: Anciens et Modernes* (Marseilles: CMR 17, 1987).

57. Marcou, *Etude sur la vie*, appendix, "Lettre VI" (n.d.), p. 453.

58. See François Bernier, *Abrégé de la philosophie de Gassendi*, 7 vols. (Paris: Fayard, 1992), reprint of the 1684 edition; and Léon Petit, "Madame de La Sablière et François Bernier," *Mercure de France* 308 (1950):670–83.

59. Marcou, *Etude sur la vie*, "Lettre XIII" (n.d.), p. 475.

60. Ibid., "Lettre XIV" (n.d.), p. 478.

61. Ibid., p. 479.

62. See Noémi Hepp, *Deux amis d'Homère au XVIIᵉ siècle: Textes inédits de Paul Pellisson et de Claude Fleury* (Paris: Klincksieck, 1970).

63. On François Cassandre, see Emmanuel Bory, "Hellénisme et Rhétorique: François Cassandre traducteur d'Aristote," in *Un classicisme ou des classicismes?* proceedings of the Colloque de Reims, edited by Georges Forestier and Jean-Pierre Néraudau (Paris: Klincksieck, 1995).

64. *Lucien, de la traduction de N. Perrot, Sr d'Ablancourt*, 2 vols. (Paris: A. Courbé, 1654), prefatory epistle, unpaginated. On the conditions of the publication and reception of this translation, see Zuber, *Les "belles infidèles,"* pp. 213–14.

65. Tallemant des Réaux, "La Marquise de Brosses et Maucroix," in *Historiettes* 2:846–53.

66. Idem, "La Fontaine," in ibid., 1:391.

67. Paris, Bibl. nat. Fr., French ms. 19142, folio 12.

68. Ibid., folio 14.

69. In *Correspondance de Nicolas Poussin*, edited by Charles Jouanny (Paris, 1911), vol. 5, *Archives de l'art français*, p. 395, letter of 17 January 1649; and p. 399, letter of 24 May 1649.

CHAPTER 3

1. Marie-Madeleine Pioche de la Vergne, comtesse de La Fayette, *Histoire de Madame Henriette d'Angleterre*, in Mme de La Fayette, *Oeuvres complètes*, edited by Roger Duchêne (Paris: François Bourin, 1990), p. 456.

2. Ronsard, *Odes* 1555, 1.1, "Au roi Henri II," stanza 7: "ce règne heureux et fortuné, / Sous qui l'heureuse destinée / Avait chanté dès mainte année / Qu'un si grand prince serait né."

3. Racine, *Oeuvres complètes* 1:982.

4. See the special issue of the review *XVIIe Siècle* 162, 1 (January–March 1989), devoted to "the Parisian mansion in the seventeenth century"; Babelon, *Demeures parisiennes;* and Alain Mérot, *Retraites mondaines, aspects de la décoration intérieure à Paris au XVIIe siècle* (Paris: Le Promeneur, 1990).

5. See Petit, "Autour du procès de Foucquet."

6. Nicole Aronson, *Mademoiselle de Scudéry ou le voyage au pays de Tendre* (Paris: Fayard, 1986).

7. Chatelain, *Le Surintendant Nicolas Foucquet*, pp. 101–34.

8. See Barbara Krajewska, *Mythes et découvertes: Le salon littéraire de Madame de Rambouillet dans les lettres des contemporains* (Paris and Tübingen, 1990).

9. La Fontaine, "Danse de l'amour," in *Le songe de Vaux*, 6: "Aminthe et Sylvie / Ce sont leurs beaux noms: / Le ciel porte envie / A mille beaux dons, / A mille trésors / Qu'ont leur esprit et leur corps" (Aminthe and Sylvie / Are their pretty names / Heaven is envious / Of a thousand fine gifts / Of a thousand treasures / Possessed by their bodies and minds).

10. See the text of Pellisson's "great show of thanks": "A Monseigneur Foucquet, Procureur général au Parlement et Surintendant des Finances," in the handy edition by Alain Viala, *L'esthétique galante: Paul Pellisson, Discours sur les Oeuvres de Monsieur Sarasin et autres textes* (Toulouse, 1989), text 5, pp. 87–95.

11. The original sumptuous manuscript is in the Dutuit collection of the Musée du Petit-Palais in Paris (cat. Rahir no. 327). It was calligraphied by Nicolas Jarry and probably bound by Florimond Badier at Foucquet's request. See the facsimile reproduction by the Société des Bibliophiles Français, with an introduction by Jean Corday (Paris, 1931); see also Claire Lesage, "Sous le signe de Fouquet"; and *Littératures classiques* 29 (January 1997), which brings together several pieces on "La Fontaine, *Adonis, Le songe de Vaux, Les amours de Psyché.*" On the relations between Marino and La Fontaine, see below, n. 19.

12. These lines, dedicated to Henry II, duc de Montmorency, are those of the 1623 edition. In 1629 they became: "Invincible Héros, dont la valeur m'étonne, / Reçois ces nouveaux fruits qui naissent de ma veine" (Invincible hero, whose valor astonishes me, / Receive these new fruits born of my vein [1.81]). See Jean Lagny, *Le poète Saint-Amant (1594–1661): Essai sur sa vie et ses oeuvres* (Paris: Nizet, 1964), pp. 74–77.

13. See above, chap. 2, nn. 22 and 23.

14. On the manuscript of *Adonis*, see above, n. 11. On the manuscript of miniatures by Jacques Bailly, see *Devises pour les tapisseries du roi*, edited by Marianne Grivel, preface by Marc Fumaroli (Paris: Herscher, 1988).

15. See Beugnot, "La figure de Mecenas," in *La mémoire du texte*, pp. 53–67.

16. On the ties between Foucquet and the religious groups, especially the Compagnie du Saint-Sacrement, which coordinated the kingdom's works of charity and mercy (at the time, social welfare was the responsibility of private groups or of the church), see chap. 4; and Dessert, *Fouquet*, chap. 7: "Fouquet et les dévots," pp. 189–96.

17. On Foucquet's family origins and the source of its fortune, see Dessert, *Fouquet*, chap. 1: "Les Fouquet avant Fouquet"; chap. 2: "François Fouquet, le père fondateur"; and chap. 3: "L'ascension de l'écureuil."

18. Paul Morand, *Foucquet ou le soleil offusqué* (Paris, 1961).

19. On Marino's influence on La Fontaine, see Marc Fumaroli, "Politique et poétique de Vénus: L'*Adone* de Marino et l'*Adonis* de La Fontaine," *Le Fablier: Revue des Amis de Jean de La Fontaine* 5 (1993):11–16; and Jürgen Grimm, "L'*Adone* de Marino et l'*Adonis* de La Fontaine: Une comparaison structurale," in *Le "dire sans dire" et le dit: Etudes lafontainiennes II* (Paris, Seattle, Tübingen: Papers on Seventeenth-Century Literature, 1996), pp. 1–11. On the poem itself, see the edition of *Adone* (1623), vol 2.1 and 2.2 of *Tutte le opere di G.B. Marino*, edited by Giovanni Pozzi (Milan: Arnoldo Mondadori, 1976; repr. Adelphi, 1990), vol. 2.1, text, vol. 2.2, commentary.

20. See Heliodorus's *Aethiopica* (another name for *Theagenes and Charicleia*). On this motif from the romance adapted by La Fontaine in *Le songe de Vaux*, see Marie-Marcelle Laplace, "L'emblème esthétique des *Ethiopiques* d'Héliodore, la bague d'ambre au chaton d'améthyste gravée," in *Poésie et lyrique antiques* (Lille, 1996), pp. 179–202.

21. See Marc Fumaroli, "Entre Athènes et Cnossos: Les dieux païens dans Phèdre," in *Revue d'histoire littéraire de la France* (1993) 1:30–61.

22. In *Le Surintendant Nicolas Foucquet* (p. 307, n. 4), Chatelain, using the manuscript catalog of Foucquet's library (Paris: Bibl. nat. Fr., French ms. 4938), shows that that library contained the works of Fletcher and Shakespeare, which reveals a curiosity on the *surintendant's* part, if not tastes that were a century ahead of their time.

23. Jacques Thuillier has recently provided a critical edition of this text for the review *Le Fablier* (no. 11, 1999). Until now, only two of Félibien's three letters have been printed, without place or date (Paris, Bibl. nat. Fr., impr. Lk7 10117). See Chatelain, *Le Surintendant Nicolas Foucquet*, p. 380, n. 2. On Foucquet's intention to "offer" Vaux to the king, see Jules Lair, *Nicolas Foucquet Procureur général, Surintendant des Finances, Ministres d'Etat de Louis XIV*, 2 vols. (Paris: Plon, 1890), 2:49–50.

24. In the "synopsis" of his poem, which shows him in a dream discovering "on all sides the pomp of a great ceremony," one of his guides tells him that "in

digging the foundations of this house . . . a case filled with precious stones was found. . . . In the middle . . . a diamond of extraordinary beauty." *Le songe de Vaux*, "Avertissement," in La Fontaine, *Oeuvres diverses*, p. 79. This is the motif of the mystic jewel borrowed from Heliodorus's *Aethiopica* (see above, n. 20).

25. On the transferral of that "model" to the early Versailles of Louis XIV, see Fumaroli, "De Vaux à Versailles: Politique de la poésie," in the exhibition catalog *Jean de La Fontaine*, pp. 14–37.

26. Louis XIV, *Mémoires pour l'instruction du Dauphin*, edited by Pierre Goubert (Paris: Imprimerie nationale, 1992).

27. See Jean Orcibal, *Louis XIV et les protestants: "La cabale des accommodeurs de religion": La caisse des conversions* (Paris: Vrin, 1951).

28. See *Adonis*, in La Fontaine, *Oeuvres diverses*, pp. 3–19 and notes pp. 797–804.

29. On the events of the festival of Vaux on 17 August 1661, see Chatelain, *Le Surintendant Nicolas Foucquet*, pp. 461–81.

30. On the relationship between Mlle de Scudéry and Pellisson, see Alain Niderst, *Madeleine de Scudéry*, esp. chap. 5, "Le monde de Foucquet (1657–1661)," pp. 335–448.

31. See Chantal Morlet-Chantalat, *La Clélie de Mlle de Scudéry, de l'épopée à la gazette: Un discours féminin de la gloire* (Paris: H. Champion, 1994).

32. Nicole Aronson, *Madeleine de Scudéry*; and esp. Roger Duchêne, "Mlle de Scudéry reine de Tendre," in *Les trois Scudéry: Actes du colloque du Havre (October 1991)*, edited by Alain Niderst (Paris: Klincksieck, 1993), pp. 625–32.

33. See *Précis de littérature française du XVIIᵉ siècle*, edited by Jean Mesnard (Paris: Presses Universitaires de France, 1990), chap. 2: "Le retour d'Astrée," pp. 47–64.

34. See Fumaroli, *Trois institutions littéraires*, pp. 111–210.

35. See Jean-Michel Pelous, *Amour précieux, amour galant (1654–1675): Essai sur la représentation de l'amour dans la littérature et la société mondaines* (Paris: Klincksieck, 1980).

36. See Linda Timmermans, *L'accès des femmes à la culture* (Paris: Champion, 1994).

37. It was the unreliable abbé de Choisy who has given currency to that legend: "He dared look upon even Mlle de La Vallière, but he soon realized that that place was taken"; he even assumed an attempt at bribery on Mme du Plessis-Bellière's part. See *Mémoires pour servir à l'histoire de Louis XIV*, edited by Georges Mongrédien (Paris: Mercure de France, 1979), p. 91.

38. On the tradition of the "précieuse," embodied in the king's entourage by Mme de Maintenon, see the edition of her correspondence with Mme de Caylus and Mme de Dangeau, *L'estime et la tendresse*, edited by Pierre Leroy and Marcel Loyau (Paris: Albin Michel, 1998).

39. Jacqueline Plantié, *La mode du portrait littéraire en France (1641–1681)* (Paris: Honoré Champion, 1994).

40. Letter from Mlle de Scudéry to Pellisson, quoted in Mongrédien, *L'affaire Foucquet*, p. 81; see the complete text of this letter of 7 September 1661, in Marcou, *Etude sur la vie et les oeuvres de Pellisson*, pp. 489–93.

41. In *La mode du portrait littéraire* (pp. 458–61), Jacqueline Plantié recognizes La Fontaine in the Anacreon of *Clélie*; see the objections made to this interpretation by Mesnard in *Les trois Scudéry*, p. 395. I support Plantié's reading.

42. Raphaël Trichet Du Fresne, *Fables diverses tirées d'Esope et d'autres auteurs* (Paris: Cramoisy, 1659). In *Le grand Cyrus*, Aesop and a few ladies are depicted making fun of Chilon, (repr. Geneva: Slatkine, 1972), 9:359–65.

43. See Plantié, *La mode du portrait littéraire*, pp. 458ff.

44. The epigraph for this section is taken from Ginette Guitard-Auviste, *Paul Morand, 1888–1976: Légende et vérité* (Paris: Balland, 1996), p. 151. The quotation is from Jean Lafond, *L'homme et son image: Morale et littérature de Montaigne à Mandeville* (Paris: H. Champion), "L'amitié selon Arnauld d'Andilly," pp. 278–80.

45. Plantié, *La mode du portrait littéraire*, pp. 459–60, quoting *Clélie*, 5:111–12.

46. Morlet-Chantalat, *La Clélie de Mlle de Scudéry*, p. 439, quoting *Clélie*, 4:1254.

47. On Pellisson's role with regard to Foucquet, see Chatelain, *Le Surintendant Nicolas Foucquet*, pp. 96ff. On the political doctrine of the novelist and her friend, see Jürgen Grimm, "Les idées politiques dans les romans de Mlle de Scudéry," in *Les trois Scudéry*, pp. 443–54.

48. On the scientific patronage of Foucquet and his wife, see Chatelain, *Le Surintendant Nicolas Foucquet*, pp. 313ff. According to Chatelain, the physician Cureau de La Chambre (father of the abbot who would give La Fontaine such a cold welcome to the Académie Française) was "the idol of précieuse society," (p. 323, n. 2). On his *Art de connaître les hommes*, dedicated to Foucquet, see Dandrey, *La fabrique des Fables*, chap. 4, "Allégorisme animalier et physiognomie comparés," pp. 167ff. This book, born in Foucquet's circle, influenced not only La Fontaine's *Fables* but also the system of Charles Le Brun, the king's painter, of "the visual expression of passions." See Jennifer Montagu, *The Expression of the Passions: The Origin and Influence of Charles Le Brun's "Conférence sur l'expression générale et particulière"* (New Haven: Yale University Press, 1994).

49. The most complete overview of Sorbière remains that of René Pintard, *Le libertinage érudit dans la première moitié du XVIIe siècle* (Paris: Boivin, 1943; repr. Geneva: Slatkine, 1983). A judgment by Conrart on his early works is quoted in Zuber, *Les "belles infidèles,"* pp. 101–2.

50. On Voiture and high-society poetry, see Alain Génétiot, *La poétique du loisir mondain de Voiture à La Fontaine* (Paris: Champion, 1996); and idem, *Les genres lyriques mondains (1630–1660)* (Geneva: Droz, 1990).

51. On the reception of Descartes's thought, esp. in the Jansenist-leaning circles of Paris, see Jean Orcibal, "Descartes et sa philosophie jugés à l'hôtel Liancourt (1669–1674)," in the collection *Descartes et le cartésianisme hollandais* (Amsterdam and Paris: Presses Universitaires de France, 1950), pp. 87–107.

Orcibal uses *Recueil de choses diverses*, subsequently published by Jean Lesaulnier in *Port-Royal insolite*.

52. On Sorbière, see above, n. 49. The treatise *De l'amitié*, published in Paris by Etienne Loyson in 1660, bears the dedication: "To Monsieur de Vaubrun, comte de Nogent, camp leader, general of the carabineers of France."

53. See the text of this dialogue by Perrault in *Recueil de divers ouvrages en prose et en vers* (Paris: Coignard, 1676). Chatelain gives an analysis of it in *Le Surintendant Nicolas Foucquet* (pp. 195 ff.), and indicates (p. 327) that Foucquet had made a sumptuous manuscript of it for his library, comparable to that of La Fontaine's *Adonis*.

54. This essay was published in *Oeuvres en prose*, edited by René Ternois, 2 vols. (Paris: Didier, 1967–68).

55. See above, n. 52. He writes in the dedication, after asserting that he was leaving all his readings there: "I have not made a reflection except on those [experiences] where I truly encountered something solid, and where someone has responded to my frankness, my tenderness, my vigilance, my firmness, and to all the other praiseworthy dispositions I have shown to those to whom I wanted to give my heart." He finds that, "even though friendship was not a thing so natural . . . it was a consequence of the state and empire under which we were born, and the politics to which we were subjected was its cause, rather than nature . . . so that we owe to civil society the birth of friendship, which distinguishes us from the other animals."

56. Pintard, *Le libertinage érudit*, p. 4.

57. See Sorbière, *De l'amitié*, pp. 36 and 57, for the two Latin quotations.

58. Ibid., p. 67.

59. It was part of that legacy that was culled in the following generation around Fénelon. See François-Xavier Cuche, *Une pensée sociale catholique: Fleury, La Bruyère, Fénelon* (Paris: Cerf, 1991), and esp. pp. 242–45, "L'amour, lien de la société."

CHAPTER 4

1. According to the account of the clerk Foucault, reported in *Mémoires sur la vie publique et privée de Fouquet, surintendant des finances*, edited by A. Chéruel, 2 vols. (Paris: Charpentier, 1862), 2:243.

2. "Elégie pour M. F[ouquet]" or "Elégie (aux Nymphes de Vaux) pour le malheureux Oronte," in La Fontaine, *Oeuvres diverses*, pp. 528–29 and notes pp. 900–901.

3. *Vocabolario degli Accademici della Crusca* (Venise, 1612), 5th ed. (Florence, 1746–1932), quoting Agnolo Firenzuola's *Prose*.

4. Antoine Furetière, *Dictionnaire universel* (Paris, 1690), with a number of successive and augmented editions.

5. Ibid., s.v. "Favori."

6. Jean-Louis Guez de Balzac, *Aristippe ou de la Cour* (Leiden: Jean Elzevier, 1658), "A la sérénissime reyne de Suède," pp. 7–20; "Discour premier," p. 34.

7. Ibid., "Discours deuxième," pp. 47 and 49.

8. Ibid., "Discours deuxième," pp. 65–66.

9. On the parallel between Louis XIV and his father, see Saint-Simon, *Mémoires;* and idem, *Traités politiques et autres écrits*, edited by Yves Coirault (Paris: Gallimard, 1996), esp. "Parallèle des trois premiers rois Bourbons," pp. 1013–1333.

10. Guillaume Budé, *De Asse*, in *Opera omnia*, 5 vols. (Basel, 1557; repr. 1966), 2:302–3.

11. [Pierre Dupuy,] "Mémoires et instructions pour servir à justifier l'innocence de Messire François Auguste de Thou," in J.-A. de Thou, *Histoire universelle*, vol. 10, "Pièces" (The Hague, 1740), p. 661. It is very probable that these "Mémoires" were known and circulated in manuscript form well before that belated publication.

12. [Pierre Dupuy,] *Histoire des plus illustres favoris anciens et modernes* (Leiden, 1660). Few copies remain of this book. On the Dupuys, see Jérôme Delatour, *Les frères Dupuy (1582–1656)*, thesis for the degree of paleographic archivist, Paris, Ecole nationale des Chartes, 1996; on the political attitude of the brothers Pierre and Jacques Dupuy, see esp. Ferretti, *Fortin de La Hoguette*.

13. On Foucquet's career and the role of Colbert, see Dessert, *Fouquet*, pp. 232–38. This overview is informed by earlier studies by the author, in particular *Argent, pouvoir et société au Grand Siècle* (Paris: Fayard, 1984).

14. On the naming of the two *surintendants*, see Chéruel, ed., *Mémoires*, pp. 226–38.

15. At stake was a plan to reestablish royal finances, but its main point was to set in place a Chambre de Justice designed to cause Foucquet's downfall. Thanks to Gourville, Foucquet learned of it and kept a copy; exhibited during the trial, it contributed toward saving Foucquet from the death penalty. See J. Hérauld de Gourville, *Mémoires*, edited by Léon Lecestre, 2 vols. (Paris, 1894), 2:153–55. Colbert's plan was published by Pierre Clément in his *Lettres, instructions et mémoires de Colbert*, 10 vols. (Paris, 1861–82), 7:164–83.

16. Mazarin supported Colbert against Foucquet in his last meetings with the king and even on his deathbed. This aspect of the drama is well explained in Mongrédien, *L'affaire Foucquet*, pp. 57–59.

17. The thesis of the "necessary sacrifice" of Foucquet as the price to be paid to cleanse the memory of Mazarin is well established by Dessert, *Fouquet*, pp. 231–39. See also Richard Bonney, "The Fouquet-Colbert Rivalry and the 'Revolution' of 1661," in *Ethics and Politics in Seventeenth-Century France*, edited by Keith Cameron and Elizabeth Woodrough (Exeter, U.K.: University of Exeter Press, 1996), pp. 107–18.

18. At the very moment of his arrest, Foucquet himself and a number of his friends still thought that the king might make him prime minister. See Mongrédien, *L'affaire Foucquet*, pp. 71–78.

19. Text in Chéruel, ed., *Mémoires*, p. 183, letter of October 1652.

20. On the "Paris of the salons" that was won over to Foucquet's side, see Niderst, "Paris des salons," in *Madeleine de Scudéry*; and Aronson, *Mademoiselle de Scudéry*, esp. chap. 21: "De Vaux-le-Vicomte à la Bastille."

21. This is what Dessert calls "the Fouquet lobby," the title of one of this chapters, pp. 167–96. See also Betty Tuba Uzman, *Kinship, Friendship, and Gratitude: Nicolas Foucquet's Patronage Network, 1650–1661*, Ph.D. diss., University of Maryland, 1989; published by UMA Dissertation Services, Ann Arbor, Michigan, 1995.

22. See ibid., appendix 4, pp. 354–62, for the text of this "Saint-Mandé plan." On the conditions under which it was composed, see Chéruel, ed., *Mémoires*, pp. 360–64.

23. L.-H. de Loménie, comte de Brienne, called Brienne the Younger, *Mémoires*, edited by P. Bonnefon, in *Société de l'Histoire de France*, 3 vols., 3:36. These same memoirs report a prior and more sober account of that session of the council, 2:59–60.

24. On the inspiration of Louis XIV's policies at its beginnings, see François Bluche, *Louis XIV* (Paris: Fayard, 1986; repr. Paris: Hachette, 1994), pp. 140–51.

25. See Dessert, *Fouquet*, pp. 48–49. There is no doubt that some people, like La Fontaine, glimpsed in this candidate of peace, the friend of artists and poets, a man capable of reviving the times of the courtly world; on this aristocratic chapter of French poetry, see Daniel Poirion, *Le poète et le prince: L'évolution du lyrisme courtois de Guillaume de Machaut à Charles d'Orléans* (Paris: Presses Universitaires de France, 1965; repr. Geneva: Slatkine, 1978).

26. The abbé de Choisy recorded that request for forgiveness in his *Mémoires*. Foucquet made several allusions to this royal pardon, which he was convinced he had obtained, in his *Défenses* and in his letters. See Chéruel, ed., *Mémoires*, 2:173.

27. On the conditions of that transaction, and the panache Foucquet put into it, see Dessert, *Fouquet*, p. 240. Contemporaries had a contradictory judgment of that sale, and Guy Patin reports that observers "suspected worse." Cited by Chéruel, ed., *Mémoires*, 2:177–78.

28. On that opposition to Colbert, see the analysis of the manuscript sources in Mongrédien, *L'affaire Foucquet*, pp. 97–116, "L'opposition naissante à Colbert."

29. The grave irregularities commited from the beginning of the procedure were troubling even to those responsible for them. See Chéruel, ed., *Mémoires*, 2:271–88, and the good summary in Mongrédien, *L'affaire Foucquet*, pp. 81–96.

30. On the "gratitude" of the France of high culture toward Foucquet, see Chatelain, *Le Surintendant Nicolas Foucquet*, pp. 482–527.

31. Dupuy, "Mémoires et instructions."

32. Ibid., p. 66.

33. On the circumstances surrounding the composition of these two pieces, see Roger Duchêne, *Jean de La Fontaine*, who supports the view that they were composed in Château-Thierry. In reality, since La Fontaine was part of the

underground staff defending Foucquet, it hardly matters where the two poems were materially composed: they were done so in close collaboration with Jannart, and even, in the case of *Ode au roi*, with Foucquet, which suggests that La Fontaine was often in Paris at Jannart's home. Jannart had moved to Quai des Orfèvres, in the Enclos du Palais de Justice. See also Petit, "Autour du procès de Foucquet."

34. Before the *surintendant*'s fall, the relations among Nicolas Foucquet (ex-pupil of the Jesuits), Port-Royal, and the Arnauld family had at times been delicate. See Chatelain, *Le Surintendant Nicolas Foucquet*, pp. 54−59.

35. In his *Etude sur la vie*, Marcou gives an analysis (pp. 211−29) of *Discours au Roy par un de ses fidèles sujets, sur le procès de M. Foucquet, ou première défense de M. Foucquet*; and of *Seconde défense de M. Foucquet, Considérations sommaires sur le procès de M. Foucquet*, and *Suite des Considérations*.

36. On the conditions of the replacement of Lamoignon by Séguier, see Mongrédien, *L'affaire Foucquet*, p. 120.

37. Ibid., pp. 114−15.

38. All these documents were collected in *Les oeuvres de M. Fouquet, ministre d'Etat, contenant son arrestation, son procès et ses défenses contre Louis XIV, roi de France*, 1st ed. (1665−68), 13 vols.; repr. 1696, 16 vols. On the effect produced by the publication of these documents during the preliminary investigation of the trial, see ibid., pp. 119 and 125.

39. This trip lasted from August to November 1663 and was the source for La Fontaine's *Relation d'un voyage de Paris en Limousin*; see also below chap. 5, n. 14.

40. Mme de Sévigné, *Correspondance*, edited by Roger Duchêne (Paris: Gallimard), vol. 1 (1972), p. 68.

41. Lefèvre d'Ormesson, *Journal*, 2:283−34. See, on this point and on the positions of historians on this question, Yves-Marie Bercé, "L'affaire Fouquet dans l'opinion de son temps et sous le regard des historiens," in the proceedings of the colloquium "La Fontaine, de Château-Thierry à Vaux-le-Vicomte," part 1: "The Early Years," 2−3 July 1992, published in *Le Fablier: Revue des Amis de Jean de La Fontaine* 5 (1993):37−42.

42. Sermon quoted in Jean Meyer, *Colbert* (Paris: Hachette, 1981), p. 79.

43. In Mme de Villedieu, *Oeuvres*, 2 vols. (Paris, 1720), act 1, scene 6, p. 163. On this work, see Perry Gethner, "Love, Self-Love and the Court in *Le Favori*," in *L'image du Souverain dans le théâtre de 1600 à 1650: Madame de Villedieu*, proceedings of Wake Forest, edited by M.R. Margitic and R. Wells (1987), pp. 407−20.

44. Ovid, *The Metamorphoses*, 6.472−73 [my translation—J.M.T.].

45. On the notion of "public" ("constellation of individuals") under Louis XIV, see Hélène Merlin, *Public et littérature en France au XVIIᵉ siècle* (Paris: Les Belles Lettres, 1994). On the coexistence, under the absolute monarchy, of a public *polis* that removed the king's subjects from any participation in political life, and of an intense private sociability, external to the court, where friendship and liberty were preserved, cultivated, and conceptualized in their order, see Daniel

Gordon, *Citizens without Sovereignty: Equality and Sociablity in French Thought, 1670–1789* (Princeton: Princeton University Press, 1994), esp. chap. 3, "The Civilizing Process Revisited," pp. 86–126. Gordon justifiably criticizes the thesis of Norbert Elias, *La société de cour* (Paris; repr. 1985), that the absolutist court was itself the only model and center for mores and manners in neoclassical France.

46. The "conspiracy" that sought to bring Foucquet to power can be seen as a final attempt to prevent the division between an administrative absolutist state and a "diverse" society living its own life, politically "represented" until then by institutions characteristic of the old kingdom. The Revocation, in suppressing the centers of Protestantism to which the Edict of Nantes had granted a political identity, encapsulated and symbolized the ambition of the state to reserve for itself the entire political realm and to leave to civil society only the art of private "conversation."

47. See Uzman, *Kinship, Friendship, and Gratitude*.

48. La Fontaine, *Oeuvres diverses*, p. 743, "A Madame de La Fayette, en lui envoyant un petit billard."

CHAPTER 5

The epigraph for this chapter is from Chateaubriand, *Oeuvres complètes* (Paris: Ladvocat, 1831), vol. 5–2:393.

1. Jacques Maritain, *Primauté du spirituel* (Paris: Plon, 1927), pp. 11–13.

2. Alexis de Tocqueville, *L'Ancien Régime et la Révolution* (Paris: Gallimard, 1967), 1–2:65.

3. The manuscript copy of Chapelain's list is in the Bibl. nat. Fr., French ms. 23045, fols. 104–129. It is reproduced in *Mélanges de littérature* (Paris: Camusat, 1726). See Henri-Jean Marin, *Livre, pouvoirs et société à Paris au XVIIᵉ siècle* (1598–1701 (Geneva: Droz, 1969), pp. 423–39; Roger Zuber, *Le classicisme*, 1660–1680 (Arthaud, 1984), pp. 68–79; and Alain Viala, *Naissance de l'écrivain*, pp. 51–84.

4. Adam, *Histoire de la littérature*, 3:10.

5. See Marc Fumaroli, "La Coupole," in *Les lieux de mémoire*, edited by Pierre Nora, vol. 2: *La nation* (Paris: Gallimard, 1986); reprinted in Fumaroli, *Trois institutions*.

6. See Louis Marin, *Le portrait du roi* (Paris: Minuit, 1981); Jean Marie Apostolidès, *Le Roi-Machine, spectacle et politique au temps de Louis XIV* (Paris: Minuit, 1981); and the biographies by Labatut, *Louis XIV roi de gloire*, and Bluche, *Louis XIV*. No one formulated the official poetics of the reign and of its legend better than Racine in "Discours prononcé à l'Académie française à la réception de MM. de Corneille et de Bergeret, le 2 janvier 1685": "In the king's history, everything lives, everything moves, everything is in action. One must simply follow it if one can and study it well, it alone. It is a continuous chain of

wondrous deeds, which he himself begins, which he himself completes, as clear and intelligible when they are executed as they are impenetrable before the execution. In a word, one miracle closely follows another. Attention is always keen, admiration always rapt; and one is no less struck by the grandeur and swiftness with which peace is made than with the speed with which conquests are made." Racine, *Oeuvres complètes*, 2:350.

7. See Ferrier-Caverivière, *L'image de Louis XIV*; and Jean-Pierre Néraudeau, *L'Olympe du Roi-Soleil* (Paris: Les Belles Lettres, 1986).

8. "Discours prononcés dans l'Académie française à la réception de M. Perrault, le 26 novembre 1671," in *Recueil de divers ouvrages en prose et en vers dédié à S.A. le prince de Conti* (Paris: J.-B. Coignard, 1675), p. 215.

9. The abbé de La Chambre, *Discours prononcé*, repr. in Mongrédien, *Recueil des textes*, p. 139.

10. Racine, *Oeuvres complètes*, 2:343–44.

11. See Jean-Michel Pelous, "Le *Voyage* de Chapelle et Bachaumont, un document sur l'état de la France et de sa littérature en 1656," in *La découverte de la France au XVIIe siècle* (Paris: CNRS, 1980), and the recent study by Normand Doiron, *L'art de voyager: Le déplacement à l'époque classique* (Quebec and Paris: Presses de l'Université de Laval/Klincksieck, 1995).

12. On Chapelle, see Georges Mongrédien, "Le meilleur ami de Molière," *Mercure de France* 329 (1957):86–109 and 242–59.

13. Chapelle and Bachaumont, *Voyage d'Encausse*, edited by Marice Sourian (Caen: L. Jouan, 1901), p. 91.

14. In a recent article, Roger Duchêne attempts to relativize the truthful character of the letters of La Fontaine and see them as only a gallant fiction, a "very successful forgery" of true letters, in which the poet *would be staging* his journey after the fact. See Duchêne, "Un exemple de lettres galantes: La *Relation d'un voyage de Paris en Limousin* de La Fontaine," *Papers on French Seventeenth-century Literature* 23 (1996): 57–71. I prefer to side with the reading of Jean-Pierre Collinet, *Le monde littéraire de La Fontaine* (Paris: Presses Universitaires de France, 1970), pp. 107–15, which is more attentive to the expression of La Fontaine's immediate sensibility in this *Relation*. See also Madeleine Defrenne, "La Fontaine à la découverte au Limousin et d'un mode d'écriture," in *La découverte de la France au XVIIe siècle*, pp. 51–58; and Normand Doiron, "Voyage galant et promenade chez La Fontaine," *XVIIe Siècle* 187 (April–June 1995):185–202.

15. That "sulk" by La Fontaine before the castle of Richelieu contrasts sharply with his taste, manifested previously, for the variety of styles in Blois. In that, he revives, in the midst of neoclassicism, the traditional "Gothic" taste. See Henri Zerner, *L'art de la Renaissance en France: L'invention du classicisme* (Paris: Flammarion, 1996), chap. 1, "Le gothique à la Renaissance." See also Claude Mignot, "Le château et la ville de Richelieu en Poitou," and John Schloder, "Richelieu mécène au château de Richelieu," in *Richelieu et le monde de l'esprit*, Sorbonne, November 1985 (Paris: Imprimerie nationale), pp. 67–74 and 115–27.

16. On this point, I echo Jean-Pierre Collinet's opening remarks in "La Fontaine mosaïste," *Le Fablier* 4 (1992):11–16. Diversity, which La Fontaine made his motto in *Contes*, is a notion whose history goes back to ancient Greece: the word *poïkilia* is already present in Homer, where it designates both the skillful variegation of woven and embroidered fabrics, artistically decorated weapons, and the ingenuity and skill of certain heroes, Prometheus and Ulysses, or certain gods, Hermes and Eros. In *The Iliad* (11.482) and in *The Odyssey* (3.163; 13.293), Ulysses is called *poïkilometes*. But the notion of *poïkilia* becomes central in Pindar's poetics: as Monique Trédé shows in *Kaïros: L'à propos et l'occasion d'Homère à la fin du IVᵉ siècle* (Paris: Klincksieck, 1992), pp. 97–105, the young Pindar compares the poet to the bee that gathers pollen here and there to make its honey, less for the sweetness of his lyricism than for its diversity. That diversity is not disorder, since the poet's taste (the art of *kaïros*) leads him to retain only the best part of the motifs offered him, and hence obtain *charis*: grace and harmony born of variety (that is the "grace even more beautiful than beauty").

All La Fontaine's poetics are to be reexamined in that light, which comes from the Pindaric Renaissance of the sixteenth century, and which passes through the Latin filter of Horace. Trédé shows as well that, for the orator Isocrates, symmetry is a beauty of a lower order than the grace of variety and its folds of meaning (p. 279), and that, for the Greek physicians, the "symmetry" of humors, ideal health, is less the object of their art than extreme "diversity," the *poïkilia* of peculiar temperaments and the troubles from which one must deliver them. That notion is also at play in the political order. In *The Republic*, Plato, opening himself to the reproaches later made him by Karl Popper, condemns democracy as a "charming, anarchical, variegated" regime (558c), whose quartermasters are the young aristocrats given over to a variety of pleasures (559e). In contrast, Polybius's *Histories* (6.3) makes a merit of the complexity (*poïkilia*) of the Roman constitution, which assures its flexibility, its capacity to adapt to the unforeseeable, and its durability. It is clear that La Fontaine, hardly a Platonist in political matters, saw too much forced "symmetry" in the absolute monarchy, and was sorry that France was not endowed, like Polybius's Rome, with a regime that drew its strength from a complex and harmonic play of various forces. (That would be the utopian project of the abbé de Saint-Pierre.) On the notion of "variegation" in the sixteenth century, see Tabourot, *Les bigarrures*, edited by Francis Goyet (Geneva: Droz, 1986); and idem, *Traités de poétique et de rhétorique de la Renaissance* (Paris: Livre de Poche, 1990). See also Wilfried Floeck, *Esthétique de la diversité: Pour une histoire du baroque littéraire en France* (Paris, Seattle, and Tübingen: Papers on Seventeenth-Century Literature, 1989).

17. [Charles Perrault], *Courses de testes et de bagues, faites par le roy et par les princes et seigneurs de sa cour en l'année 1662; à Paris, de l'Imprimerie royale, 1670.* The text given here (folios 25 verso and 26 recto) is under a beautiful engraving depicting the king on horseback, dressed as a Roman emperor. This work in large folio format is a true "documentary" of this spectacle, sumptuous in its images.

18. The work by Marc de Vulson, squire of la Colombière, is a true manual of aristocratic life and "points of honor": *Le vrai théâtre d'honneur et de chevalerie, ou le miroir héroïque de la Noblesse. Seconde partie. Contenant les combats en camp clos, les gages de bataille, les cartels de défi, les querelles, les appels, les duels, les joutes mortelles, les injures, les offenses, les satisfactions, les accords, les récompenses d'honneur, les punitions des crimes, les dégradations de noblesse et de chevalerie, les obsèques, les pompes funèbres, les tombeaux des anciens nobles et chevaliers, et plusieurs autres choses remarquables sur toutes ces matières. Avec un traité du véritable honneur et en quoi il consiste* (The true theater of honor and chivalry, or the heroic mirror of nobility. Part 2. Containing battles in the lists, gages of battle, challenges, disputes, appeals, duels, jousting to the death, insults, offenses, amends, settlements, recompenses of honor, punishment of crimes, degradation of nobility and chivalry, funerals, funeral rites, the tombs of ancient nobles and knights, and several other remarkable things on all these subjects. With a treatise on true honor and of what it consists), 2 vols. folio (Paris: Augustin Courbé, 1648); quoted from vol. 2, "Préface, servant d'avertissement à la Noblesse de France," unpaginated.

19. On the symbolics of the cock, see Michel Pastoureau, "Le coq gaulois," in *Les lieux de mémoire*, edited by Pierre Nora, vol. 3: *Les France* (Paris: Gallimard), pp. 506–39.

20. See Fumaroli's preface to the facsimile reproduction of this illuminated manuscript, Grivel, ed., *Devises pour les tapisseries*.

21. "Discours de M. L. T. touchant la vie de M. de Benserade," first paragraph, in *Oeuvres de Monsieur de Benserade*, 2 vols. (Paris: Charles de Sercy, 1697).

22. Ibid., "A Grisette, chatte de Mademoiselle Deshoulières. Sonnet," 1:[278].

23. Ibid., "Discours de M. L. T." (see above n. 21).

24. See Perrault, *Les hommes illustres* 2:182–83.

25. On Benserade's court ballets, see Christout, *Le ballet de cour*. See also Marie-Claude Canova-Green, *La Politique spectacle: Les rapports franco-anglais* (Paris, Seattle, and Tübingen: Papers on French Seventeenth-Century Literature, 1993); and Mark Franko, *Dance as Text: Ideologies of the Baroque Body* (New York: Cambridge University Press, 1993).

26. Racine, *Britannicus*, act 4, scene 4, ll. 1471–76: "Pour toute ambition, pour vertu singulière, / Il excelle à conduire un char dans la carrière, / A disputer des prix indignes de ses mains, / A se donner lui-même en spectacle aux Romains, / A venir prodiguer sa voix sur un théâtre, / A réciter des chants qu'il veut qu'on idolâtre" (For all ambition, for only virtue, / He excels at driving a chariot in the arena, / At fighting for prizes unworthy of his hands, / At presenting himself as a spectacle to the Romans, / At coming to squander his voice at the theater, / At reciting songs he wants to have worshiped). Louis Racine's anecdote is reproduced in Racine, *Oeuvres complètes* 1:29–30.

27. Isaac de Benserade, *Ballet royal de Psyché dansé par Sa Majesté en 1656. Divisé en deux parties: Dans la première sont représentées les beautés et les délices du Palais d'Amour. Et dans la seconde, l'Amour même y divertit la belle Psyché, par la*

représentation d'une partie des merveilles qu'elle a produites, in *Les oeuvres de M. de Benserade,* 2 vols. (Paris: Charles de Sercy, 1697), 2:142–72; quoted from "Première partie, Douzième entrée, de six Esprits folets," 2:161.

28. Idem, *Ballet royal de la Raillerie, dansé par Sa Majesté en 1659,* "Première entrée, Du Ris, accompagné d'une symphonie de fleurs, appelées communément par les poètes, le Ris des prairies," in ibid., pp. 207–16, quoted p. 208.

29. Idem, *Ballet des Saisons dansé par Sa Majesté à Fontainebleau en 1661,* "Quatrième entrée. Des Moissoneurs. Le Roi représentant Cérès," ibid., pp. 217–30, quoted p. 222.

30. Idem, *Ballet royal d'Hercule amoureux, dansé par Leurs Majestés en 1662,* "XVIIᵉ entrée. Le Soleil et les douze Heures du Jour. Pour le Roy, représentant le Soleil," in ibid., pp. 254–80, quoted p. 280.

31. Idem, *Ballet royal de la naissance de Vénus dansé par Sa majesté en 1665,* ibid., 2:325–56. "Seconde partie, dernière entrée. Pour le Roi, Alexandre," quoted p. 351. On the king's responsibility in the Dutch War, see Paul Sonnino, *Louis XIV and the Origins of the Dutch War* (New York: Cambridge University Press, 1988), esp. p. 61 and pp. 66–67. See also Joël Cornette, *Le roi de guerre: Essai sur la souveraineté dans la France du Grand Siècle* (Payot, 1993), esp. 1:3: "Quand une république fait naître un roi de guerre."

32. Isaac de Benserade, "Discours de réception à l'Académie française," in *Poésies de Benserade,* edited by Octave Uzanne (Paris: Librairie des Bibliophiles, 1875).

33. Molière, *Oeuvres complètes,* edited by Maurice Rat (Paris: Gallimard, 1959), 2:922–25.

34. See Roger Duchêne, *Madame de Sévigné ou la chance d'être femme* (Fayard, 1982; new ed. 1996), p. 192.

35. *Le labyrinthe de Versailles comprenant la description du Labyrinthe de Versailles par Charles Perrault avec des gravures de S. Le Clerc* (Paris: Imprimerie royale, 1676), reproduced in a facsimile edition with an afterword by Michel Conan (Editions de Moniteur, 1982). See Bassy, "Les Fables," pp. 3–26. The author hypothesizes that the plan for this labyrinth may have been outlined by Le Nôtre, Le Brun, and La Fontaine, and initially designed for the gardens of Vaux; Louis XIV then may have got hold of the plan to embellish the grounds of Versailles, eliminating the future fabulist from the project. See also Michel Conan, "Le labyrinthe de Vaux-le-Vicomte," in *Le temps des jardins* (Melun: Conseil général de Seine-et-Marne, 1992), pp. 68–71.

36. See Fumaroli, "De Vaux à Versailles, politique de la poésie," in *Jean de La Fontaine,* pp. 14–37, and the analysis of the modulations in the description of Versailles in *Les amours de Psyché* given by Boris Donné, *La Fontaine et la poétique du songe: Récit, rêverie et allégorie dans Les Amours de Psyché* (Paris: Champion, 1995), pp. 24–37.

37. On the relations between the version of the myth of Psyche given by Marino and La Fontaine's work, see Françoise Graziani, "La Fontaine lecteur de

Marino: *Les Amours de Psyché*, oeuvre hybride," *Revue de littérature comparée* (October–December 1984):389–97.

38. La Fontaine, *Les amours de Psyché*, "Livre premier," in *Oeuvres diverses*, p. 127.

39. Ibid., p. 128.

40. See the pages devoted to *Les amours de Psyché* in Collinet's *Le monde littéraire de La Fontaine*, pp. 229–84, esp. the analysis of the "aesthetic temperament" of the work as an effort to harmoniously combine different passions likely to be produced by literary discourse; and the analysis of Donné, *La Fontaine et la poétique du songe*, pp. 74–118.

41. La Fontaine, *Les amours de Psyché*, in *Oeuvres diverses*, p. 176.

42. Louis Racine, *Mémoires contenant quelques particularités sur la vie et les ouvrages de Jean Racine*, in Racine, *Oeuvres complètes*, pp. 19–120, quoted p. 47.

43. La Fontaine, *Les amours de Psyché*, in *Oeuvres diverses*, p. 184.

44. Ibid., p. 80.

45. Ibid., p. 205.

46. One will find an analysis of these ordeals and, more broadly, of the initiatory journey of Psyche in Yves Giraud, "Un mythe lafontainien: Psyché," *Studi di Letteratura Francese* 230, no. 16 (1990):48–63. See also Boris Donné, "Paysages intérieurs et espaces allégoriques dans les récits 'galants' de La Fontaine," *Revue de littératures françaises et comparées* 7 (November 1996):95–107.

47. La Fontaine, *Les amours de Psyché*, in *Oeuvres diverses*, pp. 250–51.

48. On the aesthetic reflections of *Les amours de Psyché*, see Jean Lafond, "La Beauté et la Grâce: L'esthétique 'platonicienne' des *Amours de Psyché*," *Revue d'histoire littéraire de la France* (May–August 1969):475–90.

49. Jean Dutourd, "La Fontaine, précurseur de tout," in *Domaine public* (Paris: Flammarion, 1993), pp. 170–71.

CHAPTER 6

1. La Fontaine, *Oeuvres diverses*, pp. 752–73, with notes pp. 1067–90, and pp. 727–36, with notes pp. 1045–55, for the translations of Christian texts.

2. Valery Larbaud, *Sous l'invocation de saint Jérôme* (Paris: Gallimard, 1946).

3. La Fontaine, *Oeuvres diverses*, pp. 647–49.

4. On the renaissance of the inscription between the fifteenth and seventeenth centuries, see Florence Vuilleumier, "La rhétorique du monument: L'inscription dans l'architecture en Europe au XVIIᵉ siècle," *XVIIᵉ Siècle* 156, no. 3 (1987):291–311; Pierre Laurens, *L'abeille dans l'ambre: Célébration de l'épigramme de l'époque hellénistique à la fin de la Renaissance* (Paris: Les Belles Lettres, 1989), pp. 419–61; and idem, *"Vox Lapidum": Dalla riscoperta della iscrizioni antiche all'invenzione di un nuovo stile* scrittorio" in Proceedings of the colloquium of Aquasparta and Urbino, September 1993, special issue of *Eutopia* 3, nos. 1–2 (1994).

5. See Zuber, Les "belles infidèles."

6. On Jean Loret, author of the Gazette rimée or Muse historique, see Fernand Putz's thesis, La Muse historique (1650–1655): L'univers de Jean Loret (Luxembourg, 1983).

7. See the preliminary texts ("Avertissement" and "Préface") to this first collection of Contes et nouvelles en vers, vol. 1 of La Fontaine, Oeuvres complètes, pp. 551–57.

8. La Fontaine, Oeuvres diverses, pp. 349–459.

9. Ibid., p. 357.

10. "Movimento della facoltà immaginativa, Impeto della mente, Furore, il quale eccita i poeti a comporre," § III: "E genericamente per Furore che eccita a checchessia; e più spesso applicasi con qualche aggiunto che determini, a Furore amoroso: ma è proprio più che altro di nobile scrittura." Vocabolario degli Accademici della Crusca, 5:408, s.v. "estro."

11. See esp. the prefaces edited by J.-P. Collinet for the texts of Oeuvres complètes, vol. 1; it is clearly Boccaccio's Decameron that comes first.

12. Marc Fumaroli, "La mélancolie et ses remèdes: Classicisme français et maladie de l'âme," in La diplomatie de l'esprit.

13. La Fontaine, "Préface," in Contes et nouvelles I, p. 556.

14. See Fumaroli, "La mélancolie et ses remèdes."

15. Mongrédien, Recueil des textes, pp. 78–79.

16. See Dissertation sur Joconde, lettre XII à Monsieur l'Abbé La Vayer, in Nicolas Boileau, Oeuvres complètes, edited by Antoine Adam (Paris: Gallimard, 1996), pp. 309–24.

17. La Fontaine, Oeuvres diverses, pp. 601–9.

18. On Pascal's Augustinianism, see Philippe Sellier, Pascal et saint Augustin (Paris, 1970; repr. Paris, 1995).

19. La Fontaine, Poème de la captivité de saint Malc, in Oeuvres diverses, pp. 47–61.

20. On the first imitations of Fables, especially by Furetière, see Dandrey, La fabrique, p. 29, n. 19, and more generally, J.-P. Collinet, La Fontaine en amont et en aval (Pisa: Goliardica, 1988), n. 11.

21. "A Mme de Montespan" (1678), ll. 31–32, Fables choisies mises en vers, book 7, and "Préface," part 1 (1665) to Contes et Nouvelles en vers, in La Fontaine, Fables, contes et nouvelles, pp. 248, 555, and 556.

22. See the letter of 12 February 1666 in Mongrédien, Recueil des textes, p. 79.

23. See Claire Lesage, "Comment La Fontaine édita ses fables, 1668–1694," in the exhibit catalog Jean de La Fontaine.

24. See the Brossette edition of Oeuvres de Mr. Boileau Despréaux, avec des éclaircissements historiques donnez par Lui-même, vol. 1 (Geneva: Fabri and Barrillot, 1716), pp. 189–90; and Epître I. Au Roi, remarks on line 150, in Boileau, Oeuvres complètes, edited by Antoine Adam, p. 954.

25. See Claire Lesage and Anne Duprat, "Les fables ésopiques, un genre ancien et familier," in the exhibit catalog Jean de La Fontaine, pp. 124–26. See also below, "Aesop and Orpheus."

26. On Aesop and Orpheus, see Marie-Odile Sweetser, "Un nouvel Orphée: Chant et charmes dans les *Fables*," in *Hommages à Jean-Pierre Collinet* (Dijon: Ed. Universitaires, 1992), pp. 343–54.

27. See Jean Marmier, *Horace en France au XVIIe siècle* (Paris, 1968); and more recently Guy Lenoir, "La Fontaine et Horace," in *Présence d'Horace* (Publ. de l'Univ. de Tours, 1988), pp. 137–46.

28. See "Les Fables dans la tradition humaniste," in Fumaroli, ed., *Fables*, pp. lxxix–cii, and in the bibliography under the heading "La tradition humaniste des *Fables*, Editions du XVIe et du XVIIe siècle."

29. See Marc Fumaroli, *L'âge de l'éloquence: Rhétorique et "res litteraria" de la Renaissance au seuil de l'âge classique* (Geneva: Droz, 1980; repr. Paris: Albin Michel, 1994).

30. See, most recently, Anne-Marie Lecoq, "'Qvieti et Mvsis Henrici II. Gall. R.' Sur la grotte de Meudon," in *Le loisir lettré à l'âge classique*, edited by Marc Fumaroli, Philippe-Joseph Salazar, and Emmanuel Bury (Geneva: Droz, 1996), pp. 93–115.

31. On Abstemio, see Fumaroli, "Les Fables dans la tradition humaniste," p. lxxxii.

32. See ibid., pp. lxxxix–xc.

33. On Gilles Ménage, Elvire Samfiresco's *Ménage, polémiste, philologue, poète* (Paris: L'Emancipatrice, 1902) has unfortunately never been superseded.

34. On Guillaume Colletet, see further, chap. 6, "Aesop and Horace: Bees and Their Barbs." See also P. A. Jannini, *Verso il tempo della ragione Studi e ricerche su Guillaume Colletet* (Milan: Editrice Viscontea, 1965). The same author has published Colletet's *Traités de l'épigramme et du sonnet* (Geneva: Droz, 1965).

35. *Le livre des Lumières, ou la Conduite des rois, composé par le sage Pilpay, indien, traduit en français par David Sahib d'Ispahan, ville capitale de Perse* (Paris: S. Piget, 1644). See André Miquel, "La Fontaine et la version arabe des fables de Bidpai," *Revue de littérature comparée* (January–March 1964):35–50.

36. See the line from the letter to Saint-Evremond: "I thrived in Voiture," La Fontaine, *Oeuvres diverses*, p. 674.

37. Quoted in Fumaroli, "Les Fables dans la tradition humaniste," p. xcvii.

38. Antoine Furetière, *Les paraboles de l'Evangile traduites en vers. Avec une explication morale et allégorique tirée de SS. Pères* (Paris: P. Le Petit, 1672), "Dédicace au roi," p. a–ii, recto and verso.

39. Bassy, "Les Fables."

40. See, most recently, the exhibition catalog *Les jardins de Versailles et de Trianon d'André Le Nôtre à Richard Mique* (Château of Versailles, 1992) (Paris: Réunion des Musées nationaux, 1992); and Michel Conan, "Les jardins chez La Fontaine," in the exhibition catalog *Jean de La Fontaine*, pp. 49–53.

41. Perrault, *Le labyrinthe*.

42. Quoted and glossed by Conan, "Les jardins chez La Fontaine," p. 52.

43. Trichet du Fresne, *Figures diverses*. This volume is illustrated with engravings by G. Sadeler.

44. *Trattato della pittura di Leonardo da Vinci, novamente dato in luce con la vita dell'istesso autore scritta da Raff. du Fresne* (Paris: Langlois, 1651), dedicated to Queen Christina of Sweden. See Julius von Schlosser and Otto Kurz, *La littérature artistique: Manuel des sources de l'histoire de l'art moderne*, rev. ed. (Paris: Flammarion, 1984), p. 198.

45. Trichet du Fresne, *Figures diverses*, pp. 3 and 11.

46. See Lacour-Gayet, *L'éducation*, pp. 61–65 and 239.

47. Audin, prior of Termes and of la Fage, *Fables héroïques comprenant les véritables maximes de la politique et de la morale*, 2d ed. (Paris: J. Guignard, 1660), pp. 188 and 191.

48. Ibid., p. 192.

49. François Charpentier, *La Vie de Socrate*, 2d ed. (Paris: A. de Sommaville, 1657), pp. 68–69.

50. Ibid., pp. 69–70.

51. Ibid., pp. 40–41.

52. Ibid., p. 50.

53. In addition to Montaigne's *Essays* and Bernier's *Abrégé de la philosophie de Gassendi*, see Lisa Tunick Sarasohn, "Epicureanism and the Creation of a Privatist Ethic in Early Seventeenth-Century France," in *Atoms, Pneuma, and Tranquillity: Epicurean and Stoic Themes in European Thought*, edited by Margaret J. Osler (Cambridge: Cambridge University Press, 1991), pp. 175–95.

54. See Pintard, *Le libertinage érudit*, passim.

55. Jean-Louis Guez de Balzac, *Socrate chrétien* (Paris: A. Courbé, 1652), pp. e–i, recto and verso.

56. Ibid., pp. e–iiii, recto and verso.

57. Ibid., pp. e–vi, recto and verso.

58. Ibid., p. i, recto.

59. Ibid., pp. i, recto and verso.

60. Ibid., pp. 124–25.

61. See Philippe Sellier's preface to the Bible, translated by Louis Isaac Lemaître de Sacy (Paris: Robert Laffont, 1990).

62. La Fontaine, *Oeuvres diverses*, pp. 590–95, 779–85, 939–46, and 1093–94.

63. See Fumaroli, "Rhétorique d'école et rhétorique adulte: Remarques sur la réception européenne du *Traité du Sublime* au XVIᵉ et au XVIIᵉ siècles," *Revue d'histoire littéraire de la France* 1 (1986):33–51.

64. See Mongrédien, *Recueil des textes*, p. 118 (on the little theater of the duc du Maine, see also chap. 8, n. 6).

65. Partly reprinted as *Traité de l'épigramme* and *Traité du sonnet*; see above, n. 34.

66. As already mentioned, François Maynard composed Priapeans, censored by Valentin Conrart in the collection he published, *Oeuvres de Maynard* (1646). On Maynard, see *Maynard et son temps*, proceedings of the colloquium of Toulouse, 1973 (Toulouse, 1976).

67. La Fontaine, *Oeuvres diverses*, pp. 495–96.

68. On Scarron's death, see ibid., p. 514.

69. See above, p. 306.

70. Colletet, *Traité de l'épigramme*, p. 48.

71. Ibid., p. 70.

72. Ibid., p. 54.

73. Ibid., p. 76.

74. Ibid., p. 69.

75. Ibid., p. 105.

76. Paul Pellisson, *Discours sur les oeuvres de M. Sarasin*, in *Oeuvres de Jean-François Sarasin* (Paris: Courbé, 1656), "Preface"; reproduced in Viala, *L'esthétique galante*, p. 51–74.

77. The abundance of collections of Aesopian emblems in the literature printed in France before 1661 was noted in chapter 4. The famous bibliography by Mario Praz, *Studies in Seventeenth-Century Imagery*, 2d ed. (Rome, 1964), gives an idea of the European breadth of that literary genre, at once poetic and graphic. Georges Couton has focused attention on the debt of La Fontaine's *Fables* to the form of the emblem and the genre of the collection of emblems. The publishers of *Fables* (esp. Régnier, in the collection *Les grands écrivains de la France*; and J.-P. Collinet, ed., *Oeuvres complètes*), have identified La Fontaine's sources among the authors of collections of Aesopian emblems from the sixteenth century: Haudent, Corrozet, La Perrière.

78. On Horace's aesthetics, see the thesis defended in 1996 by Anne-Marie Lathière, *Horace: Nature et poésie: Une politique justifiée par une métaphysique*, part 1: "Les textes théoriques"; part 2: "L'art horatien."

79. On the notion of symbol among the humanists and the elaboration of a symbolic repertoire during the Renaissance, see the thesis defended in December 1996 by Florence Vuilleumier, *La raison des figures symboliques à la Renaissance et à l'âge classique: Etude sur les fondements philosophiques, théologiques et rhétoriques de l'image*. In *Clélie*, Anacréon alludes to Pythagoras's *Golden Verses*.

80. On the play of the popular and familiar appearance of the utterance dissimulating a philosophical and religious meaning in Pythagoras's *Symbola*, see Vuilleumier, *La raison des figures symboliques*.

81. The structure of the *emblema triplex* elaborated in the sixteenth century presupposes an epigrammatic "soul," an image "body," and an exegetical poem that makes the meaning of the two different facets of the same symbol come through. Baudoin's Aesopian emblems, which I mentioned in chap. 4, bow to this three-fold structure. The exegesis in that author and in Claude Mignaut, the French commentator of Alciati's *Emblemata* (where Aesopian emblems play an important role), is further supplemented by a prose commentary. That tendency toward the proliferation of glosses is completely absent in La Fontaine. The soul and body of the fable are blended in the robust *obviousness* of the narrative, and the exegesis is left to the reader.

82. According to T. Schirren (*Dictionnaire de termes de la rhétorique*, s.v. "Emphase," cols. 1121–23), the theoretical notion of *emphasis* took on the modern sense of "grandiloquence" by extending to oratory its use in musical rhetoric, where it designates an emphasis of the voice to charge with meaning a word of sung text, whereas "accent" designates that same emphasis with respect to a single syllable. For the original meaning of *emphasis*, see Lausberg, *Handbuch*, 3d ed. (1990), § 578, and the Schirren entry noted above. It was thanks particularly to Quintilian that the notion entered the vocabulary of humanist literary criticism: it designates the restrained figure of thought used out of caution or propriety. In *Institutio oratoria* (9.2.65), Quintilian cites the words of Plato, who was asked if Aristippus and Cleombrotus, two of Socrates' disciples, who were known to be carousing on Aegina during the imprisonment of their master, had at least come to attend him at the hour of his death: "No, they were on Aegina." The condemnation is all the more terrible for being restrained. In this case, the *emphasis* is all the more striking in that, through an epigram by Callimachus, we know that Cleombrotus committed suicide when he read *Phaedo*, in which Plato recounts Socrates' last dialogue in prison among his faithful disciples. In another passage (*Institutio oratoria*, 8.83), Quintilian lists, among the ornaments of style, that manner of leaving understood more than one says, in order to make the thing of which one speaks more intelligible. He gives the example "One must be a man," which might well be the source of Alceste's "I want one to be a man." In the *Rhetorica ad Herennium* (67), *emphasis*, under its Latin name *significatio*, is defined as the figure of thought allowing one to discern more than is said. And in Cicero (*De oratore*, 139 and 202), *significatio* is either a virtue of style (which means more than it says) or a figure of brevity that allows one to understand many things in few words. For the sixteenth century, see Olivier Millet, *Calvin et la dynamique de la parole: Etude de rhétorique réformée* (Paris: Champion, 1992), pp. 377–82.

CHAPTER 7

The epigraph for this chapter is from Chateaubriand, *Etudes historiques*, in *Oeuvres complètes* (Ladvocat, 1831), 5–3:44.

1. In the absence of any recent study of Scarron's works, see Jean Serroy, *Roman et réalité: Les histoires comiques au XVIIᵉ siècle* (Paris: Minard, 1981); Marcel Simon, "Les *Epistres chagrines* de Scarron," *Littératures Classiques* 18 (1993); and Jean Serroy, "Scarron journaliste," *Recherches et Travaux* 48 (1995).

2. On the burlesque, see F. Bar, *Le genre burlesque en France au XVIIᵉ siècle: Etude de style* (Paris, 1960); and, more recently, I. Landy and M. Ménard, *Burlesque et formes parodiques* (1987).

3. On Pellisson and the "Round Table," see chap. 2, "A Mentor for the 'Knights-errant': Paul Pellisson."

4. See chap. 6.

5. On the interest the king took in the witty brother and sisters of Mme de Montespan, especially Mme de Thianges, see Saint-Simon, *Mémoires*, 2:473 in particular.

6. That reply by the comte de Vivonne to the king is reported by Voltaire, *Le siècle de Louis XIV*, chap. 26, "Suite des particularités et anecdotes."

7. On the legendary "wit of the Mortemarts," see ibid.

8. Mme de Sévigné to Mme de Grignan, 17 May 1676, in *Correspondance*, edited by Roger Duchêne, vol. 2 (July 1675–September 1680), pp. 293–95. The account of the meeting is on page 294.

9. Quoted by General comte de Rochechouart, in *Histoire de la Maison de Rochechouart*, 2 vols. (Paris: Allard, 1859), 2:132.

10. On Clagny, see Pierre Bonassieux, *Le château de Clagny et Mme de Montespan, d'après les documents originaux: Histoire d'un quartier de Versailles* (Paris: Picard, 1881); and Claude de Montclos, *La mémoire des ruines: Anthologie des monuments disparus en France* (Paris: Mengès, 1992), pp. 220–28.

11. On allegory in general, see Georges Couton, *Ecritures codées: Essai sur l'allégorie au XVIIe siècle* (Paris, 1991). On allegory in high-society poetry, see Genetiot, *Les genres lyriques*. On the allegorical landscape, of which the most famous are Parnassus and Mlle de Scudéry's Carte du Tendre, see, for the former: *Le Parnasse, un mythe de la République des Lettres et des Arts*, edited by Marc Fumaroli (forthcoming); for the latter, Niderst, ed., *Les trois Scudéry*, and L. Van Delft, *Littérature et anthropologie* (Paris, 1993), pp. 47–51, 69–86, and passim.

12. Gabriel Guéret, *La promenade de Saint-Cloud, dialogue sur les auteurs*, edited by François Bruys, vol. 2 of *Mémoires historiques, critiques et littéraires* (Paris, 1751; repr. Paris: G. Monval, 1888).

13. Ibid., p. 21, which uses *Recueil de pièces choisies* (The Hague, 1714); the preface of this collection indicates "it is to Chapelle—called 'La Monnoie' according to Callières—that one owes a great portion of the finest things in the comedies of Molière." On the relation between Molière and Chapelle, see Adam, *Histoire de la littérature*, pp. 214–15, 237.

14. In the absence of a major monograph that would do justice to Saint-Réal, see Jean-Paul Sermain's articles "Comment réussir auprès du prince? Une image du pouvoir absolu à la mort de Colbert: Le *Césarion* de Saint-Réal," in *Actes du XIVe Colloque du CMR 17* (Marseilles, 1985); and "Rhétorique et politique dans la seconde moitié du XVIIe siècle: Le modèle français," *Rhetorik* 10 (1991). See also the reissue of Saint-Réal's *De l'usage de l'histoire*, edited by R. Démoris and C. Meurillon (Lille: Gerl, 1980), accompanied by two studies, "Saint-Réal et l'histoire" and "Saint-Réal et Pascal."

15. Mme de Sévigné, on the fables of the second collection, 26 July and 2 August 1679, *Correspondance* 2:660–62.

16. See Jürgen Grimm, "'Quel Louvre! un vrai charnier!' La représentation de la société de cour dans les *Fables* de La Fontaine," *Littératures Classiques* 11 (January 1989):221–31.

17. See Adnan Haddad, *Fables de La Fontaine d'origine orientale* (Paris: Sedes, 1984).

18. On Mme de La Sablière, see Menjot d'Elbenne, *Madame de La Sablière;* Fumaroli, ed., *Fables*, note on *Discours à Madame de La Sablière*, pp. 935–37.

19. See Walckenaer, *Poésies diverses d'Antoine Rambouillet de La Sablière, de François de Maucroix . . .* (Paris, 1825); Tallemant des Réaux, *Historiettes*, vol. 2.

20. Satire X (1692–94), in *Contre les femmes*, edited by A. Adam, pp. 62–80, ll. 425–37, especially: "Bon, c'est cette Savante / Qu'estime Roberval, et que Sauveur fréquente. / D'où vient qu'elle a l'oeil trouble, et le teint si terni? / C'est que sur le calcul, dit-on, de Cassini, / . . . elle a dans sa gouttière / A suivre Jupiter passé la nuit entière" (Well, it's that lady scientist / esteemed by Roberval and frequented by Sauveur. / How does it happen that she is so bleary-eyed, and her color so drab? / It is because, on the calculation of Cassini, it is said, . . . she has in her gutter / spent the whole night following Jupiter).

21. Menjot d'Elbenne, *Madame de La Sablière*, p. 69.

22. To situate Mme de La Sablière's salon within the history of conversation, see Fumaroli, "La conversation," in *Trois institutions*, pp. 113–210. This salon, where philosophical debate played an important role, prefigured, under Louis XIV, that of Mme Geoffrin. It is to be noted that Mme de Lambert inherited the tradition from Mme de La Sablière (for whom she wrote a eulogy) through Bachaumont, who was the second husband of her mother and the friend of Chapelle.

23. On the cabal of princes of blood, see Saint-Simon, *Mémoires*, 1:1024–25.

24. See L. Petit, "Madame de La Sablière et François Bernier," *Le Mercure de France* 308 (1950): 670–83.

25. See Fumaroli, ed., *Fables*, note on *Discours à Madame de La Sablière*, pp. 937–39.

26. Jacques Maritain, *Trois réformateurs: Luther, Descartes, Rousseau* (Paris: Plon, 1926), p. 91.

27. La Fontaine, *Oeuvres diverses*, p. 670.

28. Letter of Jean-Baptiste Rousseau to Brossette, 14 July 1715, in *Correspondance de Jean-Baptiste Rousseau et de Brossette*, edited by Paul Bonnefon, vol. 1, 1715–1729 (Paris: E. Cornély pour la Société des textes français modernes, 1910), p. 15.

29. [Chaulieu and de La Fare], *Poésies* (Amsterdam, 1724; London, 1781; Paris, 1812). De La Fare's masterpiece, *Ode à la Paresse*, is the best example of a purely Epicurean high-society poetry, clear, nonchalant, seemingly artless: "Présent de la seule nature, / Amusement de mon loisir, / Vers aisés par qui je m'assure / Moins de gloire que de plaisir, / Coulez, enfants de ma paresse. / Mais si d'abord on vous caresse, / Refusez-vous à ce bonheur: / Dites, qu'échappés de ma veine, / Par hasard, sans force et sans peine, / Vous méritez peu cet honneur" (A present of nature alone, / Amusement of my free time, / Easy verses with which I assure myself / Less glory than pleasure, / Flow, children of my idleness. / But if someone caresses you first, / Deny yourself that happiness: / Say that, hav-

ing escaped my vein / By chance, without force and without pain, / You hardly deserve that honor).

30. De La Fare, *Mémoires et réflexions sur les principaux événements du règne de Louis XIV* (Rotterdam, 1716; Amsterdam, 1734), edited by Michaud-Poujoulat, vol. 8 (1851), p. 260.

31. Ibid.

32. "Madrigal," in *Poésies de Monsieur l'abbé de Chaulieu et de Monsieur le Marquis de La Fare* (Amsterdam: E. Roger, 1724), p. 169.

33. Mme de Sévigné, letter to her daughter, 8 November 1679, *Correspondance* 2:731.

34. Saint-Simon, *Mémoires*.

35. La Fontaine, *Oeuvres diverses*, pp. 694–719.

36. See G. Bouriquet, *L'abbé de Chaulieu* (Nizet, 1972).

37. See Chaulieu's edition of de La Fare, or Chaulieu, *Oeuvres* (Amsterdam, 1733; Paris, 1757; repr. Geneva: Slatkine, 1968).

38. La Fontaine, letter of 31 August 1687, *Oeuvres diverses*, p. 667.

CHAPTER 8

1. See the classic work by Frances Yates, *The Art of Memory* (Chicago and London: University of Chicago Press, 1966), esp. pp. 27–30 and 41–42.

2. On the rhetoric and humanist politics of praise, see O. B. Hardison, Jr., *The Enduring Monument: A Study of the Idea of Praise in Renaissance Literary Theory and Practice* (Chapel Hill: University of North Carolina Press, 1962; repr. Westport, Conn.: Greenwood Press, 1973), esp. p. 36 for the quotations by Coluccio Salutati and Lorenzo di Medici.

3. La Fontaine, *Oeuvres diverses*, pp. 682–94. This opposition between praise and flattery is ancient. See Laurent Pernot, *La rhétorique de l'éloge dans le monde gréco-romain* (Paris: Collection des Etudes Augustiniennes, 1993). Saint-Simon, for his part, underscored the king's weakness in that respect: "Praise, or better, flattery pleased him to such a point that even the crudest was well received, the basest savored even more. It was only by that path that one got close to him, and those he loved owed that love only to having felicitously come across that genre, and to never tiring of it" (*Mémoires* [1715], p. 478). See also, on the previous period, Orest A. Ranum, *Artisans of Glory: Writers and Historical Thought in the Seventeenth Century* (Chapel Hill: University of North Carolina Press, 1980).

4. La Fontaine, *Oeuvres diverses*, pp. 702–5. Let us note that, twenty-five years later, it was in that same society of the Vendômes that Voltaire earned his spurs as a poet. In the year of Louis XIV's death, the young Arouet sent Philippe de Vendôme, Grand Prior of the Temple and the duke's brother (who died in 1712), an epistle "to awaken the bantering playfulness" of that "highness of

song," where one finds again many of the themes inspired by La Fontaine, especially a certain pacifism. In that piece of verse, the young Arouet sees Francis I in a dream: "Il ne traînait point après lui / L'or et l'argent de cent provinces, / Superbe et tyrannique appui / De la vanité des grands princes; / Point de ces escadrons nombreux, / De tambours et de hallebardes; / . . . Quelques lauriers sur sa personne, / Deux brins de myrte dans ses mains, / Etaient ses atours les plus vains" (He did not drag behind him / The gold and silver of a hundred provinces, / Superb and tyrannical support / Of the vanity of great princes; / None of those numerous squadrons / Of drums and halberds; / . . . A few laurels on his person / Two sprigs of myrtle in his hands, / Were the vainest of his finery). Francis I then praises the songs of the Grand Prior, "so pretty . . . that Marot remembers them by heart," and compares himself to the prince, who, like him, "loves the arts" "and beautiful verses by preference." And the king concludes: "Except in love, in all cases / He keeps, like me, his word." Voltaire, *Oeuvres complètes* (Paris: Hachette, 1879), 9:180.

5. See Marc Fumaroli, "La Fontaine et l'Académie Française," *Le Fablier* 8 (1997).

6. On the collaboration between Molière and Lully, see the special issue of *XVIIe Siècle* devoted to this subject (*Molière- Lully* 98–99 [1973]). On the subject as a whole, see Marcelle Benoit, *Musiques de cour Chapelle, Chambre, Ecurie: Recueil de documents 1661–1733 (La vie musicale sous les rois Bourbons)* (Paris: Picard, 1971).

7. The following anecdote appears in an (anonymous) letter addressed to Bussy-Rabutin. See his *Correspondance*, edited by Ludovic Lalanne (Paris: Charpentier, 1858), 2:415–16: "As a New Year's gift, Mme de Thianges gave M. du Maine an entirely gilded room as large as a table. Above the door was written *Chambre sublime*. Outside the balusters, Despréaux, wielding a pitchfork, prevented seven or eight bad poets from approaching. Next to Despréaux was Racine, and, a little farther on, La Fontaine, whom he beckoned with his hand to approach; all these figures were miniatures made of wax, and each person depicted had given his own: they were called the sublime cabal." See Mongrédien, *Recueil des textes*, p. 118.

8. On the collaboration between La Fontaine and Lully, see Henry Prunières, *La vie illustre et libertine de Jean-Baptiste Lully* (Paris: Plon, 1929), pp. 155ff; and more generally, *Lully musicien du Soleil*, catalog of the Versailles exhibition, 1987.

9. On the collaboration between Quinault and Lully, see Jérôme de La Gorce, "Un proche collaborateur de Lully: Philippe Quinault," *XVIIe Siècle: Le tricentenaire de Lully* 161, no. 4 (October–December 1988):365–70. On the success of *Bellérophon*, see Prunières, *La vie illustre et libertine*, pp. 202–5.

10. Ibid., pp. 215 and 217.

11. The text of *Daphné* can be found in La Fontaine, *Oeuvres diverses*, pp. 361–406. The libretti composed by La Fontaine have attracted little atten-

tion from critics. One may, however, consult Collinet, *Le monde littéraire de La Fontaine*, pp. 339–47.

12. See Marc Fumaroli, *L'inspiration du poète de Poussin* (Paris: Réunion des Musées nationaux, 1989), reprinted as *L'école du silence: Le sentiment des images au XVIIe siècle* (Paris: Flammarion, 1994).

13. Evrard Titon du Tillet set out the plan for such a monument in detail in a book illustrated with numerous engravings: *Description du Parnasse françois exécuté en bronze à la gloire de France et de Louis le Grand, et à la mémoire perpétuelle des illustres poètes et des fameux musiciens françois* (Paris, 1718). See Judith Colton, *The Parnasse François: Titon du Tillet and the Origins of the Monument to Genius* (New Haven: Yale University Press, 1979).

14. "Sur la mort de M. Colbert qui arriva peu de temps après une grande maladie qu'eut le chancelier M. Le Tellier" (On the death of M. Colbert, which occurred shortly after a serious illness that Chancellor Le Tellier had): "Colbert jouissait par avance / De la place de chancelier, / Et sur cela pour Le Tellier / On vit gémir toute la France, / L'un revint, l'autre s'en alla: / Ainsi ce fut scène nouvelle, / Car la France, sur ce pied-là, / Devait bien rire. . . . Aussi fit elle" (Colbert enjoyed in anticipation / the place of chancellor, / And so, for Le Tellier / All of France moaned. / One recovered, the other went away: / Hence it was a new scene, / Since France, on that score, / Was to have a good laugh. . . . And so it did). La Fontaine, *Oeuvres diverses*, p. 638.

15. La Fontaine, *Oeuvres diverses*, pp. 638–39.

16. Anecdote reported by the abbé d'Olivet in his *Histoire de l'Académie française* (1729). See Mongrédien, *Recueil des textes*, pp. 137–38.

17. La Fontaine, *Oeuvres diverses*, p. 677.

18. Among the many studies devoted to this subject, let me recommend above all the classic book by Raymond Klibansky, Erwin Panofsky, and Fritz Saxl, *Saturn and Melancholy* (New York: Basic Books, 1964). For neoclassical France, see Marc Fumaroli, "Nous serons guéris si nous le voulons: Classicisme français et maladie de l'âme," *Le Débat* 29 (March 1984); reprinted in *La diplomatie de l'esprit*, pp. 403–39; idem, "Saturne et les remèdes à la mélancolie," in *Précis de littérature française du XVIIe siècle*, edited by Jean Mesnard (Paris: Presses Universitaires de France, 1990), pp. 29–46; and Patrick Dandrey's recent "La rédemption par les lettres dans l'occident mélancolique (1570–1670)," in *Le loisir lettré à l'âge classique*, edited by Marc Fumaroli, Philippe-Joseph Salazar, and Emmanuel Bury (Geneva: Droz, 1996), pp. 63–91.

19. La Fontaine, *Oeuvres diverses*, pp. 720–24, "A Monsieur l'abbé Verger," cited p. 720.

20. Quinault, *L'amour malade* (1676). I have not been able to verify the title and text given here. See William Brooks, *Bibliographie critique du théâtre de Quinault* (Paris, Seattle, Tübingen: Papers on French Seventeenth-Century Literature, 1988).

21. La Fontaine, *Oeuvres diverses*, pp. 633–35.

22. Saint-Simon, *Mémoires*, 3:112-14.

23. On the cycle of fables addressed to the Dauphin, see Jürgen Grimm, "'Malgré Jupiter même et les temps orageux': Pour une réévaluation du livre XII des *Fables*," in *Le pouvoir des fables, études lafontainiennes* (Paris, Seattle, and Tübingen: Papers on French Seventeenth-Century Literature, 1994), 1:161-72; and the preface and notes to Fumaroli, ed., *Fables*.

24. See Jeanne-Lydie Goré, *L'itinéraire de Fénelon: Humanisme et spiritualité* (Paris: Presses Universitaires de France, 1957).

25. The portrait of Fénelon occurs in Saint-Simon, *Mémoires* 5 (1715):144, written upon the prelate's death. Another appears ibid., 4 (1711):209-11.

26. On this subject in general, see Louis Châtellier, *L'Europe des dévots* (Paris: Flammarion, 1987).

27. La Fontaine, *Oeuvres diverses*, pp. 591-95.

28. Cited by Chatelain, *Le Surintendant Nicolas Foucquet*, p. 546.

29. See the proceedings of the colloquium of Saint-Cyr (June 1986), held on the occasion of the tricentennial of the founding of the Maison Royale de Saint Louis, published in the *Revue de l'Histoire de Versailles et des Yvelines* 74 (1990); and other papers appearing in volumes 74 (1990), 75 (1991), and 77 (1993).

30. See Picard, *La carrière de Jean Racine*, pp. 393-432.

31. See Cuche, *Une pensée sociale*.

32. On La Bruyère's social thought, see ibid.

33. On this question, see in particular the critical views of Roland Mousnier, "Les idées politiques de Fénelon," in *XVIIᵉ Siècle* (1951-52), nos. 12, 13, and 14, pp. 190-207. The name *Tables de Chaulnes* is given to the political program elaborated by Fénelon and the duc de Luynes upon the death of the Grand Dauphin.

34. See the recent edition of *Lettre à Louis XIV* procured by François-Xavier Cuche and preceded by an essay, "Un prophète à la cour," (Rezé, 1994), and above all the authoritative editions edited by Jean Orcibal, in vols. 1 and 2 of Fénelon's *Correspondance* (Paris: Klincksieck, 1972); and Jacques Le Brun, in vol. 1 of Fénelon's *Oeuvres* (Paris: Gallimard, 1983).

35. Fénelon translated many of La Fontaine's fables into Latin. See *Fables choisies de J. de La Fontaine (Fabulae Selectae J. Fontani) traduites en prose latine par F. de Salignac Fénelon Nouvelle édition critique . . .* , edited by the abbé J. Bézy (Paris: Picard, 1904).

36. See Fumaroli, "Le retour d'Astrée," in *Précis de littérature française du XVIIᵉ siècle*, pp. 47-64.

37. Studied especially in Marie-Odile Sweetser, "Conseils d'un vieux Chat à une jeune Souris: Les leçons du livre XII," *Papers on French Seventeenth-Century Literature* 23, no. 44 (1996):95-103.

38. La Fontaine, *Daphnis et Alcimadure*, in *Oeuvres complètes*, pp. 500-502.

39. See Léon Petit, *La Fontaine et Saint-Evremond ou la tentation de l'Angleterre* (Toulouse: Privat, 1953).

40. See the fine study by Bernard Beugnot, "Autour d'un texte: L'ultime leçon des *Fables*," in *Mélanges de littérature française offerts à René Pintard* (Strasbourg,

1975), pp. 291–301. The author has continued his reflections in his recent book *Loin du monde et du bruit: Le discours de la retraite au XVIIᵉ siècle* (Paris: Presses Universitaires de France, 1996).

41. See La Fontaine, *Oeuvres diverses*, p. 741.

42. Cited ibid., pp. 1062–63.

43. *Rituale romanum Pauli V*, "De sacramento extremae unctionis" (Paris, 1645).

44. On the abbé Pouget, see chap. 1, unnumbered note.

45. On *La captivité de saint Malc*, see the text by La Fontaine in *Oeuvres diverses*, pp. 49–61.

46. "Le chemin de velours, ballade sur Escobar," in La Fontaine, *Oeuvres diverses*, pp. 587–88; "Stances sur le même," pp. 588–90.

47. On La Fontaine's role in the genesis and completion of this collection, see La Fontaine, *Oeuvres diverses*, pp. 939–46, note by P. Clarac.

48. Speaking of Racan and Malherbe in the fable "The Miller, His Son, and the Ass" (3.1, ll. 9–10), La Fontaine writes: "Ces deux rivaux d'Horace, héritiers de sa Lyre, / Disciples d'Apollon, nos Maîtres pour mieux dire" (Those two rivals of Horace, heirs to his lyre, / Disciples of Apollo, our masters in short).

49. On this vast subject, see the recent work by Anne-Elisabeth Spica, *Symbolique humaniste et emblématique: L'évolution et les genres (1580–1700)* (Paris: Champion, 1996); and Marc Fumaroli, "Hiéroglyphes et lettres: La 'Sagesse mystérieuse des Anciens,' au XVIIᵉ siècle," *XVIIᵉ Siècle* 158 (January–March 1988):7–20.

50. The main lines of this story can be found in Mongrédien, *Recueil des textes*, pp. 181–83. The question of La Fontaine's conversion has been the subject of very different critical views, esp. in the first quarter of the twentieth century: see the studies cited by Mongrédien, ibid., p. 184, n. 1.

51. On the religious poet Racan, see Raymond Picard, *La poésie française de 1640 à 1680: Poésie religieuse, épopée, lyrisme officiel* (Société d'Edition d'Enseignement Supérieur, 1965), pp. 99–113; and C.K. Abraham, *Enfin Malherbe: The Influence of Malherbe on French Lyric Prosody, 1605–1674* (Lexington: University Press of Kentucky, 1971).

52. *Recueil de poésies chrétiennes et diverses* (1671), "Paraphrase du Psaume XVII Diligam te, Domine," ll. 11–30 and 81–100, in La Fontaine, *Oeuvres diverses*, pp. 591–95; cited pp. 591 and 593.

53. Opening words of "Officium defunctorum," in *Rituale parisiense ad Romani formam expressum, authoritate Illustrissimi et Reverendissimi in Christo Patris D.D. Joannis Francisci de Gondy, Parisiensis Archiepiscopi editum* (Paris: Cramoisy, 1654), pp. 173–226.

54. Letter from La Fontaine to Maucroix, 26 October 1693, in *Oeuvres diverses*, pp. 727–30. See the accounts of La Fontaine's last two years in Duchêne, *Jean de La Fontaine*, pp. 508 ff.

55. "Traduction paraphrasée de la prose *Dies irae*," stanzas 1–23 and 8, in La Fontaine, *Oeuvres diverses*, pp. 734–36; cited pp. 734 and 735. A first version of

that translation was read on 15 June 1693 during La Bruyère's and the abbé Bignon's induction into the Académie Française.

56. On La Fontaine's religion, see Léon Petit, "Troisième partie, La Fontaine converti: Le pathétique de l'heure suprême," in *La Fontaine à la rencontre de Dieu* (Paris: Nizet, 1970), pp. 155–81.

57. Maucroix, *Mémoires*, edited by Louis Paris (Reims: Société des Bibliophiles, 1842).

58. Latin version given by Fénelon to the duc de Bourgogne, 14 April 1695, in Mongrédien, *Recueil des textes*, pp. 192–93; and in the abbé Bézy, *Fables choisies J. de La Fontaine*, pp. 143–44.

Index